PETERSON'S®

MASTER THE™ SAT®

About Peterson's®

Peterson's has been your trusted educational publisher for more than 50 years. It's a milestone we're quite proud of as we continue to offer the most accurate, dependable, high-quality educational content in the field, providing you with everything you need to succeed. No matter where you are on your academic or professional path, you can rely on Peterson's for its books, videos, online information, expert test-prep tools, the most up-to-date education exploration data, and the highest quality career success resources—everything you need to achieve your education goals. For our complete line of products, visit **www.petersons.com.**

For more information, contact Peterson's, 4380 S. Syracuse St., Suite 200, Denver, CO 80237; 800-338-3282 Ext. 54229; or visit us online at **www.petersons.com.**

Peter Giebel, Editorial Manager; Lacey N. Smith, Content Editor; Michelle Galins, Book Designer; Jeff Bellomi, Editor; Chrissy Frye, Editor; Kelsie McWilliams, Contributing Editor; Laura Neff, Contributing Editor; Justin Wisner, Contributing Editor

Peterson's Master the SAT
ISBN-13: 978-0-7689-4597-3

Printed in the United States of America

10 9 8 7 6 5 4 3 2 1 25 24 23

Twenty-first Edition

CONTENTS

CONTENTS

Part III: SAT® Reading and Writing

Part IV: The SAT® Math Section

CONTENTS

Peterson's Updates and Corrections:

Check out our website at **www.petersonsbooks.com/updates-and-corrections/** to see if there is any new information regarding the test and any revisions or corrections to the content of this book. We've made sure the information in this book is accurate and up to date; however, the test format or content may have changed since the time of publication.

Credits

Excerpt from "The Sculptor's Funeral" by Willa Cather (1905)

Excerpt from "European Invasion: DNA Reveals the Origins of Modern Europeans" by Alan Cooper and Wolfgang Haak, published by *The Conversation* (March 2015)

Excerpt from *The Autobiography of Charles Darwin* by Charles Darwin (1887)

Excerpt from "My Escape from Slavery" by Frederick Douglass (1881)

Excerpt from "A Scandal in Bohemia" by Arthur Conan Doyle (1891)

Excerpt from "Snowy Mountains" by John Gould Fletcher (1922)

"Nothing Gold Can Stay" by Robert Frost (1923)

Excerpt from *The Prophet* by Kahlil Gibran (1923)

Excerpt from "Briar Rose" by Jacob and Wilhelm Grimm (1821)

Excerpt from "The Slave Mother" by Frances Ellen Watkins Harper (1854)

Excerpt from *In Ghostly Japan* by Lafcadio Hearn (1899)

Excerpt from "By Your Response to Danger" by Jenny Holzer (1980-1982)

Excerpt from "September" by Helen Hunt Jackson (1891)

Excerpt from "John Redding Goes to Sea" by Zora Neale Hurston (1912)

Excerpt from *The French Impressionists* by Camille Mauclair (1903)

Excerpt from "The Spring and the Fall" by Edna St. Vincent Millay (1923)

Excerpt from *Beyond Good and Evil* by Friedrich Nietzsche (1886)

Excerpt from "Annabel Lee" by Edgar Allen Poe (1849)

Excerpt from *The Science of Human Nature: A Psychology for Beginners* by William Henry Pyle (1917)

Excerpt from "Sonnet 18" by William Shakespeare (1609)

Excerpt from *A Daughter of the Samurai* by Etsu Inagaki Sugimoto (1925)

Excerpt from *The Outline of Science, Vol. 1* by J. Arthur Thomson (1921)

Excerpt from "When modern Eurasia was born" from University of Copenhagen – Faculty of Science, published by *ScienceDaily* (June 2015)

Excerpt from "The Time Machine" by Herbert George Wells (1895)

Excerpt from *Twilight Sleep* by Edith Wharton (1927)

Excerpt from "O Captain! My Captain!" by Walt Whitman (1865)

Review of "Overview – SSRI Antidepressants" by UK National Health Service (February 2021)

BEFORE YOU BEGIN

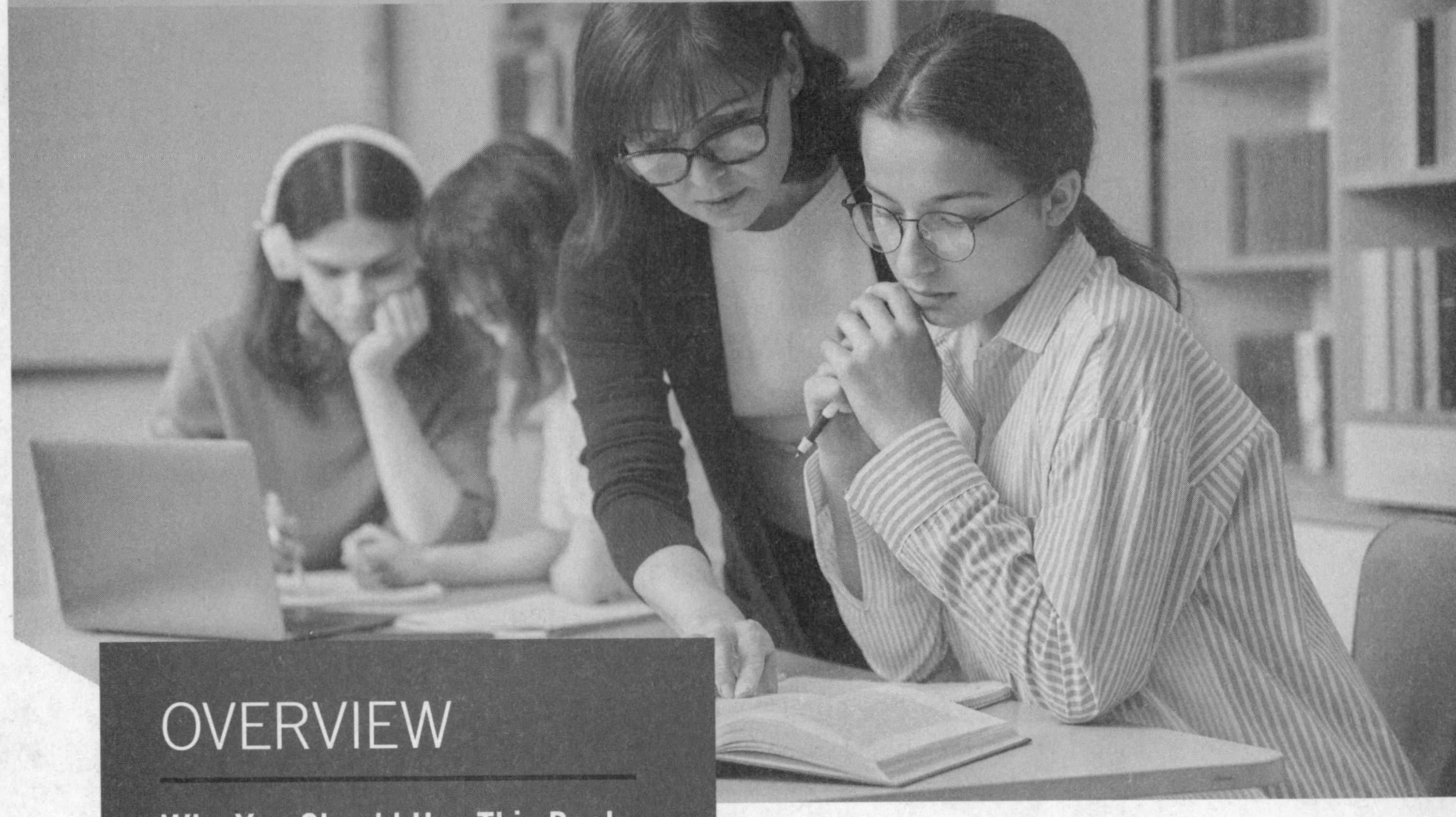

OVERVIEW

WHY YOU SHOULD USE THIS BOOK

Peterson's *Master the™ SAT®* is designed by test experts and educators to fully prepare you for test-day success. From the start of your test prep journey to your final review, this book includes an array of tools and tips to help you shine on the SAT. This helpful guide includes the following components.

ESSENTIAL TEST INFORMATION

We take the stress out of preparing for the SAT by providing all the information you'll need to know before the big day in one place—including how to register, where to go, and even what to bring on the day of the exam. We've got you covered!

COMPREHENSIVE COVERAGE OF SAT TEST FORMATS

After using this book, you'll know the structure and format of the SAT from start to finish and have all the information you'll need for success on test day.

THOROUGH TEST TOPIC REVIEW

You'll get a thorough review of every topic tested on the SAT and help with creating an effective study plan for reaching your goal score. Not only will there be no surprises on test day, but you'll also have the confidence that comes with being thoroughly prepared.

PLENTY OF REALISTIC TEST QUESTION PRACTICE

This book has parts that cover both sections of the SAT. Within each part, you'll find abundant opportunities for realistic practice with questions just like those you'll encounter during the actual test.

PRE- AND POST-TESTING TO SUPPORT ANY STUDY PLAN

Take a full-length diagnostic exam to help you determine your strengths and weaknesses and target your study time effectively. When you're close to exam day, take a practice test to see your progress and find places to target for last minute review. And if you need more practice, there are additional practice tests available through **www.petersons.com/testprep/sat.**

EXPERT TIPS, ADVICE, AND STRATEGIES

Our test prep professionals are veteran educators who know what it takes to get a top score on the SAT—you'll get the expert tools that have proven to be effective on exam day, putting you a step ahead of the test-taking competition. Consider this your inside edge as you prepare to conquer the SAT!

ACCESS TO AN ONLINE ADAPTIVE-STYLE TEST

By purchasing this book, you get access to an online adaptive-style test that simulates the adaptive design and formatting of the new Digital SAT. To register, go to **http://petersons.com/satbook** and follow the on-screen instructions.

HOW THIS BOOK IS ORGANIZED

This book has all the answers to your questions about the SAT. It contains up-to-date information, hundreds of practice questions, and solid test-taking advice. Here's how you can use it to optimize your SAT prep journey.

Familiarize Yourself with the SAT

- **Part I** contains answers to all your questions about the SAT. You'll learn what kinds of questions to expect and how they look, how the two sections that comprise the SAT are scored, and how the different modules work.
- **Part II** contains both the diagnostic test and a chapter on how to analyze your diagnostic test results. In Chapter 2, the diagnostic test simulates the format of the new Digital SAT with a standard first module but a harder second module for each test section. This better represents the challenges you need to overcome to achieve the highest scores. In Chapter 3, you'll find information on a variety of study strategies that support preparation for the SAT, including tips on using research-based study techniques to complement a variety of learning styles.

Study by SAT Subject

- **Part III** covers the Reading and Writing section of the SAT. Here, you'll find information on the section as a whole as well as guidance on mastering skills related to reading comprehension, Standard English conventions, and writing and language use. At the end of Part III, you'll find a chapter with strategies proven to help test takers perform their best on the Reading and Writing section.
- **Part IV** covers the Math section of the SAT. Here, you'll find information on the section as a whole as well as guidance on mastering skills related to fundamental math concepts, algebra, geometry, trigonometry, advanced math, data analysis, statistics, and probability. You'll also find a strategy chapter with techniques to assist you on the Math section.

Evaluate Progress and Review

- **Part V** contains a practice test. While you can take this test at any time in your study journey, we recommend using it as a post-test after reviewing content and strategy chapters. Doing so allows you to evaluate your overall progress since the diagnostic test. Furthermore, if you analyze your post-test the same way we suggest you do with the diagnostic test in Chapter 3, you'll receive useful feedback on any subjects you need to target during your final test prep review sessions. You also have access to an adaptive-style practice test online by going to **http://petersons.com/satbook.**

HOW TO USE THIS BOOK

The way this book is set up lends itself to two primary paths of study. Choose the one that works the best for your study goals.

Diagnostic Test Method

One way to use this book is to start with the diagnostic test in Chapter 2. A diagnostic test is a type of pre-test that helps you understand your strengths and weaknesses before you begin studying. It "diagnoses" the skills that need the most improvement.

In this method, you start with a diagnostic test and then you use the results of your diagnostic test to develop a study plan in Chapter 3. The diagnostic test will give you a sampling of the kinds of questions you are likely to see on the SAT, and it will show you where you might need to focus your test-prep efforts.

Once you've developed a cohesive study plan with the help of Chapter 3, you'll be prepared to work through the rest of the book in an order that suits your performance goals. You don't have to follow the book in the order it is presented in this case; instead, you can feel free to jump around between the different skills you need to practice based on the personalized study plan you created from your diagnostic test results. For instance, if your diagnostic test reveals that you did fine on geometry and trigonometry questions but really struggled with those related to statistics and

TIP

Test takers who want extra practice can find additional practice exams online. For more information, go to www.petersons.com/testprep/sat/

probability, you'll know that you need to spend more time working with Chapter 14 than with Chapter 12. In this method, you can take the practice test whenever makes the most sense for your personal goals.

Front-to-Back Method

Another way to use this book is the front-to-back method. In this method, you work through the book the way it is organized.

Start at Part I of the book and carefully read through the introductory section. This will help you understand the exam and how it's scored. Next, take a diagnostic test and analyze your results in Part II. Then, study the content sections in Parts III and IV. If you know your stronger and weaker skills, you might devote extra time to sections where you need the most improvement.

After you've reviewed the content, take a practice test in Part V. Taking a practice test will help you be more prepared on exam day. Even if you somehow don't improve

SPECIAL STUDY FEATURES

Peterson's *Master the™ SAT®* was designed to be easy to use so that you can locate the information you need. It includes several features to make your preparation easier.

Overview: Each chapter (excluding tests) begins with an overview listing the topics that will be covered in the chapter. You know immediately where to look for a topic that you need to work on.

Summing It Up: Each chapter (excluding tests) ends with a point-by-point summary that captures the most important points.

Practice Sets: In some chapters, you'll find Practice Sets that are designed to help you practice question types or specific concepts as you learn them. Use these practice exercises to ensure that you understand key concepts as they are introduced. In other chapters, you may find run-throughs of example questions in place of practice sets.

Test Yourself Exercises: In addition to Practice Sets, you'll notice that some chapters include Test Yourself sections at the end. These are similar to practice sets, but they are longer and offer you the opportunity to practice multiple new strategies or skills simultaneously. Each time you encounter a Test Yourself is an opportunity to check your progress so far and play with different strategies you've been considering for exam day.

Bonus Information

In addition, be sure to look out for the following test prep tools:

- **FYI:** *FYI* notes highlight critical information about the format of the SAT.
- **TIP:** *Tips* draw your attention to valuable concepts, advice, and shortcuts for tackling the tests or your study time.
- **ALERT:** Whenever you need to be careful of a common pitfall or test-taker trap, you'll find an *Alert.* This information reveals and helps eliminate the wrong turns many people take on the exam.

your score between the diagnostic test and practice test, the process of taking each can still help increase your score. This is because you become more familiar with the test format each time you try, which increases your confidence.

After you complete each test, review your answers with the explanations provided. If you still don't understand how to answer a certain question, you might ask a teacher or tutor for help. A review session with a friend might prove helpful, too.

EIGHT WAYS TO RAISE YOUR SCORE

When it comes to taking the SAT, some test-taking skills will help you more than others. There are concepts you can learn, techniques you can follow, and tricks you can use that will help you to perform your very best. Those strategies and tricks can be found throughout this book, but generally speaking, here are our picks for the eight best ways to raise your score:

1. **Regardless of your study plan, get started by reading Part I to familiarize yourself with the test formats.** Understanding the ins and outs of the SAT will make it easier to strategize when studying.

2. **Make sure you understand the information in Chapter 3 on effective learning and studying.** Alongside information on how to understand your diagnostic test results, we've included information on useful study techniques that support effective test prep. Make sure you understand and apply these techniques to make the most of your study time.

3. **Make sure to complete the exercises in each chapter you read.** You can do so as you go along to practice concepts right after you review them.

4. **Use your diagnostic test to plan your study time.** Spend most of your time studying concepts you struggled with, but save time to at least review familiar skills too.

5. **Revisit challenging chapters and their summaries.** Try to summarize each chapter like you were teaching the concepts to someone else. If there's one you are struggling to "teach," that's a good clue you need to review it. Making your own notes or study guides is a helpful way to reinforce concepts.

6. **After you have completed all the study sections, take your practice test.** When you go to take your practice test, make sure you are applying new test-taking strategies you've picked up, as well.

7. **During the last phase of your study, review your practice test.** Can you readily identify why questions you got wrong were wrong and how you'd answer them now? Can you spot any old mistakes you used to make and imagine what you'd do differently now that you've studied hard? This is a good way to refresh your knowledge of all the concepts you've learned and pinpoint where you can focus during any last-minute review.

8. **The night before your exam, RELAX.** You'll be prepared—you've already put in the work, so get some rest and go into your exam feeling awake and refreshed.

PETERSON'S® PUBLICATIONS

Peterson's publishes a full line of books—career preparation, education exploration, test prep, and financial aid. Peterson's books are available for purchase online at **www.petersons.com**. Sign up for one of our online subscription plans and you'll have access to our entire test prep catalog of more than 150 exams *plus* instructional videos, flashcards, interactive quizzes, and more! Our subscription plans allow you to study as quickly as you can or as slowly as you'd like.

GIVE US YOUR FEEDBACK

Peterson's publications can be found at your local bookstore and library, high school guidance offices, college libraries and career centers, and at **www.petersonsbooks.com**. Peterson's books are now also available as ebooks.

We welcome any comments or suggestions you may have about this publication. Your feedback will help us make educational dreams possible for you—and others like you.

YOU'RE WELL ON YOUR WAY TO SUCCESS

Remember that knowledge is power. We know you're eager to get to the diagnostic test and review, but taking the time in the next chapter to develop a thorough understanding of the exam from top to bottom will give you a real advantage—and put you ahead of the test-taking competition. We'll go through each section of the SAT so you'll be confident and prepared for test day success. Let's get started!

Good luck!

PART I

PREPARING FOR THE SAT®

CHAPTER

All about the SAT®

ALL ABOUT THE SAT®

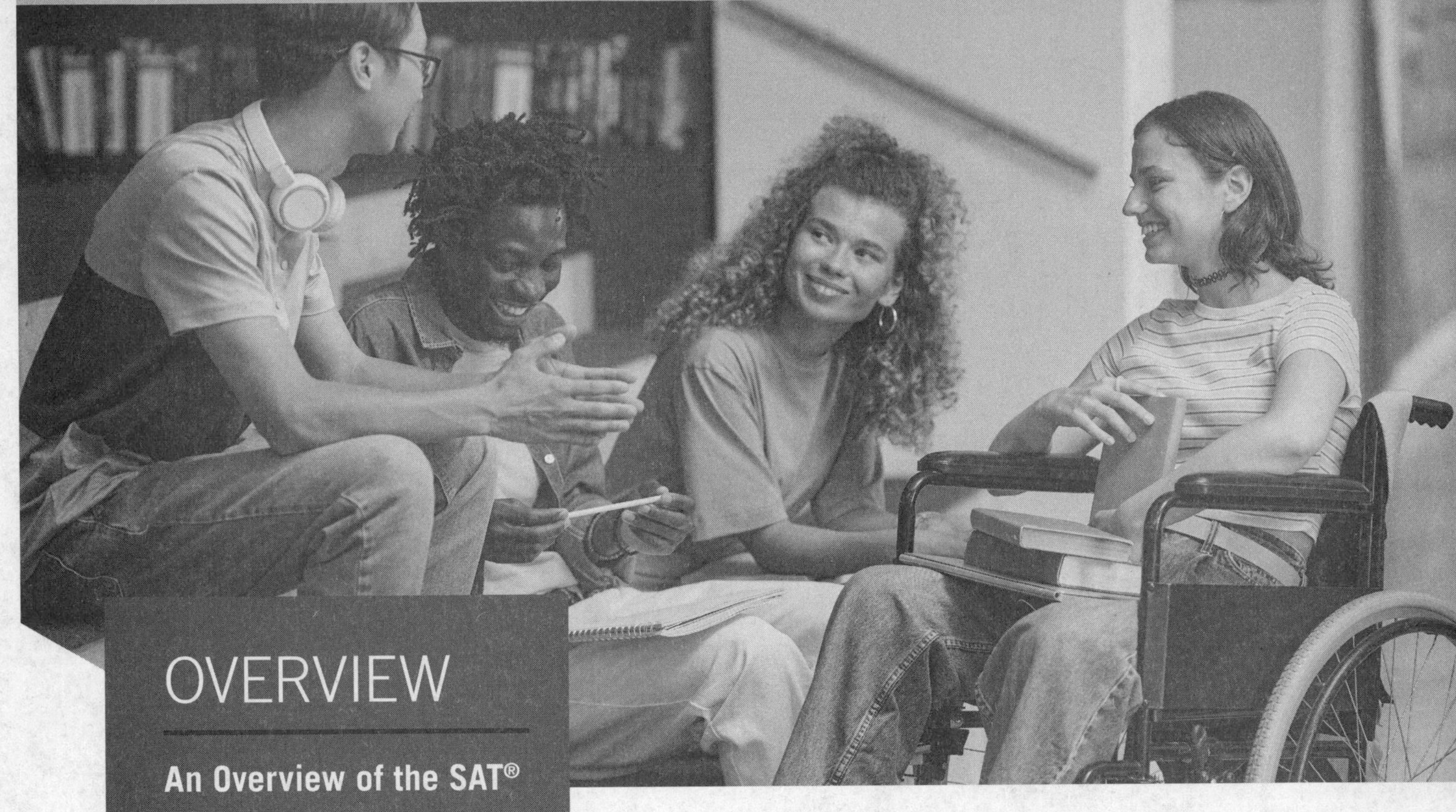

OVERVIEW

AN OVERVIEW OF THE SAT®

For almost one hundred years, the SAT Suite of Assessments has acted as a test of the skills and knowledge that students use every day—in class and in the world. The College Board—the maker of the SAT—has designed the SAT as a tool to help predict how students will perform academically as first-year college students—indicating overall college preparedness.

Before you jump straight into the review sections and test practice in the chapters that follow, it's worth your time and attention to get to know some of the SAT fundamentals first. The more you know about the exam and its different components, the more prepared you'll be on the big day, and the greater your advantage will be over other test takers. In addition, with the recent administration of the digital SAT, there are changes to the test that you need to know about before diving in.

1

Why Does the SAT Matter?

Along with your academic record (which includes your GPA, your record of extracurricular activities, and any awards, distinctions, and letters of recommendation written on your behalf), your scores on the SAT will be an important factor in your college applications. Your scores provide a single standardized means of comparison that college admissions staff will use to help determine whether you're a good fit for their school and are ready to handle college-level subject material.

If the schools you plan on applying to require the SAT, it's in your best interest to take the exam as seriously as your GPA or any other admission requirement.

Should I Take the SAT?

Each college and university has a unique set of requirements to be considered for admission—know the rules of the schools to which you plan to apply so you can determine if you need to take the SAT. As a result of the COVID-19 pandemic, fewer institutions are requiring students to submit SAT scores as part of their college applications. Even if the schools you're applying to don't require the SAT, it might be worth taking the exam as a supplement to your other application materials. The SAT can help college admissions departments gauge your academic proficiency in several key subject areas and help you demonstrate that you're ready and prepared to handle the rigors of college-level coursework.

How Has the COVID-19 Pandemic Affected SAT Scores?

The average total SAT score for the high school class of 2022 was 1050 (out of 1600), which is the lowest since the test changed its format in 2016. While it was only a slight decline compared to the average score in 2021, the College Board recognizes the impact of the COVID-19 pandemic on these results. Due to the disruptions caused by the pandemic, many students either had to postpone taking the SAT or take it under less-than-ideal circumstances. As a result, some test takers may have been unable to prepare as thoroughly as they would have liked, while others may have faced additional stress and anxiety related to the pandemic. Moreover, the shift to remote learning and the closure of schools significantly impacted students' educational experiences, which in turn likely affected their SAT scores. Some students may have contracted COVID-19, which could have limited their ability to participate fully in remote learning. Others may have experienced different obstacles, such as limited access to internet, the pressure caused by financial or caretaking responsibilities, or other distractions and sources of stress. These factors, among many others, led some colleges and universities to drop the requirement for prospective students to submit SAT scores as part of their applications. However, many institutions still require applicants to submit their SAT scores to be eligible for admission. They may also require SAT scores to qualify students for certain types of scholarships or aid.

As you review the concepts covered in this book, consider how the pandemic affected your own education. Did you thrive or struggle with the shift to remote learning? Were there certain concepts or ideas that you weren't able to fully grasp? Are there any content areas that would be helpful for you to review prior to taking the SAT? Throughout this book, we encourage you to reflect on your own learning and to identify opportunities to learn or relearn concepts that you might have missed during your education. Because the COVID-19 pandemic was such an unprecedented disruption to education and society at large, there's no shame in acknowledging areas where you could benefit from additional review time. This book is intended to be a valuable tool and reference guide to help you every step of the way.

FYI

If at any point you feel like you could benefit from more focused instruction on a given topic or if you would like additional opportunities for practice, visit www.petersons.com/testprep/sat to learn more. To access your free online adaptive-style test, go to www.petersons.com/satbook and follow the directions for registration.

THE DIGITAL SAT®

The days of bubble-lined SAT answer sheets have ended. Starting in spring 2023 for international students and spring 2024 for students in the US, the SAT is a digital adaptive test. While the need for certain testing accommodations may result in some students being able to take a paper form of the new format, the majority of students will make use of the College Board's digital delivery and testing system. Under the new procedure, students will bring and use their own approved (or a College Board-provided) digital device to take the test at SAT testing centers.

What's Changed?

Digital delivery allows the use of adaptive testing. The digital SAT uses a multistage adaptive testing (MST) method. What that means is each test section is divided into two equal-length and separately timed stages, each composed of a module of questions. The first module contains a range of easy, medium, and hard questions, in which students demonstrate their skills before continuing to the second module. The second module question levels are based on how the students perform in the first module; in general, questions are either more difficult or less difficult than those in the first module. In other

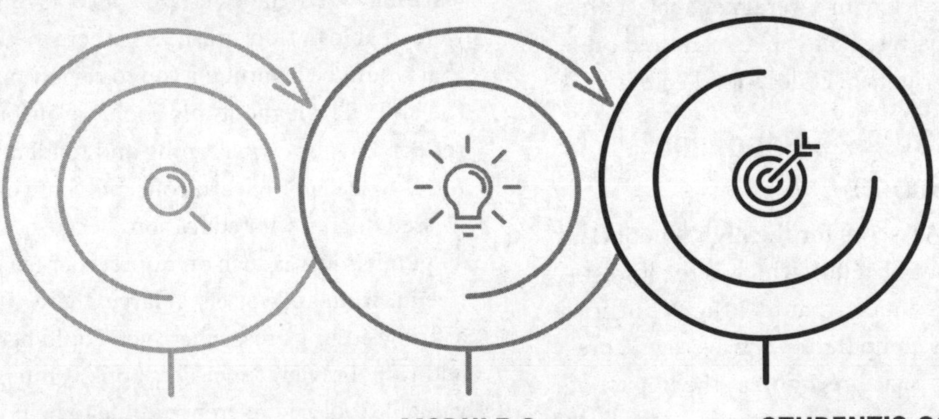
Digital SAT Adaptive Testing Model
MODULE 1
Students are given a broad mix of easy, medium, and hard questions.
MODULE 2
Students are given a targeted mix of questions of varying difficulties based on their performance in Module 1.
STUDENT'S SCORE

words, the test "adapts," presenting questions more appropriate to a student's performance level. The MST method results in shorter, more efficient tests and provides a tailored assessment experience for each student.

In addition to adaptive testing, other user-experience changes resulting from the SAT transition to a digital format include the following:

- Students and educators receive scores in days instead of weeks.
- Score reports connect students to local two-year college, workforce training program, and career option information and resources.
- The tests are more secure. A digital format assigns every student a comparable but unique test form, making answer sharing practically impossible.
- Test administration is more flexible for states, schools, and districts.

Test-specific results from the transition include:

- The test length has been reduced from 3 hours to 2 hours and 14 minutes.
- A single Reading and Writing section has replaced both the Reading and Writing and Language Tests.
    - This section features many short passages instead of just a few long texts, which will expose students to a wider range of college-level reading topics.
    - The test still includes paired passages, but only one question is associated with each passage or passage pair.
- The Math section is no longer divided into separately timed no-calculator and calculator-allowed portions.
    - Calculator use is allowed throughout the entire Math section.
    - Students can take advantage of the built-in graphing calculator in the Bluebook™ test delivery application or use their own approved calculator on test day.
    - Word problem lengths are shorter, so students can focus on demonstrating their math skills without having to navigate through longer contexts.
- Test takers have more time, on average, to answer each question, shifting the test's measures to knowledge and skills rather than test-taking speed.

The Bluebook™ Testing Application

The SAT is delivered via Bluebook, a test delivery application that you will need to download onto your device before test day. Bluebook is designed to enhance students' test-taking experience:

- In the Reading and Writing section, students can highlight and annotate text.
- A built-in graphing calculator is available throughout the entire Math section.
- Students can navigate freely through a given module to preview upcoming questions.
- Students can mark and return to an earlier question within a module as time permits.
- Students can use the interface to eliminate answer choices that they think are wrong.
- Students have access to a list of common formulas in the Math section.
- A clock counts down the time remaining in each module. If a student chooses to hide the timer, an alert sounds when 5 minutes remain in the module.

Getting ready to use Bluebook to take the SAT is a simple process. First, go to https://bluebook.app.collegeboard.org/ to download the app to your testing device and get installation instructions. The College Board recommends taking the SAT practice test in Bluebook at least two weeks before test day to allow you to familiarize yourself with the app functionality and assessment features and help you to recognize the question types you will see on test day, know how to properly enter answers, and try all the testing tools.

Five days before your test, complete a quick exam setup. The Bluebook application will confirm that your device meets all requirements, then it will download your test

Digital SAT Testing Timeline

STEP 1: Now
Download and install the Bluebook app.

01

STEP 2: Two weeks before test day
Take a full-length practice test in Bluebook.

02

STEP 3: Five days before test day
Complete exam setup in Bluebook and get your admission ticket.

03

STEP 4: On test day
Arrive on time (check your admission ticket).

04

and generate your admission ticket. You can either print your admission ticket or email it to yourself to have it handy on test day.

Using Your Testing Device

Students can take the digital SAT on a Windows laptop or tablet, a Mac laptop, an iPad, or a school-managed Chromebook. In addition, students who are taking the SAT on a weekend and do not have access to a device can request to borrow one from the College Board for use on test day. For information about requesting a device from the College Board, go to https://satsuite.collegeboard.org/digital/device-lending.

On test day, you will connect your device to the test site's internet to start and complete testing. Bluebook is designed to withstand internet outages, so if any internet connection interruption occurs during testing, you can continue taking the test without disruption. If your computer battery runs down, you can simply plug in, restart your device, and pick up where you left off—your work will be saved, and you won't lose any testing time. However, you should bring your device fully charged on test day, as there may be limited access to power outlets in the testing room.

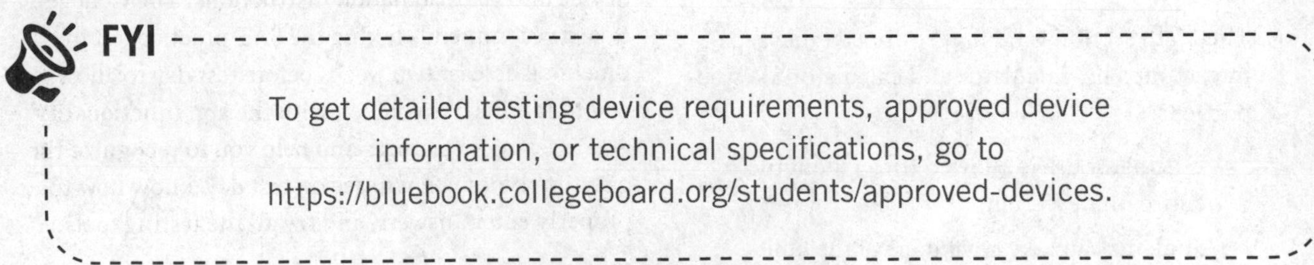

FYI
To get detailed testing device requirements, approved device information, or technical specifications, go to https://bluebook.collegeboard.org/students/approved-devices.

WHAT TO EXPECT ON THE SAT®

The SAT is designed to measure the skills and knowledge that students are learning in school that matter most for college and career readiness. The SAT consists of two sections: 1) Reading and Writing, and 2) Math. Students have 64 minutes to complete the Reading and Writing section and 70 minutes to complete the Math section.

Each section is composed of two equal-length modules of test questions. Each Reading and Writing module lasts 32 minutes, and each Math module lasts 35 minutes. Each module is separately timed, and students can move backward and forward among questions in each module during the allotted time. When time runs out on the first module of each section, the test delivery application moves students to the second module. After completing the Reading and Writing section, students will have a 10-minute break before starting the Math section.

FYI

The College Board likes to preview their questions for developing future versions of the SAT, so a small number of indistinguishable, unscored items (the "pretest" questions) are included in each section to aid with the test development process.

The total testing time for the SAT is 2 hours and 14 minutes. Here's the official SAT breakdown in the table below.

The Reading and Writing (RW) Section

The SAT Reading and Writing (RW) section focuses on key elements of comprehension, rhetoric, and language use. This section consists of 54 multiple-choice questions that measure students' college and career readiness in literacy; that is, it tests your ability to read critically; use information and ideas in texts; analyze the craft and structure of texts; revise texts to improve the rhetorical expression of ideas; and edit texts to conform to core conventions of Standard English.

SAT® BREAKDOWN

Section	Reading and Writing (RW)	Math
Format	Two-stage adaptive test design: one Reading and Writing section administered through two separately timed modules	Two-stage adaptive test design: one Math section administered through two separately timed modules
Test Length (number of operational & pretest questions)	**Module 1:** 25 operational questions and 2 pretest questions	**Module 1:** 20 operational questions and 2 pretest questions
	Module 2: 25 operational questions and 2 pretest questions	**Module 2:** 20 operational questions and 2 pretest questions
Time per Stage	**Module 1:** 32 minutes	**Module 1:** 35 minutes
	Module 2: 32 minutes	**Module 2:** 35 minutes
Total Number of Questions	54 questions	44 questions
Total Time Allotted	64 minutes	70 minutes

Each item consists of a short passage (or passage pair) and a single related question, rather a set of questions related to a longer passage. The texts you encounter on exam day represent those typically encountered in a student's first-year college coursework and will span a variety of subject areas. Questions on the Reading and Writing section represent one of four content domains: 1) Craft and Structure, 2) Information and Ideas, 3) Standard English Conventions, and 4) Expression of Ideas.

Questions from all four domains appear in each Reading and Writing section module, always in the order of Craft and Structure, Information and Ideas, Standard English Conventions, and Expression of Ideas questions. Questions within the Craft and Structure, Information and Ideas, and Expression of Ideas content domains that assess similar skills and knowledge are grouped together and arranged in order of increasing difficulty. Questions in the Standard English Conventions content domain increase in difficulty as the test progresses, regardless of the convention being tested.

Here's a brief overview of the Reading and Writing section content domain descriptions.

CRAFT AND STRUCTURE (≈28% OF RW SECTION/13–15 QUESTIONS)

These questions assess your ability to demonstrate the analysis, comprehension, reasoning, synthesis, and vocabulary skills and knowledge needed to understand and use high-utility words and phrases in context, evaluate texts rhetorically, and make connections between topically related texts.

Specific Skill/Knowledge Testing points for the Craft and Structure content domain:

- Words in Context
- Text Structure and Purpose
- Cross-Text Connections

INFORMATION AND IDEAS (≈26% OF RW SECTION/12–14 QUESTIONS)

These questions measure your knowledge and your comprehension, analysis, and reasoning skills and also assess your ability to locate, interpret, evaluate, and integrate information and ideas from texts/informational graphics (tables, bar graphs, and line graphs).
Specific Skill/Knowledge Testing points for the Information and Ideas content domain:

- Central Ideas and Details
- Command of Evidence
  - Textual
  - Quantitative
- Inferences

STANDARD ENGLISH CONVENTIONS (≈26% OF RW SECTION/11–15 QUESTIONS)

These questions evaluate your ability to edit texts to conform to core conventions of Standard English sentence structure, usage, and punctuation.

Specific Skill/Knowledge Testing points for the Standard English Conventions content domain:

- Boundaries
- Form, Structure, and Sense

EXPRESSION OF IDEAS (≈20% OF RW SECTION/8–12 QUESTIONS)

These questions assess your ability to revise texts to increase the effectiveness of written expression and meet specific rhetorical goals.

Specific Skill/Knowledge Testing points for the Expression of Ideas content domain:

- Rhetorical Synthesis
- Transitions

The Math Section

The SAT Math section focuses on proficiency in key elements of algebra, advanced math, problem-solving and data analysis, and geometry and trigonometry. This 44-question section consists of multiple-choice and student-produced response (SPR) questions that measure students' fluency with, understanding of, and ability to apply the math concepts, skills, and practices consistent with college-level work.

The SAT Math section consists of 44 multiple-choice and student-produced response (SPR) questions that measure students' fluency with, understanding of, and ability to apply the math concepts, skills, and practices consistent with college-level work. Questions from all four content domains appear in each test module. Across each module, questions increase in difficulty as the test progresses.

Here's a brief overview of the Math section content domain descriptions.

ALGEBRA
(≈35% OF MATH SECTION/13–15 QUESTIONS)

For these questions, you will be asked to analyze, create, and solve linear equations and inequalities and to analyze and solve various types of equations and systems of equations using multiple techniques.

Specific Skill/Knowledge Testing points for the Algebra content domain:

- Linear equations in one variable
- Linear equations in two variables
- Linear functions
- Systems of two linear equations in two variables
- Linear inequalities in one or two variables

ADVANCED MATH
(≈35% OF MATH SECTION/13–15 QUESTIONS)

These questions will evaluate your proficiency with the skills and knowledge necessary to progress to more advanced math courses, including an understanding of absolute value, quadratic, exponential, polynomial, rational, radical, and other nonlinear equations.

Specific Skill/Knowledge Testing points for the Advanced Math content domain:

- Equivalent expressions
- Nonlinear equations in one variable and systems of equations in two variables
- Nonlinear functions

PROBLEM-SOLVING AND DATA ANALYSIS
(≈15% OF MATH SECTION/5–7 QUESTIONS)

In these questions, you will be asked to apply quantitative reasoning to ratios, rates, and proportional relationships; demonstrate understanding and application of unit rate; and analyze and interpret one- and two-variable data.

Specific Skill/Knowledge Testing points for the Problem-Solving and Data Analysis content domain:

- Ratios, rates, proportional relationships, and units
- Percentages
- One-variable data: distributions and measures of center and spread
- Two-variable data: models and scatterplots
- Probability and conditional probability
- Inference from sample statistics and margin of error
- Evaluating statistical claims: observational studies and experiments

GEOMETRY AND TRIGONOMETRY (≈15% OF MATH SECTION/5–7 QUESTIONS)

These questions will test your ability to solve problems focusing on area and volume; lines, angles, triangles, and trigonometry; and circles.

Specific Skill/Knowledge Testing points for the Geometry and Trigonometry content domain:

- Area and volume
- Lines, angles, and triangles
- Right triangles and trigonometry
- Circles

Your Target SAT Score and Test Goals

Don't forget that you're a unique individual with unique goals for the SAT. Do not feel pressured to compete with other students—determine what your goals are for the SAT and then work toward achieving them. Depending on which colleges and universities you're applying to, you might need to aim for the best score you can get, while other schools might only require scores that fall in the middle or lower range. No matter what score you're aiming for, we'll provide tips and tricks throughout this book to help you get the score you want on the SAT.

The best path to hitting your target score on the SAT is to fully understand and become comfortable with the structure, timing, and format of the test and to make sure your skills on each test are razor-sharp. The most effective approach for SAT success is thorough practice and review with your individual strengths and weaknesses in mind. Make the most of the material presented in this book between now and test day to make your test goals a reality!

HOW THE SAT® IS SCORED

The SAT is scored on a 1600-point scale. The SAT generates three scores: a score for the Reading and Writing section, a score for the Math section, and a total score. The total score is based on a student's performance on the entire assessment and is the arithmetic sum of the two section scores. Each section score is calculated based on the number of correctly answered questions in both modules and then translated into a number between 200 and 800. Your two section scores will be added together to get your total scaled score, which will be a number between 400 and 1600.

WHEN TO TAKE THE SAT®

The SAT is typically offered on one Saturday morning in August, October, November, December, March, May, and June. Tests are also offered on select Sundays, usually the Sunday after each Saturday test date, for students who cannot take the test on Saturday due to religious observance. Students who wish to take the SAT exam on a Sunday must provide a letter printed on stationery from their house of worship explaining the religious reason for the request. An official religious leader must sign the letter.

Select the test date that works best for you and your specific goals. It is best to choose a test date at least two months ahead of the application deadlines for the institutions to which you plan to apply.

FYI

The digital SAT is designed to eliminate the need for students to rely on familiar test-taking tricks and strategies just to complete the test—now you can focus on demonstrating your skills and knowledge, not your test-taking speed.

FYI

If you elect to take the SAT during a designated SAT School Day, you will receive information from your school or school district regarding registration requirements and any fees you may need to pay. You DO NOT register for SAT School Day through the College Board. Pay careful attention to the requirements set forth by your school or district, and contact your guidance counselor with any questions that you may have.

For information related to specific test dates, registration deadlines, cancellations, and late registration, go to https://satsuite.collegeboard.org/sat/registration/dates-deadlines.

Although the digital SAT implementation greatly reduces turnaround time for receiving scores, make sure that your testing date will allow you enough time to receive your scores before you need to apply, whether that's for early decision, early action, or regular decision.

However, when you plan to take the SAT, there is something even more important than the school application deadlines: you need to select a test date that works best with your schedule. Some states—such as Colorado, Illinois, and Tennessee, among others—participate in SAT School Day, a weekday when the SAT is administered to high school juniors. And while your state may require you to take the exam on that test date, it doesn't have to be the *only* time you do so. Ideally, you should allow yourself at least two to three months to use this book to prepare. Many students like to take the test in March of their junior year, before final exams, the prom, and other end-of-the-year distractions. Taking the test in March also gives students early feedback as to how they are scoring. If they are dissatisfied with their scores, there are opportunities to take the test again in the spring or following fall. But your schedule might not easily accommodate a March testing. Or maybe you simply prefer to prepare during a different time of year. If that's the case, just pick another date.

For a complete list of key dates, registration requirements and deadlines, options regarding special circumstances, and to sign up for test update alerts, visit https://satsuite.collegeboard.org/.

REGISTERING FOR THE SAT®

Now that you have a better understanding of the structure, format, timing, and scoring of the SAT—and have determined that taking the SAT is right for you—the next important step is signing up for the test.

Online Registration

You should register for the SAT exam at least six weeks before your testing date. That way you will avoid late registration fees and increase your chances of taking the exam at your first-choice testing center.

Registering online is the quickest (and preferred) method, and you will receive immediate registration confirmation. The registration information you provide is used to create your test day admission ticket. You will need to pay by credit card, and you will need to upload a photo with your registration. The photo you submit will be compared to the photo ID you bring with you on test day. For more information, visit https://satsuite.collegeboard.org/sat/registration/online-registration.

Registration Fees

At the time of this book's printing, the fee for the SAT is $60. To determine if you are eligible for a fee waiver, visit https://satsuite.collegeboard.org/sat/registration/fee-waivers.

Students who qualify for a fee waiver may also be eligible to apply to college, send their scores, and apply for financial aid (through CSS Profile) to as many colleges as they choose, at no cost.

Registration Photo

The photo you provide when you register will be compared to the photo ID you bring with you on test day. Photos must be properly focused with a full-face view. The photo must be clearly identifiable as you, and it must match your appearance on test day.

Choose a photo that:

- Shows only you—no other people in the shot
- Shows a head-and-shoulders view, with the entire face, both eyes, and hair clearly visible (head coverings are allowed if worn for religious purposes)
- Is properly focused and has no dark spots or shadows

To see examples of acceptable photos, visit https://satsuite.collegeboard.org/sat/registration/online-registration/photo-requirements.

GETTING READY FOR TEST DAY

In addition to thoroughly preparing for each of the subject sections on the SAT, be sure to brush up on test day fundamentals and focus on getting ready for the big day—including selecting a test day and location, understanding what to expect when you arrive at your test center, and knowing what to bring and what to leave at home. Taking these steps will help you avoid surprises and reduce anxiety.

Getting ready for the SAT is essential, but getting ready for what you'll encounter on exam day is just as important to your success.

What to Expect, What to Bring, and What to Leave at Home

Test centers open at 7:45 a.m. and doors close at 8:00 a.m. unless otherwise noted on your admission ticket. Testing begins between 8:15 and 8:45 a.m., and by this time, you should be present and in your seat. Plan to arrive a little early, giving you time to relax, get

comfortable, and get settled into test-taking mode; you definitely don't want to deal with the stress of racing the clock to avoid missing the start of the test. If you arrive late, you will not be admitted to the test. Consider making a practice run to the test center in advance of test day so that you'll know just how long you'll need the morning of the exam.

When you arrive at your test center, the staff will check your photo ID and admission ticket, allow you into the room, bring you to your seat, and provide you with the required test materials. For more information about test day procedures, visit https://satsuite.collegeboard.org/digital/what-to-bring-do/what-to-expect.

Your Admission Ticket

You must have a legible copy of your admission ticket for entry into the testing center. To print your admission ticket, go into Bluebook one to five days before your test day, select your test, and complete the exam setup. The app will generate your admission ticket, which you can either print out or email to yourself. If you choose to present your admission ticket on your mobile phone, you must turn your phone in to a test administration staff member after check-in or store it away from your assigned desk during the test administration.

Your Photo ID

You will also need an acceptable form of identification that includes a photograph for admission into the testing center. The photo must be clearly identifiable as you, and it must match both your registration photo and your appearance on test day. Acceptable examples include:

- Government-issued driver's license
- Government-issued non-driver ID card
- Official school identification card (from the school you currently attend)
- Government-issued passport or US Global Entry identification card
- Government-issued military or national identification card
- SAT Student ID Form: must be prepared by the school you currently attend or a notary, if homeschooled (only accepted in US centers for students under 21 years of age)

For a detailed ID requirement checklist, visit https://satsuite.collegeboard.org/digital/what-to-bring-do/id-requirements.

Your Test Day Checklist

Make absolutely certain that you bring the following items with you on test day:

- Your fully charged testing device with the Bluebook application installed
- Your up-to-date admission ticket
- Acceptable photo ID
- Pencils or pens for scratch work
- An acceptable calculator for use on the Math section of the test (there will be an embedded graphing calculator available to use within Bluebook)
- Face covering (if required at your test center)

Do not bring the following items with you to the test room, or keep them completely silent and out of sight while taking the exam—you will absolutely not be able to use them, including during the break:

- Mobile phone (these can be used to present the admission ticket, but after check-in must be collected or stored away from desks)
- The following electronic devices: cameras, headphones/ear buds, smart watches, and fitness bands
- Reading material, textbooks, unapproved reference materials (including dictionaries and other study aids), scratch paper, and any other outside notes
- Highlighters, colored pens and pencils, or correction tape/fluid
- Compasses, rulers, protractors, or cutting devices
- Unacceptable calculators that have computer-style (QWERTY) keyboards, use paper tape, make noise, use a power cord, or can connect to the internet
- Privacy screens
- Weapons or firearms
- Separate timers of any type

FYI

Epinephrine auto-injectors (like EpiPens) are permitted without the need for accommodation approval. They must be placed in a clear bag and stored under the student's desk during testing. For policies on other medications and medical devices, contact Services for Students with Disabilities. For information about requesting accommodations, go to https://satsuite.collegeboard.org/digital/accommodations-digital-testing.

Penalties for possession of prohibited devices may include immediate dismissal from the testing site, cancellation of scores, and confiscation and content inspection of the prohibited device.

There are a few optional items you may consider bringing—they might be nice to have during the test or during the break:

- A charging cable if your testing device can't hold a charge for 3 hours or more
- A bag or backpack
- A drink or snacks (for your break)
- A backup testing device

NEXT STEPS

Okay—so now you have a better understanding of the SAT fundamentals, including the structure, format, and timing of the exam, how it's all scored, what you need to do to register, and what you should expect on the day of the exam—this is powerful information that will help set you up for success on test day.

Now it's time to move on to building your SAT study plan and making the most of the time you have between now and test day to study, practice, and review each test section as you work toward achieving your best possible scores. And remember—we'll be with you every step of the way. Let's begin!

SUMMING IT UP

- The SAT is delivered digitally via the Bluebook testing application. Students take the exam by connecting their approved device (or a school-provided device) to the internet at testing centers.
- Bluebook functions designed to enhance students' test-taking experience include:
    - Text highlighting and annotation (in the Reading and Writing section)
    - A built-in calculator with graphing capabilities (throughout the entire Math section)
    - Question preview capability
    - Question flagging for returning to review as time permits
    - Answer choice elimination
    - List of common math formulas
    - A module timer with a "5 minutes remaining" alarm
- The Bluebook testing application generates your SAT admission ticket upon student completion of the exam setup process, so be sure to complete the process one to five days before test day and print out or email your admission ticket to yourself.
- The SAT uses a multistage adaptive testing (MST) method, which divides each section of the exam into two modules. Questions in the first module are a range of easy, medium, and hard difficulty levels. The difficulty level of the questions in the second module is determined by the student's performance in the first module.
- The SAT consists of two sections: Reading and Writing, and Math, with a total of 98 questions. You will have 2 hours and 14 minutes to complete the exam.
    - The Reading and Writing section consists of 54 multiple-choice questions, each paired with a passage (or passage pair), that tests your ability to read critically; use information and ideas in texts; analyze the craft and structure of texts; revise texts to improve the rhetorical expression of ideas; and edit texts to conform to core conventions of Standard English.
    - The 44-question Math section is a combination of multiple-choice and student-generated response questions that test your knowledge of linear and nonlinear equations, linear and nonlinear functions, systems of equations, proportional relationships, unit rate, one- and two-variable data, geometry, trigonometry, statistics, and probability.

- Your scores on the SAT will be an important variable that college admissions staff will use to help determine whether or not you're a good fit for their school and are ready to handle college-level subject material.
    - For each section—Reading and Writing, and Math—the number of questions you answer correctly will be tabulated, becoming your score for that section.
    - Your scores are then converted into scale scores to give you a test score for each section that ranges from 200 (low) to 800 (high).
    - Your total scaled score is the sum of the two section scaled scores. The maximum score you can get on the SAT is 1600.
- The SAT is administered several times a year—in August, October, November, December, March, May, and June. Select the test date that works best for you.
- Register for the test online through the SAT website. During registration, you will choose where and when you will take the test. Registration fees apply.
- The photograph you provide when you register will be compared to the photo ID you bring with you on test day. The photo must be clearly identifiable as you, and it must match your appearance and photo ID on test day.
- Be aware of the items you *must* bring, items you *may* bring, and items you *should not* bring under any circumstances to the test center.
    - Your fully charged testing device, admission ticket, and an acceptable photo ID are your top three "must bring" items.
    - Penalties for possession of prohibited devices may include immediate dismissal from the testing site, cancellation of scores, and confiscation and content inspection of the prohibited device.

PART II

DETERMINING STRENGTHS AND WEAKNESSES

CHAPTER

SAT® Diagnostic Test

SAT® DIAGNOSTIC TEST

DIAGNOSTIC TEST

This diagnostic test is designed to help you recognize your strengths and weaknesses at the start of your preparation for the SAT. It covers every section of the SAT. In Chapter 3, we'll discuss how you can use your results to help guide your study time.

SAT® DIAGNOSTIC TEST ANSWER SHEET

Reading and Writing

Module 1

1. Ⓐ Ⓑ Ⓒ Ⓓ	7. Ⓐ Ⓑ Ⓒ Ⓓ	13. Ⓐ Ⓑ Ⓒ Ⓓ	19. Ⓐ Ⓑ Ⓒ Ⓓ	25. Ⓐ Ⓑ Ⓒ Ⓓ
2. Ⓐ Ⓑ Ⓒ Ⓓ	8. Ⓐ Ⓑ Ⓒ Ⓓ	14. Ⓐ Ⓑ Ⓒ Ⓓ	20. Ⓐ Ⓑ Ⓒ Ⓓ	26. Ⓐ Ⓑ Ⓒ Ⓓ
3. Ⓐ Ⓑ Ⓒ Ⓓ	9. Ⓐ Ⓑ Ⓒ Ⓓ	15. Ⓐ Ⓑ Ⓒ Ⓓ	21. Ⓐ Ⓑ Ⓒ Ⓓ	27. Ⓐ Ⓑ Ⓒ Ⓓ
4. Ⓐ Ⓑ Ⓒ Ⓓ	10. Ⓐ Ⓑ Ⓒ Ⓓ	16. Ⓐ Ⓑ Ⓒ Ⓓ	22. Ⓐ Ⓑ Ⓒ Ⓓ	
5. Ⓐ Ⓑ Ⓒ Ⓓ	11. Ⓐ Ⓑ Ⓒ Ⓓ	17. Ⓐ Ⓑ Ⓒ Ⓓ	23. Ⓐ Ⓑ Ⓒ Ⓓ	
6. Ⓐ Ⓑ Ⓒ Ⓓ	12. Ⓐ Ⓑ Ⓒ Ⓓ	18. Ⓐ Ⓑ Ⓒ Ⓓ	24. Ⓐ Ⓑ Ⓒ Ⓓ	

Reading and Writing

Module 2

1. Ⓐ Ⓑ Ⓒ Ⓓ	7. Ⓐ Ⓑ Ⓒ Ⓓ	13. Ⓐ Ⓑ Ⓒ Ⓓ	19. Ⓐ Ⓑ Ⓒ Ⓓ	25. Ⓐ Ⓑ Ⓒ Ⓓ
2. Ⓐ Ⓑ Ⓒ Ⓓ	8. Ⓐ Ⓑ Ⓒ Ⓓ	14. Ⓐ Ⓑ Ⓒ Ⓓ	20. Ⓐ Ⓑ Ⓒ Ⓓ	26. Ⓐ Ⓑ Ⓒ Ⓓ
3. Ⓐ Ⓑ Ⓒ Ⓓ	9. Ⓐ Ⓑ Ⓒ Ⓓ	15. Ⓐ Ⓑ Ⓒ Ⓓ	21. Ⓐ Ⓑ Ⓒ Ⓓ	27. Ⓐ Ⓑ Ⓒ Ⓓ
4. Ⓐ Ⓑ Ⓒ Ⓓ	10. Ⓐ Ⓑ Ⓒ Ⓓ	16. Ⓐ Ⓑ Ⓒ Ⓓ	22. Ⓐ Ⓑ Ⓒ Ⓓ	
5. Ⓐ Ⓑ Ⓒ Ⓓ	11. Ⓐ Ⓑ Ⓒ Ⓓ	17. Ⓐ Ⓑ Ⓒ Ⓓ	23. Ⓐ Ⓑ Ⓒ Ⓓ	
6. Ⓐ Ⓑ Ⓒ Ⓓ	12. Ⓐ Ⓑ Ⓒ Ⓓ	18. Ⓐ Ⓑ Ⓒ Ⓓ	24. Ⓐ Ⓑ Ⓒ Ⓓ	

Math

Module 1

1. Ⓐ Ⓑ Ⓒ Ⓓ
2. Ⓐ Ⓑ Ⓒ Ⓓ
3. ________
4. Ⓐ Ⓑ Ⓒ Ⓓ
5. Ⓐ Ⓑ Ⓒ Ⓓ
6. Ⓐ Ⓑ Ⓒ Ⓓ
7. Ⓐ Ⓑ Ⓒ Ⓓ
8. ________
9. Ⓐ Ⓑ Ⓒ Ⓓ
10. ________
11. Ⓐ Ⓑ Ⓒ Ⓓ
12. Ⓐ Ⓑ Ⓒ Ⓓ
13. Ⓐ Ⓑ Ⓒ Ⓓ
14. ________
15. Ⓐ Ⓑ Ⓒ Ⓓ
16. Ⓐ Ⓑ Ⓒ Ⓓ
17. Ⓐ Ⓑ Ⓒ Ⓓ
18. Ⓐ Ⓑ Ⓒ Ⓓ
19. ________
20. Ⓐ Ⓑ Ⓒ Ⓓ
21. Ⓐ Ⓑ Ⓒ Ⓓ
22. Ⓐ Ⓑ Ⓒ Ⓓ

Math

Module 2

1. Ⓐ Ⓑ Ⓒ Ⓓ
2. Ⓐ Ⓑ Ⓒ Ⓓ
3. Ⓐ Ⓑ Ⓒ Ⓓ
4. ________
5. ________
6. Ⓐ Ⓑ Ⓒ Ⓓ
7. ________
8. Ⓐ Ⓑ Ⓒ Ⓓ
9. Ⓐ Ⓑ Ⓒ Ⓓ
10. Ⓐ Ⓑ Ⓒ Ⓓ
11. Ⓐ Ⓑ Ⓒ Ⓓ
12. Ⓐ Ⓑ Ⓒ Ⓓ
13. Ⓐ Ⓑ Ⓒ Ⓓ
14. Ⓐ Ⓑ Ⓒ Ⓓ
15. Ⓐ Ⓑ Ⓒ Ⓓ
16. ________
17. Ⓐ Ⓑ Ⓒ Ⓓ
18. Ⓐ Ⓑ Ⓒ Ⓓ
19. Ⓐ Ⓑ Ⓒ Ⓓ
20. ________
21. Ⓐ Ⓑ Ⓒ Ⓓ
22. ________

READING AND WRITING

Module 1

27 Questions—32 Minutes

Directions: The questions in this section address a number of important reading and writing skills. Each question includes one or more passages, which may include a table or graph. Read each passage and question carefully, and then choose the best answer to the question based on the passage(s).

All questions in this section are multiple-choice with four answer choices. Each question has a single best answer.

1. All over the world, people gather for festivals to celebrate events, mark holidays, foster community, and engage in shared cultural traditions. The tendency toward festival-style gathering is common across human cultures, meaning that the world is full of beautiful festival traditions. However, cultures vary, so just as there are certain types of celebrations that appear over and over, like weddings and harvest festivals, there are others that are truly ___________.

   Which choice completes the text with the most logical and precise word or phrase?

   A. truncated

   B. nonchalant

   C. singular

   D. mysterious

2. Occasionally, scientists get creative when deciding what a group of animals should be called. This often takes the form of alliteration, such as in a flamboyance of flamingos, a caravan of camels, a wisdom of wombats, a coalition of cheetahs, a shiver of sharks, or a pandemonium of parrots. Other groups have dramatic names that ___________ the unique characteristics of the species in question, as is the case with a quiver of cobras, a murder of crows, a thunder of hippopotami, a conspiracy of lemurs, or an ostentation of peacocks.

   Which choice completes the text with the most logical and precise word or phrase?

   A. allude about

   B. allude to

   C. elude about

   D. elude to

CONTINUE

3. It might sound like an idyllic place for specters to cohabitate, but the term "ghost town" refers to a town that has long since been left abandoned or uninhabited. While buildings and other artifacts remain as proof of the life that once lit up the streets, ghost towns are generally empty, decaying, and proverbially returning to nature. There are roughly 3,800 ghost towns in the United States alone. Most were founded during gold and oil rushes or periods of thriving industrial development, then abandoned when the industries were no longer lucrative or resources ran out.

   As used in the text, what does the word "lucrative" most nearly mean?

   A. Profitable

   B. Expensive

   C. Habitable

   D. Safe

4. The following text is from Edna St. Vincent Millay's 1923 poem "The Spring and the Fall."

   In the fall of the year, in the fall of the year,
   I walked the road beside my dear.
   The rooks went up with a raucous trill.
   I hear them still, in the fall of the year.
   He laughed at all I dared to praise,
   And broke my heart, in little ways.

   As used in the text, what does the word "raucous" mean?

   A. Soft

   B. Harsh

   C. High-pitched

   D. Low-pitched

5. Nanotechnology involves designing and engineering materials with extraordinary properties due to their nano-sized dimensions, typically ranging from 1 to 100 nanometers. At this scale, quantum effects become prominent, enabling novel applications in diverse fields such as medicine, electronics, and energy. Nanoparticles, for instance, possess unique properties that make them ideal for targeted drug delivery in cancer treatments. By precisely controlling the structure and composition of nanomaterials, scientists can tailor their properties for specific applications. <u>However, alongside the immense possibilities, researchers must address challenges related to scalability, safety, and ethical considerations.</u> By pushing the boundaries of nanotechnology, scientists strive to unlock its full potential and revolutionize numerous industries.

   Which choice best states the function of the underlined sentence in the text as a whole?

   A. It defines nanotechnology in terms that are comprehensible to most people.

   B. It compares nanotechnology with related science fields.

   C. It details the ethical dilemma related to nanotechnology.

   D. It indicates the challenges for those working in the field of nanotechnology.

6. In the indigenous Ainu culture of northern Japan, oral literature serves as a means of translating history, values, legends, and stories from one generation to the next. One type of Ainu tale is called *yukar*, an epic tale in which the protagonist hero is an orphan boy. In other stories, the heroes are gods who descend from the heavens and interact with people. Sometimes, the heroes of Ainu stories are gods in animal form; many of these tales are morality tales, much like fables. The oral literature also includes stories that recount the experiences of their ancestors, either as history or as legends.

Which choice best states the main purpose of the text?

A. It delineates the origin of oral storytelling traditions in Japanese indigenous cultures.

B. It defines the term *yukar* and provides an example.

C. It summarizes the importance and background of oral storytelling traditions in the Ainu culture.

D. It praises the Ainu for pioneering unique approaches to oral storytelling.

7. In the 1950s, Rosalind Franklin made a groundbreaking discovery about the structure of DNA. Having acquired skills in both x-ray diffraction and crystallography, she pioneered a new way to apply both to the study of DNA fibers. In the process, Franklin managed to take photographs that played a pivotal role in scientists' early understanding of DNA structure. Specifically, Franklin determined that DNA had a dry crystalline form, known as the A form, and a wet form, known as the B form. Franklin's images showed the B form clearly enough to help solidify this new knowledge about DNA, but getting it also meant Franklin was exposed to more than 100 hours of x-ray radiation. <u>While there is no definitive proof, many speculate that Franklin's radiation exposure ultimately played a role in her developing terminal cancer at the young age of 37.</u>

Which choice best states the function of the underlined sentence in the text as a whole?

A. To connect an important element of Franklin's biography to the dangers inherent in her scientific research

B. To transition away from the topic of scientific discovery toward that of recounting Franklin's life

C. To clarify how DNA affects one's likelihood to develop terminal cancer

D. To provide evidence that DNA has both a dry form and a wet form

CONTINUE

8. Scholars study the phenomenon of collective memory to better understand how groups of people remember and engage with the past. Collective memory refers to the experiences and memories that are shared by a group of people and passed down through generations. In the United States, there are many public memorials to commemorate a variety of important events, like the 9/11 Memorial in New York City or the USS *Arizona* Memorial in Pearl Harbor, Hawaii. Memorials provide insight into how a country collectively remembers people and events and how those events have shaped history and national identity.

Which choice best states the main purpose of the text?

A. To critique the manner in which memorials are organized in the US

B. To discuss collective memory and its social and historical impacts, particularly in reference to the use of memorials

C. To emphasize the need for more research on the relevance of collective memory and memorials

D. To illustrate specific ways that collective memory is conveyed among a particular group of people or society

9. Plants have a huge impact on a person's mood. One study showed that when young people spend time tending to plants, it had a repressing effect on signals of stress in their bodies, such as blood pressure and cortisol levels. Plants are also known to provide people with a sense of visual escape from their everyday lives. Imagine, for instance, that you're stuck in a dreary office environment and looking at a computer screen all day. Taking a few moments to admire the fern on your desk might then give you a moment of reprieve from the environment and provide a spot of tranquility. The smell, feel, and sight of plants have also all been shown to ________.

Which choice most logically completes the text?

A. distract from other elements in the environment

B. be irrelevant

C. improve a person's overall disposition

D. contribute to negative health outcomes

10. "Snowy Mountains" is a 1922 poem by John Gould Fletcher. In the poem, the author describes majestic mountains which are being overrun by industrial society.

Which quotation from "Snowy Mountains" most effectively illustrates this claim?

A. Blue-white like angels with broad wings, / Pillars of the sky at rest / The mountains from the great plateau / Uprise.

B. The world makes war on them / Tunnels their granite cliffs, / Splits down their shining sides, / Plasters their cliffs with soap advertisements, / Destroys the lonely fragments of their peace.

C. Vaster and still more vast, / Peak after peak, pile after pile, / Wilderness still untamed, / To which the future is as was the past

D. The mountains swing along / The south horizon of the sky; / Welcoming with wide floors of blue-green ice / The mists that dance and drive before the sun.

11. Diabetes, a disease in which the body does not produce or properly use insulin to convert sugar into usable energy, is marked by elevated blood sugar levels. A glycated hemoglobin test reveals a person's average blood sugar level for the past three months. A result of 5% or more is considered high. A glycated hemoglobin reading above 7% is a strong indicator of diabetes. In a recent research effort, scientists estimated the risk of developing cardiovascular disease associated with various glycated hemoglobin levels, first among a group of non-diabetics, and then among a group of diabetics. Based on the results in the table provided, one could hypothesize that as glycated hemoglobin levels increase, the risk of cardiovascular disease generally increases for ______________.

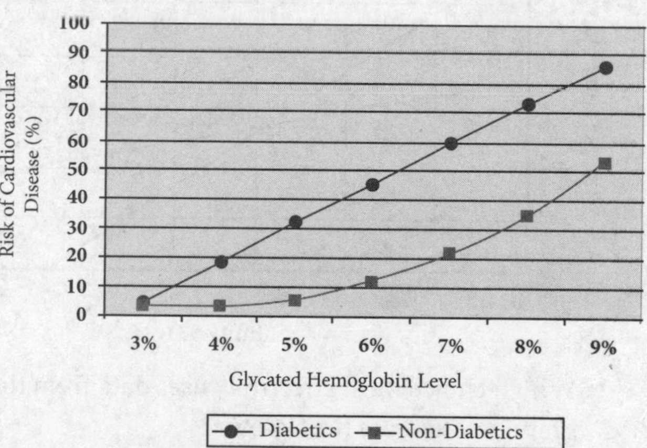

Which choice most effectively uses data from the graph to illustrate the claim?

A. diabetics but not for non-diabetics.

B. non-diabetics but not for diabetics.

C. both diabetics and non-diabetics.

D. neither diabetics nor non-diabetics.

SAT® DIAGNOSTIC TEST

CONTINUE

12. Ocean water is salt water, which means that the water contains dissolved salts and other minerals. The percentage of dissolved salts in a body of water is known as salinity. Notably, amounts of dissolved salts and minerals in ocean water contribute to ocean water's density, which is the mass of the substance per unit of volume. The greater the mass of dissolved salts, the greater the density of the ocean water. Density is also affected by temperature. Pure water, which freezes at 0°C, reaches its maximum density at around 4°C. Adding salt and other minerals to water ________

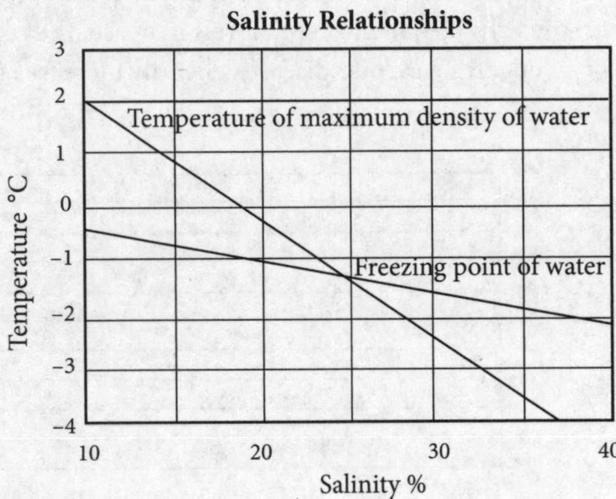

Which choice most effectively uses data from the graph to illustrate the claim?

A. increases the freezing point of water while having no effect on the temperature at which maximum density occurs.

B. increases the ambient temperature of water under normal conditions.

C. lowers both the freezing point and the temperature at which maximum density occurs.

D. increases the density of water until it reaches a point of equilibrium.

13. The following text is taken from William Henry Pyle's 1917 book *The Science of Human Nature.*

> Each science has its own particular field. Zoology undertakes to answer every reasonable question about animals; botany, about plants; physics, about motion and forces; chemistry, about the composition of matter; astronomy, about the heavenly bodies, etc. The world has many aspects. Each science undertakes to describe and explain some particular aspect. To understand all the aspects of the world, we must study all the sciences.

According to the text, botany is the study of what subject?

A. Animals

B. Plants

C. Heavenly bodies

D. Motion and forces

14. When a Cincinnati high school student named Edna Murphey set off in 1910 to market her father's antiperspirant invention as a solution for underarm sweat, she was marketing about a problem that didn't necessarily exist yet. At least, to that point, there hadn't been much concern among the general public about underarm sweat broadly speaking. Even Murphey's father had not created it for that purpose; as a surgeon, he had wanted an invention to keep sweat off his palms when operating. Edna, however, saw opportunity. She named the product Odorono, which when sounded out sounds like "Odor? Oh, no!," and began manufacturing it for sale to tourists on summer holiday after receiving an initial investment from her grandfather.

According to the text, who invented Odorono and why?

A. Edna Murphey invented Odorono because her father hated sweating at work.

B. Edna Murphey invented Odorono because she knew Americans would want a product to limit underarm sweat.

C. Edna Murphey's father invented Odorono because he was embarrassed by sweating through his clothes in the summer.

D. Edna Murphey's father invented Odorono to keep his hands from sweating when performing surgery.

15. The advent of artificial intelligence, or AI, has raised serious questions about the ethics of the technology and the safety of its use in society. Many people can reap the benefits of instantaneous information with programs like ChatGPT, but ________________ implications are ever increasing; AI can be used to simulate the skills and knowledge that humans require years to develop. Such implementations represent direct threats to the income and status of human workers. Additionally, private corporations may use AI to make decisions related to medicine, health, and employment without government oversight or regulations. Such applications of AI can put society's underserved populations at risk of more bias and discrimination, as well as reduce the perceived necessity of essential human judgment.

Which choice completes the text so that it conforms to the conventions of Standard English?

A. at what cost! The ethical

B. at what cost? The ethical

C. at what cost. The ethical

D. at what cost; the ethical

CONTINUE

16. Jean-Michel Basquiat is widely considered to be one of the most influential African American artists of the 20th century. He began his early career as the graffiti artist "Samo" in the streets of New York City in ______________ in the 1980s as his unconventional art attracted the likes of Andy Warhol and the elites of the international art scene. While some may argue his art lacks proper technique, the meaning behind the works of art speaks volumes.

Which choice completes the text so that it conforms to the conventions of Standard English?

A. the late 1970s. But rose to fame

B. the late 1970s but rose to fame

C. the late 1970s; but rose to fame

D. the late 1970s but he rose to fame

17. The Nakizumo Baby Crying Festival is an annual event that takes place in Tokyo, Japan. Translated into English, Nakizumo means "Naki Sumo," which is a hint as to what occurs at this unorthodox event. Namely, two sumo wrestlers enter a ring, each carrying a baby. The objective is to be the first sumo wrestler to get your opponent's baby to cry while also soothing your own baby to keep them from crying. While this may seem a bit bizarre from an outsider's perspective, ____________. Specifically, the festival is linked with the long-held Japanese belief that one can ensure the health of a baby by letting them occasionally cry hard. One related saying, "Naku-ko wa sodatsu," translates to "the child who cries grows up," meaning that many people in Japan see crying as essential for childhood development.

Which choice completes the text so that it conforms to the conventions of Standard English?

A. the event is steeped in a nearly 400-year-old tradition

B. the event is steeped, in a nearly 400-year-old tradition

C. the event is a nearly 400-year-old steeped tradition

D. the event is a tradition steeped in nearly 400 years

18. The Panama Canal is a manmade series of locks that connect a web of rivers and lakes across the Central American country of Panama, creating the shortest possible path linking the Atlantic and Pacific Oceans. Before the ___________ around Cape Horn, the southernmost tip of South America. This area was chosen because it has the narrowest strip of land between the two oceans. It is considered one of the greatest accomplishments in human engineering.

Which choice completes the text so that it conforms to the conventions of Standard English?

A. construction of this canal, ships were forced to travel south

B. construction of this canal ships were forced to travel south

C. construction of this canal. Ships were forced to travel south

D. construction of this canal—ships were forced to travel south

19. If you ever visit South America, there's a good chance you'll try yerba mate. Yerba mate is a tea consumed in the Southern Cone region of South America, particularly in Argentina, Brazil, Paraguay, and Uruguay. It was first used by the Guarani indigenous peoples that inhabited the same geographical area. The drink can be prepared hot or cold and ________ often enjoyed socially among friends and family from a shared drinking vessel made from a dried, hollowed out gourd with a wooden or metal straw. Certain cultural norms around enjoying the drink exist within these social groups, regions, and countries. This long-standing tradition unifies and connects people as it forms a key part of their cultural identity.

Which choice completes the text so that it conforms to the conventions of Standard English?

A. is

B. was

C. are

D. were

CONTINUE

20. Scientist Dian Fossey initially began her work with the endangered mountain gorilla in Zaire but was forced to leave because of political unrest. After that, she moved her research to another African country, Rwanda, where she established a research camp in a national park. There, she spent thousands of hours observing the behavior of gorillas. Her steadfast patience won the trust of the animals, and they __________ her presence among them. As a result, she was able to observe gorilla behaviors that had previously never been seen by humans.

Which choice completes the text so that it conforms to the conventions of Standard English?

A. began to accept

B. would be accepting

C. begin to accept

D. are beginning to accept

21. To understand the power of advertising, one need only consider the allure of the late-night infomercial. One night, laying feverish in bed, I was somehow convinced to buy a product called Confidence in a Can. The flashy commercial boasted an array of benefits and included testimonials from happy customers. After everything I heard and saw, I was interested, but I still couldn't decide whether or not I was going to make a purchase. Of course, right as those doubts sunk in, I heard the commercial narrator promising it would help me be more successful at work and in my relationships with the people in my life. Who wouldn't want that? And then the host said that if I called the toll-free number right now I could have not one but two full cans of Confidence in a Can for one low discount price—that was all __________ to hear to make the impulse buy.

Which choice completes the text so that it conforms to the conventions of Standard English?

A. I'm needing

B. I need

C. I will be needing

D. I needed

22. Sumatran tigers are a critically endangered species native to the Indonesian island of Sumatra. These majestic big cats possess distinctive dark orange fur with black stripes. They are well-adapted to the island's diverse habitats, including forests, grasslands, and swamps. ___________, habitat loss due to deforestation, illegal logging, and palm oil plantations has significantly contributed to their endangered status. Additionally, poaching for their valuable body parts and conflict with humans further threaten their survival. Efforts are underway to conserve their habitats, strengthen anti-poaching measures, and raise awareness about the importance of protecting these magnificent creatures.

Which choice completes the text with the most logical transition?

A. Well

B. Because

C. Unfortunately

D. Otherwise

23. One of the instruments that electronic music pioneer Wendy Carlos helped make famous was the Moog synthesizer. Back in 1968, she released an album called *Switched-On Bach*, on which she translated the music of classical composer Johann Sebastian Bach for the Moog. Few people had used electronic sounds to compose music before that point, so hearing Bach in this new way made Carlos a sensation. ___________, the success of the album made the Moog synthesizer one of the definitive sounds of the 1970s, as everyone who was anyone started using it in their music. Later, producers like the Italo-disco legend Giorgio Moroder and the German band Kraftwerk would help popularize genres centered on the synthesizer sound, creating a ripple effect that still resonates today; everyone from Jay-Z to Coldplay has made modern songs directly influenced by these early electronic sounds.

Which choice completes the text with the most logical transition?

A. Surprisingly

B. On the other hand

C. Lastly

D. Furthermore

CONTINUE

24. Rowers do everything that they can to maintain the speed of their boat, especially when racing. __________, races are won or lost by thousandths of a second, which can be devastating for a team that trains as hard as elite rowers usually do. They often train on the water two times a day (morning and night) and spend hours in the weight room, all in hopes of shaving even just a few fractions of a second off their times.

Which choice completes the text with the most logical transition?

A. Sometimes

B. Conversely

C. Instead

D. However

25. The ancient Mayans inhabited the area that now consists of Mexico, Guatemala, Belize, Honduras, and El Salvador. Their rich civilization flourished from the third through the ninth centuries. __________ the many notable achievements of this society was the Mayan understanding of astronomy, which was manifest not only in Mayan science but in every aspect of the culture.

Which choice completes the text with the most logical transition?

A. Plus

B. Despite

C. Among

D. Between

26. While researching a topic, a student has taken the following notes:

- From a structural engineering perspective, the Hoover Dam is one of the most impressive American infrastructure projects to date.
- Located along the Colorado River on the border between Nevada and Arizona, the hydroelectric power plant and arch-gravity dam was built in the early 1930s as the Great Depression loomed in the United States.
- The concrete structure stands over 725 feet tall and facilitates the movement of water to Lake Mead, the reservoir that supplies water to millions of people and irrigates over 2 million acres of land.
- Millions visit the Hoover Dam each year to marvel at its design, participate in recreational activities, and tour the facility.
- Its construction was largely made possible by President Herbert Hoover, for whom it is dedicated, as he understood the need for flood control and large-scale irrigation in the southwest.

The student wants to introduce the Hoover Dam to someone who is unfamiliar with the topic. Which choice most effectively uses relevant information from the notes to accomplish this goal?

A. Built in the early 1930s as the Great Depression loomed in the United States, the Hoover Dam stands over 725 feet tall and facilitates the movement of water to a reservoir called Lake Mead.

B. The Hoover Dam is a hydroelectric power plant and arch-gravity dam located along the Colorado River between Nevada and Arizona and is one of the most impressive American engineering projects to date.

C. The Hoover Dam is an impressive structural engineering project that was built in large part thanks to President Herbert Hoover, for whom it is dedicated.

D. The Hoover Dam was built in the early 1930s as the Great Depression loomed due to the need for flood control and large-scale irrigation in the southwestern United States.

CONTINUE

27. While researching a topic, a student has taken the following notes:

- Quechua is a term used to describe both a group of indigenous people and the group of languages they speak.
- The Quechua people have inhabited various regions of the Andes Mountains of South America for centuries, including the countries of Argentina, Bolivia, Chile, Colombia, Ecuador, and Peru.
- Descendants of the Incas, the Quechua have maintained much of their culture and traditions, even through colonialism and modern history.
- As a language, Quechua is still spoken among millions of people and consists of several dialects, divided by geographical regions.
- As the importance of cultural diversity continues to be recognized, Quechua has been made an official language in some countries and is also being maintained through language instruction and education programs.

The student wants to introduce the term "Quechua" to someone who is unfamiliar with it. Which choice most effectively uses relevant information from the notes to accomplish this goal?

A. *Quechua* is used to describe a group of indigenous people who have inhabited the Andes Mountains, as well as the language they speak.

B. Descendants of the Incas, the Quechua indigenous people continue to maintain their culture and traditions, including their language.

C. The Quechua language dialects are still spoken among millions of people and are also maintained through language instruction and education programs.

D. The Quechua people of South America lived for centuries in the Andean region before it was colonized and divided into independent countries.

STOP.

If you finish before time is up, you may check your work on this module only.

Do not turn to any other module in the test.

2

SAT® DIAGNOSTIC TEST

READING AND WRITING

Module 2

27 Questions—32 Minutes

Directions: The questions in this section address a number of important reading and writing skills. Each question includes one or more passages, which may include a table or graph. Read each passage and question carefully, and then choose the best answer to the question based on the passage(s).

All questions in this section are multiple-choice with four answer choices. Each question has a single best answer.

1. The following text is from Lafcadio Hearn's 1899 book *In Ghostly Japan*.

 One day he ordered some Spirit-Recalling-Incense to be procured, that he might summon her from the dead. His counsellors prayed him to forego his purpose, declaring that the vision could only intensify his grief. But he gave no heed to their advice, and himself performed the rite,—kindling the incense, and keeping his mind fixed upon the memory of the Lady Li. Presently, within the thick blue smoke arising from the incense, the outline, of a feminine form became visible. It defined, took tints of life, slowly became luminous, and the Emperor recognized the form of his beloved.

 As used in the text, what does the word "luminous" mean?

 A. Blurry

 B. Vivid

 C. Dark

 D. Odorous

2. On November 9, 1989, following the accidental and premature announcement of the opening of the Berlin Wall, thousands of East Germans flooded the Wall's six border crossings. The border guards, who had no idea what had just been broadcast on national television, were overwhelmed by the size of the crowds and flummoxed as to what to do. One crossing, Bornholmer Strasse, was located on a bridge. So many people gathered on this bridge that officials worried it would collapse; they were forced to open the gates and let the East Germans pour into West Berlin. Once the gates were opened, it wasn't long before citizens and government officials alike started dismantling the wall. Less than a year later, in October 1990, Germany was reunited as one country.

 As used in the text, what does the word "flummoxed" most nearly mean?

 A. Confused

 B. Angered

 C. Disorganized

 D. Apprised

3. The following text is taken from Kahlil Gibran's 1923 book *The Prophet*.

   Therefore let your soul exalt your reason to the height of passion, that it may sing;

   And let it direct your passion with reason, that your passion may live through its own daily resurrection, and like the phoenix rise above its own ashes.

   I would have you consider your judgment and your appetite even as you would two loved guests in your house.

   <u>Surely you would not honour one guest above the other; for he who is more mindful of one loses the love and the faith of both.</u>

   Which choice best states the function of the underlined sentence in the text as a whole?

   A. It clarifies the purpose of the simile provided in the line that precedes it.

   B. It summarizes the author's concept of reason.

   C. It critiques common misconceptions about the relationship between reason and passion.

   D. It poses a philosophical question for the reader to ponder.

4. The following text is taken from Etsu Inagaki Sugimoto's 1925 memoir *A Daughter of the Samurai*.

   The standards of my own and my adopted country differed so widely in some ways, and my love for both lands was so sincere, that <u>sometimes I had an odd feeling of standing upon a cloud in space, and gazing with measuring eyes upon two separate worlds</u>. At first I was continually trying to explain, by Japanese standards, all the [strange] things that came every day before my surprised eyes; for no one seemed to know the origin or significance of even the most familiar customs, nor why they existed and were followed. To me, coming from a land where there is an unforgotten reason for every fashion of dress, for every motion in etiquette—indeed, for almost every trivial act of life—this indifference of Americans seemed very singular.

   Which choice best states the function of the underlined portion in the text as a whole?

   A. To use figurative language to express the author's experience of navigating two cultures simultaneously

   B. To allude to the frustration the author felt about not knowing any American customs

   C. To question the purpose of engaging in American customs at all

   D. To vividly display how the author's knowledge of Japanese affected her conception of American traditions

CONTINUE

5. **TEXT 1**

The Republic of Colombia on the northwestern coast of South America is the second most biologically diverse country in the world. It is considered a "megadiverse" country on account of the heterogeneity among its endemic and non-native species. Colombia contains 59 protected areas and 314 types of coastal and inland ecosystems that host 10% of the world's biodiversity. Colombia is a geographical wonder of natural regions that give residence to various flora and fauna. The ice-capped mountains of the Andes stretch through the interior and western regions, while tropical beaches border the northern and western coastlines. The northwestern region shares its jungle with the neighboring country of Panama, yet deserts reside in the north and grassy plains overrun the east. Dense forests cover more than 50% of the mainland, including the Amazon rainforest region, which blankets the southern portion of the country.

TEXT 2

Deforestation, urbanization, overfishing, water pollution, and air pollution all contribute to the environmental crisis in Colombia. Water pollution in the country is caused by domestic and industrial waste, agricultural operations, and mining activities. Armed guerilla groups such as the FARC and ELN aim to dismantle the economic infrastructure that serves the government and the interests of multinational corporations. Since 1984, their most common tactic has involved destroying oil pipelines. As a result, oil spills have caused the contamination of land and water and the deterioration of various ecosystems.

Based on the texts, what is the relationship between Text 1 and Text 2?

A. Text 1 specifies the types of biodiversity in Colombia, and Text 2 justifies the political tactics of Colombia's guerrillas.

B. Text 1 details the impact of biodiverse species on Colombia, and Text 2 explains the effects of humans invading those species' ecosystems.

C. Text 1 praises Colombia for its protection of its ecosystems, and Text 2 criticizes large corporations for polluting them.

D. Text 1 illustrates the biodiversity and geography of Colombia, and Text 2 conveys the ways in which those ecosystems are in danger.

6. **Text 1**

Georg Wilhelm Friedrich Hegel (1770–1831) is one of the most prominent German philosophers of all time. Though his dense works are notorious for giving today's philosophy students headaches, his complex ideas were so revolutionary that they founded the basis of most modern philosophy, including serving as inspiration to prominent thinkers like Karl Marx, Søren Kierkegaard, and Michel Foucault. Hegel developed a way of thinking known as the dialectic which involved investigating how contradictions between two seemingly true things, termed a thesis and antithesis, can reveal an even higher level of truth. The process of thinking through the contradiction between thesis and antithesis and its implications was known as the "Hegelian dialectic" and the idea was that engaging in dialectical thinking helped advance knowledge over time.

Text 2

In his philosophy, Karl Marx posited that economic and social conditions were the primary drivers of historical change and that class struggle was the mechanism by which this change occurred. In doing so, Marx used the dialectic to uncover contradictions and conflicts in human society, particularly those related to power and exploitation. Similarly, Simone de Beauvoir used Hegelian dialectics in her feminist philosophy. In her influential book *The Second Sex*, de Beauvoir used the dialectic to critique the patriarchal structure of society. She argued that dialectical thinking revealed contradictions inherent in gender roles and called for the liberation of women from oppressive societal structures.

Based on the texts, how does Text 2 relate to the claims made in Text 1?

A. Text 2 provides an overview of the different ways Michel Foucault influenced Hegelian dialectics.

B. Text 2 offers examples to support the claim in Text 1 that Hegel's work influenced later thinkers.

C. While Text 1 provides an overview of Hegelian philosophy, Text 2 provides more details on Hegel's biography.

D. While Text 1 provides a definition of the Hegelian dialectic, Text 2 critiques Hegel's use of it.

CONTINUE

7. **TEXT 1**

William Shakespeare is considered a legend in the literary world because of the innovative ways that he manipulated and employed the English language, as well as the significant topics and themes of his works. Shakespeare invented hundreds of words by using English prefixes and suffixes and parts of words from other languages. Their meaning could be inferred by the audience or reader through context. He is also credited with many idiomatic expressions still used today, such as "wild goose chase" and "break the ice." Shakespeare's works often reflected topics like familial and romantic relationships, history, society, politics, and religion through perspicacious stories of love, tragedy, drama, and comedy.

TEXT 2

William Shakespeare published *Hamlet*, what is arguably his most popular play, at the beginning of the 17th century. This theatrical tragedy evokes several literary devices that scholars have been analyzing for centuries. Shakespeare demonstrates allusion by indirectly referencing certain topics or themes, such as religion and mythology. His use of dramatic irony builds up emotional tension for the audience as they learn information that certain characters of the play do not know. *Hamlet* is brimming with metaphors that depict the characters, setting, and plot. In the well-known soliloquy "To be, or not to be," the character Hamlet uses metaphor throughout his monologue. For example, he compares sleep with death: "to die, to sleep; to sleep perchance to dream."

Based on the texts, how does Text 2 relate to the claims made in Text 1?

A. Text 2 provides an overview of the different ways Shakespeare influenced language and literature while Text 1 introduces specific words the author invented.

B. Text 2 rejects the claim in Text 1 that Shakespeare's work majorly impacted literature.

C. While Text 1 provides an overview of Shakespeare's linguistic and literary innovations, Text 2 offers more details on a specific work.

D. While Text 1 provides a biography of Shakespeare's life, Text 2 compares his work with other notable writers.

8. Between 68 to 65 million years ago, the end of the Cretaceous, about 480,000 cubic miles of molten lava seeped out of cracks in the earth's crust in present-day India. The lava erupted in many separate episodes, each lasting from a few days to a year or more, and each expelling tremendous amounts of ash and toxic gases into the air. In the short term, the ash would decrease the amount of sunlight reaching the earth's surface, decreasing temperatures, inhibiting photosynthesis, and disrupting the food chain. Sulfur dioxide (SO_2) gas from the eruptions would form super-acid rain that would poison marine organisms. In the long term, after the ash settled, the carbon dioxide (CO_2) released would cause global warming. These continuing environmental stresses would have caused a gradual extinction of organisms lasting from tens to hundreds of thousands of years.

Which of the following pieces of evidence, if found, would contradict the claims in this hypothesis?

A. Isotope data from rock layers at the end of the Cretaceous show warmer temperatures than earlier in the Cretaceous.

B. Large amounts of volcanic ash are found in rock layers that are 68 to 65 million years old.

C. Shells of marine organisms from the end of the Cretaceous show acid damage.

D. Fossils of Cretaceous organisms disappear quickly over a few thousand years just before the end of the Cretaceous.

9. Some researchers argue that the discovery of fossilized reptiles equipped with feathers, wings, and beak-like snouts may be significant but more likely provides only limited support for the claim that dinosaurs evolved into birds. Convergent evolution often provides animals of very distant lineages with similar appendages. These researchers claim that it is more likely the case that birds and dinosaurs share a very distant common ancestor, perhaps from among the thecodonts. These prototypical reptiles of the late Permian survived the largest mass extinction recorded in the planet's history to bring forth many more recent lines; crocodiles, dinosaurs, pterosaurs, and birds are the most notable among these.

Which of the following pieces of evidence, if found, would offer support to the claims in this hypothesis?

A. Discovery of thecodont fossils with characteristics of modern birds and existing dinosaur fossils

B. Discovery of another possible intermediate form between dinosaurs and birds from the Jurassic Era

C. Discovery of an avian prototype dating back to before the beginning of the era of dinosaur dominance

D. A careful examination of several sets of theropod fossil remains

CONTINUE

10. The following text is taken from the story "Briar Rose" from the 1812 book *Grimms' Fairy Tales* by Jacob and Wilhelm Grimm.

> Just as eleven of them had done blessing her, a great noise was heard in the courtyard, and word was brought that the thirteenth fairy was come, with a black cap on her head, and black shoes on her feet, and a broomstick in her hand: and presently up she came into the dining-hall. Now, as she had not been asked to the feast she was very angry, and scolded the king and queen very much, and set to work to take her revenge. So she cried out, "The king's daughter shall, in her fifteenth year, be wounded by a spindle, and fall down dead." Then the twelfth of the friendly fairies, who had not yet given her gift, came forward, and said that the evil wish must be fulfilled, but that she could soften its mischief; so her gift was, that the king's daughter, when the spindle wounded her, should not really die, but should only fall asleep for a hundred years.

Which of the following claims could be logically supported by evidence from the text?

A. It was common for members of the monarchy to be given spindles as gifts.

B. The number 13 was associated with evil at the time the story was written.

C. Fairy tales by the Grimm brothers always take a patriarchal perspective.

D. Gifts in Grimm fairy tales symbolize new beginnings for the recipient.

11. Sonnet 18 is one of William Shakespeare's most famous sonnets.

Which quotation from Sonnet 18 best supports the claim that the poem's narrator believes the addressee's inner beauty will last forever?

A. Shall I compare thee to a summer's day? / Thou art more lovely and more temperate

B. Rough winds do shake the darling buds of May, / And summer's lease hath all too short a date

C. And every fair from fair sometimes declines, / By chance, or nature's changing course, untrimmed

D. But thy eternal summer shall not fade, / Nor lose possession of that fair thou ow'st

12. The rubbing between solid objects is called friction, while the rubbing between a solid object and a liquid or gas is called drag. Each produces a resistance force, measured in newtons (N), that works against the momentum of moving objects subjected to these forces. Both friction and drag produce heat. Researchers performed the following experiments to investigate the various properties of and relationships between these phenomena. Researchers placed a 10 kg box, a 30 kg box, and a 40 kg box at the top of an inclined ramp and let it slide down. A monitoring device was positioned to record the friction resistance force slowing the box's descent. The friction resistance force working against each box was recorded at the point each attained a velocity of 20 km/hr. Moreover, the level of heat generated at that point was measured. The results are noted in in the table below. The experiment demonstrated a positive correlation between ___________

Table 1

Box	Friction Resistance Force	Heat Generated
10 kg	55 N	3.5°C
30 kg	75 N	10.5°C
40 kg	85 N	14°C

Which choice most effectively uses data from the table to illustrate the claim?

A. velocity and drag.

B. weight and drag.

C. weight and heat.

D. friction and velocity.

13. The Nêhiyawak, more commonly known by English speakers as the Cree people, are the largest indigenous group in Canada. The Cree First Nations includes numerous people groups, most of whom can be divided into Woodland Cree, who live in the forests of eastern and central Canada, and Plains Cree in the northern Great Plains of western Canada. The English term "Cree" describes the common language spoken by these groups and does not necessarily tell you about the tribe with which a person identifies or the areas in which their ancestors have traditionally lived. Over 350,000 people in Canada identify as having Cree ancestry. Of those, only about 96,000 still speak the language. Consequently, efforts are being made by many to preserve the Cree language for future generations.

Which choice best states the main idea of the text?

A. Indigenous languages are in danger of disappearing unless more effort is made to preserve them.

B. The term "Cree" refers to a common language spoken by a wide range of groups.

C. The Cree First Nations comprise a range of indigenous groups who historically shared a language that many are now trying to preserve.

D. There are many different indigenous groups among Canada's First Nations, and the Cree are one of them.

CONTINUE

14. The following text is a poem from 1923 by Robert Frost entitled "Nothing Gold Can Stay."

Nature's first green is gold,
Her hardest hue to hold.
Her early leaf's a flower;
But only so an hour.
Then leaf subsides to leaf.
So Eden sank to grief,
So dawn goes down to day.
Nothing gold can stay.

Which choice best states the main idea of the text?

A. Nature can inspire both awe and fear.
B. Everything in nature has a season and a lifespan.
C. People are too obsessed with their own thoughts to notice nature.
D. Tending a garden is one of life's greatest joys.

15. Known for their long-distance running abilities, the indigenous people group known as the Tarahumara, or Rarámuri as they call themselves, have lived in the mountainous ranges of Chihuahua, Mexico, for centuries. Due to the remoteness of the mountains and valleys this group has called home, they have managed to limit their ______ they have made headlines by competing in ultra-marathon races. One of the most intriguing points about the runners is that they prefer to wear their traditional sandals, called huaraches, instead of athletic shoes.

Which choice completes the text so that it conforms to the conventions of Standard English?

A. contact with society; however more recently
B. contact with society, however, more recently
C. contact with society; however, more recently,
D. contact with society however more recently

16. Pancho Villa embodies the Mexican sentiment of perseverance and fortitude. ___________ Villa has been characterized as the "Robin Hood of Mexico." He began adulthood as a bandit, often stealing from rich landowners under Porfirio Diaz's dictatorship to feed the poor. As the Mexican Revolution evolved, Villa's enigmatic leadership as a renegade general fighting along the northern Mexico and US border captured the attention of the international press and Hollywood. His untimely assassination in 1923 after evading capture and imprisonment for years only contributes to the leader's legacy.

Which choice completes the text so that it conforms to the conventions of Standard English?

A. With his mustache being unmistakable and a gaze that was intense,

B. With his unmistakable mustache and intense gaze,

C. He had an unmistakable mustache and intense gaze,

D. His unmistakable mustache and intense gaze,

17. Spanish author Miguel de Cervantes published the iconic novel *Don Quixote de la Mancha* in two ___________. Many consider the literary work to be the first modern novel. As a result, it has had more than 140 translations and endless literary analysis over the past 400 years. The endearing characters and whimsical plot take readers on an epic journey with the main character, Don Quixote, as he pursues a knight's voyage "tilting at windmills" he believes to be giants. The novel continues to offer many potential interpretations regarding how one defines reality and fantasy. It also raises questions for literal and figurative language as well as the use of satire.

Which choice completes the text so that it conforms to the conventions of Standard English?

A. parts. The first in 1605 and the second in 1615

B. parts; the first in 1605 and the second in 1615

C. parts: the first in 1605 and the second in 1615

D. parts the first in 1605 and the second in 1615

CONTINUE

18. With popular movies like *The Book of Life* and *Coco*, the traditions and customs associated with the Day of the Dead have become more prominent in popular culture over the past decade. The popular holiday is celebrated in Mexico and extends to the United States and other Latin American countries, although the name and traditions may vary in each place. Mexico's Day of the Dead is a fusion of ancient Aztec rituals and post-colonial Catholic practices that __________ over centuries. Family and friends of deceased loved ones are remembered from November 1st to the 2nd through a variety of customs: they often clean, visit and adorn the resting place of the deceased, and will set up an altar of offerings in the home to honor and celebrate them.

Which choice completes the text so that it conforms to the conventions of Standard English?

A. had evolved

B. has evolved

C. will evolve

D. had been evolving

19. The idea of nonsense commingling with chaos and meaninglessness was central to Dada art, as was the idea that people should question what makes something a piece of art to begin with. These ideas __________ sound poems composed entirely of nonsense syllables, geometric masks meant to mimic ideas of primitivism from around the world, largely improvised dances that would later inspire much of the modern dance movement, and early experimental photography and cinema.

Which choice completes the text so that it conforms to the conventions of Standard English?

A. manifesting with

B. manifested with

C. manifesting as

D. manifested as

20. Nelson Mandela was a political activist and leader known for working to end apartheid in South Africa, being the first Black and democratically elected President of South Africa, and fighting for human rights worldwide. Apartheid, a system of legally enforced segregation and oppression of people of color by dominant minority white people in Africa, institutionally controlled South Africa from 1948 until __________ end in 1994, coinciding with Mandela's presidency. Imprisoned from 1964–1990 for his anti-apartheid activism, Mandela gained popularity for his resistance and refusal to compromise his ideologies for freedom. In 1993, he and South African President Frederik Willem de Klerk earned the Nobel Peace Prize for their joint work on political negotiations toward a democracy for all. Mandela's presidency from 1994 to 1999, as well as his social justice advocacy in the subsequent 14 years of his life, paved the way for international discourse on human rights.

Which choice completes the text so that it conforms to the conventions of Standard English?

A. they're

B. their

C. its

D. it's

21. Until recently, the most widely accepted theory about why giraffes have long necks has been that giraffes evolved in such a way to reach leaves on higher and higher trees, an adaptation that would have been crucial when drought or overgrazing meant lower foliage was picked over. While this seems like a straightforward theory, there's a catch—research has shown that giraffes don't necessarily go for the highest foliage they can reach, often seeming perfectly content to munch on lower-hanging leaves. Another theory suggests that the length of the neck was a way for male giraffes to attract mates, ______.

Which choice completes the text so that it conforms to the conventions of Standard English?

A. but female giraffes have the same average neck length. So this has largely been considered speculation

B. but, female giraffes, have the same average neck length; this has also been considered speculation, largely

C. but female giraffes have the same average neck length, so this has also largely been considered speculation

D. but, female giraffes have the same average neck length so this has also largely been considered speculation

22. One of Jane Jacobs's key contributions to urban studies was the concept of social capital. This refers to the networks of relationships and trust that exist within communities. Jacobs believed that social capital was essential for creating vibrant and resilient cities. When people know and trust each other, they are more likely to work together to solve problems and build strong local economies. ______, neighbors who know and trust one another are more likely to assist one another with tasks like repairs and childcare or by making referrals to local tradespeople. Jacobs envisioned cities wherein neighbors felt connected to one another and their neighborhood as a whole. She argued that social capital allows people to feel a sense of belonging and connection to their neighborhoods, which can lead to greater civic engagement and participation.

Which choice completes the text with the most logical transition?

A. Lastly

B. Primarily

C. In conclusion

D. For instance

CONTINUE

23. Biomimicry involves drawing inspiration from nature to solve complex engineering challenges. One major thinker in this field is Robert Full, a renowned biomechanist and engineer. Full is known for his exploration of the movement and mechanics of various animal species, particularly arthropods. By studying the locomotion strategies of creatures like cockroaches and geckos, Full has gained insights into designing robots with enhanced mobility and adaptability. ________, Full's research aims to uncover principles that can revolutionize the field of bio-inspired engineering, opening up new possibilities for advanced robotic systems and human-made designs.

Which choice completes the text with the most logical transition?

A. As a way of evolving efficient and ingenious solutions in nature

B. Just as nature has evolved efficient and ingenious solutions

C. Since he has been unable to uncover the mystery of arthropod locomotion strategies

D. Owing to his work in the field of biomimicry

24. While researching a topic, a student has taken the following notes:

- Nikola Tesla was a Serbian American scientist, inventor, and engineer during the late 19th and early 20th centuries.
- His contributions to alternating current (AC) electricity continue to be used today.
- Tesla led a number of electrical and mechanical projects, including polyphase current, high-voltage transmission, high-frequency current, and even wireless systems.
- He posthumously regained notoriety in 1960 when the term for a scientific unit of magnetic flux density was named a "tesla" to honor his work.
- Tesla has had a resurgence in popularity since the 1990s, even more so with the production of the electric vehicle with the same name.

The student wants to list Tesla's major contributions to science. Which choice most effectively uses relevant information from the notes to accomplish this goal?

A. Nikola Tesla has had a profound impact on the way we use electricity and mechanics today thanks to his research in alternating currents (making breakthroughs in polyphase and high-frequency current), high-voltage transmission, and wireless systems projects.

B. Nikola Tesla was less appreciated for his contributions to science until 17 years after his death, when the scientific unit known as a tesla was named after him.

C. The electric vehicle company Tesla has reintroduced Nikola Tesla into popular culture, more than a century after the scientist began his own work.

D. Tesla's work in the fields of electrical and mechanical engineering paved the way for major developments in technology.

25. While researching a topic, a student has taken the following notes:

- Tiananmen Square, an area in the center of Beijing, China, marks the spot where protesters were killed in 1989 during student-led demonstrations opposing China's Communist rule.
- As a more global view of politics and societies emerged in the 1980s, resistance to the heavy-handed Chinese Communist Party increased, with activists demanding more freedom.
- For several weeks, tensions rose between the government and the protesters, eventually erupting into violence as Chinese military tanks rolled into Tiananmen Square to quell protests.
- An iconic photo of a man holding grocery bags as he stands squarely in front of a line of advancing Chinese tanks acts as a powerful reminder of the events that transpired at the square.
- While the exact number is unknown, it is estimated that thousands of people died as a result of the confrontation in Tiananmen Square.

The student wants to compare the political ideologies of the two conflicting groups. Which choice most effectively uses relevant information from the notes to accomplish this goal?

A. Many people were killed in 1989 as a result of the violent confrontation in Tiananmen Square between the Chinese military and protesters.

B. Tourists from around the world who go to Beijing, China, often visit the landmark Tiananmen Square where protesters were killed in 1989 during student-led demonstrations.

C. A tragic reminder of the violence between the Chinese government and protesters is often symbolized by the iconic photo of a man holding a grocery bag in each hand as he stands squarely in front of military tanks in Tiananmen Square.

D. Tiananmen Square is a historical landmark where anti-government protesters and the Chinese military clashed during student-led demonstrations that opposed China's Communist rule and demanded more political freedom.

CONTINUE

26. While researching a topic, a student has taken the following notes:

- The ancient Egyptian pharaoh Tutankhamun, also known as King Tut, began his rule of Egypt over 3,000 years ago around the age of nine.
- The discovery of his tomb and its untouched contents at his burial site in 1922 was a modern historical event that made worldwide headlines.
- His sarcophagus was uncovered in the Valley of the Kings by a team of archaeologists led by Howard Carter, a British Egyptologist.
- The more than 5,000 artifacts found with King Tut's now-famous mummified remains, including his golden mask, offered archeologists a detailed look at the history of Egypt.

The student wants to emphasize the impact of the international attention paid to King Tut's tomb. Which choice most effectively uses relevant information from the notes to accomplish this goal?

A. British Egyptologist Howard Carter led the expedition to eventually uncover King Tut's tomb in 1922, making the event one of the most important in contemporary archaeological studies.

B. King Tutankhamun's life as an Egyptian pharaoh was resurrected through a thorough archaeological analysis of his burial site, including his tomb and more than 5,000 artifacts that accompanied him into the afterlife.

C. The discovery of King Tutankhamun's tomb and its artifacts sparked worldwide headlines in the early 20th century, renewing public interest in ancient Egypt that continues in museums and exhibits around the globe today.

D. While few may know that King Tut's reign over ancient Egypt began when he was a young child more than 3,000 years ago, many recognize his famous golden mask, as it symbolizes an important part of ancient history.

27. While researching a topic, a student has taken the following notes:

- Many people recognize the unmistakable face of Frida Kahlo, with her intense gaze and thick eyebrows, both features that are often used as parts of pop culture avatars for the artist.
- While Kahlo's enigmatic look, especially as it emerges from her various self-portraits, often inspires feminism and power, her work also conveys her life of suffering and pain.
- Kahlo, a Mexican artist who gained popularity during the first half of the 1900s, endured a terrible bus accident at the age of 18, which would lead to lifelong back surgeries and require her to remain in bed for long periods of time.
- Kahlo had a mirror installed above her bed. She used her reflection to paint many of her self-portraits, often displaying the many medical devices and anatomy that caused her pain.
- Kahlo also painted reflections on her marriage with fellow artist Diego Rivera, a tumultuous relationship that vacillated between adoration and anguish for several years.

The student wants to provide examples of the pain and suffering Kahlo endured in her life. Which choice most effectively uses relevant information from the notes to accomplish this goal?

A. Frida Kahlo is considered an icon of feminism and has also emerged as a recognizable figure in modern pop culture.

B. Frida Kahlo endured many hardships in her life, including a terrible accident that caused many medical problems and a difficult marriage that caused years of turmoil.

C. Kahlo's bedridden state allowed her ample time to paint, including many of the self-portraits she did using a mirror above her bed.

D. In her self-portraits, Kahlo's striking physical appearance intertwines with her introspection to yield complex representations of gender and identity.

STOP.

If you finish before time is up, you may check your work on this module only.
Do not turn to any other module in the test.

MATH

Module 1

22 Questions—35 Minutes

Directions: The questions in this section address a number of important math skills.

Use of a calculator is permitted for all questions.

Unless otherwise indicated:

- All variables and expressions represent real numbers.
- Figures provided are drawn to scale.
- All figures lie in a plane.
- The domain of a given function f is the set of all real numbers x for which $f(x)$ is a real number.

Reference:

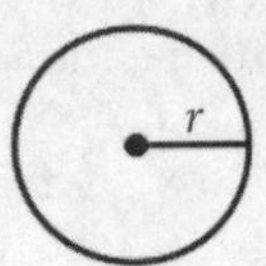

$A = \pi r^2$
$C = 2\pi r$

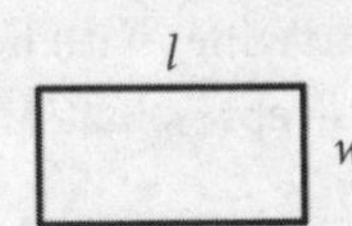

$A = lw$

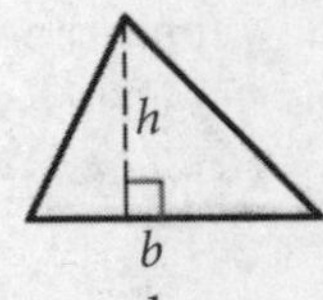

$A = \frac{1}{2}bh$

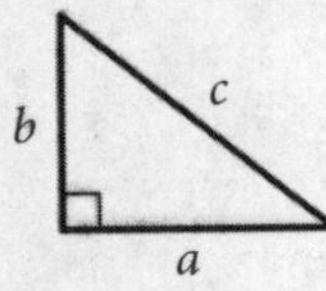

$c^2 = a^2 + b^2$

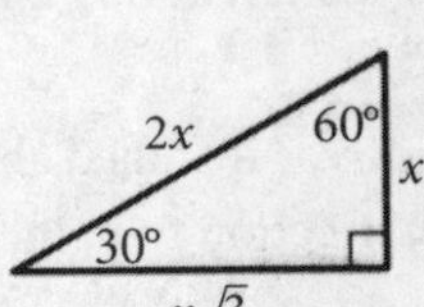

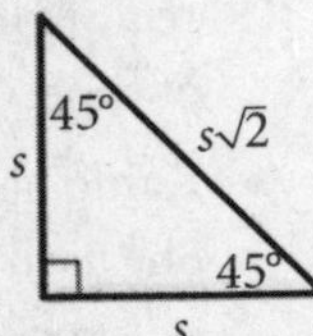

Special Right Triangles

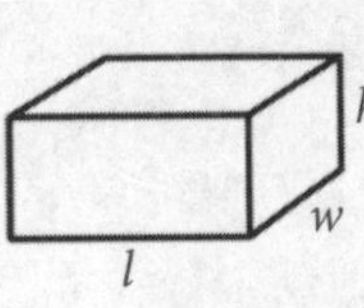

$V = lwh$

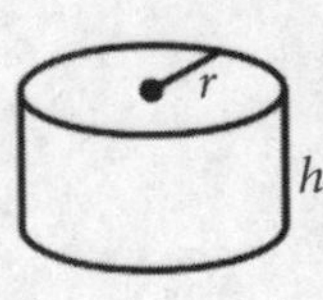

$V = \pi r^2 h$

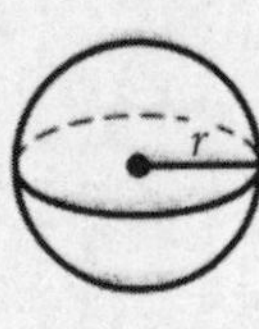

$V = \frac{4}{3}\pi r^3$

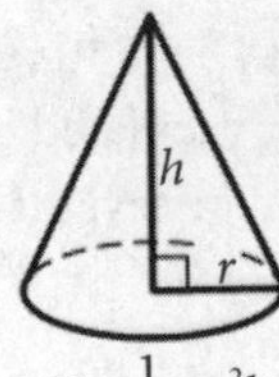

$V = \frac{1}{3}\pi r^2 h$

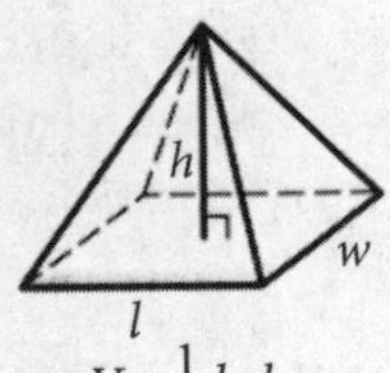

$V = \frac{1}{3}lwh$

The number of degrees of arc in a circle is 360.

The number of radians of arc in a circle is 2π.

The sum of the measures in degrees of the angles of a triangle is 180.

For **student-produced response questions**, your answer can be up to 5 characters for a positive answer and up to 6 characters (including the negative sign) for a negative answer.

If you find **more than one correct answer**, write only one answer in the blank provided.

If your answer is a **fraction** that is too long, write the decimal equivalent.

If your answer is a **decimal** that is too long, truncate it or round at the fourth digit.

If your answer is a **mixed number**, write it as an improper fraction or its decimal equivalent.

Don't include **symbols** such as a percent sign, comma, or dollar sign in your answer.

1. If $-2x + 5 = 2 - (5 - 2x)$, what is the value of x?

A. -2

B. 2

C. 3

D. 5

2. If $H(x) = 3 - 2x^2$, compute $H(x - 1)$.

A. $-2x^2 + 1$

B. $-2x^2 - 2x + 4$

C. $-2x^2 + 4x + 5$

D. $-2x^2 + 4x + 1$

3. The average weight of a medium-sized bottlenose dolphin is 400 pounds. If a particular medium-sized bottlenose dolphin weighs 110% of the average, how many pounds does the dolphin weigh?

4. During the *Apollo* 14 mission, astronaut Alan Shepard hit a golf ball on the moon. The height of the ball in meters is modeled by the function $f(t) = -0.81t^2 + 55t + 0.02$, where t is the time in seconds after the ball was hit. What does 0.02 stand for in this equation?

A. Acceleration of the ball due to gravity

B. Vertical velocity of the ball

C. Horizontal velocity of the ball

D. Height of the ball before it is hit

5.

	None	**1 to 3**	**4 or more**
Group A	8	23	19
Group B	14	21	5
Total	22	44	24

The table above shows data from demographic researchers studying the number of living siblings people have. If a person is chosen at random from Group A, what is the probability that the person has no living siblings?

A. $\frac{4}{25}$

B. $\frac{4}{11}$

C. $\frac{7}{11}$

D. $\frac{22}{25}$

CONTINUE

6. The population of a small town is growing. The town currently has 500 people. Based on the growth of the population in past years, it is estimated that the population will be 650 after 1 year. Similarly, it is estimated that after 2 years, the population will be 845, and after 3 years, the population will be 1,099. Which of the following is an expression that represents the town's population growth?

   A. 500×1.3^x

   B. $150x + 500$

   C. $500 \times (1.3)^{x-1}$

   D. $650 \times (1.3)^{x-t}$

7. The ratio of "Yes" to "No" votes at a town hall meeting regarding the installation of a new gas pipeline is 2 to 5. If there were 42 "Yes" votes, how many people, all told, voted?

   A. 105

   B. 126

   C. 147

   D. 252

8.
$$3x + y = -4$$
$$x + y = 13$$

   If (x, y) is a solution for the system of equations above, what is the value of y?

9. For what values of x, if any, does the graph of $f(x) = 2 - |4 - x|$ cross the x-axis?

   A. 4

   B. 2 and 6

   C. −2

   D. No such values

10. The surface area of a cubical cage is 1,176 square feet. What is the length of a diagonal of one of its faces, accurate to the tenths place?

11. Amy is renting a moving van for \$19.99 per day, plus an additional \$0.15 per mile. A tax of 7.5% is applied to both the daily rate and the mileage rate. Which of the following represents the total charge, y, that Amy will pay to rent the van for one day and drive it x miles?

A. $y = 19.99 + 0.075x + 0.15$

B. $y = 1.075(19.99) + 0.15x$

C. $y = 1.075(19.99 + 0.15x)$

D. $y = 1.075(19.99 + 0.15)x$

12. Line a intersects the x-axis at (3, 0) and the y-axis at (0, −2). Line b passes through the origin and does not intersect line a. Which of the following is the equation of line b?

A. $y=\frac{3}{2}x$

B. $y=\frac{2}{3}x$

C. $y=-\frac{3}{2}x$

D. $y=-\frac{2}{3}x$

13. 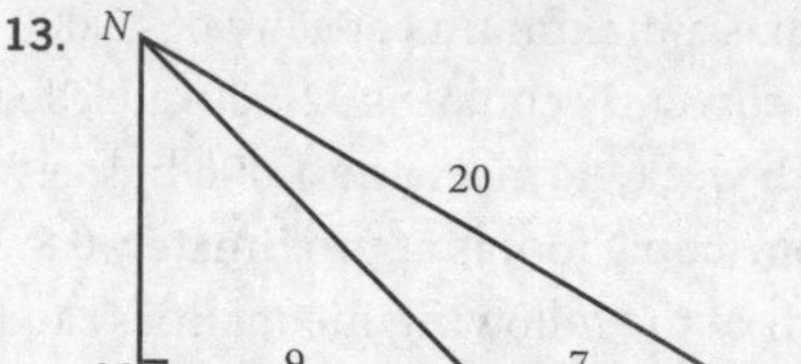

In the figure above, what is the length of NP?

A. 8

B. 9

C. 12

D. 15

14.

$$y=x^2-8x+7$$
$$y=x-1$$

If (x, y) is a solution to the system of equations above, what is a possible value of $x + y$?

15. The endpoints of a diameter of a circle are (−2, −1) and (0, −4). What is the circumference of this circle?

A. $\frac{\sqrt{13}}{2}\pi$

B. $\sqrt{13}\pi$

C. $\frac{13}{2}\pi$

D. 13π

CONTINUE

16. A grain silo has a maximum capacity of 45,000 cubic feet. It currently contains 32,500 cubic feet of grain. Each week, farmers add 1,000 bushels of grain. If one cubic foot is approximately 0.8 bushel, which of the following inequalities can be used to model the number of weeks, w, until the silo reaches its maximum capacity?

A. $32{,}500 + 1{,}250w \leq 45{,}000$

B. $32{,}500 + 800w \leq 45{,}000$

C. $32{,}500 + 1{,}250w \geq 45{,}000$

D. $32{,}500 + 800w \geq 45{,}000$

17. What is the value of a so that the points $(-a, 2)$ and $(3, 4a)$ lie on a line perpendicular to the line with the equation $x = \frac{1}{2}y - 1$?

A. $-\frac{2}{3}$

B. $\frac{1}{9}$

C. $\frac{1}{7}$

D. 4

18.

$$\frac{R_1 - R_2}{\frac{1}{R_2} + \frac{1}{R_1}} = R_2$$

Which of the following is equivalent to the equation shown above?

A. $\frac{R_1 - R_2}{R_1 + R_2} = \frac{1}{R_1}$

B. $\frac{R_1}{R_2} - \frac{R_2}{R_1} = R_2$

C. $\frac{R_1^2 - R_2^2}{R_1} = R_2$

D. $\frac{(R_1 - R_2)(R_1 + R_2)}{2} = R_2$

19. If $f(x) = 5x + 12$, what is the value of $f(p + 3) - f(p)$?

20.

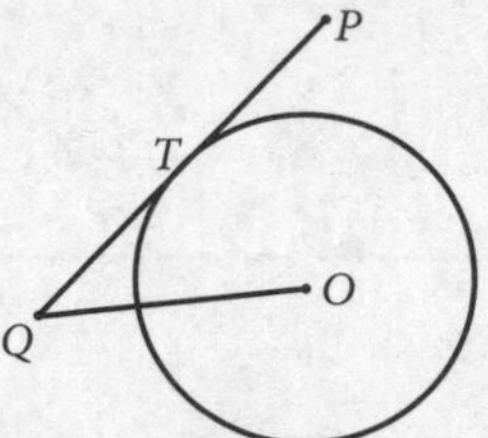

Line segment $\overline{PQ}$ is tangent to the circle with center O at point T. If T is the midpoint of $\overline{PQ}$, $OQ = 13$, and the radius of the circle is 5, what is the length of $\overline{PQ}$?

A. 10

B. 12

C. 24

D. 26

21. Fernand averaged a score of 182 for 6 games of bowling. His scores for the first three games were 212, 181, and 160. Of the remaining three games, two scores were identical, and the third was 20 points higher than one of these two games. What was the second highest score of these 6 games?

A. 173

B. 181

C. 182

D. 193

22. What is the sum of the solutions of the equation $\frac{9}{x-2}+\frac{16}{x+3}=5$?

A. –1

B. 4

C. 5

D. 6

STOP.

If you finish before time is up, you may check your work on this module only.

Do not turn to any other module in the test.

MATH

Module 2

22 Questions—35 Minutes

Directions: The questions in this section address a number of important math skills.

Use of a calculator is permitted for all questions.

Unless otherwise indicated:

- All variables and expressions represent real numbers.
- Figures provided are drawn to scale.
- All figures lie in a plane.
- The domain of a given function f is the set of all real numbers x for which $f(x)$ is a real number.

Reference:

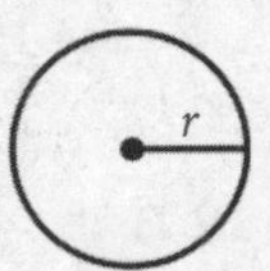

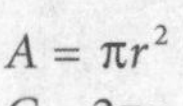

$A = \pi r^2$
$C = 2\pi r$

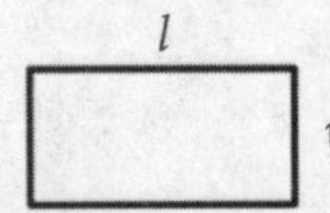

$A = lw$

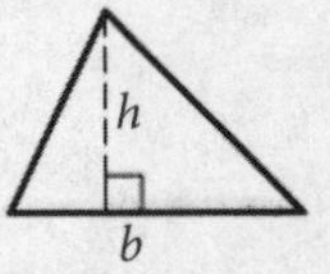

$A = \frac{1}{2}bh$

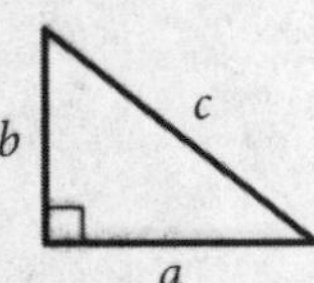

$c^2 = a^2 + b^2$

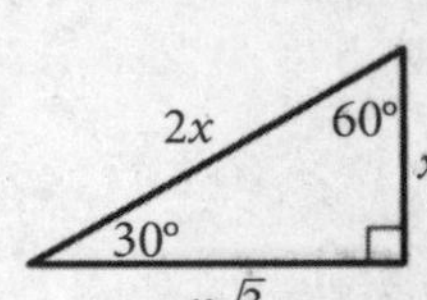

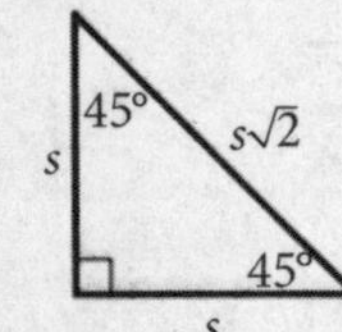

Special Right Triangles

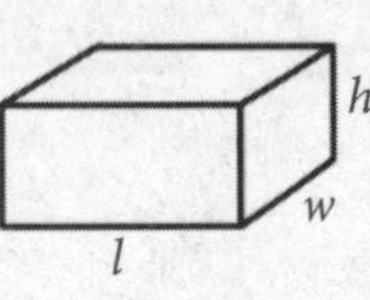

$V = lwh$

$V = \pi r^2 h$

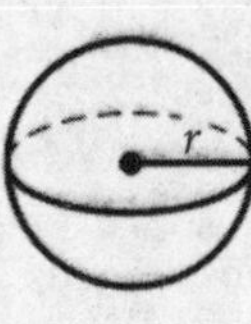

$V = \frac{4}{3}\pi r^3$

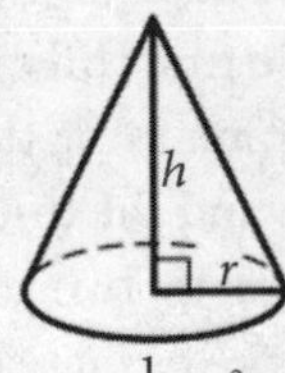

$V = \frac{1}{3}\pi r^2 h$

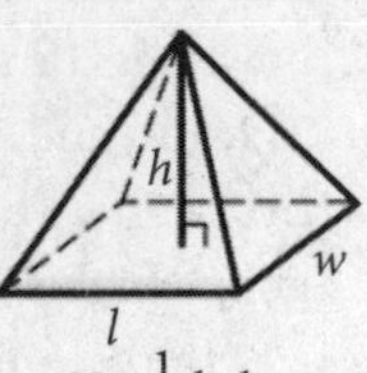

$V = \frac{1}{3}lwh$

The number of degrees of arc in a circle is 360.

The number of radians of arc in a circle is 2π.

The sum of the measures in degrees of the angles of a triangle is 180.

For **student-produced response questions**, your answer can be up to 5 characters for a positive answer and up to 6 characters (including the negative sign) for a negative answer.

If you find **more than one correct answer**, write only one answer in the blank provided.

If your answer is a **fraction** that is too long, write the decimal equivalent.

If your answer is a **decimal** that is too long, truncate it or round at the fourth digit.

If your answer is a **mixed number**, write it as an improper fraction or its decimal equivalent.

Don't include **symbols** such as a percent sign, comma, or dollar sign in your answer.

1. If $(x - 4)$ and $(x + 2)$ are factors of $f(x)$, which of the following graphs could represent the function $f(x)$?

A.
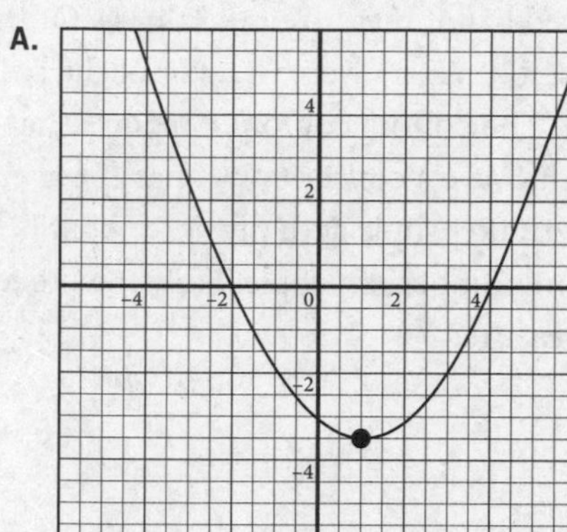

B.
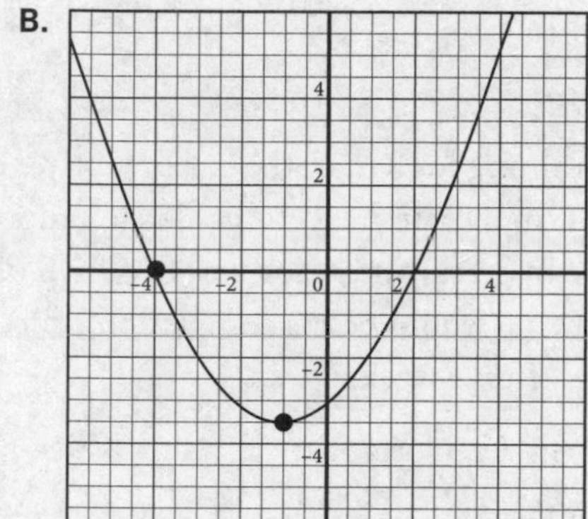

C.
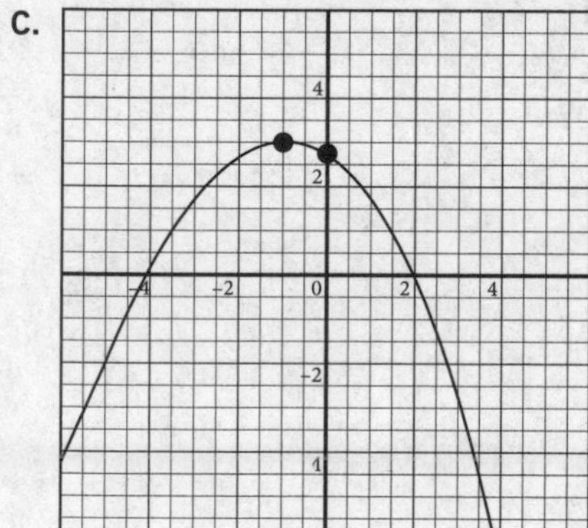

D.
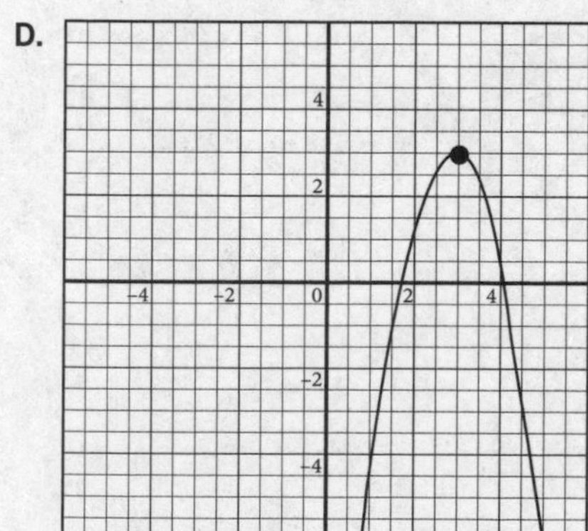

2. The Matthews family is driving to the beach, which is 480 miles away. The function that represents the distance (in miles) it takes them to get to the beach is $f(t) = 480 - 60t$, where t represents time (in hours). In this equation, t is the independent variable, and $f(t)$ is the dependent variable. At which point does the graph of the function $f(t) = 480 - 60t$ cross the x-axis?

A. (0, 480)

B. (6, 0)

C. (0, 8)

D. (8, 0)

CONTINUE

3. 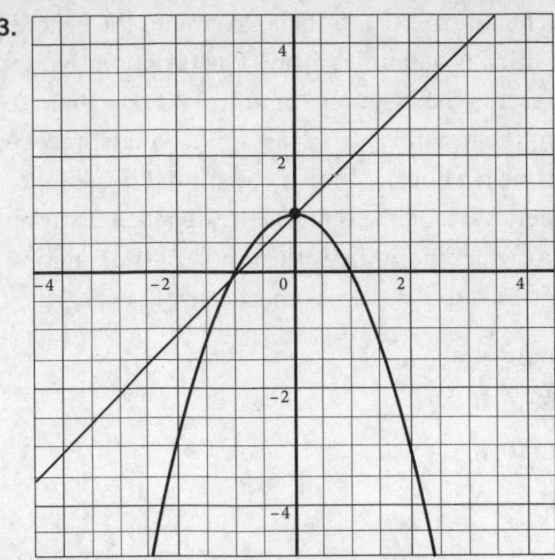

$$y = x + 1$$
$$y = -x^2 + 1$$

A system of equations and their graphs are shown above. Which of the following are solutions to the system?

A. (0, 1) and (–1, 0)

B. (0, 1) and (1, 0)

C. (–1, 0)

D. (1, 0) and (–1, 0)

4.
$$5x - 4y = 13$$
$$x + 2y = 4$$

If (x, y) is a solution of the system of equations above, what is the value of the ratio $\frac{x}{y}$?

5. A polling company surveys 625 randomly selected registered voters to determine whether a proposed ballot measure might pass. Of those surveyed, 400 voters were in favor of the ballot measure. The polling company reports that the poll results have a conservative margin of error of 4%. If 9,000 people actually vote, what is the minimum number of people likely to vote for the ballot measure?

6. Jack is training for a marathon. Currently, he runs a 5K in 29 minutes. His goal is to reduce this time by 15 seconds each week. Which of the following would be his completion time, in minutes, after w weeks?

A. $29 - 15w$

B. $29 \times 60 - 15w$

C. $29 - \frac{1}{4}w$

D. $29 + 15w$

7.

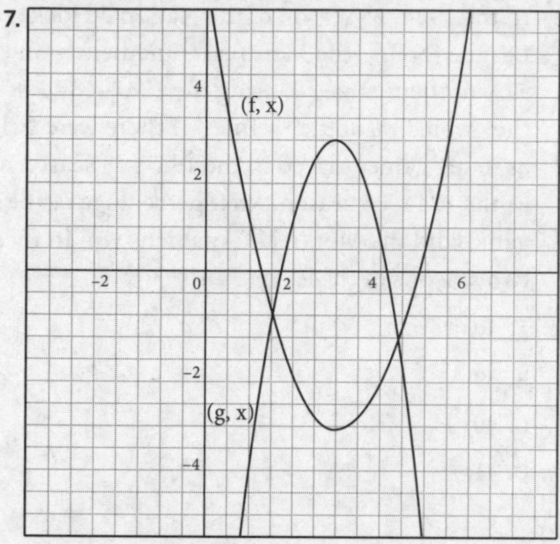

$$f(x) = (x-3)^2 - 3$$
$$g(x) = -2(x-3)^2 + 3$$

Graphs of the functions f and g are shown in the xy-plane above. For which of the following values of x does $f(x) + g(x) = 0$?

8.

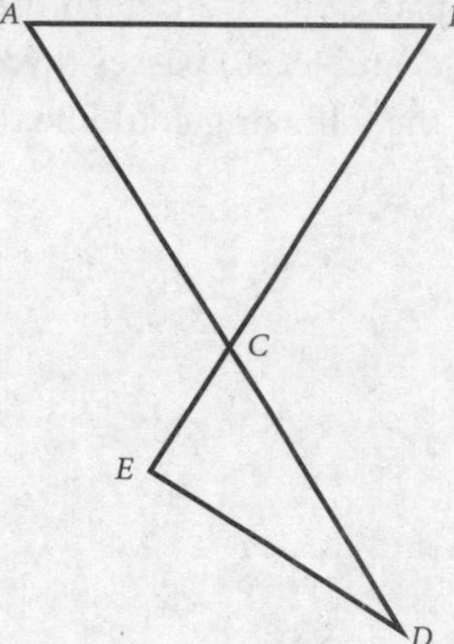

In the figure above, $AC = BC$. If $m\angle B = 50°$, what is the measure of $\angle ECD$?

A. 130°

B. 80°

C. 50°

D. 40°

9. If $f(x) = -5(2x - 1)^2 + 1$ and $g(x) = 3 - x$, which of the following equals $(f \circ g)(x)$?

A. $-(124 + 20x^2)$

B. $20x^2 - 20x + 7$

C. $4x^2 - 10x - 124$

D. $-20x^2 + 100x - 124$

CONTINUE

10. In the xy-plane, the line determined by the points $(8, c)$ and $(c, 18)$ passes through the origin. Which of the following could be the value of c?

A. 10

B. 11

C. 12

D. 13

11. A linear function $g(x)$ has x-intercept $(-3, 0)$ and y-intercept $(0, -6)$. Compute $g\left(-\frac{1}{2}\right)$.

A. −7

B. −6

C. −5

D. −2

12. In the 1924–25 season of the National Hockey League (NHL), the Montreal Canadiens won 57% of their games. During the 1947–48 season, they won 33% of their games. If there were twice as many games played in the 1947–48 season as in the 1924–25 season, what percentage of the games did the Montreal Canadiens win in these two seasons of the league?

A. 37

B. 39

C. 40

D. 41

13. An artist uses glass-blowing techniques to create glass vases. Once a vase has been made, its temperature is approximately 1,800°F. To ensure that it does not crack, it is placed in a cooling oven so that its temperature decreases slowly at a constant rate, starting at 1,800°F and ending at 60°F. After one and a half days, the temperature of the vase is 1,550°F. How many days, D, does it take for the vase to reach 60°F?

A. 7

B. 8.9

C. 10.4

D. 12

14. $$\frac{x\left(x^{-3}y^{2}\right)^{2}}{y\left(x^{2}y^{4}\right)^{-1}}=x^{a}y^{b}$$

What values of a and b make the equation true for all nonzero values of x and y?

A. $a = 3, b = 7$

B. $a = -1, b = 0$

C. $a = -3, b = 7$

D. $a = 10, b = -12$

15. In engineering, the ratio between the critical pressure p_C and initial pressures p_I of a nozzle is described by the formula $\frac{p_C}{p_I}=\left[\frac{2}{k+1}\right]^{\frac{k}{k-1}}$, where k is a physical constant related to expansion and compression. Which of the following expresses p_I in terms of p_C for $k=\frac{5}{4}$?

A. $p_I=\left(\frac{8}{9}\right)\frac{1}{p_C}$

B. $p_I=\left(\frac{9}{8}\right)^{5}p_C$

C. $p_I=\left(\frac{9}{8}\right)^{\frac{5}{16}}p_C$

D. $p_I=\left(\frac{9}{2}\right)^{5}p_C$

16. $$-3x+2y=-1$$
$$6x-by=8$$

What is the value for b that will make the system above have no solution?

17. $$A=\frac{M}{M-N}$$

What is the value of M?

A. $M=\frac{AN}{A-1}$

B. $M=\frac{AN}{1-A}$

C. $M=\frac{N}{A-1}$

D. $M=\frac{N}{1-A}$

CONTINUE

18. Yasmine owns a coffee shop and orders both coffee and tea from a wholesale supplier. The supplier will send no more than 600 kg in a shipment. Coffee beans come in packages that weigh 18.5 kg, and tea leaves come in packages that weigh 10 kg. Yasmine wants to buy at least twice as many packages of coffee as packages of tea. If c stands for the number of packages of coffee, and t stands for the number of packages of tea, which of the following systems of inequalities best represents Yasmine's order? Both c and t are nonnegative integers.

A. $18.5c + 10t \leq 600$
$c \geq 2t$

B. $18.5c + 10t \leq 600$
$2c \geq t$

C. $37c + 10t \leq 600$
$c \geq 2t$

D. $37c + 10t \leq 600$
$2c \geq t$

19. A student, who is 4 ft. 9 in. tall, is looking at their shadow as the sun sets. They measure the length of their shadow when the angle of the sun is 27.5 degrees above the horizon. A little later, the student measures their shadow again when the sun is 13.75 degrees above the horizon. What is the difference between the two shadow measurements?

A. 9.12 ft.

B. 10.29 ft.

C. 14.66 ft.

D. 19.41 ft.

20. If the expression $\frac{6x}{2x+4}$ is written in the form $3+\frac{A}{x+2}$, what is the value of A?

21.

International Market Stock

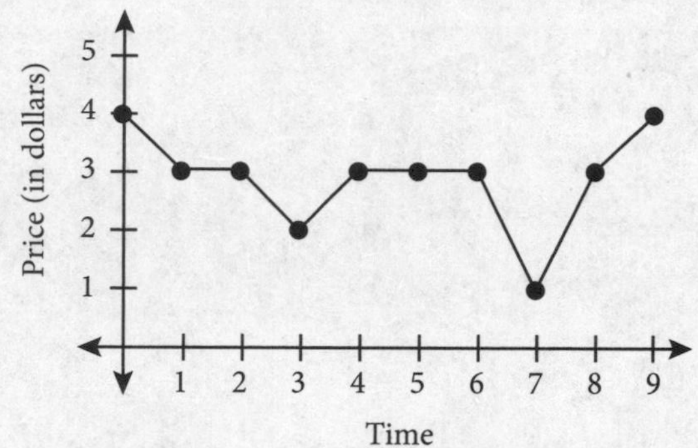

Emerging Market Stock

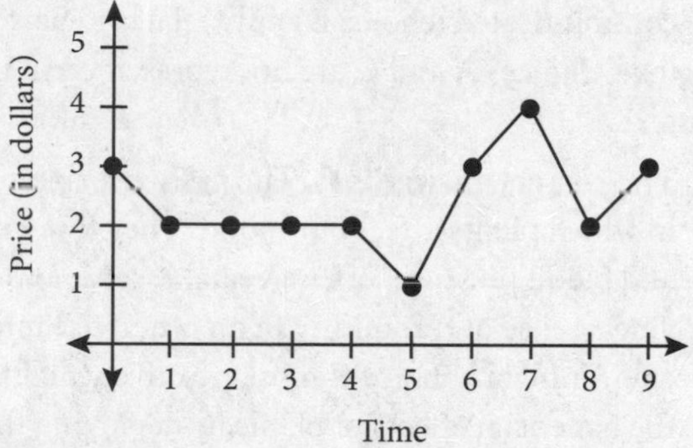

A stockbroker continually monitors the price of shares of two different stocks, one in the International Markets sector and one in the Emerging Markets sector. The values of each stock during the trading period are shown below. Here, t is time (in hours) with $t = 0$ corresponding to 7 a.m. and $t = 9$ corresponding to 4 p.m.

If the trader wanted to simultaneously sell x shares of the International Market stock and buy x shares of the Emerging Market stock, at which of the following hours would making this trade yield the largest profit?

A. 10 a.m.

B. 12 p.m.

C. 1 p.m.

D. 2 p.m.

22.

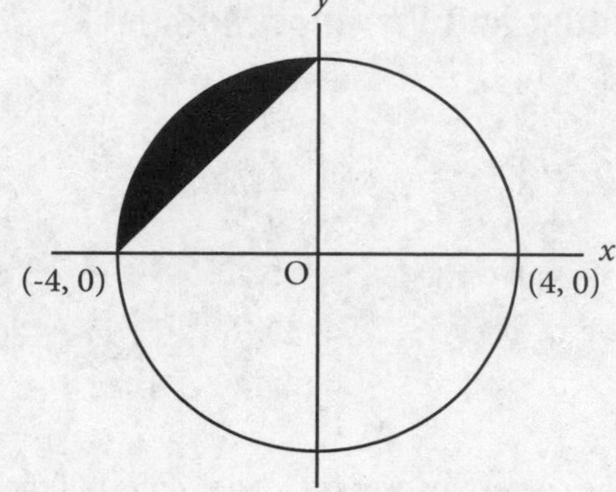

What is the area of the shaded region in the figure above?

STOP.

If you finish before time is up, you may check your work on this module only.

Do not turn to any other module in the test.

ANSWER KEY AND EXPLANATIONS

Reading and Writing: Module 1

1. C	6. C	11. C	16. B	21. D	26. B
2. B	7. A	12. C	17. A	22. C	27. A
3. A	8. B	13. B	18. A	23. D	
4. B	9. C	14. D	19. A	24. A	
5. D	10. B	15. B	20. A	25. C	

1. **The correct answer is C.** The context of the passage calls for a word that means something like "unique" or "uncommon." Only *singular* fulfills this purpose.
2. **The correct answer is B.** The context of the passage calls for a word that means something like "suggested" or "referred." *Elude* means "to avoid" or "get away from," so eliminate choices C and D. Of those that remain, *allude* + *to* is the correct idiomatic phrasal verb.
3. **The correct answer is A.** Something that is lucrative is profitable.
4. **The correct answer is B.** The term *raucous* means "harsh, loud, discordant, or dissonant."
5. **The correct answer is D.** The underlined sentence demonstrates the difficulties nanotechnology researchers encounter by using the word "challenges" and listing them as "related to scalability, safety, and ethical considerations."
6. **The correct answer is C.** The main purpose of the text is to tell the importance and history of oral storytelling traditions in the Ainu culture. The definition and example of the term *yukar* (choice B) only relate to part of the text. Choice A is too general, and choice D describes an authorial attitude missing from the objective description of Ainu oral storytelling.
7. **The correct answer is A.** The underlined sentence connects Franklin's exposure to radiation during her research to an element of her biography (dying from cancer at a young age).
8. **The correct answer is B.** The main purpose of the text is to define the term *collective memory* and its relationship with history and society, such as in the construction of memorials. The example of memorials as a way that collective memory is shared and communicated (choice D) only relates to part of the text. Choices A and C are not represented in this text.
9. **The correct answer is C.** The passage explains ways in which plants affect our mood. They lower stress and blood pressure, offer a visual escape, and provide a sense of tranquility in an otherwise mundane environment. Choice C most effectively highlights the beneficial effects of plants by deploying the word "improve" as related to a person's "disposition," meaning one's attitude or mood.
10. **The correct answer is B.** The quotation illustrates the claim that industrial society is ruining the majestic mountains with figurative language like "makes war," the idea of the mountains being split and plastered with ads, and the claim that industry "destroys the lonely fragments" of the "peace" represented by the mountains.
11. **The correct answer is C.** While the risk of cardiovascular disease increases at a more consistent rate for diabetics than for non-diabetics, it nonetheless increases for both groups as glycated hemoglobin levels increase. The upward slope of both lines attests to this fact. Choices A, B, and D all claim one or both groups do not show an increase.
12. **The correct answer is C.** The second sentence of the passage explains that the percentage of dissolved salts in a body of water is known as salinity. Since the final sentence talks about adding salt to water,

this is another way of saying that salinity increases. Knowing this, you can read the graph from left to right along the *x*-axis, noting that the lines named "Temperature of maximum density of water" and "Freezing point of water" slope downwards, indicating a decrease in both. You can then infer that adding more salt to water decreases both factors, and only choice C correctly fits this claim.

13. **The correct answer is B.** Botany is one of many scientific areas of study, each with "its own particular field." Botany, as stated by the second sentence of the passage, is differentiated from other areas of study by focusing on plants.

14. **The correct answer is D.** Edna Murphey's father invented Odorono to keep his hands from sweating when performing surgery. The text relays this information by stating "her father's antiperspirant invention" and "as a surgeon, he had wanted an invention to keep sweat off his palms when operating."

15. **The correct answer is B.** A question mark is needed at the end of the sentence because it uses the interrogative pronoun *what*, preceded by the preposition *at*, indicating a question.

16. **The correct answer is B.** The subject of the sentence is "he," referring to Basquiat. The subject takes two actions in the sentence: "He began his early career" and "rose to fame." Despite the length of the sentence and the distance between the subject "he" and the second verb "rose," no comma is necessary as the second clause is a fragment and cannot stand alone. If the sentence stated "but he rose to fame," then a comma would be placed before the coordinating conjunction *but*. Choice A creates a sentence fragment with the period. Choice C uses a semicolon to imply that the second clause is independent, similar to choice A; if it were independent, then no coordinating conjunction would need to accompany the semicolon. Choice D provides a clear subject for the verb *rose* but then fails to provide a comma before the coordinating conjunction to separate the two independent clauses.

17. **The correct answer is A.** No commas are needed in this independent clause, so you can eliminate choice B. The word order and phrasing in choices C and D change the meaning of what is stated in ways that do not match the context of the passage.

18. **The correct answer is A.** A comma is needed to separate the introductory prepositional phrase from the independent clause. Choice A provides no punctuation to separate the phrase from the clause. Choice C creates a sentence fragment by using a period. Choice D inappropriately uses an em dash to separate the independent clause from the prepositional phrase; em dashes are used to separate nonessential information that comes later in the sentence, not at the beginning.

19. **The correct answer is A.** The present tense, third person singular form of the verb "to be" should be used, *is*, because the subject is "the drink" and the topic is still relevant and active today.

20. **The correct answer is A.** As written, choices B and D contain incorrect forms of the verb "to be." Choice C uses the present tense *begin*, yet the sentence requires the past tense *began* for consistency with the rest of the paragraph. Choice A fixes the issue.

21. **The correct answer is D.** As written, choice A contains an inappropriate contraction, *I'm*, and an incorrect form of the verb "to need." Choices B and C also contain the incorrect form of the verb "to need." The sentence requires the pronoun *I* and the past tense verb *needed*; only choice D offers an appropriate combination.

22. **The correct answer is C.** The use of "unfortunately" indicates a shift in tone appropriate for the discussion of the causes of the Sumatran tiger's unfortunate endangerment, as exemplified by the factors in the animal's habitat loss.

23. **The correct answer is D.** The most logical transition is "furthermore" because it indicates that the clause that follows adds more information about Carlos's contribution to the success of the Moog synthesizer.

24. **The correct answer is A.** Context is essential when determining the appropriate conjunctive adverb to begin a sentence. Choices B, C, and D reference a contrast between the sentence the conjunctive

adverb appears in and the previous sentence—and are not appropriate here.

25. **The correct answer is C.** *Among* is the correct choice because it indicates that the Mayan understanding of astronomy was one of their many notable achievements. *Plus* (choice A) means "in addition to"—in other words, in addition to "notable achievements," the Mayans had a profound understanding of astronomy. Astronomy is one of these notable achievements, so the word choice needs to acknowledge this. *Despite* (choice B) means "in spite of," which would contradict the meaning of the sentence, and *between* (choice D) works only when there are exactly two achievements, not many.

26. **The correct answer is B.** The student introduces the topic of the Hoover Dam by providing general information as to what it is ("The Hoover Dam is a hydroelectric power plant and arch-gravity dam"), where it is ("located along the Colorado River between Nevada and Arizona"), and why it's important ("one of the most impressive engineering projects to date"). Choice A only denotes when it was built and a few features. Choice C provides anecdotes about the dam as an engineering project and its name. Choice D explains only when and why it was built.

27. **The correct answer is A.** The student introduces the term "Quechua" by stating it "is used to describe a group of indigenous people" and "the language they speak." Choices B and D give specific background information on the Quechua people, their maintenance of their culture and traditions, and the region in which they live. Choice C narrows the focus to Quechua as a language.

ANSWER KEY AND EXPLANATIONS

Reading and Writing: Module 2

1. B	6. B	11. D	16. B	21. C	26. C
2. A	7. C	12. C	17. C	22. D	27. B
3. A	8. D	13. C	18. B	23. B	
4. A	9. A	14. B	19. D	24. A	
5. D	10. B	15. C	20. C	25. D	

1. **The correct answer is B.** The word *luminous* means "vivid, lustrous, brilliant, or shining with light."

2. **The correct answer is A.** This question asks you to identify the meaning of a vocabulary term with which you might not be familiar by using the details given in the passage as context. *Flummoxed* means something like "confused, bewildered, or perplexed." As the passage states, "The border guards, who had no idea what had just been broadcast on national television, were overwhelmed by the size of the crowds and flummoxed as to what to do." If the guards were both overwhelmed and didn't have enough information to know what was happening or what to do, it would be safe to assume that they were confused. Furthermore, there are no contextual details to support the conclusion that they were angered (choice B) or disorganized (choice C). Apprised (choice D) is incorrect because it implies the guards were told what to do, which is the opposite of what happened.

3. **The correct answer is A.** The underlined sentence makes the previous sentence more understandable by explaining the simile wherein judgement and appetite are likened to two houseguests who deserve equal treatment.

4. **The correct answer is A.** The underlined sentence uses the metaphor "standing upon a cloud in space" to illustrate the author's experience of navigating two cultures (Japanese and American) at the same time, as expressed by the quotation "gazing with measuring eyes upon two separate worlds."

5. **The correct answer is D.** Text 1 illustrates the biodiversity and geography of Colombia with statistics and locations of varied natural regions wile Text 2 conveys the ways in which those ecosystems are in danger due environmental problems, including "deforestation, urbanization, overfishing, water pollution, and air pollution."

6. **The correct answer is B.** Text 2 offers examples to support the claim in Text 1 that Hegel's work influenced later thinkers. It mentions how philosophers Karl Marx and Simone de Beauvoir both used Hegelian dialectics to drive their philosophies.

7. **The correct answer is C.** Text 1 provides an overview of Shakespeare's linguistic and literary innovations, such as his contributions to the English language, invention of idiomatic expressions, and use of certain themes in his works. Text 2 offers more specific details related to Shakespeare's use of literary devices in a specific play (*Hamlet*).

8. **The correct answer is D.** According to this hypothesis, extinction occurred gradually, over the course of tens to hundreds of thousands of years. Therefore, fossil evidence of Cretaceous organisms disappearing over only a few thousand years just before the end of the Cretaceous would contradict its claims.

9. **The correct answer is A.** The hypothesis argues that dinosaurs and birds share a common ancestor. A fossil find from before the age of the dinosaurs with common features would support this view. An intermediate form between dinosaurs and birds (choice B) or an avian prototype before dinosaur dominance (choice C) would not directly support the position of a common ancestor. Examining theropod remains (choice D) does not relate to this hypothesis—instead, it discusses thecodonts.

10. **The correct answer is B.** The inference that the number 13 was associated with evil at the time the story was written can be supported by the description of the thirteenth fairy as a witch: "the thirteenth fairy was come, with a black cap on her head, and black shoes on her feet, and a broomstick in her hand." The thirteenth fairy also cast a spell in the text, which was described as an "evil wish" by the "friendly" twelfth fairy. It is also the only response that can be supported by evidence from the text.
11. **The correct answer is D.** The quotation supports the claim that the poem's narrator believes the addressee's inner beauty will last forever by comparing it to an "eternal summer" that "shall not fade," meaning it will not disappear. The narrator adds that the addressee will not "lose possession" of their inner beauty ("that fair thou ow'st").
12. **The correct answer is C.** The table indicates that as the weight of the boxes observed increases from 10 to 30 to 40 kg, the heat generated at the point the box reaches a speed of 20 km/hr increases as well. That constitutes a positive correlation between weight and heat.
13. **The correct answer is C.** The main idea of the text is that the Cree First Nations comprise a range of indigenous groups who historically shared a language that many are now trying to preserve. The danger of losing indigenous languages (choice A), the definition of the term "Cree" (choice B), and the status of the Cree as one of many different indigenous groups in Canada (choice D) relate to parts of the text and support the main idea, but they are not the main idea themselves.
14. **The correct answer is B.** The main idea of the text is that everything in nature has a season and a lifespan. The poem refers to nature in its seasons ("Nature's first green is gold" and "Her early leaf's a flower;") but indicates their fleetingness ("Her hardest hue to hold" and "But only so an hour"). Choices A, C, and D are not represented in this text.
15. **The correct answer is C.** The semicolon can be used between related independent clauses. In this instance, it is placed before a conjunctive adverb, the word *however.* In addition to the semicolon, a comma is necessary after *however* and the phrase *more recently* to separate the introductory and adverbial phrases from the rest of the second independent clause.
16. **The correct answer is B.** To introduce the independent clause that follows the question blank, a prepositional phrase can be used. Choice B uses parallel adjectives and nouns and is more concise than choice A. Choice C is an independent clause and cannot be separated from the following independent clause with just a comma. Choice D creates improper modification.
17. **The correct answer is C.** The colon is used in this sentence after the independent clause to precede a list.
18. **The correct answer is B.** The use of the present perfect in third person singular verb *has evolved* needs to agree with the predicate nominative *fusion*, making choice B the only appropriate answer. Choices A and D incorrectly imply that the fusion stopped evolving by using past perfect tense, while Choice C inaccurately uses the future tense, *will evolve*, indicating the fusion's evolution has yet to begin.
19. **The correct answer is D.** As written, choices A and C contain inappropriate use of the verb *manifesting* as it would also require a linking verb to join the participle. Both choices B and D use the required past tense form, *manifested*, yet the verb should be followed by the conjunction *as* (choice D) and not the preposition *with* (choice B).
20. **The correct answer is C.** The possessive pronoun *its* in choice C is the only logical choice since it refers to the antecedent *apartheid*, a singular noun. Choice A is a contraction of the subject *they* and the verb *are*, and choice D is a contraction of the pronoun *it* and the verb form *is*. Neither of these choices are needed in this sentence. While choice B uses a possessive pronoun, the use of the plural form makes it incorrect.

21. **The correct answer is C.** As written, choice A unnecessarily separates two independent clauses with a period and a coordinating conjunction. The word *so* is a coordinating conjunction that requires a comma to separate the two clauses, as seen in choice C. Choice B inaccurately places the adverb *largely*. Choice D places an unnecessary comma after *but* and removes punctuation between the two independent clauses.

22. **The correct answer is D.** The use of "for instance" indicates an example will be provided in relation to the previous sentence. In this case, the example is the positive outcomes of relationships among neighbors to validate the preceding statement regarding the greater likelihood of people to work together when they know each other. Choices A and C refer to a final statement, which this sentence is not. Choice B emphasizes the sentence as the passage's key point, which is also unwarranted in the context of the sentence.

23. **The correct answer is B.** The intention is to connect the solutions nature can provide with those that technology and engineering can also provide. The use of "just as" indicates the connection between the two ideas.

24. **The correct answer is A.** The sentence lists Tesla's contributions to science, including research in "alternating currents (making breakthroughs in polyphase and high-frequency current), high-voltage transmission, and wireless systems projects." Choices B and C focus on his popularity, and choice D states his importance but does not offer specifics.

25. **The correct answer is D.** The student compares the political ideologies of the two conflicting groups by using the word *clashed* and describing each group as either "anti-government" and "[demanding] political freedom" or "military" and "Communist rule." Choice A provides background information about the event. Choice B provides information describing Tiananmen Square as a popular tourist location, foregoing discussion of the parties involved in the conflict. Choice C illustrates the conflict by describing an iconic photo. While it mentions the opposing parties, it fails to speak to the nature of the conflict.

26. **The correct answer is C.** The student emphasizes the impact of the international attention paid to King Tut's tomb by using words like "worldwide headlines" and "public interest" while describing the current attraction "in museums and exhibits around the world today." Choice A focuses on the discovery of the tomb itself by Howard Carter. Choice B includes information about the tomb and its artifacts. Choice D provides biographical and historical information.

27. **The correct answer is B.** The sentence provides examples of the pain and suffering Kahlo endured in her life by using the word "many" and providing examples like her medical and marriage problems. Choice A describes her as an icon in contemporary pop culture. Choice C explains her self-portraits, and choice D focuses on her physical appearance.

ANSWER KEY AND EXPLANATIONS

Math: Module 1

1. B	**6.** A	**11.** C	**16.** A	**21.** D
2. D	**7.** C	**12.** B	**17.** B	**22.** B
3. 440	**8.** 21.5	**13.** D	**18.** A	
4. D	**9.** B	**14.** 15 or 1	**19.** 15	
5. A	**10.** 19.8	**15.** B	**20.** C	

1. **The correct answer is B.** Solve for x:

$$-2x+5=2-(5-2x)$$
$$-2x+5=2-5+2x$$
$$-2x+5=-3+2x \quad \text{Add } 2x \text{ to both sides.}$$
$$5=-3+4x \quad \text{Add } +3 \text{ to both sides.}$$
$$8=4x \quad \text{Divide by 4.}$$
$$2=x$$

2. **The correct answer is D.** Substitute the expression $x - 1$ in for x and simplify:

$$H(x-1)=3-2(x-1)^2$$
$$=3-2(x^2-2x+1)$$
$$=3-2x^2+4x-2$$
$$=-2x^2+4x+1$$

3. **The correct answer is 440.** If the dolphin weighs 110% of the average, it weighs 10% more than the average weight of 400 pounds, or $0.10 \times 400 = 40$ pounds. The dolphin weighs $400 + 40 = 440$ pounds.

4. **The correct answer is D.** When $t = 0$, the height of the ball is 0.02 m, so 0.02 represents the height of the ball before it is hit.

5. **The correct answer is A.** There are a total of $8 + 23 + 19 = 50$ people in Group A, and 8 of them have no living siblings. The probability is as follows:

$$\frac{8}{50}=\frac{4}{25}$$

6. **The correct answer is A.** The initial population of the town is 500. The rate of change between consecutive x values (1 year, 2 years, 3 years) is not constant. As a result, the expression cannot be linear, and choice B is eliminated. Determine the ratio of each year's population to the previous year's population. Comparing the population after one year to the initial population, we have: $\frac{650}{500}=1.3$

If the population is growing exponentially, then we can calculate the population after x years by multiplying the initial population by 1.3 raised to the x power. Choice A represents that calculation. (You can eliminate choice C by substituting $x = 1$ year, and choice D doesn't make sense because it introduces the undefined quantity t.)

7. **The correct answer is C.** Let x be the number of "No" votes. Set up the following proportion and solve for x:

$$\frac{2}{5}=\frac{42}{x}$$
$$2x=42(5)$$
$$x=105$$

The number of people who voted, all told, is the sum of "Yes" and "No" votes, namely $105 + 42 = 147$.

8. **The correct answer is 21.5.** First, combine the equations by subtracting $(x + y = 13)$ from $(3x + y = -4)$:

$$3x+y=-4$$
$$\underline{-(x+y=13)}$$
$$2x=-17$$
$$x=-8.5$$

Then substitute the value of x into one of the equations to solve for y:

$$-8.5+y=13$$
$$y=21.5$$

9. The correct answer is B. Solve the equation $2-|4-x|=0$. This is the same as $|4-x|=2$, which breaks down into two equations, namely $4-x=2$ and $4-x=-2$. Solving these for x yields the solutions $x=2$ and $x=6$.

10. The correct answer is 19.8. Let e be an edge of a face of this cube. The surface area is $6e^2$. Solve the following equation for e:

$$6e^2=1{,}176$$
$$e^2=196$$
$$e=14$$

Let d be a diagonal of an edge. Use the Pythagorean theorem to find d:

$$14^2+14^2=d^2$$
$$2\cdot 14^2=d^2$$
$$14\sqrt{2}=d$$
$$d\approx 19.8$$

11. The correct answer is C. The total charge that Amy will pay is the daily rate, the mileage rate, and the 7.5% tax on both. If Amy drove x miles, then the total charge is $(19.99+0.15x)+0.075(19.99+0.15x)$, which can be rewritten as $1.075(19.99+0.15x)$.

12. The correct answer is B. Since we know points on line a, we can calculate the slope of this line:

$$\frac{y_2-y_1}{x_2-x_1}=\frac{-2-0}{0-3}=\frac{2}{3}$$

Since line b does not intersect line a, it must be parallel. Thus, the two lines have the same slope: $\frac{2}{3}$. The problem tells us that line b passes through the origin, which means that it intercepts the y-axis at 0. Thus, line b can be expressed by the equation $y=\frac{2}{3}x$.

13. The correct answer is D. Notice that this figure is really two right triangles, *NMO* and *NMP*. Since *NM* is a side of both triangles, once you find its length, you can find the length of *NP*. The Pythagorean theorem is what you need:

$$NM^2+MO^2=NO^2$$
$$NM^2+(16)^2=(20)^2$$

Note that 16 and 20 are multiples of 4 and 5, respectively, so you now know that this is a 3-4-5 right triangle, which means that $NM=12$. Since you just found out that triangle *NMP* has sides of 9 and 12, it's also a 3-4-5 right triangle, so *NP* must be 15.

14. The correct answer is 15 or 1.

$$y=x^2-8x+7$$
$$y=x-1$$
$$x^2-8x+7=x-1$$
$$x^2\quad 9x+8=0$$
$$(x-8)(x-1)=0$$
$$x=8 \text{ or } x=1$$

If $x=8$, then $y=8-1=7$

If $x=1$, then $y=1-1=0$

$x+y=15$ or $x+y=1$

15. The correct answer is B. Calculate the distance between the endpoints. The length of the diameter, d, is:

$$d=\sqrt{(-2-0)^2+(-1-(-4))^2}$$
$$=\sqrt{4+9}$$
$$=\sqrt{13}$$

The circumference of a circle is $\pi d=\sqrt{13}\pi$.

16. The correct answer is A. The amount of grain added each week is 1,000 bushels. Divide 1,000 bushels by 0.8 bushels per cubic foot to obtain 1,250 cubic feet per week. So the total amount of grain in the silo is 32,500 (what is already there) plus $1{,}250w$ (the amount added each week times the number of weeks), which must be less than or equal to the volume of the silo, 45,000 cubic feet.

17. **The correct answer is B.** First, find the slope of the given line by putting it into $y = mx + b$ form:

$$2x = y - 2$$
$$y = 2x + 2$$

The slope of the given line is 2. The slope of the desired line, being perpendicular to this one, is $-\frac{1}{2}$. Use the definition of slope to set up the following equation to determine the value of a:

$$\frac{4a-2}{3-(-a)} = -\frac{1}{2}$$
$$\frac{4a-2}{3+a} = -\frac{1}{2}$$
$$2(4a-2) = -(3+a)$$
$$8a-4 = -3-a$$
$$9a = 1$$
$$a = \frac{1}{9}$$

18. **The correct answer is A.** Get a common denominator in the bottom of the left side and simplify, as follows:

$$\frac{R_1 - R_2}{\frac{1}{R_2} + \frac{1}{R_1}} = R_2$$

$$\frac{R_1 - R_2}{\frac{R_1 + R_2}{R_1 R_2}} = R_2$$

$$(R_1 - R_2)\frac{R_1 R_2}{R_1 + R_2} = R_2$$

$$\frac{R_1 - R_2}{R_1 + R_2} = \frac{\cancel{R_2}}{R_1 \cancel{R_2}}$$

$$\frac{R_1 - R_2}{R_1 + R_2} = \frac{1}{R_1}$$

19. **The correct answer is 15.** To begin:

$f(p + 3) = 5(p + 3) + 12 = 5p + 15 + 12 = 5p + 27$

Similarly:

$f(p) = 5p + 12$

Thus:

$$\begin{aligned} f(p+3) - f(p) &= 5p + 27 - (5p + 12) \\ &= 5p + 27 - 5p - 12 \\ &= 15 \end{aligned}$$

20. **The correct answer is C.** You are told that the radius of the circle is 5, and if you draw in the radius, you will create triangle OTQ. Use the fact that a tangent line to a circle is perpendicular to the radius at the point of contact to deduce that OTQ is a right angle.

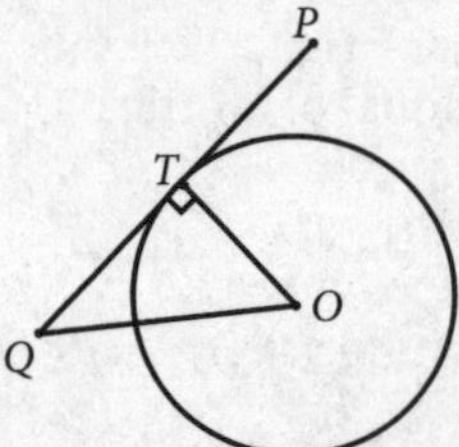

The diagram now depicts right triangle OTQ, and $OT = 5$ and $OQ = 13$. Now, use the Pythagorean theorem to determine that $TQ = 12$, as shown here:

$$OT^2 + TQ^2 = OQ^2$$
$$5^2 + TQ^2 = 13^2$$
$$25 + TQ^2 = 169$$
$$TQ^2 = 144$$
$$TQ = 12$$

Finally, since T is the midpoint of line segment $\overline{PQ}$, the entire length of the line segment is $12 + 12 = 24$.

21. **The correct answer is D.** Let x represent the score of one of the two games in which he scored identically. Then, the score of the third game is $x + 20$. Since the average of all six games is 182, solve the following equation for x:

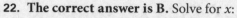

$$\frac{212+181+160+x+x+(x+20)}{6}=182$$
$$\frac{573+3x}{6}=182$$
$$573+3x=1{,}092$$
$$3x=519$$
$$x=173$$

So his six scores were 160, 173, 173, 181, 193, and 212. Therefore, the second highest score is 193.

22. The correct answer is B. Solve for x:

$$\frac{9}{x-2}+\frac{16}{x+3}=5$$
$$\left(\frac{9}{x-2}+\frac{16}{x+3}\right)(x-2)(x+3)=5(x-2)(x+3)$$
$$9x+27+16x-32=5x^2+5x-30$$
$$0=5x^2-20x-25$$
$$0=5(x+1)(x-5)$$
$$x=-1 \text{ or } x=5$$

To get the sum of the solutions, simply add –1 and 5 to get 4.

NOTES

ANSWER KEY AND EXPLANATIONS

Math: Module 2

1. A	6. C	11. C	16. 4	21. B
2. D	7. 3	12. D	17. A	22. 4.57
3. A	8. B	13. C	18. A	
4. 6	9. D	14. C	19. B	
5. 5400	10. C	15. B	20. –6	

1. **The correct answer is A.** Because the function f has $(x - 4)$ and $(x + 2)$ as factors, the function should have zeros when $x - 4 = 0$ and $x + 2 = 0$. The only graph that shows a curve that has x-intercepts at –2 and 4 is choice A.

2. **The correct answer is D.** The graph will cross the x-axis at the point where the function (that is, the y-coordinate) has a value of 0. As a result, the following equation needs to be solved:

$$480 - 60t = 0$$
$$-60t = -480$$
$$t = 8$$

Since t represents the independent variable, the point is (8, 0).

3. **The correct answer is A.** The two intersections of the graphs of the equations are at the points (0, 1) and (–1, 0). Substituting 0 for x and 1 for y makes both equations true. Also, substituting –1 for x and 0 for y makes both equations true.

4. **The correct answer is 6.** First, solve for x by multiplying the second equation by 2 so that the coefficient of y will be 4, the additive inverse (the opposite) of the y coefficient in the first equation. Add the two equations to eliminate y.

$$\begin{array}{r} 5x - 4y = 13 \\ x + 2y = 4 \\ \hline 5x - 4y = 13 \\ 2x + 4y = 8 \\ \hline 7x = 21 \\ x = 3 \end{array}$$

Then, substitute $x = 3$ into the second equation to get the value of y:

$$3 + 2y = 4$$
$$2y = 1$$
$$y = \frac{1}{2}$$

Finally, substitute $x = 3$ and $y = \frac{1}{2}$ into $\frac{x}{y}$ to get the value of the ratio:

$$\frac{x}{y} = \frac{3}{\frac{1}{2}} = 6$$

5. **The correct answer is 5400.** Of the number of voters polled, 400 of 625, or 64%, were in favor of the measure. If the margin of error is 4%, the likely population proportion will be between 60% and 68%:

60% of 9,000 total voters is (0.6)(9,000) = 5,400.

6. **The correct answer is C.** There are 60 seconds in one minute and 15 seconds equals $\frac{1}{4}$ minute. The number of minutes reduced after w weeks is $\frac{1}{4}w$. Subtracting this from 29 yields the number of minutes equal to Jack's completion time after w weeks.

7. **The correct answer is 3.** The sum of the function values is 0 when the function values for f and g are opposites. That appears to be true at $x = 3$.

Substitute in each function in the equation $f(x) + g(x) = 0$ and solve for x:

$$
\begin{aligned}
f(x)+g(x)&=0\\
(x-3)^2-3+\left(-2(x-3)^2+3\right)&=0\\
x^2-6x+9-3+\left(-2\left(x^2-6x+9\right)+3\right)&=0\\
x^2-6x+6-2x^2+12x-18+3&=0\\
-x^2+6x-9&=0\\
-(x-3)^2&=0\\
x&=3
\end{aligned}
$$

8. **The correct answer is B.** If $AC = BC$, then $m\angle A = m\angle B = 50°$.

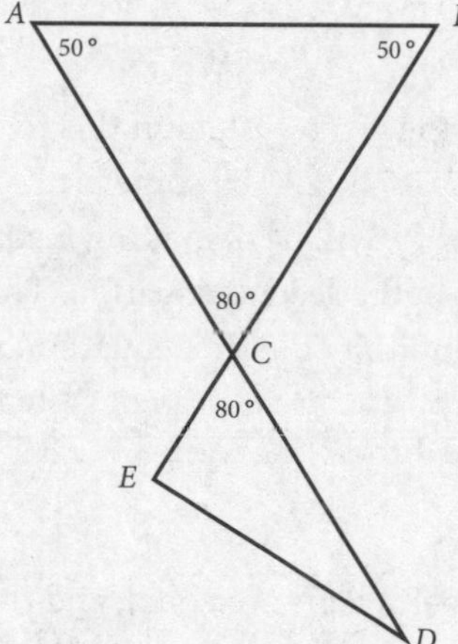

In ΔABC, $m\angle ACB = 180° - (m\angle A + m\angle B)$

So $m\angle ACB = 80°$.

Further, $m\angle ACB = m\angle ECD$ because they are opposite angles.

Therefore, $m\angle ECD = 80°$.

9. **The correct answer is D.** Compute the composition as follows:

$$
\begin{aligned}
(f\circ g)(x)&=f(g(x))\\
&=-5\left[2(3-x)-1\right]^2+1\\
&=-5\left[5-2x\right]^2+1\\
&=-5\left[25-20x+4x^2\right]+1\\
&=-125+100x-20x^2+1\\
&=-20x^2+100x-124
\end{aligned}
$$

10. **The correct answer is C.** Find the slope of the line by using one of the points from the question $(c, 18)$ and the origin $(0, 0)$: $m=\frac{18-0}{c-0}=\frac{18}{c}$. Substitute this value into the slope-intercept equation for a line along with the other point from the question $(8, c)$ and solve for c:

$$
\begin{aligned}
y&=mx+b\\
c&=\frac{18}{c}(8)+0\\
c&=\frac{144}{c}\\
c^2&=144\\
c&=12
\end{aligned}
$$

11. **The correct answer is C.** The slope is $m=\frac{0-(-6)}{-3-0}=-2$. Using this in $y = mx + b$ with the y-intercept $b = -6$ yields the equation $y = -2x - 6$. This is $g(x)$. So $g\left(-\frac{1}{2}\right)=-2\left(-\frac{1}{2}\right)-6=1-6=-5$.

12. **The correct answer is D.** The number of games that the Montreal Canadiens played is not provided, but it is given that the ratio of the number of games played in the 1947–48 season to that in the 1924–25 season is 2:1. Problems like this can be solved by plugging in real numbers. Let's say that there were 100 games in the 1924–25 season, so they won 57 of those games. In the 1947–48 season, there were twice as many games, or 200 games, so they won 33% of 200 games, or 66 games. Altogether they won 123 out of 300 games, and this fraction can be simplified to 41 out of 100, or 41%.

13. **The correct answer is C.** Using the points (0, 1,800) and (1.5, 1,550), find the equation of the line. The slope is $m=\frac{1{,}800-1{,}550}{0-1.5}=\frac{-250}{1.5}=\frac{-500}{3}$. Since the y-intercept is 1,800, the equation of the line is $y=-\frac{500}{3}x+1{,}800$. Now, determine the value of x for which this equals 60:

$$-\frac{500}{3}x+1,800=60$$
$$-\frac{500}{3}x=-1,740$$
$$x=1,740\left(\frac{3}{500}\right)$$
$$=\frac{261}{25}=10.44$$

As such, it takes approximately 10.4 days for the vase to cool. Choice A is the result of using point (1, 1,550) instead of (1.5, 1,550), choice B uses 1,550 instead of 1,800 as the y-intercept, and choice D is a significant overestimate.

14. **The correct answer is C.** Use the exponent rules to write the given expression in the desired form:

$$\frac{x(x^{-3}y^2)^2}{y(x^2y^4)^{-1}}=\frac{x^{-5}y^4}{x^{-2}y^{-3}}$$
$$=\frac{x^2y^3y^4}{x^5}=\frac{x^2y^7}{x^5}=x^{-3}y^7$$

As such, $a = -3$ and $b = 7$. Choice A has the wrong sign on the a-value. In choice B, you simplified a "power to a power" incorrectly. In choice D, you simplified the quotient of terms with the same base raised to powers incorrectly.

15. **The correct answer is B.** Substitute $k=\frac{5}{4}$ and simplify:

$$\frac{p_C}{p_I}=\left[\frac{2}{\frac{5}{4}+1}\right]^{\frac{\frac{5}{4}}{\frac{5}{4}-1}}=\left[\frac{2}{\frac{5}{4}+\frac{4}{4}}\right]^{\frac{\frac{5}{4}}{\frac{1}{4}}}$$
$$=\left[\frac{2}{\frac{9}{4}}\right]^{\frac{5}{1}}=\left[\frac{8}{9}\right]^5=\frac{8^5}{9^5}$$

Now, solve for p_I:

$$\frac{p_C}{p_I}=\frac{8^5}{9^5}$$
$$9^5p_C=8^5p_I$$
$$\frac{9^5p_C}{8^5}=p_I$$
$$\left(\frac{9}{8}\right)^5p_C=p_I$$

16. **The correct answer is 4.** In general, a system of equations that has no solution takes this form, where a, b, m, and n are constants:

$$ax+by=m$$
$$ax+by=n$$

To rewrite the given system in this form, we must multiply $-3x + 2y = -1$ by some factor so that the coefficient of x will be 6, making it equal to the coefficient in the second equation. That factor is -2. When we multiply the first equation by -2, the given system becomes this equivalent system:

$$6x-4y=2$$
$$6x-by=8$$

Now the coefficients are equal, and the y coefficients would be equal if $b = 4$. So if $b = 4$, then the system has no solution.

17. **The correct answer is A.**

$$A=\frac{M}{M-N}$$
$$A(M-N)=M$$
$$AM-AN=M$$
$$AM-M=AN$$
$$M(A-1)=AN$$
$$M=\frac{AN}{A-1}$$

18. **The correct answer is A.** Start by using the variables c for coffee beans and t for tea. The total weight, in kg, of coffee beans and tea that the wholesale supplier sends can be expressed as the weight of each package multiplied by the number of each type of package, which is $18.5c$ for coffee beans and $10t$ for tea leaves. Since the supplier will not send shipments that weigh more than 600 kg,

it follows that $18.5c + 10t \le 600$ expresses the first part of the problem. Since Yasmine wants to buy at least twice as many packages of coffee beans as packages of tea leaves, the number of packages of coffee beans should be greater than or equal to two times the number of packages of tea leaves. This can be expressed by $c \ge 2t$.

19. The correct answer is B. First, convert the height of the person to 4.75 ft. to simplify your calculations. Next, build a model of the situations to track the different components.

For the first shadow-length measurement, draw the following:

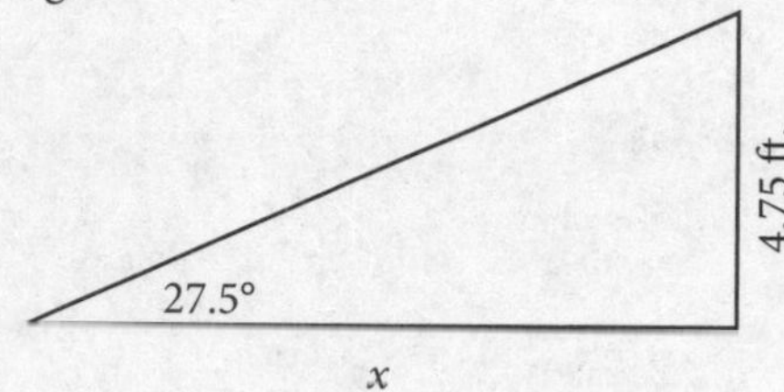

To find the length of the shadow on the ground when the sun is 27.5° from the horizon, you can do the following:

$$\tan 27.5 = \frac{4.75}{x}$$
$$x(\tan 27.5) = 4.75$$
$$x = \frac{4.75}{\tan 27.5}$$
$$x = 9.12$$

With that same setup, you can calculate the length of the shadow when the sun is 13.75° above the horizon. Proceeding through those calculations, you find that $x = 19.41$. Now subtract one value from the other to find that the difference in the length of the shadows is 10.29 ft.

20. The correct answer is –6. Simplify the ratio $\frac{6x}{2x+4}$ by factoring out the greatest common factor (2). The result is $\frac{3x}{x+2}$. Set $\frac{3x}{x+2} = 3 + \frac{A}{x+2}$ and solve.

$$\frac{3x}{x+2} = 3 + \frac{A}{x+2}$$
$$\frac{3x(x+2)}{x+2} = 3(x+2) + \frac{A(x+2)}{x+2}$$
$$3x = 3(x+2) + A$$
$$3x = 3x + 6 + A$$
$$A = -6$$

21. The correct answer is B. The strategy is to make the trade at a time when the International Market stock is worth the most and simultaneously the Emerging Market stock is worth the least. You can identify the times when the two stocks have the greatest range in value, but only when the International Market stock is higher than the Emerging Market stock. Doing so for each time would yield the following table:

t	Time	International Market Stock Price (in Dollars)	Emerging Market Stock Price (in Dollars)	Profit: International Market – Emerging Market
0	7 a.m.	4	3	1
1	8 a.m.	3	2	1
2	9 a.m.	3	2	1
3	10 a.m.	2	2	0
4	11 a.m.	3	2	1
5	12 p.m.	3	1	2
6	1 p.m.	3	3	0
7	2 p.m.	1	4	–3
8	3 p.m.	3	2	1
9	4 p.m.	4	3	1

From the table, you can see that the best time to make the trade is 12 p.m.

22. The correct answer is 4.57. To find the area of the shaded region, we first obtain the area of the circle, then find the area of the sector of the circle containing the shaded region. Because the circle is centered at the origin, the part of the circle that lies in Quadrant II is one fourth of the total circle. You can find the area of the entire circle and multiply by $\frac{1}{4}$ as follows:

$$\text{Area of Circle} = \pi r^2$$
$$\text{Area of Circle} = 16\pi$$
$$\text{Area of Sector} = \frac{1}{4}(16\pi)$$
$$\text{Area of Sector} = 4\pi \approx 12.57$$

Now, you need to subtract the area of the triangle bounded by the x- and y-axis and the shaded region, triangle OAB, from the area of the sector containing the shaded region. Triangle OAB has a height and base of 4 (the radius of the circle) and has an area of $\frac{1}{2}bh = \frac{1}{2}(4)(4) = 8$. Therefore, the area of the shaded region = 12.57 – 8 = 4.57.

SCORING CHARTS

Mark missed questions and then calculate the total number of questions you answered correctly for each question domain, module, and test section.

READING AND WRITING			
Question Domains	**Question Numbers**	**Module Totals**	**Raw Scores**
Craft and Structure	**Module 1:** 1, 2, 3, 4, 5, 6, 7, 8	**Module 1:**_______/8	_______/15
	Module 2: 1, 2, 3, 4, 5, 6, 7	**Module 2:**_______/7	
Information and Ideas	**Module 1:** 9, 10, 11, 12, 13, 14	**Module 1:**_______/6	_______/13
	Module 2: 8, 9, 10, 11, 12, 13, 14	**Module 2:**_______/7	
Standard English Conventions	**Module 1:** 15, 16, 17, 18, 19, 20, 21	**Module 1:**_______/7	_______/14
	Module 2: 15, 16, 17, 18, 19, 20, 21	**Module 2:**_______/7	
Expression of Ideas	**Module 1:** 22, 23, 24, 25, 26, 27	**Module 1:**_______/6	_______/12
	Module 2: 22, 23, 24, 25, 26, 27	**Module 2:**_______/6	
			Total Raw Score: _______**/54**

MATH			
Question Domains	**Question Numbers**	**Module Totals**	**Raw Scores**
Algebra	**Module 1:** 1, 8, 11, 12, 16, 17, 19	**Module 1:**_______/7	_______/15
	Module 2: 2, 4, 6, 10, 11, 13, 16, 18	**Module 2:**_______/8	
Advanced Math	**Module 1:** 2, 4, 6, 9, 14, 18, 22	**Module 1:**_______/7	_______/15
	Module 2: 1, 3, 7, 9, 14, 15, 17, 20	**Module 2:**_______/8	
Problem-Solving and Data Analysis	**Module 1:** 3, 5, 7, 21	**Module 1:**_______/4	_______/7
	Module 2: 5, 12, 21	**Module 2:**_______/3	
Geometry and Trigonometry	**Module 1:** 10, 13, 15, 20	**Module 1:**_______/4	_______/7
	Module 2: 8, 19, 22	**Module 2:**_______/3	
			Total Raw Score: _______/44

Use the raw-to-scaled score conversion charts on pages 117 (Reading and Writing) and 257 (Math) to see your estimated score range. Then, record the values in the table below. Combine your section totals to calculate your total SAT score.

SAT TEST SECTION AND FINAL SCORES	
Test Section	**Scaled Scores**
Reading and Writing	_______/800
Math	_______/800
SAT Total Score	**_______/1600**

CHAPTER

Using Your Diagnostic Test Results

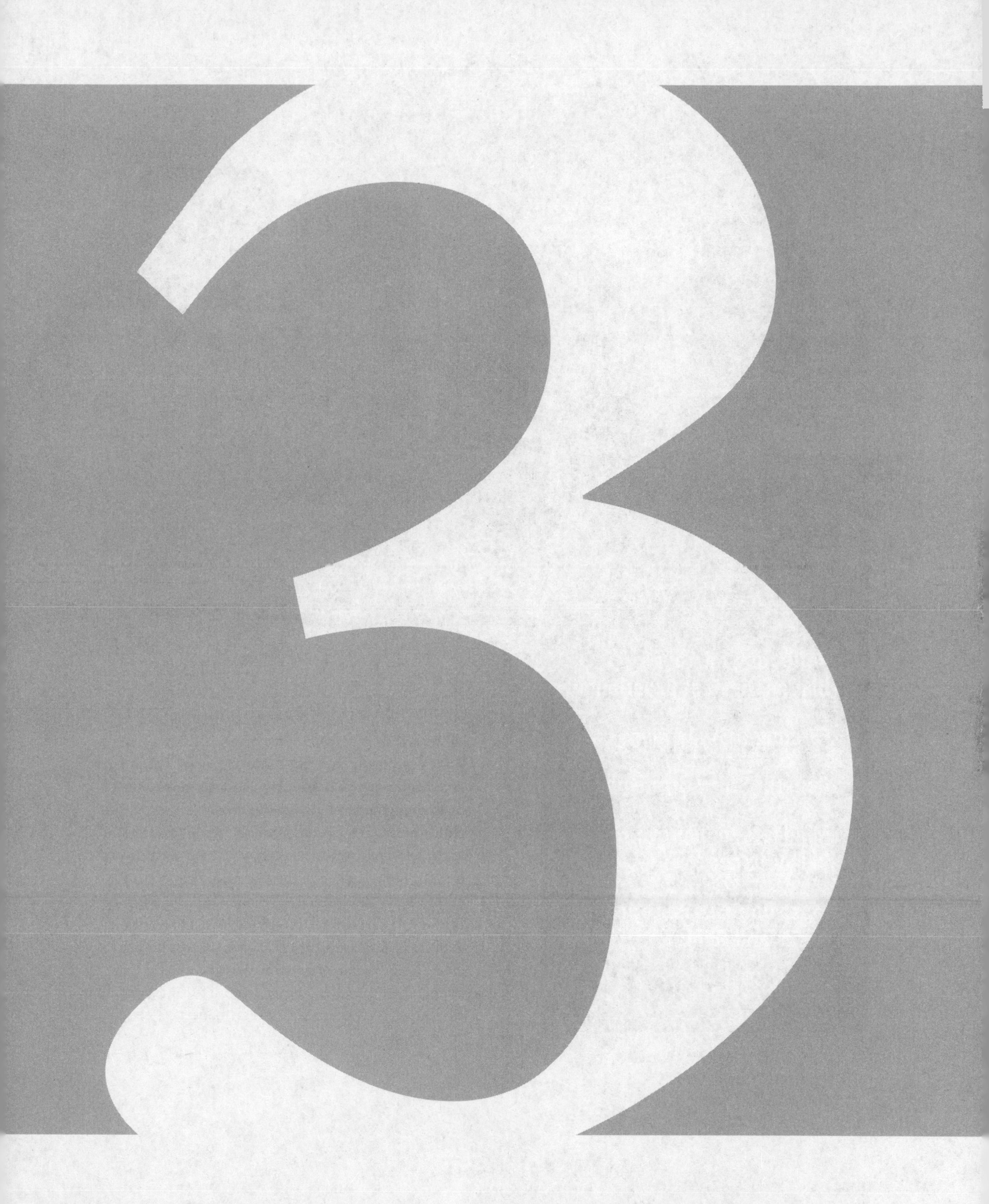

USING YOUR DIAGNOSTIC TEST

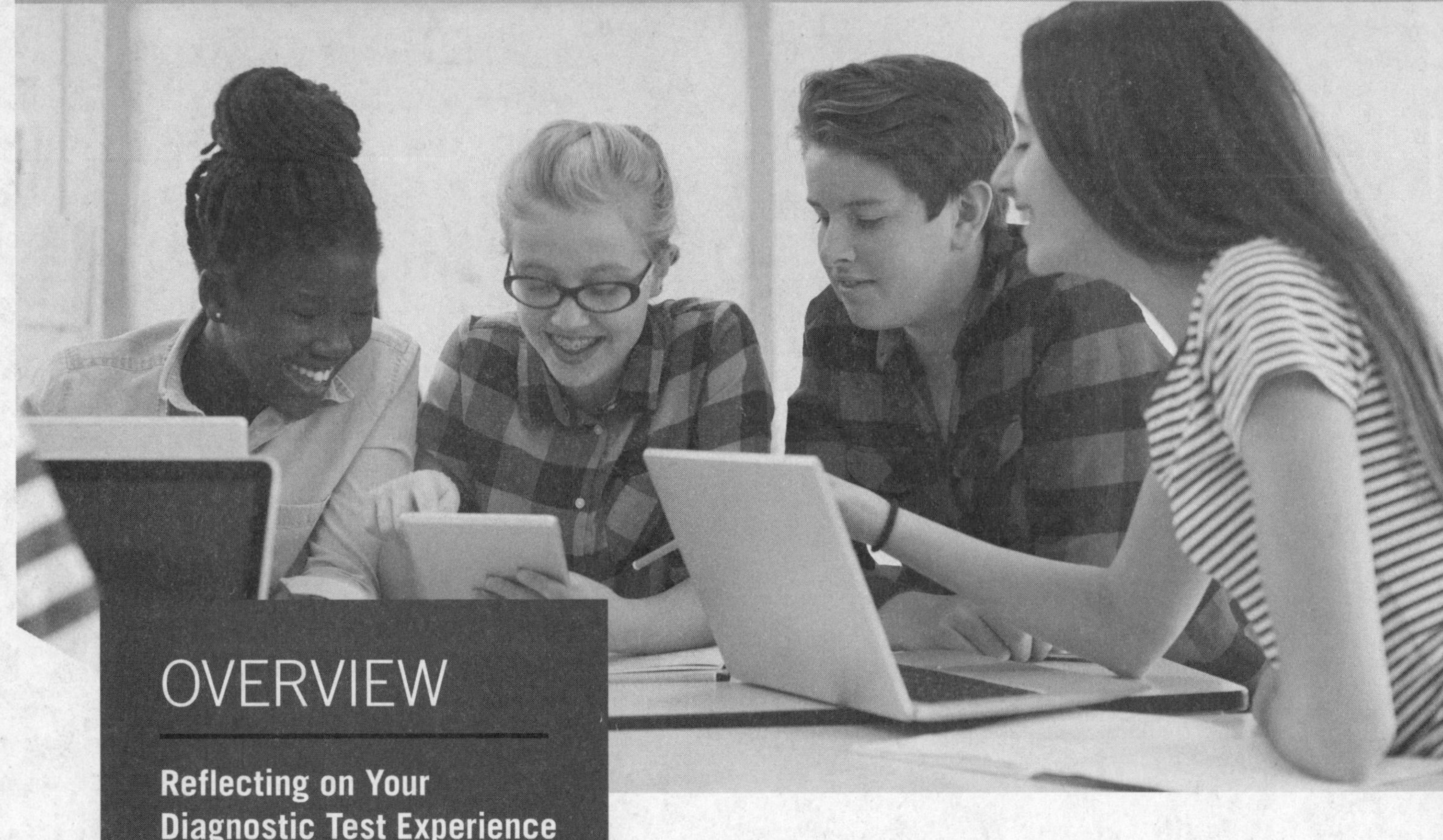

OVERVIEW

In the last chapter, you took a diagnostic test to establish a baseline for your SAT preparedness. The purpose of a diagnostic test is exactly what it sounds like—it diagnoses your strengths and weaknesses so you can make informed decisions about how you want to study going forward. In this chapter, we'll help you reflect on your performance in the diagnostic test so you can make the most of your study time while prepping for the SAT. We'll offer reflection questions to help you analyze your diagnostic test scores, discuss how to create a study plan, offer some tips to make the most of your studying, and talk about overall test strategies that can help you optimize your performance.

RESULTS 3

REFLECTING ON YOUR DIAGNOSTIC TEST EXPERIENCE

The SAT is not just about what you know. It's also about how well you apply what you know. The test places constraints on you, the test taker, and your responses to those constraints can impact your score, for better or worse. Familiarizing yourself with the test format by taking a diagnostic test is one of the first steps towards internalizing those constraints and learning how to respond to them in ways that positively impact your score. A diagnostic test like the one we included in Chapter 2 can provide you useful feedback to help meaningfully shape your test prep journey. Before we break down how to make a study plan based on your performance in individual test sections, take a moment to reflect on your overall experience during your diagnostic test.

DIAGNOSTIC TEST REFLECTION: OVERALL	
Diagnostic Test Composite Score: ___________	
Reflection Question	**Notes**
What went well for you during the diagnostic test and which skills were easiest for you to use?	
What did you struggle with during the diagnostic test or which skills were harder for you to use?	
After your experience, what are some things you might like to keep in mind as you study?	
What are some aspects of approaching the SAT for which you are most hoping to build strategies?	
What do you think are the 1–2 things you do best as a test taker?	
What 1–2 improvements could you make as a test taker that would help you most?	
Where did you run out of time? Or, on the flip side, where did you end up with extra time?	
Did you answer all the questions? If not, how many did you skip?	

Now that you've reflected on your prior experience, think about your SAT goals. For many test takers, the goal may simply be to get the best score possible in every section. However, some might prioritize improving their score in one subject that matters more for their college goals than another. Or, perhaps, there might be a minimum score a test taker is hoping to achieve to stand out to their school of choice. Maybe they've taken the SAT once before and simply want to improve upon a prior score. No matter what goals you have, it's important to keep them in mind as you study so that you can make choices that will help you achieve them.

FORMING A STUDY PLAN

Just as different people will have different score goals, different test takers will have different goals for how they spend their study time. For example, if you are a math whiz who aces every calculus test you take but you struggle a lot with reading comprehension, you may be planning to devote significantly more of your time to studying for the Reading and Writing section. Different test takers also have differing amounts of time to allot to studying for the SAT. If you have an hour a day for several months to devote to preparation, you'll probably approach things differently than someone who is trying to study as comprehensively as they can in the two weeks leading up to their exam.

Using Data to Inform Your Goals

Knowing a bit about the SAT as an exam can help guide some of the basic decisions you will need to make regarding your target score and study time. Let's start with average scores. The College Board's most recent data on average SAT scores comes from the class of 2021 and is depicted in the following table.

AVERAGE SAT SCORES (2021)	
Math	538
Reading and Writing	541
Composite	**1088**

Source: https://blog.collegeboard.org/what-is-the-average-sat-score

Another piece of data that can help you determine your personal target involves SAT score percentiles. Consider the chart that follows:

SAT SCORE PERCENTILES (2021–2022)	
Composite Score	**Percentile**
1350+	90th percentile and higher
1200+	75th percentile and higher
1040+	50th percentile and higher

Source: https://satsuite.collegeboard.org/media/pdf/understanding-sat-scores.pdf

This means that a test taker who scores a 1350 or above can assume that they performed better than 90% of test takers. If you are applying to highly competitive schools where you need to stand out, then 1350 is likely the minimum composite score you'd want to achieve. Those applying to slightly less competitive schools might consider aiming for 1200 or higher, as that will still ensure they outperform 75% or more of test takers. If you're simply hoping to perform like an average test taker or better, then scoring above 1040 is fine.

Take a moment to ask yourself the following questions:

- What are my score goals? Is there a minimum score I want to achieve?
- Given what I know about average scores and percentiles, are my score goals realistic and appropriate for the types of schools to which I am applying?
- Are my score goals even between the Math section and the Reading and Writing section or am I aiming to perform better on one or the other?
- How can I best divide my study time to address my score goals?

Once you've considered these questions, you're ready to start analyzing your diagnostic test scores in service of creating a personalized study plan.

Analyzing Your Diagnostic Test Scores

At the beginning of this chapter, we asked you to reflect on your diagnostic test as a whole. Now that you've done so and learned a bit about SAT average scores and percentiles, it's time to think about your performance in each section individually. Jot down some thoughts in the following chart or take notes independently to help you reflect.

MY DIAGNOSTIC TEST SCORES			
Minimum Composite Score Goal: ______			
Test	**Score**	**Strengths**	**Spaces for Improvement**
Reading and Writing			
Math			
Composite			

If you decided to take the SAT tomorrow without any further preparation, and you did things the exact same way, you would likely score the same as how you performed on the diagnostic test. Since you are working with this book, you likely have some amount of time to prepare for the SAT, which means you have ample opportunity to improve upon that score. Your task is, therefore, to mentally divide the amount of preparation time you have according to your study priorities. Only you can determine what the best way to do this might be. However, your diagnostic test offers helpful clues about how to do this most effectively. If you performed significantly better in one section than another, then you'll need to devote more time to preparing for the section for which you received a lower score. If your scores are pretty even, then you know you can divide your time fairly equally.

Create an Informed Study Schedule

Now that you have analyzed your diagnostic test results, you are ready to create a study plan. Let's say you had an hour a day after school for 5 weeks to study for the SAT and your diagnostic test results indicate that you should split your time evenly across subjects. At the end of the 5 weeks, you plan to take your practice test on a Saturday to see how you improved, leaving you a week before your official exam for any last-minute review based on the results of your practice test. This means you have 25 total hours to devote to studying (not including the practice test you'll take towards the end) before your practice test and 5 more for post-practice test review. You could plan to spend two days a week on Reading and Writing, two days a week on Math, and one day a week reviewing what you learned that week. Or if, for instance, you knew you needed to spend more time on Math, then you could spend three days a week on Math and two on Reading and Writing.

There are lots of ways to divide your time—the important thing is to consider how much total time you have, make a schedule, and stick to it. Creating a specific study calendar helps remind you that organized studying correlates with a better chance of meeting your score goals. Remember to include variety in your plan (so you don't get too bored with one subject or forget things you study early on) and ample chances to review skills you practiced earlier. Learning is largely about repetition, so you want to give yourself multiple opportunities to review information.

Take a moment to ask yourself the following questions. Then, come up with a study plan that works for you and your goals.

- How much total time can I commit to studying for the SAT?
- How do I want to divide that study time, based on my diagnostic performance?
- What are some of the most important skills I want to work on overall?
- What are some of the most important skills I want to work on for each section?
- When would it be most useful for me to take a practice test, given my study style?

Once you have a study plan in place, you are ready to consider how to make the most of your study time.

Setting an Environment

How and where you prep for the SAT matters. Creating optimum study conditions will help keep you focused and motivated. How you do so is largely dictated by what has worked for you in the past as well as your current life and schedule — busy students who are always on the go may have fewer options for when and where they can study, and students who have plenty of time between now and test day have more leeway. The earlier you start preparing for the SAT, the more likely you are to have wiggle room in your study schedule and to create a routine and study environment that suits your needs.

TIP

You don't have to wait to take the practice test included in this book until the end of your study time if you think it would be more beneficial to you to take it at a midpoint to check your progress. It's up to you! Remember, there's an adaptive-style practice test available at https://petersons.com/satbook.

When you're designing your perfect study environment, keep the following suggestions in mind.

- **Keep distractions to a minimum.** Your study space should be free of anything that will distract you from the task at hand. This means that cell phones, tablets, TVs, and other items that make it difficult to focus should be kept elsewhere. Many people prefer to avoid listening to music with lyrics as they can make it hard to focus.
- **Get comfortable—but not too comfortable.** Your study space should be comfortable so you can relax and focus on practice and review without fidgeting, but it shouldn't be so comfortable that you find yourself napping whenever you sit down to study. A good chair and uncluttered desk are often a better choice than lying down in bed.
- **Find a location that works for you.** Do you prepare better alone in your bedroom or in a bustling coffee shop or library? This choice is totally up to you and should be based on what has worked for you in the past. A bit of background noise can be helpful to some and distracting to others, so if you're not sure what works best for you, then experiment.
- **Adjust your lighting.** Make sure your study environment contains the right level of light to keep you engaged. Whatever lighting matches your preferences is fine—just be sure not to study in a dark place that will make you sleepy.
- **Decide if you'd rather prep alone, in a group, or both.** Studying alone may help you stay focused, but if you're struggling in a certain area, then working with others whose strengths and weaknesses complement each other may be a great way to help you improve. Studying in a group may be distracting for some while others find it difficult to avoid distractions when studying alone and need others to keep them on task. Decide for yourself which individual approach (or combination of both) works for you.
- **Find your ideal time of day.** The time of day during which you study best is an important part of your study environment. Do you work best first thing in the morning, or are you a nighttime study owl? Can you focus right after school, or do you need a bit of downtime before studying in the early evening? If possible, schedule your study sessions at the time of day that matches what naturally works best for you.
- **Fuel up.** Don't try to study on an empty tank. Make sure to approach each study session well-rested, energized, and with your hunger satiated. Keep in mind that nutritious foods tend to keep your energy levels higher for longer, while things like sugary snacks, sodas, and caffeine tend to create spikes in energy levels that will eventually send you crashing back down.
- **Gather your tools.** Make sure you have all of your most effective study tools at hand in your workspace, including this book, paper and pens/pencils, a calculator, a highlighter, and a watch or clock if you're taking a timed practice test. The last thing you want to do every time you sit down to study is waste time searching for your study tools. Also, staying organized will help keep you focused, serious, and motivated.
- **Pay attention to your mental environment.** Just as important as having the perfect physical study environment is having the right mindset during each study session. Try to leave external worries, stressors, or anxieties outside of your SAT prep since they will only drain your energy and focus. A great way to do this is to take a few minutes before each study session to relax, breathe, and clear your mind. Sometimes just a minute or two is enough and can make a big difference. When your mind is clear and free from distractions, you'll be much more likely to devote yourself to effective test preparation. Remember also that you should schedule rest days into your study calendar to give your brain time to recharge as necessary.

GENERAL STUDY STRATEGIES

Once you've made a schedule and set your environment, there are some general study strategies that can help you make the most of your prep time.

- **Don't wait until the last minute—start early!** It takes time to move things you review into long-term memory, and the more time you give yourself to learn and review different concepts, the better you'll be able to recall them on exam day. Don't cram all of your studying into the last minute; instead, come up with a reasonable study calendar early in your test prep process and stick to it.
- **Spread out your study sessions over time.** Few people are served better by a multi-hour cram session than they are a couple different shorter study sessions spread out over time. Your brain needs time to process what it's learned and then to recall it later, so spreading your studying out across multiple sessions is the best way to allow this to happen.
- **Study regularly.** People need to periodically return to information to ensure that it sticks around in memory, so studying new materials demands that learners complete a periodic review of what they've already learned. Studying regularly leading up to the date of an assessment is the best way to do this and is far more effective than cramming, which offers few opportunities to recall information learned earlier.
- **Study intensely rather than passively.** There is a documented relationship between stress and performance. Low stress situations tend to result in lower performance. High stress situations do the same. But there's a sweet spot where just the right amount of pressure and intensity can improve performance on tasks, especially when learning. For studying, this means that you are far better served by short, intense intervals of studying. Languidly skimming over notes for hours on end will do significantly less than an hour of active retrieval combined with paraphrasing, timed practice questions, or intentional mind mapping. Studying is a question of efficiency, and the most efficient and effective way to study usually involves real effort.
- **Develop active learning practices.** Active learning involves planning, monitoring, and reflecting on your learning process. Here are some tips for active learning:
    - Plan out your work time
    - Read strategically
    - Take some form of notes
    - Regularly self-assess
    - Spread out your study time
    - Keep a regular schedule
    - Create something while studying
    - Use metacognitive techniques (such as reflective questions) to think about what you've learned so far and how you learned it
- **Eliminate distractions.** Humans can multitask, just not well. Your divided attention is often the weakest of your attentive modes. To truly attend to a task, you need to be able to isolate what you're trying to learn from other stimuli; this is how you ensure that what you learn can be registered properly. One of the most significant distractors for many (but not all) people is language, whether that's lyrics to a song or a TV playing in the background. If you brain struggles to filter out other voices, remove yourself from environments with lots of noise and set your phone in another space so that you can't even see it. Remember that you won't have to do this for long periods of time. Your studying is more productive in intense bursts (an hour at a time) rather than an entire afternoon.
- **Encode new information meaningfully.** Whenever we talk about memory, we're talking about a process called encoding, wherein information moves from your senses to be stored for later use. There are any number of tricks and tips for getting information to stick around, but one of the most effective ways is what's called elaborative encoding. When you make information meaningful by connecting it to your own life and interests, the brain more easily stores that information for later use. For example, if you

practice a new math concept by thinking about a real-life situation in which you are likely to need it, you are more likely to retain the concept for later retrieval because you've encoded it in a way that holds meaning for you.

- **Divide tasks and information into chunks.** This technique can help anyone but is especially helpful for those who have focus issues. Divide topics into digestible chunks of information rather than larger blocks so you can deal with one chunk at a time. Resources (like this book) have organizational structures that may or may not suit your learning objectives. A chapter may cover a vast swath of topics that makes your studying load too great while also not necessarily aligning with what you need to know. In this case, it might be useful to focus on a given section, chart, or exercise at a time. Use different study strategies for different chunks of information to prevent getting overwhelmed. Reorganize resources in your notes and study materials based on relationships that you see, not necessarily what is prescribed by the resource itself. Consider what you can cover in the time you have for a given study session and focus only on that.
- **Vary topics and weave them together as you learn.** Alternate between topics while studying rather than dedicating time to one topic at a time. This applies to both what you review and self-quiz in your notes as well as practice questions. When you encounter different kinds of questions in sequence (say, a simple example, multiplication, division, addition, and subtraction), you have to retrieve different kinds of information and strategies to answer accurately. That cross-talk will increase connections between different topics and processes, ultimately improving your learning. While you're at it, look for connections between different fields of study. For instance, how does working on quantitative reasoning in math make it easier to answer reading questions that require you to understand quantitative data? Can studying reading comprehension provide you insights on how to answer grammar questions as well? Reflecting on these connections as you study helps solidify concepts in your mind.
- **Create new materials as you study.** To retain and understand information, you need to recall and process as well as apply topics and concepts. Learning about something isn't enough—you need exposure in different forms and in different ways. That usually means doing something with the information you're trying to learn. Often, practice tests are one of the best ways to study, but mixing your methods before you get to the practice test can have positive results. You can do this by:
    - Creating something using the new information, such as forming your own example questions or mini practice test
    - Developing a visual aid that helps you make sense of new information
    - Using different modes (auditory, visual, physical) to study
    - Seeking outside sources to expand your research and understanding
    - Creating materials that help you engage in repetitive learning (such as flashcards)
- **Regularly assess your retention and understanding.** In this book, we've included Test Yourself sections at the end of many chapters to assist you with assessing your retention and understanding as you develop new skills, but there are lots of other ways to do this as well. Periodically check in with yourself and look for ways to test or elaborate on what you've learned so far. Then, reflect on which skills you've developed well, and which may still need some improvement.
- **At the end of each study session, review and summarize what you learned.** This is yet another form of metacognition that helps you make the most of your study time. By reflecting on what you learned and summarizing new information, you are encoding that new information to give you a better chance of recalling it later. If you can't summarize a concept that you've just learned, then it's a good indicator that you should devote more time to it during a future study session.

Active Studying Techniques

The following are active studying techniques that help you to retrieve information (the basic process of remembering). These techniques help you transform what you know to create and reveal relationships that may not have been apparent before. Many of the strategies offer similar types of tasks that all capitalize on how humans learn, so your goal in reading this section should be to find strategies that suit your preferences and personal learning style. While there is some overlap, different strategies are better for different levels of thinking (gathering, processing, and/or applying). Be aware that one should generally use different strategies to meet different goals.

FLASHCARDS

What: A technique for remembering terms and concepts using index cards or online flashcard apps.

How: On one side of a set of index cards, write the names of different topics and/or procedures. On the opposite side, record definitions and steps. Read the topic/procedure name and recall the definition/steps. Check your accuracy. Set correct answers in one pile and incorrect answers in another. Continue to review cards until no cards remain in the incorrect pile, and repeat.

Why: To build conceptual understanding, you first need to know basic details. Flashcards are a great starting point for the studying process if you're struggling to remember the terms that accompany new concepts and procedures.

FEYNMAN TECHNIQUE

What: An activity for reducing complex topics to simplified statements through repeated paraphrasing and consultation of resources.

How: List the topic in question at the top of a sheet of paper or blank document on your computer. Describe the topic in terms that could be understood by an imagined audience that is unfamiliar with the topic (someone in a lower grade than you, for instance). Be sure to identify what it is, how it works, why it works that way, why it is important/what it is connected to. Avoid using technical terms and jargon. After completing a paraphrase, reread what you wrote. Identify any gaps in your understanding and consult resources as necessary. Continue to refine your paraphrase until the topic is clear—you both remember and understand the topic and could teach it to someone else.

Why: The continual simplification of complex ideas for an imagined audience requires use of a lot of higher-level thinking and that use of information is going to improve understanding and also reinforce retention through repetition.

MIND MAP/CONCEPT MAP

What: A diagram focused on displaying the hierarchical relationships between pieces of a topic—whether that's a book, a mathematical or scientific concept, a field of study, etc. A mind map makes use of both images and language to depict and relate different characteristics or parts of a topic to one another. It uses a branching system to indicate the major topic, categories or subsets of topics related to the main topic, and associated details.

How: Draw and/or label the main topic of the map in the center of a document. From the central topic, place subtopics in the space around the main topic. Stemming off the subtopics, provide important details, categories, characteristics, views, etc. Use color, arrows, images, and other diagramming features to enhance the mind map.

Why: A mind map helps you identify the key features of a topic while developing spatial and logical relationships between different features of the topic. They are especially helpful for test takers who would identify as visual learners. Mind maps capitalize on our brain's strong visual capacity while also asking us to retrieve, organize, and connect information—all higher-level processes that reinforce retention and understanding.

CORNELL NOTES/GRAPHIC NOTES

What: A multi-step note-making process: taking notes, revising notes, reviewing notes. This happens with the intent of forcing retrieval of information as soon after receiving material as possible, rather than waiting until the notes are "needed" for a test or assignment.

How: Format a document into two columns with space for a topic name at the top of the document and a gap of roughly two inches at the bottom of the document. Take notes in the right column and leave the left column blank. While reading, watching a video, or listening to a lecture, record (to the best of your ability) short complete sentences in the right-hand column that describe the topic of the reading/lesson/video/lecture. After finishing the source material, reread what you recorded—this should happen as soon after recording has finished as possible. Mark places where more information may be needed or any places of confusion. Add details that you may recall. Then, in the left-hand column, record questions (either from the material(s) or generated by you) that may be answered by the information in the right-hand column. Cover the right-hand column in some way and answer the self-generated questions without looking at the noted information. Check your accuracy and mark questions that you're unable to answer effectively. Once you've completed that initial quiz, use the gap at the bottom of the page to write a summary that describes the topic of the notes. Revisit this document to study. Read the summary and answer the questions while covering up the notes column.

Why: Revisiting information soon after your first exposure is a critical step that many students don't take, and skipping that step contributes to a lot of information loss (and thus wasted time) that could be avoided with a short review. A good note-making process requires that you revisit notes soon after taking them and regularly revisit them to maintain retention. The Cornell method has a built-in system of review in the form of questions and a format that allows you to easily quiz yourself on the content of the notes without requiring a partner. At the same time, the summary creates an easy-to-reference place to quickly get the gist of a topic without having to fully reread the entire set of notes.

EXAMPLE SENTENCES

What: A way of summarizing, simplifying, and solidifying what you've learned by clarifying it in your own words.

 **How:** Write out complete sentences describing the information acquired from your lessons. Try to write longer complex sentences (an independent and dependent clause) as they create conditions for statements. The words *but*, *because*, and *so* can also be used to create different kinds of relationships in your sentences, encouraging you to explore topics from different perspectives (*but* creates contrast, *because* shows cause, and *so* demonstrates effects).

 **Why:** A sentence is a vehicle for thought—the word literally comes from one of the Latin words for "thought." By constructing a complete sentence with a topic from your material as a subject, you're requiring yourself to construct a cohesive thought connecting knowledge and concepts that were previously foreign.

SELF-QUESTIONING

 **What:** Create questions based on the facts, concepts, and applications of learning topics.

 **How:** Imagine the act of thinking as having multiple different levels. It is essential that you be able to remember information. Once you can remember information, you need to construct meaning by developing relationships between ideas/topics. After understanding comes application, which means using information in different situations. Ask questions that require defining, listing, or identifying different ideas. Then, ask questions that compare, summarize, or classify ideas. Finally, pursue higher-level thinking by responding to, using, judging, or generating applications for the ideas.

 **Why:** Those three kinds of "thinking" encompass the cognitive processes required by most tests. If you can answer questions that demand those tasks, you know that you're prepared for your assessment. As such, you should create questions of different levels. This strategy is connected to practice tests. When practice tests are unavailable or inaccessible, you can make your own.

PRACTICE TESTS

 **What:** As the name suggests, the purpose of a practice test is to practice retrieving and using information acquired from your materials. At the same time, you can practice strategies for test taking and certain concepts.

 **How:** Find a test (or something that'll serve as a test), set a timer, and do it. One of the most important steps that most students skip when taking practice tests is evaluating how they did after. It's not just about what you got right and what you got wrong. You also need to think about why you answered incorrectly—did you misread a question, skip a strategy, forget a term, rush the answer, or misunderstand the concept? Use that reflection to identify valuable steps for what's next in your study process. If helpful, analyze your practice test using the same strategies we discussed at the beginning of this chapter for analyzing your diagnostic test.

 **Why:** Time and time again, research has shown that practice tests have a significant impact on test performance. That's largely the result of the "practice effect" wherein the act of practicing for the assessment in the form of a practice run will improve performance. It's intuitive, but many students either skip this step (not knowing where to find practice tests) or rely solely upon it (without adequately preparing beforehand or reflecting on performance afterward).

ADEPT

What: A method for expressing a topic in multiple forms, often used as a teaching technique, by creating an Analogy, Diagram, Example, Plain English definition, and a Technical definition.

How: Write the name of the topic at the top of the page or a blank document. Write a paraphrased technical definition. Then, write a plain English definition. With those definitions in mind, create an example of the topic as it is applied. Then create a visual representation of the topic. Finally, create an analogy wherein you compare the topic to something that is familiar to you and would be clear to others reading through the document. Arrange the document in the ADEPT order. Should any stage in the ADEPT process prove difficult, re-examine resources and clarify the definition of the term (consider the Feynman technique).

Why: Complexity can be broached by bridging a new topic with something more familiar. When moving through different types of communication for a new or complex topic, higher order thinking skills are deployed to grapple with examining a new idea from multiple perspectives. That serves to expand understanding and reinforce memory.

PARAPHRASING

What: State information in your own words while preserving the meaning of the original with the intent of expanding or clarifying what was stated. Consider paraphrasing a form of rewriting.

How: The mechanics of paraphrasing are not precise. You're restating something "in your own words." That means that you'll likely change the actual words used, the sentence structure, and, most importantly, add clarifying details. This means that your paraphrase can be longer than the original statement.

Why: The act of rephrasing information forces you to process what was stated or read. The cognitive load of rewriting is going to draw on far more cognitive processes than reading alone. Paraphrasing signals to your brain that this information is of greater value, which then leads to improved encoding and retention. Additionally, you're also creating a resource that you can refer to—one that may be more valuable to you than the original source. Paraphrasing is at the heart of many of these study techniques (the Feynman Method, ADEPT, Cornell Notes, Example Sentences). It's an essential skill as it is one of the easiest ways to generate activity and shift studying away from passive modes. Here is an example or paraphrasing:

EXAMPLE

Original: The Pythagorean Theorem ($a^2+b^2 = c^2$) can be used to calculate the length of the hypotenuse of a right triangle.

Paraphrase: The longest side of a triangle is called the hypotenuse. In a triangle with a 90-degree angle (a right triangle), a formula exists that lets you calculate the length of an unknown third side if you know the lengths of the other two sides. The formula is $a^2+b^2 = c^2$, where a and b represent the two shorter sides and c equals the length of the hypotenuse. If a triangle had two side lengths 3 and 4, the equation would look like $3^2+4^2 = c^2$. In that case, $a^2+b^2 = 25$. Take the square root of 25 (c^2) and you know the length of the hypotenuse equals 5.

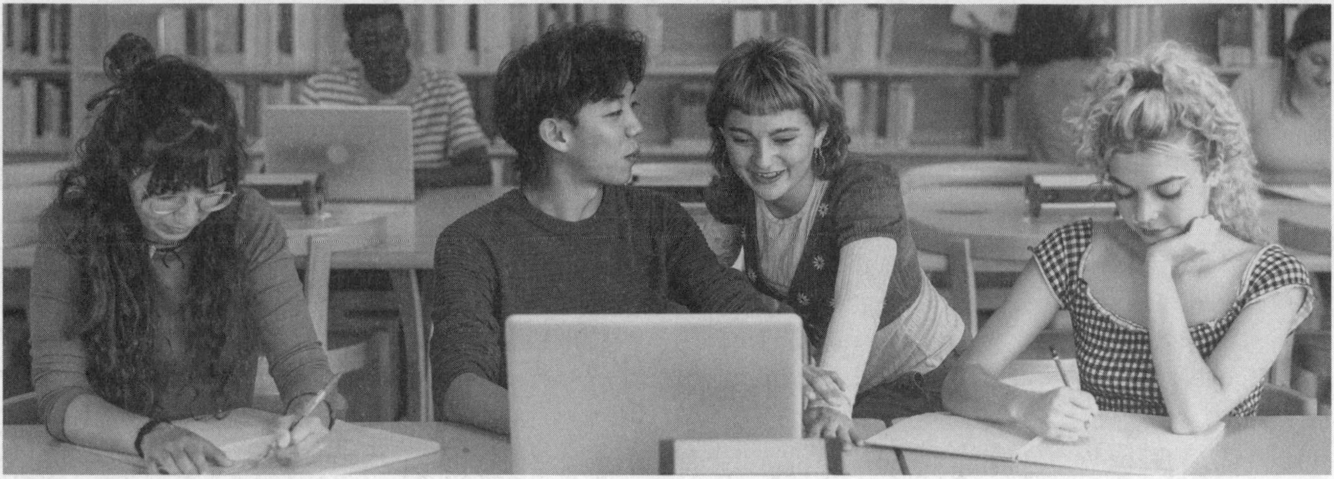

MINDSETS TO IMPROVE PERFORMANCE

Up to this point, we've discussed what it takes to create a study plan that will help you prepare for the SAT. We've also discussed different ways to study, including providing you with a number of active studying techniques that have been scientifically shown to boost performance. Now, we'll pivot to some of the overarching mindsets and strategies that can help you maximize your study time and exam performance.

Every Strategy Can Be Personalized

The two strategy chapters in this book (Chapter 8 and Chapter 15) will offer you a basic point of reference for how to approach each section of the test, but the good news is that you can alter your approach to suit your needs. Part of the reason we previously had you consider your strengths and weaknesses was so that you'll be on the lookout for the tips and strategies that will help you most. As you work through the book, play with these techniques we share and figure out which work best for you. Remember, you can personalize your approach for each individual section, not just the test as a whole.

Time Management is Paramount

While the SAT has fairly forgiving time constraints compared to other standardized tests, time management can still be a key issue for some test takers. However, if you practice with the SAT's time constraints in mind and recreate test conditions by timing yourself whenever possible, you'll find it much easier to develop techniques that help you manage your time. Wherever possible, look for ways to save yourself time without reducing accuracy. Each of the strategies chapters in this book also includes subject-specific tips for how to make the most of your time, so keep an eye out!

Keep the Stakes in Mind

You need to approach the SAT as the high stakes test that it is since it has important long-term consequences. Don't let that awareness spike your anxiety so much that you can't cope, but do be aware that each time you take the SAT matters a great deal. Depending on when your college applications are due, you may be able to take the SAT multiple times, but each time you take it is important, so you need to be thorough and focused. This is especially true if you only get one shot at it.

Build Confidence by Building Strategies

Your goal is to be as certain as possible when you answer a question. There are numerous strategies that can help you get there, many of which are in this book, but you need to know them and practice them to be able to use them. The good news is that as you become more adept at using these strategies, you will also become more confident in your ability to perform well on the SAT. Confidence correlates positively with test performance, so the act of building confidence in yourself is worthwhile in its own right as a test prep technique.

Must-Do SAT® Performance Tasks and Goals

Here are some things you can do across both sections to improve your overall performance. During the SAT, you MUST:

KNOW THE DIRECTIONS FOR EACH TEST. You'll find the SAT test directions in various places in this book. They're not going to change between now and test day. Learn them now to save time later on the real SAT.

ANSWER EVERY SINGLE QUESTION. You are not penalized for guessing on the SAT, and whenever you guess, you raise your chances of guessing correctly (especially if you eliminate obviously wrong options first). Always guess rather than leave a question blank since you can always note and review guesses later anyhow. If you're running out of time, guess on all the questions that remain.

KNOW THE QUESTION TYPES FOR EACH TEST. We will cover these in the first chapter of each part of this book that focuses on a test section.

USE ALL THE TIME YOU'RE ALLOTTED. If you finish early, take time to review questions you guessed on or go over answers again. There is no such thing as "finishing early" with the SAT—use every minute you're given!

BE CERTAIN OF YOUR ANSWERS. Don't just select an answer that seems right and call it a day. Instead, always make sure you review all the answer options and eliminate incorrect options as best you can so you can be certain of the answer you do select. When guessing, take time to eliminate answers you're pretty sure are incorrect first.

HAVE STRATEGIES FOR APPROACHING DIFFERENT KINDS OF QUESTIONS OR PASSAGES. Just like the chapters in this book can help you craft a strategy for each test section, so also can they help you craft strategies for approaching different types of questions or passages. Make sure you familiarize yourself with different question or passage strategies, especially if you struggle with a given type.

TIME YOUR PRACTICE. The Test Yourself sections and Practice Test in this book are designed to approximate SAT test conditions. If you do them timed, you will have much more information about how well you perform within the time constraints of the SAT. Then, you can develop strategies to help you meet the time constraints while also familiarizing yourself with how long a given length of time feels to you when testing.

HAVE A STRATEGY FOR EVERY SINGLE SECTION. Don't just go in blindly—plan how you want to approach each section. The chapters in this book are designed to help you make such a plan.

Test Performance Goals

Just as there are certain mindsets you can keep in mind on exam day and while studying, it's helpful to remember the following goals when testing so as to better attain those goals on exam day. These are the goals you should target when taking the SAT, including when recreating test conditions for a practice test.

- **Answer every question before time is called.** Remember, there is no penalty for guessing, so always guess rather than leave a question blank. If you are running out of time on a section, spend the last 1–2 minutes guessing on any questions that remain.
- **Have time for review.** One of your primary goals as you develop exam strategies should be to find places you can save time so that you have time to review any guesses you did make. As you finish a module, make it a goal to use your time as efficiently as possible so you have at least a few moments to review guesses. You can only review questions within your current module—you will not be able to go back to Module 1 once you begin Module 2.
- **Guess on as few questions as possible.** While it is better to guess than leave a question blank, your goal should still be to maximize the number of questions for which you give a well-considered answer. The more you work on time management, the better equipped you'll be to answer every question thoroughly.
- **Prioritize the questions you can answer with confidence.** When deciding the order in which to approach questions, prioritize the easiest questions with answers you feel confident about first, then move on to harder questions. That way, you can maximize the number of questions you're likely to get right. The digital testing environment makes it possible for you to mark questions you'd like to review.
- **Use strategies for handling different kinds of passages and questions**. By test day, you'll have spent plenty of your study time developing strategies for how to handle certain types of passages and questions, so remember to use those strategies when the time comes!

Once you've analyzed your diagnostic test scores, determined a study plan, set up an optimum study environment and routine, figured out the study techniques that will help you most, and familiarized yourself with the mindsets and performance goals that are critical for the SAT, you'll be well-prepared to jump into studying for your exam.

SUMMING IT UP

- Use the charts provided at the beginning of this chapter to reflect on your performance during the diagnostic test in Chapter 2. These self-reflection questions are designed to help you plan your study time more effectively and develop strong strategies.
- Consider the total amount of time you have to study for the SAT, then create a study calendar (or other form of study plan) that accounts for your study needs based on your analysis of your diagnostic test results.
- Studying is most effective when done in a conducive environment. Optimize your environment for studying by:
  - Minimizing distractions
  - Working somewhere comfortable (but not so cozy that you will fall asleep)
  - Finding a location that suits your learning habits
  - Adjusting background noise and lighting to increase focus
  - Making individual determinations regarding group vs. solo study
  - Studying on a "full tank" by making sure to eat and get rest ahead of studying
  - Ensuring you have all the tools you need to study ahead of time
  - Paying attention to your mental environment in addition to your physical environment
- Start early rather than waiting until the last minute, and spread study sessions out over time rather than trying to engage in long cramming sessions.
- Study regularly, actively, and with enough intensity to encode information meaningfully. When you can apply new concepts to your own life and experiences, you tend to retain them better.
- Divide tasks and information into chunks so you can address one piece of the overall puzzle at a time.
- Create new materials as you study to concretize new concepts and terms.
- Engage in regular metacognition (thinking about what you've learned and how you learned it) and regularly assess how much information you've retained, and which techniques helped you develop understanding.
- Summarize what you've learned at the end of each study session to help you encode new information and check understanding.

- Engage in some of the active study techniques outlined in this chapter, including:
  - Flashcards
  - Feynman Technique
  - Mind Mapping/Concept Maps
  - Cornell Notes/Graphic Notes
  - Example Sentences
  - Self-Questioning
  - Practice Tests
  - ADEPT
  - Paraphrasing
- Adopt mindsets that improve your performance by remembering to personalize your strategies, recognizing the importance of time management, keeping the high stakes of the test in mind (without letting anxiety take over), and building your exam confidence through strategic learning.
- When taking the SAT or any practice tests, remember the following Must-Do Items:
  - Know the directions for each section.
  - Know the question types for each section.
  - Use all the time you're allotted.
  - Answer every single question.
  - Have a strategy for each test section.
  - Have strategies for approaching different kinds of questions or passages.
  - Be certain of your answers.
  - Time your practice.
- When taking the SAT or any practice tests, remember the following test performance goals:
  - Answer every question before time is called.
  - Save time for review whenever possible.
  - Guess on as few questions as possible.
  - Prioritize questions you can answer with confidence.
  - Use strategies for different types of passages and questions.
- Take the practice test in Chapter 16 at any time that makes sense for your study schedule. When you do, feel free to return to this chapter and analyze your results the same way you did for the diagnostic test. You can also find additional practice tests at www.petersons.com/testprep/sat/ through our online SAT course.

PART III

SAT® READING AND WRITING

CHAPTER

Introduction to SAT® Reading and Writing

INTRODUCTION TO SAT® READING

OVERVIEW

- How to Study with Part III
- All about the Reading and Writing Section
- Scoring Table
- Sample Questions
- Common Challenges
- Summing It Up

As you prepare for the SAT Reading and Writing section, it's essential for you to be aware of the Reading and Writing section's layout, the nature of the questions you'll be asked to answer, and the typical challenges that test takers face. Part III offers a summary of the Reading and Writing section in this chapter. The chapters that follow include information on essential concepts you'll need to master to do well on the section. We'll also delve into specific techniques you can employ to approach questions and texts on the Reading and Writing section.

AND WRITING

4

HOW TO STUDY WITH PART III

Before we get into the details about the SAT Reading and Writing section, take some time to reflect on your experience with English as a subject. In general, English classes are designed to sharpen both your reading and writing skills in tandem, through grammar, vocabulary, composition, and reading comprehension practice. What kind of English classes did you take over the course of your high school career? Which reading and writing skills do you excel at, and which ones do you struggle with? For example, are you an ace at reading, do you enjoy researching and developing an argument, or are you an expert at grammar and mechanics? Do you find it difficult to grasp an author's point, or is reading just not something you enjoy? Are you a native speaker of English, or is English a second or third language for you? Knowing your strengths and weaknesses when it comes to reading and writing will help you narrow down how to prepare and where to focus your energy as you study for the SAT Reading and Writing section.

This chapter covers the structure of the Reading and Writing section and provides information on the types of questions you'll be given. In Chapter 5, we'll cover reading comprehension as a skill set, including giving you the opportunity to hone your skills using example passages. If you are already an ace at reading, you may only need to skim this chapter as a refresher. However, if you struggle with reading, this chapter will give you a helpful primer on the different types of reading skills you'll be tested on. If you'd like to focus on improving your English skills, then Chapters 6 and 7 will be helpful resources for you. In Chapter 6, we'll provide in-depth explanations and examples of important concepts in English grammar, usage, and mechanics. If you already have a strong grasp of English, when it comes to the organization, structure, and overall development of ideas and the intricacies of English grammar and mechanics, then feel free to just skim this chapter. In Chapter 7, we'll talk about

Self-Reflection: Reading and Writing

- Which English courses did you take in high school and which did you not take (yet)?
- Which of your high school courses helped you with your reading skills and what strategies did you learn in those courses?
- Which aspects of reading have historically been easier for you? Harder for you?
- Which reading skills require the most time and effort for you?
- What do you like to read and what do you enjoy about doing that type of reading?
- Which English concepts have historically been easier for you to understand? Harder for you to understand?
- What grammatical errors do you often find in your writing?
- Which English skills require more effort for you?
- Did you experience any conditions during your high school experience (remote learning, recovering from surgery, etc.) that could have created gaps in your reading/writing learning? If so, what topics were covered during those gaps?
- Is English your native language? If not, how has this impacted your experience learning key concepts in English?

the major skills necessary for success in answering the Expression of Ideas questions and other writing-heavy question types (like those concerning Command of Evidence) and give you an opportunity to brush up on your rhetorical knowledge and skills. In Chapter 8, we'll discuss strategies to implement on the SAT Reading and Writing section to help you do your best. Throughout each chapter, you'll find opportunities to practice your skills as you review them.

ALL ABOUT THE READING AND WRITING SECTION

The SAT Reading and Writing section is designed to assess a test taker's ability to understand and apply elements of reading comprehension and reasoning skills, rhetoric, writing practices, and the conventions of standard written English in a variety of contexts. This includes the ability to analyze and evaluate written passages and use textual evidence to assess meaning and support ideas, identify errors in writing, and make effective choices in revising and editing texts. The Reading and Writing section consists of 54 multiple-choice questions that must be completed within 64 minutes. Each test item has a short passage or passage pair (text lengths range from 25 to 150 words) and a single related question.

You can expect to see questions from four category domains in the SAT Reading and Writing section.

CRAFT AND STRUCTURE
(≈28% of RW section/13–15 questions)

You'll be asked to demonstrate skills and knowledge related to analysis, comprehension, reasoning, synthesis, and vocabulary as well as your ability to understand and use high-utility words and phrases in context, identify a text's structure and purpose, and make connections between topically related texts.

INFORMATION AND IDEAS
(≈26% of RW section/12–14 questions)

You will be tasked with displaying your comprehension, analysis, and reasoning skills and knowledge, including the ability to identify central ideas and details; and your ability to locate, interpret, evaluate, and integrate information and ideas from texts and informational graphics, such as tables, bar graphs, and line graphs.

STANDARD ENGLISH CONVENTIONS
(≈26% of RW section/11–15 questions)

You'll be asked to demonstrate your ability to edit texts to conform to core conventions of Standard English sentence structure, usage, and punctuation, including form, structure, and sense.

EXPRESSION OF IDEAS
(≈20% of RW section/8–12 questions)

You will be assessed on your ability to revise texts to increase the effectiveness of written expression and meet specific rhetorical goals, including organization and transitions.

Questions from all four domains appear in each Reading and Writing section module, always in the order of Craft and Structure, Information and Ideas, Standard English Conventions, and Expression of Ideas questions. Questions within the Craft and Structure, Information and Ideas, and Expression of Ideas content domains that assess similar skills and knowledge are grouped together and arranged in order of increasing difficulty. Questions in the Standard English Conventions content domain increase in difficulty as the test progresses, regardless of the convention being tested.

SCORING TABLE

In Chapter 2, you completed a diagnostic test to help gauge your current skills and knowledge when it comes to what's covered on the SAT. As you work through this part of the book, consider the score you're aiming for, especially if you're applying to colleges whose applicants tend to receive certain score ranges on the SAT. While the scoring method used here is a simplified version of that used on the actual SAT, we've created a table that can help you anticipate how your raw score (0–54 questions) might translate into a scaled score (200–800). Please note that this is an estimate and not an exact reflection of official SAT scoring metrics.

RAW SCORE TO SCALED SCORE CONVERSION

Raw Score	Lower Range	Upper Range
54	790	800
53	780	800
52	770	800
51	760	790
50	750	780
49	740	770
48	730	760
47	710	740
46	690	720
45	670	700
44	650	680
43	630	660
42	620	650
41	600	630
40	590	620
39	580	610
38	570	600
37	560	590
36	550	580
35	530	560
34	520	550
33	510	540
32	500	530
31	480	510
30	470	500
29	460	490
28	440	470
27	430	460
26	420	450
25	400	430
24	390	420
23	380	410
22	370	400
21	370	400
20	360	390
19	350	380
18	340	370
17	330	360
16	330	360
15	320	350
14	310	340
13	300	330
12	290	320
11	280	310
10	250	280
9	220	250
8	200	230
7	200	220
6	200	200
5	200	200
4	200	200
3	200	200
2	200	200
1	200	200
0	200	200

SAMPLE QUESTIONS

To reiterate, questions on the SAT Reading and Writing section will fall into one of four categories: Craft and Structure, Information and Ideas, Standard English Conventions, and Expression of Ideas. Throughout Part III, we'll cover these question categories in more depth along with strategies you can use on test day.

Here, we've provided four examples of questions you might encounter on the exam: The first is a Craft and Structure question; the second is an Information and Ideas question; the third is a Standard English Conventions question; and the fourth is an Expression of Ideas question. You may be given a passage with certain words or phrases underlined, or with a blank that needs to be filled in. These questions will be paired with a question stem such as the following:

- Which choice completes the text with the most logical and precise word or phrase?
- Which choice most logically completes the text?
- Which choice best describes the function of the underlined sentence in the overall structure of the text?
- Which choice completes the text so that it conforms to conventions of Standard English?

Other times, you will be asked to choose the best answer to questions related to identifying the main purpose of the text, applying data from charts and graphs to a given text and drawing conclusions, comparing the ideas of one author to another in paired passages, or effectively identifying or using given information to meet specific rhetorical goals.

EXAMPLES

In the first part of the ice cream experiment, the children were initially presented with two flavor choices: chocolate and vanilla. At each stage of the experiment, researchers introduced new flavor options until there were a total of 100. Researchers noted that past a certain point, the variety of choice became overwhelming. Students' initial enthusiasm in the first few stages was betrayed by an unexpected ________ in latter stages, to the point where many students were unable to make a choice. The researchers thus concluded that a great degree of choice does not always correlate with a greater degree of enthusiasm and negatively correlates with decisiveness, particularly as the number of choices exponentially grows.

Which choice completes the text with the most logical and precise word or phrase?

A. efficiency

B. reticence

C. sincerity

D. resilience

The correct answer is B. The word *unexpected* contradicts the word *enthusiasm* in this sentence and the context provided suggests that the word must correspond with the students' dwindling enthusiasm. Thus, *efficiency, sincerity*, and *resilience* (meaning "the ability to recover quickly") can all be eliminated since they convey enthusiasm and interest. *Reticence*, meaning "restraint" or "reserve," conveys a lack of enthusiasm.

High blood pressure is, in part, a familial disease, which could be attributed to shared genetic influences, shared environmental factors, or both. The role of one environmental factor, dietary salt, was studied at Brookhaven National Laboratory. The studies suggested that excessive ingestion of salt can lead to high blood pressure in humans and animals. Some people and some rats, however, consumed large amounts of salt without developing high blood pressure. Despite implementation of the strictest environmental factor controls in these experiments, some salt-fed animals never developed hypertension; others rapidly developed very severe hypertension followed by early death. These marked variations were interpreted as resulting from differences in genetic makeup.

Which choice best states the main idea of the text?

A. A cure for high blood pressure is possible.

B. A tendency toward high blood pressure may be inherited.

C. Research shows salt to be an environmental factor that may cause high blood pressure.

D. Some animals never develop high blood pressure.

The correct answer is C. The main point of the text is that an interplay of genetic and environmental factors influencing the development of high blood pressure exists, and that excessive ingestion of salt can be a factor. There is no mention of a cure in the paragraph, so Choice A is incorrect. Choice B is incorrect because while high blood pressure is, in part, a familial disease and thus may be inherited, that detail is not the focus of the paragraph. The fact that some animals never develop high blood pressure is too general a statement and does not tie directly into the paragraph, so choice D is incorrect.

EXAMPLE

Discarded electronic products can cause significant lead pollution risks in this ________. Old electronics are supposed to be tested for lead content. Objects with a high lead content should be treated as hazardous waste and discarded in locations other than landfills. However, one of the most common tests used to detect lead in discarded products frequently misses high lead concentrations.

Which choice completes the text so that it conforms to the conventions of Standard English?

A. country's landfill's

B. countries' landfills

C. countries landfills'

D. country's landfills

The correct answer is D. The convention being tested here is the use of plural and possessive nouns. The singular possessive noun *country's* and the plural noun *landfills* correctly indicate that there is only one country being discussed and it has multiple landfills.

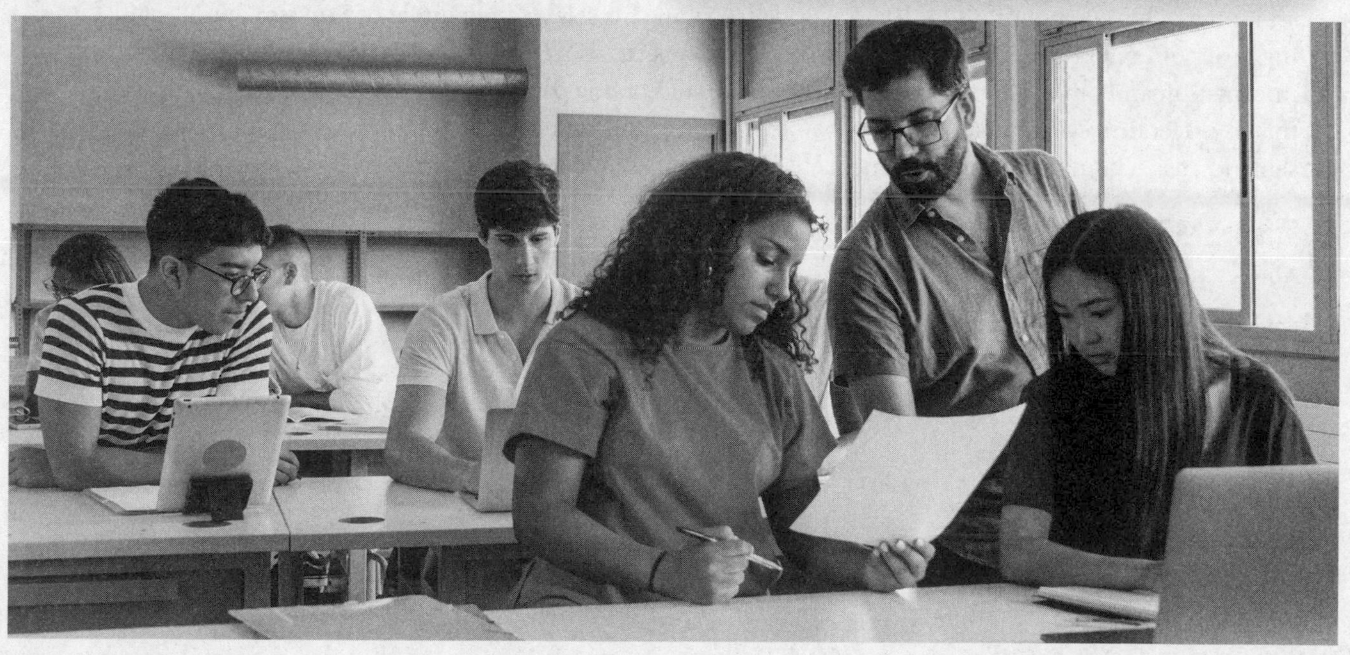

EXAMPLE

While researching a topic, a student has taken the following notes:
Andre Derain was one of the founders, along with Henri Matisse, of the Fauvism movement.

- Many art critics consider Fauvism the first 20th-century avant-garde art movement.
- André Derain was a French painter and sculptor.
- In 1906, at height of the Fauve movement, Derain produced a series of 30 paintings featuring the city of London as the subject.
- Derain later produced works connected to other twentieth-century movements as well, including Cubism, Neo-Impressionism, and Der Blaue Reiter.

The student wants to introduce this artist to an audience unfamiliar with him and his role in art history. Which choice most effectively uses relevant information from the notes to accomplish this goal?

A. French painter and sculptor André Derain, a cofounder with Henri Matisse of the Fauvism movement, created a series of 30 paintings featuring the city of London in 1906; he later produced works connected to other twentieth-century movements, including Cubism and Der Blaue Reiter.

B. André Derain cofounded Fauvism with Henri Matisse and later produced works connected to other twentieth-century movements, including Cubism and Der Blaue Reiter.

C. André Derain was a French painter and sculptor who painted 30 pictures of London and produced works connected to twentieth-century art movements such as Fauvism, Cubism, and Der Blaue Reiter.

D. Henri Matisse cofounded the Fauvism movement with French painter and sculptor André Derain; he created a series of 30 paintings featuring the city of London in 1906, and later produced works connected to other twentieth-century movements as well, including Cubism and Der Blaue Reiter.

The correct answer is A. The sentence introduces André Derain to an audience unfamiliar with the artist and some of his contributions to the art world, describing his role as a cofounder of Fauvism, his 30-painting series of London, and his involvement in later notable art movements. Choice B is missing biographical information and omits mentioning his famous series of London paintings. Choice C excludes any details that give Derain's accomplishments any context. Choice D introduces Henri Matisse as the subject of the sentence; as written, the accomplishments listed are Matisse's, not Derain's.

4

COMMON CHALLENGES

There are some common challenges that test takers encounter on the SAT Reading and Writing section.

- **Time management:** The SAT Reading and Writing section is timed, and you will have to answer 54 questions in 64 minutes. This means you'll have a little more than a minute to answer each question, but you will want to balance working at a good pace with carefully reading and analyzing the given passages and questions. We'll cover strategies for how to pace yourself while carefully approaching each question.
- **Multiple viewpoints:** Passages on the SAT Reading and Writing section may present multiple viewpoints, which can be confusing at times. As you read the passages you are given, be sure to identify the author's perspective and distinguish it from the viewpoints of other sources presented in the text.
- **Complex sentence structure and vocabulary:** Sample passages and texts on the SAT Reading and Writing section may include complex sentence structures and vocabulary. This can make it challenging to comprehend the text and answer questions accurately. We'll walk through strategies for how to approach a question when you're unsure of the correct answer. Remember that on the SAT, you won't have your points reduced for wrong answers, so there is always the option to guess if you are stuck.
- **Answer choices that seem plausible but are not the best option:** The SAT Reading and Writing section includes answer choices that can seem grammatically correct and relevant but may not be the best choice in the context of the passage or question. This can be confusing, but we'll discuss important criteria to consider as you weigh the answer choices presented to you.
- **Applying rhetorical skills:** The SAT Reading and Writing section can include questions that require you to carefully analyze the passage's purpose or draw inferences based on information from the text. These may require more time and more critical thinking than other questions focused on grammar or punctuation. If you struggle with concepts pertaining to rhetorical analysis, then Chapters 7 and 8 will be a valuable resource for you.
- **Specific grammar knowledge:** There are a lot of grammar rules and conventions in the English language. You don't need to know all of them to do well on the SAT Reading and Writing section, but there are specific rules and concepts the SAT considers imperative for every English user to know when entering college. Chapter 6 will discuss those essential conventions and concepts to provide exactly what you need to know to succeed. In addition, Chapters 7 and 8 will provide you with specific strategies for approaching language-use questions accurately and efficiently.

Consider the self-reflection exercise that was introduced at the beginning of this chapter. Have you experienced any of the challenges mentioned? Throughout this part of the book, we'll address strategies for dealing with these challenges. We'll focus on things like active reading, time management, and understanding the structure of a text to locate essential ideas and details. We'll also walk you through essential English language grammar, usage, and rhetorical skills. Reflecting on your own strengths and weaknesses, how might you need to approach studying for this section? As you progress through the remaining chapters of Part III, be mindful of the challenges we've presented here and identify any that you feel apply to you. Afterwards, review the strategies provided and assess which ones may be most effective for your unique skills, goals, and experiences.

As you go through the next four chapters, be sure to pay attention to where you struggle the most and focus on the strategies that will help you compensate for any areas where you feel less prepared or confident.

SUMMING IT UP

- The Reading and Writing section contains 54 multiple-choice questions that must be completed within 64 minutes.
- Each item consists of a short passage or passage pair (text lengths range from 25 to 150 words) and a single related question.
- SAT Reading and Writing questions fit into four domain categories: Craft and Structure, Information and Ideas, Standard English Conventions, and Expression of Ideas.
- Questions from all four domains appear in each Reading and Writing section, always in the order of Craft and Structure, Information and Ideas, Standard English Conventions, and Expression of Ideas questions. Within each domain set, excluding Standards of English Conventions, questions are arranged by testing point and then difficulty.
- Some challenges you might encounter in the SAT Reading and Writing section include time management, multiple-viewpoint passages, navigating complex vocabulary and syntax, choosing the correct and most effective answer option, applying rhetorical skills to revise the sample text, and maintaining knowledge of diverse, but specific, grammar concepts.

CHAPTER

Reading Comprehension

READING COMPREHENSION

OVERVIEW

- Reading Comprehension on the SAT®
- Eight Key Reading Skills
- Building Vocabulary to Increase Comprehension
- Summing It Up
- Test Yourself: Reading Comprehension

The SAT Reading and Writing section evaluates numerous crucial reading comprehension skills. Many of the questions examine not only how well you comprehend what you read but also how well you can interpret a given passage's meaning and the author's intent. In this chapter, we'll discuss key skills related to reading comprehension, expanding your vocabulary, and reading actively based on the questions you are given. We'll also discuss eight different categories of common reading comprehension skills, all of which are addressed in the SAT Reading and Writing section.

5

READING COMPREHENSION ON THE SAT®

In Chapter 4, we covered the different question domains addressed by the SAT Reading and Writing section as a whole. In this chapter, we'll focus specifically on the reading skills that are necessary to perform well on these questions. Note that even though we are isolating reading skills for review in this chapter, many questions will evaluate reading and writing skills simultaneously rather than focusing exclusively on one or the other at a time.

SAT Reading and Writing Passages

Passages in the SAT Reading and Writing section are most often informative (explanatory) texts. Their primary purpose is to explain a concept or inform the reader on a topic. Informative texts typically focus on explaining key details of a concept or event, defining terms, or providing the reader with information. There are also numerous literary excerpts represented in the passages. The excerpts provided may be informative or narrative in nature. In narrative texts, the purpose is to tell a story or narrate an experience. These texts may focus on providing a play-by-play of how certain actions took place; describing an object, place, person, or time period in detail; relaying information about events that have already occurred; or some combination of all three. You will also be presented with texts or questions that rely on your understanding of argumentative writing. Argumentative texts focus on making a specific argument, persuading the reader to agree with a particular point of view, or convincing the reader that the analysis provided is sound.

Since the primary task of this book is preparing you for and familiarizing you with the SAT, we've made every effort to replicate the formatting of reading passages as they appear on the official test. However, since test makers often change up their approach from year to year, be aware that the reading passages on your exam day may look slightly different than how they are presented here. If this is the case, don't worry! The key with preparing for SAT Reading and Writing is recognizing how to address certain question types when they come up and learning to pull necessary information from a given reading passage. By practicing with this book, you will be well on your way to tackling any reading passage that might come up on the SAT, no matter how it is formatted.

Reading Skills by Question Type

The questions that follow your passages are multiple-choice with four answer choices each. The four question domains covered by the SAT Reading and Writing section (Craft and Structure, Information and Ideas, Standard English Conventions, and Expression of Ideas) all address reading to some degree since every question requires you to work with a reading passage. However, questions from the Information and Ideas and Craft and Structure domains focus more on reading skills than questions from the other two domains. Yes, questions from the Expression of Ideas and Standard English Conventions domains still require you to do some reading, but they will not address reading skills directly so much as your ability to read a passage for the necessary context to complete a writing and editing task.

To help you understand which question types will address which types of reading skills and Knowledge Testing Points (KTPs), consult the chart that follows.

READING SKILLS BY QUESTION CATEGORY		
Question Domain	**Knowledge Testing Point (KTP)**	**Related Reading Skills**
Craft and Structure	Words in Context	Using contextual information to determine the meaning of a word as it is used within a text
	Text Structure and Purpose	Analyzing and determining the structure of a text as well as the primary rhetorical purpose of a given part or the text as a whole
	Cross-Text Connections	Synthesizing information from two different texts to determine the relationship between them
Information and Ideas	Central Ideas and Details	Determining main idea, finding relevant information, recognizing key details, and interpreting how the details support the main idea
	Command of Evidence (Textual)	Using textual evidence such as a fact, detail, or example to support, challenge, or respond meaningfully to a specified claim or argument
	Command of Evidence (Quantitative)	Using quantitative textual evidence such as data from an informational graphic to support, challenge, or respond meaningfully to a specified claim or argument
	Inferences	Drawing conclusions and making inferences based on information either explicitly or implicitly provided in the text
Standard English Conventions	Boundaries	Evaluating context to appropriately correct grammatical errors within a text
	Form, Structure, and Sense	
Expression of Ideas	Rhetorical Synthesis	Evaluating provided information and determining how it should be integrated when creating another text or object to accomplish a specific provided goal
	Transitions	Determining which transition word or phrase most effectively matches the context of the blank in question

One thing you'll notice as you work through this chapter is that certain types of skills, like identifying supporting details or making inferences, may pop up in questions from any one of these categories. Therefore, while it is useful to know what these categories are and it may even sometimes be helpful to pinpoint which kind of question you're looking at, your study time is usually better served breaking down reading comprehension into explicit skills that you can practice, as we do later in this chapter. Recognize the question categories by which you'll be evaluated, certainly, but also note that each category usually requires you to use a combination of reading skills simultaneously.

EIGHT KEY READING SKILLS

Since most skills are likely to come up in a variety of SAT question categories, we have split reading comprehension into eight key skills that are important to SAT test makers and represented across all question types.

Eight Key Reading Skills

The eight key reading comprehension skill sets that questions in the SAT Reading and Writing section address are as follows.

1. **Determining Main Idea:** These questions test the ability to identify the main idea of a text, including central themes or arguments, as well as to determine how that main idea relates to other elements of the text, such as structure and rhetorical purpose.

2. **Addressing Rhetorical Purpose:** These questions test the ability to determine an author's purpose for writing a given text or to adequately support the rhetorical purpose of a text to be written.

3. **Evaluating Context and Supporting Details:** These questions test the reader's comprehension of supporting details in the passage and the ability to identify contextual information related to those details through effective reading.

4. **Using Vocabulary in Context:** These questions test a reader's word comprehension and the ability to define vocabulary words or phrases based on the context in which they are used within a passage or sentence.

5. **Making Inferences:** These questions test the reader's ability to draw logical inferences and conclusions from ideas and details presented in the passage.

6. **Structure, Organization, and Logic:** These questions test the ability to identify and evaluate how a passage's organization and logic help an author meet their purpose, including the ability to recognize how a passage is structured and why.

7. **Opinion and Argument:** These questions ask readers to evaluate the rhetoric authors use to express opinions and arguments, including how that rhetoric relates to an author's point of view and mode of writing as well as their ability to support claims and counterclaims.

8. **Synthesis:** These questions ask readers to synthesize information between two passages, including recognizing the relationship between two texts and where two authors converge and contrast in their claims as well as summarizing both individual texts and their combined impact or message.

In the sections that follow, we'll discuss each of these question types, offer tips on how to address them, and give you a chance to practice your skills with SAT-like passages. At the end of this section, you'll find a graphic model demonstrating how multiple question types relate to details from a single informational passage.

Determining Main Idea

The main idea of a text is the primary point the text is trying to convey to readers. In argumentative writing, it will be the author's main opinion or argument. You can think of the main idea as the overall message an author is trying to send by writing a text. Since passages on the SAT are only a paragraph long, the main point should be evident after you complete your reading.

Questions to Ask Yourself: Main Idea

- What is the author telling me?
- What does the author want me to take away from the passage?
- What would be a good title for this passage?
- Why did the author write this passage?
- If I had to summarize this passage in one sentence, what would it be?

You can be prepared for any main idea question if you summarize the most important "takeaway" from the passage whenever you finish reading. Try and do so in a single statement, such as by completing sentences like "This passage was about ____________" or "The author wants the reader to know that ____________." Having this main idea in mind should make it easier to identify correct answers to both main idea questions and questions that are related to them, such as supporting detail questions, and questions about organization and logic.

One of the fastest ways to eliminate incorrect answers to main idea questions is by looking for choices that are either too specific or too general. To demonstrate, let's say you read a passage, and when you finish, you mentally summarize the main idea as follows: "This passage was about how squid develop over the course of their entire life." Then, you are faced with the following main idea question.

EXAMPLE

Which title best describes the main idea of the passage?

A. "Squid Mating Habits"
B. "The Life Cycle of Squid"
C. "Animals of the Ocean"
D. "The Evolution of Squid"

You are looking for the answer that is most like your summary of the passage's main idea. In this case, "The Life Cycle of Squid" does the trick. Having already identified the main idea, the correct answer should hopefully stand out the second you read it. If it doesn't, remember to check for answers that are too vague or too specific. "Squid Mating Habits" (choice A) reflects a topic that relates to the life cycle of squid and may even have been addressed in part of your passage; however, it is too specific to encompass the main idea you identified, which included the stages of a squid's entire life. Meanwhile, "Animals of the Ocean" (choice C) is far too vague to be the title of a passage that talks about squid specifically.

FYI

Even if a test question doesn't use the words "main idea," it might still be asking for the main idea. If you have identified the main idea for yourself, then you shouldn't be caught off guard no matter how the question is phrased.

Once you have eliminated options that are too specific or vague, the remaining incorrect option(s) will usually address something that either wasn't mentioned in the passage or that is slightly off topic from the passage. In this case, "The Evolution of Squid" (choice D) is related to the main idea you identified, but not directly so, since the evolution of a species is different than its life cycle.

What follows is the first of many practice sets in this chapter. Each is roughly double the length of a traditional SAT passage to allow you to answer a few questions at a time instead of just one. This way, you can evaluate your understanding of reading comprehension topics as you review them. At the end of this chapter, you'll find a longer Test Yourself section where the questions do match the SAT passage standards. Use the Test Yourself when you finish reviewing this chapter to evaluate your progress.

PRACTICE: DETERMINING MAIN IDEA

Directions: Read the passage that follows. Then, answer the accompanying questions.

The Socialist Republic of Vietnam, known more commonly as "Vietnam," is a country located along the eastern edge of Southeast Asia's mainland. With a history spanning thousands of years, Vietnam has long embraced diverse cutural elements—today, it is an intricate cultural blend of ancient traditions and contemporary influences, such as the integration of French cultural touchpoints as a result of colonization. This blending of old and new is evident not just in cultural practices but also in the spatial development of the country. For instance, in Vietnam's bustling metropolises like Ho Chi Minh City and Hanoi, traditional markets coexist with trendy shopping malls, and ancient temples stand alongside modern skyscrapers.

One key to understanding Vietnamese culture is recognizing its emphasis on the Confucian concept of filial piety as well as universal respect for elders. In Vietnamese society, the family holds a central position, and children are taught to honor and care for their parents and grandparents. This traditional value can be observed in the daily lives of Vietnamese individuals, where strong familial ties and support are highly valued. This regard for family is reflected in the value assigned to festivals, which play a vital role in Vietnamese cultural life by providing opportunities for communities to come together and celebrate their shared heritage. The Lunar New Year, known as Tet, is the most significant and widely celebrated festival in Vietnam, where families gather to pay respects to ancestors, exchange wishes for good fortune, and indulge in traditional foods.

1. Which choice best states the main idea of the text?
   - A. Vietnamese culture comes from a mix of influences, yet the commitment to family and ancestral tradition remains a major focus.
   - B. Vietnamese culture is focused entirely on the value of family and ancestral tradition.
   - C. Vietnamese culture spans thousands of years.
   - D. Today, people in Vietnam are skeptical about modernization and would rather maintain their ancestral traditions.
2. Which choice best states the main idea of the first paragraph?
   - A. The culture in Vietnam is resistant to modernization because ancient traditions and customs are so highly valued.
   - B. Family is a major focus of cultural festivals in Vietnam, such as Tet.
   - C. Vietnam's culture is rapidly modernizing and metropolises like Ho Chi Minh City and Hanoi no longer look how they once did.
   - D. Vietnam's culture is a combination of ancient and modern influences, which is reflected in areas like commerce and architecture.
3. Which choice best states the main idea of the second paragraph?
   - A. During Tet, which is the Vietnamese Lunar New Year, families gather to pay homage to their ancestors.
   - B. The metropolises in Vietnam are modernizing rapidly, so it is difficult for those who believe in ancient customs to keep up.
   - C. Two major focuses of Vietnamese culture include respect for elders and filial piety, both of which are reflected in Vietnamese festivals like Tet.
   - D. Filial piety is a Confucian concept taken from Chinese culture, and it involves observing certain cultural norms and respecting one's family heritage.

Answer Explanations

1. **The correct answer is A.** The main idea of the text is that while Vietnamese culture comes from a multitude of influences, the commitment to family is a uniting force among cultural practices. Remember to select the choice that best represents the passage as a whole. Choice B overstates the intensity of the focus on family in Vietnamese culture. Choice C is vague and represents only a small portion of the text. Choice D inaccurately interprets the text.

2. **The correct answer is D.** This paragraph focuses on the way cultural traditions in Vietnam come from both modern and ancient sources. It offers both commerce (traditional markets vs. shopping malls) and architecture (ancient temples vs. modern skyscrapers) as examples. Choices A and C misrepresent the paragraph. Choice B represents ideas from the second paragraph rather than the first.
3. **The correct answer is C.** This paragraph discusses how filial piety and respect for elders are important cultural values that are reflected in Vietnamese traditions like the Lunar New Year festival known as Tet. Choices A and D focus too intently on small aspects of the paragraph. Choice B misrepresents an idea from the first paragraph.

ADDRESSING RHETORICAL PURPOSE

Closely related to main idea questions are those that address the author's purpose for writing a passage or the purpose of a specific portion of a passage. This is called the rhetorical purpose because it relates to rhetoric, which can be defined as "the art of writing effectively." In short, the rhetorical purpose is the reason the author has written the passage. While the main idea is about *what* is in the passage—the information the author wants you to know—the rhetorical purpose is about *how* information is presented and *why* the author has chosen to express their ideas in that manner.

Questions that deal with the author's purpose are easy to spot because they usually contain the word *purpose*. An author's purpose can generally be expressed as a *to* + verb expression, with common purposes being to inform, explain, or argue. The table on the next page provides a list of verbs commonly used to describe an author's rhetorical purpose.

Questions to Ask Yourself: Rhetorical Purpose

- Why did the author write the information they did in the way they did?
- What verbs would I use to describe what the author is doing in this passage?
- Is the author trying to convince me to believe something?
- Is the author making an argument for or against a particular idea or course of action?
- Is this passage written for a particular audience?
- Is the author telling me a story?
- Why has the author chosen the words they used or phrased things the way they did?

COMMON VERBS TO DESCRIBE AN AUTHOR'S PURPOSE	
Purpose Verbs	**In a reading passage, this looks like the author. . .**
inform educate teach	. . . providing information to educate a reader on a topic, often (but not always) while gesturing to credible support.
persuade argue convince	. . . convincing the reader to agree with an opinion or point of view.
amuse entertain	. . . entertaining the reader with an interesting, inventive, or humorous topic.
compare contrast	. . . showing the similarities or differences between ideas or known facts.
describe	. . . using the five senses or other descriptive details to portray the characteristics or qualities of a topic.
explain (information) clarify break down	. . . making an idea or issue clearer through description, details, or a breakdown of how something works or occurred.
discuss examine consider	. . . examining different angles or perspectives of a topic or argument.
analyze evaluate assess	. . . conducting a detailed analysis of numerous facts, quantities, or perspectives impacting an issue or topic, most often using credible support.
critique criticize	. . . expressing disapproval for a topic, issue, or the perspective of another person.
praise celebrate	. . . expressing approval for a topic, issue, or the perspective of another person.
tell narrate explain (as a story)	. . . using a narrative (storytelling) approach to entertain, relay ideas, or explain a topic using figurative details.
quantify	. . . employing statistics, facts, and other quantifiable data to "place a number" on something that is otherwise a concept.
summarize	. . . providing a summary of a topic.

As with main idea questions, state for yourself what the author's purpose is whenever you finish reading a passage. Whatever verb you choose to describe the author's purpose (or a synonym for it) is likely to pop up in your answer options later.

To illustrate, let's say you finish reading a passage and decide that the author's purpose was to compare an alligator's typical diet with a crocodile's typical diet. Consequently, you know you're looking for an answer that includes the word *compare* or a synonym for it. You are then given a seemingly vague question:

EXAMPLE

Which choice best states the main purpose of the text?

A. To praise the historical conservation efforts of Australian regional governments in preserving saltwater crocodiles

B. To criticize the US Department of Fish and Wildlife for their response to poachers in the Florida Everglades

C. To contrast the dietary requirements of alligators and crocodiles as related to their habitats

D. To illustrate the evolutionary trajectory of large reptiles' diets

If you have already determined that the author's rhetorical purpose was to compare, you will easily spot that choice C is the correct answer, since *contrast* is used as a synonym for *compare* when discussing an author's purpose. Sometimes, two answers may seem plausible. For instance, you might convince yourself that such a comparison illustrates (choice D) the differences between the animals' diets. However, always choose the answer that *best* expresses the rhetorical purpose. *Contrast* is a more specific description of the author's purpose, which you determined was to compare the diets of two similar but different species.

The skill category most directly associated with determining rhetorical purpose is Text Structure and Purpose, which falls under the Craft and Structure question domain. However, determining the context of the passage and recognizing how the details of the text support its main idea, rhetorical purpose, structure, and logic is an important skill for every question domain. It will be important to recognize the rhetorical purpose of any text you read so that you can address issues related to numerous question types. For instance, having a strong command of the rhetorical needs of a theoretical research project will help significantly with the Rhetorical Synthesis section, and knowing the purpose of each respective text for Cross-Text Connections questions will help you more easily recognize the relationships between the texts.

TIP

If a question asks about a text's purpose, focus on the active verbs in the answer choices. Sometimes, you can automatically eliminate some incorrect choices by noting what the passage *didn't* do.

PRACTICE: ADDRESSING RHETORICAL PURPOSE

Directions: Read the passage that follows. Then, answer the accompanying questions.

Serotonin is a neurotransmitter found in serum and blood platelets. Common thinking around serotonin is that it's a "good mood" chemical that plays a vital role in regulating emotions, focus, and sleep—if you're feeling calm, happy, or at ease, it's probably because your serotonin levels are stable. In people with depression or other mental health concerns, it can be difficult to keep serotonin levels stable. When coupled with the fact that mental health disorders can also affect hormones, other neurotransmitters, and the body's physical sensations, it's clear why a medication that can help regulate serotonin would be beneficial. This is where the drug class known as Selective Serotonin Reuptake Inhibitors (SSRIs) comes in.

SSRIs work by ensuring the brain has enough serotonin even in individuals who have trouble keeping levels stable. According to the United Kingdom National Health Service (NHS), "After carrying a message, serotonin is usually reabsorbed by the nerve cells (known as 'reuptake'). SSRIs work by blocking ('inhibiting') reuptake, meaning more serotonin is available to pass further messages between nearby nerve cells." This explains the "R" and "I" in the term SSRIs; these types of drugs are reuptake inhibitors. Since there is less serotonin reuptake, more serotonin sticks around, making it easier to combat issues caused by decreased serotonin. While low serotonin isn't necessarily the cause of all mental health concerns treated by SSRIs, studies show that increasing serotonin levels is a positive therapeutic intervention for many. <u>Though SSRIs aren't without their side effects, which the NHS notes include gastrointestinal issues, feelings of dizziness or blurred vision, and a suite of symptoms related to reproductive wellness, for many who suffer from mental health struggles, the benefits of this type of therapy outweigh potential side effects.</u>

Adapted from UK National Health Service, 2021. "Overview - SSRI Antidepressants." *NHS*. February 15, 2021. https://www.nhs.uk/mental-health/talking-therapies-medicine-treatments/medicines-and-psychiatry/ssri-antidepressants/overview/.

1. Which choice best states the main purpose of the text?

A. To narrate the author's experience taking SSRIs

B. To praise SSRIs for being so effective

C. To educate the reader about what SSRIs are and how they work

D. To summarize scientific studies about the efficacy of SSRIs

2. Which choice best states the main purpose of the first paragraph?

   A. To debate the validity of SSRI research and determine if they are in fact safe

   B. To define *serotonin* in order to introduce SSRIs

   C. To consider new ways that doctors might use SSRIs to make them even more effective for patients

   D. To explain what SSRIs are and how they function in therapeutic settings.

3. Which choice best states the function of the underlined sentence in the text as a whole?

   A. To articulate the conditions under which taking an SSRI might be dangerous

   B. To critique doctors for prescribing SSRIs despite the symptoms associated with them

   C. To enumerate the symptoms associated with SSRI use by degree of severity

   D. To communicate that even though there are side effects of taking SSRIs, many patients still benefit from them

Answer Explanations

1. **The correct answer is C.** The author's purpose in this passage is to educate the reader about what SSRIs are and how they work.
2. **The correct answer is B.** In this question, you must consider the purpose of a particular paragraph. In this case, the author's purpose in the first paragraph is to define serotonin in order to explain the serotonin reuptake process in the second paragraph.
3. **The correct answer is D.** Text Structure and Purpose questions under the Craft and Structure domain will often ask about the purpose of a particular line within the text as a whole. Here, the purpose of the line is to communicate that even though there are side effects of taking SSRIs, many patients still benefit from them.

Evaluating Context and Supporting Details

Supporting details, or supporting ideas, are pieces of information that help the reader understand the author's main idea or argument. Generally, they offer background or necessary context. These sentences might provide examples, facts, statistics, quotations, related stories, descriptions, or lots of other information to support the main idea and rhetorical purpose. Any time you read through a passage for the information you need or read the sentences around a blank, you are determining the context within which a question is being asked. Context is the information you need from a text to answer a question effectively.

Quite often, questions that require you to determine the context or find supporting details won't look like language arts questions at all. Remember, though, these questions are in the Reading and Writing section, so they will never ask about anything you can't answer using the details of the reading passage(s) alone. Don't be thrown off if you get a question that looks like it's from history, science, math, or any other subject besides reading and writing. Instead, assume the question is asking about something you can answer by finding the relevant information in the text.

Questions to Ask Yourself: Context and Supporting Details

- What information does the author provide?
- How is that information used to support and explain the main idea and purpose?
- Are there any important names, concepts, or words repeated multiple times?
- How do smaller details in the passage add up to a bigger picture?
- What claims and counterclaims does the author make to support their main argument?
- What context do I need from the text to properly answer the question?

Supporting detail questions will look wildly different depending on the topic of the reading passage; in other words, don't expect to see something like "What are the supporting details in this passage?" Instead, detail questions will ask you about the passage's content. For example, if the passage is informing you about different cultural theories prominent in the field of sociology, then a details question might ask, "Which of the following is *not* a tenet of postcolonial theory?" Or "In this passage, the author compares Foucault's theories on power to..." It's your job to scan back through the passage and choose the right answer based on the details provided.

The skill category most directly associated with context and reading comprehension is Central Ideas and Details, which falls under the Information and Ideas question domain. However, determining the context of the passage and recognizing how the details of the text support its main idea, rhetorical purpose, structure, and logic is an important skill for every question domain.

PRACTICE: CONTEXT AND SUPPORTING DETAILS

Directions: Read the passage that follows. Then, answer the accompanying questions.

There are few figures from Slavic folklore considered as formidable or intriguing as Baba Yaga. Loosely translated, her name is said to mean something like "Grandmother Witch," though this only partially encompasses her folkloric characterization. Baba Yaga is also a cannibal, goddess figure, fairy godmother, trickster, and villain, popping up in stories to terrorize heroes only to inadvertently provide them with the skills or items they require to complete their journey. Perhaps most importantly, Baba Yaga is a figure who symbolizes transformation, affording her further associations with birth, death, and transitional life phases like puberty.

There are numerous telltale characteristics that let you know Baba Yaga is in a story, even when she is not mentioned by name. For one, she lives in a hut in the woods that rests on chicken legs, which act like moveable stilts to hold the hut aloft. Because the house can move around the forest and turn itself in any direction, Baba Yaga is thought to always potentially be around the corner. This status gives her a frightening mystique. Her hut is not her only means of transport, however, as she can also fly around using a mortar and pestle. Because she is associated with fertility, the mortar and pestle are said to symbolize her male and female sides. When traveling this way, she uses a broom to sweep away the tracks left behind; some scholars believe this is partially why we associate brooms with witches today. The primary way she threatens people is by kidnapping them and planning to eat them, though in most stories, they escape before she can feast.

1. Based on the text, which of the following modes of transportation does Baba Yaga use?
   - **A.** A flying broomstick
   - **B.** A mortar and pestle
   - **C.** Teleportation
   - **D.** Floating on air

2. Based on the text, which of the following is NOT a life stage with which Baba Yaga is associated?
   - **A.** Death
   - **B.** Puberty
   - **C.** Pregnancy and Childbirth
   - **D.** Adulthood

3. Based on the text, which of the following statements most accurately summarizes Baba Yaga's role in relation to the protagonists of the stories in which she appears?
   - **A.** Baba Yaga is a cannibal figure who usually eats protagonists by the end of a story.
   - **B.** Baba Yaga is a figure associated with love and infatuation, so she is often tricking protagonists into falling in love.
   - **C.** Baba Yaga is a fairy godmother figure who appears during rough situations to help protagonists with her magic.
   - **D.** Baba Yaga initially appears as a villain but usually ends up helping the characters she encounters in the end.

Answer Explanations

1. **The correct answer is B.** As the second paragraph states, in addition to having a moving hut that walks on chicken feet, "[Baba Yaga] can also fly around using a mortar and pestle."
2. **The correct answer is D.** The passage never mentions Baba Yaga being associated with adulthood.
3. **The correct answer is D.** This question relies on your ability to find necessary context clues in the passage. The passage states that Baba Yaga "often [pops up] in stories to terrorize heroes only to inadvertently provide them with the skills or items they require to complete their journey." Choice D is a fair summary of this key detail. Choice A is disproven by the last sentence in the passage. Choices B and C make unfounded inferences from small details in the text.

Questions to Ask Yourself: Vocabulary

- What does this word mean?
- If I don't know this word, can I figure out its definition based on what the passage tells me?
- Which of these answer options means the same thing or something close?
- Can I eliminate answer options that I know the meaning of and which I know are incorrect answers?

Using Vocabulary in Context

When vocabulary questions come up, you usually won't have to identify word definitions directly, as is common on other vocabulary tests. Instead, you'll be asked to identify a synonym for a word or phrase from the passage that matches the context in which it was used in the passage. Remember that a synonym is a word with the same meaning. It is not uncommon for multiple answer choices to provide possible synonyms for the word in question. You must consider how the word is used in the passage and then choose the answer that most nearly matches that same contextual meaning.

Sometimes, a question or answer option will present you with a short phrase instead of a single word, so don't be thrown off if you notice this. For instance, "in a little bit" is a perfectly suitable synonym for *soon*, even if one is a phrase and the other a word. Remember, too, that building vocabulary and studying word parts can help you tackle unknown words when you encounter them. Knowing word parts can also help you eliminate answer choices that are less likely to be correct. Towards the end of this chapter, we've provided a section called "Building Vocabulary for Reading Comprehension" to help you with this task.

Understanding an array of words and their meanings will help you with every question type on the SAT. However, there are two question categories that test

ALERT

Vocabulary-in-context questions don't always ask for the most common meaning of a word. Instead of choosing the most common definition, look for the meaning that best fits the context in which the word was used in the passage.

this skill explicitly: Words in Context (from the Craft and Structure domain) and Transitions (from the Expression of Ideas domain). For Words in Context questions, you will either need to provide a synonym for a given word or select the word that most accurately fills a blank based on the context of the passage. For Transitions questions, you'll need to select the transition that most accurately fills the blank and connects ideas in a manner that matches the relationship between the sentence or clause prior to the transition and the clause that follows it. We will discuss transitions more when we cover writing skills in Chapter 7.

PRACTICE: USING VOCABULARY IN CONTEXT

Directions: Read the passage that follows. Then, answer the accompanying questions.

The biggest of all species within the genus *Bathynomus* is the giant isopod, or *B. giganteus*. They may look like bugs, but giant isopods are not ocean insects. Rather, like crabs and shrimp, they're crustaceans. You might not expect a somewhat scary looking bottom dweller crustacean to get much love, but it seems the internet at large has given the giant isopod a new reputation. Thanks to the popularity of digital forms of communication like memes, the giant isopod has become recognizable to a wider swath of the general population, including a dedicated (1)___________of isopod fans who insist these little guys are quite cute.

Giant isopods truly are sizable; their average length is between 7.5 and 14.2 inches, but scientists have found specimens as long as 2.5 feet! Their outer shells are usually brown or a pale lilac. Some researchers speculate that isopods evolved to be so massive to withstand the ocean's immense pressure. These carnivorous scavengers typically gorge themselves on the corpses of dead animals that fall to the ocean floor but are also adapted to forgo eating for long periods of time. One interesting adaptation isopods share with felines is what's called a tapetum, meaning a reflective layer towards the back of the eye that increases their ability to see in the dark. (3)___________, this only helps giant isopods so much—they have weak eyesight and often must depend on their antennae to augment their navigational abilities.

1. Which choice completes the text with the most logical and precise word or phrase?

   A. designation

   B. subset

   C. neighborhood

   D. company

2. As used in the text, what does the word "augment" most nearly mean?

   A. Agree with

   B. Negate

   C. Camouflage

   D. Amplify

3. Which choice completes the text with the most logical transition?

   A. However

   B. Nonetheless

   C. Lastly

   D. As a result

Answer Explanations

1. **The correct answer is B.** You are looking for a word that means something like "portion" or "part." The closest synonym of your options is *subset*, which means "part of a larger group of related things."

2. **The correct answer is D.** The verb *augment* means "to amplify, strengthen, reinforce, or expand."

3. **The correct answer is A.** You are looking for a transition that illustrates a contrast between what was stated before and what was stated after—eliminate choices C and D because they do not satisfy this condition. Of the two that remain, *however* is more logical because *nonetheless* is more often used in situations where it could logically replace some version of the phrase "in spite of," such as in the sentence "The weather was cold; nonetheless, we enjoyed visiting the beach." *However* does a better job of setting up the type of contrast required by the statement in the text.

Making Inferences

An inference is a logical conclusion you can draw based on information provided to you. The information given to you can be explicit (stated directly) or implicit (not stated or stated only indirectly). On the SAT, the information needed to answer Inference questions will usually not be explicit. Instead, you are looking for a reasonable conclusion that could be drawn based on what the text does say. For instance, if the text mentioned that field geologists must often spend long periods of time camping alone or in small groups, you could infer that camping skills are *most likely* a job requirement for field geologists even if the text didn't say so directly. You don't have enough information to know if this is for sure the case, but it's a logical conclusion you could draw from what you read.

Inference questions are therefore asking you to "do something" with what you've just read. For example, you might be asked to make a prediction about what happens next or to compare ideas in two paired texts with one another. Some inference questions on the SAT may also present you with a summary of the findings from a particular study or experiment and ask you to identify which conclusion could be drawn or which claim could be supported by the information given.

Questions to Ask Yourself: Making Inferences

- What do I know, and what can I predict?
- How are ideas in the passage(s) alike and different?
- What do I know about the characters present in the story and how they feel about the situation presented?
- What am I supposed to "get" that the author isn't saying directly?
- What might I understand to be true or false after reading this passage?

5

Inference questions will sometimes be blunt and ask you "From the passage, you can reasonably infer that…" But these questions might also ask you things like "With which of these statements would the author of this passage most likely agree?" or "Based on the text, the scientist can logically conclude that…" They may also resemble supporting detail questions, such as by asking you to identify which statement *might* be true in light of another detail from the passage. Another common type of inference question on the SAT involves filling in a blank with an inference that logically completes the text.

All of these questions are asking you to infer since you can only make a logical prediction. Of all the reading comprehension abilities the SAT tests, this one relies the most on your critical thinking skills. You may have to think a little to find your answer, but remember that at their core, inference questions are asking you what you can figure out from the information you've been given. You shouldn't have to work too hard to make your answer fit.

These skills are tested directly by the Inferences skill category within the Information and Ideas question domain. You may also need to make inferences when finding textual or quantitative evidence to support certain claims, or when synthesizing information between texts or from research notes, as in the Rhetorical Synthesis skill category.

PRACTICE: MAKING INFERENCES

Directions: Read the passage that follows. Then, answer the accompanying questions.

If you were a 6-year-old headed to your first day of school in Germany, you would likely do so with a giant paper cone in tow. These cones, called *Kindertüte*, are fun-filled goodie bags containing candy, toys, school supplies, and anything else a child might need to have a joyful first day. Even though the treats are nice, the *Kindertüte* are more about celebrating and communicating to children that they are entering a new stage of life. Japanese parents do something similar, gifting their children a new backpack and sometimes a new desk to use at home to mark the first day of school. As in Germany, these presents are intended to help the child understand that they are embarking on a new chapter in their development.

Many cultures mark the first day of school with a celebration. In Kazakhstan, children start school at the age of 7. Their first day is called Tyl Ishtar, which means "Initiation into Education," and to celebrate it, parents will invite family and friends to a giant feast at their home. During this feast, the school-bound child is expected to recite the names of their grandfathers going back seven generations to honor their ancestry. Other first day celebrations are more about giving children an opportunity to get to know one another. In Saudi Arabia, the first few days of school contain no lessons, instead giving children a chance to share food and play games. In parts of Indonesia, the first day is treated as an orientation to (3)__________.

1. Which statement can most logically be inferred from the text?

   A. Children do not start school until after age 7 in Japan.

   B. There are no back-to-school traditions in the United States.

   C. Japanese and German children are culturally considered more mature once they start school.

   D. Children in Japan are commonly homeschooled.

2. Which statement can most logically be inferred from the text?

   A. Children's friendships aren't considered meaningful in Kazakhstan.

   B. Children's friendships aren't considered meaningful in Indonesia.

   C. Families in Kazakhstan have traditionally followed a patriarchal structure.

   D. Families in Indonesia have traditionally followed a matriarchal structure.

3. Which choice most logically completes the text?

   A. help children intentionally develop friendships meaningful enough to last through their schooling years

   B. ensure children recognize the importance of respecting their teachers as elders

   C. give children placement tests, so their teachers know which skills they need help with the most

   D. provide parents with as much information as possible about what they can expect from their child's first year of education

Answer Explanations

1. **The correct answer is C.** The first paragraph mentions how both Germany and Japan consider the start of school an important life stage transition for children. Consequently, it would be logical to infer that the start of school is considered an advancement in a child's maturity in these cultures.

2. **The correct answer is C.** On the first day of school, children in Kazakhstan are expected to honor their ancestors by reciting the names of their grandfathers going back seven generations. Since they must recite the names of grand*fathers*, we can infer that families in Kazakhstan have traditionally followed a patriarchal structure.

3. **The correct answer is A.** The latter half of the paragraph that contains the blank in question discusses cultures which use the first day of school as an opportunity to help children build friendships. You can therefore logically infer that the correct answer is the one which refers to children forming friendships.

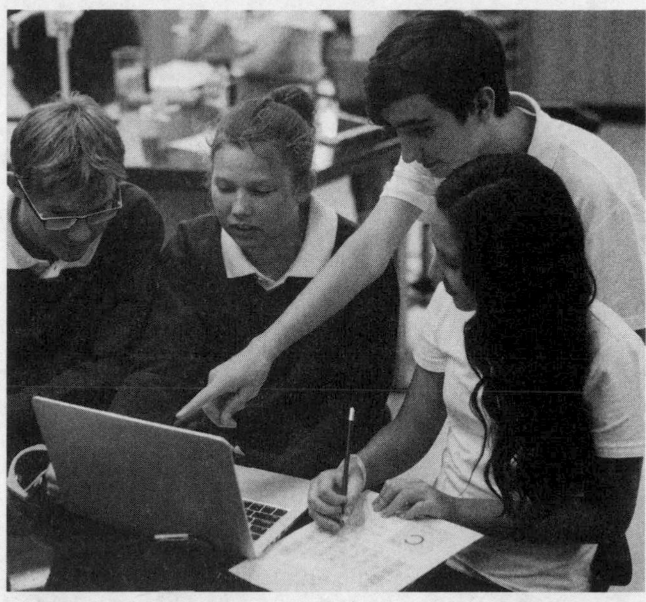

Structure, Organization, and Logic

In terms of reading, organization concerns how information in a text is arranged and how logical that arrangement is for the text's main idea and rhetorical purpose. It is also about transitions between ideas and how smoothly those transitions are executed. You can trust that each of the passages you read on the SAT will be well organized, but you should be prepared to answer questions about *how* the author chose to organize the text. You should also be prepared to identify a reasonable summary of a passage, which usually involves not just recognizing the main idea of the passage but also the sequence and structure through which the author has conveyed their message.

The term *logic* refers to a reasonable way of thinking about something using rational thought. All the reading passages you'll see should be logical, understandable, and clear. As with questions about organization, you will be tested less on whether the text is logical or not and more on what logic it uses to justify its claims or ideas. Or, as we'll discuss more in Chapter 7, you could be asked to draw a logical conclusion or justify a claim using the information presented to you in the text. It's up to you to decipher how each text is organized, how the author has logically arranged their ideas, and how the author might logically build on what is already written if they were to do so.

Questions to Ask Yourself: Structure, Organization, and Logic

- How are the ideas in this text arranged—are they in order of importance, time, or a different pattern?
- Does the author use transitions to help guide me through their argument?
- How does the organization of the passage affect its logic?
- If the passage were to continue, what might logically come next?
- What might have logically come before an excerpted passage?
- How does the author use (or fail to use) evidence to support claims and counterclaims?

Compared with other reading topics on the SAT, organization and logic are not tested as extensively as reading comprehension topics so much as writing and editing topics, which we'll discuss in more depth in Chapter 7. However, one particular type of Text Structure and Purpose (Craft and Structure) question asks you to identify the purpose of an indicated line within a text. In this case, you must be able to identify the author's purpose for the line in question with regards to the overall organization and logic of the text. Furthermore, Transitions (Expression of Ideas) questions will require you to choose a transition that logically completes the text and matches the text's organization.

PRACTICE: STRUCTURE, ORGANIZATION, AND LOGIC

Directions: Read the passage that follows. Then, answer the accompanying questions.

(1) Sometimes referred to as the Godmother of Rock n' Roll, Sister Rosetta Tharpe is an example of a Black woman who shaped history but didn't end up as famous as most of her male contemporaries. Born in Cotton Plant, Arkansas, she was the daughter of Willis Atkins and Katie Bell Nubin Atkins, a mandolin-playing singer who was also an evangelist for the Church of God in Christ. As a result of her mother's influence, Tharpe's early musical inspiration came primarily from gospel music. To aid in her mother's efforts, Tharpe began singing and playing the guitar as young as four years old.

By the time Tharpe was six years old, she was performing regularly with her mother and was adept at combining secular music styles with the gospel styles popular in religious music. While she was a gifted singer, it was Tharpe's virtuoso skill on the guitar that from such a young age paved her path to fame. (2) Not only could Tharpe easily find various chords and tones, but she was also able to manipulate the strings to produce individual notes, melodies, and riffs, as well as combine chords unexpectedly to produce new sounds. Very few women played guitar at the time, let alone young Black women, so Tharpe was something of an anomaly. (3) __________, her experimentation with the capabilities of the guitar as an instrument proved foundational to rock n' roll music as a genre.

1. Which choice best states the function of the underlined sentence in the text as a whole?
   - A. It introduces the topic of the text.
   - B. It introduces the argument that the author will make.
   - C. It provides the reader with Rosetta Tharpe's nickname.
   - D. It provides background information that is important to understand the main idea.
2. Which choice best states the function of the underlined sentence in the second paragraph as a whole?
   - A. It introduces the topic of the paragraph.
   - B. It provides evidence that elaborates on the claim made in the sentence before it.
   - C. It critiques the argument made in the sentence before it.
   - D. It summarizes the author's viewpoint on Tharpe's musical impact.
3. Which choice completes the text with the most logical transition?
   - A. Unfortunately
   - B. In light of her death
   - C. Despite her efforts
   - D. As contemporary critics note

Answer Explanations

1. **The correct answer is A.** Based on both its location within the text and its content, this is an introductory sentence. Choice B is incorrect because while the sentence introduces the topic, it does not introduce a particular argument. Choice C correctly states one aspect of the sentence but not its function in the text as a whole. Choice D is too vague—Choice A states the purpose of the sentence more directly.
2. **The correct answer is B.** For this question, you must rely on your awareness of context as well as your knowledge of how the text is organized. Since the sentence prior introduces the claim that Tharpe had "virtuoso skill on the guitar," it makes sense that the sentence in question offers evidence to support that claim. The sentence is neither introductory (choice A) nor critical of Tharpe (choice C). Choice D does not accurately reflect the text.
3. **The correct answer is D.** This is the only option which matches both the logic and organization as set up in the text—all three of the others do not make logical sense.

Opinion and Argument

When an author clarifies their own beliefs, viewpoints, or judgments, they are expressing an opinion. When an author takes a side in a debate, presents a plausible perspective on a researched subject, or tries to convince you to agree with their opinion, they are making an argument. If an author is making an argument, you should be able to identify the argument and how it's organized as well as any support given for that argument, such as related facts or examples. You should also be able to identify any claims the author makes and counterclaims they address. Conversely, if you are presented with a set of information, you should be able to recognize the plausible arguments an author could make from the given information.

ALERT

A statement being true doesn't necessarily mean it's a correct answer. Make sure that the answer choice you mark answers the question that is asked. Several answer choices might be true, but only one will be the answer to the question.

Questions to Ask Yourself: Opinion and Argument

- Is this text fact or opinion?
- What is the author's opinion and why?
- What is the author's argument?
- What strategies does the author use to convince me to agree with their argument?
- From whose perspective is the author speaking and to which intended audience?
- Does the author seem to have any bias that might cloud the logic of their argument?

On the SAT, questions of opinion and argument may come up as relates to the main idea or author's purpose. You will also likely need to address issues of opinion and argument when dealing with Text Structure and Purpose or Cross-Text Connections questions from the Craft and Structure domain. Identifying an author's opinion or argument will also prove useful on Inferences or Central Ideas and Details questions from the Information and Ideas domain. While questions about Command of Evidence from the Information and Ideas domain rely more on writing skills than reading skills, some will require you to recognize which piece of evidence best supports the argument an author is making. Finally, Rhetorical Synthesis questions from the Expression of Ideas domain (which we'll discuss in more depth in Chapter 7) will rely on your ability to craft plausible arguments from a given set of research notes. None of these question categories focus on opinion and argument exclusively, but you may need to use your comprehension skills related to opinion and argument to answer them effectively.

PRACTICE: OPINION AND ARGUMENT

Directions: Read the passage that follows. Then, answer the accompanying questions.

Teenagers today are not receiving adequate education in financial literacy, and it is having an undue impact on their adult lives. On top of that, common advice given to teenagers encourages them to embark on risky financial endeavors that they are too young to fully understand. An 18-year-old is not even considered responsible enough to purchase alcohol, yet our culture believes they have the wherewithal to make a sound and informed decision concerning five-figure student loans. If the culture isn't going to change to be less financially predatory towards young people, then school curricula must change to incorporate a far greater degree of financial literacy training before students graduate high school.

Besides it simply being the ethical thing to do in today's world, there are numerous benefits for young people who learn financial literacy starting in high school or earlier. Knowing how to make money, save money, and make wise financial decisions is empowering for teens, allowing them to feel like they're in control of their financial futures. Furthermore, not providing this type of education leaves young people anxious and ill-equipped. As Geoffrey Bellamy notes in his book *Guiding Teens Toward Financial Success*, when young people don't receive financial literacy education, "they struggle to maintain good credit scores, are unable to save enough money to buy a home or prepare for retirement, and have no idea how to invest." Equipping teens with financial literacy ensures they enter the world with more confidence and avoid falling into bad habits that will be harder to break when they're in a financial hole later. This can protect them, too, such as by making it easier for them to keep a savings fund for emergencies and making them aware of common financial pitfalls, such as gambling and pyramid schemes.

1. Which choice best states the main idea of the text?
   - **A.** Financial literacy training should begin in early adulthood.
   - **B.** Young people deserve more financial literacy training before they graduate high school.
   - **C.** Teenagers are usually bad with money.
   - **D.** It's becoming harder and harder to save money.

2. Based on the text, with which of the following statements would the author likely agree?
   - **A.** No one should ever take out student loans.
   - **B.** Credit scores are an unfair way to determine who deserves loans.
   - **C.** Teenagers should not have to pay taxes until age 18.
   - **D.** High school students should be taught how to financially plan for their retirement.

3. Which quotation from the text best expresses the author's argument?
   A. "...common advice given to teenagers encourages them to cmbark on risky financial endeavors..." (Paragraph 1)
   B. "...school curricula must change to incorporate a far greater degree of financial literacy training..." (Paragraph 1)
   C. "Knowing how to make money, save money, and make wise financial decisions is empowering..." (Paragraph 2)
   D. "Furthermore, not providing this type of education leaves young people anxious and ill-equipped." (Paragraph 2)

Answer Key and Explanations

1. **The correct answer is B.** As is often the case with argumentative passages like this one, the author summarizes their argument in the final sentence of the first paragraph: "If the culture isn't going to change to be less financially predatory towards young people, then school curricula must change to incorporate a far greater degree of financial literacy training before students graduate high school."
2. **The correct answer is D.** Since the author's main idea is that young people should get more financial literacy education before they graduate high school, you can infer that the author would agree with the idea of teaching high school students how to start planning for their eventual retirement.
3. **The correct answer is B.** The second quotation comes from the author's thesis statement, which is a type of statement that summarizes an author's argument.

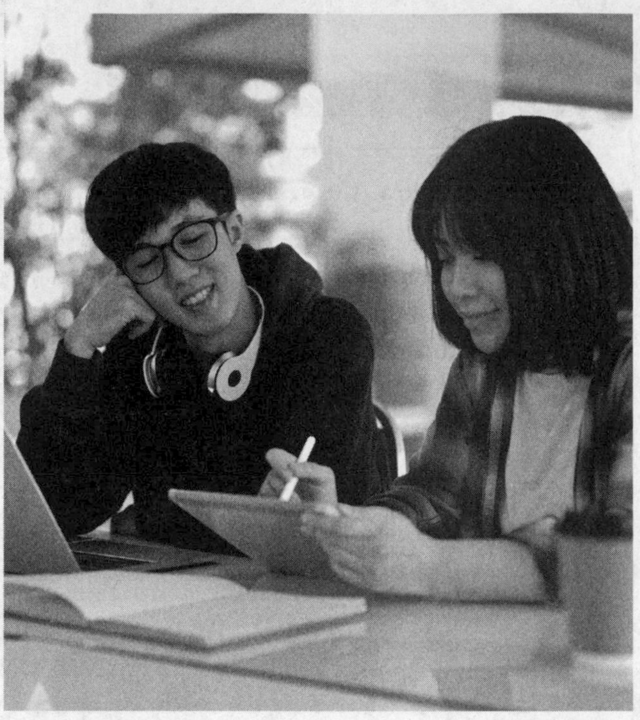

Synthesis

When you are asked to address more than one passage at a time, as you will be in Cross-Text Connections (Craft and Structure) questions on the SAT, you must use all of your other reading comprehension skills simultaneously. Paired passages are all about synthesizing information. The verb *synthesize* in this context means "to combine a number of elements into a coherent whole." Thus, your task with synthesis questions is to figure out how the passages make sense together rather than just on their own.

The good news is that when synthesizing information from multiple passages simultaneously, you're not actually reading any differently. You should approach reading the paired passages in the same way you would solo passages in any other section. The challenge lies in looking for relationships between the texts, recognizing where they agree and diverge, and practicing your inference and summary skills so you can express that relationship clearly.

If you can identify the main idea, purpose, and supporting details of each passage, you should have what you need to synthesize information between the two.

Questions to Ask Yourself: Synthesizing Information from Multiple Passages

- How would I summarize each passage individually?
- How would I summarize both passages together?
- In which ways do the authors agree and disagree?
- What are some key concepts or ideas that come up in both passages?
- How might looking at both passages give me deeper understanding than just looking at one or the other?
- If the authors of both passages were to debate each other, what topics might come up?
- How do the passages represent two different perspectives on the same topic?

PRACTICE: SYNTHESIS

Directions: Read the passages that follow. Then, answer the accompanying questions.

PASSAGE 1

The re-writing of the genetic map began in the early Bronze Age, about 5,000 years ago. From the steppes in the Caucasus, the Yamnaya Culture migrated principally westward into North and Central Europe, and to a lesser degree, into western Siberia. Yamnaya was characterized by a new system of family and property. In northern Europe the Yamnaya mixed with the Stone Age people who inhabited this region and along the way established the Corded Ware culture, which genetically speaking resembles present-day Europeans living north of the Alps today.

These new results derive from DNA analyses of skeletons excavated across large areas of Europe and Central Asia, thus enabling these crucial glimpses into the dynamics of the Bronze Age. In addition to the population movement insights, the data also held other surprises. For example, contrary to the research team's expectations, the data revealed that lactose tolerance rose to high frequency in Europeans, in comparison to prior belief that it evolved earlier in time (5,000–7,000 years ago).

PASSAGE 2

Apart from two groups already, the genomic signals clearly showed that a third—previously unsuspected—large contribution had been made sometime before the Iron Age, around 2,000 years ago. But by whom?

We have finally been able to identify the mystery culprit, using a clever new system invented by our colleagues at Harvard University. Instead of sequencing the entire genome from a very small number of well-preserved skeletons, we analysed 400,000 small genetic markers right across the genome. This made it possible to rapidly survey large numbers of skeletons from all across Europe and Eurasia.

This process revealed the solution to the mystery. Our survey showed that skeletons of the Yamnaya culture from the Russian/Ukrainian grasslands north of the Black Sea, buried in large mounds known as kurgans, turned out to be the genetic source we were missing.

1. Based on the texts, which choice best characterizes the relationship between Passage 1 and Passage 2?
   - A. Both passages show conflicting claims about the migrations.
   - B. Both passages describe different scientific methodologies.
   - C. Passage 2 provides supplementary information to Passage 1.
   - D. Passage 2 is written from a different perspective than Passage 1.

2. Based on the texts, which of the following statements could be made about scientific inquiry?
   - A. DNA evidence showed why many Europeans are lactose intolerant.
   - B. Genetic research can provide valid historical information.
   - C. Evidence showed that the Yamnaya evolved into the Corded Ware culture over time.
   - D. Scientific investigation can provide evidence about human history not obtainable through other means.

3. How do the texts illustrate the contributions of DNA evidence to scientific inquiry?
   - A. Both passages provide examples of how DNA evidence enabled scientists to fill in gaps in their knowledge about human migrations.
   - B. Both passages describe how DNA analysis is used in scientific investigations.
   - C. Both passages imply that DNA evidence can solve evolutionary questions.
   - D. Both passages show how scientists solved the mysteries of DNA evidence.

Answer Key and Explanations

1. **The correct answer is C.** When reading paired passages, you will encounter questions that ask you to examine the relationship between the passages. On your first reading, you probably noticed that the two passages do not contradict one another, nor do they show different points of view. This means you can eliminate choices A and D. Since both passages describe scientific studies and what scientists were able to learn from them, and both describe using DNA as the methodology,

choice B cannot be correct. By process of elimination, choice C must be the best answer. The second passage adds to the information in the first, which makes the information in Passage 2 supplementary to the information shown in Passage 1.

2. **The correct answer is D.** This question asks you to compare the two passages and look for a topic that is not directly discussed, but one that is implicit within it—the nature of scientific inquiry. While choices A and C are true, neither one answers the question. Choice B is also true, but it doesn't address the nature of scientific investigations; it is simply a general statement that could apply to many texts. Choice D, however, states a fact about scientific inquiry that can be gleaned from the texts. Both passages describe how scientists were able to use DNA data to answer questions they were unable to address before the use of DNA testing was available.

3. **The correct answer is A.** In paired passages, you will encounter questions that ask you to compare or contrast information presented explicitly in the passages. Both passages illustrate how DNA has been used to answer questions about human migration patterns—questions that had been unresolved before the ability to use DNA as evidence for such studies. Neither passage gives details about the actual scientific methodology as both are focused on the results, so you can eliminate choice B as a possible correct answer. Choices C and D are incorrect interpretations of the passages, so you can eliminate these choices as well.

Bringing Your Reading Comprehension Skills Together

You now know all the most important reading comprehension topics and skills that are likely to be covered on the SAT. As a reminder, these include the following:

- Determining Main Idea
- Addressing Rhetorical Purpose
- Evaluating Context and Supporting Details
- Using Vocabulary in Context
- Making Inferences
- Structure, Organization, and Logic
- Opinion and Argument
- Synthesis

The section that follows will also provide you with a primer on vocabulary expansion as relates to reading and writing skills. At the end of this chapter, you'll find a Test Yourself section to evaluate your progress on reading comprehension. In Chapter 6, we'll continue preparing you for the SAT Reading and Writing section by discussing the two question types that relate to Standard English Conventions. Then, in Chapter 7, we'll address all the writing skills you'll need to pair with the reading skills you reviewed here so that you can nail the section and bring home your best score.

Following this paragraph, you'll find a sample reading passage with a graphic illustration of how different parts of the passage relate to multiple reading comprehension skills we have discussed here. Keep in mind that you might get a question on the SAT that doesn't seem to fall into any of these categories, but don't panic! Rest assured that the information you need to answer a question will always be found in the text, so rely on the reading comprehension abilities you've built to find the right answer. If you're reading closely and actively for understanding, you can tackle any reading comprehension question that is thrown at you.

Example Reading Passage with Sample Questions

Directions: Read the passage and note how the numbered sections relate to the numbered sample questions on the opposite page. The numbers are there to help you identify how different types of questions relate to a single passage and where in the passage you would find the answer. Try to answer the questions for yourself. Then, check your answers against the answer key. As a challenge, imagine yourself in the role of an editor for this book. What sort of explanations would you write to show how and why the correct answers are correct?.

Sometimes, you can knock a vocabulary question out before you even begin reading by previewing the sentence that contains it.

Note that previewing the first and last sentence of the first and last paragraphs first would allow you to answer at least two questions before even reading the full passage!

Michelangelo Buonarroti's *David* is arguably the most famous statue in the world. Michelangelo sculpted the 17 ft. biblical figure from marble between ❶ 1501 and 1504 to grace the Pallazo Vecchio, a public square near some government buildings. ❷ Today, a replica stands in its initial location and Michelangelo's original is featured at the Galleria dell'Accademia in Florence, Italy.

❸ In his left hand, David carries a sling reminiscent of the biblical story in which he slays a giant. This detail means that Michelangelo was likely picturing David as a left-handed person. However, art historians note that ❹ it is David's right hand that presents a bigger mystery. First, it seems oversized compared to the otherwise proportionate statue. Second, the fingers appear to be curled around a mystery object. Art historians note that the veins in the right hand are prominent, suggesting that whatever David is holding, he's clutching it tightly.

There is some speculation that the oversized structure of the right hand is purely symbolic and meant to remind viewers of David having a "strong ❺ hand" in his later years as a king. Others suggest it could be as simple as David holding the stone that he will use to slay a foe with his sling. Still others suggest he could be holding a second weapon entirely. Whatever the case may be, ❻ there is no way of knowing what exactly Michelangelo imagined David gripping in his right hand, so the answer remains one of the art world's greatest mysteries.

INFERENCES

From paragraph 1, we can infer that

A. in the 16th century, all Italian art was required to have a religious context.

B. it took more than a decade to sculpt *David.*

C. *David* was not considered a masterpiece of sculpture until it was moved to a museum.

D. the government in Michelangelo's time was at least somewhat tied to the Christian church.

SUPPORTING DETAILS

Where is the original *David* located today?

A. Museo di Michelangelo

B. Pallazo Vecchio

C. Galleria dell'Accademia

D. Sistine Chapel

VOCABULARY

As used in paragraph 2, the word "reminiscent" most nearly means

A. bashful.

B. elusive.

C. critical.

D. remindful.

ORGANIZATION & LOGIC

The author's purpose in paragraph 2 is to

A. amuse the reader with an anecdote.

B. critique Michelangelo's artistic execution.

C. clarify a prominent reason that art historians still speculate about the statue.

D. narrate Michelangelo's creative process.

5 STYLE, TONE & LANGUAGE USE

The author's use of the phrase "strong hand" in paragraph 3 figuratively references the idea that David might have been a(n)

A. firm, decisive leader.

B. renowned athlete.

C. impulsive, hot-headed warrior.

D. naïve, immature monarch.

6 MAIN IDEA

The main idea of this passage is that

A. *David* is the most important statue of all time.

B. art historians remain divided as to what the David figure is holding in his right hand.

C. art historians determined that the David figure is holding a weapon in his left hand.

D. *David* is a proportionately oversized work, and its size reflects its symbolic meanings.

ANSWER KEY

1. D	2. C	3. D	4. C	5. A	6. B

BUILDING VOCABULARY TO INCREASE COMPREHENSION

Before we finish things up on the topic of reading comprehension, take a moment to consider the value of vocabulary expansion. Vocabulary and reading comprehension are closely related. You can't grow your vocabulary without reading, and you can't comprehend a text without a firm grasp of the words the author is using. To perform your best on the SAT Reading and Writing section, you'll need a strong vocabulary. Here are some ways you can build vocabulary expansion into your overall exam prep.

Keep a Word Log

First off, read material that is more challenging. The key is to find material with words that are new or unfamiliar to you.

Next, write down the words that you don't understand. Once you have a good list of unfamiliar words, look up the definitions in a dictionary and write them down for future reference. Focus on learning a few words at a time so that you can learn them well.

Third, try to use the word yourself in a sentence or in conversation. Practice using the word by creating your own sentences and writing them down in a notebook. This will help you get a sense of how to use the word in different contexts while cementing the word and its meaning into your vocabulary. Take note of the contexts in which you often see or use a word. Getting familiar with the topics and situations in which certain words are used will help you feel more confident and self-assured when you integrate new words into your vocabulary.

Study Root Words, Prefixes, and Suffixes

You can increase your vocabulary by learning about the structure of words. This will help you figure out the meanings of unfamiliar words when you encounter them.

English words have recognizable parts that often come from Latin or Greek. Generally, there are three basic types of word parts:

1. **Roots** are the basic elements of a word that determine its meaning. Many derive from Latin and Greek and must be combined with prefixes, suffixes, or both.

2. **Prefixes** attach to the beginning of a root word to alter its meaning or to create a new word.

3. **Suffixes** attach to the end of a root word to change its meaning, help make it grammatically correct in context, or form a new word. Suffixes often indicate whether a word is a noun, verb, adjective, or adverb.

Sometimes, depending on the word, it can be difficult to determine if it is a prefix or a root word. However, the key takeaway here is that certain word parts carry meaning that is recognizable no matter what the word is. Knowing the meaning of part of a word can help you infer the meaning of the word.

To aid you in your vocabulary building, we've compiled some frequently used root words, prefixes, and suffixes. These tables are by no means comprehensive, but they should help you get started on breaking down the words you see often or encounter when reading, including while preparing for your exam.

COMMON ROOTS		
Root	**Meaning**	**Example**
Aqu *Hydr*	Water	Aqueous, aquarium, hydrate, hydrotherapy
Aud	Hear	Auditory, audio, audible
Biblio	Book	Bibliophile, bibliography
Chrono	Time	Chronological, chronology
Chrom	Color	Monochromatic, chromosome
Circ	Round	Circle, circus
Geo	Earth	Geography, geomagnetic
Juris	Law	Jurisdiction, jurisprudence
Junct	Join	Conjunction, juncture
Log *Logue*	Speaking, speech	Epilogue, eulogy, dialogue
Photo	Light	Photosynthesis, photography, photon
Scribe	Write	Describe, prescribe, inscribe
Sect	Cut	Dissect, sector
Volve	Roll, turn	Involve, evolve, revolve

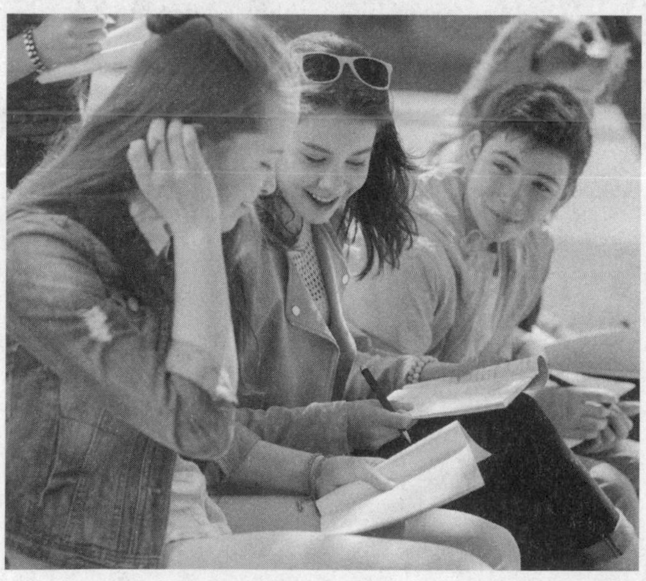

COMMON PREFIXES		
Prefix	**Meaning**	**Example**
Anti-	Against	Antifreeze, antibacterial
Bene-	Good	Benefit, benevolent
De-	Opposite	Deactivate, derail
Dis- *Dys-*	Not	Disagree, dysfunctional
En- *Em-*	Cover	Encode, embrace
Extra-	Beyond	Extraterrestrial, extracurricular
Fore-	Before	Forecast, forehead
Il- *Im-* *In-* *Ir-* *Non-* *Un-*	Not	Illegitimate, impossible, inexcusable, irregular, nonstop, nonsense, unable, undefined
Inter-	Between	Intergalactic, interpret, intermediary
Mal-	Bad, badly	Malicious, malnourished, malfunction
Mis-	Wrongly	Mistake, misinterpret, misnomer
Over-	Over, more, too much	Overlook, oversee, overachieve, overcast
Pre-	Before	Prefix, prevent, predict, prehistoric, prejudice
Re-	Again	Revision, reimagine, return
Trans-	Across	Transatlantic, transverse, transport

COMMON SUFFIXES		
Suffix	**Meaning**	**Example**
-able *-ible*	Capable	Agreeable, collectible
-al	Pertaining to	Logical, magical, criminal
-ance *-ence*	Indicating a state or condition; indicating a process or action	Clearance, ignorance, evidence, patience
-ent	Causing, promoting, or doing an action; one who causes or does something	Different, absorbent, student, agent, deterrent
-fy *-ize* *-ate* *-en*	Cause to be	Classify, diversify, realize, contextualize, create, communicate, awaken, sharpen
-ious *-ous*	Characterized by; full of	Nutritious, delicious, simultaneous, nervous
-ism	Belief, act	Catholicism, plagiarism
-ity	State or quality of being	Enmity, ability, responsibility
-less	Without	Homeless, restless, countless
-let	Small	Booklet, piglet
-or *-er* *-ist*	A person or object who is or does something	Benefactor, investigator, driver, teacher, chemist, narcissist, container
-ship	Position held	Friendship, citizenship, allyship, ownership
-tion *-sion* *-ment*	Action or instance of something	Liberation, concentration, admission, decision, achievement, bereavement
-y	Quality of	Thirsty, wintry

SUMMING IT UP

- These are the eight key reading comprehension skills you will need to use throughout the SAT Reading and Writing section:
  - Determining Main Idea
  - Addressing Rhetorical Purpose
  - Evaluating Context and Supporting Details
  - Using Vocabulary in Context
  - Making Inferences
  - Structure, Organization, and Logic
  - Opinion and Argument
  - Synthesis
- Pay attention to what the passage isn't saying. You might be asked to infer or predict something that isn't directly stated.
- If you're stumped, try to eliminate incorrect answer choices before making a guess and moving on.

TEST YOURSELF

READING COMPREHENSION

10 Questions—12 Minutes

Directions: The questions in this section address a number of important reading and writing skills. Each question includes one or more passages, which may include a table or graph. Read each question carefully, and then choose the best answer to the question based on the passage(s). All questions in this section are multiple-choice with four answer choices. Each question has a single best answer. Note that unlike the actual SAT Reading and Writing section, this test set focuses exclusively on questions related to reading comprehension—the actual exam section will have writing and grammar questions mixed in as well..

1. The following text is taken from H.G. Wells' 1895 short story "The Time Machine."

> It is a law of nature we overlook, that intellectual versatility is the compensation for change, danger, and trouble. An animal perfectly in harmony with its environment is a perfect mechanism. Nature never appeals to intelligence until habit and instinct are useless. There is no intelligence where there is no change and no need of change. Only those animals partake of intelligence that have to meet a huge variety of needs and dangers.

As used in the text, what does the phrase "partake of" most nearly mean?

A. Clash with

B. Disconnect from

C. Refuse

D. Experience

2. One cannot speak of the performance art known as tanztheater without mentioning its creator, Pina Bausch, who revolutionized the world of dance when she introduced this new form in the 1970s. Bausch created tanztheater to be a blend of dance, theater, and visual art. Unlike traditional dance forms, tanztheater combines intricate choreography with theatrical elements, narrative storytelling, and raw emotional honesty. It emphasizes how exaggerated physicality can support the exploration of human experiences and the expression of universal themes. Her most famous work, "Café Müller," premiered in 1978 and explores themes of loneliness, human relationships, and vulnerability. <u>It exemplifies tanztheater by providing Bausch's signature blend of expressive movement and spoken text as well as striking stage design that is integrated into the performance.</u> Though Bausch died in 2009, her legacy lives on as tanztheater remains one of the most enduring forms of modern dance.

Which choice best states the function of the underlined sentence in the text as a whole?

A. It provides clarity and specificity to the sentence that comes before it.

B. It introduces necessary context for the sentence that comes after it.

C. It illustrates how elements of Bausch's biography are relevant to the advent of tanztheater.

D. It defines the term "tanztheater" and explains key tenets of the art form.

3. The following text is taken from Zora Neale Hurston's 1912 short story "John Redding Goes to Sea."

> The raptures of the first few weeks over, John began to saunter out to the gate to gaze wistfully down the white dusty road; or to wander again to the river as he had done in childhood. To be sure he did not send forth twig-ships any longer, but his thoughts would in spite of himself, stray down river to Jacksonville, the sea, the wide world—and poor home-tied John Redding wanted to follow them.

Which choice best states the main purpose of the text?

A. To express John Redding's hope that he will one day get to visit Jacksonville

B. To characterize John Redding as someone who is longing to travel

C. To provide an explanation as to why John Redding likes to stand by the gate

D. To exemplify the kinds of topics John Redding liked to think about privately when visiting the river

4. **Text 1**

Denali National Park is a captivating example of the natural beauty and rich biodiversity to be found in Alaska. The park is named for North America's tallest peak, Denali, which stands at a staggering elevation of 20,310 feet. Spanning over six million acres, Denali National Park's pristine ecosystem plays host to numerous creatures who thrive despite the harsh climate, which is marked by extreme seasonal variations including short, mild summers and long, intense winters. Iconic residents of Denali include the majestic grizzly bear, the elusive grey wolf, the agile Dall sheep, and the regal Alaskan moose.

Text 2

Alaskan grizzly bears are sometimes known simply as brown bears. They are enormous creatures with remarkable adaptations that help these apex predators survive the challenging climate in Alaska. As far as physical adaptations are concerned, Alaskan grizzlies have dense fur and thick layers of fat to provide insulation against frigid temperatures. They have powerful muscles and razor-sharp claws that make them extremely efficient when hunting and foraging. Additionally, grizzly bears are opportunistic omnivores, which allows them to make the most of any resources they encounter. While they prefer certain foods (like salmon), their diet consists of any vegetation, berries, nuts, fish, and small mammals they can get their paws on, especially when food is scarce. One place where their population is especially dense (as many as 350 bears) is Denali National Park. Within the park, rangers have spotted both solitary bears and family units roaming the vast territory.

Based on the texts, which choice best characterizes how Text 2 relates to Text 1?

A. Text 2 provides significant details about one particular species while Text 1 provides an overview of the species.

B. Text 2 provides significant details about one particular geographical region while Text 1 provides an overview of the geographical region.

C. Text 2 provides significant details to help clarify and expand on a topic mentioned briefly in Text 1.

D. Text 2 critiques the claims made in Text 1, which is a simple overview of Denali National Park.

5. Cristiano Ronaldo is not only famous in his home country of Portugal—he is arguably the most famous athlete in the entire world. The soccer player, famous for playing on both Manchester United and Real Madrid as well as Portugal's World Cup team, is renowned not only for his success on the field but also for his charisma and philanthropy, which is reflected in the numerous charities, hospitals, children's organizations, disaster relief efforts, and other worthy causes who can call him a donor. As one of Portugal's most successful athletes, Ronaldo is both an inspiration and a role model, having garnered numerous individual awards and accomplished an array of record-breaking athletic feats. Many fans feel that his working-class origins and personal history, which includes heart surgery at age 15, are proof that hard work can pay off if you're truly dedicated.

Which choice best states the main idea of the text?

A. Cristiano Ronaldo is the primary reason that soccer has become such a beloved pastime in Portugal.

B. There are many athletes who are better at soccer than Cristiano Ronaldo, but none of them are as famous or philanthropic.

C. Cristiano Ronaldo is a prominent cultural figure in Portugal not only as an athlete but also as a philanthropist and role model.

D. Cristiano Ronaldo grew up working class, so he had to work twice as hard as anyone else to get where he is today.

6. Orcas are formidable hunters—both their highly adaptive hunting habits and collaborative social structures contribute to their status as the ocean's apex predators. Orcas deploy exceptional communication skills to cooperate when hunting. One such method involves herding prey into compact groups using a synchronized series of tail slaps and vocalizations. This coordinated effort isolates weaker individuals, making them vulnerable to swift attacks. Even larger prey (seals, sea lions, other whales) are no match for their unparalleled ingenuity. Orcas also possess a remarkable ability to exploit local environmental conditions. For instance, in areas with shallow water, some orcas use a technique called "wave washing" that involves generating waves to wash seals off ice floes, making it easier to hunt them. Similarly, orcas often use a stealth approach wherein they deploy their distinctive black and white coloring as deep ocean camouflage to surprise unsuspecting prey.

According to the text, which of the following most accurately summarizes the purpose of wave washing?

A. It provides an easy method for herding prey into compact groups.

B. It helps orcas communicate between family members while hunting.

C. It allows orcas to camouflage against the backdrop of the deep ocean.

D. It pushes seals off of ice floes to make them easier for orcas to hunt.

7. Holi, also known as the festival of colors, has its origins in ancient India. Each spring celebrants gather for the festival, which is intended to mark the victory of good over evil and to celebrate the arrival of a new season. Festivities take place throughout the world, but the largest Holi celebrations take place in the Indian cities of Mathura and Vrindavan. These two cities are significant because of their relationship to the Hindu god Lord Krishna—Mathura is where Krishna was born, and Vrindavan is where Krishna spent his childhood. During the festival, people gather in open spaces, armed with colored powders and water. Laughter fills the air as participants playfully throw and smear vibrant hues onto each other, all while music, dance, and traditional folk performances add energy to the festive atmosphere.

   Which choice can most logically be inferred from the text?

   A. Honoring the Hindu god known as Krishna is an important part of Holi.

   B. Krishna is the most important deity in all of Hinduism.

   C. Holi is the most important festival in all of Hinduism.

   D. Hindus consider smearing one's body in different colors a sacred ritual.

8. Among Kenya's many tribes is the Samburu people, who live in the arid regions of northern Kenya. The Samburu are skilled herders who are adept at raising cattle, sheep, and goats. Consequently, livestock plays a central role in their economy, providing milk, meat, and hides for trade and consumption. The Samburu are a communal tribe whose day-to-day life is centered around *manyattas*, which are traditional homesteads consisting of circular huts made from mud, grass, and wood. Each manyatta houses an extended family unit that works together to support one another. This shared commitment to kinship and community is reflected in Samburu traditions. For instance, the Samburu possess a rich oral history that involves passing down stories, folklore, rituals, and traditional artistic practices (__________) from one generation to another. Even as the world modernizes, the Samburu remain committed to preserving their cultural identity and ancestral customs.

   Which choice most logically completes the text?

   A. the official language is Samburu

   B. like beadwork and jewelry making

   C. their social structure is hierarchical

   D. such as Shamans and warriors

9. The Harbin Ice Festival is a winter celebration in Harbin, China, that has taken place between early January and late February every year since 1985. Set against the snowy backdrop of Harbin's frigid climate, the festival showcases an array of stunning ice sculptures meticulously crafted by skilled artisans. These icy masterpieces, illuminated by vibrant lights, transform the entire city into a dazzling winter wonderland. __________, the festival features performances (such as a figure skating showcase) and tournaments for different ice sports.

   Which choice completes the text with the most logical transition?

   A. Additionally
   B. By contrast
   C. In summation
   D. Nevertheless

10. The Faroe Islands are an archipelago situated in the North Atlantic Ocean, halfway between Norway and Iceland. Owned by the Kingdom of Denmark, these eighteen rocky islands are home to a unique blend of Nordic traditions and seafaring culture. Known for their dramatic landscapes, the Faroe Islands boast towering cliffs, rugged mountains, and cascading waterfalls. Visitors are drawn to admire the puffin colonies that dot the cliffs, making tourism a large income generator for the local economy. Resources from the sea also drive the economy on the Faroe Islands. Owing to their location and relative isolation, Faroe Island cuisine reflects a coastal lifestyle, with a strong emphasis on delicacies like fermented lamb and dried fish. __________, whaling remains nonetheless common on the islands for both industrial and dietary uses, as whales are abundant in the area. Seals and various species of seabirds also thrive in the surrounding waters.

    Which choice completes the text with the most logical transition?

    A. Likely founded by Vikings
    B. Because of the association with Nordic traditions
    C. As a result of their remote location
    D. Though a controversial practice throughout most of the world

Answer Key and Explanations

1. D	**3.** B	**5.** C	**7.** A	**9.** A
2. A	**4.** C	**6.** D	**8.** B	**10.** D

1. **The correct answer is D.** The word *partake* means "to take part in" or "participate in." As used in the text, the term *experience* is closest in meaning. If you were unsure, you could participate in a process of elimination by recognizing that all the other choices would convey the opposite of what is stated.
2. **The correct answer is A.** The sentence prior to the indicated sentence introduces a work called "Café Müller," and the sentence in question explains how "Café Müller" exemplifies tanztheater. Consequently, the sentence in question provides clarity and specificity to the sentence that precedes it.
3. **The correct answer is B.** Only choice B summarizes what can be inferred by the way John is characterized in this scene. The passage states that John frequently leaves the house to stare down the road or visit the river, that he imagines floating down the river to Jacksonville, and that he was "home-tied," all of which suggest that he is longing to travel. Choices A and D mischaracterize small details from the excerpt. Choice C is not supported by the text.
4. **The correct answer is C.** Text 1 is an overview of Denali National Park that mentions grizzly bears as one of the many species adapted to live there. Text 2 then goes into great detail about grizzly bears and their adaptations, including mentioning there are many grizzlies in Denali National Park. Therefore, Text 2 provides significant details to help clarify and expand on a topic mentioned in Text 1. All of the other options characterize one or both texts incorrectly.
5. **The correct answer is C.** If you didn't recognize that choice C does the best job of summarizing the text, you could use a process of elimination to recognize that all the other choices exaggerate or misstate some aspect of the text.
6. **The correct answer is D.** The text directly states that wave washing "involves generating waves to wash seals off ice floes, making it easier to hunt them."
7. **The correct choice is A.** The only answer that can be fully supported by the text is choice A, since the detail about the largest Holi celebrations taking place in cities associated with Krishna makes the idea that Krishna is important to Holi a logical inference. Choices B and C overemphasize Krishna and Holi's roles. While people do smear vibrant hues on each other during Holi, there is nothing to suggest that the practice is considered sacred (choice D).
8. **The correct answer is B.** Since the blank in question is between parentheses, you are looking for a statement that provides extra information on what was mentioned directly prior, which is "traditional artistic practices." The only answer that refers to traditional artistic practices is choice B.
9. **The correct answer is A.** The sentence that follows the blank provides additional information on the Harbin Ice Festival, so *additionally* is the most appropriate choice.
10. **The correct answer is D.** The use of the phrase "remains nonetheless common" suggests that the transition might need to set up a contrast to the acceptance of whaling on the Faroe Islands. Only choice D fulfills this task.

CHAPTER

Standard English Conventions

STANDARD ENGLISH CONVENTIONS

OVERVIEW

Many of the questions on the SAT Reading and Writing section will test your skills as relates to the conventions of Standard English. Fittingly, these questions fall under the "Standard English Conventions" testing domain, which accounts for approximately 11–15 questions (or ~26%) of the Reading and Writing section on the SAT. These questions, as their name implies, ask you to find errors in written English according to standard conventions. To perform well, you need a thorough (but not comprehensive) understanding of English grammar, sentence structure, punctuation, verb tense, usage, and agreement. This chapter will provide you with a refresher on the essential conventions of standard written English that the SAT commonly assesses. You'll find multiple opportunities throughout the chapter to practice the conventions as you review them.

6

STANDARD ENGLISH CONVENTIONS QUESTIONS

Within the Standard English Conventions question domain, there are two primary sub-categories of questions: 1) Boundaries; and 2) Form, Structure, and Sense.

Boundaries questions primarily address a test taker's ability to edit a text to ensure complete sentences. Questions might address the placement of words or punctuation within a sentence and the joining of different types of clauses. The primary goal with these types of questions is to form a complete sentence or set of sentences.

Form, Structure, and Sense questions primarily address a test taker's ability to edit a text in a manner that ensures correct use of the conventions of Standard English. Questions might address agreement, verb tense, verb aspect, preposition placement, or anything else that relates to using Standard English effectively. These questions differ from Boundaries questions in that they focus less on the grammatical completeness of a sentence or text and more on how effectively the test taker can use the conventions of Standard English to communicate ideas effectively.

In the sections that follow, we have divided Standard English convention topics into four categories according to the types of grammar issues they help test takers address: Grammar, Sentence Structure and Formation, Punctuation, and Verbs, Usage, and Agreement. Note that each section addresses issues that could be relevant to either Standard English Conventions question type.

GRAMMAR

The rules of grammar govern the ways in which parts of speech are organized in a sentence. There are rules concerning word endings, word order, and which words may be used together. You must know the parts of speech to follow the rules of grammar.

PARTS OF SPEECH

Type	Definition	Examples
Noun	A person, place, thing, or idea	teacher, city, desk, democracy
Pronoun	Substitute for a noun	he, they, ours, those
Adjective	Describes a noun	warm, quick, tall, blue
Verb	Expresses action or a state of being	yell, interpret, feel, are
Adverb	Modifies a verb, an adjective, or another adverb	fast, slowly, friendly, well
Conjunction	Joins words, sentences, and phrases	for, and, nor, but, or, yet, so
Preposition	Shows position in time or space	in, during, after, behind

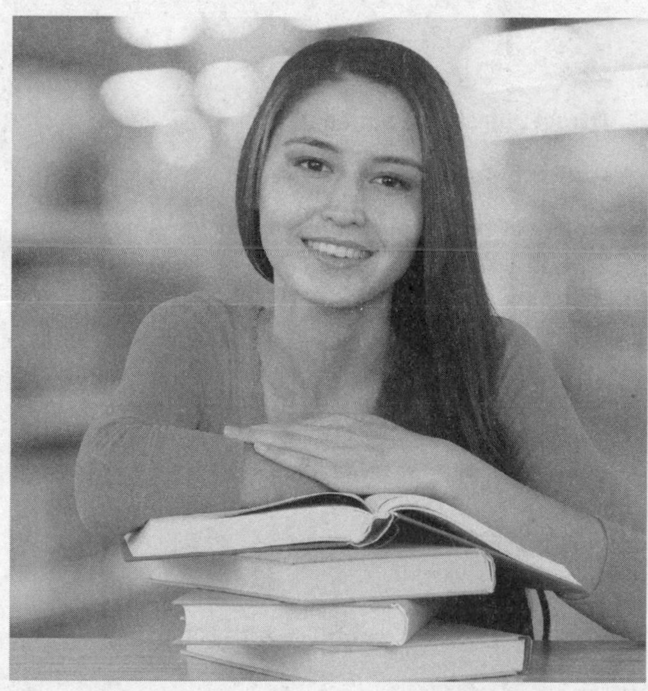

Nouns

A noun is a person, place, thing, or idea. There are different kinds of nouns:

- **Common nouns** are general, such as house, person, street, or city.
- **Proper nouns** are specific, such as White House, Fernando, Main Street, or New York.
- **Collective nouns** name groups, such as team, crowd, organization, or Congress.

Nouns have cases:

- A noun is in the **nominative case** when it is the subject of the sentence.

EXAMPLE

Giorgio joined the band.

- A noun is in the **objective case** when it is the direct object, indirect object, or object of the preposition.

EXAMPLES

Direct object: She built a *treehouse*.

Indirect object: Joel sent *Marco* a message.

Object of the preposition: The fairies danced around *Jasmine*.

- **Possessive case** is the form that shows possession.

EXAMPLE

The *queen's* crown was filled with rubies.

Pronouns

A pronoun is a substitute for a noun. The antecedent of the pronoun is the noun that the pronoun replaces. A pronoun must agree with its antecedent in gender, person, and number. There are several kinds of pronouns:

- **Demonstrative pronoun:** this, that, these, those
- **Indefinite pronoun:** anyone, anybody, everyone, nobody, several, some, someone, somebody
- **Interrogative pronoun:** who, which, what
- **Personal pronoun:** I, you, we, me, him, she, us, they

Verbs

A verb expresses action or a state of being. There are four major kinds of verbs: transitive, intransitive, linking, and auxiliary or helping verbs.

- **Transitive verbs** are action verbs and always have a direct object. In other words, there's something receiving the action of a transitive verb.

EXAMPLES

The dog *broke* her tooth.

The teacher *discussed* the effects of nuclear radiation.

- **Intransitive verbs** are action verbs with no direct object. Some verbs can be either transitive or intransitive depending on their usage.

EXAMPLES

The vase *broke*.

Misha *cried*.

- **Linking verbs** indicate a state of being and have no action. These verbs serve to link the subject to additional descriptive information. Examples include *is, are, was, were, be, been, am, smell, taste, feel, look, seem, become*, and *appear*. Sometimes, the verbs listed here can be linking, auxiliary, or action verbs depending on their usage.

EXAMPLES

I *am* here.

He *looks* nervous.

She *is* sick.

The food *tasted* delicious.

- **Auxiliary verbs** or **helping verbs** are used with an infinitive or participle to create a verb phrase. Auxiliary verbs always need a primary verb to function. Examples of auxiliary verbs include all forms of the verbs *to be, to have, to do*, and *to keep*, as well as *can, could, may, might, must, ought to, shall, will, would*, and *should*.

EXAMPLES

I *am having* a glass of water.

She *might go* to the store.

Alex *should study* harder.

Adjectives

An adjective describes a noun. Adjectives can answer questions like:

- "Which one?"
- "What kind?"
- "How many?"

There are three uses of adjectives:

- A **noun modifier** is usually placed directly before the noun it describes.

EXAMPLE

He is a *tall* man.

- A **predicate adjective** follows a linking verb and modifies the subject.

EXAMPLES

She is *happy*.

I feel *terrible*.

- An **article** or **noun marker** points to a noun. The articles are *the, a*, and *an*.

EXAMPLE

The teacher took *a* vacation to *an* island.

Adverbs

An adverb modifies a verb, an adjective, or another adverb and can answer questions like:

- "Why?"
- "How?"
- "Where?"
- "When?"
- "To what degree?"

Adverbs should not be used to modify nouns. Many adverbs are easy to identify because they end in *-ly*. But there are other adverbs that do not have this ending.

EXAMPLES

He *quickly* jumped over the hole.

I am doing *well*.

The water swirled *clockwise* down the drain.

Adverbs can also operate like conjunctions when they are serving as conjunctive adverbs. Conjunctive adverbs act as transitions, indicating relationships between sentences. They are used to begin independent clauses, which are essentially complete sentences.

EXAMPLE

The motorcyclist lost control and collided with a tree; *however*, he was able to stand and walk away from the crash.

In the preceding example, the word *however* is used at the beginning of the second complete sentence to establish the contrasting relationship with the sentence before. Other examples of conjunctive adverbs include the following: *additionally, alternatively, certainly, consequently, meanwhile*, and *furthermore*.

Conjunctions

A conjunction joins words, sentences, and phrases. There are multiple kinds of conjunctions: coordinating conjunctions, subordinating conjunctions, and correlative conjunctions.

Coordinating conjunctions link together things that are of equal importance. The best way to remember the coordinating conjunctions is with the acronym FANBOYS. FANBOYS stands for the following: for, and, nor, but, or, yet, so.

EXAMPLES

She *and* I went to the park.

I wanted to play video games, *but* my mom said it was time to leave.

Subordinating conjunctions link together a dependent clause and an independent clause. Common subordinating conjunctions include the following: *after, although, because, before, despite, since, though, until, whether*, and *while*.

Correlative conjunctions are pairs of conjunctions. When the first of the pair appears in a sentence so too then must the second. For instance, *neither/nor* is a correlative pair.

EXAMPLE

Neither John *nor* his children wanted to move to the new city.

Other correlative conjunctions you may see on the SAT include the following: *either/or, such/that, not only/but also, both/and*, and *whether/or*.

TIP

For coordinating conjunctions, remember the acronym **FANBOYS:**

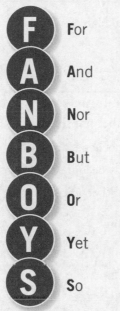

For

And

Nor

But

Or

Yet

So

Conjunctions connect ideas together. If you're using a comma to separate two complete sentences, you also need one of the FANBOYS.

Prepositions

A preposition shows position in time or space. Common prepositions are words like *around*, *in*, *over*, *under*, *during*, *after*, and *behind*. A preposition starts a prepositional phrase that usually shows the relationship between a noun or pronoun and the rest of the information in the sentence.

EXAMPLES

The dog sleeps *under the bed.*

She stood up *during the presentation.*

After the meeting, Dr. Smith changed her policy.

As we'll mention again when we discuss Verbs, Usage, and Agreement, sometimes the only way to know which preposition is correct in a given phrase is through idiomatic awareness of how the preposition is linked to a given verb and when.

What follows is the first of a few practice sets you'll find in this chapter. These are there to help you check your understanding of key skills related to Standard English Conventions on the SAT. While each passage on the actual SAT exam will relate to only a single question, we have included three per passage in each of these practice sets to make it easy to work with a few skills simultaneously. At the end of the chapter, you'll have a Test Yourself section that will follow the conventions of SAT passages more closely and mimic test conditions more directly. Use the practice sets to check your understanding as you learn. Use the Test Yourself set at the end to evaluate your progress after you finish reviewing the chapter.

Practice Set 1: Grammar

Directions: Read the passage that follows. Then, for each numbered blank, answer the following question:

Which choice completes the text so that it conforms to the conventions of Standard English?

According to the journals the forest rangers found, winter in the Beartooth Range had only (1) __________ for the aging mountain man. Soon, he would be 84. He wrote that he now (2) __________ the weather's changes first in his joints and that the wet, cold air made him red in the cheeks and hoarse in the throat, even when he was bundled up inside. His children had been bothering him to move out of that tiny cabin in the woods and into one of their homes closer to a proper town, but he was stubborn and wouldn't hear of it. He had built that cabin with his own two hands, and he wasn't about to abandon (3) __________ just because the blizzards were getting harder to endure with each passing year. If this was to be his last winter, he wrote, then so be it.

1. **A.** recent become difficult
   B. recent become difficulty
   C. recently become difficult
   D. recently become difficultly

2. **A.** is feeling
   B. feels
   C. felt
   D. was to feel

3. **A.** it
   B. them
   C. us
   D. him

Answer Explanations

1. **The correct answer is C.** *Recent* is incorrect because the verb *become* must be modified by an adverb rather than an adjective—you can eliminate choices A and B. Choice D incorrectly uses the adverb form of *difficult* by adding *-ly*.

2. **The correct answer is C.** Based on the context of the passage, the correct verb choice will be a transitive verb in the simple past tense to align with the use of *wrote* and *made* elsewhere in the sentence. Only choice C offers an appropriate choice.

3. **The correct answer is A.** *It* is the proper singular pronoun to refer to the antecedent *cabin*.

6

SENTENCE STRUCTURE AND FORMATION

Understanding the parts of speech is fundamental to good writing and editing, but so is understanding how to combine the parts of speech to form effective sentences. On the SAT, sentence structure and formation plays an especially key role in addressing Boundaries questions. Understanding sentence structure in English requires you to be an expert on two related concepts: complete sentences and sentence fragments.

A complete sentence is called an independent clause. An independent clause possesses a subject (something that completes an action) and a verb (the action), and the clause expresses a complete thought. For example, "My SAT Reading and Writing score will improve." That's a complete sentence—an independent clause. It has a subject ("My SAT Reading and Writing score") and a verb ("will improve.") It also expresses a complete thought.

Sentence fragments are essentially incomplete sentences—they are missing one or more of the key ingredients for a sentence: a subject, a verb, or the expression of a complete thought.

A kind of sentence fragment you'll encounter regularly within answer options for these questions is a dependent clause. Dependent clauses are used to add information to independent clauses, often expanding on the conditions under which the action of the independent clause will occur. A dependent clause has a subject and a verb, but it doesn't express a complete thought. For instance, "When I learn the conventions of Standard English" is not a complete sentence—it's a dependent clause. It has a subject ("I") and a verb ("learn"), but it doesn't express a complete thought. "When I learn the conventions of Standard English" . . .what happens then? It can't stand on its own, but we can address the error by combining it with an independent clause to produce a complete sentence: "When I learn the conventions of Standard English, my SAT Reading and Writing score will improve."

Adding the dependent clause to the independent clause not only creates a complete sentence for the dependent clause but also adds information to the independent clause, creating a more sophisticated sentence structure and specific idea. That's just one possible sentence type in English. In this type of Standard English Convention question on the SAT Reading and Writing section, you will need to be able to recognize and address structural issues related to four different kinds of sentences, as demonstrated in the graphic on this page.

Compound, complex, and compound-complex sentences can technically have as many clauses as you want, as long as they are connected and punctuated correctly.

Sentence Fragments

As we mentioned in the last section, every sentence must have a subject (something to do the action) and a verb or predicate (the action) and express a complete idea. When all those items are present, you get an independent clause. If a group of words is missing

Four Types of Sentences

01 **SIMPLE SENTENCE** (an independent clause)

02 **COMPOUND SENTENCE** (two independent clauses joined together)

03 **COMPLEX SENTENCE** (an independent clause and at least one dependent clause)

04 **COMPOUND-COMPLEX SENTENCE** (at least two independent clauses and one dependent clause)

one of these elements, then it is called a sentence fragment or an incomplete sentence. If the group of words has a subject and verb but doesn't express a complete thought, it's a specific type of incomplete sentence called a dependent clause. When issues with joining clauses and forming complete sentences appear on the SAT, you'll need to rely on your knowledge of how to correct sentence fragments and complete incomplete sentences.

There are two ways to correct incomplete sentences.

1

Add the fragment to the sentence that precedes it or the sentence that follows.

Incorrect: Zoologists and wildlife biologists study animals and other wildlife. Including how they interact with their ecosystems.

Correct: Zoologists and wildlife biologists study animals and other wildlife, including how they interact with their ecosystems.

Explanation: The fragment is added to the sentence that precedes it by inserting a comma.

Incorrect: By studying animal behaviors. Wildlife biologists seek to understand how animals interact with their ecosystems.

Correct: By studying animal behaviors, wildlife biologists seek to understand how animals interact with their ecosystems.

Explanation: The fragment is added to the sentence that follows it by inserting a comma. (The fragment now serves as a prepositional phrase that modifies the rest of the sentence.)

2

Add a subject and/or verb to the fragment.

Incorrect: Considerable time studying animals in their natural habitats.

Correct: Wildlife biologists may spend considerable time studying animals in their natural habitats.

Explanation: A subject (*wildlife biologists*) and verb (*may spend*) are added to the fragment.

Run-Ons and Comma Splices

Complete sentences must be separated by a period, a comma and a coordinating conjunction, or a semicolon. A run-on sentence occurs when a writer fails to use either end-stop punctuation to divide complete thoughts or suitable conjunctions to join two ideas. When two independent clauses are joined only by a comma, you have an error called a comma splice.

The following rules will help you avoid and fix run-on sentences and comma splices.

1

Divide the sentence using periods.

Incorrect: Zoologists need a bachelor's degree for entry-level positions a master's degree or Ph.D. is often needed for advancement.

Correct: Zoologists need a bachelor's degree for entry-level positions. A master's degree or Ph.D. is often needed for advancement.

Explanation: Inserting a period between *positions* and *A* corrects the run-on sentence by creating two independent clauses.

2

Create a compound sentence by joining independent clauses using a coordinating conjunction such as *and*, *but*, or *so*.

Incorrect: Zoologists need a bachelor's degree for entry-level positions, a master's degree is often needed for advancement.

Correct: Zoologists need a bachelor's degree for entry-level positions, but a master's degree is often needed for advancement. (Remember that a comma is required when you use a coordinating conjunction to join two independent clauses.)

Explanation: Adding the coordinating conjunction *but* eliminates the comma splice and connects the two independent clauses correctly.

3

Create a complex sentence by adding a subordinating conjunction—such as *because*, *although*, or *while*—making one of the independent clauses a dependent clause.

Incorrect: Zoologists need only a bachelor's degree for entry-level positions a master's degree is often needed for advancement.

Correct (option 1): Zoologists need only a bachelor's degree for entry-level positions although a master's degree is often needed for advancement.

Explanation: Adding the conjunction *although* between the two independent clauses corrects the run-on sentence by changing the second clause to a dependent clause and creating a complex sentence. (In general, commas are not required when the dependent clause follows the independent clause.)

Correct (option 2): Although a master's degree is often needed for advancement, zoologists need only a bachelor's degree for entry-level positions.

Explanation: Adding the conjunction *although* before the second independent clause and then moving the entire clause to the beginning of the sentence corrects the run-on sentence. (A comma is required when the dependent clause precedes the independent clause.)

4

Use a semicolon when ideas in two independent clauses are closely related in meaning.

Incorrect: Zoologists and wildlife biologists study how animals and other wildlife interact with their ecosystems, these scientists work outdoors or in offices or laboratories.

Correct: Zoologists and wildlife biologists study how animals and other wildlife interact with their ecosystems; these scientists work outdoors or in offices or laboratories.

Explanation: Inserting a semicolon between the two independent clauses corrects the comma splice and creates a compound sentence.

Coordination and Subordination

Coordinating and subordinating conjunctions are used to join phrases and clauses and form compound and complex sentences.

COMMON CONJUNCTIONS	
Coordinating conjunctions	**Subordinating conjunctions**
and, but, for, nor, or, so, yet	after, although, as, as if, because, before, even if, even though, if, if only, rather than, since, that, though, unless, until, when, where, whereas, wherever, whether, which, while

Basic Rule of Coordinating Conjunctions

Coordinating conjunctions are used to add items to a list and join independent clauses to make compound sentences. With items in a list, the last item in the list should be preceded by a coordinating conjunction.

Independent clauses: There was a Treaty of Paris signed in 1763. There was also one signed in 1783. There was another signed in 1919.

Joined: There were Treaties of Paris signed in 1763, 1783, and 1919.

When two clauses are joined, if the second remains an independent clause, a comma must be used before the coordinating conjunction. The coordinating conjunction signals that each clause carries the same weight while also creating a relationship between the ideas (additive, contrasting, or causal).

Independent clauses: There was a Treaty of Paris signed in 1763. There was also one signed in 1783.

Joined: There was a Treaty of Paris signed in 1763, but there was another Treaty of Paris signed in 1783.

Basic Rule of Subordinating Conjunctions

Subordinating conjunctions are added to an independent clause to make it a dependent clause.

A dependent clause establishes a place, a time, a reason, a condition, a concession, or a comparison for the independent clause—some form of extra information that clarifies the action of the independent clause. Dependent clauses have a subject and a verb but don't express a complete thought, usually as indicated by a subordinating conjunction. A subordinating conjunction signals that the dependent clause needs (or *depends* on) an independent clause to be grammatically correct. This also means that dependent clauses are subordinate to the information in the independent clause—meaning they're less important (offering extra information) and

TIP

Remember that an independent clause is just a complete sentence. It has a subject and a verb and expresses a complete thought.

preceded by a subordinating conjunction. Dependent clauses can come before or after an independent clause, but if they're before, they must be separated from the independent clause by a comma. Review the list of subordinating conjunctions to identify dependent clauses more quickly. Let's look at some examples of subordinating conjunctions used to create dependent clauses.

Independent clauses: A tax on imported goods from another country is called a tariff. A tax on imported goods from another country to protect a home industry is called a protective tariff.

Joined: A tax on imported goods from another country is called a tariff while a tax on imported goods from another country to protect a home industry is called a protective tariff.

Here, the subordinating conjunction *while* was added to the second independent clause. The resulting dependent clause is then joined to the end of the first independent clause without using any punctuation.

A subordinating conjunction can also be used at the beginning of a sentence. The resulting dependent clause must be joined to an independent clause and separated by a comma.

Independent clauses: A tax on imported goods from another country is called a tariff. A tax on imported goods from another country to protect a home industry is called a protective tariff.

Joined: While a tax on imported goods from another country is called a tariff, a tax on imported goods from another country to protect a home industry is called a protective tariff.

Modifier Placement

A modifier is a word, phrase, or clause that adds detail to a sentence. To avoid confusion, modifiers should be placed as close as possible to the things they modify. Examples of different modifiers are underlined in the sentences below.

1

Example 1: <u>Within the field of marine biology</u>, employment is <u>highly</u> competitive.

Explanation: The phrase "within the field of marine biology" modifies the subject of the sentence, which is *employment.* The word *highly* modifies our understanding of the competitive nature of finding employment.

2

Example 2: The <u>abundant</u> supply of <u>marine</u> scientists far exceeds the demand, and the number of <u>government</u> jobs is <u>limited</u>.

Explanation: *Abundant* modifies *supply. Marine* modifies *scientists. Limited* modifies our understanding of the number of jobs. *Government* modifies *jobs.*

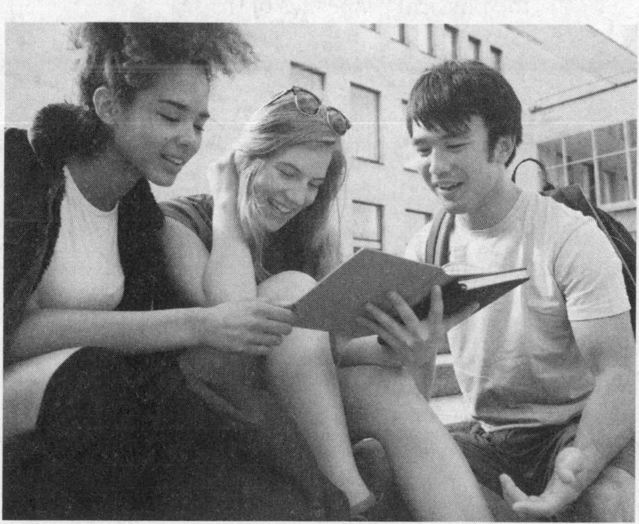

When the subject of a modifier is unclear or is not included in the sentence, it is considered a dangling modifier.

Incorrect: Not realizing that the job title "marine biologist" rarely exists in the real world, *marine biology* is a term recognized by most people. (What is the first phrase modifying?)

Possible revision: Not realizing that the job title "marine biologist" rarely exists in the real world, most people recognize the term *marine biology*.

Misplaced modifiers occur when a modifier is poorly placed and doesn't express the writer's intent accurately.

Incorrect: The term *marine biologist* is used to almost describe all of the disciplines and jobs that deal with the study of marine life, not just those that deal with the physical properties of the sea.

Possible revision: The term *marine biologist* is used to describe almost all of the disciplines and jobs that deal with the study of marine life, not just those that deal with the physical properties of the sea.

Parallel Structure

Parallel structure is the repetition of a grammatical form within a sentence. When things are parallel, they are moving in the same direction. Parallel structure is a hallmark of effective writing and is often used to emphasize ideas and present compared items in an equal light. Coordinating conjunctions are often used in parallel constructions.

Nonparallel structure: As a child, George Washington Carver enjoyed reading, learned about plants, and he made art.

Parallel structure: As a child, George Washington Carver enjoyed reading, learning about plants, and making art.

In the first sentence, "George Washington Carver enjoyed reading" leads the reader to expect that the next items in the list will also be gerunds (verbs that end in *-ing* but act as nouns). However, the next items in the list are not in the same form: "learned about plants" is in the past tense while "he made art" is an independent clause. To resolve the issue with parallel structure, we need to pick one form of the word and stick to it. The easiest and most concise fix is to change the last two items to gerunds to match the first item, *reading*.

Issues with parallel structure are most noticeable in lists of things. Note that parallel structure applies to other parts of speech as well. To be grammatically correct, items being compared should be the same part of speech and fit the structure of the sentence.

Active Vs. Passive Voice

Voice, as related to sentence structure, tells us whether the subject of a sentence is the actor (active) or is acted upon (passive). In formal writing, active voice is generally preferred because it is more immediate and places the reader closer to the action. Passive voice can be the better choice when you want to emphasize what received the action (e.g. "I was hit by a car" vs. "A car hit me."). The SAT will almost always prefer active voice to passive construction in questions where voice is a concern, so recognizing passive voice can be a good way to eliminate less precise answer options.

Passive voice example: The cherry tree was chopped down by George Washington.

Active voice example: George Washington chopped down the cherry tree.

Practice Set 2: Sentence Structure

Directions: Read the passage that follows. Then, for each numbered blank, answer the following question:

Which choice completes the text so that it conforms to the conventions of Standard English?

Neon, a noble gas, possesses unique chemical qualities that make it valuable in various industrial applications. Known for its vibrant, reddish-orange glow when electrically charged, neon is frequently used in lighting, particularly neon signs. Its ability to emit light efficiently, (1) ___________, makes it a popular choice for illuminating displays and (2) ___________ advertising. Additionally, neon's inert nature and stability make it suitable for cryogenic applications, like cooling scientific equipment and preserving biological samples. Neon is also (3) ___________ as a gain medium to amplify light. Despite its scarcity in the atmosphere, neon's distinct properties have found important roles in several industrial sectors, demonstrating its versatility and utility.

1. **A.** much without consuming energy
   B. without much consuming energy
   C. without consuming much energy
   D. without energy consuming much

2. **A.** highlighting
   B. highlight
   C. to highlight
   D. to be highlighting

3. **A.** used in lasers, where it serves
   B. used; in lasers, where it serves
   C. used in lasers. Where it serves
   D. used. In lasers, where it serves

Answer Explanations

1. **The correct answer is C.** This question addresses the test taker's ability to correctly place the modifier *much* before the noun it modifies, *energy*.

2. **The correct answer is A.** This question simultaneously evaluates parallel structure and verb usage. Here, you want the form of *highlight* that matches the form of the verb that precedes it, *illuminating*. The term *highlighting* is therefore most appropriate.

3. **The correct answer is A.** This is a Boundaries question related to the formation of clauses. If you look closely, all three incorrect answers contain sentence fragments. Only choice A correctly forms a complete sentence.

PUNCTUATION

Like the other conventions of good writing, punctuation helps you communicate more effectively. Punctuation includes commas, semicolons, em dashes, parentheses, colons, and apostrophes, among other punctuation marks. Both of the question types within the Standard English Conventions domain may require you to recognize effective punctuation. Here, we'll prioritize the most important punctuation you'll need to remember.

The Comma

We use commas for a lot of things, but for the SAT, focus on separating the following:

- Independent clauses that are connected by a coordinating conjunction
- Introductory clauses and phrases
- Dependent and independent clauses
- Items in a series
- Nonessential and parenthetical elements
- Coordinate adjectives

Let's look at some examples:

- To separate independent clauses connected by a coordinating conjunction

EXAMPLE

Toni Morrison's first novel was published in 1970, and it received a rave review from *The New York Times*.

- To set off introductory clauses and phrases

EXAMPLE

The year after winning her Nobel Prize, Toni Morrison published the novel *Jazz*.

- To separate a leading dependent clause from an independent clause

EXAMPLE

While she was praised for her writing style and range of emotion, Toni Morrison was also celebrated for the attention she drew to racial tension in the past and present of the United States.

- To separate three or more items in a list

EXAMPLE

In a span of 15 years, Toni Morrison won a National Book Critics Circle Award, the Pulitzer Prize, and the Nobel Prize for Literature.

If you pay attention to punctuation, it's likely you've noticed that not everyone puts the serial or Oxford comma before the *and* when separating three or more items in a list. In recent years, a lot of writing (especially online) has ignored the serial comma, but its absence or presence can affect what a sentence means. In 2018, a missing Oxford comma in a Maine labor law cost a dairy company in the state $5 million dollars in a lawsuit with its employees. Increasingly, using the Oxford comma is considered preferable punctuation, and you will see it (or see it missing) in questions from the SAT Reading and Writing section.

- To separate nonessential and parenthetical elements from the main clause

EXAMPLES

Toni Morrison, who won the Nobel Prize in Literature in 1993, was a Professor Emeritus at Princeton University.

Last night, Toni Morrison began her lecture, titled "The Future of Time: Literature and Diminished Expectations," with a meditation on the nature of time and the human perception of progress.

- To separate coordinate adjectives that precede the noun they describe

EXAMPLE

Toni Morrison was described as a fun, entertaining speaker.

When you have at least two adjectives describing a noun (e.g., "The tall, funny man" or "The cold and windy weather"), you can separate the adjectives with a comma when their order can be reversed or when the conjunction *and* can be placed between them while still preserving the meaning of the phrase. If reversing the order or adding *and* disrupts the meaning of the phrase (e.g., "The giant hockey players" as "The hockey giant players" or "The giant and hockey players"), no comma is needed.

The Semicolon

A semicolon may be used to separate two complete ideas (independent clauses) in a sentence when the two ideas have a close relationship and are *not* connected with a coordinating conjunction.

EXAMPLE

"Inalienable rights" are basic human rights that many believe cannot and should not be given up or taken away; life, liberty, and the pursuit of happiness are some of those rights.

The semicolon is often used between independent clauses connected by conjunctive adverbs such as *consequently, therefore, also, furthermore, for example, however, nevertheless, still, yet, moreover,* and *otherwise.*

TIP

Nonessential and parenthetical elements provide extra information that is not necessary for the meaning or grammatical correctness of a sentence. Commas, parentheses, and em dashes serve similar purposes; the difference between them is one of emphasis. On the SAT, you will not likely be asked to choose between these three marks as that is often a stylistic decision. If a question presents them in different answer choices, there are likely other errors present to help you eliminate choices.

EXAMPLE

In 1867, critics thought William H. Seward foolish for buying the largely unexplored territory of Alaska for the astronomical price of $7 million; however, history has proven that it was an inspired purchase.

A word of caution: Do not use a semicolon between an independent clause and a phrase or subordinate clause.

 **Incorrect:** While eating ice cream for dessert; Clarence and Undine discussed their next business venture.

 **Correct:** While eating ice cream for dessert, Clarence and Undine discussed their next business venture.

Similar to serial commas, semicolons are used to separate items in a list but only when the items themselves contain commas.

EXAMPLE

Some kinds of biologists study specific species of animals. For example, cetologists study marine mammals, such as whales and dolphins; entomologists study insects, such as beetles and butterflies; and ichthyologists study wild fish, such as sharks and lungfish.

The Em Dash

Em dashes are used to set off parenthetical material that you want to emphasize. Dashes interrupt the flow of your sentence, thereby calling attention to the information they contain. An em dash always precedes the nonessential information, so the aside must start later in the sentence.

EXAMPLES

Many consider Toni Morrison—winner of both the Pulitzer and Nobel Prizes in Literature—to be one of the greatest writers of her generation.

Benjamin Franklin's many intellectual pursuits—from printmaking to politics—exemplify his eclectic personality.

Em dashes can also be used to rename a nearby noun. Typically, a comma would be used to set off this information, but since it includes commas already, use an em dash.

EXAMPLE

Benjamin Franklin—a printer, writer, inventor, and statesman—was the son of a soap maker.

An em dash also indicates a list, a restatement, an amplification, or a dramatic shift in tone or thought.

EXAMPLE

Eager to write for his brother's newspaper, young Benjamin began submitting letters to the editor under the pseudonym Silence Dogood—they were a hit!

The Colon

The colon is used to precede a list, a long quotation, or a statement that illustrates or clarifies the earlier information. A colon can be used only after an independent clause.

EXAMPLES

There are only three nations that have successfully landed spacecraft on the moon: the Soviet Union, the United States, and China.

In the United States, there are three branches of government: the Executive, the Legislative, and the Judicial.

Use colons only after independent clauses. Most commonly, that means that you won't use colons after a verb. Further, no introductory or connecting information should occur before or after a colon, such as *and* or *including*.

Incorrect: The Louisiana Purchase included territory that would become: Montana, South Dakota, Nebraska, Kansas, Oklahoma, Arkansas, Louisiana, and Missouri.

Correct: The Louisiana Purchase included territory that would become many of today's states: Montana, South Dakota, Nebraska, Kansas, Oklahoma, Arkansas, Louisiana, and Missouri.

The Apostrophe

Apostrophes usually serve one of two purposes:

1. To indicate a contraction—the omission of one or more letters: Place the apostrophe exactly where the missing letters occur.

   Examples:

   can't = cannot

   it's = it is

   we're = we are

2. To indicate the possessive case of nouns: If the noun does not end in *s*—whether singular or plural—add an *'s*; if the noun ends in *s* simply add the *'*. Some writers like to add *'s* to all nouns, even those that already end in *s*, but the SAT will default to *s'*, except for proper nouns.

   Example 1: The impact of Allen Ginsberg's poem "Howl" on the cultural landscape of the United States cannot be overstated.

   Example 2: A car's headlights are typically wired in parallel so that if one burns out the other will keep functioning.

   Example 3: The women's club sponsored many charity events.

   Example 4: Charles Mingus's skill as a jazz musician is widely recognized.

ALERT

Do not use apostrophes with possessive pronouns such as *yours, hers, ours, theirs,* and *whose,* which indicate possession already.

End-of-Sentence Punctuation

There are three types of punctuation used to end a sentence: the period, the question mark, and the exclamation mark.

1

A period is used at the end of a sentence that makes a statement.

Example: In 1620, the Pilgrims in Plymouth signed the Mayflower Compact.

2

A question mark is used after a direct question. A period is used after an indirect question.

Direct Question: Were *The Federalist Papers* written by James Madison, John Jay, or Alexander Hamilton?

Indirect Question: Profession Mahin wanted to know if you knew who wrote *The Federalist Papers.*

3

An exclamation mark is used after an expression that shows strong emotion or issues a command. It may follow a word, a phrase, or a sentence.

Example: Koko the gorilla knew more than 1,000 sign-language signs and could communicate with humans. Amazing!

Unnecessary Punctuation

Unnecessary punctuation can break a sentence into confusing and illogical fragments. Here are some common mistakes to look out for.

- Don't use a comma alone to connect independent clauses. This is called a comma splice.

Incorrect: Toni Morrison grew up in an integrated neighborhood, she did not become fully aware of racial divisions until she was in her teens.

Possible revision: Toni Morrison grew up in an integrated neighborhood and did not become fully aware of racial divisions until she was in her teens.

- Don't use a comma between compound elements that are not independent clauses.

Incorrect: In 1998, Oprah Winfrey, and Danny Glover starred in a film adaptation of Morrison's novel *Beloved.*

Possible revision: In 1998, Oprah Winfrey and Danny Glover starred in a film adaptation of Morrison's novel *Beloved.*

- Do not use an apostrophe when making a noun plural.

Incorrect: In 2006, *The New York Times Book Review* named *Beloved* the best American novel published in the last 25 year's.

Possible revision: In 2006, *The New York Times Book Review* named *Beloved* the best American novel published in the last 25 years.

Practice Set 3: Punctuation

Directions: Read the passage that follows. Then, for each numbered blank, answer the following question:
Which choice completes the text so that it conforms to the conventions of Standard English?

Pollinators, such as bees, butterflies, and hummingbirds, rely on certain plants to survive and thrive. These plants are called pollinator-friendly plants. They come in different types and (1) __________. Some popular pollinator-friendly plants include brightly colored flowers like (2) __________. These flowers produce nectar and pollen, which are the main sources of food for pollinators. Additionally, native plants like milkweed, lavender, and coneflowers are great choices as they have adapted to the local environment and attract a wide range of pollinators. Trees and shrubs like cherry, apple, and butterfly bush are also (3) __________ food and nesting sites. By planting these pollinator-friendly plants, we can create a welcoming habitat for our buzzing friends and help ensure their survival.

1. A. shapes but they all have one thing; in common, they provide essential food and shelter for pollinators
   B. shape's but they all have one thing in common: they provide essential food and shelter for pollinator's
   C. shapes, but, they all have one thing in common: they provide essential food and shelter, for pollinators
   D. shapes, but they all have one thing in common: they provide essential food and shelter for pollinators
2. A. sunflowers, marigolds, zinnias
   B. sunflowers, marigolds, and zinnias
   C. sunflowers, marigolds and zinnias
   D. sunflowers marigolds and zinnias
3. A. important—they offer both
   B. important, they offer: both
   C. important, they offer both
   D. important, they offer both;

Answer Explanations

1. **The correct answer is D.** One must use a comma after *shapes* and before the coordinating conjunction *but*; consequently, you can eliminate choices A and B. Choice C can be eliminated because it adds numerous unnecessary commas, leaving you with choice D.
2. **The correct answer is B.** Each of the elements in this simple list should be separated by commas, and the coordinating conjunction *and* should precede the final item in the list.
3. **The correct answer is A.** Only choice A correctly uses punctuation (an em dash, in this case) to separate two related independent clauses.

VERBS, USAGE, AND AGREEMENT

In addition to English grammar, sentence structure, and punctuation, you will encounter questions in the Reading and Writing section that focus on the ways in which Standard English conventions are used to convey meaning. There are any number of particular things that are done in English not because they follow a strict grammatical rule but because they are how a majority of fluent English speakers use English on a day-to-day basis. Put simply, Standard English makes sense to most people who speak English fluently. To address this aspect of Standard English Conventions testing, we'll review proper use of verbs as well as agreement, which describes using both verbs and pronouns in ways that match the meaning of phrases and sentences. You may notice some topics we've already covered (like agreement between pronouns and their antecedents) appear again in this section as relates to proper language use. Questions from either of the Standard English Conventions domain's subtopics may address these concepts.

Verb Tense

Use the same verb tense whenever possible within a sentence or paragraph. Do not shift from one tense to another unless there is a valid reason for doing so.

Incorrect: The Magna Carta *was* signed in 1215 by King John of England and *has been* the first document of its kind to limit the power of the British monarchy.

Correct: The Magna Carta *was* signed in 1215 by King John of England and *was* the first document of its kind to limit the power of the British monarchy.

Naturally, different verb tenses have different forms, but you will see some overlap. For example, even though the sentences "He was tall" and "He was running" both use the verb *was*, the former is a simple past tense verb while the latter is in a tense called the past progressive—*was* acts as a helping verb attached to the word *running*. Complete verbs can be individual words or consist of a helping verb (often a form of "to be," "to have," or "to do") and a main verb or participle. Look out for those small verbs to decide which choice is best for the passage.

When to Use the Perfect Tenses

Knowing when to choose between the simple (past, present, and future) and perfect tenses can be challenging since those choices often depend on the author's intended meaning. However, other information presented in the sentence, like prepositional phrases or other modifiers, can help you decide which tense makes the most sense.

- Use *present perfect* for an action begun in the past and extended to the present.

Example: Scientists at NASA *have seen* an alarming increase in the accumulation of greenhouse gases.

Explanation: In this case, *scientists at NASA saw* would be incorrect. What they *have seen* (present perfect) began in the past and extends to the present.

ALERT

Different verb tenses have different forms, and there may be some overlap. It's important to select the choice that is the best for the passage.

- Use *past perfect* for an action begun and completed in the past before some other past action.

Example: Despite their preparations, Lewis and Clark *had never encountered* the kinds of challenges that awaited them before their expedition.

Explanation: In this case, *never encountered* would be incorrect. The action *had never encountered* (past perfect) is used because it is referring to events prior to their expedition.

- Use *future perfect* for an action begun at any time and completed in the future.

Example: When the American astronauts arrive, the Russian cosmonauts *will have been* on the International Space Station for six months.

Explanation: In this case, although both actions occur in the future, the Russian cosmonauts *will have been* on the space station before the American astronauts *arrive*. When there are two future actions, the action completed first is expressed in the future perfect tense.

Common Verbs and Their Tenses

Refer to the following chart to familiarize yourself with some common verbs and their tenses.

COMMON VERBS AND THEIR TENSES*

Infinitive	Present	Past	Future	Present Perfect	Past Perfect	Future Perfect
to ask	ask	asked	will ask	have asked	had asked	will have asked
to be	am	was	will be	have been	had been	will have been
to become	become	became	will become	have become	had become	will have become
to begin	begin	began	will begin	have begun	had begun	will have begun
to come	come	came	will come	have come	had come	will have come
to do	do	did	will do	have done	had done	will have done
to eat	eat	ate	will eat	have eaten	had eaten	will have eaten
to feel	feel	felt	will feel	have felt	had felt	will have felt
to find	find	found	will find	have found	had found	will have found
to get	get	got	will get	have gotten	had gotten	will have gotten
to give	give	gave	will give	have given	had given	will have given
to go	go	went	will go	have gone	had gone	will have gone
to grow	grow	grew	will grow	have grown	had grown	will have grown
to have	have	had	will have	have had	had had	will have had
to hear	hear	heard	will hear	have heard	had heard	will have heard

COMMON VERBS AND THEIR TENSES*						
Infinitive	**Present**	**Past**	**Future**	**Present Perfect**	**Past Perfect**	**Future Perfect**
to hide	hide	hid	will hide	have hidden	had hidden	will have hidden
to keep	keep	kept	will keep	have kept	had kept	will have kept
to know	know	knew	will know	have known	had known	will have known
to leave	leave	left	will leave	have left	had left	will have left
to like	like	liked	will like	have liked	had liked	will have liked
to look	look	looked	will look	have looked	had looked	will have looked
to make	make	made	will make	have made	had made	will have made
to meet	meet	met	will meet	have met	had met	will have met
to put	put	put	will put	have put	had put	will have put
to say	say	said	will say	have said	had said	will have said
to see	see	saw	will see	have seen	had seen	will have seen
to sleep	sleep	slept	will sleep	have slept	had slept	will have slept
to speak	speak	spoke	will speak	have spoken	had spoken	will have spoken
to study	study	studied	will study	have studied	had studied	will have studied
to take	take	took	will take	have taken	had taken	will have taken
to think	think	thought	will think	have thought	had thought	will have thought
to walk	walk	walked	will walk	have walked	had walked	will have walked
to want	want	wanted	will want	have wanted	had wanted	will have wanted
to work	work	worked	will work	have worked	had worked	will have worked
to write	write	wrote	will write	have written	had written	will have written

*Note: For consistency, all verbs are conjugated in the first-person singular.

Pronoun Case

Pronouns substitute for nouns in sentences. Every pronoun must have a clear antecedent (the noun that it replaces), have the same number as the antecedent (singular or plural), share the same perspective or person (1st, 2nd, or 3rd), and be in the proper pronoun case for its use in the sentence (subjective, objective, possessive).

EXAMPLES

George Washington was born on February 22, 1732, in Pope's Creek, Virginia; *he* was the first American president.

Did you know that Besty Ross and George Washington both went to the same church? *It* was called Christ Church, and *it* was located in Philadelphia.

The following pronoun chart may prove useful:

PRONOUNS				
Number	**Person**	**Subjective Case**	**Objective Case**	**Possessive Case**
Singular	1st person	I	me	mine
	2nd person	you	you	yours
	3rd person	he, she, it, who	him, her, it, whom	his, hers, whose
Plural	1st person	we	us	ours
	2nd person	you	you	yours
	3rd person	they, who	them, whom	theirs, whose

A pronoun must agree in number with its antecedent, using a singular or plural pronoun of the correct person and case.

Incorrect: George Washington was among the seven figures that were key to the formation of the United States government, the Founding Fathers, because *they* shaped and served the country's executive branch. (What is the antecedent for the marked pronoun? George Washington or Founding Fathers?)

Correct: George Washington was among the seven figures that were key to the formation of the United States government, the Founding Fathers, because *he* shaped and served the country's executive branch. (The pronoun needs to be in the third-person singular in the subjective case in order to agree with the antecedent *George Washington*.)

Incorrect: George Washington issued two vetoes successfully during his two presidential terms. One was issued in his first term, and the other was issued after he left office. Congress was unable to overturn *it*. (What was Congress unable to overturn?)

Correct: George Washington issued two vetoes successfully during his two presidential terms. One was issued in his first term, and the other was issued after he left office. Congress was unable to overturn *them*. (The pronoun needs to be third-person plural in the objective case to agree with the antecedent *two vetoes* and work with the grammar of the sentence.)

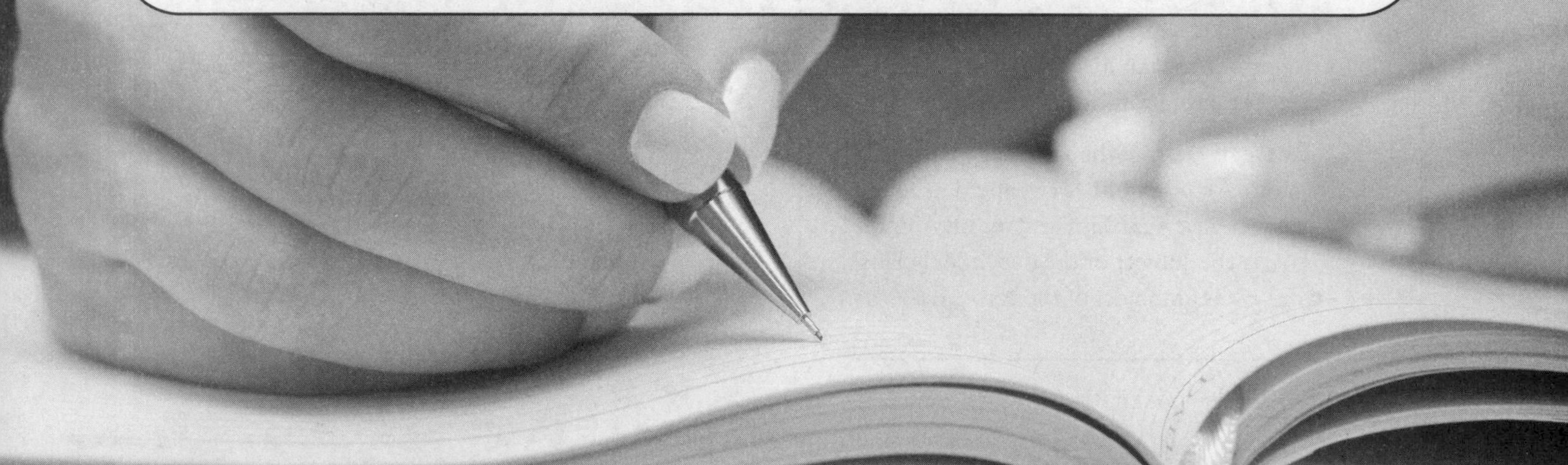

A pronoun uses the *subjective* case when it is the subject of the sentence or when it renames the subject as a subject complement.

Incorrect: One story of the American flag's creation says George Ross, Robert Morris, and *him* asked Betsy Ross to sew the first flag.

Correct: One story of the American flag's creation says George Ross, Robert Morris, and *he* asked Betsy Ross to sew the first flag. (*He* is part of the compound subject of the sentence and stands in for George Washington.)

Incorrect: *Him* is George Washington.

Correct: *He* is George Washington. (*He* renames the subject.)

If a pronoun is the object of a verb or preposition, it is placed in the *objective* case.

Incorrect: Washington placed a lot of trust in Benedict Arnold. In 1780, George Washington gave command of West Point to *he*.

Correct: Washington placed a lot of trust in Benedict Arnold. In 1780, George Washington gave command of West Point to *him*.

Incorrect: Despite the fact that *us* turned in our American history paper late, our teacher gave Franklin and *I* an A grade.

Correct: Despite the fact that *we* turned in our American history paper late, our teacher gave Franklin and *me* an A grade. (*We* is the subject of the dependent clause, and *me* is an object of the verb *gave*.)

Avoid ambiguity and confusion by making sure that the antecedent of the pronoun is clear. The presence of multiple nouns that share the same gender and number means that the sentence must clarify which antecedent is being referred to.

Incorrect: At the height of his career, Frank Lloyd Wright told an architectural scholar that *he* thought *his* work was improving. (Is Wright talking about his own work or the work of the scholar?)

Correct: At the height of his career, Frank Lloyd Wright told an architectural scholar that he thought *his own* work was improving.

Incorrect: Frank Lloyd Wright and his wife Olgivanna founded a school for aspiring artists in Spring Green, Wisconsin, where *they* could "learn by doing." (Does *they* refer to the Wrights or the artists?)

Correct: Frank Lloyd Wright and his wife Olgivanna founded a school in Spring Green, Wisconsin, where aspiring artists could "learn by doing."

Possessive Determiners

When a pronoun expresses ownership, it is placed in the possessive case. An absolute possessive pronoun can stand on its own without needing a noun to follow it to be clear. Absolute possessive pronouns are *mine*, *yours*, *his*, *hers*, *its*, *ours*, and *theirs*.

EXAMPLES

The watch is *mine*.

That one is *his*.

Theirs are broken.

A possessive pronoun that identifies, specifies, or quantifies the noun it precedes is called a possessive determiner. Possessive determiners are *my, your, his, her, its, our,* and *their.*

EXAMPLES

It's *my* watch.

That's *her* watch.

Their watches are broken.

Pronoun-Antecedent Agreement

A pronoun agrees with its antecedent in both person and number.

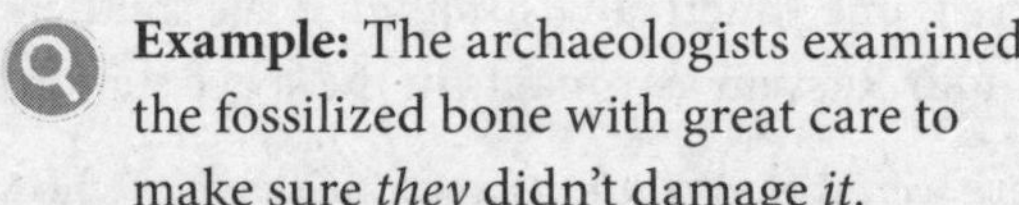

Example: The archaeologists examined the fossilized bone with great care to make sure *they* didn't damage *it.*

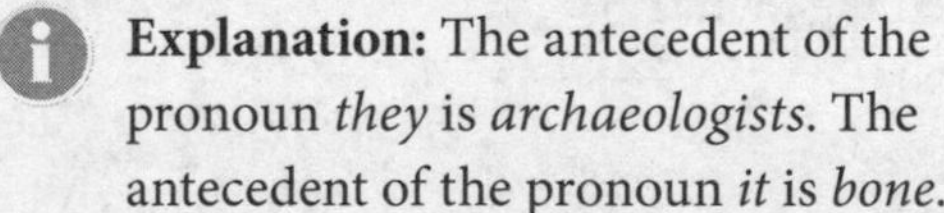

Explanation: The antecedent of the pronoun *they* is *archaeologists.* The antecedent of the pronoun *it* is *bone.*

Remember to use a singular verb when you refer to indefinite pronouns such as *everyone, everybody, each, every, anyone, anybody, nobody, none, no one, one, either,* and *neither.* Some indefinite pronouns—*any, more, most, some*—will be singular or plural as dependent on usage. The pronouns *both, many, others,* and *several* will always need a plural verb for agreement.

EXAMPLES

Although Union High School's male lacrosse players operate as a team, each knows it's *his* (not *their*) responsibility to arrive on time and in uniform.

Despite the fact that many of the women came from wealthy families, everyone who attended the Seneca Falls conference on women's rights risked *her* (not *their*) life and reputation.

When the programmers were questioned, none could be certain if it was *his* or *her* (not *their*) mistake that caused the computer network to crash.

TIP

Increasingly in everyday English usage, the word *their* is considered an acceptable substitute for *his* or *her* when the gender of an individual is unknown (also *them* for *him* or *her* and *they* for *he* or *she*). However, the SAT is all about Standard English usage, so stick with the phrases *his or her, he or she,* or *him or her* when the antecedent for a pronoun is singular and gender is unclear.

Subject-Verb Agreement

A verb agrees in number with its subject. A singular subject takes a singular verb. A plural subject takes a plural verb.

EXAMPLES

Coral reefs are an important part of the marine ecosystem.

My teacher believes that *coral reefs are* an important part of the marine ecosystem.

Let's take a look at another example.

Example: Choose the correct verb (*is, am, are*):

Booker T. Washington, Frederick Douglass, and W.E.B. DuBois ________ all important historical figures.

Explanation: Remember that the verb must agree with the subject. Since the subject is plural—subjects joined by *and* are plural—a plural verb is needed.

The correct response is:

Booker T. Washington, Frederick Douglass, and W.E.B. DuBois *are* all important historical figures.

Sometimes, the subject comes after the verb, but the rule still applies.

Example: Choose the correct verb (*is, are*):

While the lecture has lasted two hours already, there ________ still three more speakers.

Explanation: The correct choice is *are* since the subject *speakers* is plural and requires a plural verb.

There is one major exception to this rule. When the sentence is introduced by the word *there* and the verb is followed by a compound (double) subject, the first part of the subject dictates whether the verb should be singular or plural.

EXAMPLES

There *is* one American *astronaut* in the shuttle and four Russian astronauts in the space station.

There *were* seven *students* and one teacher who attended the field trip.

When compound subjects are joined by *either/or* or *neither/nor*, the verb agrees with the subject closest to the verb.

Examples:

Neither the violinist nor *the other musicians have had* much experience performing for an audience.

Neither you nor *I am* willing to make the sacrifices required of a professional musician.

Explanation: In the first example, *musicians* (plural) is closest to the verb; in the second example, *I* (singular) is closest to the verb.

TIP

Indefinite pronouns—such as *anyone, everyone, someone, no one,* and *nobody*—are singular and require singular verbs. Others are plural—such as *both, few, many,* and *several*. The number of some indefinite pronouns will depend on context.

Sometimes, a word or a group of words may come between the subject and the verb. The verb still must agree with the simple subject, and the simple subject is never part of a prepositional phrase.

Example: Stephen King, the author of hundreds of best-selling novels, novellas, and short stories, *is* also a guitarist and singer in a band.

Explanation: The simple subject is *Stephen King*, a singular noun. The verb must be *is*.

The SAT will often use verbs that are next to plural nouns but agree with a singular noun located earlier in the sentence. Work to identify which noun is performing the action, not just what's nearby.

Example: Choose the correct verb (*was, were*):

The causes of the deterioration of the coral reef ________ not known until recently.

Explanation: The simple subject is *causes*; "of the deterioration of the coral reef" is a prepositional phrase. Since the subject is plural, the plural verb *were* is required. The correct answer is *were*.

Collective Nouns

Collective nouns present special problems. A collective noun names a group of people or things. Although usually singular in form, it is treated as either singular or plural according to the sense of the sentence.

TIP

The third person singular of most present-tense verbs ends in *–s*. For other forms, consider the following: I, we *speak* (first person); you *speak* (second person); he, she, it *speaks* (third person singular). Examples: He *runs*. She *jogs*. It *jumps*. The man *sees*. Eric *laughs*. The child *walks*. They *run*.

- A collective noun is treated as singular when members of the group act, or are considered, as a unit.

EXAMPLE

The *student council* is raising money for new vending machines in the cafeteria.

A collective noun is treated as plural when the members act, or are considered, as multiple individuals.

EXAMPLE

After one of the longest and most fabled droughts in baseball history, the *Boston Red Sox have* finally overcome the "Curse of the Bambino" to win another World Series.

COMMON COLLECTIVE NOUNS			
assembly	commission	crowd	minority
association	committee	department	number
audience	company	family	pair
band	corporation	firm	press
board	council	group	public
cabinet	counsel	jury	staff
class	couple	majority	United States

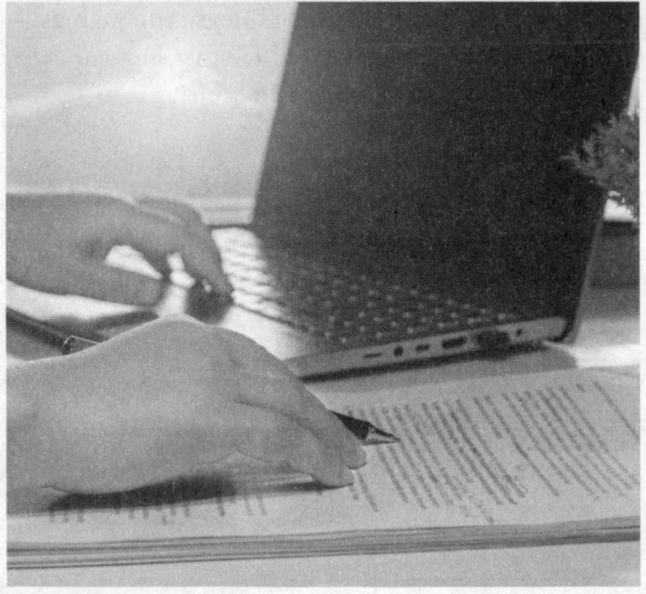

Idiomatic Prepositional Usage

Like many languages, English is full of idioms. Idioms are phrases that are peculiar to not only a particular language but also to a time and place. There's no strict logic or rule behind their usage; they simply are typically used and understood in particular ways. For SAT Standard English Conventions questions, you'll most likely encounter idioms as related to the use of prepositions. In English, there are prepositions that are used in some ways and not others. Often, prepositions, through everyday usage, are attached to other words, creating some stock phrases. This is called idiomatic prepositional usage.

Consider the following: You wait *for* (not *about*) a bus, and when it arrives, you get *on* (not *in*) the bus. You may have had to stand *in* the rain (not *under* it). If you had decided to call a taxi or get a Lyft instead of waiting, when it arrives, you would get *in* the car. Those are largely idiomatic usages of prepositions. Why you get *on* a bus versus getting *in* is very much up for debate. You'll simply find that certain words in English always take a certain preposition. For more examples, one may look at, look in, look through, etc. However, one always disagrees *with* rather than disagrees *against*, or has scorn *for* rather than scorn *at*.

> The young man assured the elderly woman that he had no intention to encroach against the latter's interest in bidding on the vintage desk.

According to idiomatic usage, the word *intention* should be followed by the preposition *of*. Because the preposition *of*, like all prepositions, must have an object, and the object must be a noun or pronoun, the verb *encroach* must also be changed to a noun form—the gerund (*-ing* construction) *encroaching*. The fully corrected sentence then reads as follows:

> The young man assured the elderly woman that he had no intention of encroaching on the latter's interest in bidding on the vintage desk.

Encroach *on* rather than encroach *against*—yet another idiom.

These questions can be challenging as they depend on your sense of English, not necessarily how well you understand it. The more immersed you are in English via reading, writing, and other media, the more natural these questions will feel and the harsher improper prepositional usage will be on your ear.

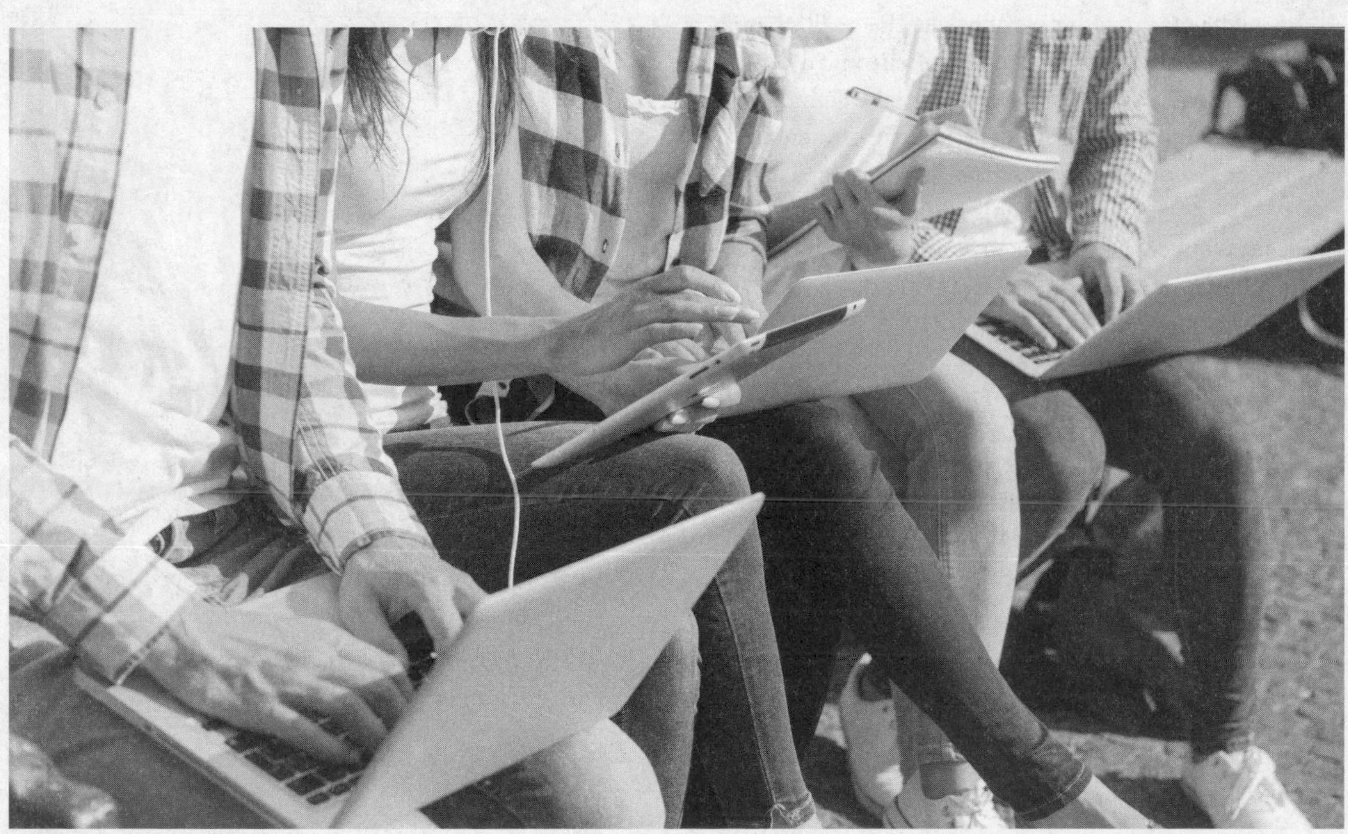

Practice Set 4: Verbs, Usage, and Agreement

Directions: Read the passage that follows. Then, for each numbered blank, answer the following question:

Which choice completes the text so that it conforms to the conventions of Standard English?

Opinions regarding vegan diets vary widely, even as the practice has become more common in recent decades. Critics (1) __________ that vegan diets may be deficient in certain nutrients, such as vitamin B-12, iron, and omega-3 fatty acids, which are primarily found in animal products. (2) __________ also express concerns about the potential challenges of obtaining sufficient protein and maintaining a well-rounded diet. On the other hand, proponents of vegan diets emphasize the health benefits, including reduced risk of chronic diseases, improved digestion, and potential weight loss. They applaud the ethical and environmental considerations of veganism, citing compassion (3) __________ animals and sustainability as compelling reasons to embrace this lifestyle choice.

1. **A.** will have argued
   B. will argue
   C. argue
   D. argued
2. **A.** It
   B. We
   C. They
   D. Their
3. **A.** for
   B. about
   C. with
   D. on

Answer Explanations

1. **The correct answer is C.** This is a verb usage question. Since critics express these ideas in the present, the present tense *argue* is the most appropriate choice.
2. **The correct answer is C.** The pronoun in question must refer to the antecedent *critics*; therefore, the best choice is *they*.
3. **The correct answer is A.** This question evaluates your ability to use the correct preposition in a phrase that idiomatically conforms to conventions. In Standard English, one typically has compassion *for* someone or something, rather than compassion about, with, or on someone or something.

SUMMING IT UP

- Knowing the parts of speech is critical for understanding the conventions and rules of grammar:
    - A **noun** is a person, place, thing or idea.
    - A **pronoun** is a substitute for a noun.
    - An **adjective** describes a noun.
    - A **verb** expresses action or a state of being.
    - An **adverb** modifies a verb, an adjective, or another adverb.
    - A **conjunction** joins words, sentences, and phrases.
    - A **preposition** shows position in time or space.
- The following list summarizes the key conventions you need to remember to edit for SAT Standard English Conventions questions effectively:
    - **Sentence Structure and Formation**
        - **Fragments:** Every sentence must have a subject and a verb and express a complete idea.
        - **Run-Ons and Comma Splices:** Connect complete sentences with proper punctuation.
        - **Combining Independent Clauses:** Use periods, a comma + coordinating conjunction (FANBOYS), or a semicolon; you can also make an independent clause dependent with a subordinating conjunction to link sentences.
        - **Combining Dependent and Independent Clauses:** Place a comma after a dependent clause at the beginning of a sentence.
        - **Misplaced Modifiers:** Place modifiers (adjectives, adverbs, prepositional phrases) as close to the word they're modifying as possible.
        - **Parallel Structure:** Keep verbs and phrases in the same grammatical form when writing sentences.
    - **Punctuation**
        - **Commas:** Separate independent clauses with a comma and a coordinating conjunction (FANBOYS); add a comma after an introductory phrase or leading subordinate clause; separate items in lists of three or more (including before the *and* before the final item); place commas around nonessential information to separate it from the main clause of a sentence.

- **Em dashes:** Indicate nonrestrictive or nonessential information with em dashes; these tangents, asides, and parenthetical statements follow em dashes and must be closed by another em dash—unless they finish the sentence.
- **Semicolons:** Separate related independent clauses and items in a list where the items have commas with a semicolon.
- **Colons:** Indicate the start of a list, a quotation, or emphasis with a colon; colons must be preceded by an independent clause.
- **Apostrophes:** Indicate possession with an *'s* (or just an apostrophe after a noun that ends in an *s*) or signal the contraction of two words into one (*they* + *are* = *they're*).
- **End-Stop Punctuation:** End statements and indirect questions with periods; use question marks to end direct questions; end statements that indicate strong emotion or commands with an exclamation point.

◦ **Verbs, Usage, and Agreement**

- **Verb Tense:** Keep consistent verb tense within sentences and paragraphs unless otherwise justified.
- **Perfect Tense Verbs:** The perfect tenses are used for actions begun and completed at different times. Whether the tense is past, present, or future perfect will depend on when the action is completed.
- **Common Verbs and Their Tenses:** In English, most verbs change in predictable ways when shifted from tense to tense; however, there are also irregular verbs (such as *eat, get, give, go,* etc.) that will have more significant changes in the past and perfect tenses.
- **Pronoun Case:** The pronoun you choose depends on the situation the pronoun is going to be used in. Personal pronouns change case depending on whether they are the subject or object of an action. Determine first if the pronoun is performing (subject) or receiving the action (object).
- **Possessive Determiners:** An absolute possessive pronoun (*mine, yours, his, hers*) can stand on its own without a noun preceding it. A possessive pronoun (*my, your, his her, its, our, their*) that quantifies the noun it precedes is a possessive determiner.
- **Pronoun-Antecedent Agreement:** A pronoun must agree with its antecedent (the word it replaces) in number, person, and gender (where applicable).
- **Subject-Verb Agreement:** Verbs must agree in number with their subjects.
- **Collective Nouns:** Collective nouns describe a group of things but are treated as singular when it comes to subject-verb and pronoun agreement.
- **Idiomatic Prepositional Usage:** In English, certain situations will demand the use of certain prepositions. These are not fixed grammar rules so much as conventions of everyday English usage.

STANDARD ENGLISH CONVENTIONS

10 Questions—12 Minutes

Directions: The questions in this section address a number of important reading and writing skills. Each question includes one or more passages, which may include a table or graph. Read each question carefully, and then choose the best answer to the question based on the passage(s). All questions in this section are multiple-choice with four answer choices. Each question has a single best answer. Note that unlike the actual SAT Reading & Writing section, this test set focuses exclusively on questions from the Standard English Conventions question domain.

1. The diverse breeds of dogs we see today are the result of centuries of selective breeding. Humans have selectively bred dogs for specific traits, such as size, coat type, and temperament, to serve various purposes. This process began ______ early humans domesticated wolves. They selectively bred the wolves that displayed desired traits, gradually creating different types of dogs, which we now refer to as breeds.

   Which choice completes the text so that it conforms to the conventions of Standard English?

   A. thousands of years ago when
   B. thousands of years ago, when
   C. thousands of years ago; when
   D. thousands of years ago. When

2. At its core, artificial intelligence (AI) refers to a machine's ability to simulate human intelligence and perform tasks that typically require human cognition. Machine learning, a crucial aspect of AI, enables computers to analyze vast amounts of data and learn from patterns, improving their performance over time. ______ a subset of machine learning, utilizes artificial neural networks to mimic the human brain's intricate structure. This allows machines to process complex information, recognize speech, and even make autonomous decisions. AI has the potential to reshape industries like healthcare, finance, and transportation, but it also raises ethical considerations regarding privacy, bias, and job displacement.

   Which choice completes the text so that it conforms to the conventions of Standard English?

   A. Deep learning,
   B. Deep learning:
   C. Deep learning;
   D. Deep learning

3. Ancient China was a land of remarkable inventions. One significant invention was paper, which revolutionized communication and knowledge preservation. It was made from mulberry bark and allowed for the creation of books, making information accessible to a wider audience. Another remarkable invention was the __________ greatly aided navigation. By using Earth's magnetic field, sailors and explorers could accurately determine their direction, leading to safer and more successful journeys. The invention of gunpowder also originated in ancient China. Initially used for fireworks, it later transformed warfare around the world. Lastly, the ancient Chinese were skilled in creating intricate and durable porcelain, which became highly sought after for its beauty and practicality.

   Which choice completes the text so that it conforms to the conventions of Standard English?

   A. compass which
   B. compass, which
   C. compass: which
   D. compass. Which

4. __________ for his contributions to the field of tropical medicine. His research on snake venoms led to the development of antivenoms to treat snakebites, saving countless lives in snakebite-endemic regions. Picado's innovative techniques for venom extraction and antivenom production revolutionized the field. His studies on tropical diseases also contributed to advancements in understanding and treating conditions like malaria and Chagas disease.

   Which choice completes the text so that it conforms to the conventions of Standard English?

   A. Peruvian scientist Clodomiro Picado is best known
   B. Peruvian scientist, Clodomiro Picado is best known
   C. Peruvian scientist, Clodomiro Picado, is best known
   D. Peruvian scientist, Clodomiro Picado, is best known,

5. Early iterations of music festivals can be traced back to ancient civilizations, where communal gatherings and celebrations often included music and performance. In ancient Greece, for instance, the city of Athens hosted the Panathenaic Festival, a grand event featuring musical contests and performances. Similarly, in medieval Europe, troubadours and minstrels would travel from town to town, entertaining crowds with their songs and stories during festivals and fairs. These events were not ________ such gatherings served as a means of cultural exchange and brought communities together through shared musical experiences. While the formats and styles of music festivals have evolved over time, the essence of celebrating music and fostering communal bonds remains a timeless tradition that continues to captivate audiences around the world.

Which choice completes the text so that it conforms to the conventions of Standard English?

A. simple concerts though

B. simple concerts, though

C. simple concerts, though,

D. simple concerts, though;

6. Audre Lorde, a trailblazing figure in American literature and activism, left an indelible mark on the world with her powerful works and unwavering advocacy. One of her most prominent works is *The Cancer Journals*, a memoir in which she candidly explores her own battle with breast cancer. Through her personal journey, Lorde fearlessly delves into themes of illness, body image, and the intersections of race, gender, and sexuality. She challenges conventional notions of femininity and confronts the inherent injustices within healthcare systems. Lorde's introspective and unflinching writing not only sheds light on her own experiences but also sparks vital conversations about power dynamics, resilience, and the importance of self-expression. ________ groundbreaking contributions continue to resonate, inspiring readers to question societal norms and fight for social justice.

Which choice completes the text so that it conforms to the conventions of Standard English?

A. She

B. Her

C. Our

D. Their

7. One intriguing concept from the field of herpetology, the study of reptiles and amphibians, is that of autotomy. Autotomy refers to the ability of certain animals to ___________ body parts intentionally as a defense mechanism. For instance, lizards like the Mediterranean gecko can detach their tails when threatened, distracting predators and allowing the gecko to escape. This remarkable adaptation is possible due to specialized muscles and fracture planes that facilitate quick detachment. The autotomized body part often regenerates over time, enabling the animal to recover from the encounter. Autotomy exemplifies the incredible strategies employed by herpetological species for their survival in diverse environments.

Which choice completes the text so that it conforms to the conventions of Standard English?

A. shed or detach

B. shedding or detach

C. shed or detaching

D. shedding or detaching

8. Wangari Maathai, an influential figure in Kenyan culture, made significant cultural contributions through her environmental and social activism. As the founder of the Green Belt Movement, Maathai advocated for sustainable development, women's rights, and conservation. Her efforts in promoting tree planting, environmental education, and community empowerment earned her recognition, including the Nobel Peace Prize. Maathai's work not only revitalized Kenya's natural landscapes but also inspired a generation of environmentalists and activists worldwide. Her legacy continues to shape cultural attitudes toward the environment, social justice, and women's empowerment, leaving an enduring impact on Kenyan society and beyond. Many today still agree ___________ Maathai's hopeful vision for Kenya's future.

Which choice completes the text so that it conforms to the conventions of Standard English?

A. in

B. for

C. with

D. from

9. Computer chips, like integrated circuits, undergo a complex manufacturing process. It begins with creating a silicon wafer, coating it with layers of specialized materials, and ___________ them to form components. After testing and quality assurance, the chips are separated, packaged, and integrated into devices. This precise and intricate process combines engineering, chemistry, and advanced technology to produce the powerful computer chips we rely on today.

   Which choice completes the text so that it conforms to the conventions of Standard English?

   A. pattern
   B. to pattern
   C. will pattern
   D. patterning

10. Based on the grief and longing associated with the aftermath of Abraham Lincoln's assassination, ___________. In the poem, Whitman writes, "O Captain! my Captain! our fearful trip is done, / The ship has weather'd every rack, the prize we sought is won." These lines symbolize the end of a tumultuous journey, with the "Captain" representing Lincoln and the ship representing the United States. Whitman mourns the loss of a beloved leader, juxtaposing triumph with sorrow. The repeated refrain reflects the poet's deep admiration and personal connection to Lincoln while also embodying the collective mourning of a nation.

    Which choice completes the text so that it conforms to the conventions of Standard English?

    A. the emotional tensions of a critical moment in American history are captured in Walt Whitman's iconic poem "O Captain! My Captain"
    B. Walt Whitman's iconic poem "O Captain! My Captain" captures the emotional tensions of a critical moment in American history
    C. Walt Whitman wrote the iconic poem "O Captain! My Captain" to capture the emotional tensions of a critical moment in American history
    D. a critical moment of emotional tensions in American history is captured in Walt Whitman's iconic poem "O Captain! My Captain"

Answer Key and Explanations

1. A	**3.** B	**5.** D	**7.** A	**9.** D
2. A	**4.** A	**6.** B	**8.** C	**10.** B

1. **The correct answer is A.** The word *when* is being used as a subordinating conjunction so no punctuation is necessary to separate it from the clause that precedes it.
2. **The correct answer is A.** The phrase "a subset of machine learning" modifies the subject "deep learning" but is not essential to the grammatical structure of the sentence. Therefore, it needs to be offset by commas. Choices B and C use inappropriate punctuation in place of a comma, and choice D omits the comma.
3. **The correct answer is B.** Since the dependent clause that begins with *which* adds additional information to the independent clause that came before it, it should be preceded by a comma.
4. **The correct answer is A.** This question evaluates the use of punctuation between titles and proper nouns, what can be described here as apposition. No punctuation is needed to set off the proper noun "Clodomiro Picado" from the title used to describe him, "Peruvian scientist," since Picado's name is essential information that identifies the "Peruvian scientist" in question.
5. **The correct answer is D.** To answer this question, it's helpful to recognize that *though* is acting as a supplementary word ending one clause rather than a conjunction beginning another. Immediately, this observation allows you to eliminate choices A and B, which use *though* as a clause-starting conjunction. From there, evaluate the clause that follows the blank to determine that it is an independent clause. As such, your most appropriate option is to separate it from the given phrase with a semicolon.
6. **The correct answer is B.** The antecedent to which the pronoun in question must refer is "Audre Lorde," and a possessive pronoun is required. Consequently, choice B is the only appropriate option.
7. **The correct answer is A.** Since the full phrase "to ___________ body parts intentionally" requires the infinitive form (*to* + verb), parallel structure dictates that both verbs should match this form, as in choice A.
8. **The correct answer is C.** This question relies on your recognition of the idiomatic prepositional use of *with* alongside the verb *agree.*
9. **The correct answer is D.** Parallel structure dictates that the verb in question should follow the pattern of the other two verbs in the list (*creating* and *coating*), meaning that the gerund (*-ing*) form of the verb "to pattern" is most appropriate.
10. **The correct answer is B.** This choice ensures that the introductory participial phrase "Based on the grief and longing associated with the aftermath of Abraham Lincoln's assassination" appears immediately before the noun phrase it modifies, "Walt Whitman's iconic poem 'O Captain! My Captain.'"

CHAPTER

Writing and Language Use

WRITING AND LANGUAGE USE

OVERVIEW

Now that you've reviewed reading comprehension skills and brushed up on the conventions of Standard English, let's turn our attention toward writing, language use, and other rhetorical skills. The SAT Reading and Writing section integrates writing-focused question types that rely on your ability to plan a text or edit existing writing according to your understanding of the given text's purpose, main idea, and structure. In this section, we'll discuss the writing skills you'll need to analyze language use, demonstrate command of text- and graphic-based evidence, synthesize research materials, and edit texts for precision, logic, and sense.

7

WRITING AND LANGUAGE USE ON THE SAT®

While some questions on the Reading and Writing section will address writing skills directly (such as Rhetorical Synthesis questions within the Expression of Ideas domain), you will most likely have to handle a number of questions that address both reading and writing skills simultaneously. These questions might ask you to choose an answer that most effectively completes an indicated blank or which represents information from the text most efficiently and correctly. In answering these questions, you should always keep in mind the clarity and concision of the reading passage and choose options that are going to make the passage most effective.

Writing Skills by Question Type

The questions that follow your passages are multiple-choice with four answer choices each. Of the four question domains covered by the SAT Reading and Writing section (Information and Ideas, Craft and Structure, Standard English Conventions, and Expression of Ideas), the Expression of Ideas domain covers writing and language use skills most directly. In other domains, you may be called upon to think like a writer or to put yourself in the author's shoes to determine which answer is correct. As we did before for reading skills, we have included a chart that delineates the specific writing and language use skills that are most important for each Knowledge Testing Point within the four Reading and Writing domains.

TIP

On the SAT, you will need to supplement your writing and editing skills with a deep understanding of how reading comprehension relates to good writing. As you work on writing skills, don't be afraid to refresh your knowledge of reading comprehension by reviewing Chapter 5!

WRITING AND LANGUAGE USE SKILLS BY QUESTION CATEGORY		
Question Domain	**Knowledge Testing Point (KTP)**	**Related Writing and Language Use Skills**
Craft and Structure	Words in Context	Using contextual information to determine which word best fits the context of what has already been written
	Text Structure and Purpose	Recognizing the choices an author makes when organizing a text and determining the purpose of those rhetorical choices
	Cross-Text Connections	Evaluating the similarities and differences between two writers' approaches to a subject
Information and Ideas	Central Ideas and Details	Recognizing the structure of a piece of writing so you can locate key information
	Command of Evidence (Textual)	Recognizing how one might use textual evidence from the passage to support a claim
	Command of Evidence (Quantitative)	Recognizing how one might use quantitative evidence from the passage to support a claim
	Inferences	Figuring out which claims an author could reasonably make based on the information given
Standard English Conventions	Boundaries	Editing a piece of writing to avoid errors related to the completion of clauses
	Form, Structure, and Sense	Editing a piece of writing to avoid errors in form and structure or to ensure the text makes logical sense
Expression of Ideas	Transitions	Determining which transition word or phrase most effectively matches the context for the blank in question
	Rhetorical Synthesis	Evaluating provided information and determining how it could best be used to write another analytical, informative, or argumentative text or perform another educational task

KEY WRITING AND LANGUAGE USE SKILLS

There are four specific question types that deal with writing and language use skills most directly. In Chapter 5, we divided your study topics by reading skill rather than question type. For writing and language use, however, we'll first focus on the questions that deal with writing most directly. Then, we'll offer some tips for using rhetorical skills with all other question types.

Command of Evidence Questions

There are two types of Command of Evidence questions within the Information and Ideas testing domain: Command of Evidence (Textual) and Command of Evidence (Quantitative). While the purpose of both question types is to determine how well a test taker can use information from a given text to produce another text, such as the topic sentence for an essay, the reading methods required for both differ. Textual command

of evidence questions require test takers to read a text and determine which words, phrases, or sentences from the text can support a given idea or inference. Quantitative command of evidence also requires you to use evidence from the text to support a given idea or inference; however, rather than gathering support from the words in the text alone, you will also need to read a graphic (such as a chart, table, or graph) that contains quantitative information. Because of the nature of these questions, certain subjects lend themselves to either type. For instance, literature and humanities topics (such as philosophy or art history) are quite common with textual command of evidence questions. By contrast, because of the quantitative nature of the question type, natural sciences and social sciences tend to be the subject of quantitative command of evidence questions more often.

The key to answering these questions is evaluating what's being asked and how it relates to the text as a whole. For instance, if you are asked to choose a piece of evidence that defends a claim the author makes, you are going to need different textual or quantitative evidence than you might if you were trying to offer a definition or introduce a topic. Figure out the rhetorical purpose (the reason the author wrote the text) and how the question you're given relates to that purpose in order to home in on the correct answer.

Here is an example of a textual command of evidence question.

EXAMPLE

"Annabel Lee" is an 1849 poem by Edgar Allen Poe. In the poem, Poe suggests that the death of a girl he loved in childhood still affects him as an adult, writing, ___________

Which quotation from "Annabel Lee" most effectively illustrates the claim?

A. "It was many and many a year ago, / In a kingdom by the sea, / That a maiden there lived whom you may know, / By the name of Annabel Lee"

B. "She was a child and I was a child, / In this kingdom by the sea, / But we loved with a love that was more than love"

C. "But our love it was stronger by far than the love / Of those who were older than we- / Of many far wiser than we-"

D. "For the moon never beams without bringing me dreams / Of the beautiful Annabel Lee; / And the stars never rise but I see the bright eyes / Of the beautiful Annabel Lee"

The correct answer is D. In this line, Poe is figuratively expressing that he cannot see the moon or stars without thinking of his memories of Annabel Lee. Consequently, it's a way of noting that even as an adult, he still dreams of and has memories of her.

Now, compare the prior example with the following, which is an example of a quantitative command of evidence question.

NEW YORK CITY CENSUS DATA ON RACIAL DEMOGRAPHICS, 2000–2010						
Indicated Mutually Exclusive Race/ Hispanic origin	**2000 Census Population Number**	**2000 Census % of Total Population**	**2010 Census Population Number**	**2010 Census % of Total Population**	**2000–2010 Number Change**	**2000–2010 % Change**
White nonhispanic	2,801,267	35.0	2,722,904	33.3	-78,363	-2.8%
Black/African American nonhispanic	1,962,154	24.5	1,861,295	22.8	-100,859	-5.1%
Asian nonhispanic	780,229	9.7	1,028,119	12.6	247,890	+31.8%
American Indian and Alaska Native nonhispanic	17,321	0.2	17,427	0.2	106	+0.6%
Native Hawaiian and Other Pacific Islander nonhispanic	2,829	0.0	2,795	0.0	-34	-1.2%
Some Other Race nonhispanic	58,775	0.7	57,841	0.7	-934	-1.6%
Two or More Races nonhispanic	225,149	2.8	148,676	1.8	-76,473	-34.0%
Hispanic origin	2,160,554	27.0	2,336,076	28.6	175,522	+8.1%
TOTAL POPULATION	**8,008,278**	**100.0**	**8,175,133**	**100.0**	**166,855**	**+2.1%**

Source: www.nyc.gov/assets/planning/download/pdf/data-maps/nyc-population/census2010/pgrhc.pdf

EXAMPLE

Some sociological researchers studying race in New York City have observed notable demographic shifts since the beginning of the 21st century. Specifically, they note that the Asian nonhispanic population in NYC (which was 14.2% of the total population according to the 2020 census) has been growing at a much more rapid rate than other racial demographics in the city. For instance, when looking at the 2000 and 2010 census data for comparison, it's clear that __________. Many researchers posit that a driving force behind this demographic expansion is the arrival of students and recent college graduates from China, South Korea, and other east Asian countries of origin. This demographic subset is also driving some of the spatial changes in various NYC boroughs; for instance, the once industrial area of Long Island City has transformed into a housing district due in part to the steady arrival of new Asian immigrants.

Which choice most effectively uses data from the table to complete the example?

A. the number of those identifying as White nonhispanic has slowly been shrinking since 2000, when they accounted for 35% of the population

B. the Asian nonhispanic population showed a much larger increase than other populations, meaning this trend has continued for at least two decades

C. there aren't nearly as many Asians who identify as having two or more races of origin

D. the Native Hawaiian and Other Pacific Islander population is by far the smallest racial demographic represented in New York City

The correct answer is B. While each of the choices relates to the data in the graphic, only choice B correctly connects that data to the context provided by the text.

As you can see, the aim of both question types is similar, and, in both cases, you'll need to rely on your reading comprehension skills to figure out the context and determine which evidence most effectively supports a given claim. However, the act of building arguments through command of evidence is ultimately a writing skill, so you'll need to think like a writer to handle these questions effectively.

Transition Questions

Transition questions are one of the most straightforward types of writing questions on the SAT. In these questions, your job is to determine which transition word or phrase fits best in an indicated blank. In some cases, these questions may function essentially like vocabulary questions in that you will need to know the meaning of each transition word or phrase you're given in order to determine which fits best. Other times, you'll be given a set of longer transitional clauses from which to choose and must determine which best fits the context of the given text.

Remember that a transition links two pieces of information together. While reading the whole text is important for determining context, you'll want to pay particular attention to the sentences before and after the indicated blank. By recognizing the relationship between them, you'll be better prepared to determine the correct transition that can indicate that relationship.

To assist you in preparing for these questions, we've included a chart of some of the most common types of transitions with example words and phrases for each. Note that while many transitions come at the beginning of a sentence, some happen at the beginning of independent clauses or otherwise in the middle of a sentence. Examples of mid-sentence use are also included.

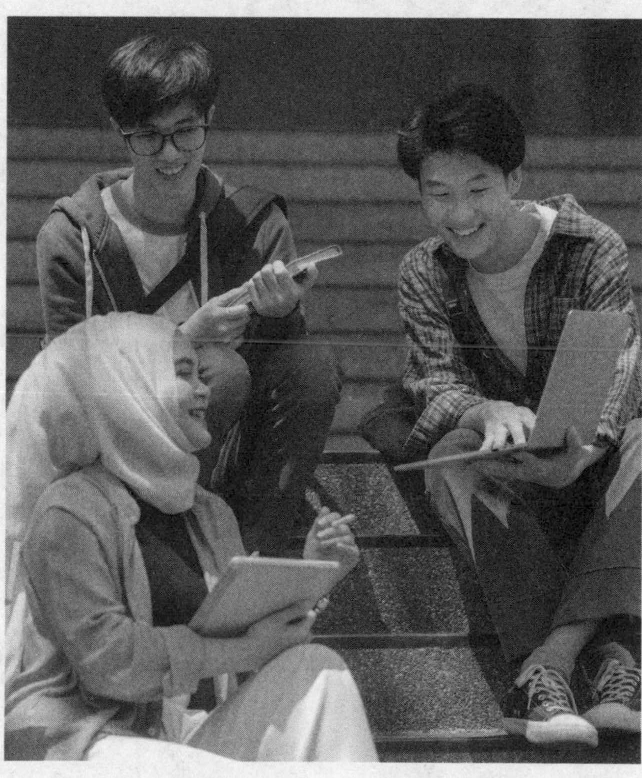

COMMON TRANSITION WORDS AND PHRASES		
Purpose of Transition	**Example Words/Phrases**	**Example Sentences**
To introduce new ideas or add to/agree with topics that have already been introduced	• additionally • coupled with • equally important • first, second, third, etc. • further • furthermore • in addition (to) • likewise • moreover • similarly	• **First**, one must understand how the structure of DNA affects genetics. • **Furthermore**, these same observations were noted at another dig site 20km away. • The question of municipal water usage is **equally important** to the discussion of local conservation efforts.
To communicate the writer's opposition to or a limit placed upon a given idea or phrase	• as much as • by contrast • conversely • despite • notwithstanding • on the contrary • on the other hand • that said • while	• **Despite** new evidence, the theory remains the most prevalent in the field. • The question of parental input is, **conversely**, overemphasized in research on childhood literacy development. • **As much as** Sushmita had hoped to sleep in, the birds noisily nesting outside her window had other plans.
To show a cause-and-effect relationship or communicate the conditions that influence a circumstance or idea	• as a result • as long as • because of • consequently • due to • hence • in case • in effect • since • unless • then • therefore	• I am going fishing later, **hence** the tackle box and gear. • **Consequently**, commuters were unable to reliably predict when the late trains would finally arrive. • Tina was upset **because of** the letters she'd found in her brother's drawer. • **Therefore**, it's important for schools to invest adequate funds into arts and music programs.

COMMON TRANSITION WORDS AND PHRASES		
Purpose of Transition	**Example Words/Phrases**	**Example Sentences**
To set up an example, fact, piece of evidence, or other form of support for another concept	• by all means • especially • explicitly • for this reason • indeed • in fact • in other words • markedly • notably • remarkably • significantly • to clarify • to reiterate	• The new model is **by all means** a notable improvement on prior models. • **In other words**, those who wish to master a new skill should expect to devote numerous hours to practicing it. • **Indeed**, Portugal was the first European nation to get actively involved in the Transatlantic slave trade.
To communicate the time at which an event occurred or the timing of one event in relation to another	• after • all of a sudden • at the present moment • before • finally • frequently • in the meantime • in the past • meanwhile • momentarily • now • occasionally • often • once • suddenly • then • today	• I was distracted, **momentarily**, by a high-pitched shriek emitting from the far-off woods. • **Today**, the James Webb Space Telescope is known for producing the clearest images of far-off galaxies. • **All of a sudden**, the doorbell rang. • **In the past**, people knew a lot more about the Dewey decimal system; **now,** most use computers to locate books and don't know much about how the system works.

COMMON TRANSITION WORDS AND PHRASES		
Purpose of Transition	**Example Words/Phrases**	**Example Sentences**
To help the writer communicate a conclusion or final idea on a topic	• by all means • especially • explicitly • for this reason • indeed • in fact • in other words • markedly • notably • remarkably • significantly • to clarify • to reiterate	• **In any event**, the festival proved a success despite a series of unfortunate technical mishaps. • **Altogether**, there are numerous factors that contribute to a feeling of loneliness, not all of them psychological. • This means that the industry as it once was is, **effectively**, over. • Mourning can be defined, **in short**, as the act of expressing deep sorrow or grief.

Here is an example of a transition question.

EXAMPLE

Ancient plumbing systems date back thousands of years, showcasing remarkable ingenuity in early civilizations. The ancient Egyptians, for example, developed complex systems to transport water through canals and pipes made from baked clay. The Indus Valley civilization constructed intricate sewage and drainage systems, complete with underground toilets and wastewater management. __________, the Roman engineering marvels of aqueducts enabled the distribution of water across vast distances, supplying public baths, fountains, and private residences. These early plumbing systems played a vital role in maintaining public health, sanitation, and daily life, laying the groundwork for the sophisticated plumbing infrastructure we rely on today.

Which choice completes the text with the most logical transition?

A. Similarly

B. Nonetheless

C. At present

D. Based on these findings

The correct answer is A. The sentence prior explains what was done in the Indus Valley before giving an example of a type of ancient plumbing that was conducted elsewhere. An appropriate transition will signal that the subsequent sentence contains information that is similar in nature to what was previously stated.

Rhetorical Synthesis Questions

In Chapter 5, you learned that synthesis involves combining ideas or elements from two different sources to form a cohesive whole. In rhetorical synthesis questions, your task is to identify which piece of writing most effectively synthesizes provided research notes to complete a particular type of task. Each question will provide you with multiple bullet points containing a student's research notes on a given topic. It will also provide you a statement that generally begins with "The student wants to…" and then clarifies what the student would like to do with the research notes. You must then choose the answer that best responds to the student's indicated task. For example, you might be asked which option best summarizes or introduces a topic, which best supports a given piece of evidence, or which best combines information from the research to make a logical inference.

You will need to use your reading skills when evaluating the research notes, but it is your writing skills that will allow you to answer these questions effectively. Imagine yourself as the student tasked with completing whatever prompt the question mentions. Of the choices you're given, which would be most useful to you? If you think like a writer when approaching these questions, then they'll be much easier to answer. Evaluate what the student's purpose might be in synthesizing the research information for a new piece of writing, then choose the answer that best assists with that synthesis.

Here is an example of a Rhetorical Synthesis question.

EXAMPLE

While researching a topic, a student has taken the following notes:

- The Amazon rainforest has lost approximately 17% of its total area over the past 50 years.
- Deforestation in the Amazon rainforest is primarily driven by activities such as agriculture, logging, and infrastructure development, often linked to the expansion of cattle ranching and soybean cultivation.
- The consequences of deforestation in the Amazon region include the loss of biodiversity, destruction of indigenous communities' livelihoods, and increased greenhouse gas emissions.
- Deforestation disrupts the delicate balance of the Amazon ecosystem, leading to soil erosion, altered rainfall patterns, and decreased water quality in rivers and streams.
- Efforts to combat deforestation in the Amazon include the establishment of protected areas, stricter law enforcement, sustainable land management practices, and support for local communities' rights and involvement in conservation initiatives.

The student wants to argue that deforestation of the Amazon rainforest has human consequences. Which choice most effectively uses relevant information from the notes to accomplish this goal?

A. Since the Amazon rainforest has lost as much as 17% of its total area in the past 50 years, it's clear that the time to act on deforestation is now.

B. Soil erosion is one of the biggest problems caused by deforestation since it is caused by altered rainfall patterns and contributes to decreased water quality.

C. Both the indigenous communities that live in the Amazon rainforest and those who rely on the Amazon river as a source of clean water have been negatively impacted by widespread deforestation.

D. Stricter law enforcement would be one way to combat the devastation caused by rampant deforestation in the Amazon rainforest.

The correct answer is C. While all choices use information from the research notes, only one of the answers directly addresses the human consequences of deforestation in the Amazon rainforest.

Using Rhetorical Skills on Reading-Intensive Questions

Now that we've addressed the four types of questions that focus on your abilities as a writer and editor, let's discuss how to use your rhetorical skills to enhance your understanding of reading-intensive questions. The primary way to do this is to mentally put yourself in the shoes of whoever wrote the text you are addressing and consider the following questions:

- Why did the author write this text?
- Why did they structure their text the way they did?
- What sort of "signposts" have they given me as a reader to navigate their text?
- What context have they provided for me to "do something" (like form a response, make an inference, or summarize an idea) with the text?

If you can recognize why an author wrote the text the way they did and the reasoning behind the language they chose to express their idea, you will be better suited to answer questions about the text. This quick set of rhetorical questions will enhance your understanding of the text and supplement your reading comprehension and grammar skills.

SUMMING IT UP

- Questions from the Expression of Ideas question domain deal with writing skills most directly, but you will encounter numerous questions from all four domains that ask you to use reading and writing skills simultaneously.
- Questions involving Command of Evidence will require you to determine which textual or quantitative evidence from a text could be used to fulfill a particular writing task, such as providing a relevant example or defending a claim.
- Transition questions require you to evaluate the context of the text as well as the sentences before and after an indicated blank in order to determine which transition word or phrase most effectively completes the text.
- Rhetorical Synthesis questions require you to evaluate a set of research notes and then choose the option that best fulfills an indicated rhetorical purpose using the research notes.
- If you think like a writer when evaluating a text, it will be easier to address reading and grammar questions.

TEST YOURSELF

WRITING AND LANGUAGE USE

10 Questions—12 Minutes

Directions: The questions in this section address a number of important reading and writing skills. Each question includes a passage, which may include a table or graph. Read each question carefully, and then choose the best answer to the question based on the text. All questions in this section are multiple-choice with four answer choices. Each question has a single best answer. Note that unlike the actual SAT Reading and Writing section, this test set focuses exclusively on questions that are primarily related to writing and language use—the actual exam section will have questions that focus more directly on reading and grammar as well.

1. In a research paper, a student argues that wind turbines are one of the most important economic investments a municipality can make to reduce local reliance on fossil fuels and the costs associated with their extraction and use.

   Which quotation from a work by an environmental scientist would best illustrate the student's claim?

   A. "Wind turbines, harnessing the power of the wind to generate electricity, have gained prominence in helping municipalities transition to clean energy."

   B. "Wind power is a clean energy source, emitting zero air pollutants and producing no harmful byproducts or carbon dioxide during operation."

   C. "Once the initial investment is made, the operational costs of wind turbines are relatively low, leading to more stable energy prices and reduced reliance on the fluctuating costs associated with fossil fuels."

   D. "Investing in wind turbines provides municipalities with numerous economic benefits."

2. "September" is an 1891 sonnet by Helen Hunt Jackson that uses color to emphasize the autumnal mood.

   Which quotation from "September" best illustrates this claim?

   A. "In yellow, still lie fields where wheat was reaped; And yellow still the corn sheaves, stacked among / The yellow gourds"

   B. "The purple grape,—last thing to ripen, late / By very reason of its precious cost"

   C. "O Heart, remember, vintages are lost / If grapes do not for freezing night-dews wait"

   D. "Think, while thou sunnest thyself in Joy's estate, / Mayhap thou canst not ripen without frost!"

3.

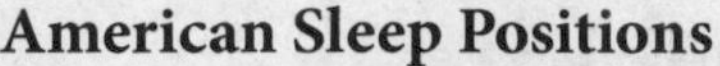

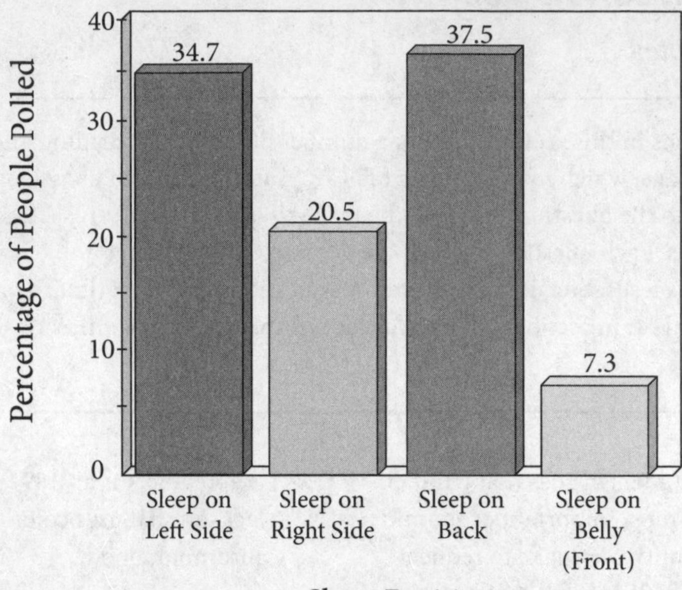

A sleep institute wanted to conduct a study to determine how Americans prefer to sleep. To do so, they sent researchers to busy areas in five major American cities (New York City, Seattle, Chicago, Dallas, and Miami) and had them interview 200 passersby each, for a total of 1000 respondents. Each respondent answered the question "How do you sleep most commonly?" and was given four answer options: on the left side, on the right side, on the back, or on the belly (front). The results of the poll showed that ____________. Furthermore, of those respondents, the left side was far more common than the right. Consequently, the sleep institute concluded that developing products to support the body in this position (such as ergonomic pillows and leg supports) might help reduce the incidence of sleep related ailments, including soft tissue injuries stemming from prolonged weight on the shoulder.

Which choice most effectively uses data from the graph to complete the example?

A. the majority of Americans sleep on their back

B. the majority of Americans sleep on either their right or left side

C. the majority of Americans sleep on their left side

D. far fewer Americans sleep on their belly than in any other position

4.

TABLE 1			
Beewolf	# of Offspring	Average number of honeybees fed to each offspring	Density of Flight Muscle Mitochondrial Membranes (f/cc)
A	22	3	78
B	7	1	9
C	35	4	168
D	12	2	30
E	5	1	6
F	29	4	140

Mitochondria are the source of energy within every living cell. Scientists conducted studies on a wasp species known as the European beewolf to investigate the mitochondria's role in species survival. In the first study, the species showed a positive correlation between amount of mitochondrial energy output and density of flight muscle mitochondrial membranes. The second study aimed to compare the relationship between beewolf feeding and breeding habits and the mitochondrial output of parent beewolves as measured by the density of their flight muscle mitochondrial membranes. Researchers noted that beewolves attack larger honeybees, which they sting, paralyze, and then feed to their young. The researchers tracked the breeding and hunting activities of six beewolves and compiled their findings, along with their analysis of each beewolf's flight muscle mitochondrial membrane density, in Table 1.

Which choice best uses data from the table to summarize the study's findings?

A. Beewolves with denser flight muscle mitochondrial membranes tended to have more offspring and feed each of them more.

B. Beewolves with denser flight muscle mitochondrial membranes tended to have fewer offspring but fed each of them more.

C. Beewolves with less dense flight muscle mitochondrial membranes tended to have more offspring but fed each of them fewer honeybees.

D. Beewolves with less dense flight muscle mitochondrial membranes tended to have more offspring but fed them about as much as beewolves with denser flight muscle mitochondrial membranes.

5. The science behind color variegation in plants, which is characterized by leaves displaying multiple colors or patterns, lies in a combination of genetic and environmental factors. Genetic mutations can disrupt the chlorophyll production process, resulting in patches or streaks of different pigments. ____________, variations in light exposure can influence variegation patterns. Leaves receiving more direct sunlight tend to exhibit stronger pigmentation, while shaded areas may appear paler. Horticulturalists and breeders have capitalized on this phenomenon, selectively cultivating and hybridizing variegated plant species. As a result, an extensive assortment of stunning variegated house plants now graces homes and gardens worldwide, showcasing the beauty of nature's genetic surprises.

   Which choice completes the text with the most logical transition?

   A. Moreover

   B. To reiterate

   C. In the meantime

   D. In conclusion

6. One of the prominent ways that people around the world interact with Japanese popular culture is through video games. ____________, Keita Takahashi created a game called *Katamari Damacy* that introduced a fresh and unconventional gameplay concept to the world. Players controlled a tiny prince who rolled a magical sticky ball, known as a "katamari," to collect various objects scattered throughout real-world settings. As objects are collected, the ball grows larger, eventually reaching outrageous sizes. The game's simple yet addictive mechanics, combined with its quirky sense of humor and frequent nods to Japanese cultural objects, resonated with players of all ages and quickly established the game as a cult classic with worldwide recognition. The game's success led to sequels, spin-offs, and even merchandise, further cementing its status in Japanese gaming history.

   Which choice completes the text with the most logical transition?

   A. In the early 2000s

   B. However

   C. As a result

   D. On the contrary

7. In the late 19th century, a pharmacist named John Pemberton concocted a new tonic in his laboratory. Little did he know that this beverage would go on to revolutionize the world of soft drinks. Coca-Cola, as it came to be known, was first introduced as a patent medicine that claimed to alleviate fatigue and headaches. However, it wasn't until the marketing genius of Asa Candler in the early 20th century that Coca-Cola's true potential was unlocked. Candler successfully positioned the drink as a symbol of American patriotism, associating it with the spirit of youth and freedom. ___________, Coca-Cola became an emblem of American culture.

Which choice completes the text with the most logical transition?

A. Despite these criticisms

B. Thanks to John Pemberton

C. Owing to its distinct caramel color

D. Through iconic advertisements and sponsorships

8. While researching a topic, a student has taken the following notes:

- Zheng Yi Sao (1775–1844) was a powerful female pirate from China who commanded a fleet of hundreds of ships during the early 19th century.
- She played a significant role in the Red Flag Fleet, a notorious pirate organization that controlled the waters of the South China Sea.
- Zheng Yi Sao implemented a strict code of conduct among her pirates, which included rules against stealing from the local population and harsh punishments for breaking the code.
- Under Zheng Yi Sao's leadership, the Red Flag Fleet grew into a formidable force, successfully challenging and defeating both Chinese and European naval forces.
- Zheng Yi Sao negotiated a peaceful retirement, securing her wealth and power, and even married her former rival, Cheung Po Tsai, establishing a pirate dynasty.

The student wants to introduce Zheng Yi Sao to someone who is unfamiliar with her. Which choice most effectively uses relevant information from the notes to accomplish this goal?

A. When Zheng Yi Sao retired, she was able to enjoy her vast riches with her spouse, Cheung Po Tsai, who had been her rival previously.

B. Did you know that not all pirates were men? For instance, Zheng Yi Sao was a Chinese woman pirate who lived in the 19th century.

C. During the nineteenth century, a group known as the Red Flag Fleet controlled the South China Sea and were considered very formidable thanks to their strong leader.

D. One of the most notorious pirates of her time, Zheng Yi Sao was a powerful 19th century leader known for her strict code of conduct, the formidability of her fleet, and the renown and riches she secured before her retirement.

9. While researching a topic, a student has taken the following notes:

- The Serengeti boasts iconic wildlife species such as lions, elephants, giraffes, zebras, and cheetahs, creating a thriving ecosystem.
- Endangered species, including the black rhinoceros and African wild dog, inhabit the Serengeti, highlighting the importance of conservation efforts in preserving their populations.
- Conservation organizations and national parks collaborate to protect endangered species by implementing anti-poaching measures, habitat restoration, and community education programs.
- The Serengeti supports a wide variety of plant life, from acacia trees and grasses to seasonal wildflowers, providing essential habitats and food sources for the diverse animal species that call the region home.
- Bird enthusiasts are drawn to the Serengeti for its rich avian diversity with over 500 species recorded, including raptors, waterbirds, and colorful migratory birds.

The student wants to explain the types of conservation efforts being made to protect the Serengeti. Which choice most effectively uses relevant information from the notes to accomplish this goal?

A. Conservation efforts are important in the Serengeti because many animals remain endangered, including the African wild dog and the black rhinoceros.

B. It's important to conserve plant life in the Serengeti because much of the plant life acts as an essential habitat for the animals who live there, including over 500 species of birds.

C. Many are fighting to conserve the Serengeti by restoring habitats, creating education programs for the community, and enacting anti-poaching measures to protect critically endangered species like the black rhinoceros.

D. Lions, giraffes, elephants, zebras, cheetahs, African wild dogs, black rhinos, and over 500 species of birds all need to be protected in the Serengeti through conservation efforts.

10. While researching a topic, a student has taken the following notes:

   - Cats possess a remarkable ability to problem-solve and adapt to new situations, indicating their cognitive prowess.
   - Studies have shown that cats can form complex social bonds, not only with humans but also with other cats and animals.
   - Research suggests that cats have a sophisticated communication system, utilizing vocalizations, body language, and scent marking to convey their intentions and emotions.
   - Cats exhibit various hunting strategies, from solitary stalking to cooperative hunting in certain species, displaying their strategic thinking and coordination.
   - Recent studies have explored the effects of environmental enrichment on cats, revealing that mentally stimulating environments enhance their overall well-being and cognitive abilities.

   The student wants to argue that cats demonstrate emotional intelligence. Which choice most effectively uses relevant information from the notes to accomplish this task?

   A. Environmental enrichment helps cats a lot by stimulating their minds and enhancing their cognitive function.

   B. In addition to their ability to form complex social bonds with humans and other animals, cats have numerous ways to convey what they are feeling to others using vocalizations, body language, and even scent.

   C. When cats hunt, they can do so on their own or by coordinating with other cats, which shows that they can think strategically and collaboratively.

   D. Since cats can communicate, it's possible for them to work together, such as when they are hunting or problem-solving.

Answer Key and Explanations

1. C	3. B	5. A	7. D	9. C
2. A	4. A	6. A	8. D	10. B

1. **The correct answer is C.** Start by eliminating choices A and B since they do not address the economic benefits of wind turbines. Of the two choices that remain, choice D is far too vague to effectively support the student's claim. Choice C is correct because it offers specific information about the economic benefits of wind turbines, including the fact that they are cheap to operate after an initial investment, result in more stable energy prices, and remove a municipality's reliance on fossil fuels, which tend to have fluctuating prices.

2. **The correct answer is A.** Neither choice C nor choice D mention colors, so you can eliminate them immediately. The difference between choices A and B is that choice B uses the color purple in a literal way (to describe the color of a grape) rather than in a figurative way. Only choice A supports the claim that the poet uses color (in this case yellow) to emphasize the autumnal mood of the poem.

3. **The correct answer is B.** To answer this question correctly, you must first recognize that the sentence following the blank concerns side sleepers—this allows you to eliminate choices A and D. Note that while choice A might seem like a correct statement at first glance since it represents the largest bar on the graph, the context of the reading passage suggests that the author's conclusion stems from combining the groups represented by the left side sleepers and right side sleepers to assert that side sleepers as a group are most common. This combination is accurately represented by choice B. Choice C is inaccurate given the graph.

4. **The correct answer is A.** As demonstrated by beewolves C and F as well as the relatively smaller numbers correlated with beewolves B and E, the most logical conclusion from the data is that beewolves with denser flight muscle mitochondrial membranes tend to have more offspring and feed each of them more honeybees than beewolves with less dense flight muscle mitochondrial membranes do.

5. **The correct answer is A.** This question sets up a relationship between one fact and an additional fact. The only choice that means something like "additionally" is *moreover.*

6. **The correct answer is A.** The transition "In the early 2000s" does the best job of introducing the emergence of Takahashi's game since it tells us when these events occurred. All of the other potential transitions set up relationships that do not logically unite the sentence in question and the one that came before it.

7. **The correct answer is D.** The sentence prior to the blank in question mentions Asa Candler's use of advertising to change the image of Coca-Cola. "Through iconic advertisements and sponsorships" helps connect Candler's efforts to the claim that "Coca-Cola became an emblem of American culture."

8. **The correct answer is D.** While both choice B and choice D introduce Zheng Yi Sao, only choice D integrates important characteristics about her as a figure into this introduction. Your job is to choose the most effective option and choice D does a better job at fulfilling the task of introducing Zheng Yi Sao than does choice B. Neither choice A nor choice C would make an effective introduction for Zheng

Yi Sao since they focus on different details of her biography rather than explaining who she was as a historical figure.

9. **The correct answer is C.** Every answer touches on conservation in the Serengeti; however, only choice C fulfills the task of explaining different measures conservationists are taking to protect the region.

10. **The correct answer is B.** Choices A, C, and D focus on specific cognitive abilities mentioned in the research notes, but none address emotional intelligence. Only choice B relates to cats' emotional intelligence since it conveys that cats can not only bond with other creatures but also communicate their emotional state.

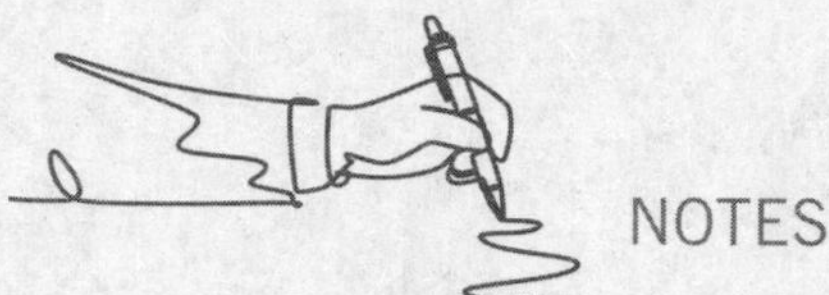

NOTES

CHAPTER

Reading and Writing Tips and Strategies

READING AND WRITING TIPS AND

OVERVIEW

Performing well in the SAT Reading and Writing section modules is a delicate balance of knowledge (English grammar and conventions), skill (your reading comprehension), and strategy (how you approach different passages and question structures). When any one of those components is lacking, getting through the section on time and with high accuracy can be challenging. We've spent the last few chapters helping you review various aspects of reading comprehension, English grammar, and language use. Now, we'll take you through some strategies that can help you make the most of your time in the Reading and Writing modules. We'll review some key facts about the design and structure of the section while also discussing a general process for working through questions and passages. With that information on hand, we'll then revisit specific questions from Chapter 2 so you can see a deep dive of how specific question structures can be approached strategically to improve accuracy and time management.

STRATEGIES 8

REFLECTING ON YOUR DIAGNOSTIC TEST SCORE

Now is a good time to flip back to the diagnostic test in Chapter 2 and your analysis of it in Chapter 3. Take a few moments to reflect on your score and performance when you started studying. You can do so in your head, take notes on your own, or use this table to jot down some ideas.

DIAGNOSTIC TEST REFLECTION: READING AND WRITING	
RW Diagnostic Section Score: ___________	**RW Section Scoring Goal:**___________
Reflection Question	**Notes**
What went well for you during the diagnostic test, and which skills were easiest for you to use?	
What did you struggle with during the diagnostic test, or which skills were harder for you to use?	
Did you feel rushed? Did you have time left over?	
How close were you to your goal?	
After reviewing reading and writing skills in the last few chapters, what are some things you might like to keep in mind as you study further?	
What are some aspects of approaching this section for which you are hoping to build strategies?	

Now, take a moment to consider your goals for the SAT Reading and Writing test. If you are hoping to land a spot at a top university, then you should be shooting for the highest score possible. That said, not everyone has the lofty goal of achieving a perfect score. Instead, you may be simply hoping to raise your score over a prior attempt or attain a score above the average for a given university. Whatever your goal, keep it in mind as you explore the strategies that follow. How well you want to do should direct how rigorously you pursue and practice these strategies.

It's important to note, though, that you're not stuck with your goal after you select it. Your goal should evolve as you continue to build your skills and practice. Just make sure, for Reading and Writing in particular, that you're using your goal to direct how you approach the section and develop your personal approach to reading passages and answering questions.

GENERAL SAT® READING AND WRITING TIPS AND STRATEGIES

Doing well with tests of reading and writing skills comes down to strong time management and strong critical thinking. Moving quickly and thinking thoroughly are often at odds with one another, but they are entirely possible within the constraints of the SAT Reading and Writing section if you understand how the test is formatted, know what your goals are, keep some general advice in mind, and make use of a step-by-step process to work through each question.

SAT Reading and Writing Section Key Details

To efficiently and effectively move through the SAT Reading and Writing modules, it helps to know some specific details about the test section. If you know how the test is structured, its time constraints, and the kinds of questions you'll encounter, you can make better choices about how to spend your time and think through questions. Consider the following as you build your general and question-specific strategies while reading this chapter.

- In each module, you have 32 minutes to answer 27 questions—roughly 70 seconds per passage and question.
- Each passage (or passage set) is accompanied by only one question.
- The passages are relatively short, generally no longer than 150 words.
- Using the Bluebook interface, you can annotate passages, cross out answers, and mark questions for later review.
- You'll encounter an almost equal number of each question type within each module.
- Some questions may come up more often in one module over another. For instance, Cross-Text Connections questions are more common in the second module, while the first module is likely to contain slightly more Standard English Conventions questions.
- Within each module, the question domains are presented in the following order: Craft and Structure, Information and Ideas, Standard English Conventions, Expression of Ideas.
- Within each domain set, excluding Standard English Conventions, questions will proceed in a particular order of skills, and within each skill set, questions will go from easier to harder.
- If you perform well with the first module, then the second module, on average, will be harder. If you perform poorly with the first module, the second module, on average, will be easier.
- Your score is capped below a certain level if you end up in the easier second module (perhaps as low as 600) because of how many questions you have already missed for the section.
- Answering around 60% of the questions correctly (about 34 questions) will put you around the average score for test takers.
- Certain question domains and skills will only refer to part of the passage.
- There is always an excellent reason why one answer is better than the other three answers.

SAT Reading and Writing Goals

To maximize your performance in the Reading and Writing section, you want to manage your time in a particular way and try to accomplish certain feats with each question. Aiming for each of the following goals will put you on a path to higher scores.

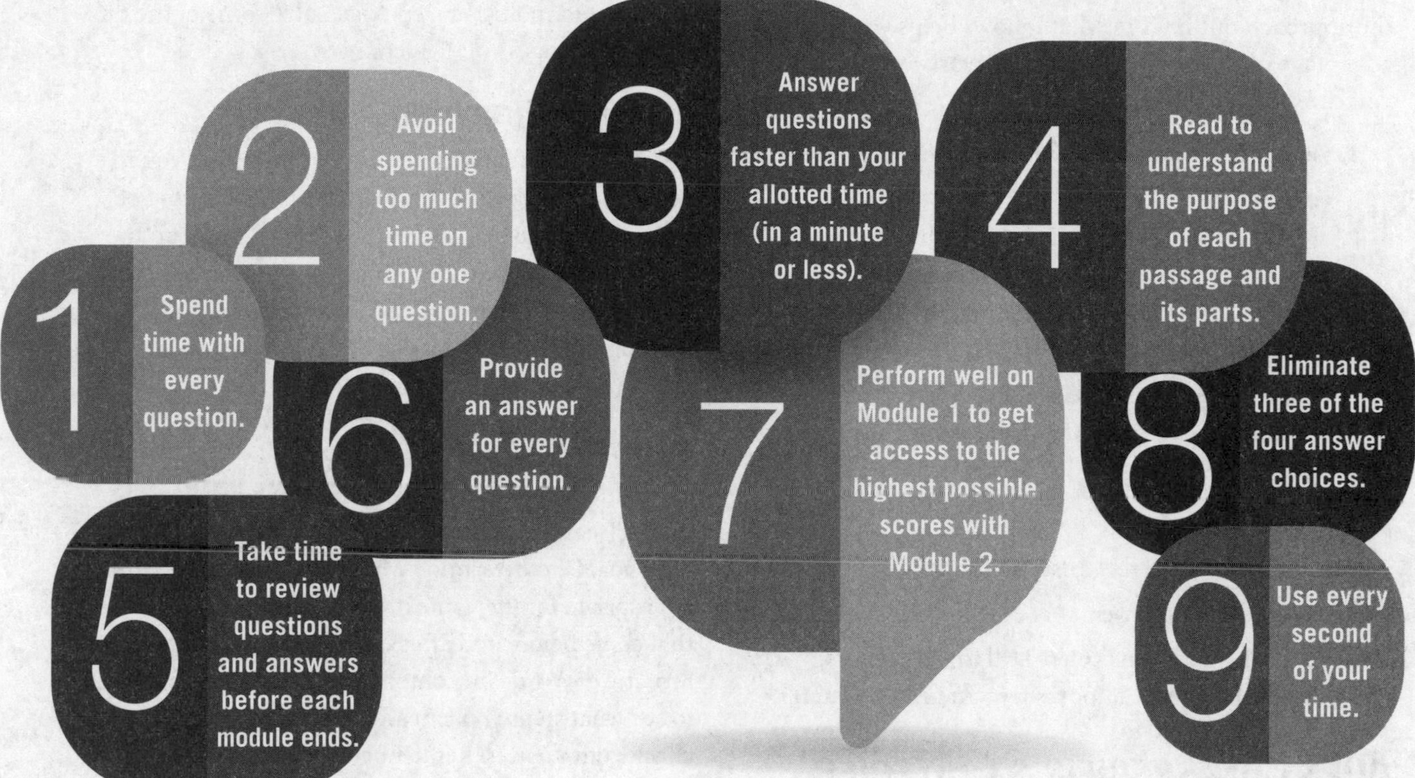

1
Spend time with every question.
2
Avoid spending too much time on any one question.
3
Answer questions faster than your allotted time (in a minute or less).
4
Read to understand the purpose of each passage and its parts.
5
Take time to review questions and answers before each module ends.
6
Provide an answer for every question.
7
Perform well on Module 1 to get access to the highest possible scores with Module 2.
8
Eliminate three of the four answer choices.
9
Use every second of your time.

SAT Reading and Writing Advice

The SAT presents questions in particular ways. Keep the following advice in mind as you work through the section to dodge answer choices that can hurt your score.

- Beware of extreme words in answer choices (like *never, always, all, none*); such usage must match the scope of claims in the passage.
- Scrutinize answer choices with terms that are reused from the passage; such answer choices aren't necessarily wrong, nor are they necessarily right.
- Reading the first and last sentences of a passage can give you a decent understanding of the passage's main idea.
- Work quickly but take the time to reread something when you don't understand.

FYI

As you'll see with the question-specific strategies, this step-by-step process is flexible so as to accommodate some of the specific choices the SAT makes for different question types. Some questions may have you add or remove a step from this process in order to exploit or compensate for how some question domain skills are tested.

SAT Reading and Writing Question Steps

When dealing with SAT Reading and Writing questions, it helps to have a step-by-step process that you can follow for most, if not all, questions. While specific question types may require you to modify these steps, the approach outlined in what follows helps you take advantage of the question format to work as quickly as you can without making careless errors.

1. Read the question first to determine what you're looking for in the passage.
2. Read strategically, reading as much as is needed to answer the question (sentences indicated by the question blank, underlining, or question reference, etc.).
3. Read more of the passage if necessary to clarify meaning (before and after relevant information, etc.).
4. Reread the question.
5. Predict the answer.
6. Eliminate incorrect answers.
7. Record your answer.
8. If after those steps you're still unsure, guess, mark the question for review, and return later.

QUESTION-SPECIFIC STRATEGIES

Each question domain in the SAT Reading and Writing modules asks you to demonstrate a variety of different skills, never limiting your work to either specific aspects of the passages (word choice, graphics, grammar, transitions) or your understanding of the broader meaning of what you read. To work at those different levels of understanding, you can consider how different question structures guide your time and attention in different ways. Often, the question type and structure will tell you to read more or less of the passage, allowing you to optimize your time and attention without taking in information that won't help you answer the question. To answer certain question types well, you may also find that removing or completing an additional step in the general question process from earlier in the chapter can help you avoid wasting time or energy. The following strategies are sequenced in the order that the relevant questions would appear in each module. Use the walkthroughs of these sample questions (appearing again from Chapter 2) to see how you can work through questions strategically based on their objectives. Each question walkthrough will guide you through the step-by-step process but offer some specific insights and modified steps that solve some of the different challenges you'll encounter.

Craft and Structure

Recall that Craft and Structure questions ask you to perform three tasks: demonstrate understanding of words and phrases in context, identify text structure and purpose, and make connections between texts. As the first questions in each SAT Reading and Writing module, you'll need to make quick decisions about how much you read and for what purpose.

Words in Context

Craft and Structure: Words in Context questions are the SAT equivalent of vocabulary questions. As such, your goal is to determine what words or phrases are appropriate for the context of the sentence (and those that come before and after). Let's look at a Craft and Structure: Words in Context question from Chapter 2 to see what steps you can add to the general process to check your answer. Remember, always start by reading the question to see what your objective is.

EXAMPLE

All over the world, people gather for festivals to celebrate events, mark holidays, create community, and engage in shared cultural traditions. The tendency towards festival-style gathering is common across human cultures, meaning that the world is full of beautiful festival traditions. However, cultures vary, so just as there are certain types of celebrations that appear over and over, like weddings and harvest festivals, there are others that are truly ___________.

Which choice completes the text with the most logical and precise word or phrase?

A. truncated

B. nonchalant

C. singular

D. mysterious

Start by reading the question (step 1). From there, you know that your goal is to complete the sentence with one of the available answer choices. Only one choice is acceptable given the context of the sentence. You have time to read the entire passage, but for a Words in Context question, you can first focus on just the relevant sentence (step 2): "However, cultures vary, so just as there are certain types of celebrations that appear over and over, like weddings and harvest festivals, there are others that are truly ___________." In this case, the sentence in question, and the sentence before, can offer a variety of clues. The sentence with the blank starts with the word *however*, indicating that what follows contrasts with a preceding idea. In continuing to read the sentence, you can see the two ideas that are juxtaposed are that "festival-style gathering is common across human cultures," further demonstrated by the phrase "certain types of celebrations [. . .] appear over and over" in the indicated sentence, and "cultures vary." If the context were still not clear, you could read the entirety of the passage to try and clarify (step 3).

With the indicated relationship clear, to complete the phrase "there are other [celebrations] that are truly," (step 4) you know you'll be dealing with a word that indicates uniqueness to build on the noted variety of cultures (step 5).

Now that you've predicted an answer, you can review the choices and eliminate those that do not fit the desired meaning (step 6). Choices A, B, and D do not represent the expected meaning. Although you've eliminated answers, for a Words in Context question, you should reread the sentence with your choice in place (question-specific step): "However, cultures vary, so just as there are certain types of celebrations that appear over and over, like weddings and harvest festivals, there are others that are truly *singular*." Does the meaning of the sentence align with the meaning of the passage? Yes. If you feel certain, you can record your answer (step 7) and move on. Otherwise, you should input your best guess, mark the question for review, and return after answering the other questions in the module (step 8).

Text Structure and Purpose

For Craft and Structure: Text Structure and Purpose questions, your focus is on determining what underlined sentences contribute to the text. In most instances, you're considering the following question: "If I were to delete this sentence, what would I no longer understand?" Let's look at a question from Chapter 2 to apply this thinking.

EXAMPLE

Nanotechnology involves designing and engineering materials with extraordinary properties due to their nano-sized dimensions, typically ranging from 1 to 100 nanometers. At this scale, quantum effects become prominent, enabling novel applications in diverse fields such as medicine, electronics, and energy. Nanoparticles, for instance, possess unique properties that make them ideal for targeted drug delivery in cancer treatments. By precisely controlling the structure and composition of nanomaterials, scientists can tailor their properties for specific applications. <u>However, alongside the immense possibilities, researchers must address challenges related to scalability, safety, and ethical considerations.</u> By pushing the boundaries of nanotechnology, scientists strive to unlock its full potential and revolutionize numerous industries.

Which choice best states the function of the underlined sentence in the text as a whole?

- **A.** It defines nanotechnology in terms that are comprehensible to most people.
- **B.** It compares nanotechnology with related science fields.
- **C.** It details the ethical dilemma related to nanotechnology.
- **D.** It indicates the challenges for those working in the field of nanotechnology.

In reading the question, you know that you can focus your attention, at least at first, on the underlined sentence. When you read the underlined sentence, you see that it talks about what researchers also need to focus on beyond possibilities. The items described include "scalability, safety, and ethical considerations." In reading more of the passage, to learn what possibilities, scalability, safety, and ethics are connected to, the first sentence tells you that the subject of this passage is nanotechnology. Now consider the following question: if you were to delete this sentence, what would you no longer understand about nanotechnology? Without this sentence, it would not be clear that while the possibilities for nanotechnology are exciting, there are potential issues. Your answer choice should state as much. In evaluating the answer choices, you can eliminate choices A and B as the term *nanotechnology* is not defined (or even used in the indicated sentence), nor is the technology compared to anything else. While choice C references an "ethical dilemma," capitalizing on the language from the passage, the sentence more broadly "indicates the challenges" (choice D), rather than focusing on a specific ethical issue. You can eliminate choice C and select choice D.

Cross-Text Connections

Craft and Structure: Cross-Text Connections questions are all about developing understanding of two texts and making sure that not only are they summarized appropriately by your answer choice but also that any relationship is properly expressed. For questions such as this, your primary consideration may be how much you read of the passages to minimize your time expenditure. Let's look at a passage set and question from Chapter 2.

EXAMPLE

Text 1

The Republic of Colombia on the northwestern coast of South America is the second most biologically diverse country in the world. It is considered a "megadiverse" country on account of the heterogeneity among its endemic and nonnative species. Colombia contains 59 protected areas and 314 types of coastal and inland ecosystems that host 10% of the world's biodiversity. Colombia is a geographical wonder of natural regions that give residence to various flora and fauna. The ice-capped mountains of the Andes stretch through the interior and western regions, while tropical beaches border the northern and western coastlines. The northwestern region shares its jungle with the neighboring country of Panama, yet deserts reside in the north and grassy plains overrun the east. Dense forests cover more than 50% of the mainland, including the Amazon rainforest region, which blankets the southern portion of the country.

Text 2

Deforestation, urbanization, overfishing, water pollution, and air pollution all contribute to the environmental crisis in Colombia. Water pollution in the country is caused by domestic and industrial waste, agricultural operations, and mining activities. Armed guerilla groups such as the FARC and ELN aim to dismantle the economic infrastructure that serves the government and the interests of multinational corporations. Since 1984, their most common tactic has involved destroying oil pipelines. As a result, oil spills have caused the contamination of land and water and the deterioration of various ecosystems.

Based on the texts, what is the relationship between Text 1 and Text 2?

A. Text 1 specifies the types of biodiversity in Colombia, and Text 2 justifies the political tactics of Colombia's guerrillas.

B. Text 1 details the impact of biodiverse species on Colombia, and Text 2 explains the effects of humans invading those species' ecosystems.

C. Text 1 praises Colombia for its protection of its ecosystems, and Text 2 criticizes large corporations for polluting them.

D. Text 1 illustrates the biodiversity and geography of Colombia, and Text 2 conveys the ways in which those ecosystems are in danger.

When a question is accompanied by two passages, you will in some way be asked to establish a relationship between the two texts. In order to select an appropriate answer choice, you'll need to be able to summarize each passage. You have enough time to read each passage, but you could also read the first and last sentence of each passage to get a decent idea of the primary focus of each. Here, the first sentence of Text 1 tells you that the paragraph will most likely be related to Colombia's biodiversity and environment. The last sentence follows up by discussing one of the major biomes of the country. The first sentence of Text 2 tells you about the kinds of problems plaguing the environments of Colombia. The last sentence focuses on a specific environmental issue (oil spills) and its effects. Make note (mental or otherwise) of each passage's focus. In selecting an answer choice that describes the relationship of these texts, any choices that do not accurately describe the overall topics of the passages can be eliminated. You may need to read more of the passage to confirm your selection, but you should be able to eliminate some choices. In reading through the choices, while some seem plausible because of how they use terms from the passage, only choice D aligns with what you read.

Information and Ideas

Information and Ideas questions draw on your ability to comprehend and use central ideas, supporting details, and evidence to come to reasonable conclusions. That means that these questions depend on your understanding of all aspects of a passage, making strategy challenging. For strategy, you're making decisions about how you approach reading the passage. Keep in mind that while you do have adequate time to read the entirety of the passage, you can potentially gain time for other questions by trying to read strategically, as discussed in the following sections.

Central Ideas and Details

An Information and Ideas: Central Ideas and Details question is all about how well you understand the passage, whether the main idea or its supporting details. Sometimes, you can glean the necessary information for a question just by reading the first and last sentences of a passage (similar to what you saw for Craft and

Structure: Cross-Text Connections), but sometimes, you'll simply need to read the entire passage. How much you read will depend on the structure of the passage and your reading comprehension abilities. In general, though, you can start with less and read more as needed to answer the question.

EXAMPLE

Scholars study the phenomenon of collective memory to better understand how groups of people remember and engage with the past. Collective memory refers to the experiences and memories that are shared by a group of people and passed down through generations. In the United States, there are many public memorials to commemorate a variety of important events, like the 9/11 Memorial in New York City or the USS *Arizona* Memorial in Pearl Harbor, Hawaii. Memorials provide insight into how a country collectively remembers people and events and how those events have shaped history and national identity.

Which choice best states the main purpose of the text?

A. To critique the manner in which memorials are organized in the US

B. To discuss collective memory and its social and historical impacts, particularly in reference to the use of memorials

C. To emphasize the need for more research on the relevance of collective memory and memorials

D. To illustrate specific ways that collective memory is conveyed among a particular group of people or society

Recall the general process for approaching SAT Reading and Writing questions. Start by reading the question. The question tells you that you're interested in the overall purpose of the text. As you've seen with some other question types, you can get a sense of the overall purpose of a text by turning to the first and last sentences. Here, you see mention of collective memory (first sentence) as well as memorials (last sentence). The purpose of the text, even if we don't read more of the passage, should in some way connect these concepts. In examining the answer choices, choices B and C both reference collective memory and memorials. Choice B emphasizes that this is a discussion of these two concepts. Choice C describes the passage as focusing on a call for more research into the concepts. Choice B could be safe, but in order to be certain, you might need to read the rest of the passage. Notice that you're only turning to the rest of the passage when you need more information to eliminate a competing answer choice. In reading through the passage, the intervening sentences define collective memory and provide examples of specific monuments in the United States. Neither proposes a call for further research. The answer is choice B.

Command of Evidence

Information and Ideas: Command of Evidence questions can be quantitative or textual in nature. A textual Command of Evidence question may describe a piece of writing and an observation about its content. From there, you would be expected to select from among the answer choices the best quotation (presumptively from the cited text) that would support such a claim. Additionally, textual Command of Evidence questions can also ask you to select answers that would support given statements or hypotheses. For a quantitative question, you may be presented with a passage that is accompanied by a table, graph, or diagram. You must then complete the passage with information that aligns with the data provided. That means analyzing the data to find relationships. Let's look at a quantitative Command of Evidence question from Chapter 2 in action.

EXAMPLE

Ocean water is saltwater, which means that the water contains dissolved salts and other minerals. The percentage of dissolved salts in a body of water is known as salinity. Notably, amounts of dissolved salts and minerals in ocean water contribute to ocean water's density, which is the mass of the substance per unit of volume. The greater the mass of dissolved salts, the greater the density of the ocean water. Density is also affected by temperature. Pure water, which freezes at 0°C, reaches its maximum density at around 4°C. Adding salt and other minerals to water __________

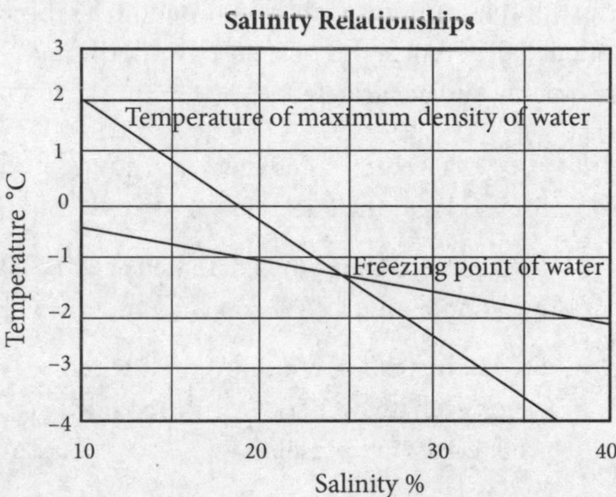

Which choice most effectively uses data from the graph to illustrate the claim?

- **A.** increases the freezing point of water while having no effect on the temperature at which maximum density occurs.
- **B.** increases the ambient temperature of water under normal conditions.
- **C.** lowers both the freezing point and the temperature at which maximum density occurs.
- **D.** increases the density of water until it reaches a point of equilibrium.

The question tells you that you need to focus on the information from the graph to answer appropriately. To start, instead of reading the passage, you'll examine the graphic for its title, axis and figure labels, scale, and relationships. The graph, according to its title, describes "Salinity Relationships." On the *x*-axis you see "Salinity %," and on the *y*-axis you see "Temperature °C." From those labels, you know that the graph will depict the relationship between salinity and temperature. Plotted on the graph are two lines; the upper line represents the "Temperature of maximum density of water" and the lower line is the "Freezing point of water." You see that both lines slope downward from left to right. Those negative slopes mean that as the percentage of salinity increases, the temperature of the maximum density of water and the freezing point of water decrease. With that analysis, you should have an adequate understanding of the data to answer whatever claim the passage is making. In referring to the question blank in the passage now, you see the following statement: "Adding salt and other minerals to water __________." Based on your analysis, you know that greater salinity in water (adding salt) decreases both the temperature of maximum density and the freezing point. Your answer choice should speak to those conclusions. As you read through the answer choices, you'll be able to eliminate choice A (does not represent the data), choice B (is unrelated to the data), and choice D (is unrelated to the data). Choice C aligns with your analysis of the graph and is thus correct.

Inferences

For Information and Ideas: Inference questions, your answer choice must logically follow from the information in the passage. That can mean a combination of fitting the context of the sentence as well as the purpose of the passage as a whole. In essence, you're using the following construction in your thinking: "If what the passage states is true, then it makes sense that. . ." This means that you'll need a thorough understanding of the whole passage, or most of the passage, to draw your inference. Let's work through an example.

EXAMPLE

Plants have a huge impact on a person's mood. One study showed that when young people spend time tending to plants, it had a repressing effect on signals of stress in their bodies, such as blood pressure and cortisol levels. Plants are also known to provide people with a sense of visual escape from their everyday lives. Imagine, for instance, that you're stuck in a dreary office environment and looking at a computer screen all day. Taking a few moments to admire the fern on your desk might then give you a moment of reprieve from the environment and provide a spot of tranquility. The smell, feel, and sight of plants have also all been shown to __________.

Which choice most logically completes the text?

A. distract from other elements in the environment

B. be irrelevant

C. improve a person's overall disposition

D. contribute to negative health outcomes

After reading the question, you see that you're being asked to infer what should come next in the passage given the information presented prior to the blank. It's possible that reading just a sentence before and after the blank (just before in this case) can shed enough light on the passage subject to help you, but you have the time to read the whole passage, and inference questions may require more information for you to make an accurate selection. Reading through the paragraph, you see claims that plants impact a person's mood, reduce stress, and provide "a sense of visual escape," all benefits. Based on that information, it would be reasonable to predict that the last sentence will also speak to more positive effects, unless there's a transition that indicates a forthcoming contrasting statement. No such transition is present, so the discussion should continue from the previous sentences.

Choices B and D state that plants either have no effect or cause negative effects, neither of which would align with the statements and driving purpose of the passage: to state the positive effects the presence of plants has on people.

Additionally, it has already been stated that the sight of plants offers a "reprieve from the environment," so stating that the "sight of plants [has] also been shown to distract from other elements in the environment" (choice A) would be redundant. You've eliminated all the choices but choice C, which also aligns with your prediction, matching both the tone and purpose of the passage.

Standard English Conventions

Standard English Conventions questions are the most different from the other question types that you encounter in the SAT Reading and Writing section. Because of their unique goals, you'll want to be thinking about a different series of steps to work through them quickly and accurately.

Step 1. Read the question.

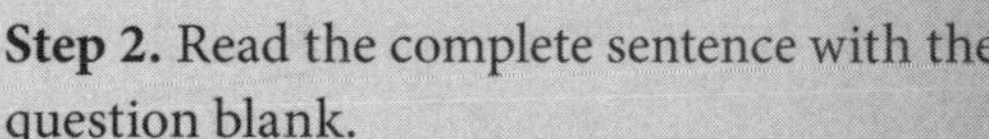

Step 2. Read the complete sentence with the question blank.

Step 3. Instead of making a prediction, check each answer choice so you know what errors are present.

Step 4. Eliminate all answer choices that are not grammatically correct as any grammatical issue disqualifies an answer choice.

Step 5. If you have multiple answers still remaining, consider their relevance to the passage (is critical information cut off grammatically, etc.?).

Step 6. Read more from the passage as necessary to justify your choice.

Step 7. Reread the sentence with your answer choice in place.

Step 8. Mark any uncertain answers to review before time expires.

Boundaries

Standard English Conventions: Boundaries questions focus your attention on the ways in which clauses are joined together. You won't know that's the focus of the question until you start examining the answer choices. But as you move through the steps for a Standard English Conventions question, you would then focus your attention on determining whether the clauses indicated represent complete sentences or fragments. Those properties will be the primary determining factor of what punctuation you use.

EXAMPLE

Known for their long-distance running abilities, the indigenous people group known as the Tarahumara, or Rarámuri as they call themselves, have lived in the mountainous ranges of Chihuahua, Mexico, for centuries. Due to the remoteness of the mountains and valleys this group has called home, they have managed to limit their ___________ they have made headlines by competing in ultra-marathon races. One of the most intriguing points about the runners is that they prefer to wear their traditional sandals, called huaraches, instead of athletic shoes.

Which choice completes the text so that it conforms to the conventions of Standard English?

A. contact with society; however more recently

B. contact with society, however, more recently

C. contact with society; however, more recently,

D. contact with society however more recently

After you have read the question, just as you would with any other question in the SAT Reading and Writing section, you would then read the entire sentence in which the question blank appears. Because this is a Standard English Conventions question, you need to understand the entire sentence to make choices about proper English grammar and conventions. Here you have a longer sentence that appears to have multiple subjects and verbs. When we look at the answer choices, we see a variety of ways that these clauses are being connected together with a few forms of punctuation and the word *however.*

Next, you'll evaluate whether each option is grammatically correct and keep or eliminate it. Choice A uses a semicolon before *however,* which is appropriate, but there's no punctuation around the phrase *more recently,* which creates two problems as both *however* and *more recently* should be separated from the main clause by commas. Choice B uses commas around *however,* but in this case, *however* is starting a new sentence ("however. . .they have made headlines by competing in ultra-marathon races."), so we need to signal that this clause is separate from the clause before. A comma is insufficient for that purpose. Choice C uses a semicolon to separate the new clause and also some commas around the phrase *more recently,* signaling that the phrase is nonessential information for the grammar of the sentence. That works, so we'll keep it. Choice D lacks any punctuation; we can eliminate it. That leaves us with choice C. Reread the sentence with that choice inserted: "Due to the remoteness of the mountains and valleys this group has called home, they have managed to limit their *contact with society; however, more recently,* they have made headlines by competing in ultra-marathon races." That appears to establish proper boundaries between the clauses and separate the conjunctive adverb *however* and the phrase *more recently* to establish clear modification.

Form, Structure, and Sense

Standard English Conventions: Form, Structure, and Sense questions examine your ability to make choices for grammar and conventions that are consistent with language elsewhere in the passage. That means, particularly when dealing with pronouns and verb tense, that you're looking elsewhere in the passage to find justification for your choice.

EXAMPLE

Nelson Mandela was a political activist and leader known for working to end apartheid in South Africa, being the first Black and democratically elected President of South Africa, and fighting for human rights worldwide. Apartheid, a system of legally enforced segregation and oppression of people of color by dominant minority white people in Africa, institutionally controlled South Africa from 1948 until ________ end in 1994, coinciding with Mandela's presidency. Imprisoned from 1964–1990 for his anti-apartheid activism, Mandela gained popularity for his resistance and refusal to compromise his ideologies for freedom. In 1993, he and South African President Frederik Willem de Klerk earned the Nobel Peace Prize for their joint work on political negotiations toward a democracy for all. Mandela's presidency from 1994 to 1999, as well as his social justice advocacy in the subsequent 14 years of his life, paved the way for international discourse on human rights.

Which choice completes the text so that it conforms to the conventions of Standard English?

A. they're

B. their

C. its

D. it's

After you see that this is a Standard English Conventions questions, you can read the entire sentence with the question blank. The sentence establishes the definition of *Apartheid*, the parties involved, relevant locations, and a date range. In evaluating the answer choices, your goal then becomes to establish who or what ended in 1994 and what is the best pronoun to use in place of the name. You would be able to eliminate choices A and D as they are contractions that stand for *they are* and *it is*, respectively. Contractions are not appropriate grammatically in this case. Going back into the sentence, you can reduce its complexity by reading it as "Apartheid [. . .] institutionally controlled South Africa from 1948 until ________ end in 1994." By dropping the nonessential phrase after the word *Apartheid*, it is easier to see that we are looking for a possessive pronoun that agrees with the antecedent *Apartheid*. In this instance, the antecedent for the pronoun is all the way back at the beginning of the sentence. The only appropriate choice is *its*, choice C. Reread the sentence with your choice and you get the following: "Apartheid, a system of legally enforced segregation and oppression of people of color by dominant minority white people in Africa, institutionally controlled South Africa from 1948 until *its* end in 1994, coinciding with Mandela's presidency."

Expression of Ideas

Expression of Ideas questions ask test takers to achieve specific rhetorical goals, whether by crafting a sentence from discordant pieces or by appropriately representing relationships between statements to express certain rhetorical positions. Answering these questions effectively means identifying relationships, whether between a question's stated rhetorical purpose and related elements in a hypothetical student's notes (Rhetorical Analysis questions) or the connection between two successive sentences.

Transitions

Expression of Ideas: Transitions questions are all about signaling the relationship between two related statements with the ultimate goal of creating a smooth and logical flow of ideas. Transitions can fall into a variety of categories, including contrasting, additive, emphatic, or temporal, among others. To meet your objective, you need to identify the relationship between statements and then select a representative transition word or phrase. Making those decisions requires context but not always the entire passage. You can often get away with just reading a little before and a little after the question blank. It also helps to reread the sentence with the transition in place before moving on. Let's walk through an example.

EXAMPLE

One of Jane Jacobs's key contributions to urban studies was the concept of social capital. This refers to the networks of relationships and trust that exist within communities. Jacobs believed that social capital was essential for creating vibrant and resilient cities. When people know and trust each other, they are more likely to work together to solve problems and build strong local economies. ____________, neighbors who know and trust one another are more likely to assist one another with tasks like repairs and childcare or by making referrals to local tradespeople. Jacobs envisioned cities wherein neighbors felt connected to one another and their neighborhood as a whole. She argued that social capital allows people to feel a sense of belonging and connection to their neighborhoods, which can lead to greater civic engagement and participation.

Which choice completes the text with the most logical transition?

A. Lastly

B. Primarily

C. In conclusion

D. For instance

The question tells you that you're looking for a transition. You'll need to read a little before the sentence with the transition and should read a little after as well to see what ideas you're trying to bridge. In doing so, you see the following statements: "When people know and trust each other, they are more likely to work together to solve problems and build strong local economies" and "neighbors who know and trust one another are more likely to assist one another with tasks like repairs and childcare or by making referrals to local tradespeople." The first sentence sets up a conditional statement: when people know each other, they help each other. The second sentence establishes that neighbors who know each other may assist with "repairs or childcare." The sentence following the transition is acting as an example for the claim in the preceding sentence. You can eliminate choices A and C as they speak to concluding statements. That cannot be the case because multiple sentences still remain in the passage. Choice B is an emphatic transition that would convey that the statement following the transition is the "primary" way that people work together to solve problems. However, the context of the passage does not support that. Choice D is all that remains; it both aligns with the prediction and is the only choice remaining. Reread the two sentences with the transition in place to check: "When people know and trust each other, they are more likely to work together to solve problems and build strong local economies. *For instance*, neighbors who know and trust one another are more likely to assist one another with tasks like repairs and childcare or by making referrals to local tradespeople." That reads well. Move on to the next question.

Rhetorical Analysis

Expression of Ideas: Rhetorical Analysis questions establish a series of notes around a common topic and then ask you to select an answer that synthesizes those notes to achieve a specific rhetorical purpose. The primary challenge is then to establish what types of statements you would expect to see to properly achieve a specific rhetorical purpose. Sometimes, that can mean sifting through the student's notes and annotating relevant information. At other times, you may be able to work only from the answer choices.

EXAMPLE

While researching a topic, a student has taken the following notes:

- From a structural engineering perspective, the Hoover Dam is one of the most impressive American infrastructure projects to date.
- Located along the Colorado River on the border between Nevada and Arizona, the hydroelectric power plant and arch-gravity dam was built in the early 1930s as the Great Depression loomed in the United States.
- The concrete structure stands over 725 feet tall and facilitates the movement of water to Lake Mead, the reservoir that supplies water to millions of people and irrigates over 2 million acres of land.
- Millions visit the Hoover Dam each year to marvel at its design, participate in recreational activities, and tour the facility.
- Its construction was largely made possible by President Herbert Hoover, for whom it is dedicated, as he understood the need for flood control and large-scale irrigation in the southwest.

The student wants to introduce the topic of the Hoover Dam to someone who is unfamiliar with the topic. Which choice most effectively uses relevant information from the notes to accomplish this goal?

A. Built in the early 1930s as the Great Depression loomed in the United States, the Hoover Dam stands over 725 feet tall and facilitates the movement of water to a reservoir called Lake Mead.

B. The Hoover Dam is a hydroelectric power plant and arch-gravity dam located along the Colorado River between Nevada and Arizona and is one of the most impressive American engineering projects to date.

C. The Hoover Dam is an impressive structural engineering project that was built in large part thanks to President Herbert Hoover, for whom it is dedicated.

D. The Hoover Dam was built in the early 1930s as the Great Depression loomed due to the need for flood control and large-scale irrigation in the southwestern United States.

After reading the question, you know that your answer should effectively synthesize notes that can explain some of the basics of the Hoover Dam. In this situation, your choice should answer questions like "What is the Hoover Dam?" and "Why is it important?" If your choice does not specify that information, it is likely that it has not effectively achieved the student's intended rhetorical purpose.

With that goal in mind, you may be able to pivot away from reading the passage first and instead read through the answer choices to eliminate unlikely answers. Depending on the nature of the answer choices, this approach may be more effective in certain cases.

Let's examine the answer choices for this question to see:

- Choice A makes it clear when the dam was constructed, its size, and its purpose: to facilitate the movement of water from Lake Mead.
- Choice B establishes the mechanics of the dam, its location, and its significance to American engineering.
- Choice C speaks to the dam's reputation and the origin of its name.
- Choice D mentions when the dam was built and why it was built.

Multiple answer choices provide some of the key points that would be needed to talk to someone who is unfamiliar with the structure. You can eliminate choices C and D with some certainty as they lack discussion of what type of dam the Hoover is or how it works. But to decide between choices A and B, you'll need to read through the student's notes.

As you go through the test, you can use the Bluebook annotation tool to highlight parts of the bullet points that could be used to, as the question states, "introduce the topic of the Hoover Dam to someone who is unfamiliar with the topic."

That could mean highlighting the following:

- First bullet: one of the most impressive American infrastructure projects
- Second bullet: Colorado River [. . .] border between Nevada and Arizona, the hydro-electric power plant and arch-gravity dam [. . .] early 1930s
- Third bullet: 725 feet tall [. . .] Lake Mead
- Fourth bullet: Millions visit [. . .] each year
- Fifth bullet: flood control and large-scale irrigation

Your answer choice should include elements of the different bullet points, but they need to be combined in the most effective way possible.

In comparing choices A and B again, you may notice some things. Choice A focuses on the concept of controlling the flow of water. Such a detail is implied by virtue of the definition of a dam. What only choice B makes clear is that the dam is also a hydro-electric powerplant and arch-gravity design. That information would provide an unfamiliar reader with a greater understanding as to the basic details of the Hoover Dam while also establishing where the dam is located and its significance in American engineering. Choice B is correct.

SUMMING IT UP

- Some of the SAT Reading and Writing section's formatting and constraints can help you make decisions about how you work through the test:
    - You have about 70 seconds to answer each question in each module. You should use all of your time in each module but try to work a little faster on each question so that you have time to review your guesses or uncertain answers before time expires. Getting to that point is helped by using a step-by-step question process, practicing reading quickly, and learning what information will help you answer the different types of questions.
    - Each passage (or passage set) is accompanied by only one question. You have enough time to read each passage fully, but certain question types can often be answered by reading only parts of the passage. Refer back to the Question-Specific Strategies section for specific situations.
    - The Bluebook app lets you annotate passages, cross out answers, and mark questions for later review. Familiarize yourself with these features before test day and use them to track information on the test.
    - The different question domains and types have set orders within each module. There's almost an equal number of each type. Within each domain skill set, with the exception of Standards of English Conventions, questions will progress from easier to harder. For instance, the first Words in Context question will be easier than the last Words in Context question.
    - If you perform well on Module 1, Module 2 will be harder on average. To get the highest score possible, make sure you work hard in Module 1.

- Use a step-by-step approach to work through different questions. A lot of the time, you'll be able to take the following steps, but you can adjust this process based on what question type you're dealing with and your own personal strengths and weaknesses.
    1. Read the question to determine what information you're looking for.
    2. Read the information referenced by the question.
    3. Read more of the passage if needed to clarify meaning or context.
    4. Reread the question.
    5. Predict the answer (for most questions).
    6. Eliminate incorrect answers.
    7. Record your answer.
    8. If after those steps you're still unsure, guess, mark the question for review, and return later.
- To achieve your highest possible score, aim to do the following as you work through the Reading and Writing section:
    - Spend time with every question, but don't get stuck on any one question.
    - Provide an answer for every question.
    - Use every second of your time in the section.
    - Work to eliminate three of the four answer choices.
    - Review your answers before the module ends.
    - Be careful with answers with extreme words like *always*, *never*, *all*, and *none*.
    - Carefully examine answers that reuse language from the passage.
    - Make use of the first and last sentences of passages to get a quick, but rough, idea of the passage's main idea.
    - Reread when you don't understand the purpose of a word, phrase, sentence, or passage as a whole.

PART IV

THE SAT® MATH SECTION

CHAPTER

Introduction to SAT® Math

INTRODUCTION TO SAT® MATH

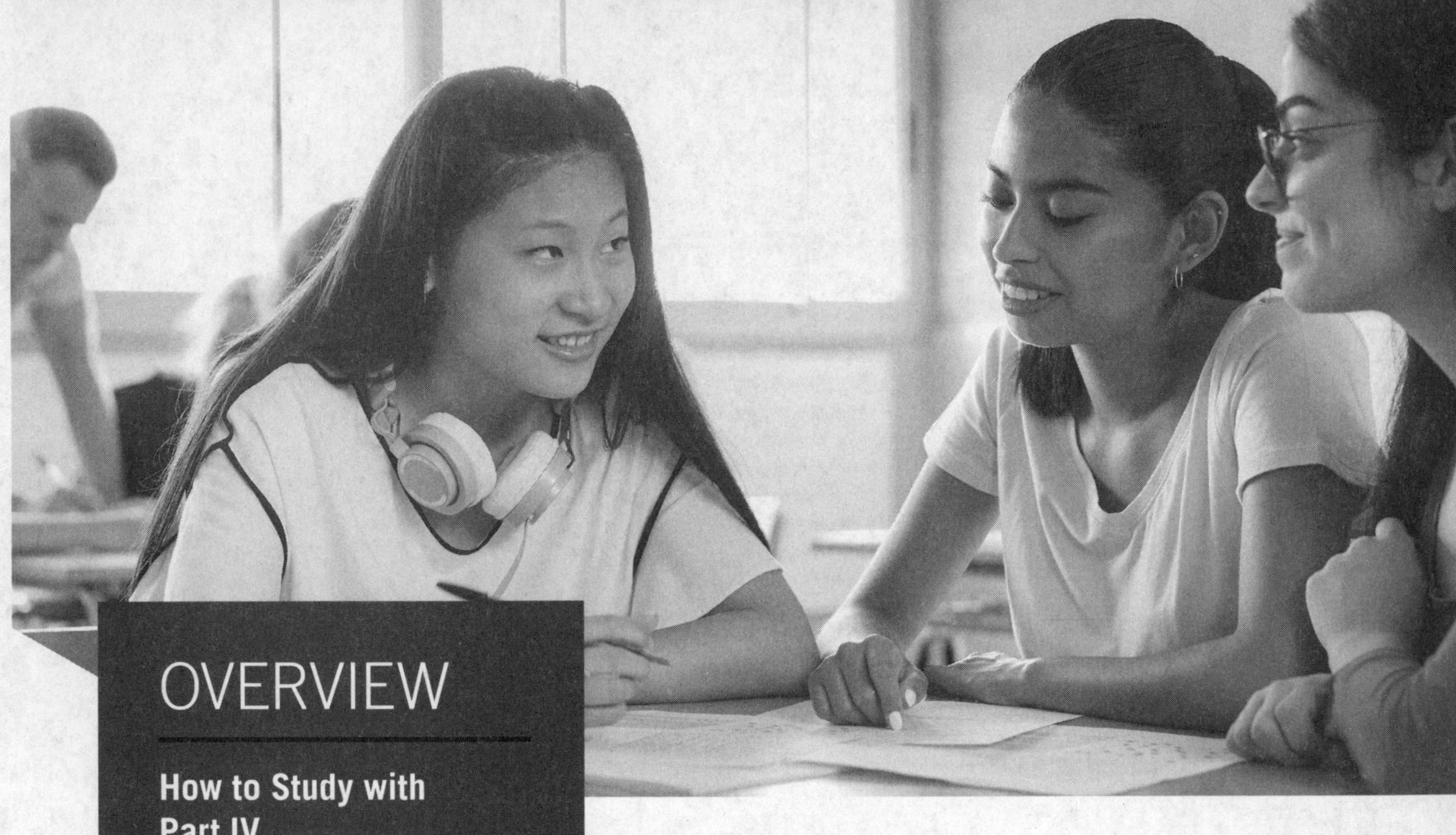

OVERVIEW

To adequately prepare for the Math section of the SAT, you'll want to familiarize yourself with the structure of the Math section, the types of questions you'll be presented with, the skills you'll be tested on, and some common challenges test takers face. In this chapter, we'll go over the basic information about the test, including what's on it and how it's structured, along with some example questions.

HOW TO STUDY WITH PART IV

Before delving into the details about the test itself, reflect on your experiences as a student of math. What sort of math classes have you taken throughout your high school career? Which kinds of math skills do you enjoy using, and which skills do you struggle with?

9

For example, have you excelled at working with equations in algebra but struggled with trigonometric ratios in geometry? Before getting started with this part of the book, it's important for you to know your own strengths and weaknesses when it comes to math. That way, you can focus your energy on the math concepts that are either challenging for you or the concepts that will make the biggest difference in your score. Regardless of your path, you can make steady improvements as you prepare for the Math section of the SAT.

FYI

Calculators are permitted throughout the entire Math section of the SAT. The testing application provides a built-in graphing calculator, but you may also bring an approved personal calculator. Please see the calculator policy on the SAT website to make sure your calculator meets the required specifications. In general, as long as your calculator does not have internet or printout capabilities, it will be valid for use. Standard accepted models include the Texas Instruments TI-83 and TI-84 graphing calculators.

Self-Reflection: Math

- Which math courses did you take in high school, and which have you not taken (yet)?
- Which math concepts have historically been easier for you to understand?
- Which math concepts have historically been harder for you to understand?
- Did you experience any conditions during your high school experience (remote learning, recovering from surgery, etc.) that could have created gaps in your math learning? If so, what topics were covered during those gaps?
- Which math skills require more effort for you, and how does this inform your studying and learning?
- What math skills can make the biggest difference for your SAT score?

This chapter provides an overview of the SAT Math section and what you can expect. In Chapter 10, we'll talk about fundamental math skills, which will help remind you of the mathematical basics that serve test takers across the different math question domains. In Chapter 11, we'll focus on algebraic concepts. In Chapter 12, we'll cover concepts and skills in geometry and trigonometry. In Chapter 13, we'll prepare you for higher math, with a focus on nonlinear equations and functions, the focus of the Advanced Math question domain. In Chapter 14, we'll discuss both probability and statistics. If you feel pretty confident in your math skills and have already taken a lot of advanced math classes, you might find yourself skimming through these skill chapters. Otherwise, you'll want to review each chapter closely, focusing first on skills you've already learned before moving on to build new skills. You can also use your diagnostic testing results to guide

you to essential areas of improvement. Finally, in Chapter 15, we'll cover some skills and strategies you can use to do your best on the Math section of the SAT.

ALL ABOUT THE MATH SECTION

The Math section is designed to measure students' knowledge of critical college and career readiness skills in math. The Math section consists of two modules, each comprised of 22 questions, to be answered within 35 minutes; in other words, there are 44 questions in total, and students have 70 minutes to complete the entire section. Across each module, questions are arranged from easiest to most difficult. The questions are divided between multiple-choice and student-produced response (SPR) formats and may be presented as in-context questions (word problems) that address science, social studies, or other real-world topics. Questions on the SAT Math section will fall into one of four content domains: 1) Algebra, 2) Advanced Math, 3) Problem-Solving and Data Analysis, and 4) Geometry and Trigonometry.

The question categories are explained as follows.

ALGEBRA
(≈35% of Math section/13–15 questions)

These questions focus on your ability to analyze, create, and solve linear equations and inequalities, and to analyze and solve various types of equations and systems of equations using multiple techniques.

Specific Skill/Knowledge Testing Points for the Algebra content domain:

- Linear equations in one variable
- Linear equations in two variables
- Linear functions
- Systems of two linear equations in two variables
- Linear inequalities in one or two variables

ADVANCED MATH
(≈35% of Math section/13–15 questions)

These questions require you to demonstrate the skills and knowledge necessary to progress to more advanced math courses, including an understanding of absolute value, quadratic, exponential, polynomial, rational, radical, and other nonlinear equations.

Specific Skill/Knowledge Testing Points for the Advanced Math content domain:

- Equivalent expressions
- Nonlinear equations in one variable and systems of equations in two variables
- Nonlinear functions

FYI

With the shortened SAT Math section length, students have, on average, 1.59 minutes to spend on each question, in contrast to the 1.38 minutes allotted in the paper-based version.

PROBLEM-SOLVING AND DATA ANALYSIS (≈15% of Math section/5–7 questions)

In these questions, you will be asked to apply quantitative reasoning to ratios, rates, and proportional relationships; demonstrate understanding and application of unit rate; and analyze and interpret one- and two-variable data.

Specific Skill/Knowledge Testing Points for the Problem-Solving and Data Analysis content domain:

- Ratios, rates, proportional relationships, and units
- Percentages
- One-variable data: distributions and measures of center and spread
- Two-variable data: models and scatterplots
- Probability and conditional probability
- Inference from sample statistics and margin of error
- Evaluating statistical claims: observational studies and experiments

GEOMETRY AND TRIGONOMETRY (≈15% of Math section/5–7 questions)

These questions test your ability to solve problems focusing on area and volume; lines, angles, triangles, and trigonometry; and circles.

Specific Skill/Knowledge Testing Points for the Geometry and Trigonometry content domain:

- Area and volume
- Lines, angles, and triangles
- Right triangles and trigonometry
- Circles

SCORING TABLE

In Chapter 2, you completed a diagnostic test to help gauge your current skills and knowledge when it comes to what's covered on the SAT. As you work through this part of the book, consider the score you're aiming for, especially if you're applying to colleges whose applicants tend to receive certain score ranges on the SAT. While the scoring table used here is a simplified version of that used on the actual SAT, we've created a table that can help you anticipate how your raw score (0–44 questions) might translate into a scaled score (200–800). Please note that this is an estimate and not an exact reflection of official SAT scoring metrics.

RAW SCORE TO SCALED SCORE CONVERSION

Raw Score	Lower Range	Upper Range
44	790	800
43	780	800
42	770	800
41	760	790
40	750	780
39	740	770
38	730	760
37	710	740
36	690	720
35	670	700
34	650	680
33	620	650
32	600	630
31	590	620
30	570	600
29	560	590
28	550	580
27	530	560
26	510	540
25	500	530
24	480	510
23	470	500
22	460	490

21	440	470
20	420	450
19	390	420
18	380	410
17	370	400
16	360	390
15	350	380
14	340	370
13	330	360
12	320	350
11	300	330
10	290	320
9	280	310
8	250	280
7	220	250
6	200	220
5	200	210
4	200	200
3	200	200
2	200	200
1	200	200
0	200	200

TYPES OF MATH QUESTIONS

Approximately three-fourths of the Math section questions are in multiple-choice (MC) format with four options; the remaining questions are in the student-produced response, or SPR, format. For SPR format, students must enter their responses to the questions in the test delivery platform.

Multiple-Choice Questions

Multiple-choice math questions on the SAT are easier than those on the math tests you take in class because the answers are right there in front of you. As you know from taking other standardized tests, multiple-choice questions always give you the answer. You just have to figure out which answer is the correct one. So even if you aren't sure and have to guess, you can use estimating to narrow your choices and improve your odds. Some multiple-choice questions ask to solve a given equation or system of equations, while others are presented in the form of word problems. Some include graphs, charts, or tables that you will be asked to interpret. All of the multiple-choice questions have four answer choices. These choices are arranged in order when the answers are numbers, usually from smallest to largest, but occasionally from largest to smallest.

Student-Produced Response Questions

Student-produced response (SPR) questions are so named because you must do the calculations and find the answer on your own; there are no multiple-choice answers from which to choose. Unlike multiple-choice questions, for which there is only one correct response listed among the answer choices, SPR questions may have more than one correct answer. However, students are instructed to provide only one answer per question. Additionally, the answers to SPR questions can only be numeric values—no symbols or equations are required.

Many students are intimidated by SPR questions. However, SPR questions test the exact same mathematical concepts as the multiple-choice questions. The differences are that there are no answer choices with which

DISTRIBUTION OF MC AND SPR QUESTION FORMATS ACROSS CONTENT DOMAINS

Format	Algebra	Advanced Math	Problem-Solving/ Data Analysis	Geometry/ Trigonometry	Total
MC	10–11	10–11	4–5	4–5	28–32
SPR	3–4	3–4	1–2	1–2	8–12

to work, and there are a few rules to remember about entering your answers to get the credit you deserve for solving the problem correctly. You will be prepared for the math concepts, so here's what you need to keep in mind when entering your responses.

- If you find more than one correct answer, enter only one correct answer.
- You can enter up to 5 characters for a positive answer and up to 6 characters (including the negative sign) for a negative answer.
- If your answer is a fraction that doesn't fit in the provided space, enter the decimal equivalent.
- If your answer is a decimal that doesn't fit in the provided space, enter it by truncating or rounding at the fourth digit.
- If your answer is a mixed number, $\left(\text{e.g., } 3\frac{1}{2}\right)$, enter it as an improper fraction (7/2) or its decimal equivalent. (3.5).
- Don't enter symbols such as percent signs, commas, or dollar signs.

SPR QUESTION ANSWER FORMS

Answer	Acceptable entry	Unacceptable entry: will not receive credit
1.5	1.5	11/2
	1.50	1 1/2
	3/2	
$\frac{2}{3}$	2/3	0.66
	.6666	.66
	.6667	0.67
	0.666	.67
	0.667	
$-\frac{1}{3}$	−1/3	−.33
	−.3333	−0.33
	−0.333	

SAMPLE QUESTIONS

Here we've presented four sample questions. The first is an Advanced Math: Nonlinear Functions question, the second is a Problem-Solving and Data Analysis: Probability SPR question, the third is an Algebra: Linear Inequalities question, and the fourth is a Geometry and Trigonometry: Right Triangles SPR question.

EXAMPLE

If $f(x) = 1 - 2^x$, which of the following equals $f(2x + 3)$?

A. $1 - 8(4^x)$

B. $1 - 16^{2x}$

C. $1 - 32^x$

D. $-4^x - 7$

The correct answer is A. Calculate as follows:

$$\begin{aligned} f(2x+3) &= 1-2^{2x+3} \\ &= 1-2^{2x}\left(2^3\right) \\ &= 1-\left(2^2\right)^x \cdot 8 \\ &= 1-4^x \cdot 8 \\ &= 1-8\left(4^x\right) \end{aligned}$$

In a ring toss game, 200 bottles are labeled on the bottom with S, M, L, or XL to indicate the prize size; 110 bottles are labeled S, 60 labeled M, 25 labeled L, and 5 labeled XL. What is the probability of a person winning either an M or L prize?

Answer: ______

The correct answer is 0.425. Because you're looking for the probability of getting the ring around the neck of either an M or L bottle, you can combine the numbers of medium and large prizes. Then, divide the sum of the number of medium prizes and number of large prizes by the total number of bottles to get the probability:

$$\frac{60+25}{200}=\frac{85}{200}=\frac{17}{40}=0.425$$

To cater meals, Esayari Inn charges a $115 set-up fee plus $9.75 per person. Miranda has a budget, *b*, from her company and wants to plan a holiday brunch using Esayari. Which of the following inequalities will help Miranda calculate how much money she needs for brunch for *p* people?

A. $115p > b - 9.75$

B. $9.75b \leq b - 115 + p$

C. $9.75p + 115 \leq b$

D. $115 + 9.75p > b$

The correct answer is C. Each person, *p*, will cost $9.75, so the expression for total cost based on the number of people is 9.75*p*. The set-up fee is $115, so that must be added to the total cost: $9.75p + 115$. This total must be less than or equal to the budget *b*, so $9.75p + 115 \leq b$. In choice A, you did not apply the two dollar amounts to the correct quantities. Choice B should not have a *p* on the right side, and the first term should be 9.75*p*, not 9.75*b*. Choice D has the wrong inequality sign.

If the length of the hypotenuse of a right triangle is 5 and the length of one of the legs is 4, what is the length of the other leg?

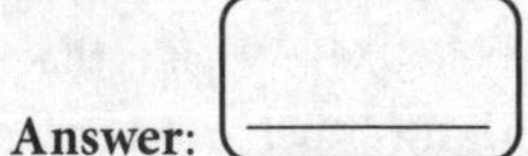

The correct answer is 3. If you recognized that the sides given fit the ratio of a 3-4-5 right triangle, you would immediately know that the length of the remaining leg is 3. If you did not realize this, you could use the Pythagorean theorem to solve for the length of the unknown side. The Pythagorean theorem says that for right triangles, $(\text{hypotenuse})^2 = (\text{leg } 1)^2 + (\text{leg } 2)^2$. In this case, $5^2 = 4^2 + x^2$, which simplifies to $25 = 16 + x^2$. Thus, $9 = x^2$, and $x = 3$.

COMMON CHALLENGES

Some common challenges test takers experience on the Math section of the SAT include the following:

- **Time management:** Even though the time allotted per question has been extended a bit, you still will need to work quickly and not get bogged down on any one problem. As such, it'll be important to be aware of your own skills and what math concepts you haven't encountered yet in your education. This will help you recognize when you might need to guess on a specific question.
- **Understanding the problem:** Some test takers may struggle to understand the wording of the questions, identify the important information needed to solve the problem, or determine the goal of the question. This can lead to errors and frustration. We'll provide helpful strategies for how to navigate complex problems later on in this part of the book.
- **Selecting the appropriate method:** There are often multiple ways to solve a problem on the Math section of the SAT, and test takers may struggle to choose the most efficient or effective method. This can result in lost time and incorrect answers. We'll discuss tools for how to solve problems in simple and efficient ways in Chapter 15.
- **Algebraic manipulation:** Algebraic manipulation is a key component of the Math section of the SAT, and many students struggle with this concept. This can make it difficult to solve certain types of problems, especially those that involve equations or systems of equations. If you struggle with algebraic equations, focus your studies on Chapter 11.
- **Geometry:** Geometry is another area that can be challenging for some students on the Math section of the SAT. This is especially true for students who have not taken a geometry course recently or who struggle with spatial reasoning. If this is one area you struggle with, pay close attention to Chapter 12.

Look back at your responses to the self-reflection exercise at the beginning of this chapter. Do any of your responses overlap with the common challenges we've covered here? If so, how might you focus your time and energy knowing where you excel and where you struggle with math? Remember, use this part of the book in the way that makes the most sense for you. Be mindful of where you can simply brush up on your existing skills, where you should focus your time and attention to improve, and which concepts or skills are more advanced than where you're currently at in your math education.

SUMMING IT UP

- The SAT Math section consists of 44 questions split into two modules, each consisting of 22 questions. Students have 70 minutes to complete the entire section. Two types of questions are presented in the section: multiple-choice, where you will choose the correct answer for the four answer choices provided, and student-produced response, where you must enter your response to the questions.
- Questions on the Math section of the SAT will fall into one of four content domains: 1) Algebra, 2) Advanced Math, 3) Problem-Solving and Data Analysis, and 4) Geometry and Trigonometry.
- A built-in graphing calculator is available in the Bluebook test delivery application for use throughout the entire Math section. If you prefer to use a personal calculator, see the SAT website for guidelines on acceptable calculators for test day.
- Some challenges you might encounter on the SAT Math section include managing your time, navigating complex problems, approaching certain math concepts like algebra or geometry, and using the most effective method for solving a problem. As you go through the next six chapters in this part, don't feel obligated to read every chapter word for word. Instead, focus your attention on where you struggle the most and master the strategies that will help you compensate for any areas where you feel less prepared or confident.

CHAPTER

Fundamental SAT® Math Skills

FUNDAMENTAL SAT® MATH SKILLS

OVERVIEW

The following concepts represent fundamental math knowledge that students typically acquire throughout middle school and their high school careers. Some of these concepts are directly tested by the SAT while others form the foundation of knowledge for different test domains. For instance, ratios, proportions, and percentages will come up as part of the Problem-Solving and Data Analysis domain. At the same time, ratios and proportional thinking may factor into certain Geometry and Trigonometry questions. The basics of working with lines and linear expressions may be directly needed for Algebra domain questions while also serving to help you answer Advanced Math and Geometry and Trigonometry questions.

10

In some way, you will need to use the information that follows to answer questions accurately and efficiently in the SAT Math modules. Mastery of this information is essential to improving your performance and achieving higher scores. In conjunction with the results from your Chapter 2 Diagnostic Test, determine which concepts you need to review. Use example questions throughout the chapter to assess your understanding and use the Test Yourself at the end of the chapter to identify any areas for further review.

NUMBERS AND OPERATIONS

To perform well with SAT math questions, you need to develop (or just review) the vocabulary and basic operations that will come to play a role in most of the questions on the test in some way or another. The following section will discuss different types of numbers, mathematical properties, order of operations, factors and multiples, prime numbers, exponents and roots, fractions, and absolute value.

Number Types

In math, various terms exist to describe the array of numbers used for counting and calculations. The ability to distinguish whole numbers, integers, and rational and irrational numbers can keep you from selecting incorrect answer choices on your exam.

TYPES OF NUMBERS		
Number Type	**Definition**	**Examples**
Whole Numbers	Positive numbers, including 0	0, 1, 2, 73, 546
Integers	All whole numbers and negative numbers—excluding decimals and fractions	–54, –6, 0, 9, 43
Rational Numbers	Numbers that result from dividing two integers	$\frac{1}{3}, \frac{3}{5}, -\frac{7}{3}$
Irrational Numbers	All real numbers that are not rational numbers; have nonterminating, nonrepeating decimals	pi (π) $\sqrt{2} = 1.41421356237...$ $\sqrt{3} = 1.73205080756...$

Properties and Identities

When studying math, it's important to understand how properties describe the behavior of numbers in certain situations. Properties and identities in math are rules that have been proven over time to be consistent. Knowing these can help simplify the process of solving problems because you can count on the fact that certain things will always function in predictable ways. To add to your confidence on your exam, become thoroughly familiar with the rules in this section, and commit to memory as many properties and rules as possible.

Here's a list of properties and identities along with definitions and examples. You may need to refer to this section as we get into more advanced math in the next two chapters, such as when solving algebraic equations.

PROPERTIES AND IDENTITIES		
Name	**Definition**	**Example**
Commutative Property	In addition and multiplication, order does not affect outcome	$7 + 8 = 8 + 7$ $3 \times 5 = 5 \times 3$
Distributive Property	Given an equation, $a(b + c)$, you can distribute the value of a to the value inside the parentheses	$7(2 + 8) = 7 \times 2 + 7 \times 8 = 14 + 56 = 70$
Associative Property	In addition and multiplication, changing how numbers are grouped will not change the result	$2(5 \times 4) = 5(2 \times 4) = 4(2 \times 5)$ $3 + (5 + 2) = 2 + (3 + 5) = 5 + (2 + 3)$
Identity Property	Any number added to zero will not change; any number multiplied by 1 will not change	$15 + 0 = 15$ $15 \times 1 = 15$
Reflexive Property	A number is always equal to itself	$a = a$
Symmetric Property	If $a = b$, then $b = a$	If $x = 10$, then $10 = x$
Transitive Property	If $a = b$ and $b = c$, then $a = c$	If $a = b$ and $b = 3 + 4$, then $a = 3 + 4$
Substitution Property	If $a = b$, then a can be substituted for b	If $a = 7$ and $b = 7$, then $a + 3 = 10$ and $b + 3 = 10$
Additive Identity	Any variable added to zero will remain unchanged	$x + 0 = x$
Multiplicative Property of Zero	Any number multiplied by zero equals zero	$1 \times 0 = 0$ $4{,}962 \times 0 = 0$
Multiplicative Inverse	Any number multiplied by its reciprocal will equal 1	$2 \times \frac{1}{2} = 1$ $12 \times \frac{1}{12} = 1$

Operations with Signed Numbers

Signed numbers are multiplied as any other numbers would be, with the following exceptions:

The product of two negative numbers is positive.

$(-3) \times (-6) = +18$

The product of two positive numbers is positive.

$(+3.05) \times (+6) = +18.30$

The product of a negative and positive number is negative.

$\left(+4\frac{1}{2}\right) \times (-3) = -13\frac{1}{2}$

$(+1) \times (-1) \times (+1) = -1$

As with multiplication, the division of signed numbers requires you to observe three rules.

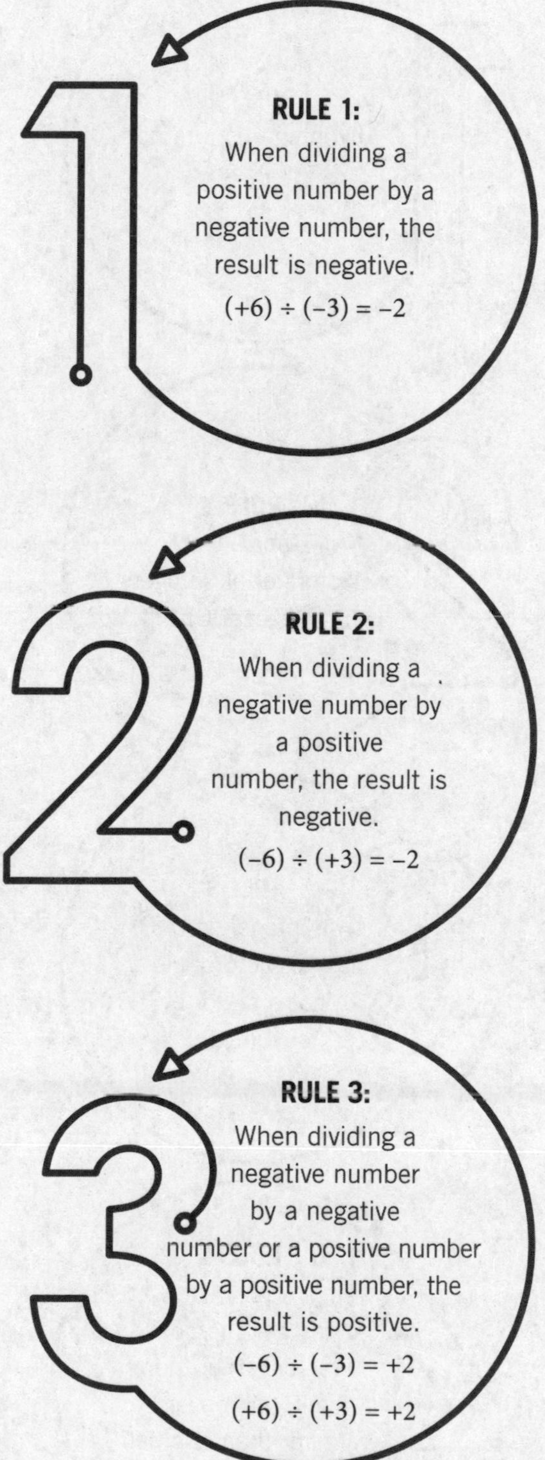

RULE 1:
When dividing a positive number by a negative number, the result is negative.
(+6) ÷ (−3) = −2
RULE 2:
When dividing a negative number by a positive number, the result is negative.
(−6) ÷ (+3) = −2
RULE 3:
When dividing a negative number by a negative number or a positive number by a positive number, the result is positive.
(−6) ÷ (−3) = +2
(+6) ÷ (+3) = +2

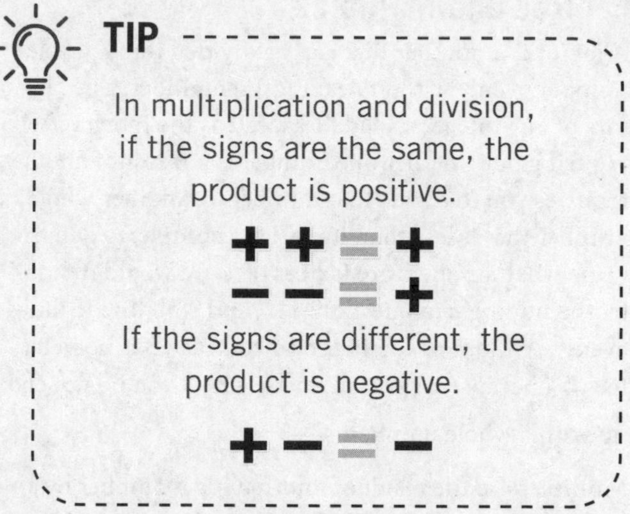

TIP
In multiplication and division, if the signs are the same, the product is positive.
+ + = +
− − = +
If the signs are different, the product is negative.
+ − = −

Order of Operations

One of the most important things to know when solving math problems is where to start. You will often encounter problems that have a series of operations to perform. Fortunately, there are rules to explain what goes first. We call these rules the order of operations. The order of operations ensures that, by solving operations in this order, you'll always be able to arrive at the same correct solution. At this stage of mathematics, there are only four rules to know. They are as follows:

1. Solve operations within parentheses first, starting with the innermost parentheses.
2. Solve operations with exponents and square roots next.
3. Solve multiplication and division from left to right.
4. Solve addition and subtraction from left to right.

These rules inform where you should start when performing calculations. They are often summarized with the acronym PEMDAS (Parentheses, Exponents, Multiplication, Division, Addition, Subtraction). As you work through problems, note each step carefully to ensure you don't miss any operations along the way.

Factors and Multiples

A factor is a number that can be divided into a whole number evenly without leaving a remainder. The factors of any integer include 1 as well as the integer itself. Figuring out whether one number is a factor of another requires you to divide that number by another whole number that is less than itself. For example, to determine what numbers are factors of 4, we would divide 4 by the numbers in question: 1, 2, and 4 all divide into 4 evenly, without a remainder. In contrast, 3 is not a factor of 4 because when you divide 4 by 3 you do not end up with a whole number: $4 \div 3 = 1\frac{1}{3}$.

Multiples are the result of multiplying a number by an integer. Finding a list of multiples can be as simple as selecting a number and working through a series of multiplication equations.

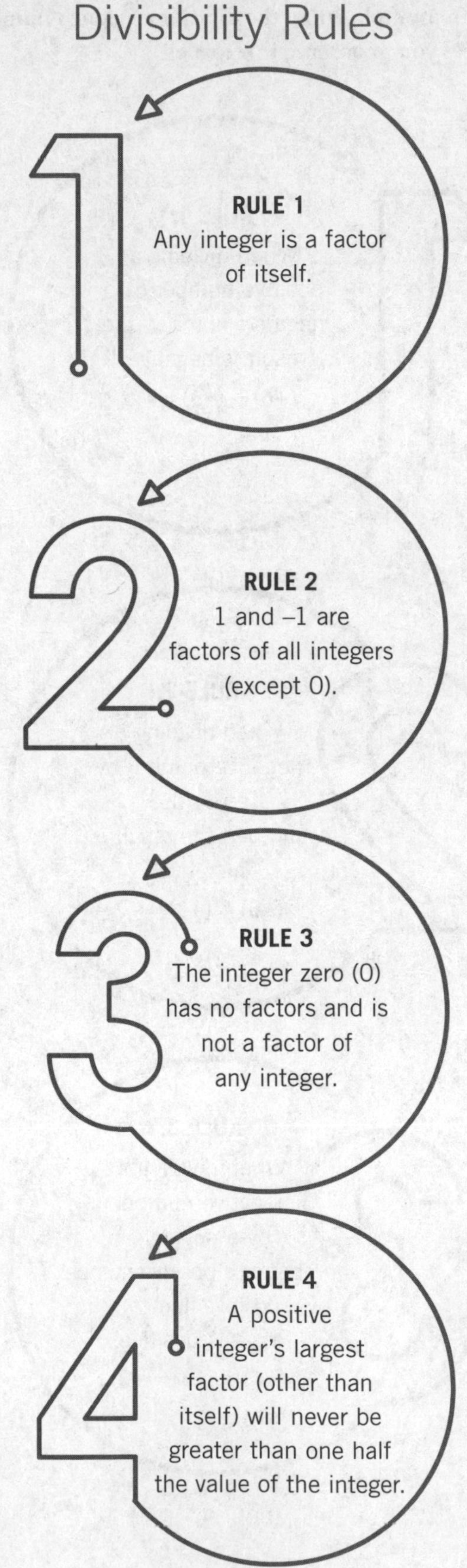

Divisibility Rules
RULE 1
Any integer is a factor of itself.
RULE 2
1 and –1 are factors of all integers (except 0).
RULE 3
The integer zero (0) has no factors and is not a factor of any integer.
RULE 4
A positive integer's largest factor (other than itself) will never be greater than one half the value of the integer.

EXAMPLE

What are the first four multiples of the number 2, starting with the integer 1?

Solution

$$1 \times 2 = \mathbf{2}$$

$$2 \times 2 = \mathbf{4}$$

$$3 \times 2 = \mathbf{6}$$

$$4 \times 2 = \mathbf{8}$$

Starting with the integer 1, the first four multiples of the number 2 are **2, 4, 6, 8.**

Note that multiples **must** be the result of multiplying a number by an integer. For instance, this means that a number multiplied by a fraction would **not** result in a multiple for that number. Since 0 is in fact an integer, this does mean that you can use it to find a multiple of any number. The result simply is always 0.

Rules about Factors

1. Complementing factors are multiples. If f is a factor of n, then n is a multiple of f. For example, 8 is a multiple of 2 for the same reason that 2 is a factor of 8: because $8 \div 2 = 4$, which is an integer.
2. A prime number is a positive integer that is divisible by only two positive integers: itself and 1. Zero (0) and 1 are not considered prime numbers; 2 is the first prime number. Here are all the prime numbers less than 50:

   2 3 5 7

   11 13 17 19

   23 29

   31 37

   41 43 47

There are certain tests you can run for divisibility, as seen in the following chart:

TEST FOR DIVISIBILITY	
To test if a number is divisible by:	**Check to see:**
2	if it is even
3	if the sum of the digits is divisible by 3
4	if the number formed by the last two digits is divisible by 4
5	if its last digit is a 5 or 0
6	if it is even and the sum of the digits is divisible by 3
8	if the number formed by the last three digits is divisible by 8
9	if the sum of the digits is divisible by 9
10	if its last digit is 0

As you can see, factors, multiples, and divisibility are different aspects of the same concept.

Greatest Common Factor

The term *greatest common factor* (GCF) refers to the largest number that can be factored into two numbers cleanly (that is, without a remainder). For example, the greatest common factor of 10 and 15 is 5. For 10 and 20, the GCF is 10. How did we get those answers? Let's look at a pair of numbers.

If you are asked to find the greatest common factor of 16 and 32, you can start by listing out the factors of each.

16: 1, 2, 4, 8, **16**

32: 1, 2, 4, 8, **16**, 32

Here, we can easily see that the greatest common factor is the number 16.

TIP

Don't be confused by the term *Greatest Common Divisor,* as the terms *divisor* and *factor* have the same meaning. They are both numbers that can divide into something.

There may be number pairs, like (7, 13), that don't have any factors other than 1 in common. When this happens, the numbers can be described as "relatively prime." Remember that a prime number is a number that is only divisible by itself and 1.

Least Common Multiple

The term *least common multiple* (LCM) refers to the smallest whole number into which each number in a list divides evenly. For example, the GCF of {18, 36, 63} is 9, and the LCM of {18, 36, 63} is 252.

You'll need to find the least common multiple when you need to add or subtract fractions with different denominators, as you'll need each to have the same denominator to be able to add them together. However, you will likely use greatest common factor to reduce or simplify the result. To find a common multiple, you can multiply the listed values together. But to find the least common multiple, you'll need to make a list of the different multiples for each number in the set or use prime factorization, which is discussed in the next section.

Prime Numbers and Factorization

Prime numbers are divisible by only two integers, themselves and 1. Another way of saying this is to state that a prime number only has two multiples: itself and 1. 11 is a prime number since the only integers that evenly divide into 11 are 11 and 1. Notice that 1 is not a prime number since it has one multiple (1×1) and not two.

It is a good idea to be familiar with the smaller prime numbers because you might need them at your fingertips for a problem. Here are the first ten: 2, 3, 5, 7, 11, 13, 17, 19, 23, and 29.

Any integer that is not prime can be written as a product of prime numbers in only one way. This product is known as the *prime factorization* of the integer. In order to factor an integer into primes, we take the integer and write it as a product of two smaller integers. If either or both of these smaller integers is not prime, write it as a product of smaller integers. Keep going until there are only prime numbers in the product. Note that sometimes you will have a choice as to how to factor a number. For example, if you are trying to factor 30 into primes, you can begin by writing $30 = 2 \times 15$ or $30 = 5 \times 6$. Regardless of the choices that you make, you will always end up with the same prime factorization.

Suppose we began by writing $30 = 2 \times 15$. The factor 2 is prime, but 15 is not. Therefore, we must break 15 down into $15 = 3 \times 5$. Thus, the prime factorization of 30 is $2 \times 3 \times 5$. We say that 30 has three distinct prime factors: 2, 3, and 5.

Consider the prime factorization of 48. Note that $48 = 6 \times 8$. The integer 6 can be further broken down into 2×3, while 8 can be broken down into $2 \times 2 \times 2$. Thus, the prime factorization of 48 is $2 \times 2 \times 2 \times 2 \times 3$; i.e., $48 = 2^4 \times 3$. The number 48 has two distinct prime factors, 2 and 3. The factor 2 appears four times, and the factor 3 appears only once.

Prime factorization can be used to find the least common multiple in a group of numbers. Consider the LCM of 40 and 75. You can multiply them together to find a common multiple of 3,000. But they have a lower common multiple, their LCM. It can be found by taking the numbers through prime factorization. The number 40 has as its prime factors $2 \times 2 \times 2 \times 5$. The number 75 has prime factors of $3 \times 2 \times 5 \times 5$. Write those factors in their exponent forms. So, the factors of 40 become $2^3 \times 5^1$, and the factors of 75 become $3^1 \times 2^1 \times 5^2$. Then take the unique factors with the highest powers and multiply them together. In this case, you would multiply $2^3 \times 5^2 \times 3^1$. That equals 600, the LCM of 40 and 75. If you wanted to find the LCM of 40, 75, and 540, you would use the same process. You would end up with the following: $3^3 \times 2^3 \times 5^2$, or 5,400.

Exponents

An exponent represents the number of times that a number (referred to as the "base number") is multiplied by itself. In the exponential number 2^4, the base number is 2 and the exponent is 4. To calculate the value of 2^4 means to multiply 2 by itself 4 times: $2^4 = 2 \times 2 \times 2 \times 2 = 16$. An exponent is also referred to as a power, meaning you can express the exponential number 2^4 as "2 to the 4th power."

There are numerous rules for working with exponents with different operations. Use the following table as a guide:

RULES FOR EXPONENTS	
Product	$a^m a^n = a^{m+n}$
Product of a power	$(a^m)^n = a^{mn}$
Quotient to a power	$\left(\frac{a}{b}\right)^n = \frac{a^n}{b^n}$
Quotient	$\frac{a^m}{a^n} = a^{m-n}$
Zero exponent	$a^0 = 1$
Negative exponent	$a^{-n} = \frac{1}{a^n}$
Inversion	$\left(\frac{a}{b}\right)^{-n} = \left(\frac{b}{a}\right)^n$
Fractional powers	$a^{\frac{m}{n}} = \sqrt[n]{a^m}$

Here is an example that demonstrates several of these rules:

Simplify the expression: $\left(\frac{x^2y^4}{x^{-1}y}\right)^{-2}$

Apply the rules for exponents within the parentheses and then apply the –2 power. Note that a variable with no exponent is assumed to have an exponent of 1:

$$\begin{aligned}\left(\frac{x^2y^4}{x^{-1}y}\right)^{-2} &= \left(x^{2-(-1)}y^{4-1}\right)^{-2} \\ &= \left(x^3y^3\right)^{-2} \\ &= x^{-6}y^{-6} \\ &= \frac{1}{x^6y^6}\end{aligned}$$

Here are some common errors when working with exponents. Keep these issues in mind when studying for the SAT:

COMMON ERRORS WITH EXPONENTS	
Error	**Interpretation**
$-a^2 \neq (-a)^2$ $(-1)a^2 \neq (-a)(-a)$	If the negative sign is outside the parentheses of a quantity being squared, then the square does not apply to it.
$(a+b)^n \neq a^n + b^n$	The power of a sum is not equal to the sum of the powers.
$\frac{a^n}{b^m} \neq \left(\frac{a}{b}\right)^{n-m}$	You cannot write the quotient of terms with different bases raised to different powers as a single quotient raised to a power.
$a^n \bullet b^n \neq (a \bullet b)^{n+m}$	You cannot write the product of terms with different bases raised to different powers as a single product raised to a power.

PRACTICE

Which of the following is equivalent to $(-4x^3)^2$?

A. $16x^6$

B. $-16x^6$

C. $8x^6$

D. $-4x^5$

The correct answer is A. For this problem, it is important to remember the rules of exponents. When a product is raised to a power, each of the terms must be raised to that power. So $(-4x^3)^2$ is equal to $(-4)^2 \times (x^3)^2$. When a power is raised to another power, you multiply the exponents. So $(-4)^2 \times (x^3)^2$ is equal to $(-4)^2 \times (x^6)$. Now evaluate: $(-4)^2 \times (x^6) = 16 \times (x^6) = 16x^6$.

Roots and Radicals

The square root of a number n is a number that you "square" (multiply it by itself, or raise to the power of 2), to obtain n. The radical sign signifies square root and looks like this: $\sqrt{\ }$. A simple example of a square root is $2 = \sqrt{4}$ (the square root of 4) because 2×2 (or 2^2) $= 4$.

The cube root of a number n is a number that you raise to the power of 3 (multiply by itself twice) to obtain n. You determine higher roots (for example, the "fourth root") in the same way. Except for square roots, the radical sign will indicate the root to be taken. For example:

$2 = \sqrt[3]{8}$ (the cube root of 8) because $2 \times 2 \times 2$ (or 2^3) $= 8$

$2 = \sqrt[4]{16}$ (the fourth root of 16) because $2 \times 2 \times 2 \times 2$ (or 2^4) $= 16$

Roots can be expressed using fractional exponents. The following notation is used:

$$\sqrt{a} = a^{\frac{1}{2}}$$

$$\sqrt[3]{a} = a^{\frac{1}{3}}$$

$$\vdots$$

$$\sqrt[n]{a} = a^{\frac{1}{n}}$$

Using the exponent rules, we have the more general definition:

$$\sqrt[n]{a^m} = (a^m)^{\frac{1}{n}} = a^{\left(m \cdot \frac{1}{n}\right)} = \left(a^{\frac{1}{n}}\right)^m = a^{\frac{m}{n}}$$

For instance:

$$8^{\frac{2}{3}} = \left(8^{\frac{1}{3}}\right)^2 = (2)^2 = 4$$

$$16^{\frac{3}{2}} = \left(16^{\frac{1}{2}}\right)^3 = 4^3 = 64$$

The following are useful properties of radicals to master before you take the SAT.

TIP

A common error is to apply the radical to each individual term of a sum. Note that the square root of a sum is not the sum of the square roots. In this example, note that $-6\sqrt{5} + 4\sqrt{7} \neq (-6+4)\sqrt{5+7}$. The same goes for cube roots.

PROPERTIES OF RADICALS	
Radical Rule (in symbols)	**Interpretation**
$\left(\sqrt{a}\right)^2 = a$ $\left(\sqrt[3]{a}\right)^3 = a$	Raising an *n*th root to the *n*th power gives back the original radicand.
$\sqrt{a \cdot b} = \sqrt{a} \cdot \sqrt{b}$, when a ≥ 0 and b ≥ 0.	The square root of a product is the product of the square roots.
$\sqrt{\frac{a}{b}} = \frac{\sqrt{a}}{\sqrt{b}}$, when a ≥ 0 and b > 0.	The square root of a quotient is the quotient of the square roots.
$\frac{1}{\sqrt{a}} = \frac{1}{\sqrt{a}} \cdot \frac{\sqrt{a}}{\sqrt{a}} = \frac{\sqrt{a}}{a}$, when a > 0.	You can clear a square root from the denominator of a fraction by multiplying the numerator and denominator of the fraction by the square root. (This is often called "multiplying by the conjugate" or "rationalizing the denominator.")
If $0 < a < b$, then $\sqrt{a} < \sqrt{b}$.	If *a* is less than *b*, then you can take the square root on both sides of the inequality without having to reverse the sign.

To simplify an integer under a radical, you can break it into its factors. The initial factors you choose will affect how many steps you need in order to reach a simplified form. Observe the following example factored in several different ways.

$$\sqrt{72} = \sqrt{2 \cdot 36} = \sqrt{2 \cdot 2 \cdot 18} = \sqrt{2 \cdot 2 \cdot 2 \cdot 9} = 2\sqrt{2 \cdot 9} = 2 \cdot 3\sqrt{2} = 6\sqrt{2}$$
$$\sqrt{72} = \sqrt{2 \cdot 4 \cdot 9} = \sqrt{2} \cdot \sqrt{4} \cdot \sqrt{9} = \sqrt{2} \cdot 2 \cdot 3 = 6\sqrt{2}$$
$$\sqrt{72} = \sqrt{3 \cdot 24} = \sqrt{3 \cdot 3 \cdot 8} = 3\sqrt{2 \cdot 4} = 3 \cdot 2\sqrt{2} = 6\sqrt{2}$$
$$\sqrt{72} = \sqrt{9} \cdot \sqrt{8} = 3\sqrt{4 \cdot 2} = 3 \cdot 2\sqrt{2} = 6\sqrt{2}$$
$$\sqrt{72} = \sqrt{2 \cdot 36} = 6\sqrt{2}$$

Note that selecting a factor that is a perfect square will allow you to reduce the amount of work you need to perform. In the first example, if we had not continued the prime factorization, we would have been able to simplify to $6\sqrt{2}$ after the first step (36 is a perfect square).

If the terms you want to add have the same radical parts, just add or subtract the coefficients:

$$2\sqrt{5} - 6\sqrt{5} =$$
$$(2-6)\sqrt{5} = -4\sqrt{5}$$

However, terms that have different radical parts cannot be combined:

$$3\sqrt{5} + 4\sqrt{7} - 9\sqrt{5} =$$
$$(3-9)\sqrt{5} + 4\sqrt{7} = -6\sqrt{5} + 4\sqrt{7}$$

Here is another example that involves a rational expression:

Simplify $\frac{56\sqrt{7}}{28\sqrt{42}}$.

For this example, you can apply the rules of multiplying fractions to simplify this expression:

$$\frac{56\sqrt{7}}{28\sqrt{42}} = \frac{2 \cdot \cancel{28}\sqrt{7}}{\cancel{28}\sqrt{7 \cdot 6}} = \frac{2\cancel{\sqrt{7}}}{\cancel{\sqrt{7}} \cdot \sqrt{6}} = \frac{2}{\sqrt{6}}$$

Then, you can rationalize the denominator (removing its root symbol) by multiplying the numerator and denominator by $\sqrt{6}$:

$$\underbrace{\frac{56\sqrt{7}}{28\sqrt{42}} = \frac{2}{\sqrt{6}}}_{\text{From above}} = \underbrace{\frac{2}{\sqrt{6}} \cdot \frac{\sqrt{6}}{\sqrt{6}}}_{\text{Rationalizing the denominator}} = \frac{2\sqrt{6}}{6} = \frac{\sqrt{6}}{3}$$

Estimating roots, such as $\sqrt{47}$ and $\sqrt[3]{11}$, can be tricky. For instance, it's not easy to compute $\sqrt{47}$. In a case like this, you can determine numbers with more obvious square roots on either side of 47.

You know that $6^2 = 36$ and that $7^2 = 49$. Further, you know that $36 < 47 < 49$. Therefore, you know $\underbrace{\sqrt{36}}_{=6} < \sqrt{47} < \underbrace{\sqrt{49}}_{=7}$, so that $6 < \sqrt{47} < 7$. The answer to $\sqrt{47}$ must lie somewhere between 6 and 7.

PRACTICE

Suppose that x, y, and z are positive real numbers. Which of the following is equivalent to the expression $\sqrt{8x^8y^2z^3}$?

A. $16x^3yz\sqrt{z}$

B. $2x^4yz\sqrt{2z}$

C. $8x^2y\sqrt{z^3}$

D. $4xyz$

The correct answer is B. Two properties are at play here, namely $\sqrt{a \cdot b} = \sqrt{a} \cdot \sqrt{b}$ and $\sqrt{a^2} = a$ whenever a > 0. The idea is to express the radicand as a product of squared terms and everything that is left over. Employing that strategy, we see that:

$$\begin{aligned}\sqrt{8x^8y^2z^3} &= \sqrt{2} \cdot \sqrt{4} \cdot \sqrt{\left(x^4\right)^2} \cdot \sqrt{y^2} \cdot \sqrt{z^2} \cdot \sqrt{z} \\ &= \sqrt{2} \cdot 2 \cdot \left(x^4\right) \cdot y \cdot z \cdot \sqrt{z} \\ &= 2 \cdot x^4 \cdot y \cdot z \cdot \sqrt{2} \cdot \sqrt{z} \\ &= 2 \cdot x^4 \cdot y \cdot z \cdot \sqrt{2z} \\ &= 2x^4yz\sqrt{2z}\end{aligned}$$

Fractions

A fraction is a part of a whole. For instance, there are 10 dimes in a dollar, so one dime is one-tenth of a dollar—one of ten equal parts. The fraction to represent one-tenth is written $\frac{1}{10}$. The top number of a fraction is called the numerator, and the bottom number is called the denominator. The denominator tells you how many equal parts the object or number is divided into, and the numerator tells you how many parts are represented.

$$\frac{3}{4}\begin{matrix}\leftarrow \text{numerator} \rightarrow \\ \leftarrow \text{denominator} \rightarrow\end{matrix}\frac{7}{8}$$

A proper fraction is one in which the numerator is less than the denominator. An improper fraction is one in which the numerator is the same as or greater than the denominator. $\frac{3}{5}$ is a proper fraction, but $\frac{5}{3}$ is an improper fraction. Sometimes, you will see an integer and a fraction together. This is called a mixed number, such as $2\frac{3}{5}$.

Here is a quick reference chart that shows how to handle arithmetic operations involving fractions. You can bookmark this page and come back to it if you get caught on a fraction problem and are unsure of the rules and how to apply them.

TIP

Need an easy way to remember which part of a fraction is which? Use alliteration to remember that the **d**enominator goes **d**own at the bottom.

OPERATIONS WITH FRACTIONS		
Arithmetic Operation	**Rule (in Symbols)**	**Interpretation**
Adding/ Subtracting	$\frac{a}{b} \pm \frac{c}{d} = \frac{ad \pm cb}{bd}$	When fractions have different denominators, first find a common denominator. Apply it to the fractions and then add or subtract the numerators.
Simplifying/ Reducing	$\frac{a \cdot c}{b \cdot c} = \frac{a}{b}$	You can cancel like factors in the numerator and denominator of a fraction to reduce it to lowest terms.
Multiplying by –1	$-\frac{a}{b} = \frac{-a}{b} = \frac{a}{-b}$	When multiplying a fraction by –1, you can multiply either the numerator or the denominator by –1, but NOT both.
Multiplying	$\frac{a}{b} \cdot \frac{c}{d} = \frac{ac}{bd}$	When multiplying two fractions, you can simply multiply their numerators and their denominators.
Dividing	$\frac{a}{b} \div \frac{c}{d} = \frac{a}{b} \cdot \frac{d}{c} = \frac{ad}{bc}$ $\frac{\frac{a}{b}}{\frac{c}{d}}$ means $\frac{a}{b} \div \frac{c}{d}$	When dividing two fractions, start by converting the quotient into a multiplication problem.

There are several errors test takers often make when working with fractions. You can prevent yourself from choosing incorrect answers when working with fractions on the SAT by observing the following rules.

COMMON ERRORS WITH FRACTIONS	
Error	**Comment**
$\frac{a}{b+c} \neq \frac{a}{b} + \frac{a}{c}$	You cannot pull a fraction apart as a sum of two fractions when the sum occurs in the denominator.
$\frac{a}{b} + \frac{c}{d} \neq \frac{a+c}{b+d}$	When adding fractions, do not simply add the numerators and denominators. First, get a common denominator.
$\frac{a}{a+b} \neq \frac{\not{a}}{\not{a}+b}$	You cannot cancel terms that are the same in the numerator and denominator. You can only cancel factors common to both.

Reciprocals

When working with fractions (or any numbers), you may need to find a fraction's reciprocal. Reciprocals can be boiled down to flipping something over. Defined, a reciprocal is $\frac{1}{x}$ where x is the number in question. For example, the reciprocal of $5 = \frac{1}{5}$ or 0.2 as a decimal. The following are numbers and their reciprocals:

$$17 = \frac{1}{17}$$

$$100 = \frac{1}{100}$$

$$42 = \frac{1}{42}$$

One thing to think about with a whole number is that 17 is the same as $\frac{17}{1}$. Keep that in mind not only with reciprocals but any time you have a mix of whole numbers and fractions. Finding the reciprocal of a fraction requires flipping the numerator and denominator. For example, to find the reciprocal of $\frac{4}{5}$, you flip the fraction over to get $\frac{5}{4}$.

Simplifying Fractions

A fraction can be simplified to its lowest terms if its numerator and denominator share a common factor. Here are a few simple examples:

$$\frac{6}{9} = \frac{\cancel{(3)}(2)}{\cancel{(3)}(3)} = \frac{2}{3}$$

(you can "cancel" or factor out the common factor 3)

$$\frac{21}{35} = \frac{\cancel{(7)}(3)}{\cancel{(7)}(5)} = \frac{3}{5}$$

(you can factor out the common factor 7)

Before you perform any operation with a fraction, always check to see if you can simplify it first. By reducing a fraction to its lowest terms, you will also simplify whatever operation you perform on it.

Adding and Subtracting Fractions

To add or subtract fractions with the same denominators, combine the numerators and keep the common denominator.

EXAMPLE

Find the difference between $\frac{7}{8}$ and $\frac{3}{8}$.

Solution

$\frac{7}{8} - \frac{3}{8} = \frac{4}{8}$ and simplified, $\frac{4}{8} = \frac{1}{2}$.

To add or subtract fractions with different denominators, you must first find the lowest common denominator, also known as the least common multiple. A common denominator is a number that can be divided by the denominators of all the fractions in the problem without a remainder. Finding the lowest common denominator is important to ensure that you have the simplest fraction.

EXAMPLE

Add the fractions $\frac{1}{4}$ and $\frac{1}{3}$.

Solution

Multiply the denominators to get $4 \times 3 = 12$. 12 can be divided by both 4 and 3:

$\frac{1}{4}$ is equivalent to $\frac{3}{12}$

$\frac{1}{3}$ is equivalent to $\frac{4}{12}$

To maintain equivalence, each numerator must be multiplied by the value used to reach the common denominator. We can now add the fractions because we have written equivalent fractions with a common denominator.

$$\frac{3}{12} + \frac{4}{12} = \frac{7}{12}$$

Therefore:

$$\frac{1}{4} + \frac{1}{3} = \frac{7}{12}$$

Seven-twelfths is in its simplest form because 7 and 12 do not have a whole number (other than 1) by which they are both divisible.

Multiplying and Dividing Fractions

When multiplying fractions, multiply numerators by numerators and denominators by denominators.

$$\frac{3}{5}\times\frac{4}{7}\times\frac{1}{5}=\frac{3\times4\times1}{5\times7\times5}=\frac{12}{175}$$

Try to work with numbers that are as small as possible.

You can make numbers smaller by dividing out common factors. Do this by dividing the numerator of any one fraction and the denominator of any one fraction by the same number.

$$\frac{\overset{1}{\cancel{3}}}{{}_{2}\cancel{4}}\times\frac{\overset{1}{\cancel{2}}}{{}_{3}\cancel{9}}=\frac{1\times1}{2\times3}=\frac{1}{6}$$

In this case, we divided the numerator of the first fraction and the denominator of the second fraction by 3, while the denominator of the first fraction and the numerator of the second fraction were divided by 2.

To divide by a fraction, multiply by the reciprocal of the divisor.

$$\frac{3}{16}\div\frac{1}{8}=\frac{3}{\cancel{16}_{2}}\times\frac{\overset{1}{\cancel{8}}}{1}=\frac{3}{2}=1\frac{1}{2}$$

Mixed Numbers and Improper Fractions

As noted earlier, a mixed number consists of a whole number along with a fraction. The number $4\frac{2}{3}$ is an example of a mixed number. Before combining fractions, you might need to convert mixed numbers to improper fractions (a fraction where the numerator is larger than the denominator). To convert, follow these three steps:

Multiply the denominator of the fraction by the whole number.

Add the product to the numerator of the fraction.

Place the sum over the denominator of the fraction.

For example, here's how to convert the mixed number $4\frac{2}{3}$ to an improper fraction:

$$4\frac{2}{3}=\frac{(3)(4)+2}{3}=\frac{14}{3}$$

To add or subtract mixed numbers, you can convert each one to an improper fraction, then find their lowest common denominator and combine them. Alternatively, you can add together the whole numbers, and add together the fractions separately.

A fraction that has a numerator greater than the denominator is an improper fraction. Examples of improper fractions include $\frac{3}{2}$, $\frac{12}{7}$, and $\frac{9}{5}$. Improper fractions can also be in their simplest forms when the numerator and denominator cannot be divided evenly by a number other than 1.

Improper fractions can be represented as mixed numbers and vice versa. Below are a few examples of how to rename a mixed number as an improper fraction.

EXAMPLES

Rename $2\frac{1}{4}$ as an improper fraction.

Solution

The whole number 2 contains 8 fourths, or $\frac{8}{4}$.

Add $\frac{1}{4}$ to it to write the equivalent fraction $\frac{9}{4}$.

Rename $\frac{9}{4}$ as a mixed number.

Solution

Divide the numerator by the denominator and use the remainder (R) as the fraction numerator:

$$9 \div 4 = 2\text{ R}1 \text{ or } 9 \div 4 = 2\frac{1}{4}$$

Absolute Value

A number line is a convenient way of illustrating the position of real numbers with respect to zero. The integers 7 and –7 are both 7 units away from 0, even though they exist on either side of 0. For any real number *a*, we use the absolute value of *a*, denoted $|a|$, to measure the distance between *a* and 0. Since distance is a nonnegative quantity, the definition has two parts:

$$|a| = \begin{cases} a, \text{ if } a \geq 0 \\ -a, \text{ if } a < 0 \end{cases}$$

For instance, $|8| = 8$ and $|-8| = -(-8) = 8$. This definition works for any type of real number: integers, fractions, decimal numbers, or irrational numbers.

The following are some useful properties of absolute value you should master before taking the SAT:

ABSOLUTE VALUE PROPERTIES

Property (in symbols)	Property (in words)
$\lvert a\rvert = b$ whenever $a = b$ or $a = -b$	The real numbers b and $-b$ are both $\lvert b\rvert$ units from the origin.
$\lvert a \bullet b\rvert = \lvert a\rvert \bullet \lvert b\rvert$	The absolute value of a product is the product of the absolute values.
$\left\lvert \frac{a}{b} \right\rvert = \frac{\lvert a\rvert}{\lvert b\rvert}$, whenever $b \neq 0$	The absolute value of a quotient is the quotient of the absolute values when the denominator does not equal 0.

Remember, when *a* and *b* have opposite signs, $|a + b| \neq |a| + |b|$. For example, $|-5 + 4| \neq |-5| + |4|$. The correct way of simplifying $|-5 + 4|$ is by first simplifying the whole expression inside the absolute value bars (much like parentheses). Then, when there is a single number enclosed by the absolute value bars, compute the absolute value. So $|-5 + 4| = |-1| = 1$. This is not equivalent to $|-5| + |4|$, which equals 9.

RATIOS, PROPORTIONS, RATES, DECIMALS, AND PERCENTAGES

Fundamental to math thinking, whether dealing with basic calculations or higher-level math, are the concepts of ratios and proportions, which embody part-to-whole thinking. On the SAT, ratios, proportions, and percentages can be tested under the domain of Problem-Solving and Data Analysis; however, the principles may also be vital to answering questions in Algebra, Advanced Math, and Geometry and Trigonometry.

Ratios

A ratio is a comparison of one quantity *x* to another quantity *y*, expressed as a fraction $\frac{x}{y}$, or sometimes using the notation *x*:*y* (read "*x* to *y*"). In plain English, this is interpreted as, "For every *x* of one type, there are *y* of the second type."

For example, if there are 3 girls to every 1 boy in a class, we say that the ratio of girls to boys is 3:1, or 3 to 1, and write the fraction $\frac{3}{1}$. Similarly, if there are 5 dogs for every 2 cats in an animal shelter, we say that the ratio of dogs to cats is 5:2, or 5 to 2, and write the fraction $\frac{5}{2}$. We could have instead described the ratio as 2 cats for every 5 dogs and said the ratio of cats to dogs is 2:5, writing the fraction as $\frac{2}{5}$. This conveys the same information. However, since $\frac{2}{5} \neq \frac{5}{2}$, the two ratios are not equal. The order in which the quantities appear in a ratio is important because we represent the ratio as a fraction.

Proportions

A proportion is an equation relating two ratios. In symbols, a proportion is expressed by setting two fractions equal to each other, say $\frac{a}{b} = \frac{c}{d}$. This establishes a relationship between the two fractions or ratios. Proportions arise when solving many different types of problems—for example, you'll use them in problems that ask you to change units of measurement and find side lengths of similar triangles.

Proportion problems are formulated when one ratio is known and one of the two quantities in an equivalent ratio is unknown. Since you can express any ratio as a fraction, you can set two equivalent ratios (also called proportionate ratios) equal to each other as fractions. For instance, the ratio 16:28 is proportionate to the ratio 4:7 because $\frac{16}{28}=\frac{4}{7}$.

If one of the four terms is missing from the equation (the proportion), you can solve for the missing term using the following method:

01 **Simplify the known fraction, if possible.**

02 **Cross multiply the numbers you know.**

03 **Divide the product by the third number you know.**

For example, if the ratio 10:15 is proportionate to 14:*x*, you can find the missing number by first setting up the following proportion:

$$\frac{10}{15}=\frac{14}{x}$$

Reading the ratio 10:15 as a fraction, simplify it to $\frac{2}{3}$.

$$\frac{2}{3}=\frac{14}{x}$$

Then, cross multiply both sides:

$$3\times 14=2x$$

$$42=2x$$

Finally, divide both sides by the coefficient of *x*, which is 2 in this case:

$$\frac{2x}{2}=\frac{41}{2}$$

$$x=21$$

Therefore, the ratio 10:15 is equivalent to the ratio 14:21. You'll often encounter proportion problems as word problems. Word problems will require you to parse out the numbers and then set up the ratios so that they are proportionate in order to solve for the missing term.

PRACTICE

Suppose there are 2 hockey sticks for every 5 pucks in the storage room. If the last count was 60 pucks, how many hockey sticks are in the storage room?

A. 8

B. 12

C. 18

D. 24

The correct answer is D. Let *h* denote the number of hockey sticks in the storage room. Here, we know that there are 2 hockey sticks for every 5 pucks. We know that there's a total of 60 pucks, but we don't know how many hockey sticks there are. However, because the number of hockey sticks is proportional to the number of pucks, we can scale up the ratio we do know to solve for the number of hockey sticks. Set up the proportion as follows:

$$\frac{2}{5}=\frac{h}{60}$$

$$5h=120$$

$$h=24$$

PRACTICE

The ratio of butter to chocolate chips in a cookie recipe is 2:3. If $2\frac{1}{4}$ cups of butter are used, how many cups of chocolate chips are used?

A. $\frac{2}{3}$

B. $1\frac{1}{2}$

C. 3

D. $3\frac{3}{8}$

The correct answer is D. Set up a proportion to determine the number of cups of chocolate chips needed for the recipe, setting this unknown equal to x. Cross multiply to solve for *x*:

$$\frac{2}{3}=\frac{2\frac{1}{4}}{x}$$

$$\frac{2}{3}=\frac{\frac{9}{4}}{x}$$

$$2x=3\left(\frac{9}{4}\right)$$

$$2x=\frac{27}{4}$$

$$x=\frac{27}{8}=3\frac{3}{8}$$

Rates of Speed, Time, and Distance

The basic formula used in solving problems for distance is:

$D=RT$ (Distance = Rate × Time)

You can use this same formula to find rate (speed) and time.

To find rate, use $R=\frac{D}{T}$ (Rate = Distance ÷ Time).

To find time, use $T=\frac{D}{R}$ (Time = Distance ÷ Rate).

PRACTICE

An aircraft flies 600 miles in 5 hours. At what rate did it complete the trip?

A. 80 mph

B. 90 mph

C. 120 mph

D. 200 mph

The correct answer is C. Here you're provided distance and time, and you're asked to determine the rate at which the distance of 600 miles can be covered in 5 hours. With the formula for calculating rate, you can see that distance will be divided by time. This creates a unit rate with the unit label of miles per hour, specifying how much distance can be covered per unit of time (every hour). Dividing the total distance by the total travel time $\left(\frac{600 \text{ miles}}{5 \text{ hours}}\right)$ yields a rate of 120 miles per hour (mph), communicating that for every hour of flight time, the aircraft will travel 120 miles.

A driver is traveling from Denver, CO, to Laramie, WY. The distance between these two cities is 128 miles. If the driver goes straight there without stopping and drives at a rate of 60 mph the entire time, about how long will it take them to get to Laramie?

A. 2 hours

B. 2.5 hours

C. 3 hours

D. 3.5 hours

The correct answer is A. Here, we are given two of the variables we need: rate and distance. This means we need to solve for time. To solve for time, we'll use the $T=\frac{D}{R}$ and plug in the values we know.

Here, we know that the driver is traveling at a rate of 60 mph. We also know that the drive is 128 miles total. If we plug the values into our formula, we get:

$$T = \frac{128 \text{ miles}}{60 \text{ miles per hour}}$$

If we divide 128 miles by 60 mph, we get 2.13 hours (notice how the shared units—miles—cancel). Note that this is **not** the same as 2 hours and 13 minutes, but we generally know that it will take the driver a little over 2 hours to make the drive.

Rates Involving Other Units

Not all rates are related to speed. Rates can involve any kind of units. You may see a question related to money. For example, if you earn $30.00 in 2 hours, your rate is $15.00 per hour. The rate in a money problem represents a unit amount—such as a salary (dollars per hour) or an individual price (cost per item).

When you solve these questions, your rate formula will look like this:

$$\text{Rate (unit amount)} = \frac{\text{Total amount}}{\text{Number of units}}$$

This calculation will yield the unit rate. If you find the unit rate first, you'll be able to scale it easily to find whatever equivalent you need. Try out the sample question we've provided here.

PRACTICE

If a 20-ounce bottle of juice costs $1.80, what is the cost for three ounces of juice?

A. $0.09

B. $0.11

C. $0.18

D. $0.27

The correct answer is D. To solve this problem, you must first identify the three pieces of the problem:

$$\begin{aligned} \text{Number of units} &= 20 \text{ ounces} \\ \text{Total amount} &= \$1.80 \\ \text{Unit amount (cost per ounce)} &= ? \end{aligned}$$

Then, plug the known values into the rate formula and use it to solve for the unit amount.

$$\begin{aligned} \text{Rate (unit amount)} &= \frac{\text{Total amount}}{\text{Number of units}} \\ &= \frac{\$1.80}{20 \text{ ounces of juice}} \\ &= \$0.09 \text{ per ounce of juice} \end{aligned}$$

The cost per ounce of juice is $0.09, which is choice A. This dollar-to-ounce value is the unit rate. However, you've been asked to find the cost of 3 ounces of juice, not just one. You'll need to multiply the unit rate by the total number of units you need. That total will be $0.27, choice D.

Decimals

A fraction that has a denominator that is either 10 or a power of 10 is called a *decimal fraction* or simply a *decimal*. You are already familiar with the shorthand notation used to express decimal fractions:

$$\frac{7}{10} = 0.7, \frac{37}{100} = 0.37, \frac{59}{1{,}000} = 0.059, \frac{4{,}139}{10{,}000} = 0.4139$$

As noted in the previous section, when a problem involves fractions, it is sometimes easier to change each fraction into a decimal.

Percentages

A percentage (%) is a fraction or decimal number written in a different form, specifically as a number out of 100. A percentage expressed as a fraction is the number divided by 100. As an example, there are 100 cents in a dollar. One percent of $1.00, then, is one cent. Using decimal notation, we can write one cent as $0.01, five cents as $0.05, twenty-five cents as $0.25, and so forth. Instead of saying that 25 cents equal 25 hundredths of a dollar, though, we use the word *percent* and the form 25%. The decimal number 0.25 as a percentage, then, can be written as 25% as well.

The information in this section will help you understand the relationship between decimals, fractions, and percentages and how to convert numbers from one form to another.

Converting between Decimals, Fractions, and Percentages

You can find a percentage with the following equation: $\text{percentage} = \left(\frac{\text{part}}{\text{whole}}\right) \times 100$. That equation can be flipped around algebraically to find that $\text{part} = \text{whole} \times \left(\frac{\text{percentage}}{100}\right)$ or $\text{whole} = \text{part} \div \left(\frac{\text{percentage}}{100}\right)$.

TIP

There's a shortcut for finding a certain percentage of a number. Here are some examples: 5% of 50 is the same as 50% of 5: 2.5. 3% of 150 is the same as 150% of 3: 4.5. 10% of 60 is the same as 60% of 10: 6. You can use this trick to flip around some percentage problems if it makes the math easier.

Here are some examples that demonstrate how to convert between decimals, fractions, and percentages.

To change a decimal to a percentage, multiply by 100 and add the % sign.

$$0.25 = 0.25 \times 100 = 25\%$$

The fraction bar in a fraction means "divided by." To change a fraction to a decimal, follow through on the division.

$$\frac{4}{5} = 4 \div 5 = 0.8$$

To change a fraction to a percentage, multiply by 100, simplify, and add the percent sign (%).

$$\frac{1}{4} \times 100 = \frac{100}{4} = 25\%$$

To change a percentage to a decimal, remove the percent sign (%) and divide the number by 100.

$$25\% = \frac{25}{100} = 0.25$$

To change a percentage to a fraction, remove the % sign and use that number as your numerator, with 100 as your denominator, and simplify.

$$25\% = \frac{25}{100} = \frac{1}{4}$$

Percentage is not limited to comparing other numbers to 100. You can divide any number into hundredths and talk about percentage. Similarly, we can find a percentage of any number we choose by multiplying it by the correct decimal notation. For example:

Five percent of 50: $0.05 \times 50 = 2.5$

Three percent of 150: $0.03 \times 150 = 4.5$

Ten percent of 60: $0.10 \times 60 = 6$

Solving Percentage Problems

A question involving percentages might involve one of these three tasks:

Finding the percentage of a number

Finding a number when a percentage is given

Finding what percentage one number is of another

Regardless of the task, three distinct values are involved: the part, the whole, and the percentage. Often, the problem will give you two of the three numbers, and your job is to find the missing value. To work with percentages, use the following formula:

$$\text{percentage} = \frac{\text{part}}{\text{whole}} \times 100$$

Once again, to know any two of those values allows you to determine the third.

Finding the Percentage

30 is what percent of 50?

In this question, 50 is the whole, and 30 is the part. Your task is to find the missing percent:

$$\begin{aligned}\text{percentage} &= \frac{30}{50} \times 100 \\ &= 60\%\end{aligned}$$

Finding the Part

What number is 25% of 80?

In this question, 80 is the whole, and 25 is the percentage. Your task is to find the part:

$$25\% = \frac{\text{part}}{80} \times 100$$

In this situation, it can be helpful to change the percentage into its decimal form (.25), which then lets you drop the 100 from the equation so you can represent the percentage as a fraction, in this case $\frac{25}{100}$. That gives us a new form of the equation:

$$\frac{25}{100} = \frac{\text{part}}{80}$$

To solve for the missing part, cross multiply 25 and 80 and 100 with the missing part. That yields the following:

$$\begin{aligned}100(\text{part}) &= 25(80) \\ 100(\text{part}) &= 2{,}000 \\ \text{part} &= \frac{2{,}000}{100} \\ \text{part} &= 20\end{aligned}$$

25% of 80 is 20. Because of the values used, there are any number of ways you could have come to that solution faster, such as by simplifying the left fraction to $\frac{1}{4}$, or calculating 80 ÷ 4 or 80 × .25, but it's important that you see the full process. Let's look at how you can streamline your work in the next example.

Finding the Whole

An example of a question that requires you to find the whole might be something like "75% of what number is 150?"

In this question, 150 is the part, and 75 is the percentage. Your task is to find the whole. Here's the streamlined equation:

$$\frac{75}{100} = \frac{150}{\text{whole}}$$

Here, you can simplify the fraction on the left to $\frac{3}{4}$ and then cross multiply:

$$\begin{aligned}\frac{3}{4} &= \frac{150}{\text{whole}} \\ \text{whole}(3) &= 150(4)\end{aligned}$$

Then, multiply the two diagonally situated numbers you know:

$$150 \times 4 = 600$$

Finally, divide 600 by 3, which equals 200.

75% of 200 is 150

PRACTICE

1% of 200 is what percentage of 40?

A. 0.2

B. 2

C. 5

D. 10

The correct answer is C. 1% of 200 is 1/100, or 0.01, of 200. Multiply 200 by 0.01. That is equivalent to 2. Then divide 2 by 40, which yields 5%. Using decimal notation, we write one-tenth of one percent as 0.001, the decimal number for one thousandth. If you remember that a percent is one hundredth of something, you can see that one tenth of that percent is equivalent to one thousandth of the whole.

Percent Increase and Decrease

The percentage of increase or decrease is found by putting the amount of increase or decrease over the original amount and renaming this fraction as a percentage. Percent-change can involve various quantities, including tax, interest, profit, discount, or weight.

EXAMPLES

Over a five-year period, the enrollment at South High dropped from 1,000 students to 800. Find the percentage of decrease.

Solution

$$\frac{1{,}000-800}{1{,}000}=\frac{200}{1{,}000}=\frac{20}{100}=20\%$$

A company normally employs 100 people. At one point, the company lost 20% of its employees. By what percentage must the company now increase its staff to return to full capacity?

Solution

$$20\%=\frac{1}{5} \rightarrow \frac{1}{5}\bullet 100=20$$

The company now has 100 – 20 = 80 employees. If it then increases its staff by 20, the percentage of increase is $\frac{20}{80}=\frac{1}{4}$, or 25%.

A discount is usually expressed as a percent of the marked price that will be deducted from the marked price to determine the sale price.

EXAMPLES

A store offers a television set marked at $340 less discounts of 10% and 5%. Another store offers the same television set also marked at $340 with a single discount of 15%. How much does the buyer save by buying at the better price?

Solution

In the first store, the initial discount means the buyer pays 90%, or $\frac{9}{10}$, of $340, which is $306. The additional 5% discount means the buyer pays 95% of $306, or $290.70. Note that the second discount must be figured on the first sale price. Taking 5% off $306 is a smaller amount than taking the additional 5% off $340. The second store will therefore have a lower sale price. In the second store, the buyer will pay 85% of $340, or $289, making the price $1.70 less than in the first store.

Bill's Hardware offers a 20% discount on all appliances during a sale week. If a customer takes advantage of the sale, how much must the customer pay for a washing machine marked at $280?

Solution

Long Method
$20\% = \frac{1}{5}$
$\frac{1}{5} \cdot 280 = \$56$ discount
$\$280 - \$56 = \$224$ sale price
The danger inherent in this method is that $56 is sure to be among the multiple-choice answers.

Shorter Method
If there is a 20% discount, the customer will pay 80% of the marked price.
$80\% = \frac{4}{5}$
$\frac{4}{5} \cdot 280 = \$224$ sale price

Taxes are a percentage of money spent or money earned. A scenario involving taxes will likely involve a percentage increase.

EXAMPLE

Washington County collects a 7% sales tax on automobiles. If the price of a car is $8,532 before taxes, what will this car cost once sales tax is added in?

Solution

Find 7% of $8,532 to determine tax and then add it to $8,532. This can be done in one step by finding 107% of $8,532.

$$\begin{array}{r} \$8{,}532 \\ \times \quad 1.07 \\ \hline 59724 \\ +\ 85320 \\ \hline \$9{,}129.24 \end{array}$$

PRACTICE

A computer originally priced at $500 is discounted by 10%, then by another 10%. What is the price of the computer after the second discount, to the nearest dollar?

A. $400

B. $405

C. $425

D. $450

The correct answer is B. After the first 10% discount, the price was $450 ($500 minus 10% of $500). After the second discount, which is calculated based on the $450 price, the price of the computer is $405 ($450 minus 10% of $450).

A positive number x is increased by 20 percent, and the result is then decreased by 30 percent. The final result is equal to which of the following?

A. x decreased by 50 percent

B. x decreased by 16 percent

C. x decreased by 10 percent

D. x increased by 10 percent

The correct answer is B. Begin by plugging in 100 for x. If 100 is increased by 20 percent, the result is 120. This number is then decreased by 30 percent. Thirty percent of 120 is 36, so the final result is 120 – 36 = 84. This is the same as decreasing 100 by 16 percent.

BASIC ALGEBRA

Fundamentally, algebra is the manipulation of mathematical symbols. More than likely, your familiarity with the topic stems from solving for unknowns by applying various rules and procedures. On the SAT, you'll need to apply your skills for both lower-level algebra (algebraic expressions, linear equations, and inequalities) as well as more advanced math (functions, nonlinear equations, and more). Regardless of the complexity of the algebra, you'll need to apply the following principles to break down and work with algebraic expressions and equations.

Expressions and Equations

So far, you've already seen plenty of mathematical expressions, defined as containing at least two values with some math operator used between them. Algebraic expressions, however, are usually used to form equations—the goal is to set two expressions equal to one another. When we're talking about algebraic expressions, know that a term is any coefficient, variable, or combination of a coefficient and a variable. In equations, at least one of the terms will be a variable—a letter such as x or y that represents a number that can vary. It does not need an exponent, but if it has one, it must be a non-negative exponent. A coefficient is the number that multiplies with a variable, such as the 2 in $2y$.

Standard Form

Standard form is something you've been using since you learned how to write numbers. Write the number one hundred: 100. That is standard form—the usual way you'd write a number. In addition to being the way you've written numbers all your life, standard form is also an agreed upon method of writing an equation. The standard form for equations has a couple of rules you need to know.

Always set an equation equal to 0. Example: $x = 7$ should have everything on the left of the equal sign, and 0 on the right: $x - 7 = 0$ is standard form.

Order terms starting with the highest exponent. Example: $7x^3 + 3x^6 - 5 + 4x^2$ should start with the highest exponent: $3x^6 + 7x^3 + 4x^2 - 5$.

Writing equations in standard form makes it easier to locate information because it is presented in a consistent order. When an equation is in standard form, you'll know what to expect and how to proceed with isolating and solving for the variable.

Evaluating Expressions and Equations through Substitution

You know that expressions can have terms, coefficients, variables, and exponents. When putting expressions into standard form, you'll often be simplifying the expression. Expressions can be simplified by combining like terms. Like terms must have the same variable (or lack thereof) and the same power (e.g., 3 and 4, $3x$ and x, $4y^7$ and $253y^7$). Sometimes, though, you'll not only be given an expression but also a value that can be substituted in for a variable to evaluate the expression. For instance, if you were told to evaluate the expression $4x^2 + 3x$ when $x = 3$, you would substitute 3 for each instance of x.

PRACTICE

Evaluate the equation $y = 4x + 5$ when $x = -3$.

A. –7

B. –3

C. –1

D. 9

The correct solution is A. Plug –3 in for x and then find the resulting value for y:

$$\begin{aligned} y &= 4x + 5 \\ y &= 4(-3) + 5 \\ y &= -7 \end{aligned}$$

The answer is $y = -7$.

Expressions in Word Problems

One of the more challenging parts of algebra is translating words that describe a math scenario into symbols.

When creating an algebraic expression, equation, or inequality that describes a relationship between one or more quantities, you must first identify what the unknowns are and how many of them you have. Use a different letter for each unknown. Then, identify common words and phrases (*is, of, less than, greater than,* etc.) and translate them, piece by piece, into algebraic expressions.

Let's look at some examples:

A number is three less than two times another number: $x = 2y - 3$

The square of the sum of two numbers is greater than 4: $(x + y)^2 > 4$

The sum of two numbers is twice the product of two other numbers: $x + y = 2wz$

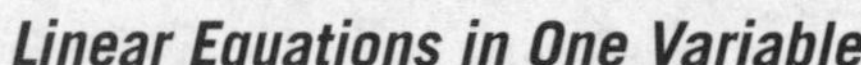

Linear Equations in One Variable

As we've mentioned, algebraic expressions are usually used to form equations in which two expressions are set equal to each other. Equations contain at least one variable, most often x or y (though variables can be represented by any letter). Most equations you'll see on the test are linear equations. In linear equations, the variables x and y don't come with exponents, and they can be graphed along the x- and y-axis of a coordinate plane.

To find the value of a linear equation's variable is to solve the equation. To solve any linear equation containing only one variable, your goal is always the same: isolate the variable on one side of the equation. To accomplish this, you may need to perform one or more of the operations listed at the bottom of this page for both sides of the equation.

Whatever operation you perform on one side of an equation you must also perform on the other side; otherwise, the two sides won't be equal. Performing any of these operations on both sides does not change the equality; it merely restates the equation in a different form.

Simplifying Equations

Sometimes, you need to simplify one or both sides of an equation before you can undo what's been done to the variable. This can be done through various means depending on the nature of the expression. In general, you'll combine like terms and then isolate the target variable to one side of the equation, using standard order of operations, to reach its solution.

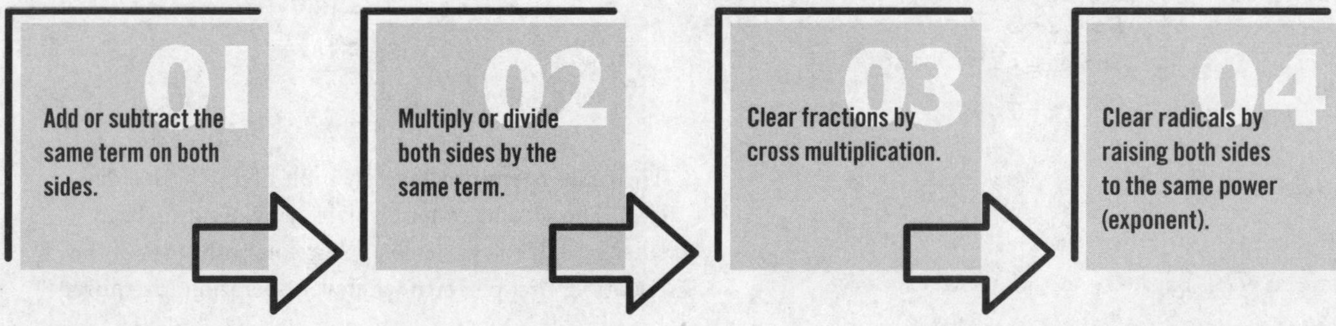

Performing Operations to Isolate the Variable
01
Add or subtract the same term on both sides.
02
Multiply or divide both sides by the same term.
03
Clear fractions by cross multiplication.
04
Clear radicals by raising both sides to the same power (exponent).

PRACTICE

Simplify $3(x - 2) - 2x = 8$.

A. –14

B. –6

C. 2

D. 14

The correct answer is D. Simplify any parts of the equation, remembering to follow the order of operations (PEMDAS). First, multiply the expression in parentheses by 3.

$$3x - 6 - 2x = 8$$

Then, combine like terms containing the variable x.

$$3x - 6 - 2x = 8$$
$$x - 6 = 8$$

To undo the subtraction of 6, add 6 to both sides.

$$x - 6(+6) = 8(+6)$$
$$x = 14$$

Simplification Methods

Here is a more detailed rundown of several simplification methods.

To find the value of the variable (to solve for x, y, or any other variable), you may need to either add a term to both sides of the equation or subtract a term from both sides. What follows are examples for each operation.

Adding the same number to both sides:

$$x - 2 = 5$$
$$x - 2 + 2 = 5 + 2$$
$$x = 7$$

Subtracting the same number from both sides:

$$y + 3 = 7$$
$$y + 3 - 3 = 7 - 3$$
$$y = 4$$

The first system isolates x by adding 2 to both sides. The second system isolates y by removing 3 from both sides.

The objective is to isolate the variable. To do this, like terms must be combined until the variable stands alone on one side of the equation. The following example isolates x by subtracting $\frac{3}{2}$ from both sides, then combining like terms and dividing by –1 to make the variable positive:

$$\frac{3}{2} - x = 12$$
$$\frac{3}{2} - \frac{3}{2} - x = 12 - \frac{3}{2}$$
$$-x = 10\frac{1}{2}$$
$$x = -10\frac{1}{2}$$

In some cases, solving for x (or y) requires that you either multiply or divide both sides of the equation by the same term. What follows are two examples.

Multiplying both sides by the same number:

$$\frac{x}{2} = 14$$
$$2 \cdot \frac{x}{2} = 14 \cdot 2$$
$$x = 28$$

Dividing both sides by the same number:

$$3y = 18$$
$$\frac{3y}{3} = \frac{18}{3}$$
$$y = 6$$

The first system isolates x by multiplying both sides by 2. The second system isolates y by dividing both sides by 3. If the variable appears on both sides of the equation, first perform whatever operation is required to position the variable on just one side—either the left or the right. The next system positions both x-terms on the left side by subtracting $2x$ from both sides:

$$16-x=9+2x$$
$$16-x-2x=9+2x-2x$$
$$16-3x=9$$

Now that x appears on just one side, the next step is to isolate it by subtracting 16 from both sides, and then divide both sides by –3:

$$16-3x=9$$
$$16-3x-16=9-16$$
$$-3x=-7$$
$$\frac{-3x}{-3}=\frac{-7}{-3}$$
$$x=\frac{7}{3}$$

PRACTICE

Solve $2(x + 1) = -10$.

A. –11

B. –6

C. –5

D. 5

The correct answer is B. First use the distributive property to eliminate the parentheses:

$$2(x+1)--10$$
$$2x+2=-10$$

Next, subtract 2 from each side:

$$2x+2-2=-10-2$$
$$2x=-12$$

Now simplify by dividing each side by 2:

$$\frac{2x}{2}=\frac{-12}{2}$$
$$x=-6$$

BASIC GEOMETRY

You have likely already encountered the terms *point*, *line*, *line segment*, *ray*, and *angle* throughout your education. Those terms form the foundation of geometry. In this section, we will explore those terms in the context of fundamental knowledge for answering the SAT Geometry and Trigonometry domain questions and examine key concepts around basic geometric shapes, as well as the fundamental principles of coordinate geometry.

Points and Lines

A *point* is defined as having no size of its own, and only a position. On the SAT, a point is typically represented by a dot and named by using a capital letter. The graphic below depicts point A.

A *line* is a continuous set of points. It only has one dimension—length—and has no width of its own. Lines can be named in several ways. Sometimes, a letter is placed next to a drawing of the line, and the line is named using this letter. For example, the following figure is a picture of line l.

Lines are also commonly named by putting a double-headed arrow over any two of the points on the line. For example, the figure below is a picture of line $\overleftrightarrow{AB}$.

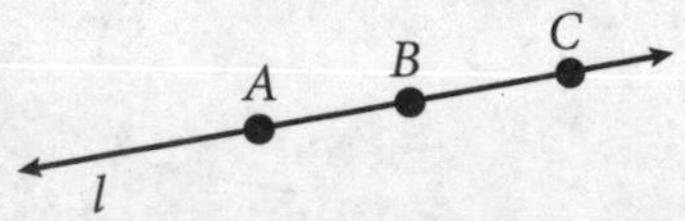

Note that, since the point C is also on this line, the line could just as well have been called line $\overleftrightarrow{AC}$ or line $\overleftrightarrow{BC}$. Also note that it is standard to put arrowheads on the ends of lines to indicate that the line extends in both directions forever.

A *line segment* is the portion of line between two of its points, which are called the *endpoints* of the line segment. A line segment is named by placing a bar over its endpoints. For example, the figure below depicts line segment $\overline{PQ}$.

Note that, while $\overleftrightarrow{AB}$ and $\overleftrightarrow{AC}$ refer to the same line, $\overline{AB}$ and $\overline{AC}$ refer to different line segments. Line segment $\overline{AB}$ runs between points A and B, while line segment $\overline{AC}$ runs between points A and C.

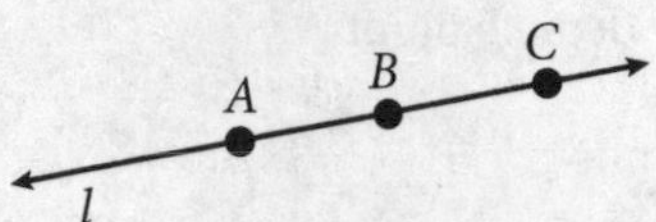

Unlike a line, which is of infinite length, a line segment is of finite length. The length of a line segment is indicated by writing its two endpoints next to each other. For example, based on the figure below, $\overline{EF} = 12$.

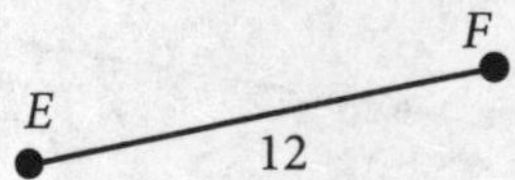

If two line segments have the same length, they are said to be *congruent*. There is a special symbol for congruence, which may be used on the SAT. The symbol is ≅. Thus, if $\overline{BC}$ and $\overline{EF}$ have the same length, that is, if $BC = EF$, we write $\overline{BC} \cong \overline{EF}$.

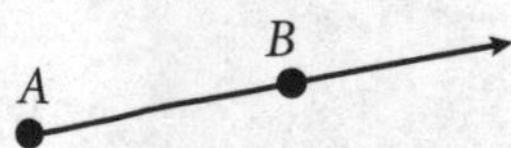

A *ray* is a portion of a line, beginning at one point on the line, called the endpoint, and extending infinitely in one direction. A ray is indicated by writing the endpoint of the ray next to another point on the ray and placing a one-headed arrow over it. For example, the figure above depicts $\overrightarrow{AB}$.

Graphing Basics

To start, let's review the coordinate plane. The coordinate plane (or grid) is divided into four sections. Each section is called a quadrant. The two number lines that divide the grid into quadrants are called the x-axis (the horizontal axis) and the y-axis (the vertical axis). The center of the grid, where the two axes meet, is called the origin. Any point on the plane has two coordinates that indicate its location relative to the axes. The points that are drawn on the grid are identified by ordered pairs. In ordered pairs, the x-coordinate is always written first. The ordered pair for the origin, in the middle of the grid, is (0, 0).

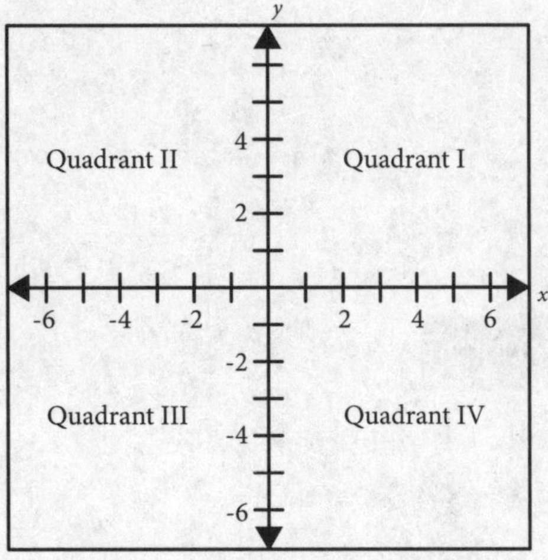

The quadrants of a grid are named in counter-clockwise order, beginning with the first quadrant in the upper right corner. For any point in the first quadrant, the coordinates are positive. The quadrant in the top left is called the second quadrant. For any point in the second quadrant, the x-coordinate is negative, but the y-coordinate is positive. The quadrant in the lower left is called the third quadrant. In the third quadrant, both coordinates are negative. The quadrant in the lower right is called the fourth quadrant, and in the fourth quadrant, the x-coordinate is positive, and the y-coordinate is negative.

On the following graph, the x-coordinate of point A is 3. The y-coordinate of point A is 2. The coordinates of point A are given by the ordered pair (3, 2). Point B has coordinates (–1, 4). Point C has coordinates (–4, –3). Point D has coordinates (2, –3).

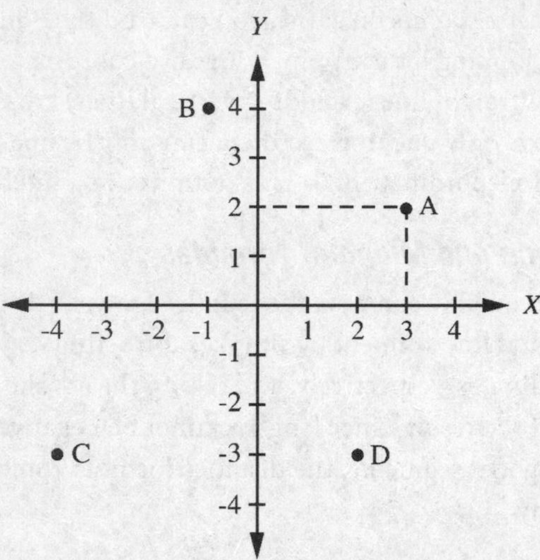

To graph a point whose coordinates are given, first locate the x-coordinate on the x-axis, then from that position, move vertically the number of spaces indicated by the y-coordinate.

Equations of Lines and Graphing

In a coordinate plane, a line can be defined by the equation $y = mx + b$. This is called the slope-intercept form. In this equation, you can see the following:

- The variable m is the slope of the line (its steepness).
- The variable b is the line's y-intercept (where the line crosses the y-axis).
- The variables x and y are the coordinates of any point on the line. Any (x, y) pair defining a point on the line can substitute for the variables x and y.

For a line with an equation of $y = 3x + 2$, the line has a positive slope of 3 and a y-intercept of 2. Let's review these terms and learn more about working with the slope-intercept equation.

Slope

Slope is a ratio that describes the steepness of a line.

$$\text{slope } (m) = \frac{\text{rise}}{\text{run}}$$

$$= \frac{\text{vertical change}}{\text{horizontal change}}$$

$$= \frac{\text{change in } y}{\text{change in } x}$$

To find the slope of a line from a graph, count the spaces from one point on the line to another.

PRACTICE

Determine the slope of the line below.

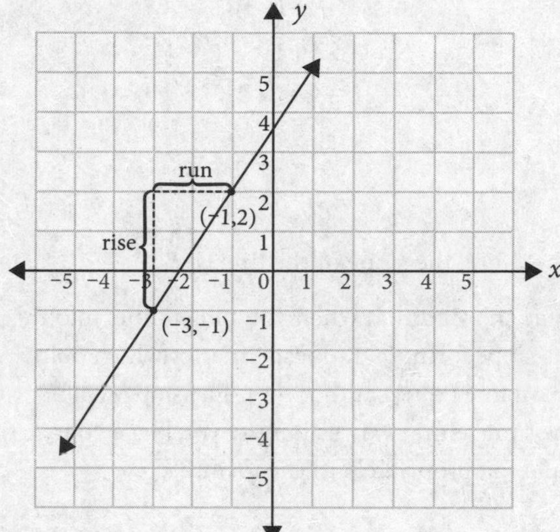

A. $\frac{1}{3}$

B. $\frac{1}{2}$

C. $\frac{2}{3}$

D. $\frac{3}{2}$

The correct answer is D. On the graph shown, count the vertical spaces and the horizontal spaces from (–3, –1) to (–1, 2).

$$\text{Slope} = \frac{\text{vertical change}}{\text{horizontal change}} = \frac{3}{2}$$

The slope of the line is $\frac{3}{2}$.

You can also calculate slope without a graph if you know two points on a line. You can find the slope of the line using the formula for slope (m):

$$m = \frac{y_2 - y_1}{x_2 - x_1}$$

If a line passes through points (–3, –1) and (–1, 2), let (x_1, y_1) be (–3, –1) and (x_2, y_2) be (–1, 2). Plug these values into the slope formula:

$$\begin{aligned} m &= \frac{y_2 - y_1}{x_2 - x_1} \\ &= \frac{2-(-1)}{-1-(-3)} \\ &= \frac{2+1}{-1+3} \\ &= \frac{3}{2} \end{aligned}$$

Therefore, the slope of the line is $\frac{3}{2}$.

Keep in mind that when you plug points into the slope formula, it doesn't matter which point you name (x_1, y_1) and (x_2, y_2). The slope will be the same either way as long as you place your values appropriately in the formula.

Y-Intercepts

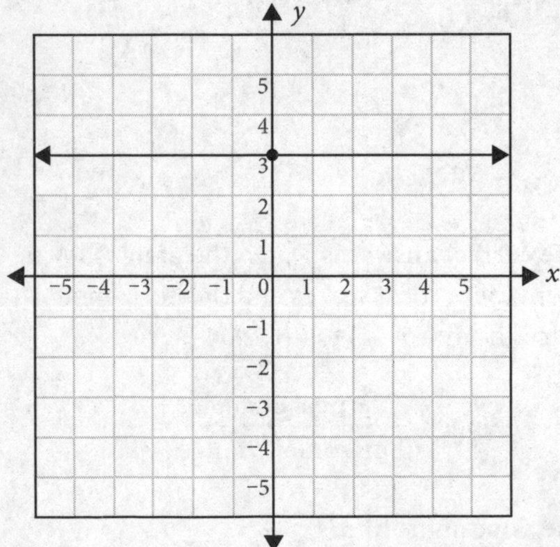

The y-intercept of a line is the y-coordinate of the point where the line crosses the y-axis. The coordinates of the y-intercept are $(0, y)$. The y-intercept of the line shown is 3, since the line crosses the y-axis at (0, 3).

In any set of points on a line, you can find the y-intercept by looking for the point with an x-coordinate of 0. Each straight line (excluding vertical lines) crosses the y-axis only one time, so there can only be one point with an x-coordinate of 0. This point is the y-intercept.

Distance and Midpoint Formulas

You can quickly compute the length of any vertical or horizontal line segment by simply subtracting its y- or x-coordinates, respectively, and taking the absolute value of the result (since length cannot be negative). For diagonal segments, the distance formula comes in handy.

The distance between two points $P(x_1, y_1)$ and $Q(x_2, y_2)$ is $\sqrt{(x_2 - x_1)^2 + (y_2 - y_1)^2}$.

Likewise, the midpoint of the line segment with endpoints $P(x_1, y_1)$ and $Q(x_2, y_2)$ is the point with coordinates $\left(\frac{x_1 + x_2}{2}, \frac{y_1 + y_2}{2}\right)$.

Often, the problems on the SAT Math section that involve the distance and midpoint formulas are word problems, such as the following questions.

PRACTICE

Suppose that $P(-1, 6)$ is one of the endpoints of a line segment $\overline{PQ}$ and that its midpoint is $M(4, -5)$. What is point Q?

A. (9, –16)

B. (– 5, 11)

C. (5, –11)

D. $\left(\frac{3}{2}, \frac{1}{2}\right)$

The correct answer is A. Since we do not know the coordinates of Q, let's call that point (x, y); we must determine the values of both x and y. Using the midpoint formula, we can express the midpoint of $\overline{PQ}$ as $\left(\frac{-1+x}{2}, \frac{6+y}{2}\right)$. Since we are given that the midpoint is (4, –5), we know that $\frac{-1+x}{2}=4$ and $\frac{6+y}{2}=-5$. Solving each of these yields $x = 9$ and $y = -16$. Hence, the coordinates of Q are (9, –16).

A map is laid out in the standard (*x*, *y*) coordinate plane. How long in units is the path from City A located at (4, 11) to City B located at (8, 9), given that the path is a straight line between the cities?

A. 2 units

B. $\sqrt{6}$ units

C. $2\sqrt{5}$ units

J. 6 units

The correct answer is C. You can use the distance formula to find the straight-line distance between any two points in the (*x*, *y*) plane.

$$\begin{aligned} d &= \sqrt{(x_1-x_2)^2+(y_1-y_2)^2} \\ &= \sqrt{(4-8)^2+(11-9)^2} \\ &= \sqrt{-4^2+2^2} \\ &= \sqrt{16+4} \\ &= \sqrt{20} \\ &= 2\sqrt{5} \end{aligned}$$

ANGLES

Angles are classified according to their measure. Angle units are expressed in degrees (and often radians when studying trigonometry), and the notation *m*∠ (name of angle) is used to denote the measure of a given angle.

See the following page for the various angle characterizations you need to know.

It's not only important that you understand individual angle classifications but also how pairs of angles relate to each other. Knowing these relationships will help you determine angle values in figures and perform more complex calculations.

Take a look at the image on page 295 and the table that follows. You may be presented with a figure on the SAT exam that has some angle values provided and then will ask you to determine some missing values in order to solve a problem. We suggest that you review and memorize these angle relationships until they're second nature to you—they are likely to come in handy when you take the test.

ANGLE TYPES		
Term	**Illustration**	**Definition**
Acute Angle	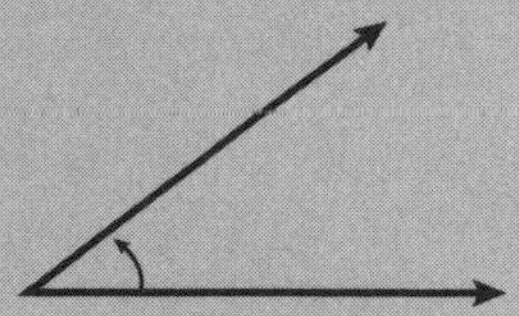	An angle with a measure between 0 and 90 degrees
Right Angle		An angle with a measure of 90 degrees
Obtuse Angle	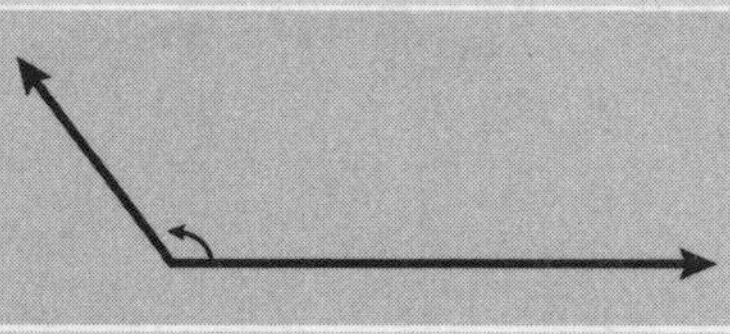	An angle with a measure between 90 and 180 degrees
Straight Angle	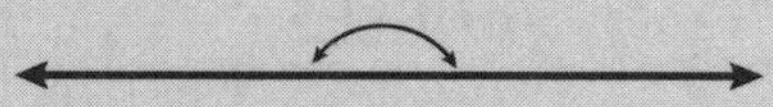	An angle with a measure of 180 degrees
Complementary Angles	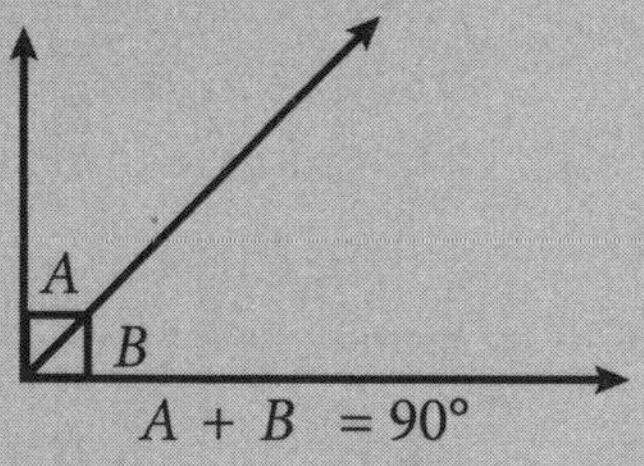 A, B; $A + B = 90°$	Two angles with measures that sum to 90 degrees
Supplementary Angles	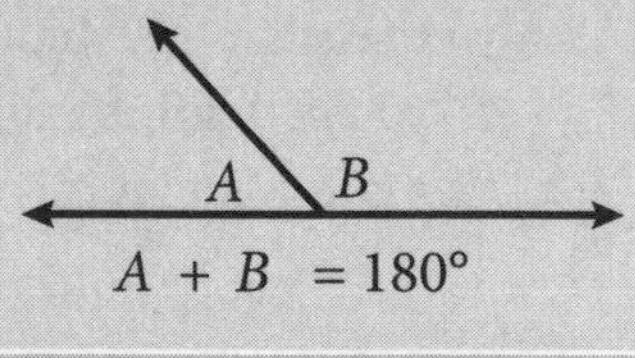 A, B; $A + B = 180°$	Two angles with measures that sum to 180 degrees
Congruent Angles	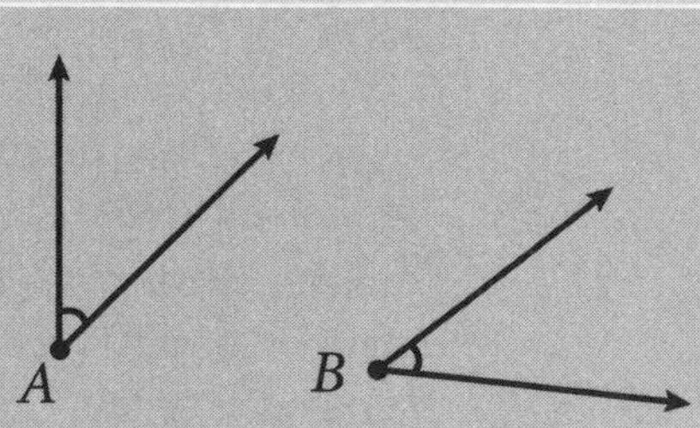 A, B	Two angles that have the same measure

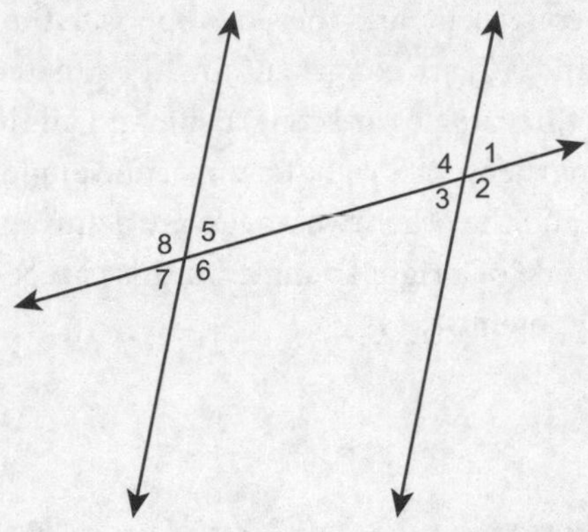

Term	Examples from Diagram
Corresponding Angles	$\angle 1$ and $\angle 5$, $\angle 3$ and $\angle 7$ In a diagram such as the one above, if the lines are parallel then corresponding angles are congruent.
Adjacent Angles	$\angle 1$ and $\angle 2$, $\angle 6$ and $\angle 7$
Vertical Angles	$\angle 1$ and $\angle 3$, $\angle 6$ and $\angle 8$ Vertical angles are always congruent.
Alternate Interior Angles	$\angle 4$ and $\angle 6$, $\angle 3$ and $\angle 5$ In a diagram such as the one above, if the lines are parallel, then alternate interior angles are congruent.

Remember: typically, parallel lines are denoted by two vertical hash marks, like 1||2. Congruence is generally denoted by a single hash mark.

If two lines cut by a transversal are NOT parallel, then pairs of corresponding angles and pairs of alternate interior angles are *not* necessarily congruent.

PRACTICE

Points A, D, and E lie on the same line in the figure below. What is the $m\angle BEC$?

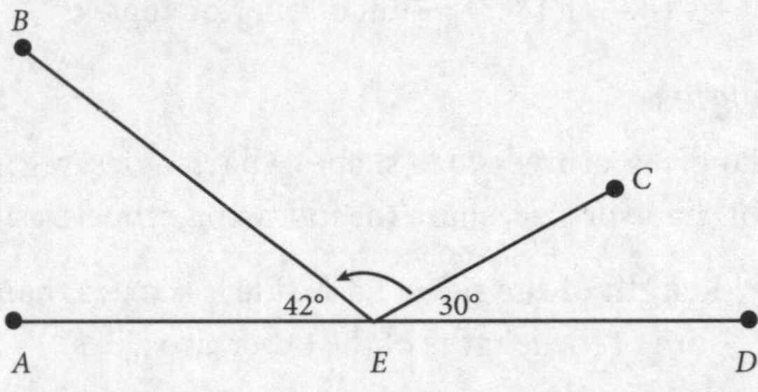

A. 60°

B. 48°

C. 90°

D. 108°

The correct answer is D. In the diagram, the three angles form a straight line, and therefore, their measures must sum to 180°.

$$m\angle AEB + m\angle BEC + m\angle CED = 180°$$
$$42° + m\angle BEC + 30° = 180°$$
$$m\angle BEC = 180° - 42° - 30°$$
$$= 108°$$

Polygons

Polygons include all closed two-dimensional figures formed only by line segments. Remember these two reciprocal rules about polygons:

If all angles of a polygon are congruent (equal in degree measure), then all sides are congruent (equal in length).

If all sides of a polygon are congruent (equal in length), then all angles are congruent (equal in degree measure).

A polygon in which all sides are congruent and all angles are congruent is called a regular polygon.

You can use the following formula to determine the sum of all interior angles of *any* polygon with angles that each measure less than 180° (n = number of sides):

$$(n - 2)(180°) = \text{sum of interior angles}$$

Triangles

A triangle is a three-sided shape. All triangles, regardless of shape or size, share the following properties:

- **Length of the sides:** Each side is shorter than the sum of the lengths of the other two sides.
- **Angle measures:** The measures of the three interior angles total 180°.
- **Angles and opposite sides:** Comparative angle sizes correspond to the comparative lengths of the sides opposite those angles. For example, a triangle's largest angle is opposite its longest side. (The sides opposite two congruent angles are also congruent.)

The next figure shows three particular types of triangles.

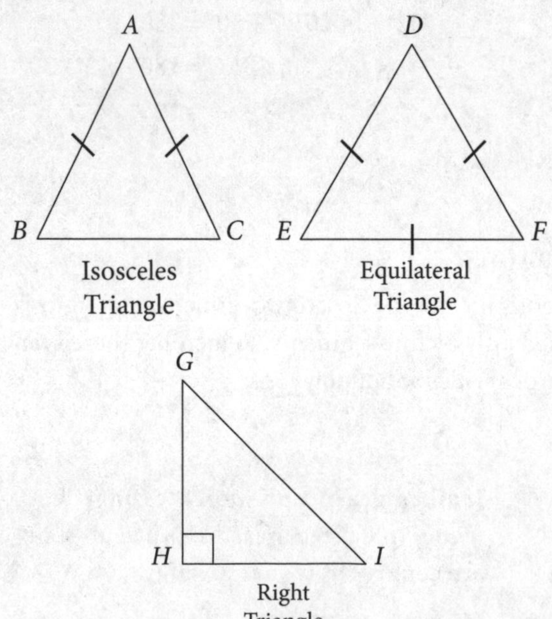

An isosceles triangle is one in which two sides (and two angles) are congruent. In the figure shown, angle B and angle C are congruent, and the sides opposite those two angles, AB and AC, are congruent. In an equilateral triangle, all three angles are congruent, and all three sides are congruent. In a right triangle, one angle is a right angle, and the other two angles are acute angles. The longest side of a right triangle (in this case, GI) is called the hypotenuse.

PRACTICE

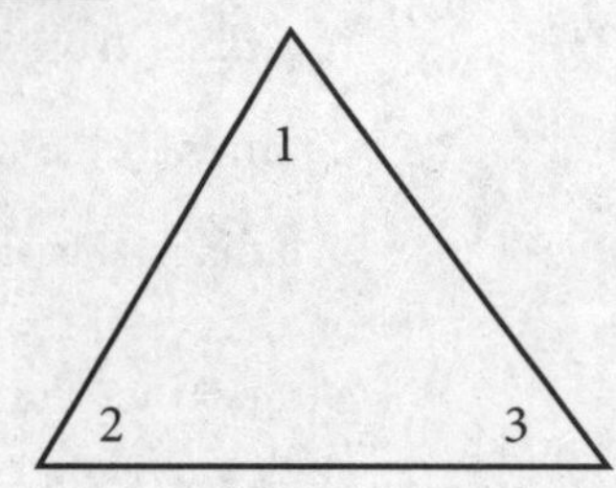

Note: Figure is not drawn to scale.

Given that $m\angle 2 = 60°$, which of the following is true?

A. $m\angle 1 + \angle 3 > 180°$

B. $m\angle 1 + \angle 3 = 120°$

C. $m\angle 1 = \angle 3$

D. $m\angle 1 > m\angle 3$

The correct answer is B. Choices B, C, and D might be true in some cases, depending upon the exact measurements of $\angle 1$ and $\angle 3$. The only answer that is true no matter the measures of $\angle 1$ and $\angle 3$ is the one in which their sum is equal to 120°.

Right Triangles and the Pythagorean Theorem

In a right triangle, one angle measures 90° and each of the other two angles measures less than 90°. The Pythagorean theorem describes the relationship among the sides of any right triangle and can be expressed by the equation $a^2 + b^2 = c^2$. As shown in the next figure, the letters a and b represent the lengths of the two legs (the two shortest sides) that form the right angle, and c is the length of the hypotenuse (the longest side, opposite the right angle).

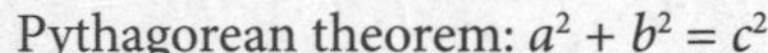

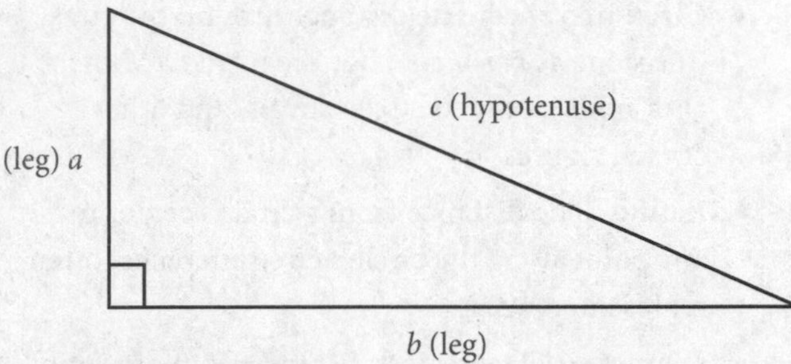

For any right triangle, if you know the length of two sides, you can determine the length of the third side by applying the Pythagorean theorem.

Quadrilaterals

A quadrilateral is a figure in a plane with four sides, each of which is a line segment. There are several common quadrilaterals (e.g., square, rectangle, parallelogram, rhombus, trapezoid) that arise in solving practical problems. As four-sided shapes, each has an internal angle measure of 360 degrees. See the following table for a comparison of properties of common quadrilaterals.

Congruency and Similarity

Two geometric figures that have the same size and shape are said to be congruent. The symbol for congruency is ≅. Two angles are congruent if their degree measure (size) is the same. Two line segments are congruent if they are equal in length. Two triangles are congruent if the angle measures and sides are all identical in size. (The same applies to figures with more than three sides.)

If a two-dimensional geometric figure, such as a triangle or rectangle, has exactly the same shape as another one, then the two figures are similar. Similar figures share the same angle measures, and their sides are proportionate (though not the same length).

COMMON QUADRILATERALS

Property	Rectangle	Square	Parallelogram	Rhombus	Trapezoid
All sides are equal length		✔		✔	
Opposite sides are equal length	✔	✔	✔	✔	(nonparallel sides in isosceles trapezoids)
Opposite sides are parallel	✔	✔	✔	✔	(only the bases)
All angles are equal	✔	✔			
Opposite angles are equal	✔	✔	✔	✔	
Sum of two adjacent angles is 180 degrees	✔	✔	✔	✔	(base and leg angles)
Diagonals bisect	✔	✔	✔	✔	
Diagonals are perpendicular		✔		✔	

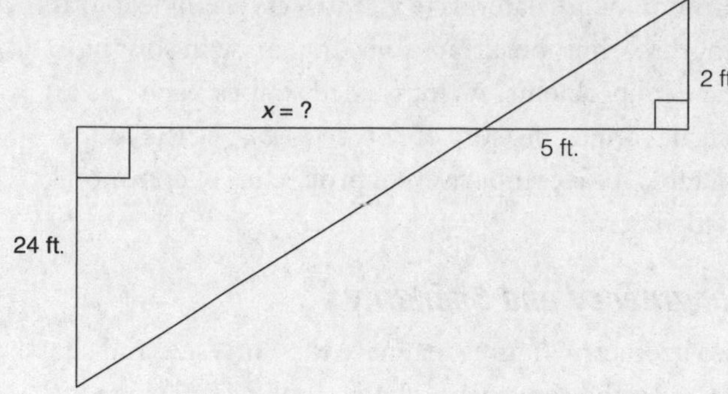

These two triangles are similar. They share an angle and both have right angles. Thus, their third angles must be equal. Because their angles are equal, their sides must be proportional. The ratio 2:5 is the same as 24:x. By creating a proportion, you can solve for x and find the missing side length as 60 ft.

PRACTICE

In the figure below, triangles BCA and DEF are similar. What is the length of segment EF?

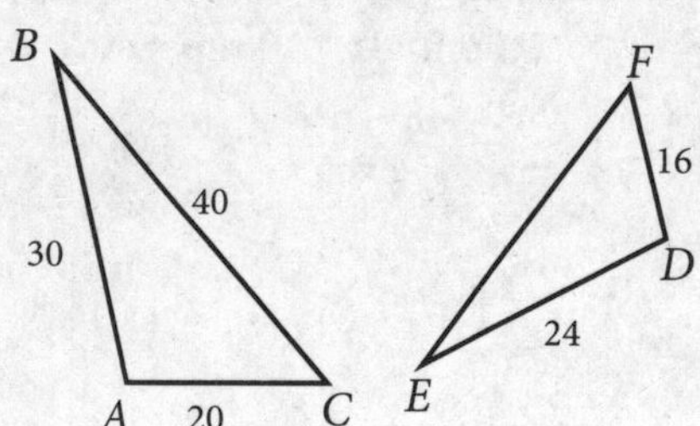

A. 28

B. 30

C. 32

D. 36

The correct answer is C. Set up a proportion between similar sides:

$$\frac{24}{30}=\frac{x}{40}$$
$$30x=960$$
$$x=32$$

Circles

Let's review some key terms related to the geometry of circles before exploring some additional characteristics of the shape.

- **Circumference:** The distance around the circle (the same as *perimeter*, but the word *circumference* applies only to circles, ovals, and other curved figures)
- **Radius:** The distance from a circle's center to any point along the circle's circumference, often represented by r
- **Diameter:** The greatest distance from one point to another on the circle's circumference (twice the length of the radius) through the center point of the circle, often represented by d
- **Chord:** A line segment connecting two points on the circle's circumference (a circle's longest possible chord is its diameter, passing through the circle's center)
- **Pi (π):** This Greek letter represents the ratio between a circle's circumference and its diameter; for all circles, the circumference divided by the diameter is π, approximated as 3.14 or $\frac{22}{7}$.

As previously noted, a circle's diameter is twice the length of its radius. The next figure shows a circle with radius 6 and diameter 12.

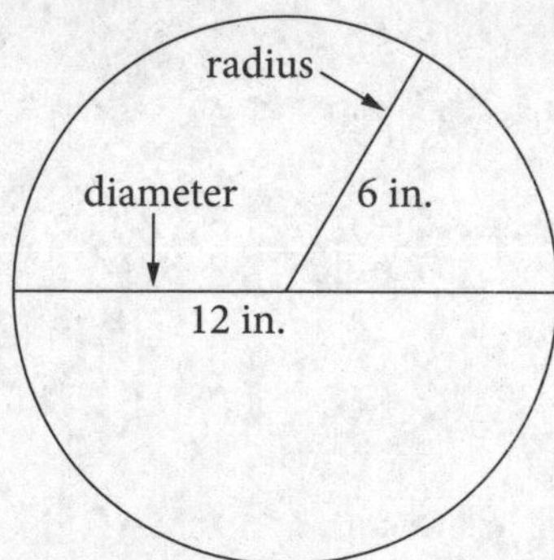

For most questions related to circles, you'll apply one, or possibly both, of two basic formulas involving circles (r = radius, d = diameter):

$$\text{Circumference} = 2\pi r, \text{ or } \pi d$$

$$\text{Area} = \pi r^2$$

With the circumference and area formulas, all you need is one value—area, circumference, diameter, or radius—and you can determine all the others. Based on the circle shown, which has a diameter of 12:

Radius = 6

Circumference = 12π

Area = $\pi(6)^2 = 36\pi$

Perimeter and Area of Planar Regions

The perimeter of a region in the plane is the "distance around." The area of a region in the plane is the number of unit squares needed to cover the shape. The following are some standard perimeter and area formulas with which you should be familiar.

PERIMETER AND AREA FORMULAS

Region	Illustration	Perimeter Formula	Area Formula
Square	s, s, s, s	$P = 4s$	$A = s^2$
Rectangle	l, w	$P = 2l + 2w$	$A = l \times w$
Triangle	h, b	Sum the three lengths of the triangle.	$A = \frac{1}{2} b \cdot h$
Circle	r	The perimeter of a circle is called the circumference; it's found with two common expressions: $C = 2\pi r = \pi d$	$A = \pi r^2$
Arcs and Sectors of Circles	r, θ	Arc length: $P = \left(\frac{\theta}{360°}\right) \cdot 2\pi r$	Sector area: $A = \left(\frac{\theta}{360°}\right) \cdot \pi r^2$

PRACTICE

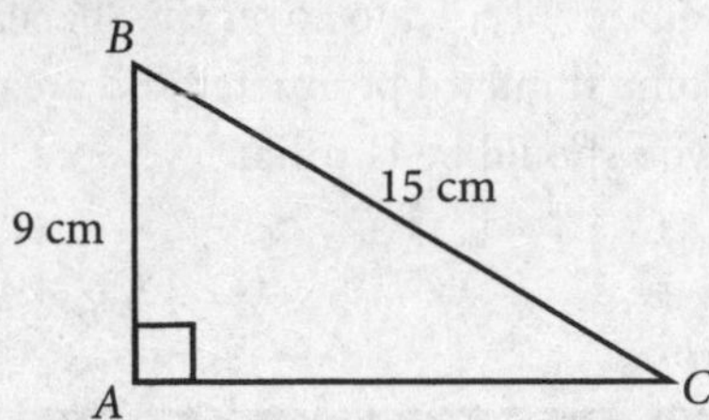

What is the area of right triangle ABC in square centimeters?

A. 12

B. 36

C. 54

D. 108

The correct answer is C. The area of a triangle is $\frac{1}{2}bh$. We already know the height of the triangle, 9 centimeters. To find the base, use the Pythagorean theorem:

$$9^2 + AC^2 = 152$$
$$81 + AC^2 = 225$$
$$AC^2 = 144$$
$$AC = 12$$

Since the base of the triangle is 12, the area of the triangle is $\frac{1}{2}(12)(9) = 54$ square centimeters. Choice B is the perimeter of the triangle, in centimeters. Choice D is double the area, which may result from forgetting the $\frac{1}{2}$ in the area formula.

Which of the following answers represents the area of a circle with diameter 20 inches?

A. 16π in.^{2}

B. 64π in.^{2}

C. 100π in.^{2}

D. 400π in.^{2}

The correct answer is C. The formula for the area of a circle is $A = \pi r^2$, where r is the radius of the circle. Since the diameter of the circle is given as 20 inches, we can find the radius by dividing the diameter by 2: $r = 20/2 = 10$ inches. So, the area of the circle is $A = \pi(10)^2 = 100\pi$ in.^{2}. Choice A is the area of a circle with a radius of 4 inches, not 10 inches. Choice B is the area if the circle had a radius of 8 inches, meaning the diameter would have to be 16 inches. Choice D indicates a diameter of 40 inches.

Surface Area and Volume of Solids

Two measures of interest for three-dimensional solids are surface area and volume. Conceptually, to compute the surface area of a solid, the solid is dissected and flattened out so that it can be visualized as a combination of recognizable figures whose areas can be computed using known formulas. The volume of a solid in space is the number of unit cubes needed to fill it. The following table details formulas for the surface area and volume of some common solids.

SURFACE AREA AND VOLUME FORMULAS			
Solid	**Illustration**	**Surface Area Formula**	**Volume Formula**
Cube	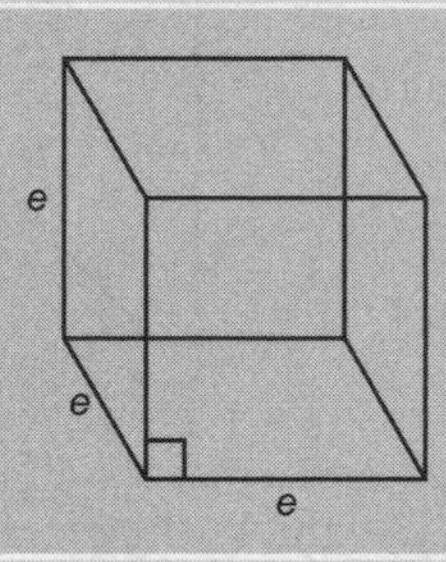 e e e	$SA = 6e^2$	$V = e^3$
Rectangular Prism	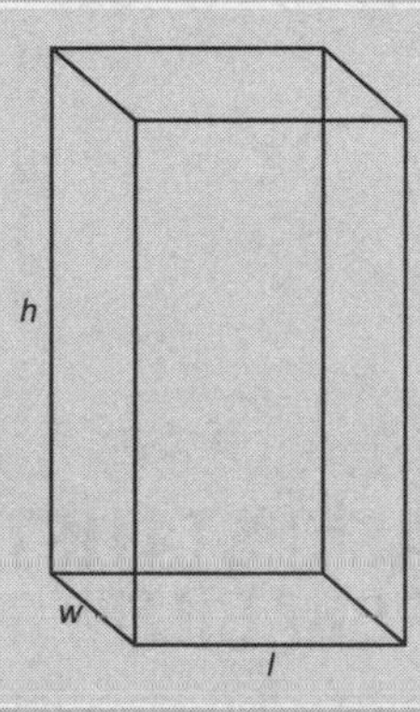 h w l	$SA = 2(lw + lh + wh)$	$V = lwh$
Circular Cone	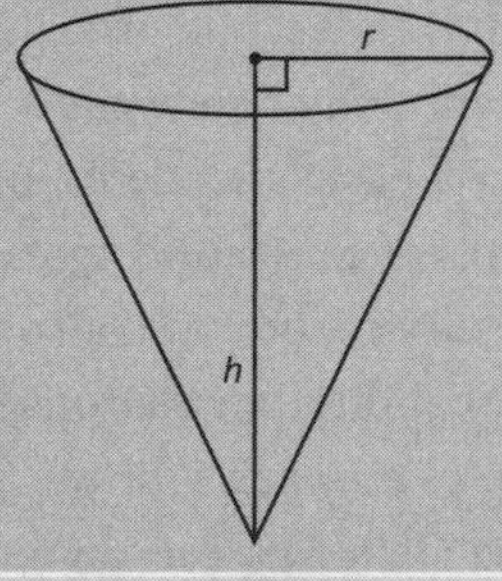 r h	$SA = \pi r^2 + \pi r\sqrt{r^2 + h^2}$	$V = \frac{1}{3}\pi r^2 h$
Circular Cylinder	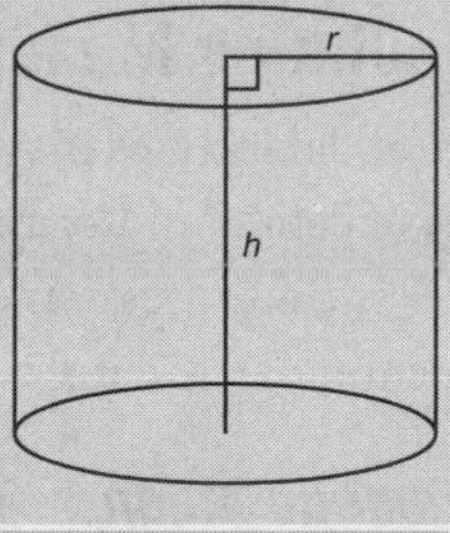 r h	$SA = 2\pi r^2 + 2\pi rh$	$V = \pi r^2 h$
Sphere	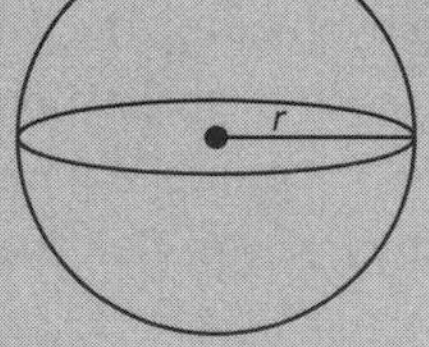 r	$SA = 4\pi r^2$	$V = \frac{4}{3}\pi r^3$

PRACTICE

Find the volume of a right rectangular prism with dimensions 5 in., 9 in., and 6 in.

A. 39 in.^{3}

B. 59 in.^{3}

C. 240 in.^{3}

D. 270 in.^{3}

The correct answer is D. The volume formula for a rectangular prism is $V = l \times w \times h$. After plugging in the given values, the volume of this rectangular prism is 270 in^3.

If the surface area of a cube is 150 square inches, what is the length of the diagonal of one of its faces?

A. 5 inches

B. $\sqrt{10}$ inches

C. $2\sqrt{5}$ inches

D. $5\sqrt{2}$ inches

The correct answer is D. Think about what a cube looks like and what you are being asked to find. The diagonal of a face of a cube is the hypotenuse of a right triangle whose legs are both edges, *e*, of the cube. So it can be found using the Pythagorean theorem if you know *e*. You must use the given information about the surface area to find *e*. The surface area of a cube with edge *e* is $6e^2$. Setting that equal to 150 and solving for *e* yields the following:

$$6e^2 = 150$$
$$e^2 = 25$$
$$e = 5$$

As such, a face of the cube looks like this:

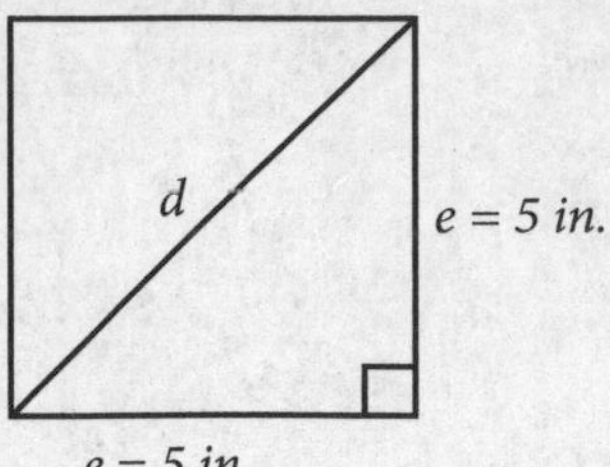

Use the Pythagorean theorem to find *d*:

$$d^2 = 5^2 + 5^2 = 50$$
$$d = \sqrt{50}$$
$$d = 5\sqrt{2}$$

BASIC STATISTICS AND PROBABILITY

Statistics is the analysis of data to determine patterns and trends while probability is the assessment of the likelihood of an event occurring. You'll need to demonstrate basic knowledge of statistics by finding measures of center and spread (mean, median, and mode). Additionally, you'll also need to be familiar with basic probability calculations for one or multiple events. Both topics may arise for the SAT Math's Problem-Solving and Data Analysis domain.

Calculating Measures of Center

A set of data values may be summarized using measures of center and/or measures of spread. Measures of center include mean, median, and mode and represent the center of the data.

Arithmetic Mean

An average or arithmetic mean is a value that is computed by dividing the sum of a set of terms by the number of terms in the collection. To find the average (arithmetic mean) of a group of *n* numbers, simply add the numbers and divide by *n*. Consider the following problem.

PRACTICE

Find the average (arithmetic mean) of 32, 50, and 47.

A. 26

B. 32

C. 43

D. 50

The correct answer is C.

$$\frac{32+50+47}{3}=43$$

Median and Mode

In order to find the median of a group of numbers, list the numbers in numerical order from smallest to largest. The median is the number in the middle. For example, the median of the numbers 3, 3, 5, 9, and 10 is 5. The median and the arithmetic mean are not the same. In this problem, for example, the arithmetic mean is $30 \div 5 = 6$.

If there is an even number of numbers, the median is equal to the arithmetic mean of the two numbers in the middle. For example, to find the median of 3, 3, 5, 7, 9, and 10, note that the two middle numbers are 5 and 7. The median, then, is $\frac{5+7}{2}=6$.

The mode of a group of numbers is simply the number that occurs most frequently. Therefore, the mode of the group of numbers 3, 3, 5, 7, 9, and 10 is 3. If all of the numbers in a group only appear once, then there is no mode. A data set can have more than one mode.

PRACTICE

What is the median of the following group of eight numbers?

2, 7, 8, 9, 9, 9, 10, and 10

A. 2

B. 8

C. 9

D. 10

The correct answer is C. Since this data set has an even number of data values, the median is the arithmetic mean of the two numbers in the middle. These numbers are both 9, so the median is $\frac{9+9}{2}=9$. Note that the mode is also 9.

Probability

Probability refers to the likelihood of an event occurring (or not occurring). By definition, probability ranges from 0 to 1. Probability is never negative, and it is never greater than 1. Here's the basic formula for determining probability:

$$\text{Probability}=\frac{\text{desired outcomes}}{\text{total number of possible occurrences}}$$

Probability can be expressed as a fraction, a percent, or a decimal number. The greater the probability, the greater the fraction, percent, or decimal number and the greater the likelihood of the event occurring.

Determining Probability (Single Event)

Probability plays an integral role in games of chance, including many casino games. In the throw of a single die, for example, the probability of rolling a 5 is "one in six," or $\frac{1}{6}$, or $16\frac{2}{3}\%$. Of course, the probability of rolling a certain other number is the same. A standard deck of 52 playing cards contains 12 face cards.

The probability of selecting a face card from a full deck is $\frac{12}{52}$ or $\frac{3}{13}$. The probability of selecting a queen from a full deck is $\frac{4}{52}$, or $\frac{1}{13}$, as a full card deck would contain four queen cards. To calculate the probability of an event NOT occurring, just subtract the probability of the event occurring from 1.

PRACTICE

A bag contains only white, yellow, and purple cubes. There are a total of 40 cubes in the bag, and the probability of NOT selecting a yellow cube is $\frac{3}{4}$. How many yellow cubes are in the bag?

A. 4

B. 5

C. 8

D. 10

The correct answer is D. If the probability of NOT selecting a yellow cube is $\frac{3}{4}$, then the probability of selecting a yellow cube is $1-\frac{3}{4}=\frac{1}{4}$. Let x represent the number of yellow cubes in the bag. Set up the following proportion to solve for x:

$$\frac{1}{4}=\frac{x}{40}$$
$$40=4x$$
$$10=x$$

Therefore, there are 10 yellow cubes in the bag.

Determining Probability (Two Events)

To determine probability involving two or more events, it is important to distinguish probabilities involving independent events from an event that is dependent on another one.

Two events are independent if neither event affects the probability that the other will occur. The events may involve the random selection of one object from *each of two or more groups.* Alternatively, they may involve randomly selecting one object from a group, then *replacing* it and selecting again (as in a "second round" or "another turn" of a game).

In either scenario, to find the probability of two events BOTH occurring, multiply their individual probabilities together:

probability of event 1 occurring × probability of event 2 occurring
=
probability of both events occurring

For example, assume that you randomly select one letter from each of two sets: {A, B} and {C, D, E}. The probability of selecting A and C = $\frac{1}{2}\times\frac{1}{3}=\frac{1}{6}$.

To calculate the probability that two events will not both occur, subtract the probability of both events occurring from 1.

Now let's look at dependent probability. Two distinct events might be related in that one event affects the probability of the other one occurring—for example, randomly selecting one object from a group, then selecting a second object from the same group without replacing the first selection. Removing one object from the group increases the odds of selecting any particular object from those that remain.

For example, assume that you randomly select one letter from the set {A, B, C, D}. Then, from the remaining three letters, you select another letter. What is the probability of selecting both A and B? To answer this question, you need to consider each of the two selections separately.

In the first selection, the probability of selecting either A or B is $\frac{2}{4}$. But the probability of selecting the second of the two is $\frac{1}{3}$. Why? Because after the first selection, only *three* letters remain from which to select. Since the question asks for the odds of selecting both A and B (as opposed to either one), multiply the two individual probabilities: $\frac{2}{4}\times\frac{1}{3}=\frac{2}{12}$, or $\frac{1}{6}$.

10

SUMMING IT UP

- Multiple SAT Math domains rely on keen understanding of numbers and operations; ratios, proportions, and percentages; algebra; geometry; and probability and statistics. Improving your SAT Math score requires a firm grasp of these fundamental mathematical concepts.
- Numbers and Operations topics represent fundamental math vocabulary and procedures for performing basic operations—whether for working with basic calculations, fractions, exponents, absolute value, and more.
  - The greatest common factor (GCF) of two whole numbers *n* and *m* is the largest whole number that divides into both *n* and *m* evenly. The least common multiple (LCM) of two whole numbers *n* and *m* is the smallest whole number into which both *n* and *m* divide.
  - The proper order of operations is PEMDAS: parentheses, exponents, multiplication and division (from left to right), and addition and subtraction (from left to right).
  - If *b* and *n* are natural numbers, then $b^n = \underbrace{b \times \ldots \times b}_{n \text{ times}}$. Here, *b* is called the base and *n* is the exponent.
  - The square root of a nonnegative real number *a* is another number *b* whose square is *a*, that is $b^2 = a$. In such case, we write $\sqrt{a} = b$. A cube root of a real number *a* is another number *b* whose cube is *a*, that is $b^3 = a$. In such case, we write $\sqrt[3]{a} = b$.
  - The absolute value of *a*, denoted $|a|$, measures the distance between *a* and 0.
- Ratios, Decimals, Proportions, Rates, and Percentages represent ways of thinking about part-to-whole relationships. These concepts are all related and can be necessary in various SAT Math questions.
  - A ratio is a comparison of one quantity *x* to another quantity *y*, expressed as a fraction $\frac{x}{y}$, or sometimes using the notation *x*:*y*. In words, this is interpreted as, "for every *x* of one type, there are *y* of the second type."
  - A proportion is an equation relating two ratios. In symbols, a proportion is expressed by setting two fractions equal to each other, say $\frac{a}{b} = \frac{c}{d}$.
  - The word *percent* means "per hundred." A percentage is used to express the number of parts out of a whole of 100.
- Basic Algebra concepts will appear in questions throughout the SAT Math section to assess your ability to manipulate basic expressions and equations whether for simple algebra or more advanced math.
  - An algebraic expression is an arithmetic combination of terms. All of the rules (exponent rules, order of operations, etc.) and properties of arithmetic (commutative property, associative property, etc.) apply to algebraic expressions.

- Linear equations are equations in which the variable is raised to the first power. The process of solving linear equations involves simplifying various expressions by clearing fractions and using the order of operations and the distributive property of multiplication in order to get the variable on one side of the equation.
- A variable is an unknown quantity represented by a letter, like x, y, or z; a constant is a real number whose value does not change.
- Like terms are two or more terms that have the same variables and powers.

- Basic Geometry concepts—such as knowledge of points, lines, angles, polygons (properties as well as calculations for area and volume)—along with coordinate geometry will be used in various combinations for Geometry and Trigonometry domain questions.
  - Points are defined positions on a plane, and they are often seen in both coordinate grids and planar figures.
  - Lines are sequences of points that have indefinite lengths. Line segments have definite end points.
  - Coordinate grids are divided into four quadrants, and points placed in these quadrants are given x and y coordinates.
  - Quadrant I assigns positive x and y coordinates. Quadrant II assigns negative x and positive y coordinates. Quadrant III assigns negative x and y coordinates. Quadrant IV assigns positive x and negative y coordinates.
  - The distance and midpoint formulas can be used to determine the distance between two points and the exact middle point of a line/line segment, respectively.
  - The slope of a line is its steepness, calculated by dividing the rise (vertical change) over the run (horizontal change).
  - Angles are classified according to their "size" or measure; the units in which this is expressed are degrees or radians. An angle with a measure between 0 and 90 degrees is acute.
  - An angle with a measure of 90 degrees is a right angle.
  - An angle with a measure between 90 and 180 degrees is obtuse.
  - An angle with a measure of 180 degrees is a straight angle.
  - Two angles with measures that sum to 90 degrees are complementary; two angles with measures that sum to 180 degrees are supplementary.
  - Two angles that have the same measure are congruent. Vertical angles are always congruent.
  - A right triangle is one that has a right angle; an acute triangle is one in which all three angles are acute; an obtuse triangle has one obtuse angle.

- An equilateral triangle is one in which all three sides have the same length; an isosceles triangle has at least two sides with the same length; a scalene triangle has three sides of different lengths.
- The triangle sum rule says that the sum of the measures of the three angles in any triangle must be 180. The triangle inequality says that the sum of the lengths of any two sides of a triangle must be strictly larger than the length of the third side.
- The Pythagorean theorem states that for a right triangle with legs a and b and hypotenuse c, $a^2 + b^2 = c^2$.
- Two triangles ΔABC and ΔDEF are congruent if all three corresponding pairs of angles are congruent AND all three corresponding sides are congruent. Two triangles ΔABC and ΔDEF are similar if the ratios of the three pairs of corresponding sides are the same; that is, $\frac{AB}{DE} = \frac{BC}{EF} = \frac{AC}{DF} = k$, where k is a positive number.
- The area formula for a triangle with base b and height h is $A = \frac{1}{2} b \cdot h$.
- Two quadrilaterals of the same type are congruent if their corresponding sides are all congruent, and they are called similar if the four ratios of their corresponding sides are equal.
- The perimeter of a square with side length s is $P = 4s$. The area of a square with side length s is $A = s^2$.
- The perimeter of a rectangle with length l and width w is $P = 2l + 2w$. The area of a rectangle with length l and width w is $A = lw$.
- The circumference of a circle with radius r (or diameter $d = 2r$) is $C = 2\pi r = \pi d$. The area of a circle with radius r is $A = \pi r^2$.
- The volume of a cube with side length s is $V = s^3$.
- The volume of a rectangular box with side lengths l, w, and h is $V = lwh$.
- The volume of a cylinder with base radius r and height h is $V = \pi r^2 h$.

- Basic Statistics and Probability concepts will appear as related to Problem-Solving and Data Analysis domain questions to check your understanding of basic measures of center (mean, median, and mode) and your grasp of how to calculate simple probability.
    - The probability of an event is a number between 0 and 1 that describes the percent chance that the event has of occurring.
    - To compute the mean of a list of numbers, simply add the numbers and divide by how many numbers are added: $\text{mean} = \frac{\text{sum of values}}{\text{number of values}}$.
    - Median is the middle value of a set of numbers when they are arranged in order from lowest to highest. Mode is the value that appears most in a set of numbers.

FUNDAMENTAL SAT® MATH SKILLS

12 Questions—19 Minutes

Directions: The questions in this section address a number of important math skills.

Use of a calculator is permitted for all questions.

Unless otherwise indicated:

- All variables and expressions represent real numbers.
- Figures provided are drawn to scale.
- All figures lie in a plane.
- The domain of a given function f is the set of all real numbers x for which $f(x)$ is a real number.

Reference:

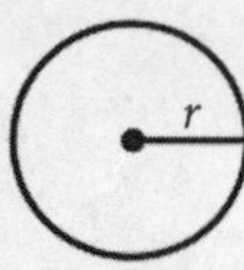

$A = \pi r^2$
$C = 2\pi r$

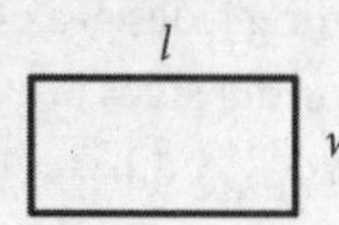

$A = lw$

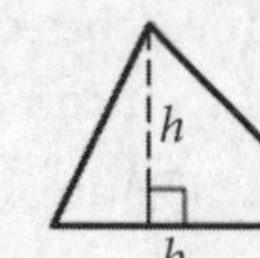

$A = \frac{1}{2}bh$

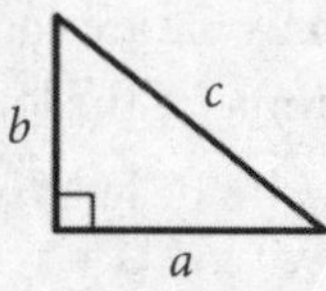

$c^2 = a^2 + b^2$

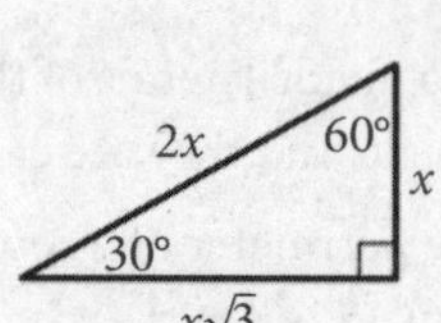

Special Right Triangles

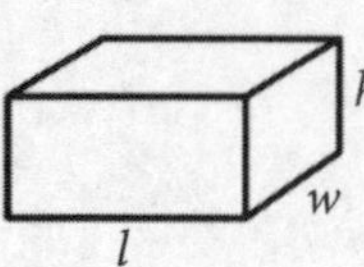

$V = lwh$

$V = \pi r^2 h$

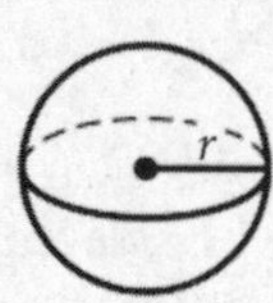

$V = \frac{4}{3}\pi r^3$

$V = \frac{1}{3}\pi r^2 h$

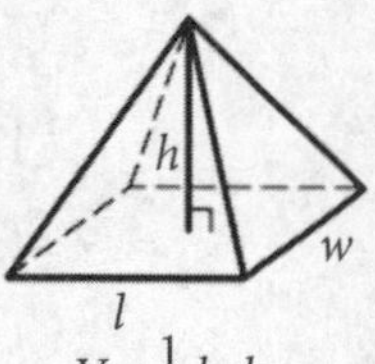

$V = \frac{1}{3}lwh$

The number of degrees of arc in a circle is 360.

The number of radians of arc in a circle is 2π.

The sum of the measures in degrees of the angles of a triangle is 180.

1. A board game involves a spinner with congruent sections numbered 1 through 25. On a given spin, the spinner has an equal chance of landing on any number. What is the probability that the spinner will land on a number that is divisible by 3?

A. $\frac{17}{25}$

B. $\frac{8}{25}$

C. $\frac{7}{25}$

D. $\frac{3}{25}$

2. Phillip answered 4 of the 35 questions on his driving exam incorrectly. What percentage of the questions did Phillip answer correctly?

A. 89%

B. 77%

C. 23%

D. 13%

3. Increasing a positive number by 40% and then decreasing the result by 30% is the same as which of the following?

A. Increasing the original number by 10%

B. Decreasing the original number by 12%

C. Increasing the original number by 2%

D. Decreasing the original number by 2%

4. If $3x + 2 = 9x + 14$, what is the value of $4x^3$?

A. 0

B. –2

C. –24

D. –32

5. What is the value of $m^2 - 6mn^3 + n$ when $m = -2$ and $n = -1$?

A. –17

B. –13

C. –9

D. 9

6. A lab technician took a measurement of new rainfall once a day during a five-day work week. The table below indicates how many inches of new rainfall were recorded on each day.

Day	Inches of New Rainfall
Monday	1.0
Tuesday	1.5
Wednesday	0
Thursday	1.0
Friday	0.5

What is the average number of inches per day for this work week?

A. 0

B. 0.8

C. 1

D. 4

7. Assume $a > 0$. Which of these expressions represents the distance between the points $P(-a, 2a)$ and $Q(-3a, -2a)$?

A. $2a$ units

B. $a\sqrt{2}$ units

C. $2a\sqrt{5}$ units

D. $2a^2$ units

8. The measure of angle A is 6 degrees less than twice the measure of angle B. If angles A and B are complementary, what is the measure of angle A?

A. 28°

B. 32°

C. 58°

D. 62°

9.

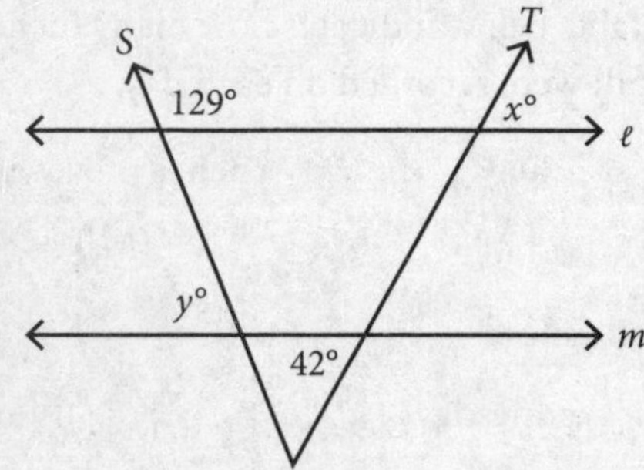

Assume lines l and m are parallel in the diagram. What is the value of $y + x$?

A. 42

B. 51

C. 93

D. 189

10. Which expression represents the length of CD in the rectangle $ABCD$?

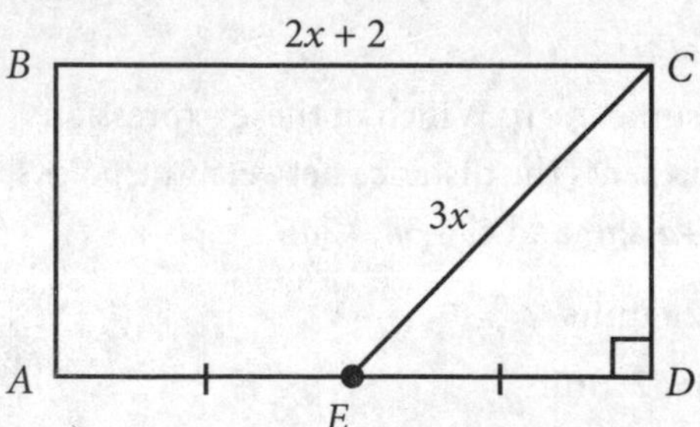

A. $2x - 1$

B. $4x + 1$

C. $8x^2 - 2x - 1$

D. $\sqrt{8x^2 - 2x - 1}$

11. What is the value of x in the equation $-\frac{1}{3}\left(3-\frac{4}{3}x\right)=-3x$?

A. $\frac{9}{7}$

B. $\frac{9}{23}$

C. $\frac{9}{31}$

D. $-\frac{9}{23}$

12. What is the sum of the polynomials $4ab^3 + 3a^2b^3$ and $-a^2b - 2a^2b^3$?

A. $4ab^3 - a^2b + 5a^2b^3$

B. $3ab^3 + a^2b^3$

C. $4ab^3 - a^2b + a^2b^3$

D. $4ab^3 + a^3b + 5a^3b^3$

ANSWER KEY AND EXPLANATIONS

1. B	3. D	5. C	7. C	9. C	11. C
2. A	4. D	6. B	8. C	10. D	12. C

1. **The correct answer is B.** There are a total of 25 numbers on the wheel, so we must determine how many of these 25 numbers are divisible by 3. Writing them down, we see that 3, 6, 9, 12, 15, 18, 21, and 24 are precisely the numbers from 1 to 25 that are divisible by 3. Since there are 8 of them and 25 numbers in all, the probability that the number on which the spinner lands is divisible by 3 is $\frac{8}{25}$.

2. **The correct answer is A.** If Phillip answered 4 of the 35 questions incorrectly, then he answered 35 – 4 = 31 correctly. By definition, the percentage is equal to $\frac{\text{part}}{\text{whole}} \times 100$. So Phillip answered $\frac{31}{35} \times 100$ of the questions correctly, which is 89%.

3. **The correct answer is D.** Let x represent some number. Increasing the number by 40% produces the new number $(1 + 0.40)x = 1.40x$. Now, decreasing this result by 30% means subtracting 30% of $1.40x$ from $1.40x$: $(0.30)(1.40x) = 0.42x$, and subtracting this from $1.40x$ yields $0.98x$. Comparing this to the original number x shows that the end result is $0.02x$ less than x. You could have decreased the number by 2% to arrive at the same result.

4. **The correct answer is D.** First, solve the given equation for x:

$$\begin{aligned} 3x+2&=9x+14 \\ 2&=6x+14 \\ -12&=6x \\ -2&=x \end{aligned}$$

Now, evaluate $4x^3$ at $x = -2$ to get $4(-2)^3 = 4(-8) = -32$.

5. **The correct answer is C.** Plug the given values of m and n into the expression and evaluate:

$$\begin{aligned} m^2-6mn^3+n&=(-2)^2-6(-2)(-1)^3+(-1) \\ &=4-6(-2)(-1)-1 \\ &=4-12-1 \\ &=-8-1 \\ &=-9 \end{aligned}$$

6. **The correct answer is B.** Remember that $\text{average} = \frac{\text{sum of values}}{\text{number of values}}$. To find the average number of inches of rainfall per day for this data, divide the total number of inches of rainfall for the week by the number of days, 5:

$$\frac{(1.0+1.5+0+1.0+0.5)}{5}=\frac{4.0}{5}=0.8$$

So the mean daily rainfall is 0.8 inches.

7. **The correct answer is C.** In this situation, you'll need to use the distance formula. Applying the formula and simplifying yields the following:

$$\begin{aligned} \sqrt{(-a-(-3a))^2+(2a-(-2a))^2}&=\sqrt{(-a+3a)^2+(2a+2a)^2} \\ &=\sqrt{(2a)^2+(4a)^2} \\ &=\sqrt{4a^2+16a^2} \\ &=\sqrt{20a^2} \\ &=2a\sqrt{5} \end{aligned}$$

8. **The correct answer is C.** Since you are given how two angles are related but do not know the measure of either one, you need to call one of them x. Since angle A is defined in terms of angle B, the better choice is to give the name x to the measure of angle B. Then, the measure of angle A is $2x - 6$.

Being complementary angles, the sum of their measures is 90°. This gives the equation $x + (2x - 6) = 90$. Solve for x, as follows:

$$\begin{aligned} x+(2x-6)&=90 \\ 3x-6&=90 \\ 3x&=96 \\ x&=32 \end{aligned}$$

Recall that x represents angle B. You still need to solve for angle A. Measure of angle A is $2(32) - 6 = 58°$.

9. **The correct answer is C.** The strategy here is to fill in the missing angles using various facts about how corresponding angles and vertical angles are related, as well as supplementary angles. Do so in the order shown in the diagram below, starting with the circled number 1 and proceeding to circled number 4:

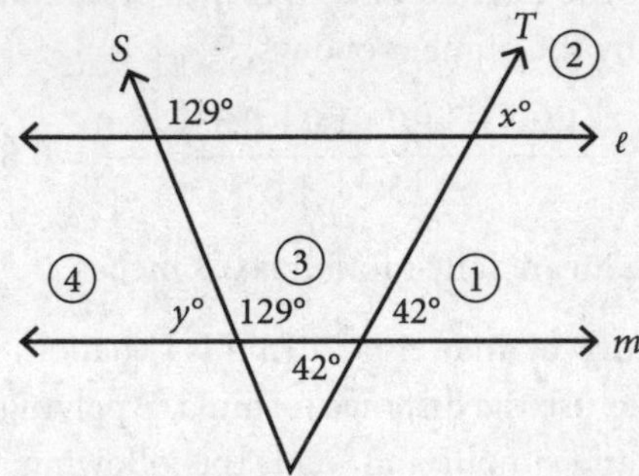

Step 1: Vertical angles are always congruent. So this angle measures 42°.

Step 2: Since lines l and m are parallel, you can use line T as a transversal. Then, corresponding angles are congruent, so the angle x has a measure of 42°.

Step 3: Since lines l and m are parallel, you can use line S as a transversal. Then, corresponding angles are congruent, so this angle has a measure of 129°.

Step 4: This angle is supplementary to angle 3, so it measures $180° - 129° = 51°$.

Thus, $x = 42$ and $y = 51$. So $x + y = 93$.

10. **The correct answer is D.** Break the problem down into smaller steps. Here is the thought process: if you had the length of ED, then you could use the Pythagorean theorem to find CD. Segments AE and ED have the same number of hash marks, which means they are congruent. Since $ABCD$ is a rectangle, AD and BC are congruent. Then, ED must be half the length of BC, or $\frac{1}{2}(2x+2)=x+1$. Now you can use the Pythagorean theorem to find ED:

$$\begin{aligned} (EC)^2&=(CD)^2+(ED)^2 \\ (3x)^2&=(CD)^2+(x+1)^2 \\ (CD)^2&=(3x)^2-(x+1)^2 \\ (CD)^2&=9x^2-(x^2+2x+1) \\ (CD)^2&=8x^2-2x-1 \\ CD&=\sqrt{8x^2-2x-1} \end{aligned}$$

11. **The correct answer is C.** Generally, getting rid of fractions in an equation as soon as possible is preferable. Here, multiply both sides by –3 to get rid of the leftmost fraction on the left side:

$$\begin{aligned} (-3)\cdot-\frac{1}{3}\left(3-\frac{4}{3}x\right)&=(-3)\cdot(-3x) \\ 3-\frac{4}{3}x&=9x \end{aligned}$$

Now, multiply both sides by 3 again to get rid of the remaining fraction:

$$\begin{aligned} 3\cdot\left(3-\frac{4}{3}x\right)&=3\cdot(9x) \\ 9-4x&=27x \end{aligned}$$

Now add $4x$ to both sides to gather the x terms on one side of the equation $9 = 31x$; make sure you do not subtract it, or you will get choice B. Finally, divide both sides by the coefficient of x to get $x=\frac{9}{31}$.

12. **The correct answer is C.** Do not be thrown by the variables—simply combine like terms. In the expression $(4ab^3 + 3a^2b^3) + (-a^2b - 2a^2b^3)$, there are two multiples of a^2b^3. Since $3a^2b^3 + (-2a^2b^3) = a^2b^3$, the entire expression simplifies to $4ab^3 - a^2b + a^2b^3$.

CHAPTER

Algebra

ALGEBRA

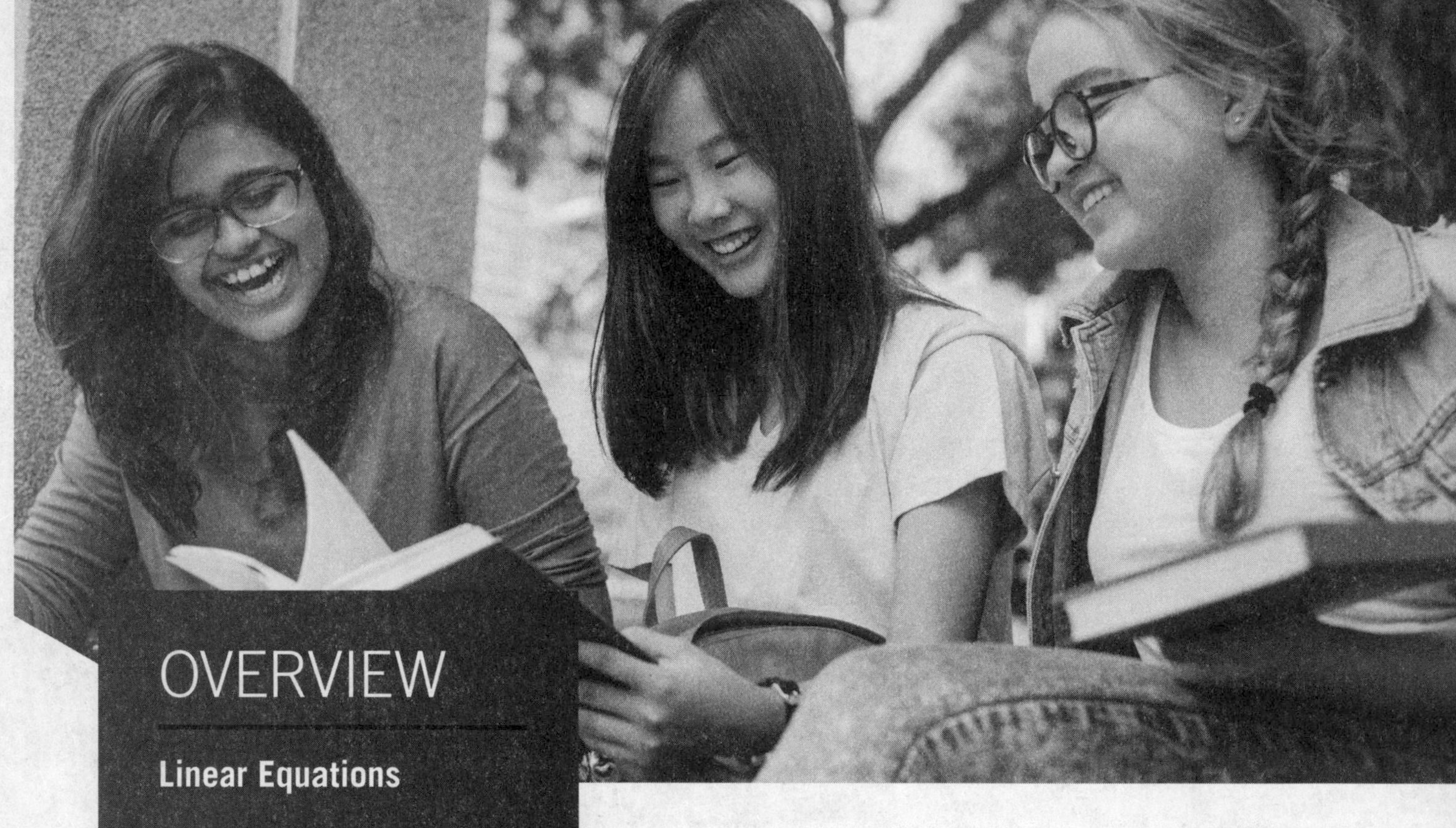

OVERVIEW

- Linear Equations
- Systems of Linear Equations
- Linear Inequalities
- Summing It Up
- Test Yourself: Algebra

The SAT Math section's Algebra domain represents 35% of the questions across both Math modules. The questions test your ability to work with linear equations in a variety of situations and forms. You need to be able to, as stated by the College Board, "interpret, create, use, represent, and solve" linear equations and inequalities, whether in one or two variables, isolated, or as part of a system. The following chapter offers further insight into linear equations, graphing, and modeling of different situations. Use the examples and practice questions throughout the chapter and the Test Yourself at the end of the chapter to assess your understanding of the different Algebra domain skills and testing points.

11

LINEAR EQUATIONS

A linear equation represents two algebraic expressions set equal to each other wherein the highest power is 1 and there are one or two variables. Linear equations are used to represent constant change in values and, when graphed in a coordinate plane, represent straight lines. The ability to work with linear equations—their points and forms—is critical to success with the SAT Math Algebra domain. The following sections revisit concepts introduced in Chapter 10 and expand on them to cover the various situations related to these fundamental algebraic equations.

Linear Equations in One and Two Variables

Recall that a basic linear equation will have at least one variable. It can appear in the form $Ax + B = 0$, wherein A and B are real numbers and x is a variable. The process for solving a linear equation with one variable is to perform operations so as to isolate the variable and set it equal to a value. For the linear equation $3x - 1 = 8$, you would add one to both sides and then divide by 3 to arrive at the solution $x = 3$. Such an equation could then be graphed on a coordinate plane to yield a vertical line that crosses the x-axis at 3.

Linear equations can also be presented with two variables in the form $Ax + By + C = 0$, wherein A, B, and C are real number coefficients of the variables x and y. The equation can be arranged in terms of x or y. The solution to a linear equation with two variables is any coordinate pair that would satisfy the equation. Thought of another way, any point that would fall onto the line of the equation when it is graphed in a coordinate plane is a solution. Examine the following linear equation: $3x - y = 8$. You have two variables, x and y, a coefficient of 3 for x and -1 for y. They are set equal to 8. Just as you would isolate the variable for a simple linear equation, so too would you do that for an equation with two variables. This time, let's isolate y:

$$\begin{aligned} 3x - y &= 8 \\ -y &= 8 - 3x \\ y &= -8 + 3x \\ y &= 3x - 8 \end{aligned}$$

This equation could then be graphed on the coordinate plane. The corresponding line would cross the y-axis at -8. The line would rise from left to right with a point at $(1, -5)$ and then another at $(2, -2)$. The line would also travel through point $(-1, -11)$. You can plug each of those sets of points into the original equation, and each one will make the equation true.

Those are the basics of linear equations, but for the SAT Math section, you'll also need to be familiar with graphing linear equations and representing various situations.

Graphing Linear Equations

Take a look at the following two-variable linear equation:

$$y = 2x + 1$$

Imagine you wanted to determine what points would be on that line if it were graphed. To do that, you can start with $x = 0$. When you substitute 0 for x, you know the corresponding y value will be 1. You can continue to substitute each point on the x-axis to determine each corresponding value for y, resulting in the following table:

x	y
0	1
1	3
2	5
3	7
4	9

You can make similar determinations about the solutions to the equation by using the different elements of the equation. When examining the equation, the 2 signifies the slope of the line—the steepness from one point to the next. The 1 is the y-intercept of the line—where the line intersects the y-axis. Those values tell you that at $x = 0$, $y = 1$. From $x = 0$ to $x = 1$, the slope of 2 means the corresponding y point will rise 2 and run 1 from the x-value, resulting in 3.

Regardless of how you find the points in the table, when they are plotted, you see the following graph.

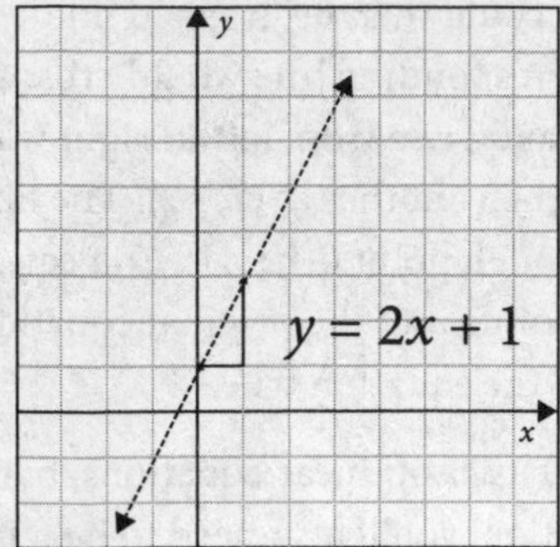

That linear equation is currently in the form $y = mx + b$, what is called the slope-intercept form. Each variable represents a key facet of the graphed line. The x and y represent corresponding points on the line. The b represents where the line crosses the y-axis, the y-intercept. The m is the slope of the line, which measures how steep the line is. A line that increases from left to right has a positive slope, and a line that decreases from left to right has a negative slope. A horizontal line has a slope of 0 since it is "flat," and a vertical line has an undefined slope.

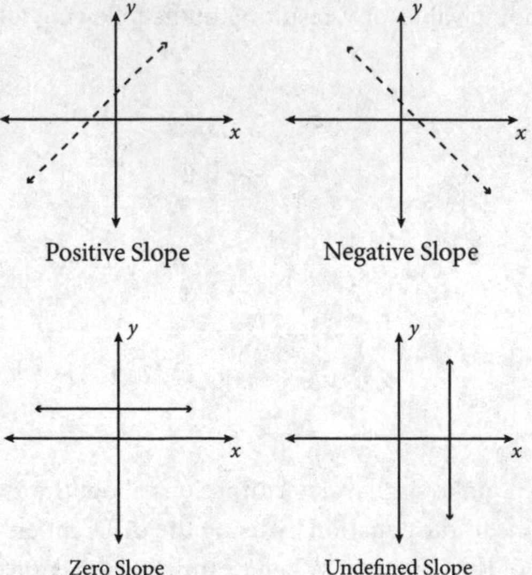

If (x_1, y_1) and (x_2, y_2) are any two points on a line, the slope is given by the formula:

$$m = \frac{(y_2 - y_1)}{(x_2 - x_1)}$$

For example, if a line contains the points (5, 7) and (3, 4), the slope would be $m = \frac{7-4}{5-3} = \frac{3}{2}$. A slope of $\frac{3}{2}$ represents the fact that for every 2 units moved horizontally along the x-axis, the line rises vertically 3 units.

An equation of degree one that contains the variables x and/or y raised to the first power, but no higher, will always have a straight line as its graph.

Let's look at a series of examples demonstrating different methods for graphing linear equations as dependent on the initial information provided.

EXAMPLES

Write the equation of the line containing the point (2, 1) and having slope 5.

Solution

Begin by taking the slope-intercept form $y = mx + b$ and substituting $m = 5$ to obtain $y = 5x + b$. To determine the value of the y-intercept b, substitute the coordinates of the point (2, 1) into the equation.

$$\begin{aligned} y &= 5x + b \quad \text{Substitute } (2, 1). \\ 1 &= 5(2) + b \quad \text{Solve for } b. \\ 1 &= 10 + b \\ -9 &= b \end{aligned}$$

Therefore, the equation of the line is $y = 5x - 9$.

What is the line represented by the equation $2x + 5y = 12$?

Solution

Write this equation in slope-intercept form.

$$2x + 5y = 12 \quad \text{Subtract } 2x \text{ from both sides.}$$
$$5y = -2x + 12 \quad \text{Divide both sides by 5.}$$
$$y = -\frac{2}{5}x + \frac{12}{5}$$

Therefore, the slope of the line is $-\frac{2}{5}$, and the y-intercept is $\frac{12}{5}$. Here is the graph of this line.

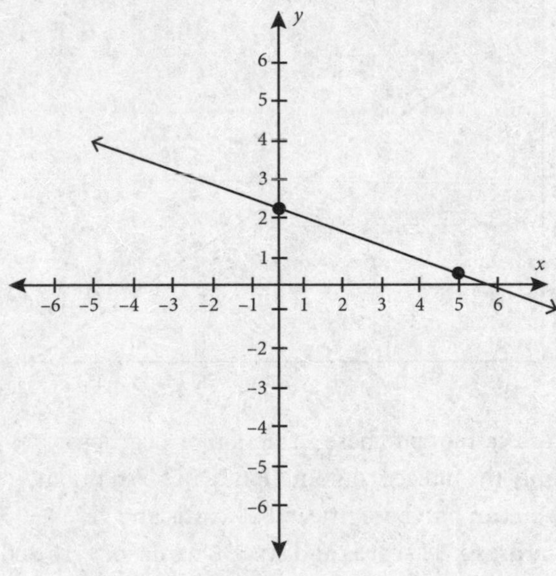

Graph the function $f(x) = 2x + 5$.

Solution

First, recognize that this is a linear equation. The notation $f(x) = 2x + 5$ translates to $y = 2x + 5$. Then, recognize that the slope is 2 and the y-intercept is (0, 5). To graph this function, first graph the point (0, 5). Then move up 2 units and then to the right 1 unit. This location is (1, 7). Starting at (0, 5) again, go down 2 units and then to the left 1 unit. This location is (–1, 3). Connect these points to form the graph of the function $f(x) = 2x + 5$.

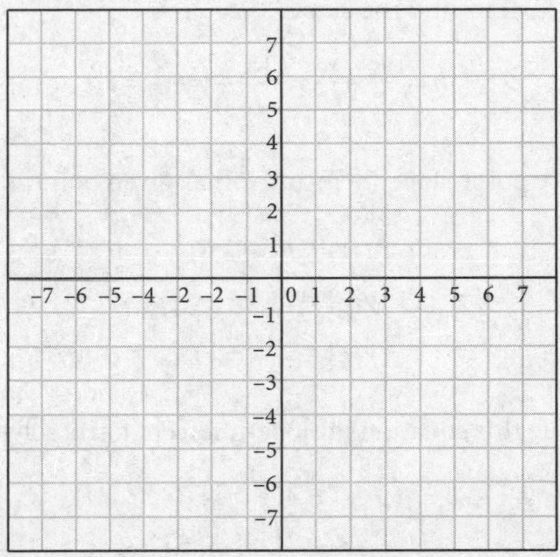

You can write an equation of a line from a graph given any two points on the line. First, use the two points to find the slope. Then use the point–slope form of an equation of a line: $y - y_1 = m(x - x_1)$. As an example, consider the following graph.

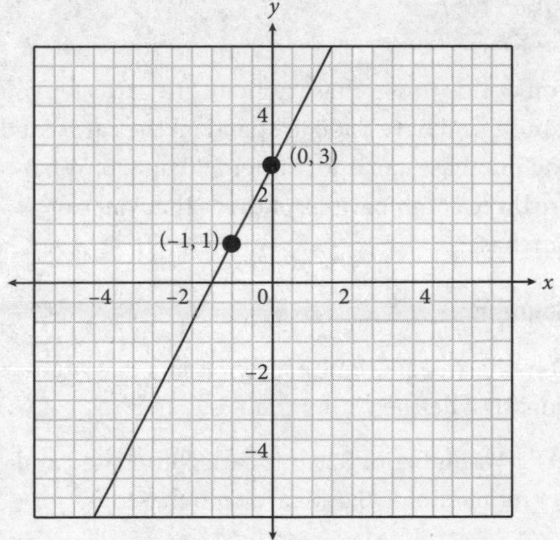

You need to first find the slope using two points on the line.

The slope formula is $m=\frac{y_2-y_1}{x_2-x_1}$. Use the points (0, 3) and (–1, 1) to find the slope.

$$m=\frac{y_2-y_1}{x_2-x_1}=\frac{1-3}{-1-0}=\frac{-2}{-1}=2$$

Use the point-slope form and either given point.

$$\begin{aligned}y-y_1&=m(x-x_1)\\y-1&=2(x-(-1))\\y-1&=2(x+1)\end{aligned}$$

To write this equation in slope-intercept form, solve for *y*.

$$\begin{aligned}y-1&=2(x+1)\\y&=2(x+1)+1\\y&=2x+2+1\\y&=2x+3\end{aligned}$$

Here's an example of how to write an equation of a line from a word problem and then graph the equation using the intercepts.

EXAMPLE

You decide to purchase holiday gift cards for your family. You have $300 to spend on the cards, and you purchase cards for either $20 or $30. What are three combinations of cards that you can purchase?

Solution

To write an equation that represents this situation, first define your variables.

Let x = number of $20 gift cards purchased and y = number of $30 gift cards purchased.

Now write an equation to represent the situation.

$$20x + 30y = 300$$

Use the intercepts to draw the graph.

$$\begin{aligned}20x+30y&=300\\20(0)+30y&=300\\30y&=300\\y&=10\end{aligned}$$

$$\begin{aligned}20x+30y&=300\\20x+30(0)&=300\\20x&=300\\x&=15\end{aligned}$$

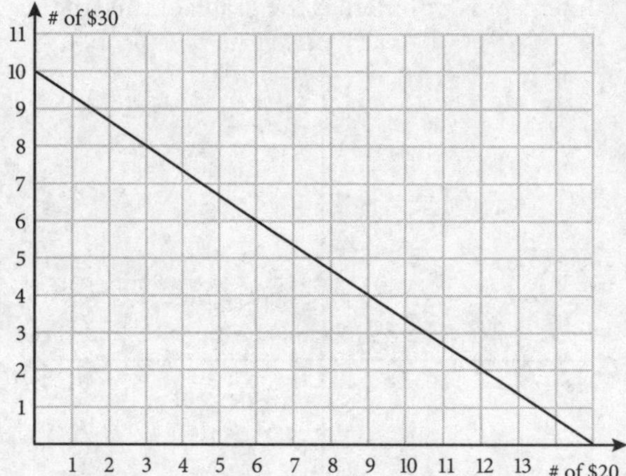

You cannot purchase a fraction of a card, so only the integer combinations can be solutions. You can purchase fifteen $20 cards and zero $30 cards, six $20 cards and six $30 cards, or zero $20 cards and ten $30 cards.

Although the question only asked for three answers, the other possible combinations are twelve $20 gift cards and two $30 gift cards, nine $20 gift cards and four $30 gift cards, and three $20 gift cards and eight $30 gift cards.

Types of Linear Equation Problems

Here are some other common SAT math problems that ask you to find the equation of a line, along with the best method of attack for each.

LINEAR EQUATION PROBLEM TYPES AND METHODS	
Problem Type	**Method of Attack**
1. Given a point and a slope (either written or by way of a graph), determine the equation of the line.	Use the point-slope formula.
2. Given two points on a line (either written or by way of a graph), determine the slope or the equation of the line.	First, find the slope of the line. (If this is what the question asks for, you are done.) Use the point-slope formula to find its equation.
3. Given a table of points that describe a linear relationship between variables x and y, determine the equation of the line.	Use any two of the points to find the slope. Then, use any of the points from the table with the slope to find the equation of the line.
4. Given a scenario in which two quantities are related linearly, find the equation of the line, or determine the value of one of the variables given the value of the other.	Identify one quantity as the input (x) and the other as the output (y). Typically, the input variable x is the quantity you change; the output variable y is the quantity you observe. Extract information from the description—either two points or a point and slope.

For all of the problem types listed in the table, depending on the way the choices are listed, you might then need to put the equation into slope-intercept form or standard form.

PRACTICE

What is the equation of a line that has a slope of –2 and passes through point (1, 5)?

A. $y = -2x - 1$

B. $y = -2x - 5$

C. $y = -2x + 7$

D. $y = 5x + 1$

The correct answer is C. Start with the slope-intercept equation and substitute in the values $m = -2$, $x = 1$, and $y = 5$. Then, solve for b.

$$\begin{aligned} y &= mx + b \\ 5 &= -2(1) + b \\ 5 &= -2 + b \\ 5 + 2 &= b \\ 7 &= b \end{aligned}$$

The slope-intercept form of the equation of the line is $y = -2x + 7$.

If given two points on a line, you'll use the same process, but first you'll need to find the slope using the slope formula. From there, you'll substitute in coordinates for one point and the slope into the slope-intercept form to find the y-intercept.

PRACTICE

Suppose that the points (1, –5) and (2, –1) lie on a line. Which of the following is the equation of this line?

A. $y = x - 8$

B. $y = 4x - 9$

C. $y = 4x + 9$

D. $y = x + 8$

The correct answer is B. First, determine the slope:

$$\text{slope} = m = \frac{-5-(-1)}{1-2} = 4$$

Using the point (2, –1) with the point-slope formula, the equation of the line passing through these two points is $y - (-1) = 4(x - 2)$. This is equivalent to $y = 4x - 9$.

Linear Functions and Applications

A linear function is a particular notation for a linear equation, taking the form $y = f(x) = mx + b$. Just as when graphing a linear equation, a linear function will have a slope and a y-intercept.

Example of Two Different Lines:

$f(x) = -2x + 2$ and $f(x) = 3x - 2$

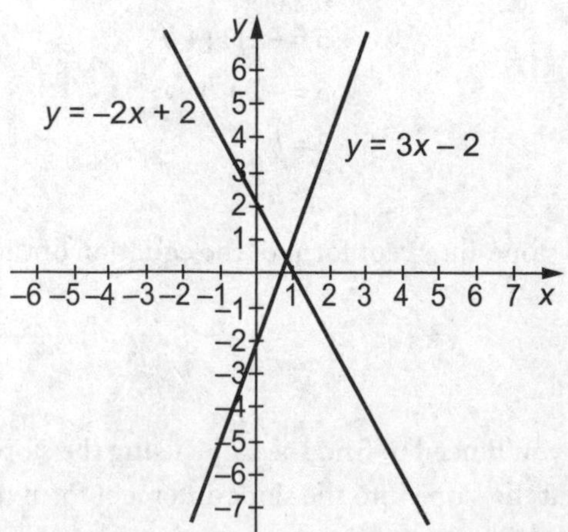

Typically, when a function is graphed, the independent variable is graphed along the x-axis, and the dependent variable is graphed along the y-axis. The set of x values over which a function occurs is called its domain. The set of y values for a function is called its range. Let's look at an example of a function graph.

EXAMPLE

In the town of Kenmore, a taxi ride costs $2.50 plus an extra $0.50 per mile. Write a function that represents the cost of taking a taxi ride, using x to represent the number of miles traveled.

Solution

If a ride costs $0.50 per mile, then the cost for x miles will be 0.50x$. Add this to the initial fee of $2.50 per ride.

$$C(x) = \$2.50 + 0.50x$$

The taxi ride function is a linear function. In order to graph this function, you must first determine the domain. Note that the domain must consist of non-negative numbers. Next, determine a few values that satisfy the rule for the function. For example, when $x = 0$, $C(0) = 2.50 + 0.50(0) = \$2.50$. A few additional simple computations will lead to the following table of values.

x	$C(x)$
0	$2.50
1	$3.00
2	$3.50
3	$4.00

If these points are plotted on a graph, you will see that they all lie on the same line. The entire graph of the taxi ride cost function follows.

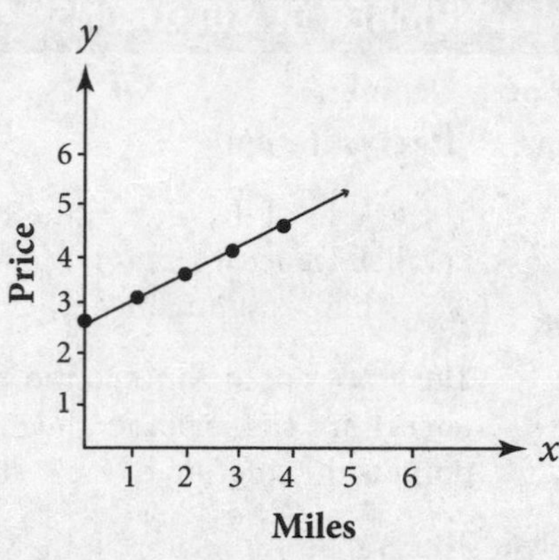

Let's look at some additional examples of real-world applications of linear functions.

EXAMPLE

In order to manufacture a new car model, a car-maker must initially spend \$750,000 to purchase the equipment needed to start the production process. After this, it costs \$7,500 to manufacture each car. In this case, what is the cost function that associates the cost of manufacturing cars to the number of cards manufactured?

Solution

The cost function is $C(x) = 7{,}500x + 750{,}000$, where x represents the number of cars manufactured, and $C(x)$ represents the cost of x cars. For example, the cost of making 7 cars is $C(7) = 7{,}500(7) + 750{,}000 = 52{,}500 + 750{,}000 =$ \$802,500.

The previous cost function is a linear function with $b = 750{,}000$ and $m = 7{,}500$. What is the domain of this function? Note that even though nothing has been said specifically about the domain, the only values that make sense as domain values are the non-negative integers 0, 1, 2, 3, 4, 5 . . . . In such a situation, assume that the domain contains only the values that make sense.

EXAMPLES

Using the cost function for the carmaker discussed in the previous example, how much would it cost to make 24 cars?

Solution

To solve this, you need to determine the value of $C(24)$.

$$\begin{aligned} C(24) &= 7{,}500(24) + 750{,}000 \\ &= 180{,}000 + 750{,}000 = \$930{,}000 \end{aligned}$$

Using the same cost function, determine how many cars could be made for \$990,000.

Solution

In this problem, you are told that the value of $C(x)$ is \$990,000, and you need to find the value of x. To do this, solve the equation:

$$\begin{aligned} 990{,}000 &= 7{,}500(x) + 750{,}000 \\ 240{,}000 &= 7{,}500x \\ 32 &= x \end{aligned}$$

Therefore, for \$990,000, 32 cars can be manufactured.

You purchased shorts for \$8 per pair, plus a shirt for \$6. Write a function that represents the cost of your purchases, where x represents the number of pairs of shorts you purchase. How much did you spend if you purchased 5 pairs of shorts?

Solution

$$f(x) = 8x + 6$$

Let $x = 5$, so $f(5) = 8(5) + 6 = 46$.

EXAMPLE

A bus pass has a starting value of \$60. Each ride costs \$2.50. Write a function that represents the remaining balance on the bus pass, where x represents the number of rides taken. How much money is left on the pass after 12 rides?

Solution

$$f(x) = 60 - 2.5x$$

Let $x = 12$, so $f(12) = 60 - 2.5(12) = 30$.

There is \$30 remaining on the pass after 12 rides.

SYSTEMS OF LINEAR EQUATIONS

A system of equations is a set of two or more (usually just two) equations that share a set of variables.

Here's an example of a system of linear equations:

$$2y + 7x = 24$$
$$y + 3x = 12$$

The solution to a system of equations with two variables is an ordered pair of numbers. The ordered pair is a solution to both equations in the system, representing the intersection point between the two equations if they were graphed in a coordinate plane.

For example, the solution to the system of equations above is (0, 12). With ordered pairs, the first number is the value for x and the second is the value for y. By substituting these numbers for the variables into both equations, you can check to make sure they work:

$$2(12) + 7(0) \rightarrow 24 + 0 = 24$$
$$12 + 3(0) \rightarrow 12 + 0 = 12$$

There are only three situations that can occur when trying to find the solution to a system, as shown in the following table.

NUMBER OF SOLUTIONS

Number of Solutions	Geometric Interpretation
0	The graphs of the lines in the system are parallel. Hence, there is no point that is on both lines simultaneously.
1	The graphs of the lines in the system intersect in a single point. The intersection point is the solution of the system.
Infinitely many	The graphs of the lines in the system are exactly the same. Every point on the line is a solution of the system.

Given a system of equations, there are two different methods for finding the values of the two variables: the substitution method and the elimination method.

The Substitution Method

To solve a system of two equations using the substitution method, follow these steps (we'll use x and y here):

1. In *either* equation, isolate one variable (x) on one side.
2. Substitute the expression that equals x in place of x in the other equation.
3. Solve that equation for y.
4. Now that you know the value of y, plug it into either equation to find the value of x.

Consider these two equations:

Equation A: $x = 4y$

Equation B: $x - y = 1$

In equation B, substitute 4*y* for *x*, and then solve for *y*:

$$\begin{aligned} 4y - y &= 1 \\ 3y &= 1 \\ y &= \frac{1}{3} \end{aligned}$$

To find *x*, substitute $\frac{1}{3}$ for *y* into either equation. The value of *x* will be the same for both.

Equation A:

$$x = 4\left(\frac{1}{3}\right) = \frac{4}{3}$$

Equation B:

$$x - \frac{1}{3} = 1$$
$$x = \frac{4}{3}$$

PRACTICE

$$\begin{cases} x = 2y - 14 \\ y = 5x + 1 \end{cases}$$

What is the value of *x* + *y* if the pair (*x*, *y*) satisfies the system above?

A. 3

B. 6

C. 9

D. 15

The correct answer is C. Substitute the expression for *y* given by the second equation in for *y* in the first equation and solve the result for *x*:

$$\begin{aligned} x &= 2(5x+1) - 14 \\ x &= 10x + 2 - 14 \\ x &= 10x - 12 \\ 12 &= 9x \\ \frac{4}{3} &= x \end{aligned}$$

Plug in this *x*-value into the second equation to determine the value of *y*:

$$y = 5\left(\frac{4}{3}\right) + 1 = \frac{23}{3}$$

Thus, $x + y = \frac{4}{3} + \frac{23}{3} = \frac{27}{3} = 9$

If $x - 4y = -2$ and $2x + y = 23$, what is the value of $5xy$?

A. 10

B. 30

C. 50

D. 150

The correct answer is D. Let's apply the substitution method. Solve the first equation for *x* to get $x = 4y - 2$ and substitute this in for *x* in the second equation to get $2(4y - 2) + y = 23$. Solving for *y* yields $8y - 4 + y = 23$, which is equivalent to $9y = 27$, so $y = 3$. Plugging this value back into the first equation yields $x = 4(3) - 2 = 10$.

The final step here is to evaluate the expression $5xy$ using $x = 10$ and $y = 3$ (since these are the only values of *x* and *y* for which both equations hold simultaneously). Doing so yields $5(10)(3) = 150$.

The Elimination Method

Another way to solve for two variables in a system of two equations is with the elimination method, sometimes also referred to as the addition-subtraction method. Here are the steps:

1. "Line up" the two equations by listing the same variables and other terms in the same order. Place one equation above the other.
2. Make the coefficient of *either* variable the same in both equations (you can disregard the sign) by multiplying every term in one of the equations.
3. Add the two equations, or subtract one equation from the other, to eliminate one variable.
4. As needed, substitute the value of one variable into one of the equations to solve for the value of the second variable.

Consider these two equations:

Equation A: $x = 3 + 3y$

Equation B: $2x + y = 4$

In equation A, subtract $3y$ from both sides, so that all terms in the two equations "line up":

Equation A: $x - 3y = 3$

Equation B: $2x + y = 4$

To solve for y, multiply each term in Equation A by 2, so that the x-coefficient is the same in both equations:

Equation A: $2x - 6y = 6$

Equation B: $2x + y = 4$

Subtract Equation B from Equation A, thereby eliminating x, and then isolate y on one side of the equation:

$$\begin{array}{r} 2x - 6y = 6 \\ \underline{-2x - y = -4} \\ 0x - 7y = 2 \\ -7y = 2 \\ y = -\frac{2}{7} \end{array}$$

Then, substitute that solution into one of the equations and solve for the value of the other variable. In this case, $x = \frac{15}{7}$.

PRACTICE

$$\begin{cases} 3y+2x=-4 \\ 2y-x=16 \end{cases}$$

What is the value of y^2 if the pair (x, y) satisfies the system above?

A. 8

B. 16

C. 28

D. 49

The correct answer is B. Multiply the second equation by 2:

$$2(2y-x)=2(16)$$
$$4y-2x=32$$

Then add the result to the first equation to eliminate x:

$$\begin{aligned} 3y+2x&=-4 \\ 4y-2x&=32 \\ \hline 7y&=28 \\ y&=4 \end{aligned}$$

Hence $4^2 = 16$.

Speedy Rent-A-Car charges $45 a day plus $0.60 per mile driven to rent a car. Zippy Rental charges $40 a day plus $0.70 per mile driven to rent a car. After how many miles would it cost the same amount to rent a car from either Speedy Rent-A-Car or Zippy Rental?

A. 25 miles

B. 50 miles

C. 75 miles

D. 100 miles

The correct answer is B. The system of equations that represents the cost of renting a car from the places is:

Speedy Rent-A-Car: $y = 45 + 0.6x$

Zippy Rental: $y = 40 + 0.7x$

Rewrite the equations so that you can eliminate the y variable.

$$-45=0.6x-y$$
$$40=-0.7x+y$$

Add the second equation to the first to eliminate the y variable:

$$\begin{aligned} -45&=0.6x-y \\ 40&=-0.7x+y \\ \hline -5&=-0.1x \end{aligned}$$

When simplified, $x = 50$. Therefore, 50 is the number of miles it would take for the cost (y) of both rental companies to be equal.

$$\begin{cases} 3x+y=1 \\ -3x+4y=9 \end{cases}$$

Determine the value of $\frac{y}{x}$ if the pair (x, y) satisfies the system above.

A. -6

B. $-\frac{2}{3}$

C. 2

D. $\frac{8}{3}$

The correct answer is A. Add the two equations to eliminate x:

$$\begin{aligned} 3x+y&=1 \\ -3x+4y&=9 \\ \hline 5y&=10 \\ y&=2 \end{aligned}$$

Plug this into the first equation for y and solve for x:

$$3x+2=1$$
$$3x=-1$$
$$x=-\frac{1}{3}$$

Thus $\frac{y}{x}=\frac{2}{-\frac{1}{3}}=2(-3)=-6$.

Applications of Systems

Systems of linear equations can be used to model a variety of real-world scenarios. Not every problem will require you to find the value of each variable in the system, though. Sometimes you'll use substitution or elimination to find one value or the difference between values. Regardless of your goals, you'll need to start by writing out two equations that translate the words of the problem to the symbols of mathematics. From there, you can solve for the indicated variable using whatever method is most efficient or effective for reaching the answer.

What follows here are a variety of scenarios that use systems to model things mathematically. When working through the examples, strive to set up each system and determine which method is most appropriate for the situation and the goal of the question.

EXAMPLES

Computer Connect, Inc. makes and sells computer parts. The material for each part costs \$3.00 and sells for \$12.75 each. The company spends \$1,200 on additional expenses each month. How many computer parts must the company sell each month in order to break even?

Solution

The break-even point is when the income equals the expenses. The first equation $12.75x = y$ represents the income. The second equation $3x + 1,200 = y$ represents expenses.

$$\begin{aligned} y &= 12.75x \\ y &= 3.00x + 1,200 \end{aligned}$$

Subtract the second equation from the first.

$$\begin{array}{r} y = 12.75x \\ \underline{y = 3.00x + 1,200} \\ 0 = 9.75x - 1,200 \end{array}$$

Solve for x:

$$\begin{aligned} -9.75x &= -1,200 \\ x &= \frac{-1,200}{-9.75} \\ x &\approx 123.08 \end{aligned}$$

To break even, the company would have to sell at least 124 computer parts.

Jordan and Alex are planning a vacation. They plan to spend some of the time in Naples, Florida, and the rest of their time in Key West. They estimate that it will cost \$250 per day in Naples and \$325 per day in Key West. They plan to vacation a total of 8 days and have a budget of \$2,375. How many days should they spend in each city?

Solution

To write the equations, let x = the number of days in Naples and y = the number of days in Key West. The first equation $x + y = 8$ represents the total number of days on vacation. The second equation, $250x + 325y = 2,375$, represents total cost.

The system of equations is:

$$\begin{aligned} x + y &= 8 \\ 250x + 325y &= 2,375 \end{aligned}$$

Solve the system by multiplying the first equation by 325 and then subtract the second equation from the first.

$$\begin{array}{r} 325x + 325y = 2,600 \\ \underline{250x + 325y = 2,375} \\ 75x = 225 \\ x = 3 \end{array}$$

You know that $x + y = 8$ and $x = 3$. Thus, $y = 5$. The couple can spend 3 days in Naples and 5 days in Key West.

EXAMPLES

Mr. Green took his four children to the local craft fair. The total cost of their admission tickets was \$14. Mr. and Mrs. Molina and their six children had to pay \$23. What was the cost of an adult ticket to the craft fair, and what was the cost of a child's ticket?

Solution

Expressing all amounts in dollars, let x = cost of an adult ticket and let y = cost of a child's ticket.

For the Greens: $x + 4y = 14$

For the Molinas: $2x + 6y = 23$

The goal of the substitution method is to solve one equation for one variable in terms of the other and then substitute that solution into the second equation. So we solve the first equation for x, because that is the simplest one to isolate:

$$\begin{aligned} x+4y&=14 \\ x&=14-4y \end{aligned}$$

Then substitute into the second equation:

$$\begin{aligned} 2x+6y&=23 \\ 2(14-4y)+6y&=23 \end{aligned}$$

This gives us one equation in one unknown that we can solve:

$$\begin{aligned} 28-8y+6y&=23 \\ -2y&=-5 \\ y&=2.5 \end{aligned}$$

Now that we know $y = 2.5$, we substitute this into $x = 14 - 4y$ to get $x = 14 - 4(2.5) = 4$. Thus, the adult tickets were \$4 each, and the children's tickets were \$2.50 each.

Paul and Denise both do some work after school for their neighbors. Two weeks ago, Paul worked 6 hours, Denise worked 3 hours, and they earned a total of \$39. Last week, Paul worked 12 hours, Denise worked 5 hours, and they earned a total of \$75. What is each one's hourly wage?

Solution

Let x = Paul's hourly wage, and let y = Denise's hourly wage.

For the first week: $6x + 3y = 39$

For the second week: $12x + 5y = 75$

The idea of the method of elimination is that adding equal quantities to equal quantities gives a true result. So we want to add some multiple of one equation to the other one so that if we add the two equations together, one variable will be eliminated. In this case, it is not hard to see that if we multiply the first equation by –2, the coefficient of x will become –12. Now when we add the two equations, x will be eliminated.

$$\begin{aligned} -12x-6y&=-78 \\ 12x+5y&=75 \\ \hline -y&=-3 \end{aligned}$$

Since $y = 3$, we can now substitute this into either of the two equations. Let's use the first:

$$\begin{aligned} 6x+3(3)&=39 \\ x&=5 \end{aligned}$$

Thus, Denise makes only \$3 per hour while Paul gets \$5.

EXAMPLES

Movie tickets are $13.50 for adults and $8 for senior citizens. On Saturday night, a total of 436 adults and senior citizens attended, and the movie theater collected $4,885 from these adults and senior citizens. How many senior citizens were at the movie theater?

Solution

To solve the problem, you must write two different equations using the data in the question. Let *a* be the number of adults and *s* represent senior citizens.

$$a + s = 436$$

From the question, you also know that $a \times \$13.50$ represents the total amount the movie theater collected for adult tickets and $s \times \$8$ is the total amount collected for senior citizen tickets. Together these dollar amounts total $4,885.

$$13.5a + 8s = 4,885$$

Solve using elimination by multiplying the first equation by –8 to eliminate one of the variables during addition of the equations:

$$(-8)(a+s)=(-8)(436)$$
$$-8a+-8s = -3,488$$

Add the equations:

$$\begin{array}{r} -8a-8s=3,488 \\ +13.5a+8s=4,885 \\ \hline 5.5a=1,397 \\ a=254 \end{array}$$

If 254 adults attended, then 436 – 254 = 182 senior citizens were at the movie theater.

A supermarket places two orders for regular and extra-large packages of paper towels. The first order had 48 regular and 120 extra-large packages and cost $644.40. The second order had 60 regular and 40 extra-large and cost $338. What is the difference in cost between a regular and extra-large package of paper towels?

Solution

Write two equations using the data given in the question. Use *r* to represent a regular package of paper towels and *e* to represent an extra-large package.

$$48r+120e=644.40$$
$$60r+40e=338$$

Multiply the bottom equation by –3 to eliminate *e*:

$$(-3)(60r+40e)=(-3)(338)$$
$$-180r-120e=-1,014$$

Add the two equations:

$$\begin{array}{r} 48r+120e=644.4 \\ +-180r-120e=-1,014 \\ \hline -132r=-369.6 \\ r=2.8 \end{array}$$

The price of a regular package of paper towels is $2.80. To find the price of an extra-large package, substitute 2.8 into one of the equations:

$$(48)(2.8)+120e=644.4$$
$$120e=510$$
$$e=4.25$$

The difference in cost between an extra-large package and a regular package of paper towels is:

$$\$4.25 - \$2.80 = \$1.45$$

11

Graphing Systems of Linear Equations

When graphing a system of linear equations, you'll take the same approach that you take when graphing a single linear equation, but you'll repeat the process for both lines in order to find their point of intersection. The point of intersection for a graphed system of linear equations is the solution for the system.

Let's look at an example.

EXAMPLE

Solve the following system of equations by graphing:

$$\begin{cases} 3x - y = 1 \\ 4x - 2y = -1 \end{cases}$$

Solution

First, solve both equations for *y*. Doing so puts the equations into slope-intercept form, which is the form from which it is easiest to graph a line.

$$\begin{cases} y = 3x - 1 \\ y = 2x + \frac{1}{2} \end{cases}$$

The first line has *y*-intercept (0, –1) and slope of 3, while the second line has y-intercept of $\left(0, \frac{1}{2}\right)$ and a slope of 2. The graphs are as follows:

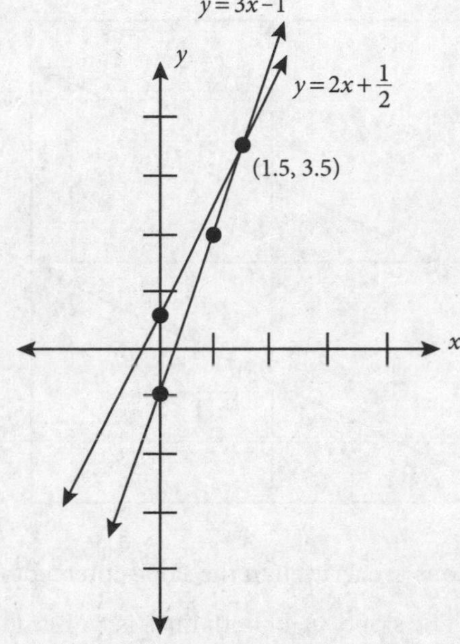

The intersection point of the graphs is the solution of the system, coordinates $x = \frac{3}{2}$ and $y = \frac{7}{2}$.

Parallel Lines

Two lines in the same plane are parallel if they do not intersect. The slopes of lines can be used to determine whether two lines are parallel. Two lines are parallel if they have the same slope, *m*.

Let's look at an example. The following graph displays the equations $y=\frac{1}{2}x+2$ and $y=\frac{1}{2}x-3$.

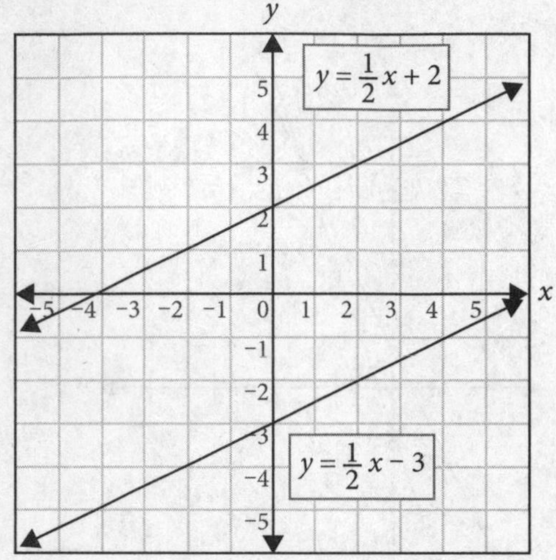

Both equations are written in the slope-intercept form, $y = mx + b$. The slope, *m*, of both lines is $\frac{1}{2}$. Because these two lines have the same slope, they are parallel lines.

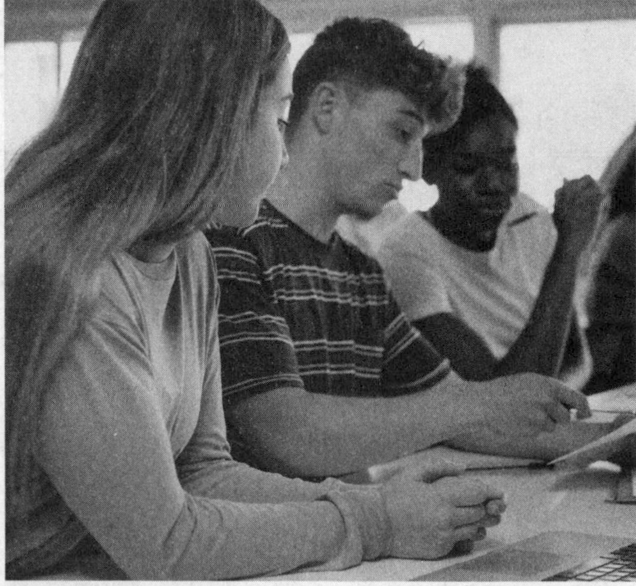

PRACTICE

The graph of which of the following equations is parallel to the line shown?

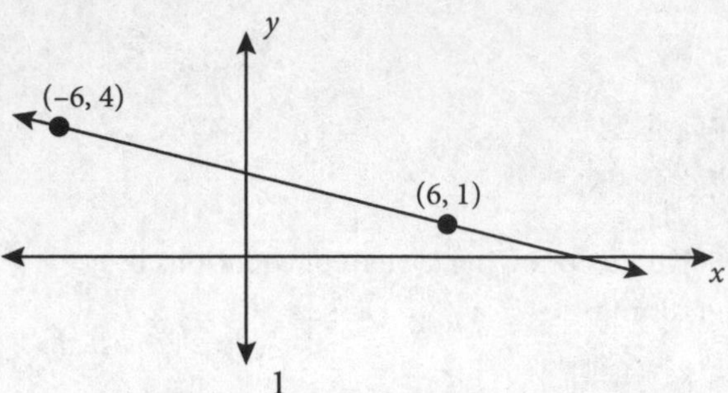

A. $y=4x-\frac{1}{4}$

B. $4x - y = -2$

C. $4y + x = 2$

D. $2x - 8y = 1$

The correct answer is C. The slope of the line shown is $m=\frac{4-1}{-6-6}=-\frac{1}{4}$. Any line with this same slope must be parallel to the one shown. Note that the equation in choice C can be written as $y=-\frac{1}{4}x+\frac{1}{2}$ and so must be parallel to the one shown. Choices A and B are incorrect because the slope of the lines is 4, making the lines perpendicular to the line shown. Choice D is incorrect because the slope of this line is $\frac{1}{4}$, not $-\frac{1}{4}$ as the one shown.

PRACTICE

Suppose the system $\begin{cases} x+ky+1=4x \\ -3x=5-2y \end{cases}$ has no solution.

What must be the value of k?

A. –2
B. 2
C. $\frac{1}{2}$
D. $-\frac{1}{2}$

The correct answer is B. The only way a linear system can have no solution is for the two lines to be parallel, which means they have the same slope. In order to determine the value of k, put each of the lines into slope-intercept form and equate the slopes:

$$x+ky+1=4x \Rightarrow ky=3x-1 \Rightarrow y=\frac{3}{k}x-\frac{1}{k}$$

$$-3x=5-2y \Rightarrow -5-3x=-2y \Rightarrow y=\frac{3}{2}x+\frac{5}{2}$$

In this form, the slopes of the lines are $\frac{3}{k}$ and $\frac{3}{2}$. Setting them equal and solving for k yields $k=2$. This is the only value for which these two lines are parallel.

Perpendicular Lines

Two lines are perpendicular if they intersect to form right angles. The slopes of two perpendicular lines are negative reciprocals of each other. This means that the product of the slopes equals –1.

For example, look at the graphs of equations $y=-2x+2$ and $y=\frac{1}{2}x-3$:

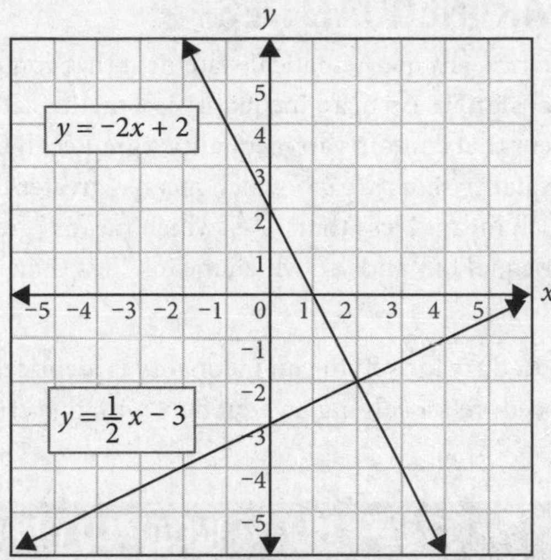

These two lines have slopes of –2 and $\frac{1}{2}$. The slopes are negative reciprocals of each other because –2 multiplied by $\frac{1}{2}$ equals –1. Therefore, these two lines are perpendicular.

PRACTICE

A line passing through the point (–1, 4) is perpendicular to the line passing through (–3, 2) and (–3, –5). What is the equation of the line passing through (–1, 4)?

A. $y=x+5$
B. $y=4$
C. $9x+2y=5$
D. $x=-1$

The correct answer is B. The given line is vertical since it passes through two points that have the same x-coordinate. As such, a line that is perpendicular must be horizontal. Since it passes through the point (–1, 4), its equation must be $y=4$. In choices A and C, you used the point (–1, 4) when computing the slope of the given line, but it does not pass through this point. Choice D is parallel to the given line.

LINEAR INEQUALITIES

An equation is a mathematical statement that contains an equal sign. In turn, an inequality is a mathematical statement that contains an inequality sign. Recall that the inequality signs are ">" which means "greater than," "<" which means "less than," "≥" which means "greater than or equal to," and "≤" which means "less than or equal to."

The procedure for solving an inequality is identical to the procedure for solving an equation, with one crucial difference. When solving an inequality, whenever you divide or multiply both sides by a negative number, you must "reverse" the inequality sign. If the sign originally was "less than," <, it will become "greater than," >, after dividing or multiplying by a negative number. Similarly, if the sign was ≤, it will become ≥, and vice versa.

Problems involving inequalities come in different varieties on the SAT. The following table gives typical forms in which these questions are asked, along with some suggestions about how to approach them.

INEQUALITY PROBLEM TYPES AND METHODS

Problem Type	Method of Attack
Solve a given inequality, where the answer choices are given symbolically.	Solve the inequality as you would a linear equation, being careful with the inequality sign. The final step will have the variable on one side and a number on the other.
Solve a given inequality, where the choices are given graphically on the number line.	Solve the inequality as you would a linear equation, being careful with the inequality sign. Once you have the variable on one side and a number on the other, match that to the correct picture. Check whether each circle over its correct numerical value is open or closed.
You are given a ray on the number line and are asked to identify which of the inequalities listed is its solution set.	If the pictured ray has a closed circle at its endpoint, you can discard any of the choices involving a strict inequality (that is, one with < or >). Likewise, if there is an open circle on the endpoint of the ray, discard any of the choices involving a ≤ or ≥ sign. To distinguish among the remaining choices, choose an extreme x-value (very large or very small) that is in the graphed ray, plug it into the inequalities, and see which one it satisfies.
You are given a verbal description whose translation into symbols results in an inequality, and you are asked for the solution set.	Translate the verbal scenario into an inequality, and solve as above. Carefully track the use of the phrases "less than" and "greater than" as multiple answer choices may have the correct values but the wrong inequality signs.

PRACTICE

When 2 times a number x is decreased by 8, the result is less than 20. Which of the following represents the solution set of this relationship?

A. $x < 2$

B. $x < 6$

C. $x < 14$

D. $x < 28$

The correct answer is C. First, translate the given information into an inequality: $2x - 8 < 20$. Now solve the inequality for x:

$$\begin{aligned} 2x-8 &< 20 \\ 2x &< 28 \\ x &< 14 \end{aligned}$$

Sometimes, you will be asked to solve a double inequality, as in the following example.

EXAMPLES

Determine the solution set for the double inequality $-4 < 8 - 3x < 20$.

Solution

The strategy behind solving such inequalities is to get the variable in the middle by itself. To do that here, simply subtract 8 from all parts of the inequality, and then divide all parts by –3. When you perform this division, make certain to switch both signs since you are working with a negative number:

$$\begin{aligned} -4 < 8-3x &< 20 \\ -12 < -3x &< 12 \\ 4 > x &> -4 \end{aligned}$$

The last line is the solution set and can be written equivalently as $-4 < x < 4$.

Solve for x: $\frac{-5x}{9} \le -15$

Solution

The best first step to solve this equation would be to multiply both sides by 9. Since 9 is a positive number, the inequality sign remains as it is.

$$\begin{aligned} -5x &\le -15(9) \\ -5x &\le -135 \end{aligned}$$

The next step is to divide both sides by –5, and since this number is negative, the inequality sign must be reversed.

$$\frac{-5x}{-5} \ge \frac{-135}{-5}$$

This becomes $x \ge 27$, which is the solution to the inequality. The value of x, therefore, can be 27 or any number larger.

PRACTICE

Given $4y \le 84 \le 5y$, how many different possible integers values for y are there?

A. 2

B. 3

C. 4

D. 5

The correct answer is D. The key to this problem is being able to interpret the compound inequality given in the problem statement: $4y \le 84 \le 5y$. This inequality is telling us that 84 is somewhere between the value of $4y$ and $5y$. In other words, we are being told that both $4y \le 84$ and $84 \le 5y$ must be true. In order to determine the biggest value y can have, solve the inequality $4y \le 84$. If we divide both sides by 4, we determine that $y \le 21$. Therefore, y can be no larger than 21. To determine the smallest value that y can have, solve $84 \le 5y$. Dividing both sides by 5 gives us the inequality $16.8 \le y$, which means that the smallest y can be is 17. Since y must be an integer, the possible values for y are 17, 18, 19, 20, and 21. There are 5 possible values for y.

If $q > 6$, which of the following is *not* true?

A. $q - 4 < 2$

B. $q + 5 > 11$

C. $2q > 12$

D. $-q < -6$

The correct answer is A. One way to solve this problem is to solve each of the answer choice inequalities for q. Note that multiplying both sides of choice D by –1 yields $q > 6$ since multiplying by a negative reverses the inequality. Subtracting 5 from both sides of choice B yields $q > 6$. Dividing both sides of choice C by 2 yields $q > 6$.

Graphing Inequalities on a Number Line

The solutions of an inequality with one variable can be graphed on a number line.

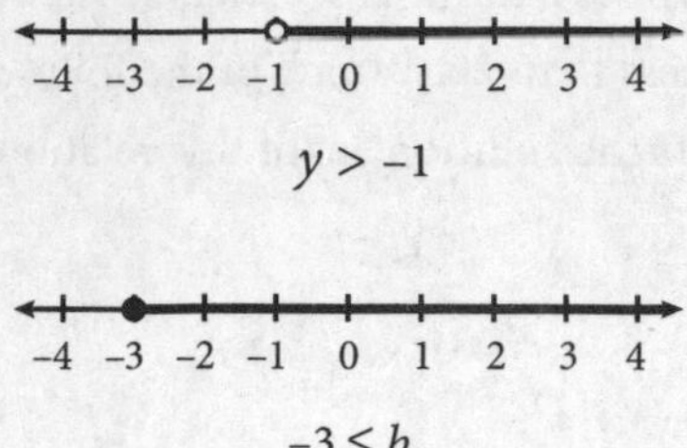

The solutions of the inequality $y > -1$ are all the real numbers that are greater than –1. Since –1 is not greater than –1, the graph of $y > -1$ contains an open dot to show that –1 is not a solution. The bold portion of the number line to the right of the open dot shows that all real numbers to the right of –1 are solutions.

Since –3 is included in the set of solutions for the inequality, $-3 \le b$, the graph of $-3 \le b$ contains a closed dot to show that –3 is a solution. Since $-3 \le b$ is the same as $b \ge -3$, the bold portion of the number line to the right of the closed dot shows that –3 and all real numbers to the right of –3 are solutions.

Another distinguishing factor of linear inequalities in contrast to linear equations is that the solution set of an inequality (that is, the set of real numbers that satisfies the inequality) contains infinitely many values, unless the inequality is bounded on both ends. The solution set is often depicted on a number line, as follows.

PLOTTING LINEAR INEQUALITIES

Linear Inequality	Picture on Number Line
$x < a$	
$x \le a$	
$x > a$	
$x \ge a$	
$a \le x \le b$	
$a < x < b$	
$-\infty < x < \infty$	

Graphing Inequalities in a Coordinate Plane

Graphing linear inequalities requires that you determine points on the line and what side of the line should be shaded to indicate what other points satisfy the inequality. Consider the following example word problem.

EXAMPLE

Charlene, a professional landscaper, purchased x small plants for \$3 each and y large plants for \$5 each. She spent no more than \$30.

Solution

This situation can be represented with the inequality $3x + 5y \le 30$, where 3 represents the price for each small plant (x), and 5 is the price for each large plant (y). Combined, these amounts must be less than or equal to \$30. To graph this inequality, you need to put it into slope-intercept form, as follows:

$$3x + 5y \le 30$$
$$5y \le 30 - 3x$$
$$y \le -\frac{3}{5}x + 6$$

As such, the slope of the line is $-\frac{3}{5}$, and the y-intercept is 6.

The following graph displays the inequality.

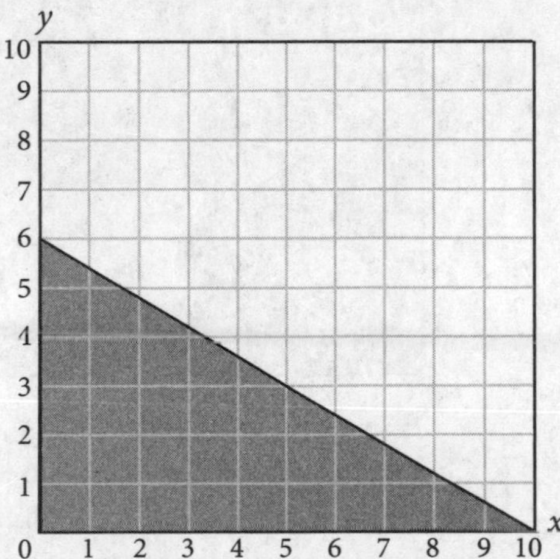

Since Charlene cannot purchase a negative number of plants, only positive values for x and y are shown. Any point in the shaded area or on the line represents a reasonable solution to the inequality.

Now, let's look at this example in greater depth by breaking down the graphing process into the necessary steps.

Graph the line for the equation $3x + 5y = 30$. Find the y-intercept by substituting 0 for x in the equation:

$$\begin{aligned} 3(0)+5y &= 30 \\ 5y &= 30 \\ y &= 6 \end{aligned}$$

Now find the x-intercept:

$$\begin{aligned} 3x+5(0) &= 30 \\ 3x &= 30 \\ x &= 10 \end{aligned}$$

Plot (0, 6) and (10, 0) and the line connecting them. Use a solid line as points along the line still satisfy the inequality (less than or equal to). If the inequality sign were less than or greater than, the line would be dashed.

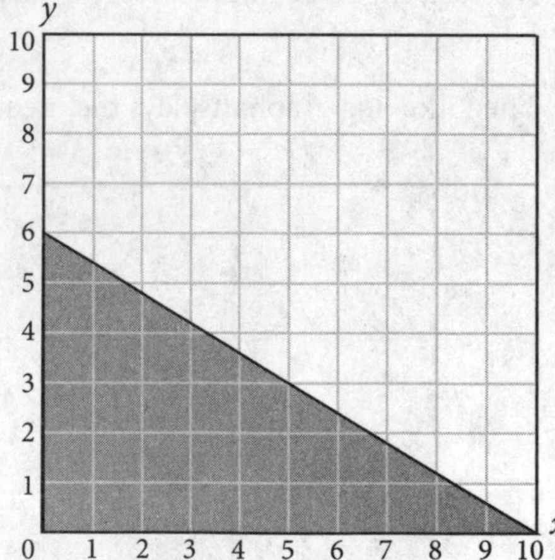

Choose a test point that is not on the line to decide which side of the line is shaded. If the values of the point make the inequality true, then shade the side the point is on. For example, using (0, 0) and substituting:

$$\begin{aligned} 3(0)+5(0) &\leq 30 \\ 0 &\leq 30 \end{aligned}$$

The point (0, 0) makes the inequality true. So, shade the side of the line containing this point.

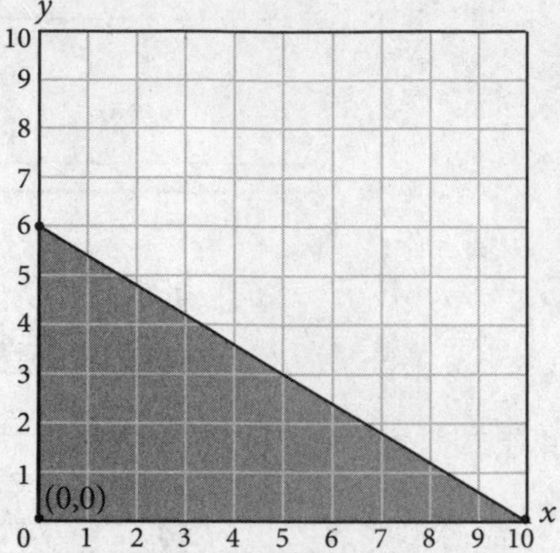

The points (3, 2), (5, 3), and (4, 5) are plotted on the graph. The point (3, 2) is in the shaded region, and the point (5, 3) is on the line. These points represent a reasonable number of small and large plants that the landscaper could have purchased. The point (4, 5) is not in the shaded region. It does not represent a reasonable solution.

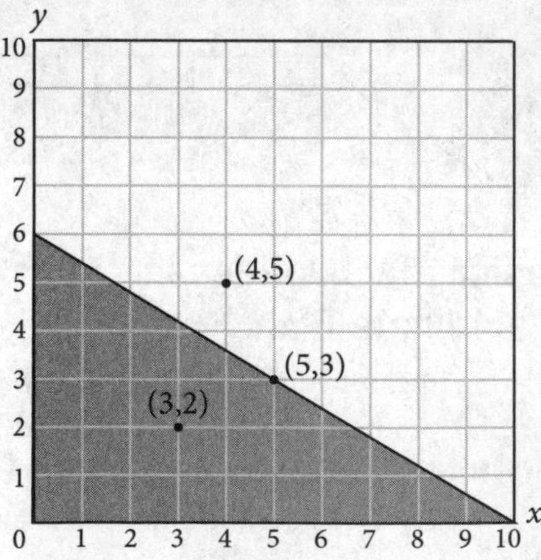

PRACTICE

What is the solution set for the inequality $y \geq 4x - 2$?

A.

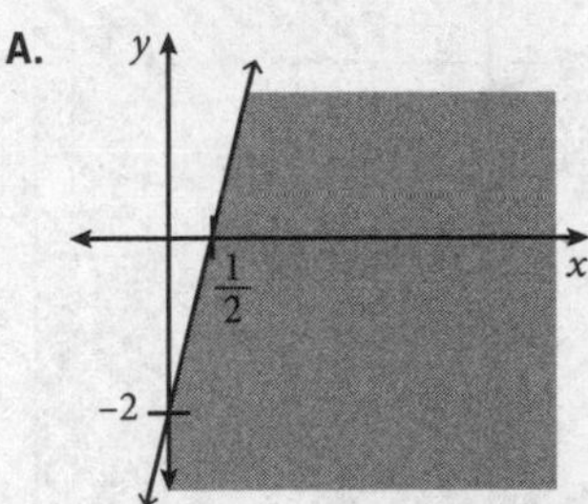

B.

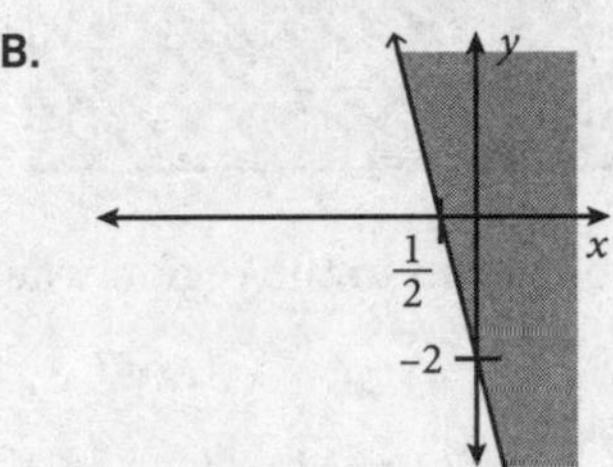

C.

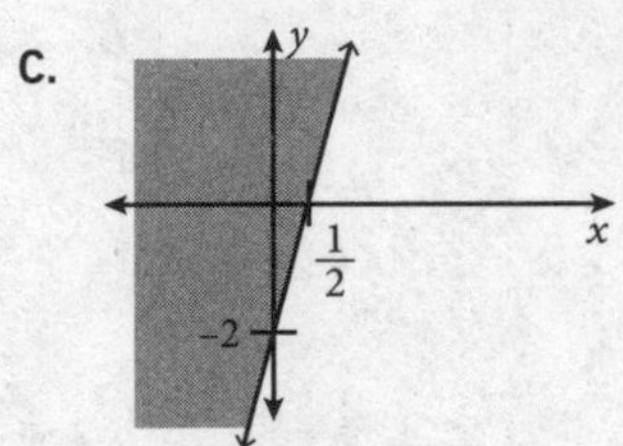

D.

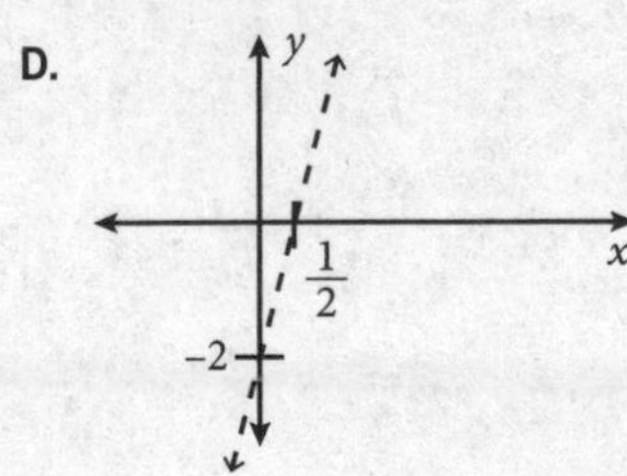

The correct answer is C. The line must be solid, not dashed, since the inequality sign includes "equals"; so, you can discard choice D. You must shade above the line since the inequality is of the form "$y \geq$"; thus, you can discard choice A. Now, it's between choices B and C. Note that the slope of the line in choice B is −4, not 4. Choice B can be discarded, leaving choice C as the answer.

Solving Systems of Inequalities by Graphing

Systems of inequalities are solved using the same methods as systems of equations. You can graph a system of linear inequalities in the coordinate plane. The solution of the system is where the graphs of the inequalities overlap. Recall that an inequality with a < or > sign is graphed as a dashed line, while an inequality with a ≤ or ≥ is graphed with a solid line. A solid line shows that answers along the line are included in the solution set for that inequality.

EXAMPLES

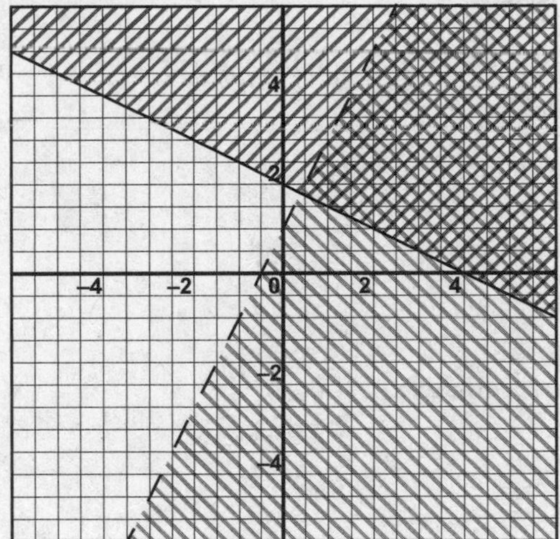

What system of inequalities is represented by the graph shown above?

Solution

First, write the inequality that represents the region bounded by the solid line, using two points along the line and the slope-intercept formula $y = mx + b$, replacing the equal sign with a comparison symbol.

$$y \geq -0.5x + 2$$

Then write the inequality that represents the region bounded by the dashed line.

$$y < 2x + 1$$

The graph shows the intersection of the system:

$$y \geq -0.5x + 2$$
$$y < 2x + 1$$

Any point both to the right of the dashed line and on or above the solid line is a solution to the system.

Solve the system of inequalities by graphing:

$$x + 2y \leq 8$$
$$3x - y \geq 3$$

Solution

First solve each inequality for y to rewrite each in slope-intercept form:

1st inequality: $x + 2y \leq 8$

$$2y \leq -x + 8$$
$$y \leq -\frac{1}{2}x + 4$$

2nd inequality: $3x - y \geq 3$

$$-y \geq -3x + 3$$
$$y \leq 3x - 3$$

Then graph each inequality.

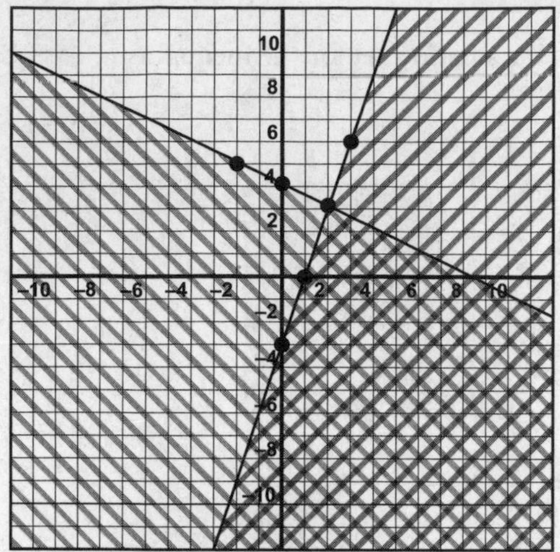

The solution set can be found in the region where the graphs overlap.

11

SUMMING IT UP

- Linear equations can have one or two variables but will have no power higher than one. The standard forms for linear equations are $Ax + B = 0$ and $Ax + By + C = 0$.
- To find the value of a variable in a linear equation, work to isolate the variable on one side of the equation by reversing operations for both sides of the equation.
- The slope-intercept form for a linear equation is $y = mx + b$, where m is the slope of the line $\left(\frac{y_2 - y_1}{x_2 - x_1}\right)$ and b is the y-intercept. When graphing lines, mark the y-intercept, and use the slope to rise the number of points indicated by the numerator of the slope and run the number of points indicated by the denominator of the slope.
- Lines with positive slopes rise from left to right. Lines with negative slopes fall from left to right.
- The point-slope form for a linear equation is $y - y_1 = m(x - x_1)$, which can help you find the slope of a line and a point the line passes through.
- A system of linear equations is a pair of linear equations involving x and y that must be satisfied at the same time. To solve a system means to identify ordered pairs (x, y) that satisfy both equations—not just one, but both! A linear system can have 0, 1, or infinitely many solutions, which can be determined using the elimination method or substitution method.
- Parallel lines have the same slope. A system with parallel lines will have no solutions.
- The equations for perpendicular lines have negative reciprocals for slopes.
- If the lines in a system of equations are the same line, there will be an infinite number of solutions.
- Linear inequalities can be solved by using the same basic strategy used to solve linear equations, with the additional step of flipping the inequality sign whenever both sides of the inequality are multiplied or divided by a negative real number.
- To graph a system of linear inequalities, graph the lines the same way you would linear equations. For an inequality sign, use a dashed line, signifying that points on the line are not solutions. For a less-than-or-equal to or greater-than-or-equal to sign, use a solid line, signifying that points on the line are possible solutions. Once both inequalities are graphed, test points that make the inequalities true. The overlapping regions of two graphed inequalities represent the set of points that makes both inequalities true.

TEST YOURSELF

ALGEBRA

12 Questions—19 Minutes

Directions: The questions in this section address a number of Algebra domain skills.

Use of a calculator is permitted for all questions.

Unless otherwise indicated:

- All variables and expressions represent real numbers.
- Figures provided are drawn to scale.
- All figures lie in a plane.
- The domain of a given function *f* is the set of all real numbers *x* for which *f* (*x*) is a real number.

1. If (x, y) satisfies the following system, what is the value of x^y?

$$\begin{cases} x-2y=-1 \\ y-2x=5 \end{cases}$$

A. $-\frac{1}{3}$

B. $\frac{1}{9}$

C. $\frac{1}{3}$

D. 3

2. For what real number a does the following system have no solution?

$$\begin{cases} \frac{x}{3}=ay \\ \frac{y}{a}=3x \end{cases}$$

A. $-\frac{1}{3}$ and $\frac{1}{3}$

B. –3 and 3

C. –1 and 1

D. 0 only

3. For what real number a, if any, does the following system have infinitely many solutions?

$$\begin{cases} a(x+y)=3 \\ y+x=-2 \end{cases}$$

A. There is no such value of a.

B. –2

C. $-\frac{3}{2}$

D. 1

4. If $\frac{1}{4}y-\frac{1}{12}=\frac{5}{8}y+\frac{3}{4}$, then what is the value of $\frac{1}{y}$?

A. 20

B. 11

C. $-\frac{9}{20}$

D. –11

5. Determine the solution set for the inequality $\frac{2}{3}\left(6x-\frac{1}{2}\right)-2(2-x)\leq-\frac{1}{3}$

A.
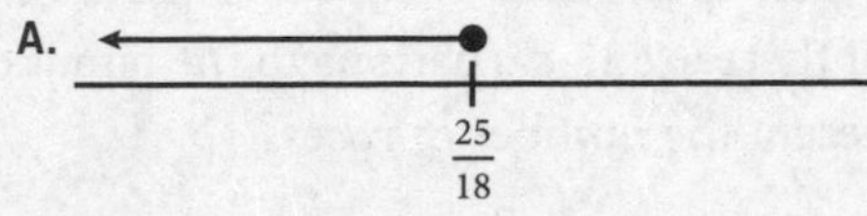

B.
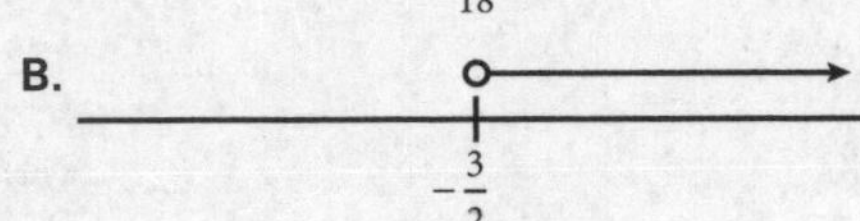

C.
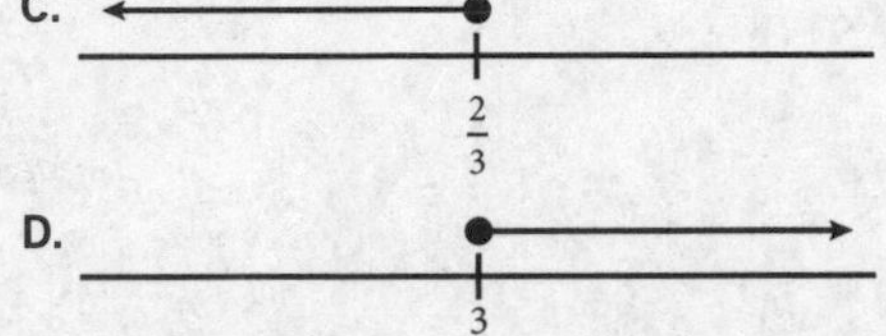

D. $\frac{3}{2}$

6. What is the value of z in the equation $3 - 2z = 9 + 4z$?

A. –1

B. 0

C. 3

D. 6

7. Membership to Iron Gym costs \$40 per month plus a \$30 registration fee. The monthly cost is deducted automatically from your account. If your starting balance is \$350, how many months will you be able to go to the gym before you have to add money to your account?

A. 6

B. 7

C. 8

D. 9

8. Lauren started a small wreath-making business. She earns \$50 per wreath that she sells. She purchased \$1,500 worth of materials when she started the business. How many wreaths must she sell to break even?

A. 15

B. 30

C. 45

D. 60

9. Solve for x: $\frac{2x+9}{7}=\frac{3x+8}{2}$

A. –3

B. $-\frac{38}{17}$

C. $\frac{17}{38}$

D. 3

10. $\begin{cases} y+\frac{3}{4}x=1 \\ y=-\frac{3}{4}x-1 \end{cases}$

What is the solution to the system shown?

A. $x = 0, y = -1$

B. $x = 0, y = 1$

C. Infinitely many solutions

D. No solution

11. Andi can work a total of no more than 35 hours per week at her two jobs. She earns \$30 per hour giving music lessons and \$45 per hour working as a life coach. She must earn at least \$800 per week. Which system of inequalities can be used to determine the pairs of the number of hours spent at each job that would enable her to earn at least \$800?

A. $\begin{cases} 35(x+y) \geq 800 \\ x+y \leq 35 \end{cases}$

B. $\begin{cases} x+y \leq 35 \\ 35x+45y \geq 800 \end{cases}$

C. $\begin{cases} x+y \geq 35 \\ 35x+45y \geq 800 \end{cases}$

D. $\begin{cases} x \leq 35 \\ y \geq 800 \end{cases}$

12. You want to order a bouquet of flowers that contains roses and carnations. You have only \$48 to spend. Roses cost \$3 each, and carnations cost \$1.25 each. How many roses can be in the bouquet if there are 18 carnations in the bouquet? Let r represent the number of roses.

A. $r \geq 8$

B. $r \leq 9$

C. $r \leq 8$

D. $r \geq 9$

ANSWER KEY AND EXPLANATIONS

1. A	**3.** C	**5.** C	**7.** C	**9.** B	**11.** B
2. A	**4.** C	**6.** A	**8.** B	**10.** D	**12.** C

1. **The correct answer is A.** When solving a linear system, you often have your choice of method to use. Whenever at least one of the equations has a variable with coefficient 1, a good strategy is to solve that equation for the variable and substitute it into the other equation. That is the method we will proceed with to solve this system. To start, solve the first equation for x to get $x = 2y - 1$. Then, substitute this expression in for x in the second equation to get the following equation involving only y: $y - 2(2y - 1) = 5$.

   Solve this equation for y:

$$\begin{aligned} y-2(2y-1)&=5 \\ y-4y+2&=5 \\ -3y+2&=5 \\ -3y&=3 \\ y&=-1 \end{aligned}$$

   Plug –1 in for y in your initial substitution to get the corresponding value of x:

$$x = 2(-1) - 1 = -2 - 1 = -3$$

   Finally, the value of $x^y = (-3)^{-1} = \frac{1}{-3} = -\frac{1}{3}$

2. **The correct answer is A.** Without knowing how to attack the problem, choice D can be eliminated off the bat because the second equation is not defined when $a = 0$. The key to this problem is knowing that two lines that are parallel do not intersect; so a linear system containing such lines has no solution. Lines are parallel if they have the same slope.

   Using these facts, the strategy is to write the two equations in the form $y = mx$. Then, equate the slopes and solve for a. The equations in this system can be written as follows:

$$\frac{x}{3} = ay \Rightarrow x = 3ay \Rightarrow y = \left(\frac{1}{3a}\right)x$$

$$\frac{y}{a} = 3x \Rightarrow y = (3a)x$$

   Equating the slopes yields the equation $\frac{1}{3a} = 3a$. Solve for a, as follows:

$$\begin{aligned} \frac{1}{3a} &= 3a \\ 9a^2 &= 1 \\ a^2 &= \frac{1}{9} \\ a &= \pm\sqrt{\frac{1}{9}} \\ a &= \pm\frac{1}{3} \end{aligned}$$

3. **The correct answer is C.** For a linear system to have infinitely many solutions, the equations must be multiples of each other. Dividing both sides of the first equation by a yields the equivalent system:

$$\begin{cases} x+y=\frac{3}{a} \\ y+x=-2 \end{cases}$$

   Since the left sides are identical, the only way these two equations are multiples of each other is if the right sides are equal. That is, $\frac{3}{a} = -2$. Solving for a yields $a = -\frac{3}{2}$ (choice C).

4. **The correct answer is C.** Multiply both sides of the equation by the LCD, 24, to eliminate the fractions. Then solve the equation for y:

$$\frac{1}{4}y - \frac{1}{12} = \frac{5}{8}y + \frac{3}{4}$$
$$24\cdot\left(\frac{1}{4}y - \frac{1}{12}\right) = 24\cdot\left(\frac{5}{8}y + \frac{3}{4}\right)$$
$$6y - 2 = 15y + 18$$
$$-20 = 9y$$
$$-\frac{20}{9} = y$$

Therefore, $\frac{1}{y} = -\frac{9}{20}$

5. **The correct answer is C.** You solve a linear inequality just as you would an equation. The only caveat is that if you multiply or divide both sides of the inequality by a negative number you must reverse the inequality sign. To start, first apply the distributive property to simplify the left side. Then, isolate the x-terms to the left side:

$$\frac{2}{3}\left(6x - \frac{1}{2}\right) - 2(2 - x) \leq -\frac{1}{3}$$
$$4x - \frac{1}{3} - 4 + 2x \leq -\frac{1}{3}$$
$$6x - \frac{13}{3} \leq -\frac{1}{3}$$
$$6x \leq 4$$
$$x \leq \frac{4}{6}$$
$$x \leq \frac{2}{3}$$

All real numbers to the left of and including $\frac{2}{3}$ are in the solution set (choice C).

6. **The correct answer is A.**

$$3 - 2z = 9 + 4z$$
$$3 = 9 + 6z$$
$$-6 = 6z$$
$$-1 = z$$

7. **The correct answer is C.**

$$40x + 30 = 350$$
$$40x = 320$$
$$x = 8$$

8. **The correct answer is B.** Let x be the number of wreaths Lauren needs to sell to break even. Then $50x = 1{,}500$. Divide both sides by 50 to get $x = 30$.

9. **The correct answer is B.**

$$\frac{2x + 9}{7} = \frac{3x + 8}{2}$$
$$2(2x + 9) = 7(3x + 8)$$
$$4x + 18 = 21x + 56$$
$$-17x = 38$$
$$x = -\frac{38}{17}$$

10. **The correct answer is D.** Substitute the expression for y given by the second equation into y in the first equation to obtain the equation $\left(-\frac{3}{4}x - 1\right) + \frac{3}{4}x = 1$. This is equivalent to the false statement $-1 = 1$. This system has no solution.

11. **The correct answer is B.** Let x be the number of hours spent giving music lessons and y the number of hours spent working as a life coach. Since the total number of hours worked in one week cannot exceed 35, we have the inequality $x + y \leq 35$. Next, the amount earned working x hours giving music lessons is $35x$ dollars, and the amount earned working y hours as a life coach is $45y$ dollars. The sum of these two amounts must be at least \$800. This gives the inequality $35x + 45y \geq 800$. The desired system is given in choice B.

12. The correct answer is C.

$$
\begin{aligned}
3r + 1.25c &\le 48 \\
3r + 1.25(18) &\le 48 \\
3r + 22.5 &\le 48 \\
3r &\le 25.5 \\
\frac{3r}{3} &\le \frac{25.5}{3} \\
r &\le 8.5
\end{aligned}
$$

There can only be at most 8 roses in the bouquet.

CHAPTER

Geometry and Trigonometry

GEOMETRY AND TRIGONOMETRY

OVERVIEW

SAT Math questions that emphasize geometry topics will fall into the Geometry and Trigonometry domain, which accounts for 15% of the test section's total questions. The Geometry and Trigonometry questions require test takers to demonstrate understanding of area, volume, congruence, triangles, circles, trigonometry, and more. Some of those topics were referenced in Chapter 10, but here you'll finder a greater depth of material and more specific geometry concepts. Use your results from Chapter 2 Diagnostic Test to determine which concepts you need to review. Use the example scenarios and questions throughout the chapter to assess your understanding. At the end of the chapter is a Test Yourself, which you can use to identify any areas for further review.

12

2D SHAPES

In Chapter 10, you saw some basic geometry concepts as related to polygons, specifically related to determining area and perimeter. Here, we'll review those ideas and also look at some more specialized concepts related to polygons (including triangles) and circles.

Triangles

Recall that all triangles obey the triangle sum and triangle inequality rules. The triangle sum rule says that the sum of the measures of the three angles in any triangle must be 180°. The triangle inequality says that the sum of the lengths of any two sides of a triangle must be strictly larger than the length of the third side.

Triangles come in all different sizes and are classified using their angles and sides. The following tables provide some essential terms and examples.

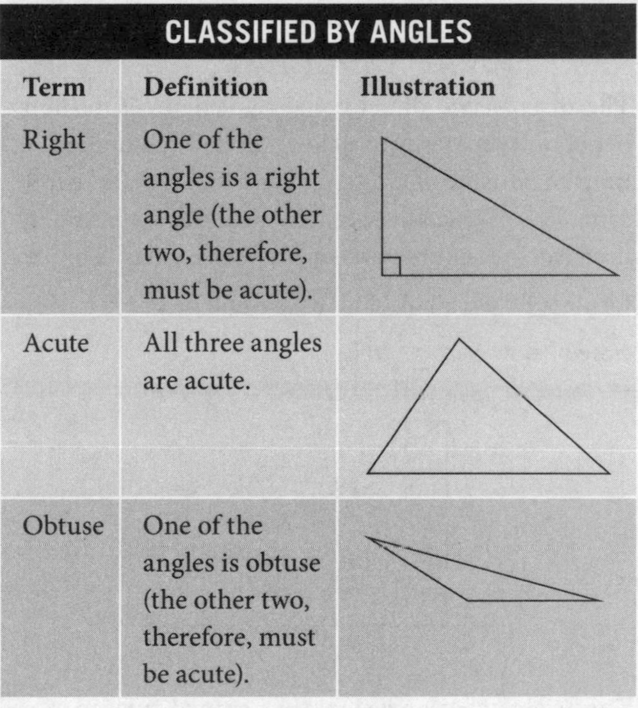

CLASSIFIED BY ANGLES

Term	Definition	Illustration
Right	One of the angles is a right angle (the other two, therefore, must be acute).	
Acute	All three angles are acute.	
Obtuse	One of the angles is obtuse (the other two, therefore, must be acute).	

CLASSIFIED BY SIDES

Term	Definition	Illustration
Equilateral	All three sides have the same length; that is, all three sides are congruent.	
Isosceles	At least two sides have the same length; that is, at least two sides are congruent.	
Scalene	All three sides have different lengths.	

Let's put some of these rules into practice with this sample problem.

PRACTICE

What is the measure of angle *DEF*?

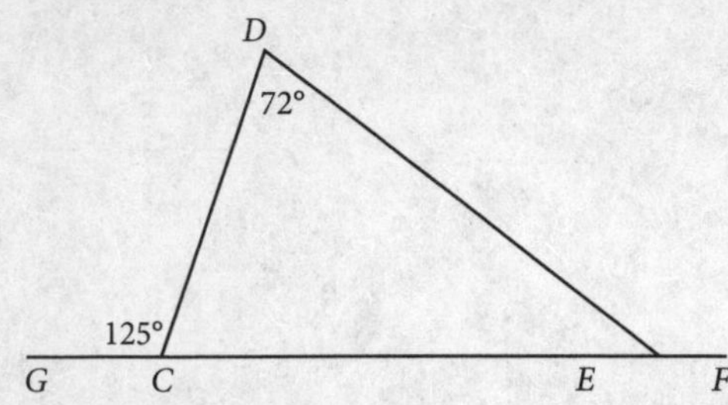

A. 127°

B. 125°

C. 108°

D. 90°

The correct answer is A. Angle *DCE* is supplementary to angle *DCG*, so its measure is 180° – 125° = 55°. The interior angles of a triangle sum to 180°, so the measure of angle *DEC* is 180° – 55° – 72° = 53°. Finally, angle *DEF* is supplementary to angle *DEC*, so its measure is 180° – 53° = 127°.

Congruent and Similar Triangles

We say two triangles *ABC* and *DEF* are congruent if all three corresponding pairs of angles are congruent and all three corresponding sides are congruent. Always identify corresponding sides of two triangles using the order in which their vertices (i.e., points where two sides meet) are written. As noted here in our description, vertex *A* corresponds to vertex *D*, *B* to *E*, and *C* to *F*.

Congruent triangles have the same perimeter and area.

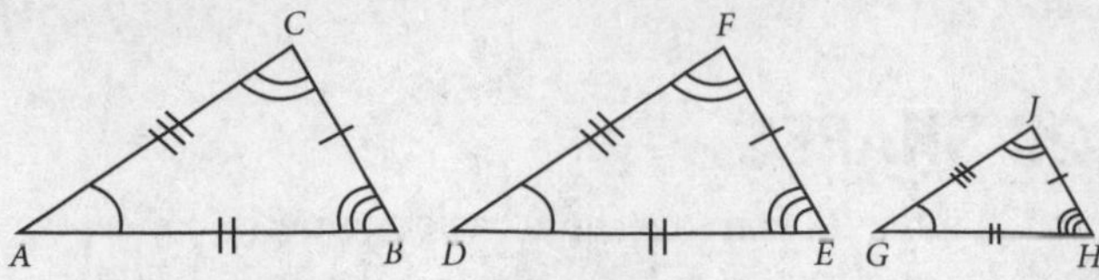

ΔABC is congruent to ΔDEF and similar to ΔGHJ.

Two triangles *ABC* and *GHJ* that are not congruent can still be proportional to each other in the sense that the ratios of the three pairs of corresponding sides are the same—that is, $\frac{AB}{GH} = \frac{BC}{HJ} = \frac{AC}{GJ} = k$, where k is a positive number.

In such cases, we say triangles *ABC* and *GHJ* are similar. Note that corresponding angles in two similar triangles must be congruent.

Perimeter and Area of Triangles

The perimeter of a triangle is the sum of the lengths of its three sides. Often, a question will require you to compute the perimeter of a right triangle, but you will not explicitly be given the lengths of all the sides. In such a case, do not forget that you have the Pythagorean theorem.

The area of a two-dimensional plane figure is the number of unit squares needed to cover it. The standard units of measure of area are square inches, square feet, square yards, etc.; the metric system is also commonly used (square centimeters, square meters, etc.). The area formula for a triangle with base b and height h, as illustrated below, is $A = \frac{1}{2} b \cdot h$.

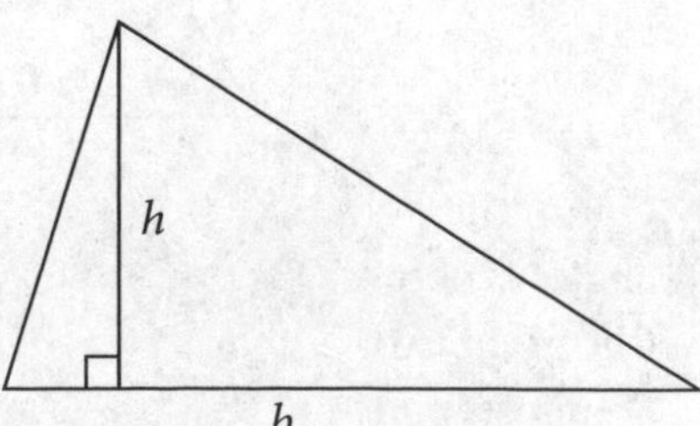

The height of a triangle must be perpendicular to its base. That means there are three possible pairings of heights with bases for any triangle—each base has its own height.

Take a look at some problems similar to what you may see on the SAT that deal with the area and perimeter of right triangles.

PRACTICE

The open area in front of a museum is a square lawn bordered by footpaths 250 feet long on each side. The museum plans to create a diagonal footpath that would connect the northwest corner of the lawn to the southeast corner of the lawn. Approximately how many feet shorter would the new path be than the shortest possible route on the existing footpaths?

A. 500

B. 354

C. 250

D. 146

The correct answer is D. The current paths require a trip of 500 feet (250 feet for each of the two sides one must travel along to get from one corner to the other). A diagonal path would form a 45°–45°–90° isosceles right triangle with the existing paths being its legs. As such, the length of the diagonal path would be $250\sqrt{2}$ feet, or approximately 354 feet. The new path would shorten the route by approximately $500 - 354 = 146$ feet.

A certain triangle has sides of lengths 50, 120, and 130 centimeters. If a similar triangle has a perimeter of 1,500 centimeters, what is the length (in centimeters) of the triangle's shortest side?

A. 50

B. 130

C. 250

D. 600

The correct answer is C. The two triangles are similar, so their sides are in proportion. The first triangle has a perimeter of $50 + 120 + 130 = 300$ centimeters. The second triangle has a perimeter that is 5 times this: 1,500 centimeters. Thus, the sides of the second triangle are exactly 5 times as long as the sides of the first triangle: 250, 600, and 650 centimeters. So, the length of the shortest side is 250 centimeters.

Right Triangles and the Pythagorean Theorem

The lengths of the sides of right triangles are always related by the Pythagorean theorem. Consider the right triangle shown here:

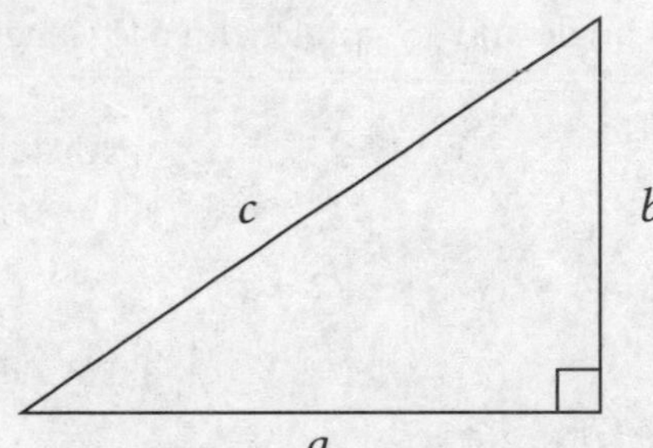

The sides with lengths *a* and *b* are called legs, and the side opposite the right angle is the hypotenuse. The hypotenuse is the longest side of a right triangle. The Pythagorean theorem says that $a^2 + b^2 = c^2$.

This relationship between the legs and hypotenuse can take on specific forms for triangles of specific side lengths and angle measures. Two common right triangles have sides that measure 3-4-5 and 5-12-13, or multiples thereof. Be on the lookout for these Pythagorean triples—recognizing them within a problem can make calculating a missing side easier. You'll also want to be on the lookout for two special right triangles: 30-60-90 and 45-45-90 triangles; the numbers indicate the triangles' angle measures.

45-45-90 Triangle

A 45-45-90 right triangle, also called an isosceles right triangle because of its interior angle measures, has a specific relationship between its side lengths, as seen in the following diagram.

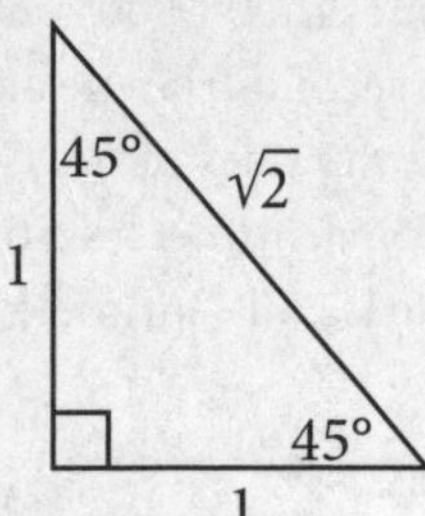

The hypotenuse of a 45-45-90 triangle will always be the length of the leg multiplied by $\sqrt{2}$. Whether the leg opposite one of the 45° angles is 1 or x or 27, the hypotenuse will always have the same relationship. You can see this using the Pythagorean theorem with a triangle with a right angle and 45° angle with a leg length of x:

$$x^2 + x^2 = c^2$$
$$2x^2 = c^2$$
$$x\sqrt{2} = c$$

30-60-90 Triangle

Similar to an isosceles right triangle, the 30-60-90 right triangle also has specific relationships among its side lengths.

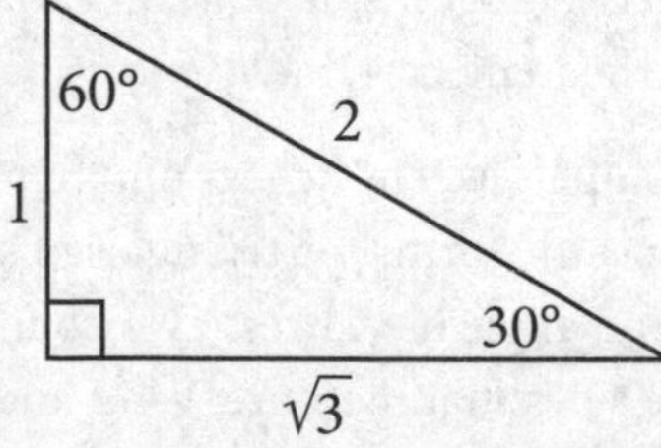

The side length relationships in a 30-60-90 triangle can also be generalized since all triangles of that type are geometrically similar and thus have the same ratio between sides. The hypotenuse's length will always be twice as much as the side length opposite the 30° angle. The side opposite the 60° angle will always be the shortest leg multiplied by $\sqrt{3}$.

Memorizing these relationships can bring some added proficiency to your work with geometry questions in the SAT Math section. You may find that by recognizing these kinds of special right triangles you'll be able to answer some complex triangle questions with exceptional speed.

PRACTICE

What is the area in square inches of a right triangle with one side length of 27 inches and a hypotenuse of 45 inches?

A. 972

B. 486

C. 192

D. Cannot be determined from the given information

The correct answer is B. To find the area of a right triangle, you'll need to find the length of both legs. You can use the Pythagorean theorem, but you may also notice that this triangle is a multiple of a 3-4-5 right triangle: 3(9) = 27 and 5(9) = 45. Thus the missing leg length is 4(9) = 36. Since it is a right triangle, the legs serve as the base and height. The area is half the product of its legs: $\frac{1}{2}(27)(36) = 486$ square inches.

Which of the following sets of triangle side lengths represents a right triangle?

A. 4-5-6

B. 5-12-14

C. $\sqrt{2}, \sqrt{2}, 1$

D. $\sqrt{3}, 3, 2\sqrt{3}$

The correct answer is D. Without access to angle measures, you can use the Pythagorean theorem to determine whether the side lengths of a triangle result in a right triangle. However, in this situation, instead of using the Pythagorean theorem to check each answer choice, you can first look for side length relationships that may indicate the presence of a special right triangle or Pythagorean triple. Choices A and B are close to the 3-4-5 and 5-12-13 right triangles, but they have some sides increased to a value that doesn't result in satisfaction of the Pythagorean theorem. Choice C resembles one of the relationships of a special right triangle but has switched the lengths of the legs and the hypotenuse. This leaves choice D. When examined, you can see that this is a 30-60-90 right triangle with the shortest leg being $\sqrt{3}$ (opposite the 30° angle), the second leg being $\sqrt{3}\cdot\sqrt{3}=3$, and the hypotenuse as twice the length of the shortest leg, $2\sqrt{3}$.

Rectangles, Parallelograms, and Other Polygons

Any closed geometric figure with straight line segments for sides is called a polygon (including triangles, quadrilaterals, and more). It is possible to draw a polygon with one or more interior angles greater than 180°, as illustrated in the figure below.

However, if all the interior angles in the polygon are less than 180°, we have a convex polygon. The sum of the angle measurements in any convex polygon is $180(n - 2)$, where n is the number of vertices. Thus, for a triangle, $n = 3$, and the sum is 180°. For a quadrilateral (a four-sided figure), $n = 4$, and the sum is 360°. For a pentagon (a five-sided figure), $n = 5$, and the angle sum is 540°, and so on.

To find the perimeter of a polygon (the distance around the figure), simply add together the lengths of all the sides. Of course, it may require some thinking to determine each length. To find its area, connect the vertices by line segments to divide the polygon into triangles; then sum the areas of the triangles. See the following example.

EXAMPLE

Find the area of figure *ABCDE*.

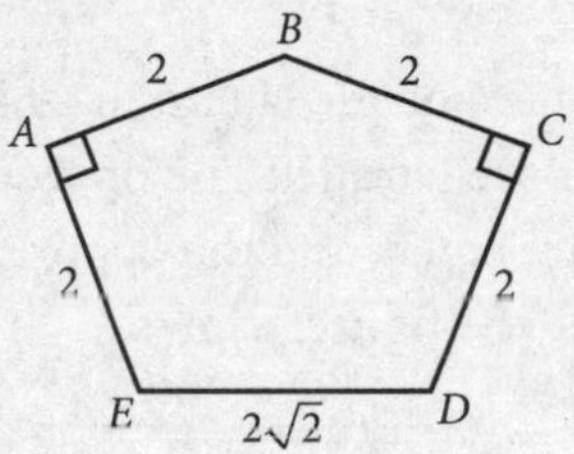

Solution

Drawing *BE* and *BD* divides the region into three triangles as shown. Triangles *BAE* and *BCD* are both 45°-45°-90° right triangles, making $BE = BD = 2\sqrt{2}$.

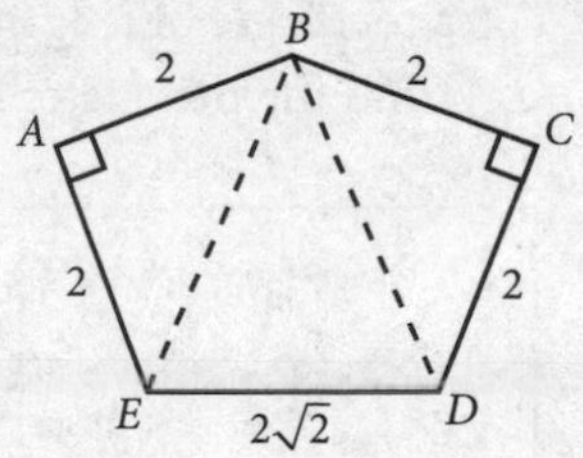

This makes the central triangle an equilateral triangle. The area of each of the two outer triangles is 2. Together, the outside triangles have an area of 4. The center triangle has a base whose length is $2\sqrt{2}$. If you draw the altitude from *B* to the midpoint of *ED*, you create two 30°-60°-90° right triangles with a shorter leg whose length is $\sqrt{2}$. This makes the height $\sqrt{6}$

(recall that the side opposite the 60° angle in this type of special right triangle is the shorter leg multiplied by $\sqrt{3}$). This yields an area of $\frac{\sqrt{2}\sqrt{6}}{2}=\frac{\sqrt{12}}{2}=\frac{2\sqrt{3}}{2}=\sqrt{3}$. Because that area represents only half the area of the central triangle, you must multiply it by 2, resulting in $2\sqrt{3}$. Adding together the areas of all of the triangles in the polygon, the total area is then $4+2\sqrt{3}$, or approximately 7.46.

A parallelogram is a quadrilateral in which the pairs of opposite sides are parallel. The opposite angles in a parallelogram are equal, and the opposite sides are of equal length (see the figure below).

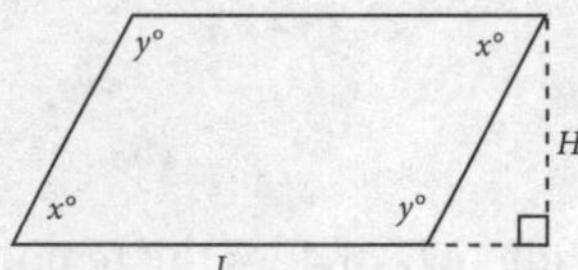

The area of a parallelogram is determined by its length times its height; that is, $A = LH$, as labeled in the diagram.

If the angles in the parallelogram are right angles, we have a rectangle. For a rectangle of length L and width W, the area is $A = LW$, and the perimeter is $P = 2L + 2W$.

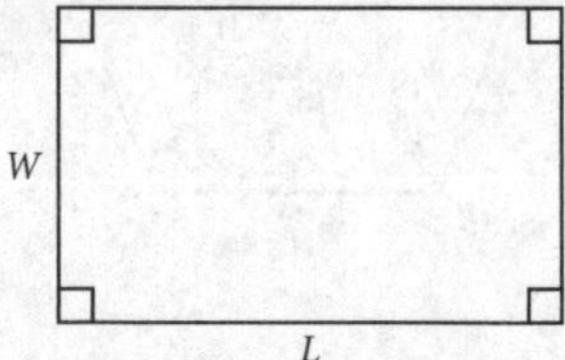

For example, the area of a rectangular garden that is 20 yards long and 10 yards deep is (20)(10) = 200 square yards. However, to put a fence around the same garden (that is, around its perimeter) requires 2(20) + 2(10) = 60 running yards of fencing. These relatively easy formulas can be used to get you to think about more complex situations using compound shapes, as seen in the following example.

EXAMPLE

If sod comes in 4 × 4 foot squares costing $3.50 per square, how much will it cost to sod the lawn shown (all distances indicated in feet)? You may assume that all angles that appear to be right angles are right angles.

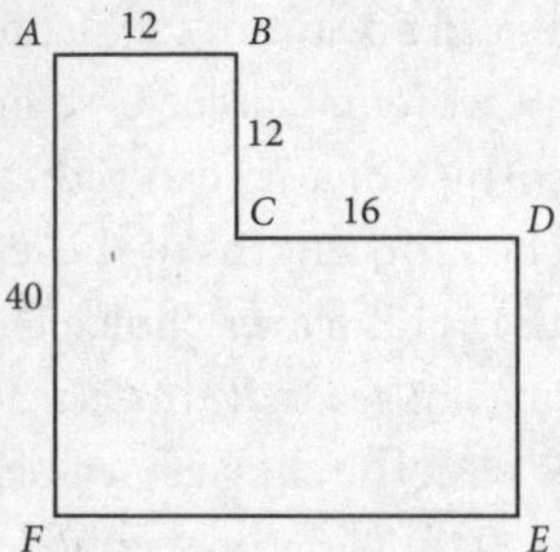

Solution

Completing the rectangle as shown in the figure below, we see that the large rectangle *AGEF* is 40 × 28 = 1,120 square feet.

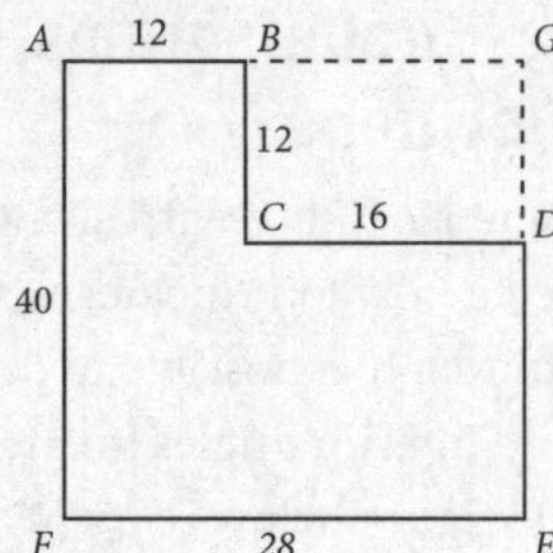

The lesser rectangle *BGDC* is 12 × 16 = 192 square feet. Hence, the area that must be sodded is 1,120 – 192 = 928 square feet. Now, each 4 × 4 foot piece of sod is 16 square feet. Therefore, we need 928 ÷ 16 = 58 squares of sod at $3.50 each. The total cost is (58)(3.50) = $203.

Circles

The set of all points in the plane that are a given distance r from a fixed-point P is a circle. Here is the basic terminology involving circles you should know before you take the SAT. Most of these are sure to surface on the exam, so you should absolutely memorize these definitions.

12

CIRCLE TERMINOLOGY		
Term	**Definition**	**Illustration**
Center	The point P equidistant from all points on the circle	P
Radius	The common distance r that points on the circle are from the center	r
Diameter	A line segment that passes through the center of the circle and has endpoints on the circle (its length is twice the radius)	P
Central Angle	An angle formed between two radial segments	
Arc	A portion of the circle that lies between two points	
Sector	The portion of the inside of a circle that lies between two radial segments	

You will use these terms when configuring values of circles, as in the following formulas. Circumference and area of circles are the formulas that come up most frequently on the SAT.

CIRCLE FORMULAS		
Term	**Definition**	**Illustration**
Circumference of a Circle	Since the diameter d is $2r$, there are two expressions for this formula: $C = 2\pi r = \pi d$	r
Length of an Arc of a Circle	$P = \frac{\theta}{360°} \cdot 2\pi r$	θ, r
Area of a Circle	$A = \pi r^2$	r
Area of a Sector of a Circle	$A = \frac{\theta}{360°} \cdot \pi r^2$	θ, r
Equation for a Circle in the Coordinate Plane	$(x - h)^2 + (y - k)^2 = r^2$, where (h, k) is the circle's center and r is the radius	(0,0); $x^2 + y^2 = 1$

TIP

Notice that the formulae for arc length and sector area actually represent two proportional relationships. If you were to make each side of the equations a ratio, $\frac{P}{2\pi r}=\frac{\theta}{360°}$ and $\frac{A}{\pi r^2}=\frac{\theta}{360°}$, you would see that you have two part-to-whole relationships (the arc length or sector area compared to the circumference or total area, respectively, and the angle measure of the arc or sector and the total angle measure of the circle).

Problems involving circles come in different varieties, but they all generally involve using the same formulas. Sometimes, you will be given a diameter instead of a radius, or you will be given an area of a sector or the perimeter of an arc and then be asked to identify the radius or diameter. The key is to be flexible with using the formulas in various ways, depending on what information is provided.

PRACTICE

The length of the radius of circle A is 4 times as long as the radius of circle B. If the radius of circle B is x units, what is the area (in square units) of circle A?

A. $16x$

B. $\frac{x}{16}$

C. $\frac{x}{4}$

D. $16\pi x^2$

The correct answer is D. The radius of circle A is $4x$. So its area is $\pi(4x)^2 = 16\pi x^2$.

Sector Area

The area of a sector of a circle is the product of the ratio $\frac{\text{measure of the arc}}{360°}$ and the area of the circle.

For example, if the radius of a circle is 3 cm and the measure of the arc is 60°, then the area of the sector is $\frac{60°}{360°}\bullet\pi(3)^2=\frac{9\pi}{6}=\frac{3\pi}{2}\text{cm}^2$.

$$\text{Area of sector } AOB=\frac{m\widehat{AB}}{360}\bullet\pi r^2$$

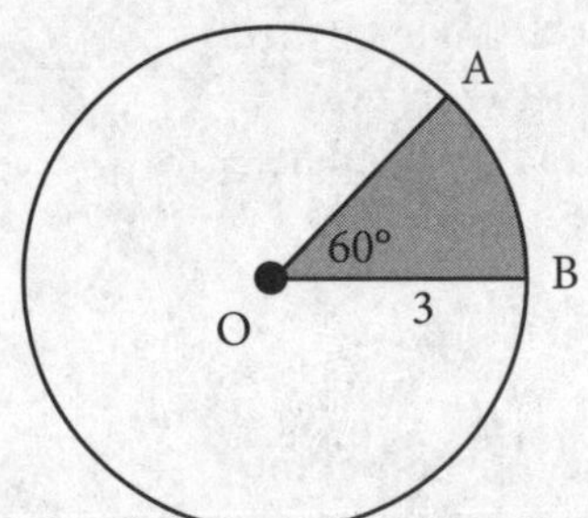

PRACTICE

What is the area of the shaded region in the circle shown below?

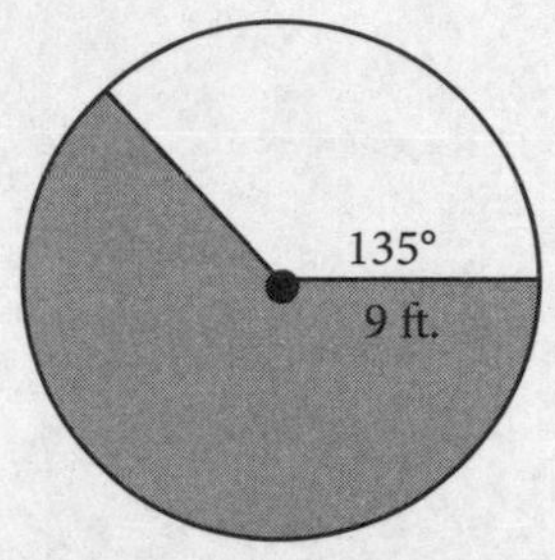
135°
9 ft.

A. 27π square feet

B. 81π square feet

C. $\frac{243}{8}$ square feet

D. $\frac{405\pi}{8}$ square feet

The correct answer is D. The central angle corresponding to the shaded region is $360 - 135 = 225$ degrees. So the area of the shaded region is $\frac{225}{360} \cdot \pi \cdot (9)^2 = \frac{405\pi}{8}$ square feet.

Arc Length

An arc is a portion of the circumference of a circle, as indicated by the shading in the example shown. Recall that the circumference of a circle, C, is the distance around the circle, which is found by multiplying the length of the radius, r, by 2π: $C = 2\pi r$. The length of an arc is determined by the central angle which creates the arc. Arc length is typically represented by the variable s. The measure of the central angle of a circle is typically represented by the Greek letter theta, which is θ. You can create a proportion as follows to solve for the arc length: $\frac{s}{C} = \frac{\theta}{360}$, where s represents the arc length and C represents the circumference of the circle. However, if the measure of the central angle is given in radians (or a question is looking for you to convert degrees to radians, as seen later in this chapter), you can simplify the formula for finding the arc length.

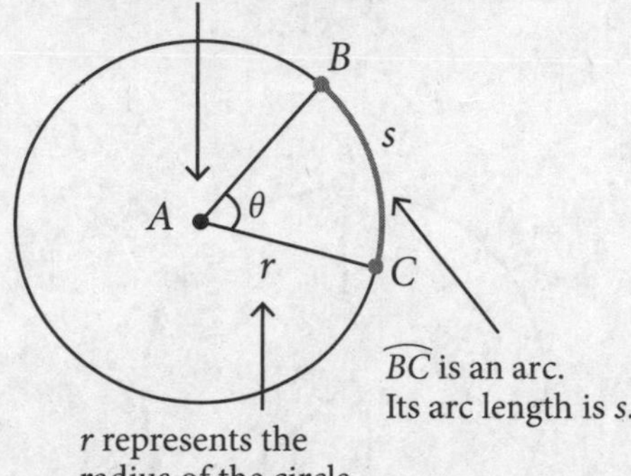
$\angle BAC$ is a central angle of the circle. Its measure is θ.
B
s
A
θ
r
C
$\widehat{BC}$ is an arc. Its arc length is s.
r represents the radius of the circle.

The radian measure θ of a central angle of a circle is defined as the ratio of the length of the arc, s, opposite of the central angle, to the radius r of the circle:

$$\theta = \frac{s}{r}$$

To find the arc length, multiply the radius of the circle by the measure of the central angle in radians:

$$s = r\theta$$

When given an angle in radian measure, substitute the angle in radians for θ, and multiply it by the radius of the circle.

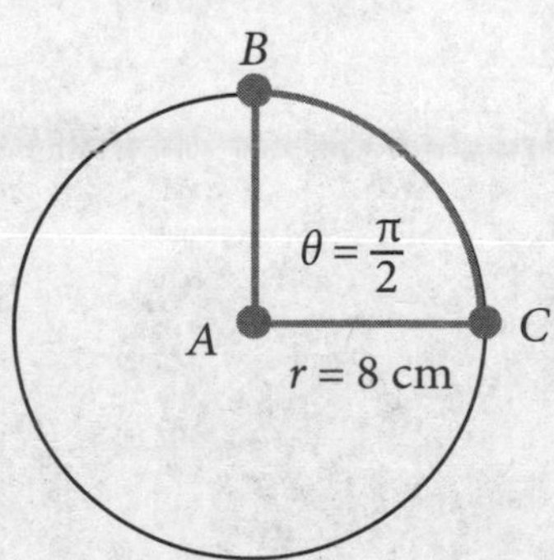
B
$\theta = \frac{\pi}{2}$
A
C
$r = 8$ cm

$$s = \frac{\pi}{2} \cdot 8 = 4\pi \approx 4(3.14)$$
$$= 12.56 \text{ cm}$$

If the central angle measure is given in degrees, you can change the angle to radians first and then use the arc length formula.

The formula for finding the arc length, when an angle is given in degrees, is:

$$s = r\theta \cdot \frac{\pi}{180^\circ}$$

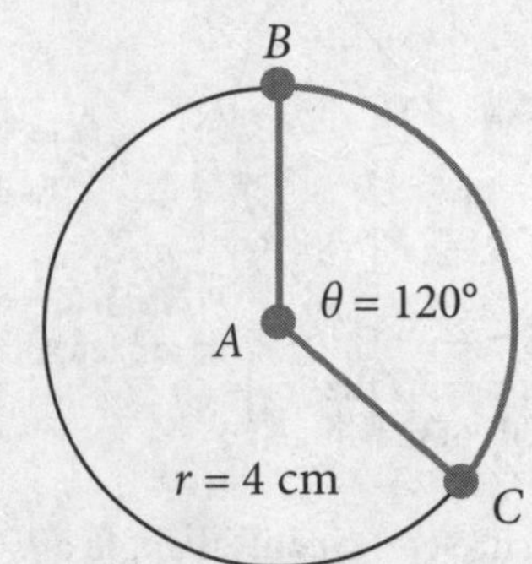

$$s = 4 \cdot 120^\circ \cdot \frac{\pi}{180^\circ} = \frac{8}{3}\pi = \frac{8}{3}(3.14)$$
$$\approx 8.38 \text{ cm}$$

In this situation, you may also notice that the central angle is one third of the total angle measure of the circle. Thus, the arc length will be one third of the circumference of the circle. Circumference is $2\pi r$ or πd, so the arc length can quickly be determined to be $\frac{8\pi}{3}$. If answer choices are provided in terms of π, one method for determining arc length may be faster than the other.

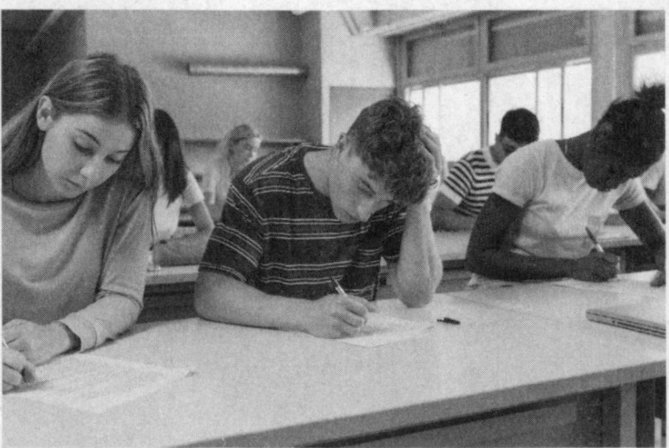

PRACTICE

A circle P has a radius of 6 and an arc s. The central angle of arc s is 60°. What is the length of arc s?

A. $\frac{\pi}{3}$

B. $\frac{\pi}{2}$

C. π

D. 2π

The correct answer is D. You have two methods to solve for the arc length s. You can use a proportion between the circle's angles and the arc length and circumference. Or you can use the arc length formula after converting the central angle to radians. We'll demonstrate both. First, let's look at the proportion between the angles and length measures of the circle.

$$\frac{\text{central angle}}{\text{total circle angle}} = \frac{\text{arc length}}{\text{circumference}}$$

$$\frac{60^\circ}{360^\circ} = \frac{s}{C}$$

$$\frac{1}{6} = \frac{s}{12\pi}$$

$$6s = 12\pi$$

$$s = 2\pi$$

If you were to convert the central angle to radians, your calculations would look like the following:

$$s = r\theta \frac{\pi}{180^\circ}$$

$$s = 6(60^\circ)\frac{\pi}{180^\circ}$$

$$s = \frac{6\pi}{3}$$

$$s = 2\pi$$

12

RIGHT TRIANGLE TRIGONOMETRY

Now, we'll look at trigonometric ratios and their application to right triangles in geometry. Trigonometric ratios were defined, in part, to identify the lengths of sides of a right triangle when one side and one angle (instead of two sides) are known. The names of these six ratios, with their abbreviations, are as follows:

TRIGONOMETRIC FUNCTIONS

Trigonometric Function	Abbreviation
Cosine	cos
Sine	sin
Tangent	tan
Secant	sec
Cosecant	csc
Cotangent	cot

If given on the SAT, you will likely see the abbreviated form of the name.

The Three Basic Trigonometric Ratios

The three basic trigonometric ratios are sine, cosine, and tangent. You can find the sine, cosine, or tangent of an acute angle (θ) in a right triangle with the following ratios.

$$\text{Sin } \theta = \frac{\text{Opposite}}{\text{Hypotenuse}}$$

$$\text{Cos } \theta = \frac{\text{Adjacent}}{\text{Hypotenuse}}$$

$$\text{Tan } \theta = \frac{\text{Opposite}}{\text{Adjacent}}$$

There are, in fact, three more ratios that are also used with trigonometric calculations: secant, cosecant, and cotangent.

Finding Trigonometric Ratios

Use SOH, CAH, TOA to remember how to find each ratio.

Consider $\angle B$:

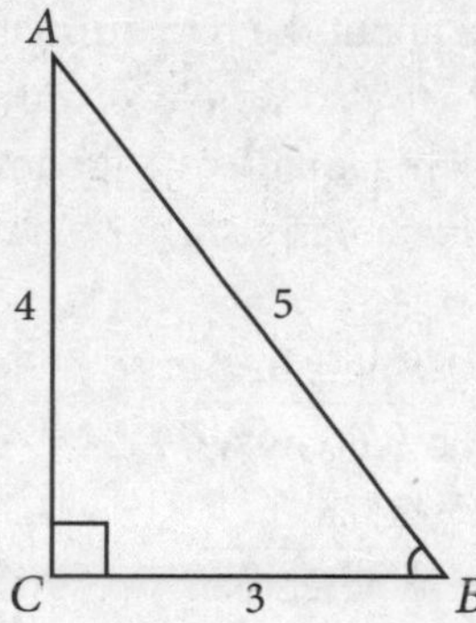

The side opposite or across from $\angle B$ is $\overline{AC}$.

The side adjacent or next to $\angle B$ is $\overline{CB}$.

The hypotenuse of the right triangle is $\overline{AB}$.

Find the trigonometric ratios.

Sine of $\angle B$

To find the sine of $\angle B$ think SOH:

$$\sin B = \frac{\text{Opposite}}{\text{Hypotenuse}} = \frac{AC}{AB} = \frac{4}{5}$$

Cosine of $\angle B$

To find the cosine of $\angle B$ think CAH:

$$\cos B = \frac{\text{Adjacent}}{\text{Hypotenuse}} = \frac{CB}{AB} = \frac{3}{5}$$

Tangent of $\angle B$

To find the tangent of $\angle B$ think TOA:

$$\tan B = \frac{\text{Opposite}}{\text{Adjacent}} = \frac{AC}{CB} = \frac{4}{3}$$

The measure of angle B will correspond to each of those ratios. If you were to use a calculator to find the inverse of $\sin B = \frac{4}{5} \left(\sin^{-1}\left(\frac{4}{5}\right)\right)$ or the inverses of $\cos B = \frac{3}{5}$ or $\tan B = \frac{4}{3}$, they would all reveal that angle B measures 53.13 degrees. If you input sin 53.13, you would get a ratio of 0.8, or $\frac{4}{5}$, the relationship between the opposite side and the hypotenuse.

SOH, CAH, TOA is an easy way to remember how to use the three basic trigonometric functions. In the case that you are asked about the remaining three functions on the SAT, there are also simple formulas to memorize. See the following for all six trigonometric ratios and their related formulas:

$$\sin\theta = \frac{\text{opposite}}{\text{hypotenuse}}$$

$$\cos\theta = \frac{\text{adjacent}}{\text{hypotenuse}}$$

$$\tan\theta = \frac{\text{opposite}}{\text{adjacent}} = \frac{\sin\theta}{\cos\theta}$$

$$\cot\theta = \frac{\text{adjacent}}{\text{opposite}} = \frac{\cos\theta}{\sin\theta} = \frac{1}{\tan\theta}$$

$$\sec\theta = \frac{\text{hypotenuse}}{\text{adjacent}} = \frac{1}{\cos\theta}$$

$$\csc\theta = \frac{\text{hypotenuse}}{\text{opposite}} = \frac{1}{\sin\theta}$$

Unknown Lengths

If one side length and one angle measurement of a right triangle are known, all remaining sides and angle measurements can be found. Since the trigonometric ratios of most angles are irrational, a calculator (in degree mode) can be used.

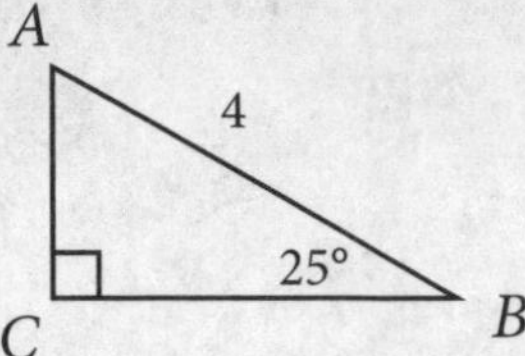

In right triangle ABC, $AB = 4$ and $\angle B$ measures 25°.

Side AC is opposite to angle B and we know the hypotenuse, so use the sine ratio:

$$\frac{AC}{4} = \sin 25 \rightarrow AC = 4\sin 25° \approx 1.7$$

Side BC is adjacent to angle B and we know the hypotenuse, so use the cosine ratio:

$$\frac{BC}{4} = \cos 25° \rightarrow BC = 4\cos 25° \approx 3.6$$

If the hypotenuse is unknown but the measure of a leg and one angle is known, the solution process is very similar. The only difference is the ratio that is used and the location of the unknown in the equation.

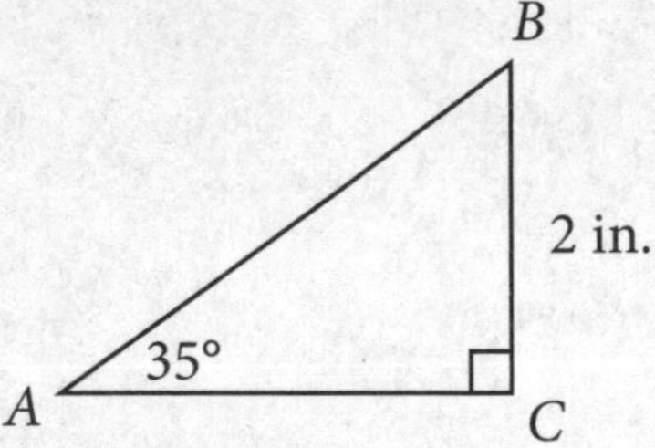

In triangle ABC, $BC = 2$ in. and angle A measures 35°.

Side AC is adjacent to angle A and we know the opposite side, so use the tangent ratio:

$$\frac{\text{opp}}{\text{adj}} : \frac{2}{AC} = \tan 35° \rightarrow AC = \frac{2}{\tan 35°} \approx 2.9 \text{ in.}$$

Side AB is the hypotenuse and side BC is opposite angle A, so use the sine ratio:

$$\frac{\text{opp}}{\text{hyp}} : \frac{2}{AB} = \sin 35° \rightarrow AB = \frac{2}{\sin 35°} \approx 3.5 \text{ in.}$$

The problems related to trigonometry on the SAT Math section come in two main varieties:

01 **Compute a trigonometric function or determine a side of a triangle using given information.**

02 **Solve a word problem that can be modeled using a right triangle.**

Let's take a look at two sample SAT-type trigonometry problems.

PRACTICE

A 95-foot cable attached to the top of a telephone pole is anchored to the ground. If the wire rises at a 64° angle from the ground, how tall is the telephone pole (in feet)?

A. 95 tan 64°

B. 64 cos 95°

C. 95 cos 64°

D. 95 sin 64°

The correct answer is D. As shown in the diagram below, the height of the telephone pole, x, is opposite a 64° angle, and the hypotenuse of the triangle is 95 feet.

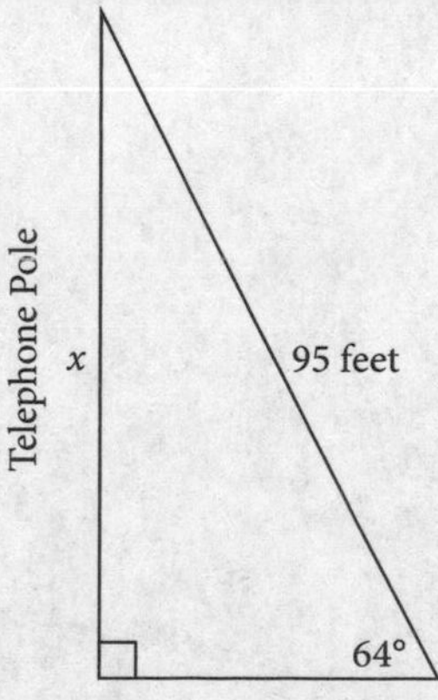

Since sine equals $\frac{\text{opposite}}{\text{hypotenuse}}$, we get the formula $\frac{x}{95} = \sin 64°; x = 95 \sin 64°$.

In right triangle ABC, $\sin A = \frac{1}{2}$. What is the value of $\cos A$?

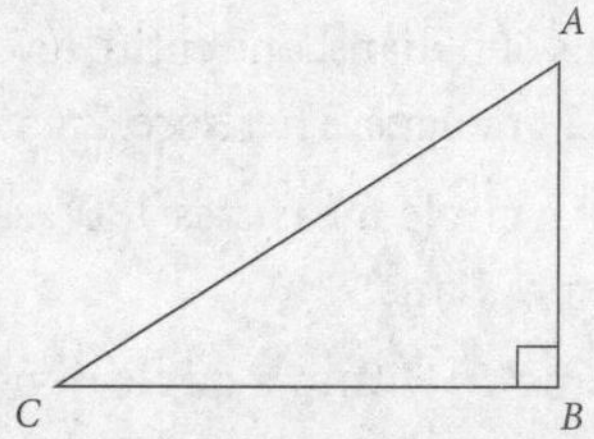

A. $\sqrt{3}$

B. 2

C. $\frac{\sqrt{3}}{3}$

D. $\frac{\sqrt{3}}{2}$

The correct answer is D. Remember that sine is $\frac{\text{opposite}}{\text{hypotenuse}}$ and that cosine is $\frac{\text{adjacent}}{\text{hypotenuse}}$. From what is given, $\frac{CB}{AC} = \frac{1}{2}$. We label the lengths of CB and AC in the triangle:

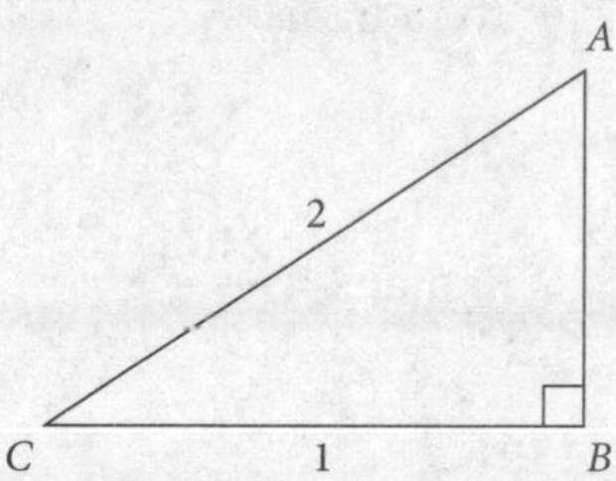

To find the cosine of angle A, you need to know the length of the side adjacent to it, namely segment AB. Since the length of a leg of this triangle is related to the length of its hypotenuse in the ratio of 1:2, remember from earlier in this chapter that this is a 30-60-90 right triangle, whose three sides are related in the ratio of $1 : \sqrt{3} : 2$. Therefore, $AB = \sqrt{3}$, so $\cos A = \frac{\sqrt{3}}{2}$.

Degrees and Radians

There are two ways in which angles can be measured: degrees and radians.

Converting Degrees to Radians

While degree measures are frequently used, a radian measure is helpful in that it relates to the circumference of a circle and trigonometric functions.

- One entire revolution of a circle is equivalent to 360°. In terms of radians, one entire revolution is equivalent to 2π radians. Therefore, 2π radians = 360°.
- Half of a circle measures 180°, so half of 2π radians is π radians.
- Since angles within a circle divide the entire 2π radians proportionally, simple proportions can be used to convert an angle given in degrees to an angle in radians.

The formula for converting a measure given in degrees to a measure in radians is:

$$\text{Radians} = \frac{\text{Degrees}}{180^\circ} \cdot \pi$$

EXAMPLE

Convert 240° to radians.

Solution

$$\begin{aligned}\text{Radians} &= \frac{240^\circ}{180^\circ} \cdot \pi \\ &= \frac{4}{3}\pi \\ 240^\circ &= \frac{4}{3}\pi \text{ radians}\end{aligned}$$

Converting Radians to Degrees

Just as an angle measure given in degrees can be converted into an equivalent angle measure in radians, an angle measure in radians can be converted into an equivalent degree measure. The formula for converting radians to degrees is:

$$\text{Degrees} = \frac{180^\circ}{\pi} \cdot \text{Radians}$$

EXAMPLE

Convert $\frac{5\pi}{6}$ radians to degrees.

Solution

$$\frac{180^\circ}{\pi} \cdot \frac{5\pi}{6} = 150^\circ$$

$$\frac{5\pi}{6} \text{ radians} = 150^\circ$$

SUMMING IT UP

- Any closed geometric figure with straight line segments for sides is called a polygon.
- A right triangle is one that has a right angle; an acute triangle is one in which all three angles are acute; an obtuse triangle has one obtuse angle.
- An equilateral triangle is one in which all three sides have the same length; an isosceles triangle has at least two sides with the same length; a scalene triangle has three sides of different lengths.
- The triangle sum rule says that the sum of the measures of the three angles in any triangle must be 180°. The triangle inequality says that the sum of the lengths of any two sides of a triangle must be strictly larger than the length of the third side.
- The Pythagorean theorem states that for a right triangle with legs a and b and hypotenuse c, $a^2 + b^2 = c^2$.
- Two triangles ΔABC and ΔDEF are congruent if all three corresponding pairs of angles are congruent and all three corresponding sides are congruent. Two triangles ΔABC and ΔDEF are similar if the ratios of the three pairs of corresponding sides are the same; that is, $\frac{AB}{DE} = \frac{BC}{EF} = \frac{AC}{DF} = k$, where k is a positive number.
- The area formula for a triangle with base b and height h is $A = \frac{1}{2}b \cdot h$.
- There are some triangles with special relationships between sides and angles that, when recognized, can simplify your calculations: 3-4-5 and 5-12-13 right triangles, as well as 30-60-90 and 45-45-90 right triangles.
- The circumference of a circle with radius r (or diameter $d = 2r$) is $C = 2\pi r = \pi d$. The area of a circle with radius r is $A = \pi r^2$.
- Part of a circle's circumference is called an arc; the length of an arc can be found with the following formula: $P = \frac{\theta}{360°}\pi 2r$, where θ represents the measure of the central angle of the arc and r is the radius of the circle.
- Part of a circle's area is called a sector; the area of a sector can be found with the following formula: $A = \frac{\theta}{360°}\pi r^2$, where θ represents the measure of the central angle of the sector and r is the radius of the circle.
- To graph a circle in the coordinate plane, use the following formula: $(x - h)^2 + (y - k)^2 = r^2$, where (h, k) is the center of the circle.
- Trigonometric ratios are used to identify the lengths of sides of a right triangle when one side and one angle (instead of two sides) are known. There are six trigonometric ratios: cosine (cos), sine (sin), tangent (tan), secant (sec), cosecant (csc), and cotangent (cot).

- Trigonometric ratios for right triangles are defined as follows:

$$\sin\theta = \frac{\text{opposite}}{\text{hypotenuse}} \text{ and } \csc\theta = \frac{\text{hypotenuse}}{\text{opposite}} = \frac{1}{\sin\theta}$$
$$\cos\theta = \frac{\text{adjacent}}{\text{hypotenuse}} \text{ and } \sec\theta = \frac{\text{hypotenuse}}{\text{adjacent}} = \frac{1}{\cos\theta}$$
$$\tan\theta = \frac{\text{opposite}}{\text{adjacent}} \text{ and } \cot\theta = \frac{\text{adjacent}}{\text{opposite}} = \frac{1}{\tan\theta}$$

- Angles can be measured in two ways: degrees and radians. Radians often arise when dealing with circles and trigonometry. You can convert between degree and radian measures using the following formula: $\text{Radians} = \frac{\text{Degrees}}{180^\circ} \cdot \pi$.

TEST YOURSELF

GEOMETRY AND TRIGONOMETRY

10 Questions—16 Minutes

Directions: The questions in this section address a number of important Geometry and Trigonometry math concepts.

Use of a calculator is permitted for all questions.

Unless otherwise indicated:

- All variables and expressions represent real numbers.
- Figures provided are drawn to scale.
- All figures lie in a plane.
- The domain of a given function f is the set of all real numbers x for which $f(x)$ is a real number.

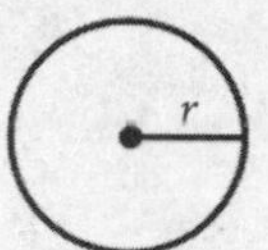

$A = \pi r^2$
$C = 2\pi r$

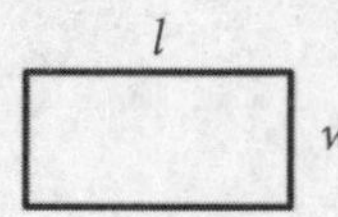

$A = lw$

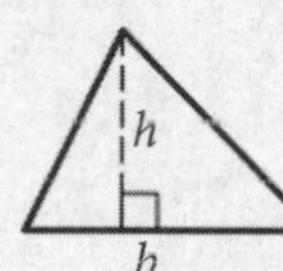

$A = \frac{1}{2}bh$

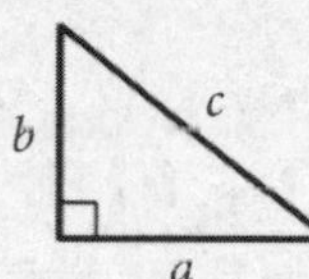

$c^2 = a^2 + b^2$

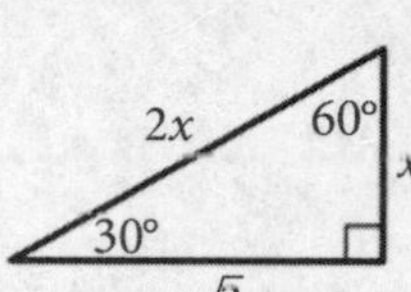

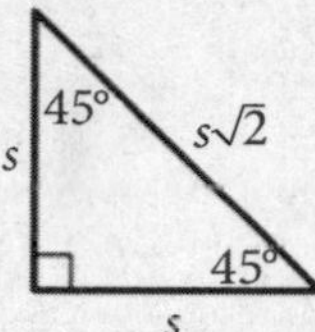

Special Right Triangles

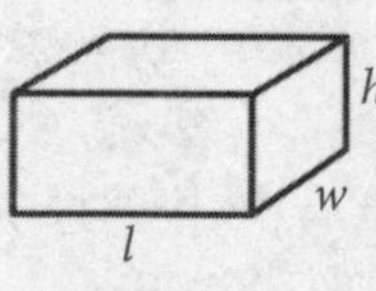

$V = lwh$

$V = \pi r^2 h$

$V = \frac{4}{3}\pi r^3$

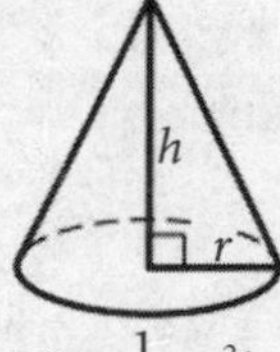

$V = \frac{1}{3}\pi r^2 h$

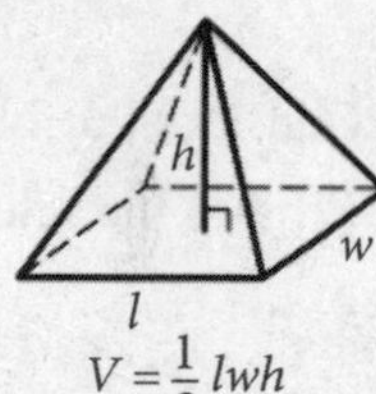

$V = \frac{1}{3}lwh$

Reference:

The number of degrees of arc in a circle is 360.

The number of radians of arc in a circle is 2π.

The sum of the measures in degrees of the angles of a triangle is 180.

1.

A rectangle of length $(w + 6)$ inches and width $(w - 1)$ inches is shaded, except for a square region of side length $(w - 3)$ inches. What is the area of the shaded region, in terms of w?

A. $w^2 + 5w - 6$

B. $w^2 + 4w - 9$

C. $2w^2 + 11w + 3$

D. $11w - 15$

2.

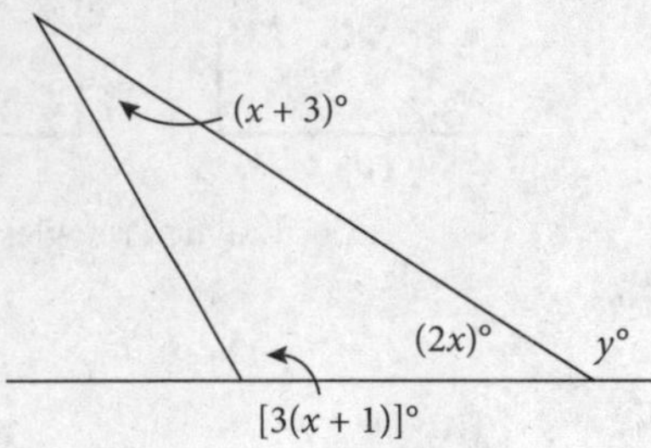

Consider the following triangle:

What is the value of $x + y$?

A. 29

B. 58

C. 122

D. 151

3.

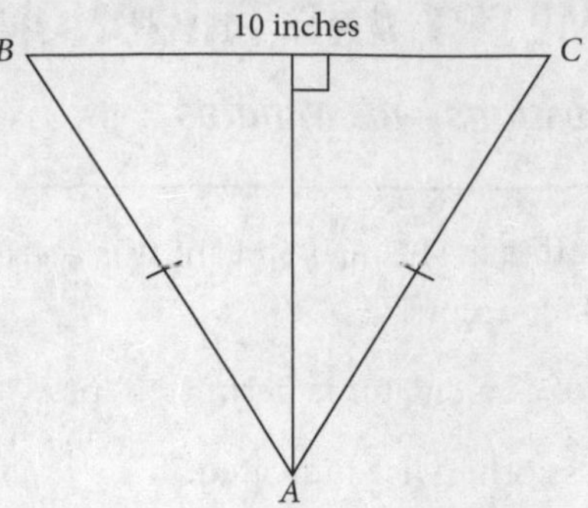

Which of these expressions represents the height of triangle ABC?

A. $\sqrt{y^2 + 25}$ inches

B. $\sqrt{y^2 - 25}$ inches

C. $y + 5$ inches

D. $y^2 + 25$ inches

4.

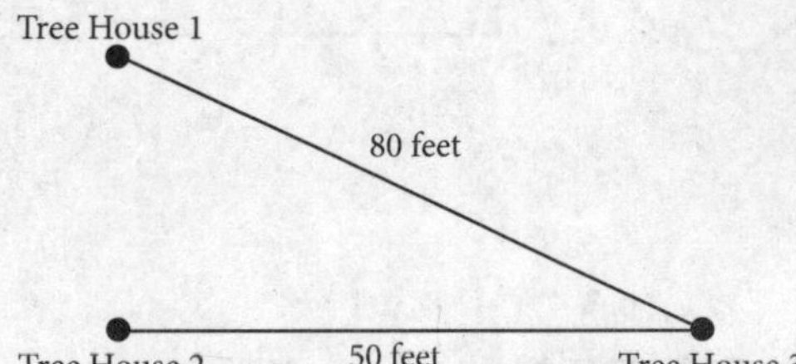

A family builds three tree houses in the backyard and connects them with bridges, as shown:

Assuming Tree House 1 is directly across from Tree House 2, which of these expressions represents the length of the bridge connecting these two tree houses?

A. $80^2 - 50^2$ feet

B. $80 - 50$ feet

C. $\sqrt{50^2 + 80^2}$ feet

D. $\sqrt{80^2 - 50^2}$ feet

5.

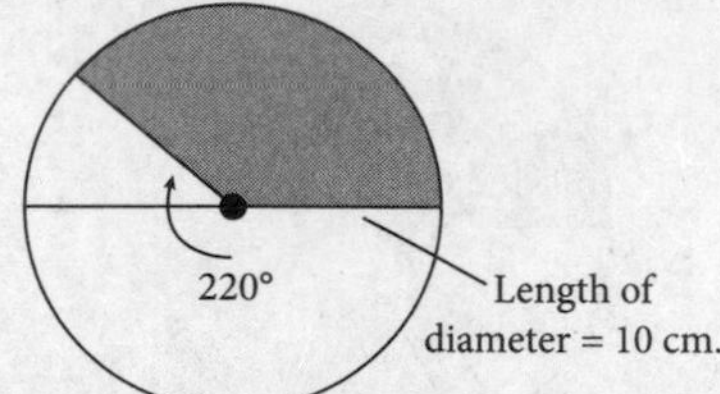

What is the length, S, of the arc of the circle corresponding to the shaded sector?

A. $\frac{9}{35}\pi$ cm.

B. $\frac{\pi}{4}$ cm.

C. $\frac{11}{9}\pi$ cm.

D. $\frac{35}{9}\pi$ cm.

6.

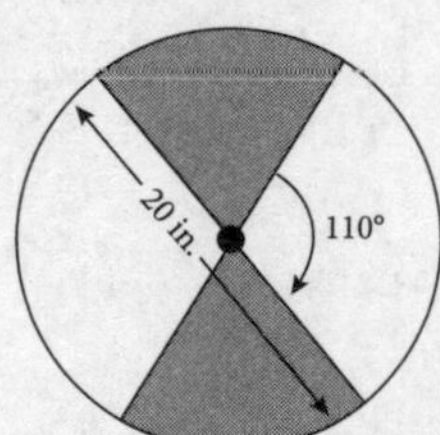

What is the area of the shaded region?

A. $\frac{175}{9}\pi$ square inches

B. $\frac{275}{9}\pi$ square inches

C. $\frac{350}{9}\pi$ square inches

D. $\frac{550}{9}\pi$ square inches

7. The circumference of circle A is three times the circumference of circle B. What is the ratio of the area of circle B to the area of circle A?

A. 1:3

B. 3:1

C. 1:9

D. 1:6

8.

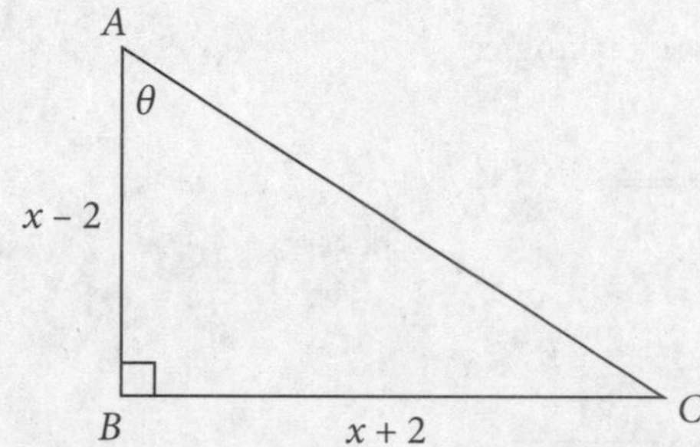

What is the value of $\sin\theta$ in triangle ABC?

A. −1

B. $\frac{(x+2)^2}{2x^2+8}$

C. $\frac{2\sqrt{x^2+8}}{x+2}$

D. $\frac{2x}{x^2-4}$

9.

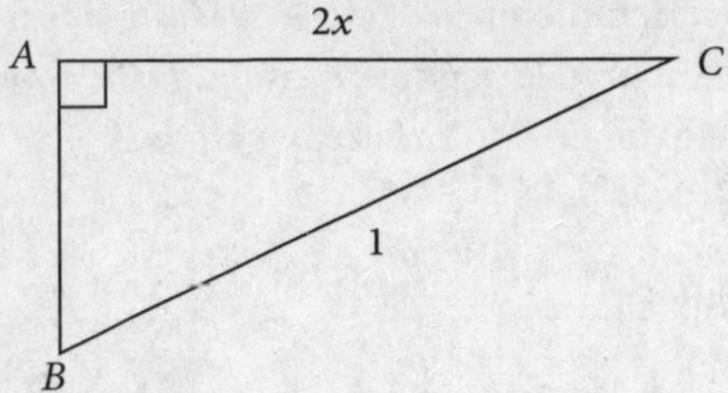

Let $0 < x < \frac{1}{2}$. Compute sec(*B*) + csc(*C*) for the following triangle:

A. $\frac{2}{\sqrt{1-4x^2}}$

B. $\frac{1}{x}$

C. $\frac{1}{2x}+\frac{1}{\sqrt{1-4x^2}}$

D. $2\sqrt{1-4x^2}$

10.

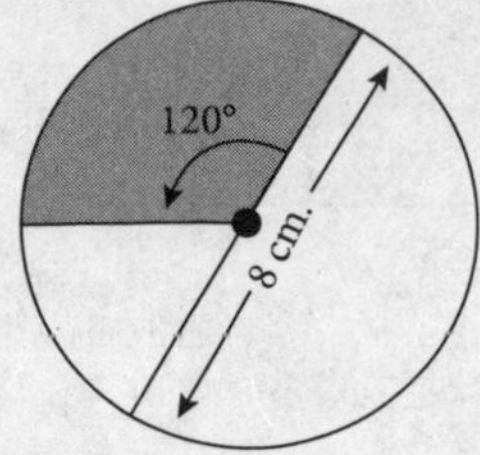

What is the radian measure of the central angle of the shaded sector?

A. $\frac{\pi}{3}$

B. $\frac{5\pi}{6}$

C. $\frac{2\pi}{3}$

D. $\frac{3\pi}{4}$

ANSWER KEY AND EXPLANATIONS

1. D	3. B	5. D	7. C	9. A
2. D	4. D	6. C	8. B	10. C

1. **The correct answer is D.** First label all the dimensions in the figure:

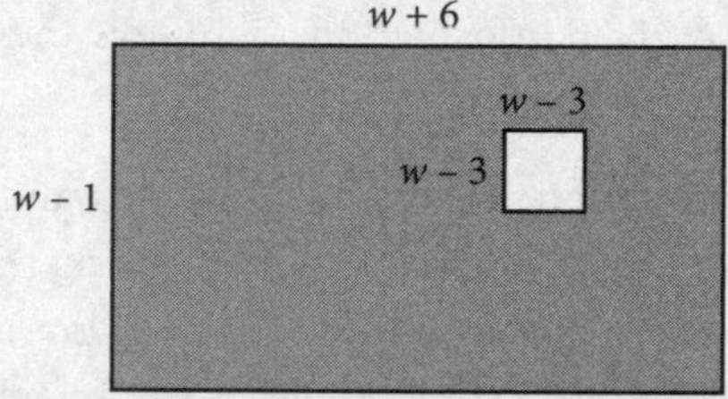

In order to find the shaded area, we need to subtract the area of the inner square from the area of the outer rectangle. The area of the outer rectangle is:

$$(w + 6)(w - 1) = w^2 + 5w - 6$$

and the area of the inner square is:

$$(w - 3)^2 = w^2 - 6w + 9$$

Subtracting these, we get:

$$w^2 + 5w - 6 - (w^2 - 6w + 9)$$
$$w^2 + 5w - 6 - w^2 + 6w - 9$$
$$11w - 15$$

2. **The correct answer is D.** This problem involves two main notions—the triangle sum law and the notion of supplementary angles. To begin, the sum of the measures of the three angles inside the triangle is 180°. This leads to the equation $(x + 3) + 3(x + 1) + 2x = 180$. Solve for x as follows:

$$\begin{aligned}(x+3)+3(x+1)+2x&=180\\ x+3+3x+3+2x&=180\\ 6x+6&=180\\ 6x&=174\\ x&=29\end{aligned}$$

Next, you need to find y. To do so, note that the adjacent angles with measures $2x$ and y are supplementary. Since $2x = 2(29) = 58$, it follows that $y = 180 - 58 = 122$. Hence, $x + y = 29 + 122 = 151$.

Pay attention to the goal of the question. Choice A is the value of x, and choice C is the value of y. Choice B is $2x$.

3. **The correct answer is B.** First note that ABC is an isosceles triangle. As such, the bisector from vertex A to side BC must be perpendicular. So we have the following updated diagram:

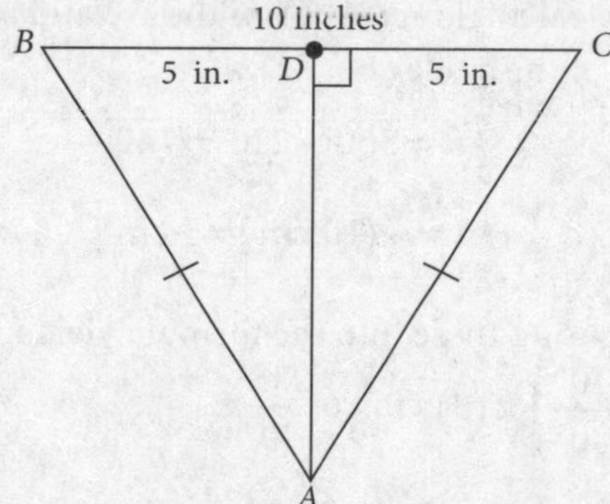

The height of triangle ABC is the length of segment AD. Use the Pythagorean theorem to find:

$$\begin{aligned}(AD)^2 + 5^2 &= y^2\\ (AD)^2 &= y^2 - 25\\ AD &= \sqrt{y^2 - 25}\end{aligned}$$

4. **The correct answer is D.** First, you should complete the given drawing by connecting Tree House 1 to Tree House 2; this forms a right triangle, as shown:

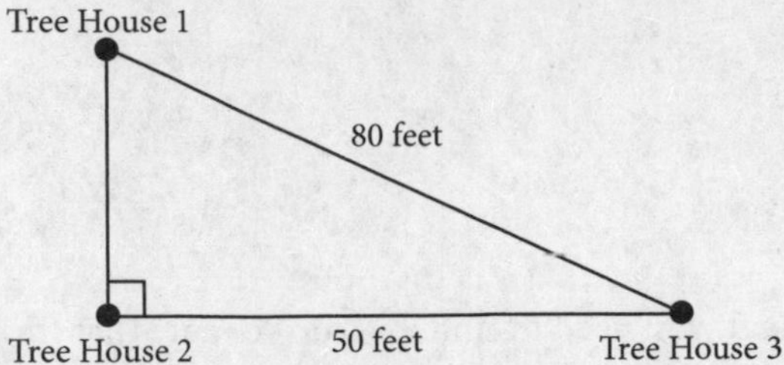

Use the Pythagorean theorem to find its length, s. Keep in mind that this side is a leg of the triangle, not the hypotenuse. As such, we see that $s^2 + 50^2 = 80^2$, so that $s = \sqrt{80^2 - 50^2}$ feet.

5. **The correct answer is D.** This problem asks you to plug in given values, but it requires that you know the formula for arc length and can identify the parts. The formula is $S = \left(\frac{\theta}{180°}\right)\pi(r)$, where θ is the central angle across from the arc and r is the radius of the circle.

$$\theta = 360° - 220° = 140°$$

$$r = \frac{1}{2}(10 \text{ cm}) = 5 \text{ cm}$$

Substituting these into the formula yields $S = \left(\frac{140°}{180°}\right)\pi(5)$ cm., or $\frac{35}{9}\pi$.

6. **The correct answer is C.** The region is comprised of two distinct sectors. Since their central angles are vertical angles, these angles are congruent, so the sectors have the same area. You only need to find the area of one of the sectors and then double it. To find the area of one of these sectors, you need the radius and the central angle. Notice that the angle corresponding to one of the two congruent unshaded sectors is 110°. Since the combination of one unshaded sector and one shaded sector comprises half the circle, it follows that the central angle for a shaded sector is 180° – 110° = 70°. Since the diameter is 20 inches, the radius is 10 inches. The area of one shaded sector is $(10)^2\pi\left(\frac{70°}{360°}\right)$ square inches. Doubling this yields the area of the shaded region as $200\pi\left(\frac{70°}{360°}\right)$ square inches, or $\frac{350}{9}\pi$ square inches.

7. **The correct answer is C.** This problem requires the use of knowledge from two different subjects: number systems and geometry. To begin, you must find the relationship between the radii of the two circles. Use the given information about how the circumferences are related to do so.

The circumference of circle A is $2\pi r_A$, and the circumference of circle B is $2\pi r_B$. Using the first sentence of the problem yields $2\pi r_A = 3(2\pi r_B)$. Dividing both sides by 2π shows that $r_A = 3r_B$. To get the ratio of the areas in the correct form, you must express them using multiples of a single radius. To this end, observe the following:

Area of circle $A = \pi r_A^2 = \pi(3r_B)^2 = 9(\pi r_B^2) = 9 \cdot$ area of circle B

So the ratio of "area of circle B" to "area of circle A" is 1:9.

8. **The correct answer is B.** Your goal is to find the value of sin θ. Sin is represented by the ratio $\frac{\text{opposite}}{\text{hypotenuse}}$. In the case of triangle ABC, you know the opposite side from θ is $x + 2$. You still need the hypotenuse of ABC. Use the Pythagorean theorem to find it:

$$(x-2)^2 + (x+2)^2 = (AC)^2$$
$$x^2 - 4x + 4 + x^2 + 4x + 4 = (AC)^2$$
$$2x^2 + 8 = (AC)^2$$
$$\sqrt{2x^2 + 8} = AC$$

Therefore,

$$\sin\theta = \frac{x+2}{\sqrt{2x^2+8}}$$

However, this is not among the answer choices. You'll need to rationalize the denominator, resulting in $\frac{(x+2)^2}{2x^2+8}$.

9. **The correct answer is A.** You need all three sides of the triangle to compute these quantities. Use the Pythagorean theorem to find the missing side:

$$(AB)^2 + (AC)^2 = (BC)^2$$
$$(AB)^2 + (2x)^2 = 1$$
$$(AB)^2 = 1 - 4x^2$$
$$AB = \sqrt{1-4x^2}$$

Now, compute the two quantities in the given expression.

$$\sec B = \frac{1}{\cos B} = \frac{BC}{AB} = \frac{1}{\sqrt{1-4x^2}}$$
$$\csc C = \frac{1}{\sin C} = \frac{BC}{AB} = \frac{1}{\sqrt{1-4x^2}}$$

Then, add the two quantities:

$$\sec B + \csc C = \frac{2}{\sqrt{1-4x^2}}$$

10. **The correct answer is C.** The central angle of the shaded sector is 120 degrees. You want the angle units in radians. To convert the degree measure to radians, simply multiply 120 by $\frac{\pi}{180}$ which equals $\frac{2\pi}{3}$. Multiplying by $\frac{\pi}{360}$ would result in choice A.

CHAPTER

Advanced Math

ADVANCED MATH

OVERVIEW

The SAT Math section's Advanced Math domain represents 35% of the questions across the Math modules. The questions test your ability to work with nonlinear equations and functions in a variety of situations and forms. You need to be able to, as stated by the College Board, "rewrite, fluently solve, make strategic use of structure, and create" equations that involve absolute values; quadratics; exponential, rational, and radical expressions; polynomials; and other nonlinear components. That may mean working to create equivalent expressions, finding solutions for nonlinear equations and systems, and applying knowledge related to nonlinear functions. Use the examples and practice questions throughout the chapter and the Test Yourself at the end of the chapter to assess your understanding of Advanced Math domain skills and testing points.

13

POLYNOMIALS AND FACTORING

Polynomials and factoring represent key concepts for working with algebraic expressions, equations, and inequalities. These concepts will appear for the Advanced Math domain questions on the SAT. The following section will focus on key terms and methods involved in combining and separating, or factoring, terms in algebra.

Polynomials

A polynomial is one or more terms, each having a variable with a whole number (0, 1, 2, ...) as an exponent. A term is:

- a number (such as 2 or 4.99 or $\frac{2}{3}$ or $\sqrt{20}$)
- a variable (such as x or k)
- any combination of numbers and variables without an operation symbol (such as $5x$, $k\sqrt{3}$, abc, $\frac{h}{2}$, or $15mn^2$)

Terms make up expressions (such as $5x + 3$) and equations (such as $5x + 3 = 23$), and they also are the building blocks of polynomials, as seen here:

- $4x^6$
- $m^2 - 5m + 7$
- $9 - 2t^3$
- 17

Even the number 17 counts as a polynomial due to the implied existence of a variable and exponent. From the laws of exponents, a number with an exponent of zero is equal to 1. So, you could look at 17 in the following way: $17x^0$. This would be equivalent to 17(1) and therefore equals 17.

The following are some examples of sequences that may appear to be polynomials but are in fact in violation of some central rules.

- $\frac{3}{c}$ (This is a rational expression and not a polynomial.)
- $\sqrt{5x}$ (This is a radical expression and not a polynomial.)
- $6y^{-3}$ (This expression contains a negative exponent, equivalent to a rational expression.)
- $3x^2 - 7x^{\frac{1}{2}}$ (This expression likewise contains a non-whole number exponent.)

For now, let's look at an example of a more complex polynomial.

$$x^4 + 14x^3 + 15x - 7$$

This polynomial has four terms: x^4, $14x^3$, $15x$, and -7. If we focused on the second term, we have a coefficient (14), a variable (x), and an exponent (3). If you wanted to read this out loud, you'd say, "fourteen x to the third power" or "fourteen x cubed."

Simplifying Polynomials

We remember that there are several methods to consider when simplifying linear equations, and these rules still apply to polynomials of varying lengths. One of the most important aspects is combining like terms, and this can become quite complex when dealing with polynomials. However, there are clear steps and techniques that you can memorize.

In short, simplifying polynomials means organizing and combining like terms to make a polynomial as easy to read as possible. This includes putting a polynomial into standard form. Let's look at a sample polynomial that has not been simplified:

$$2x + 4x^2 - 13 + 7x - x^2 + x - 3$$

To simplify, first gather like terms:

$$4x^2 - x^2 + 2x + 7x + x - 13 - 3$$

Then, combine like terms:

$$4x^2 - x^2 = 3x^2$$

$$2x + 7x + x = 10x$$

$$-13 - 3 = -16$$

Finally, write out the expression in standard form:

$$3x^2 + 10x - 16$$

This is much easier to read—and make sense of—than the original expression.

Adding and Subtracting Polynomials

If you have two polynomials and you want to combine them through addition or subtraction, the steps are similar to what you've done already. Let's take a look:

$$(11x^2 + 14 + 3x) + (-3x^2 + 2x + 6)$$

Since you have two polynomials inside of parentheses connected by addition, the first step is to remove the parentheses:

$$11x^2 + 14 + 3x + -3x^2 + 2x + 6$$

From here, gather terms and simplify:

$$11x^2 - 3x^2 + 3x + 2x + 14 + 6$$

The resulting polynomial is:

$$8x^2 + 5x + 20$$

Let's look at the same set of polynomials when we subtract one from the other. The process is essentially the same, except that you need to pay careful attention to number signs.

$$(11x^2 + 14 + 3x) - (-3x^2 + 2x + 6)$$

Now that you're subtracting one polynomial from the other, remove the parentheses and distribute the negative sign to the terms inside the second set of parentheses:

$$(11x^2 + 14 + 3x) + (3x^2 - 2x - 6)$$

Remove the parentheses, gather like terms, and combine to simplify:

$$11x^2 + 14 + 3x + 3x^2 - 2x - 6$$

$$11x^2 + 3x^2 + 3x - 2x + 14 - 6$$

$$14x^2 + x + 8$$

Multiplying Monomials

Remember that a monomial is a polynomial with only one term. For example, $7x$ is a monomial. $2y^2$ and $1{,}784{,}921t^{45}$ are also monomials. Multiplying monomials gives us the chance to combine two terms that are not alike, such as $3x^2$ and $6x^4$. First, let's review the operation of multiplying exponents.

$$3x^2\,(6x^4)$$

As with any polynomial equation, it's easier to solve after simplifying. With two monomials, break each monomial into its component parts:

$$3 \times 6 \text{ and } x^2 \bullet x^4$$

The first portion requires standard multiplication:

$$3 \times 6 = 18$$

As for the exponents, when you are asked to multiply, remember that if they have the same base, you will add the exponents. Therefore, $3x^2 \bullet 6x^4 = 18x^6$.

Multiplying a Polynomial and a Monomial

When multiplying a polynomial and a monomial, distribution is the key. Here is a sample expression:

$$2(x^2 + 7x + 4)$$

The first step is to distribute the 2 to the terms in the trinomial (a polynomial with three terms):

$$(2 \bullet x^2) + (2 \bullet 7x) + (2 \bullet 4)$$

Finish multiplying and then add the terms together to present the polynomial in standard form:

$$2x^2 + 14x + 8$$

Note that even though you can factor 2 out of each term, $2x^2 + 14x + 8$ is the simplified answer. Factoring out the 2 would bring us back to the original mononomial and polynomial of $2(x^2 + 7x + 4)$.

Multiplying Binomials (FOIL)

Let's start with a situation involving two binomials:

$$(4x + 3)(2x + 9)$$

These binomials need to be multiplied together. To multiply binomials, you'll use a process called FOIL. FOIL is a mnemonic that stands for First, Outer, Inner, Last. It describes the order in which you multiply terms.

Start with the first terms: $4x$ and $2x$, and multiply them together:

$$4x \bullet 2x = 8x^2$$

Then, multiply the outer terms, $4x$ and 9:

$$4x \bullet 9 = 36x$$

Continue following FOIL. Next, multiply the inner terms:

$$3 \bullet 2x = 6x$$

Then, multiply the last terms:

$$3 \bullet 9 = 27$$

Combine:

$$8x^2 + 36x + 6x + 27$$
$$= 8x^2 + 42x + 27$$

While you could have also used standard distribution to multiply the polynomial, tracking what you've multiplied can become challenging, especially as the number of terms in your polynomials grows. The mnemonic FOIL serves to remind you of the distributive property of multiplication.

There are cases wherein you can factor a trinomial (seen in the previous example) to produce two binomials. Here are some examples of algebraic expressions that can also be factored:

$$4x + 2y = 2 \cdot (2x + y)$$

$$xz - bz = z \cdot (x - b)$$

Factoring Numbers and Variables Out of Expressions

In some cases, all of the numbers in a polynomial can be factored out. Here is a simple example:

$$4x - 4z$$

There are two terms: $4x$ and $4z$. Each of these terms has a 4 in it, so each of these terms is divisible by 4. It also is the case that 4 is the largest possible term that is factorable. Dividing $4x$ by 4 leaves x, and dividing $4z$ by 4 leaves z. So, factoring out the 4 produces the following:

$$\begin{aligned} 4x - 4z &= 4(x) - 4(z) \\ &= 4 \cdot (x - z) \\ &= 4(x - z) \end{aligned}$$

For some expressions, a number can be factored out, but not the entire number. In these instances, you have to first pull out a factor of the number in question. Consider the following example:

$$9xy - 6ab$$

The number 6 can't be factored out because 6 doesn't divide evenly into 9. Similarly, 9 can't be factored out as 9 doesn't divide evenly into 6. However, both numbers have a common factor: 3. This means that you can factor 3 out of both terms:

$$9xy = 3(3xy)$$
$$6ab = 3(2ab)$$

As a result, the whole expression becomes:

$$9xy - 6ab = 3(3xy - 2ab)$$

In addition to numbers, variables can also be factored out of expressions. If the same variable occurs in every term, it can be factored out. Look at the following expression:

$$11a - 5ab$$

There are no common factors for 11 and 5. However, both $11a$ and $5ab$ contain a factor of a. Therefore, you can factor out the variable, leaving the numbers as they are:

$$11a - 5ab = a(11 - 5b)$$

Sometimes, both a number and a variable can be factored out of an expression. Since the process for factoring out variables is essentially the same as it is for factoring out numbers, these operations can be done together under certain circumstances—as in the following example.

$$8xyz - 4yb$$

Factor out the number first. Both 8 and 4 are divisible by 4, so:

$$8xyz - 4yb = 4(2xyz - yb)$$

Now, look at the variables in the parentheses. Since there is a y in both terms inside the parentheses, it can be factored out. Pull the y outside the parentheses:

$$4(2xyz - yb) = 4y(2xz - b)$$

Sometimes, you can factor an entire term from an expression. There are situations in which this might result in an unexpected change, as the following example illustrates.

$$4x + x$$

In this expression, an x can be factored out of both terms. Note that factoring an x away from the second term leaves a 1. It does not simply remove the x entirely.

$$4x + x = x(4 + 1)$$

Factoring Trinomials

Factoring a trinomial is essentially the same as multiplying binomials but in reverse. Let's look at the standard form of a trinomial and an example:

$$Ax^2 + Bx + C$$

$$x^2 + 5x + 6$$

When factoring a trinomial, the goal is to build two binomials that, when you use FOIL, recreate the trinomial.

Here's what you will see:

$$x^2 + 5x + 6 = (x + a)(x + b)$$

Let's expand the right side of this equation:

$$\begin{aligned} x^2 + 5x + 6 &= (x + a)(x + b) \\ &= x^2 + ax + bx + ab \\ &= x^2 + (a + b)x + ab \end{aligned}$$

What you see here is true for any trinomials that can be factored. You're looking for the values of a and b that multiply to make the C term of the standard form but also add up to the B term. In the example, ab must equal 6 and $a + b$ must equal 5.

We start by factoring the constant, 6.

$$6 \times 1$$

$$3 \times 2$$

Now, $6 \times 1 = 6$ but $6 + 1 = 7$. Try another pair of factors. What about 3×2?

$$3 \times 2 = 6$$

$$3 + 2 = 5$$

The numbers look correct, but test them in the expression to be sure.

$$a = 3,\ b = 2$$

$$\begin{aligned} x^2 + 5x + 6 &= (x + a)(x + b) \\ &= (x + 3)(x + 2) \\ &= (x)(x) + (x)(2) + (3)(x) + (3)(2) \\ &= x^2 + 2x + 3x + 6 \\ &= x^2 + 5x + 6 \end{aligned}$$

Our original trinomial was $x^2 + 5x + 6$, so $(x + 2)(x + 3)$ would suffice as an answer. If the trinomial was set equal to 0 (as an equation), you would then solve for the roots (where the trinomial would intersect the x-axis if graphed) and the algebra would yield –2 and –3.

Let's look at another example. What if you are told to factor the following trinomial?

$$5x^2 + 35x + 50$$

To start, look to see if there are any common factors among 5, 35, and 50. The greatest common factor of these three numbers is 5. So, factor out a 5 from each term:

$$5(x^2 + 7x + 10)$$

From here, factor the trinomial like you did in the first example:

$$5\left(x^2+7x+10\right)=(x+a)(x+b)$$

$$a+b=7$$

$$ab=10$$

We can factor 10 as 10 and 1 or 5 and 2. Since we need the factors of the C term to add to 7, we would select 5 and 2. Substitute 5 and 2 for the a and b terms and you have your answer:

$$5(x+5)\ (x+2)$$

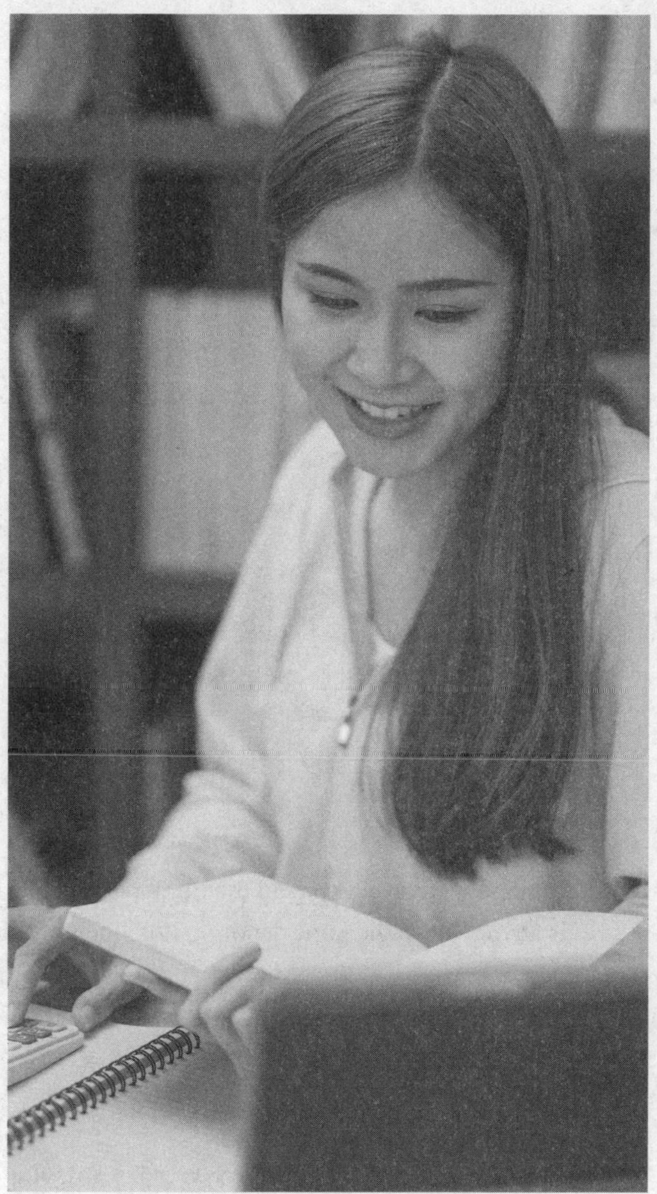

PRACTICE

Compute: $-2(2 - x^2) + x^2(x - 4) - 2x(1 - 4x)$

A. $x^3 - x^2 - 6x - 8$

B. $x^3 + 4x^2 - 2x - 4$

C. $x^3 - 6x^2 + 2x + 4$

D. $x^3 + 6x^2 - 2x - 4$

The correct answer is D. This problem is all about making proper use of the distributive property and keeping track of negative signs. All distractor choices are the results of making an error in one or both. To begin, apply the distributive property on all three products to get the following:

$$-2(2 - x^2) + x^2(x - 4) - 2x(1 - 4x) =$$
$$-4 + 2x^2 + x^3 - 4x^2 - 2x + 8x^2$$

Make certain to multiply each term in the parentheses by the factor outside.

Next, gather like terms (meaning terms with the exact same variable parts) and add their coefficients. It's convenient to underline like terms using the same marking to ensure you do not miss any:

$$-4 + \underline{2x^2} + x^3 \underline{- 4x^2} - 2x + \underline{8x^2} = x^3 + \underline{6x^2} - 2x - 4$$

RATIONAL EXPRESSIONS

Rational expressions employ many of the rules that govern working with fractions. The math here is similar to what you have already seen—you simply add, subtract, multiply, and divide polynomials like you did before and cancel like factors in the top and bottom as you would when simplifying a fraction involving only numbers.

Here are a few examples that you can use to practice these techniques.

EXAMPLES

Simplify: $\frac{8x^2+2x-3}{1-2x}$

Solution

First, factor the numerator and see if anything can be canceled in the top and bottom:

$$\frac{8x^2+2x-3}{1-2x}=\frac{(4x+3)(2x-1)}{-(2x-1)} \text{ Factor.}$$

$$=\frac{(4x+3)\cancel{(2x-1)}}{-\cancel{(2x-1)}} \text{ Cancel like factors}$$

$$=-(4x+3)$$

Note that we factored a –1 out of the denominator. Always be on the lookout for negatives when factoring—a common error (and likely one of the incorrect answer choices) is a final expression that drops the –1.

Add and simplify: $\frac{2x-4}{x^2-1}+\frac{3-x}{x^2-1}$

Solution

In this case, we can simply add the numerators while keeping the denominator the same because the two fractions already have the same denominator. Then, we simplify the result as much as possible:

$$\frac{2x-4}{x^2-1}+\frac{3-x}{x^2-1}=\frac{2x-4+3-x}{x^2-1} \text{ Combine the fractions.}$$

$$=\frac{x-1}{x^2-1} \text{ Simplify.}$$

$$=\frac{\cancel{x-1}}{\cancel{(x-1)}(x+1)} \text{ Factor and cancel like factors in top and bottom.}$$

$$=\frac{1}{x+1}$$

Multiply and simplify: $\frac{2x^2+2x}{x^2-4}\cdot\frac{x+2}{x^2-1}$

Solution

First, factor all expressions and then cancel those common to the top and bottom:

$$\frac{2x^2+2x}{x^2-4}\cdot\frac{x+2}{x^2-1}=\frac{2x\cancel{(x+1)}}{(x-2)\cancel{(x+2)}}\cdot\frac{\cancel{x+2}}{\cancel{(x+1)}(x-1)}=\frac{2x}{(x-2)(x-1)}$$

Do not multiply the numerators and the denominators before factoring. Doing so can create a situation that is much more difficult to simplify.

Subtract and simplify: $\frac{x}{5-2x}-\frac{1}{2+x}$

Solution

First, find a common denominator—remember, you can't add or subtract without one. You can simply multiply the denominators already present: $(5 - 2x)(2 + x)$. Express both fractions using this denominator, and then combine and simplify:

$$\frac{x}{5-2x}-\frac{1}{2+x}=\frac{x(2+x)}{(5-2x)(2+x)}-\frac{5-2x}{(5-2x)(2+x)}$$
$$=\frac{x^2+2x}{(5-2x)(2+x)}-\frac{5-2x}{(5-2x)(2+x)}$$
$$=\frac{x^2+2x-5+2x}{(5-2x)(2+x)}$$
$$=\frac{x^2+4x-5}{(5-2x)(2+x)}$$
$$=\frac{(x+5)(x-1)}{(5-2x)(2+x)}$$

Note that the final expression cannot be simplified further since there are no factors common to the top and the bottom.

PRACTICE

Simplify the following rational expression:

$$\frac{x^2-y^2}{5x-5y}$$

A. $\frac{x-y}{5}$

B. $\frac{5}{x+y}$

C. $\frac{x+y}{5}$

D. $\frac{1}{5}$

The correct answer is C. First, factor both the numerator and denominator of the fraction, and then cancel any common factors:

$$\frac{x^2-y^2}{5x-5y}=\frac{\cancel{(x-y)}(x+y)}{5\cancel{(x-y)}}=\frac{x+y}{5}$$

TIP

If you are asked to divide two rational expressions, the process is practically identical to multiplication, with the additional step of first rewriting the division problem as a multiplication problem, just as with division of numerical fractions.

QUADRATICS

Quadratics take their name from *quad*, meaning "square," because in quadratics, the variable is squared. These sorts of equations come up in many real-life scenarios including those related to designing spaces or objects, calculating area, determining an object's speed, evaluating profits and loss, and much more.

What Is a Quadratic Equation?

In the prior section, you learned how to go about multiplying two binomials together. The resulting expression of such an operation is a special type of polynomial (often a trinomial) called a quadratic function. Simply put, a quadratic function includes one or more variables that are squared (x^2) and contains no exponents greater than this.

When set in standard form, a quadratic equation looks like the following:

$$ax^2 + bx + c = 0$$

In this particular equation type, a must be any real number other than 0. Likewise, when applicable, b and c are also real numbers. Not all quadratic equations contain a constant at the end (c), and they do not necessarily need a second x variable attached to a b coefficient. What is important is the presence of a squared variable, and these sets of restrictions allow for unique mathematical operations and graphs. We will cover them throughout this section.

Here are some examples of quadratic equations (trinomials):

$$x^2 + 2x + 3 = 0$$
$$3x^2 - 5x = -6$$
$$x^2 + 6x = 0$$
$$2x^2 - 8 = 0$$

The Quadratic Formula

In the Polynomials and Factoring section earlier in this chapter, we looked at how to factor trinomials (a form that quadratic functions often take). Not all quadratics can be factored, though. There is another method of solving for the roots of quadratic equations that can always be used: the quadratic formula.

Once again, a quadratic can be expressed in standard form as follows:

$$ax^2 + bx + c = 0$$

Remember that x is the variable, a and b are coefficients, and c is a constant. Those values can be arranged in the quadratic formula as follows:

$$x = \frac{-b \pm \sqrt{b^2 - 4ac}}{2a}$$

Notice that this formula uses a sign for plus or minus in the numerator, and this is because quadratics have two solutions, as we've previously seen. By plugging in all known values for a general quadratic into this formula, you can solve for both solutions. When graphing a quadratic, the result will be a parabola, which is a u-shaped graph that opens upwards or downwards. The two solutions to the quadratic formula are the values of x that satisfy the quadratic. When these values are real numbers, they indicate where the arms of the parabola cross the x-axis—the roots of the equation.

Let's take the following general quadratic as an example:

$$x^2 + 6x + 8 = 0$$

In this case, $a = 1$ (as the coefficient is assumed to be 1), $b = 6$, and $c = 8$. Plugging what we have into the quadratic formula will result in this equation:

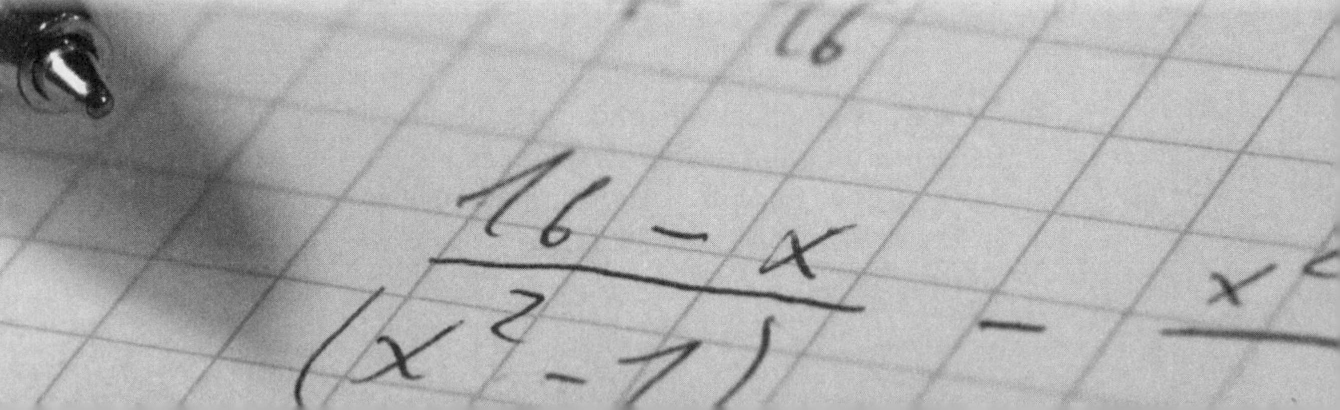

$$x = \frac{-6 \pm \sqrt{6^2 - 4(1)(8)}}{2(1)}$$
$$x = \frac{-6 \pm \sqrt{36-32}}{2}$$
$$x = \frac{-6 \pm \sqrt{4}}{2}$$
$$x = \frac{-6 \pm 2}{2}$$
$$x_1 = \frac{-8}{2} = -4$$
$$x_2 = \frac{-4}{2} = -2$$

Since we have to both add and subtract 2 from –6 before dividing by 2, we are left with two solutions:

–4 and –2

These will be the points where the resultant parabola crosses the x-axis.

The Discriminant

The part of the quadratic formula that is underneath the square root symbol is called the discriminant ($b^2 - 4ac$). Evaluating the discriminant tells you whether a quadratic equation has two real roots, one real root, or no real roots. Let's look at some examples of how the discriminant changes for each scenario.

Positive Discriminant

If the discriminant is positive, the equation has two real roots. In other words, the equation has two different solutions.

The discriminant of the equation $2x^2 + x - 1 = 0$ is:

$$b^2 - 4ac = 1^2 - 4(2)(-1)$$
$$b^2 - 4ac = 1 + 8$$
$$b^2 - 4ac = 9$$

Since 9 is positive, the equation has two real roots. (If you looked at the whole quadratic formula, not just the discriminant, you'd see that the roots are –1 and $\frac{1}{2}$.)

Discriminant Is Zero

If the discriminant is zero, the equation has one real root.

The discriminant of the equation $x^2 - 2x + 1 = 0$ is:

$$b^2 - 4ac = (-2)2 - 4(1)(1)$$
$$b^2 - 4ac = 4 - 4$$
$$b^2 - 4ac = 0$$

The discriminant is zero, so this equation has one real root.

Negative Discriminant

If the discriminant is negative, the equation has no real roots. This is because the discriminant is under a square root symbol, and the square root of a negative number is an imaginary number, not a real number.

The discriminant of the equation $2x^2 + x + 1 = 0$ is:

$$b^2 - 4ac = 12 - 4(2)(1)$$
$$b^2 - 4ac = 1 \quad 8$$
$$b^2 - 4ac = -7$$

Since –7 is negative, the equation has no real roots, only imaginary roots.

PRACTICE

Assume $m > 0$. Which of the following conditions on m guarantees that the equation $2m^2 - \sqrt{m}x + (m-1) = 0$ has two imaginary solutions?

A. $m > 1$

B. $m > \frac{9}{8}$

C. $m < \frac{9}{8}$

D. $-8m^2 - 1 < 0$

The correct answer is B. The sign of the discriminant, or the radicand of the radical part of the quadratic formula, is all you need to determine the nature of the solutions of a quadratic equation. The discriminant for a quadratic equation of the form $ax^2 + bx + c = 0$ is $b^2 - 4ac$.

Applying this to the given equation yields the expression and simplifying yields:

$$\left(-\sqrt{m}\right)^2 - 4(2m)(m-1) = m - 8m(m-1)$$
$$= m - 8m^2 + 8m = -8m^2 + 9m$$

Choices A and D are both results of making errors by not identifying the discriminant formula correctly, or not applying the distributive property when simplifying. If the discriminant is negative, then the equation has imaginary solutions. This yields the condition $-8m^2 + 9m = m(9 - 8m) < 0$.

Since m is assumed to be positive, this expression will be negative only if the other factor, $9 - 8m$, is negative. That is, $9 - 8m < 0$, which is equivalent to $m > \frac{9}{8}$. Choice C will guarantee two distinct real solutions.

Completing the Square

When working with quadratics, you'll encounter certain situations where you will want to take a quadratic in standard form and find the maximum and minimum values of the function. To do that, you can perform a series of operations referred to as "completing the square."

The goal is to get a quadratic in standard form ($ax^2 + bx + c = 0$) into the form $a(x + h)^2 + k = 0$ where $h = \frac{b}{2a}$ and $k = c - \frac{b^2}{4a}$. The values of h and k represent the vertex of a graphed quadratic. That information can then also lead you to the quadratic's roots. You can see this in the following work with the standard form equation.

$$ax^2 + bx + c = 0$$
$$x^2 + \frac{b}{a}x + \frac{c}{a} = 0$$
$$x^2 + \frac{b}{a}x = -\frac{c}{a}$$
$$x^2 + \frac{b}{a}x + \left(\frac{b}{2a}\right)^2 = -\frac{c}{a} + \left(\frac{b}{2a}\right)^2$$
$$\left(x + \frac{b}{2a}\right)^2 = -\frac{c}{a} + \left(\frac{b}{2a}\right)^2$$
$$\left(x + \frac{b}{2a}\right)^2 + \frac{c}{a} - \left(\frac{b}{2a}\right)^2 = 0$$
$$a\left(x + \frac{b}{2a}\right)^2 + c - \frac{b^2}{2a} = 0$$

Look at the following quadratic as it is taken through the process for completing the square. By the end, you're able to identify the vertex of the quadratic and the real roots of the quadratic.

$$6x^2 - x - 2 = 0$$
$$6\left(x - \frac{1}{12}\right)^2 - 2 - \frac{1}{24} = 0$$
$$6\left(x - \frac{1}{12}\right)^2 - \frac{49}{24} = 0$$
$$6\left(x - \frac{1}{12}\right)^2 = \frac{49}{24}$$
$$\left(x - \frac{1}{12}\right)^2 = \frac{49}{144}$$
$$x - \frac{1}{12} = \pm\sqrt{\frac{49}{144}}$$
$$x = \frac{1}{12} \pm \frac{7}{12} = \frac{2}{3}, -\frac{1}{2}$$

LITERAL EQUATIONS

An equation that contains more than one variable is known as a literal equation. For example, $xy + z = t$ is a literal equation, as it contains four variables: x, y, z, and t. It is not possible to "solve" this equation and find the actual values of these variables. However, it is possible to rewrite the equation in a number of different ways. In its present form, the equation is said to be "solved" for t, since the variable t appears by itself on one side of the equation only, and all other terms appear on the other side.

If you were asked to solve this equation for z, you would need to rewrite the equation in such a way that z appeared by itself on one side of the equation only, and the other variables appeared on the other side. Solving for z is quite straightforward. You simply need to treat all of the other variables as if they were constants and apply the rules for manipulating equations discussed in the previous section. Thus, starting with $xy + z = t$, simply remove the term xy from the left by subtracting it from the right. The equation solved for z would be $z = t - xy$.

Suppose you were asked to solve the equation $xy + z = t$ for x. It takes two steps to do this. Starting with $xy + z = t$, begin by moving z from the left by subtracting it from the right. This would give you $xy = t - z$. Remove the y from the left by dividing the right by y. This gives you $x = \frac{t-z}{y}$, and you have successfully solved the equation for x.

PRACTICE

If $5p = xy^2$, which of the following is equal to $5px$?

A. xy

B. y^2

C. $(xy)^2$

D. x^2y

The correct answer is C. Recall that we are allowed to "do the same thing" to both sides of an equation at any time. Perhaps the quickest way to solve this problem is to multiply both sides by x. This would give us the $5px$ we want. In fact, starting with $5p = xy^2$, if we multiply both sides by x, the result is $5px = xy^2(x)$. This means that $5px = x^2y^2$. Thus, $5px = (xy)^2$.

If $p = \frac{q^4}{r^2}$, what is the value of $\frac{1}{q^4}$?

A. $\frac{p}{r^2}$

B. $\frac{r^2}{p}$

C. pr^2

D. $\frac{1}{pr^2}$

The correct answer is D. In this problem, we are given a literal equation and asked to solve it for $\frac{1}{q^4}$. Note that the expression q^4 appears on the top of the fraction on the right. An efficient way to solve this problem is to rewrite the equation by inverting both sides to get $\frac{1}{p} = \frac{r^2}{q^4}$. We can now divide both sides by r^2 to get $\frac{1}{r^2p} = \frac{1}{q^4}$.

FUNCTIONS

Functions are used to discuss and evaluate how one variable, known as an independent variable, relates to another variable, known as a dependent variable.

Let D and R be any two sets of numbers, where the set D is called the domain of the function, and the set R is called the range. A function is a rule that assigns to each element of D one and only one element of R. It can be specified by listing all of the elements in the first set next to the corresponding elements in the second set or by giving a rule or a formula by which elements from the first set can be associated with elements from the second set.

As an example, let set $D = \{1, 2, 3, 4\}$ and set $R = \{5, 6, 7, 8\}$. The diagram below indicates a particular function, f, by showing how each element of D is associated with an element of R.

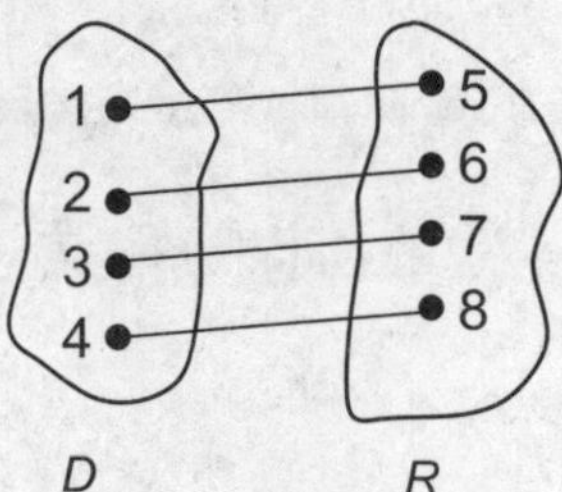

This diagram shows that the domain value of 1 is associated with the range value of 5. Similarly, 2 is associated with 6, 3 is associated with 7, and 4 is associated with 8. To express the function f in words, one might say that f is the function that assigns to each domain value x the range value $x + 4$.

Typically, the letter x is used to represent the elements of the domain and the letter y is used to represent the elements of the range. This convention enables us to write the equation $y = x + 4$ to express the rule of association for the function above. Note that as soon as a domain value x is selected, a range value y is determined by this rule. For this reason, x is referred to as the independent variable, and y is called the dependent variable (since it is determined by the independent variable).

Often, the rule of association for a function is written in function notation. In function notation, the symbol $f(x)$, which is read "f of x," is used in place of y to represent the range value. Therefore, the rule for our example function can be written $f(x) = x + 4$. For example, if you were asked to determine which range value was associated with the domain value of 3, you would compute $f(x) = f(3) = 3 + 4 = 7$. Note that, in this notation, the letter f is typically used to stand for "function," although any other letter could be used in its place. So, for instance, this rule could also be written as $g(x) = x + 4$.

Consider the notation of functions in the following examples.

EXAMPLES

Using function notation, write the rule for a function that associates, to each number in the domain, a range value that is 7 less than 5 times the domain value.

Solution

$$f(x) = 5x - 7$$

Use $f(x) = 5x - 7$ to determine the range value that is associated with a domain value of -12.

Solution

$$f(-12) = 5(-12) - 7 = -60 - 7 = -67$$

If $f(x) = 8x + 9$, determine the value of $f(5), f(q), f(p^2)$, and $f(r + 3)$.

Solution

$$f(5) = 8(5) + 9 = 40 + 9 = 49$$

In the same way, to determine the value of $f(q)$, simply substitute q for the value of x in the rule for $f(x)$.

Therefore, $f(q) = 8q + 9$.

Similarly, $f(p^2) = 8(p^2) + 9 = 8p^2 + 9$.

Similarly, $f(r + 3) = 8(r + 3) + 9 = 8r + 24 + 9 = 8r + 33$.

PRACTICE

If $f(x)=x^2-\sqrt{x}$, what is $f(x + 4)$?

A. $x^2-\sqrt{x}+4$

B. $x^2+16-\sqrt{x+4}$

C. $x^2+8x+20-\sqrt{x}$

D. $x^2+8x+16-\sqrt{x+4}$

The correct answer is D. Some test takers confuse the variable used to define the function, namely x, and the expression by which they are to compute the function, namely x + 4. To remove this confusion, replace the x in the definition of the function with a box (or a place holder). In other words, $f(x)=x^2-\sqrt{x}$ really means:

$$f(\square)=\square^2-\sqrt{\square}$$

Whatever is inside the parentheses is what goes into each of those boxes. So:

$$f(\boxed{x+4})=\boxed{x+4}^2-\sqrt{\boxed{x+4}}$$

This will help you to avoid the common error of just "adding 4" to the function as in choice A. Now, simplify the expression:

$$\begin{aligned} f(x+4) &= (x+4)^2-\sqrt{x+4} \\ &= (x+4)(x+4)-\sqrt{x+4} \\ &= x^2+8x+16-\sqrt{x+4} \end{aligned}$$

Two critical errors that often occur here are (1) not FOILing $(x + 4)^2$, as in choice B, and (2) distributing the radical to both terms of the sum, as in choice C.

OPERATIONS AND FUNCTIONS

Functions can be added, subtracted, multiplied, and divided. Function operations work just like operations on expressions. The notation for these operations can be found in the following table.

FUNCTION OPERATIONS	
Sum of f and g	$(f+g)(x)=f(x)+g(x)$
Difference of f and g	$(f-g)(x)=f(x)-g(x)$
Product of f and g	$(f \bullet g)(x)=f(x) \bullet g(x)$
Quotient of f and g	$\left(\frac{f}{g}\right)(x)=\frac{f(x)}{g(x)}$
Composite function	$(f \circ g)(x)=f(g(x))$

The composite function is an important operation to remember because it allows you to find the function of another function. In this case, the input becomes the function as a whole instead of a value for x, demonstrated as follows:

- $h(f(x))$
- $f(g(x))$
- $g(h(x))$

EXAMPLES

Find $(f \circ g)(x)$ for $f(x) = 2x - x^2$ and $g(x) = x + 1$.

Solution

Replace each x in $f(x)$ with $g(x)$, then replace $g(x)$ with $x + 1$ and simplify.

$$\begin{aligned}(f \circ g)(x) &= f(g(x)) = 2(g(x)) - (g(x))^2 \\ &= 2(x+1) - (x+1)^2 \\ &= 2x + 2 - (x^2 + 2x + 1) \\ &= 2x + 2 - x^2 - 2x - 1 \\ &= -x^2 + 1\end{aligned}$$

Find $(f \circ g)(x)$ for $f(x) = 4x^2 - 6$ and $g(x) = x + 4$?

Solution

Replace each x in $f(x)$ with $g(x)$, then replace $g(x)$ with $x + 1$ and simplify.

$$\begin{aligned}(f \circ g)(x) &= f(g(x)) = 4(g(x))^2 - 6 \\ &= 4(x+4)^2 - 6 \\ &= 4((x+4)(x+4)) - 6 \\ &= 4(x^2 + 4x + 4x + 16) - 6 \\ &= 4(x^2 + 8x + 16) - 6 \\ &= 4x^2 + 32x + 64 - 6 \\ &= 4x^2 + 32x + 58\end{aligned}$$

GRAPHING FUNCTIONS

On the following page are graphs of some of the most common functions you will encounter on the SAT.

Note that when you have a graph of a function, you can figure out if an x-value belongs to the domain of f by determining if an ordered pair with that x-value belongs to the graph of f. You should be familiar with the following features of the graph of a function $y = f(x)$:

- The minimum of f is the smallest y-value in the range of f; it is the y-value of the lowest point on the graph of f.
- The maximum of f is the largest y-value in the range of f; it is the y-value of the highest point on the graph of f.
- f is decreasing if its graph falls from left to right as you progress through the interval from left to right.
- f is increasing on an interval if its graph rises from left to right as you progress through the interval from left to right.
- An x-intercept of f is a point of the form $(x, 0)$. You determine the x-intercepts of a function by solving the equation $f(x) = 0$.
- A y-intercept of f is the point $(0, f(0))$.

All of the functions in the table to the right can be moved within the coordinate plane using horizontal and vertical translations and reflections, defined as follows. Here, let h and k stand for positive real numbers.

TRANSFORMATIONS OF FUNCTIONS

New Function	Graphing the Function By Translation or Reflecting the Graph of $y = f(x)$
$F(x) = f(x) + k$	Translate the graph of $y = f(x)$ k units vertically upward.
$F(x) = f(x) - k$	Translate the graph of $y = f(x)$ k units vertically downward.
$F(x) = f(x - h)$	Translate the graph of $y = f(x)$ h units to the right.
$F(x) = f(x + h)$	Translate the graph of $y = f(x)$ h units to the left.
$F(x) = -f(x)$	Reflect the graph of $y = f(x)$ over the x-axis.

FUNCTION FAMILIES	
Function	**Typical Graphs**
Linear Functions $f(x) = mx + b$	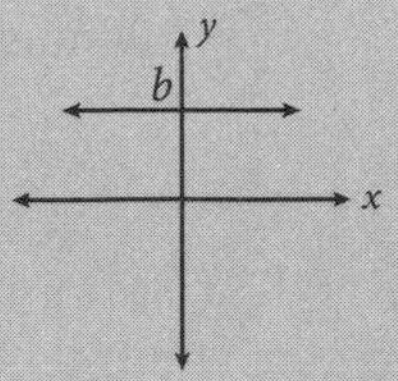 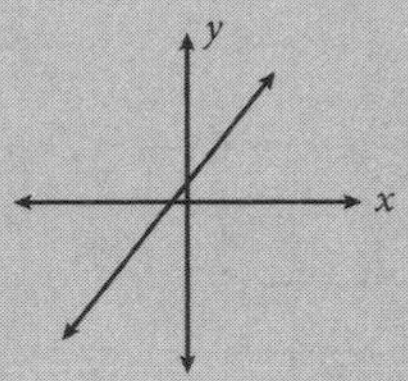 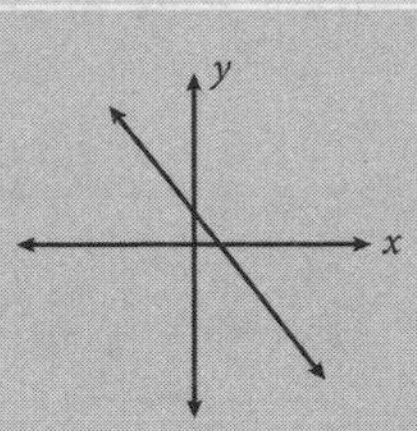
Quadratic Functions $f(x) = a(x - h)^2 + k$	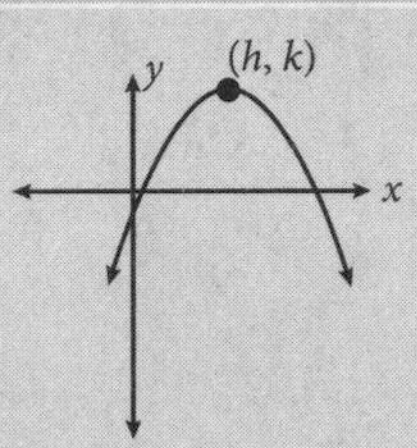 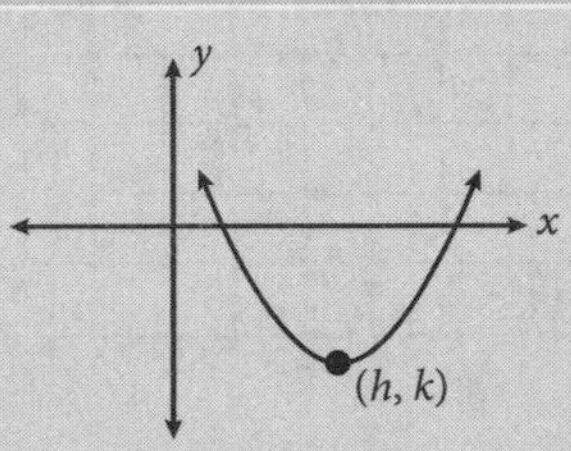 The graph is called a parabola. The vertex is the point (h, k). Note that the maximum or minimum value of a parabola occurs at the vertex
Cubic Function $f(x) = x^3$	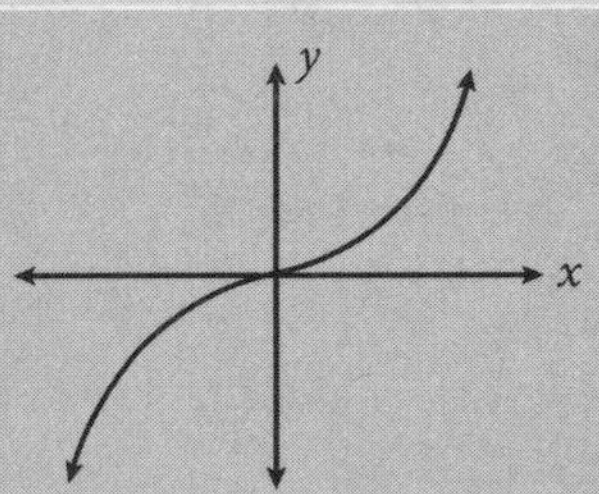
Absolute Value Function $f(x) = \|x\|$	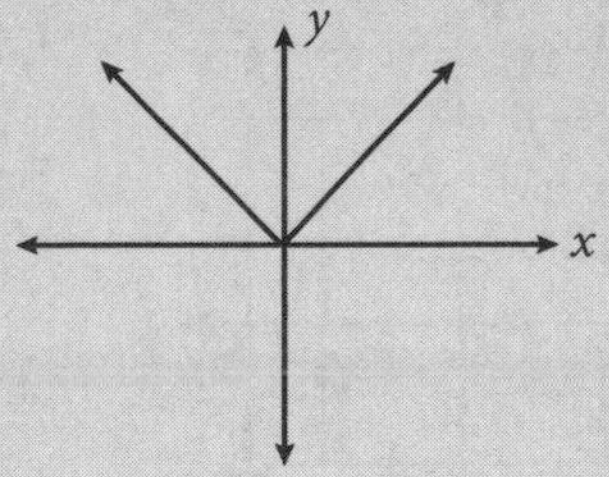 More generally, if h and k are positive numbers, then the graph of $g(x) = \|x - h\| + k$ is obtained by moving the graph to the right h units and up k units.
Square Root Function $f(x) = \sqrt{x}$	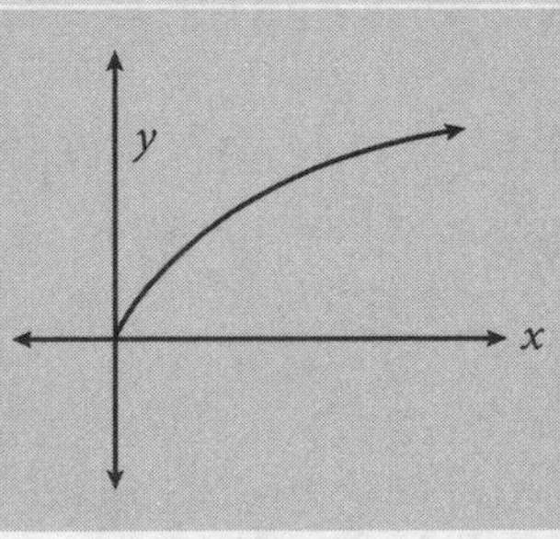

Here is a visual example:

The graph shown, $f(x) = x^2$, is the parent function for all quadratic functions.

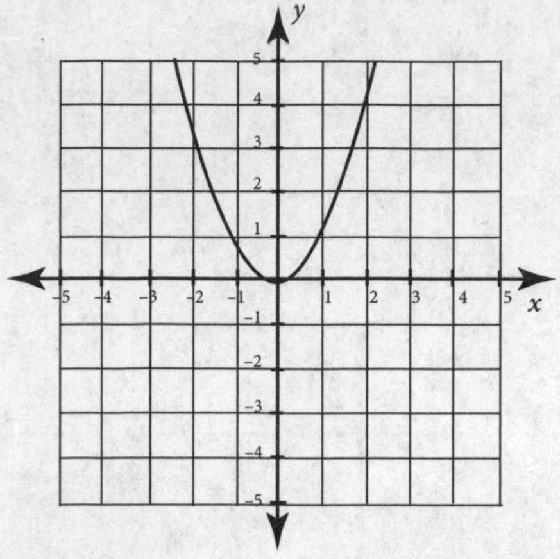

Now let's compare the parent function to a function of the same degree.

EXAMPLES

Compare $f(x) = 2x^2$ to $f(x) = x^2$.

Solution

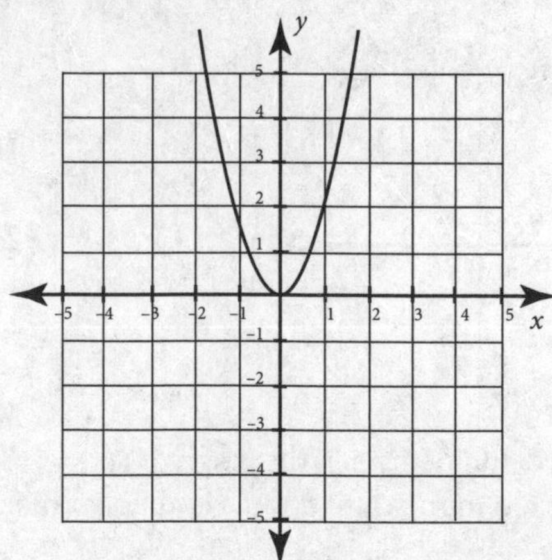

The graphs $f(x) = 2x^2$ and $f(x) = x^2$ both open up, have (0, 0) as their vertices, and have the same axis of symmetry $x = 0$. The graph $f(x) = 2x^2$ is narrower than the graph of $f(x) = x^2$.

How does the graph $f(x) = x^2 + 2$ compare to the parent function $f(x) = x^2$?

Solution

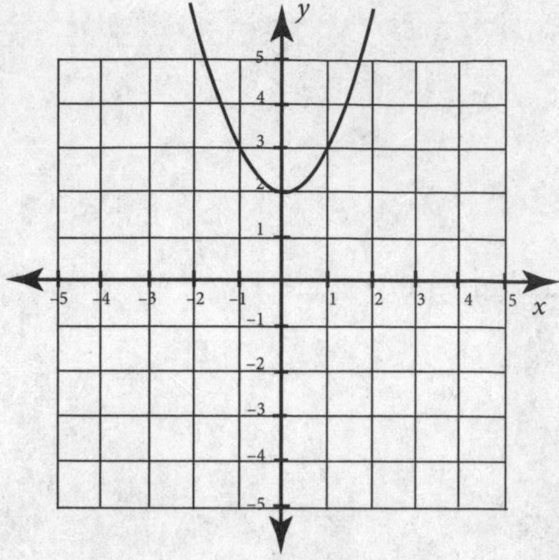

The graph $f(x) = x^2 + 2$ is two units higher than $f(x) = x^2$. The function $f(x) = x^2$ has been shifted up 2 units. The shifting, or translating, of a function is called a transformation.

To move a function up, add a value b to the function:

$$f(x) = x^2 + b.$$

To move a function down, subtract a value b from the function:

$$f(x) = x^2 - b.$$

Translate the function $f(x) = x^2$ two units to the left.

Solution

To translate the parent function two units to the left, add 2 to the x term before squaring it, resulting in $f(x) = (x + 2)^2$.

The function $f(x) = (x + 2)^2$ looks like the following:

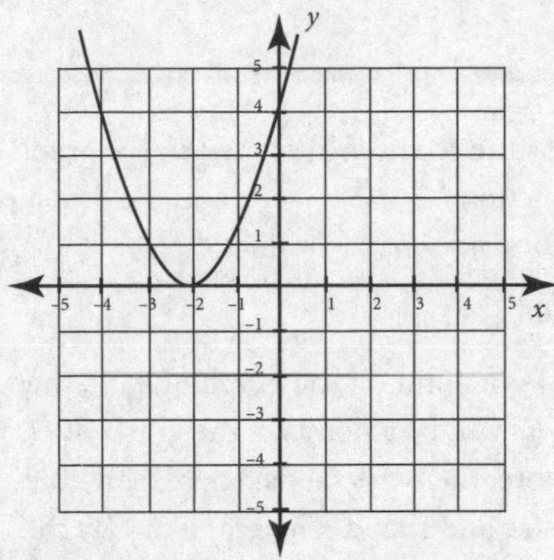

The graph has been shifted to the left 2 units.

TYPES OF FUNCTIONS

There are numerous types of functions beyond linear functions (as seen in Chapter 11) that you may be asked to work with in either their original or inverse forms for Advanced Math domain questions. A family of functions is a group of functions with similar characteristics. The parent function is the most basic function in a family.

Quadratic Functions

Recall that a quadratic function is any function of the form $f(x) = ax^2 + bx + c$ where a, b, and c are real numbers. The shape of the graph of a quadratic function is called a parabola. It reaches a maximum or minimum height called the vertex.

Example of a Quadratic:

$f(x) = x^2 + 3$

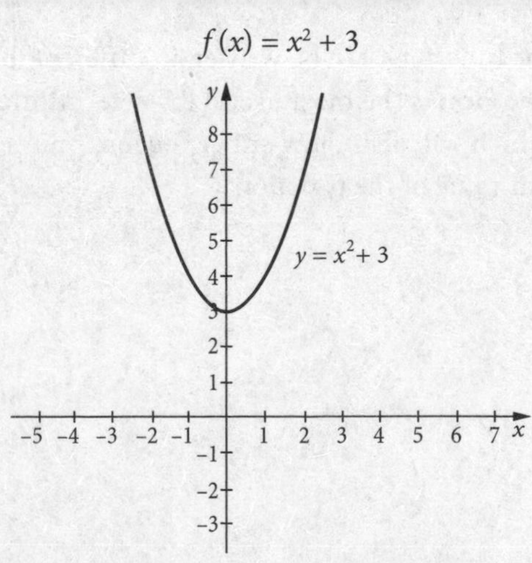

To determine what the graph of a quadratic function looks like, consider the graph of the quadratic function $R(x) = 40{,}000x - 2{,}000x^2$. Negative numbers must be excluded from the domain. A few computations lead to the table here.

x	$R(x)$
0	0
3	102,000
5	150,000
9	198,000
10	200,000
11	198,000
15	150,000
17	102,000
20	0

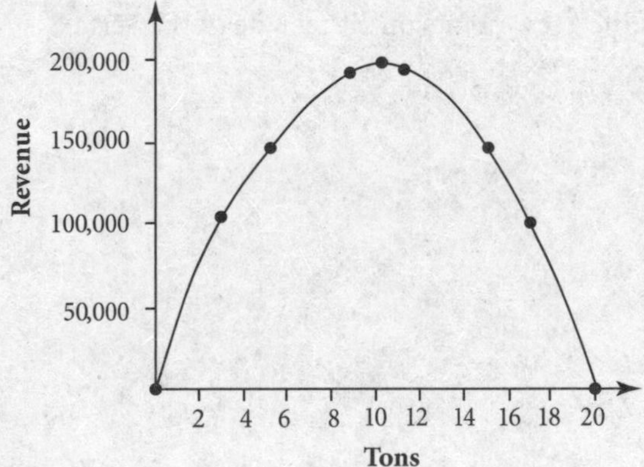

The graph of $R(x)$ is shown above, and this parabola is said to "open down." The highest point, or vertex, on the parabola is (10, 200,000).

Recall that the general form of a quadratic function is $f(x) = ax^2 + bx + c$. In general, the graph of any quadratic function will be a parabola. If $a > 0$, the parabola will "open up," and if $a < 0$, the parabola will "open down." If the parabola opens up, its vertex is the minimum value of the function, and if the parabola opens down, its vertex is the maximum value of the function.

The coordinates of the vertex of a parabola are

$$\left[\frac{-b}{2a},\ f\left(\frac{-b}{2a}\right)\right].$$

EXAMPLES

Sketch the graph of the function $f(x) = x^2 - x - 2$.

Solution

Since the function is quadratic, the graph will be a parabola. Note that the value of a, the number in front of the x^2-term is 1, so the parabola opens up. The x-coordinate of the minimum point is $x = \frac{-b}{2a} = \frac{-(1)}{2(1)} = \frac{1}{2}$, and the y-coordinate of this point is

$$f\left(\frac{1}{2}\right) = \left(\frac{1}{2}\right)^2 - \frac{1}{2} - 2$$
$$= \frac{1}{4} - \frac{1}{2} - 2$$
$$= -2\frac{1}{4}$$

In order to sketch a parabola, it is helpful to determine a few points on either side of the vertex.

x	$f(x)$
–2	4
–1	0
0	–2
1	–2
2	0
3	4

The graph is shown here.

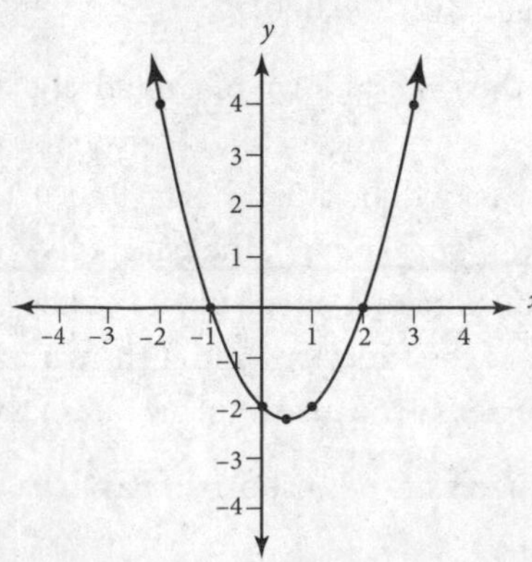

What is the relationship between the graph of the function $h(x) = ax^2 + bx$ and the graph of the function $j(x) = ax^2 + bx + 7$?

Solution

If (x, y) is a point on the graph of $h(x)$, then $(x, y + 7)$ will be a point on the graph of $j(x)$. Therefore, the two graphs have exactly the same size and shape. The graph of $j(x)$ can be obtained by taking the graph of $h(x)$ and "lifting" each point 7 units, that is, increasing the y-coordinate of each point by 7.

Find the minimum value reached by the function $f(x) = x^2 - 6x + 1$.

Solution

The minimum value is reached when:

$$x = -\frac{b}{2a} = \frac{6}{2} = 3$$

Evaluate the function for 3 to find the minimum value:

$$f(3) = 3^2 - 6(3) + 1 = 9 - 18 + 1 = -8$$

Thus, the vertex is at (3, –8), and the minimum value reached by the function is –8.

Quadratic functions can be written in different forms. The *vertex form* is the most useful for determining the vertex, which will also show either the maximum or minimum value of the function.

The vertex form of a quadratic function is $y = a(x - h)^2 + k$, where the x-coordinate of the vertex is h and the y-coordinate of the vertex is k.

For example, in the function $y = (x - 3)^2 - 2$, the vertex is located at $(3, -2)$. This also means that the axis of symmetry is $x = 3$ and the minimum value of the function is -2.

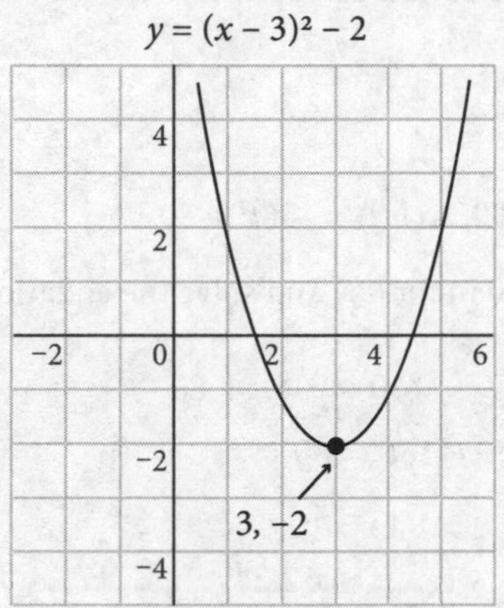

The *factored form* of a quadratic function is the most useful for identifying the roots of the function. The factored form of a quadratic function is $y = a(x - r_1)(x - r_2)$, where r_1 and r_2 are the roots of the function. The roots may also be referred to as the x-intercepts of the graph or the zeros of the function.

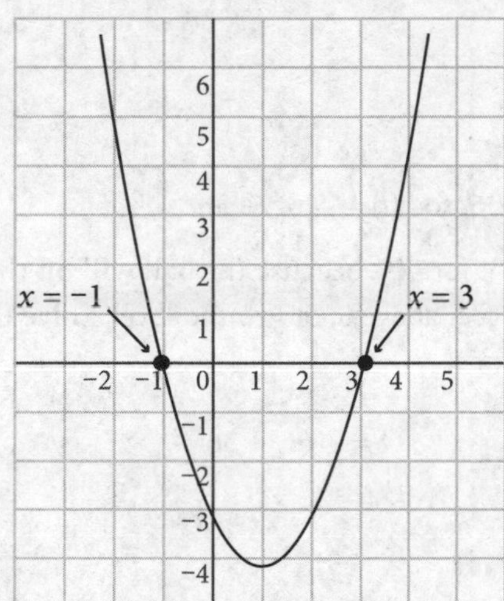

In the example shown, the quadratic function $y = x^2 - 2x - 3$ can be rewritten as $y = (x - 3)(x + 1)$, because:

$$\begin{aligned}(x-3)(x+1) &= x^2 + x - 3x - 3 \\ &= x^2 - 2x - 3\end{aligned}$$

The roots of the function are then $x = 3$ and $x = -1$ (notice the change of sign). The following steps show why this works:

- When $x = 3$, $y = (3 - 3)(3 + 1) = (0)(4) = 0$
- When $x = -1$, $y = (-1 - 3)(-1 + 1) = (-4)(0) = 0$

PRACTICE

What is the equation of the parabola graphed below?

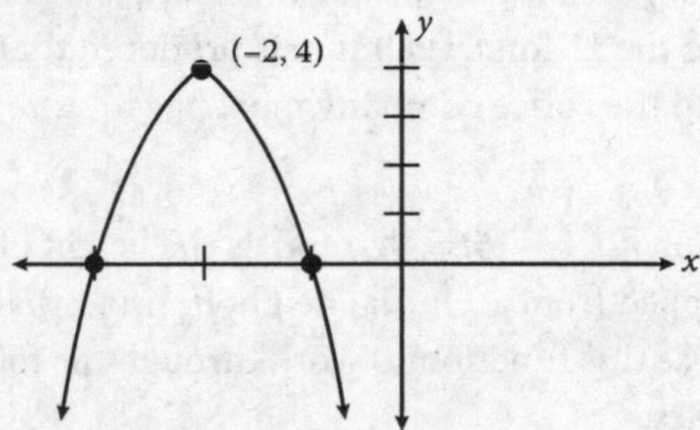

A. $f(x) = -4x^2 - 16x - 12$

B. $f(x) = -x^2 - 2x + 3$

C. $f(x) = -x^2 + 4x + 3$

D. $f(x) = 4x^2 - 16x - 12$

The correct answer is A. Examine each function. The graph opens downward, which means that the coefficient of x^2 must be negative, so you can eliminate choice D immediately. Select an expression and factor. Start with choice A:

$-4x^2 - 16x - 12 = -4(x^2 + 4x + 3) = -4(x + 3)(x + 1)$.

This equals zero at $x = -3$ and $x = -1$; as shown, the y-intercept is -12; the parabola opens downward because the coefficient of x^2 is negative. Therefore, this is the equation of the graph shown.

Applications of Quadratic Functions

Quadratic functions can also be used to model certain real-world happenings. To understand these functions better, suppose a coffee manufacturer has a revenue function given by $R(x) = 40{,}000x - 2{,}000x^2$, where x represents the amount of coffee produced in tons per week. Let's consider some of the values for this function.

- If $x = 0$, $R(x) = 40{,}000(0) - 2{,}000(0)^2 = 0$ represents the obvious fact that if no coffee is produced, there is no revenue.
- That $R(1) = 40{,}000 - 2{,}000 = 38{,}000$ tells that the revenue from 1 ton of coffee is \$38,000.
- Similar computations show that $R(10) =$ \$200,000 and $R(11) =$ \$198,000.

Note that the revenue is smaller if 11 tons of coffee are produced than if 10 tons are produced. There are a number of possible reasons for this. Perhaps, for example, at the 11-ton level, more is produced than can be sold, and the coffee company must pay to store the overage.

The function $h(t) = -16t^2 + h_0$ models the height of an object dropped from an initial height h_0 (in feet) after t seconds. Use this function to work through the following examples.

EXAMPLES

An object is dropped from the roof of a building that is 80 ft. tall. How long will it take the object to hit the ground? Round your answer to the nearest hundredth of a second.

Solution

$h(t) = -16t^2 + h_0$

Here $h_0 = 80$, so $h(t) = -16t^2 + 80$.

Substitute 0 in for $h(t)$ and solve the equation for t.

$$\begin{aligned} 0 &= -16t^2 + 80 \\ 16t^2 &= 80 \\ t^2 &= 5 \\ t &\approx \pm 2.24 \end{aligned}$$

Suppose you drop a ball from a window that is 36 ft. above the ground and it lands on a porch that is 4 ft. above the ground. How long does it take for the ball to land on the porch? Round your answer to the nearest hundredth of a second.

Solution

$h(t) = -16t^2 + h_0$

Here $h_0 = 36$, so $h(t) = -16t^2 + 36$.

Substitute 4 for $h(t)$, because the ball will hit the porch at 4 feet above 0, or ground level. Solve the equation for t.

$$\begin{aligned} 4 &= -16t^2 + 36 \\ 16t^2 &= 32 \\ t^2 &= 2 \\ t &\approx \pm 1.41 \end{aligned}$$

It will take approximately 1.41 seconds for the object to land on the porch.

13

Exponential Functions

The graph of an exponential function $f(x) = b^x$ has a horizontal asymptote of the x-axis—that is, $y = 0$. If the base is a whole number, the graph rises rapidly on the right. If the base is a fraction or decimal, the graph falls quickly from left to right.

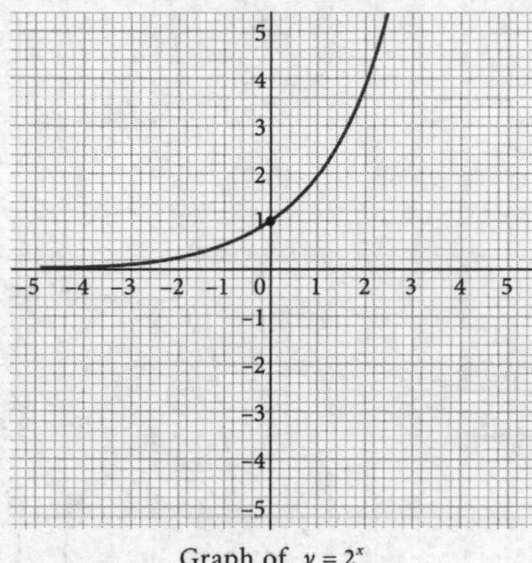

Graph of $y = 2^x$

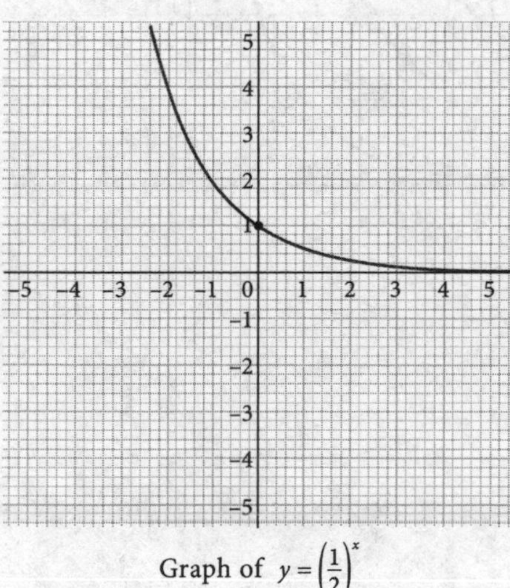

Graph of $y = \left(\frac{1}{2}\right)^x$

Consider the graph of the exponential function $f(x) = 5{,}250(0.9)^x$, where $f(x)$ is the value of a jet ski in dollars after x years.

The initial value of the jet ski is \$5,250 and the percent of decrease per year is 10%. The graph of $f(x)$ is a curve that falls from left to right and gets less and less steep as x increases. The x-axis is a horizontal asymptote.

x	$f(x)$
0	5,250
1	4,725
5	3,100
8	2,260
12	1,482.8
15	1,080
25	339.21

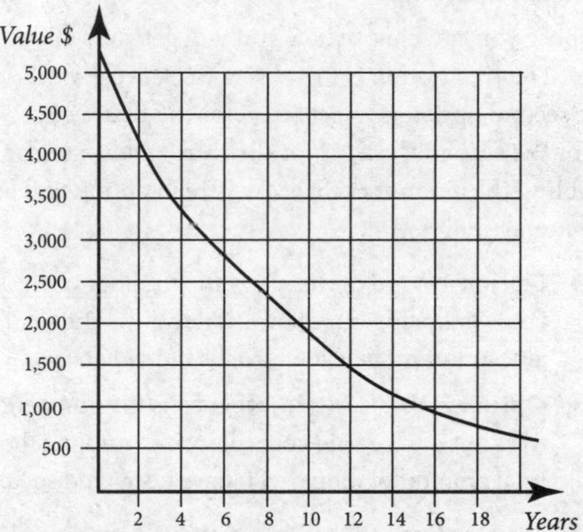

Applications of Exponential Functions

If $a > 0$ and $b > 1$, then the function $f(x) = ab^x$ is an exponential growth function and b is called the growth factor. If $a > 0$ and $0 < b < 1$, then the function $f(x) = ab^x$ is an exponential decay function and b is called the decay factor.

An exponential growth function can model the number of students in a high school. Suppose the number of students in 2011 is given by $f(x) = 1{,}250(1.13)^x$, where x is the number of years since 2011. Let's consider some of the values for this function. If $x = 0$, then $f(x) = 1{,}250(1.13)^0 = 1{,}250$ represents the student population in 2011. If $x = 1$, then $f(x) = 1{,}250(1.13)^1 = 1{,}413$ represents the student population after 1 year. Similar computations show that $f(x) = 1{,}596$ when $x = 2$ and $f(x) = 2{,}303$ when $x = 5$.

An exponential decay function can model the value of an automobile. Suppose the value of the automobile is given by $f(x) = 35{,}000(0.85)^x$, where x is the number of years since the automobile was purchased. Let's consider some of the values for this function. If $x = 0$, then $f(x) = 35{,}000(0.85)^0 = 35{,}000$ represents the value of the automobile at the time of purchase. If $x = 2$, then $f(x) = 35{,}000(0.85)^2 = 25{,}287.50$ represents the value of the automobile after 2 years. Similar computations show that $f(x) = 15{,}529.69$ when $x = 5$ and $f(x) = 3{,}057.40$ when $x = 15$.

Comparing Linear and Exponential Growth Functions

Suppose you can choose how you will get your allowance. The first option is to get \$5 a week every week. The second option is to get \$0.50 for the first week, \$1 for the second week, \$2 for the third, and so on, by doubling the amount each week. Which option will pay you more?

- **Option 1:** $y = 5x$, where x is the number of weeks you were paid your allowance and y is the total amount of money you have been paid so far.
- **Option 2:** $y = (0.5)(2)^{x-1}$, where x is the number of weeks you were paid your allowance and y is the total amount of money you have been paid so far.

As you can see from the tables, Option 1 pays more until the 8th week. After that, Option 2 will always pay more since you are doubling a larger number.

Option 1: $y = 5x$

x (week)	1	2	3	4	5	6	7	8	9	10
y (total)	5	10	15	20	25	30	35	40	45	50

Option 2: $y = (0.5)(2)^{x-1}$

x (week)	1	2	3	4	5	6	7	8	9	10
y (total)	0.5	1	2	4	8	16	32	64	128	256

Option 1 is a linear function that is increasing at a constant rate, and Option 2 is an exponential function that is increasing rapidly as x gets bigger. You would choose Option 2 to be paid the most.

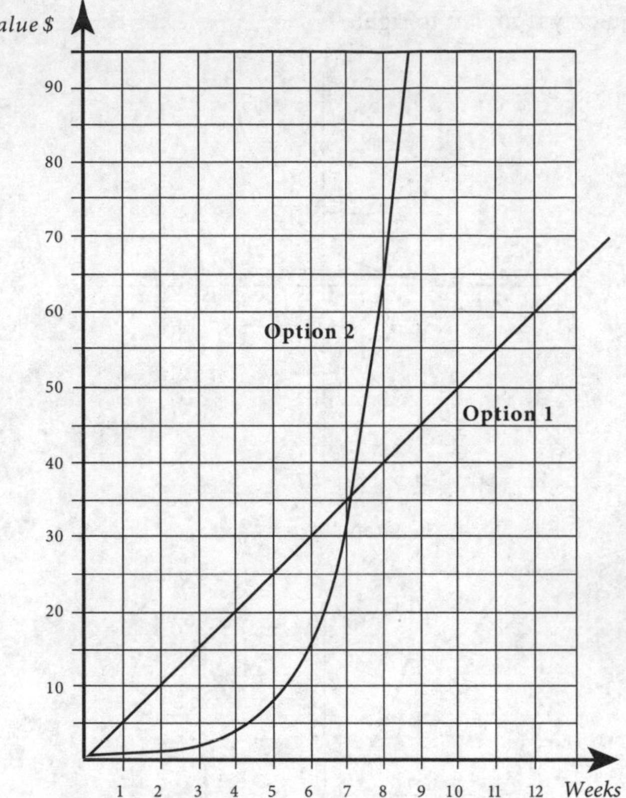

Polynomial Functions

Polynomial functions have the same form as polynomial expressions. Polynomial functions have variables taken to a power, are multiplied by some coefficient, and then are added together. For example, $f(x) = -x^3 + 4x^2 - x$. Technically, both linear functions and quadratic functions are polynomial functions. But they have special properties, as shown in the previous sections. We will focus on polynomials where the degree (highest power) is 3 or greater.

The graphs of polynomial functions are curves with turning points where they change direction.

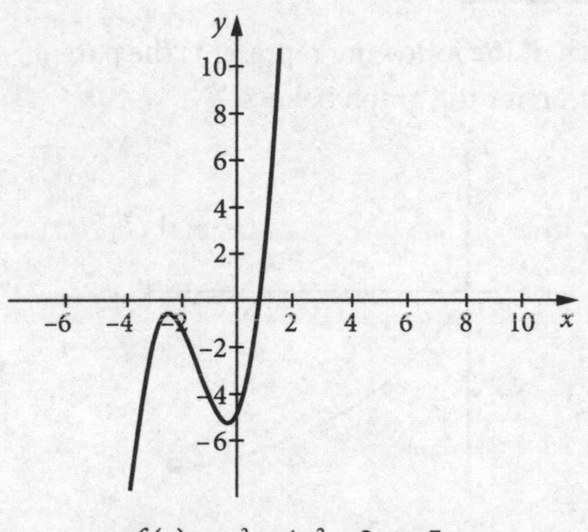

$f(x) = x^3 + 4x^2 + 2x - 5$

The number of turning points is equal to the degree minus 1. The polynomial function shown in the figure has a degree of 3 and two turning points.

The end behavior of a polynomial function can be determined by the degree of the polynomial and the coefficient of the highest degree term. The following table explains these properties.

POLYNOMIAL FUNCTION PROPERTIES

Degree	Sign of the Highest Degree Term	End Behavior
Even	Positive	Rises on both left and right
Even	Negative	Falls on both left and right
Odd	Positive	Falls on left, rises on right
Odd	Negative	Rises on left, falls on right

In the previous example, the polynomial function has an odd degree and a positive coefficient for the highest degree term.

Rational Functions

Rational functions are similar to rational expressions. Their domain is determined by the denominator. When the denominator is zero, the value is not included in the domain. Further, rational functions have asymptotes. The function approaches these lines but never crosses them.

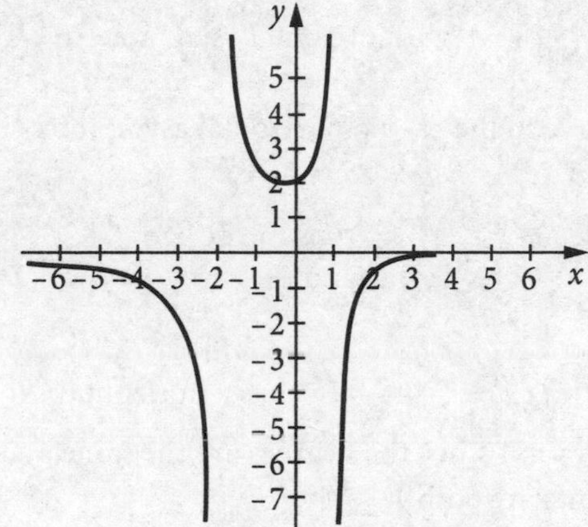

Graph of $f(x) = \dfrac{x-4}{x^2+x-2}$, with two vertical asymptotes and one horizontal asymptote

To find the vertical asymptotes of a rational function, find all values where the denominator is 0 but the numerator is not 0.

EXAMPLE

Find all vertical asymptotes of the function $f(x) = \dfrac{x^2-x-2}{x^2-2x-3}$.

Solution

$$f(x) = \frac{x^2-x-2}{x^2-2x-3} = \frac{(x+1)(x-2)}{(x+1)(x-3)}$$

The denominator is 0 whenever $x = -1$ or 3. However, -1 also makes the numerator 0, so the only vertical asymptote is $x = 3$.

Horizontal asymptotes are found by looking at the degrees of the highest degree terms. The following table shows the rules for this.

HORIZONTAL ASYMPTOTE PROPERTIES

Degrees of the terms	Horizontal asymptote
The same	y = the ratio of the coefficients Ex: $y=\dfrac{2x^3-4}{5x^3}$ has the horizontal asymptote $y=\dfrac{2}{5}$
Higher degree in the numerator	No horizontal asymptote
Lower degree in numerator	$y = 0$ is the horizontal asymptote

The function $f(x)=\dfrac{x^2-x-2}{x^2-2x-3}$ has a horizontal asymptote of $y = 1$ since the degrees are the same and the coefficients are both 1.

Radical Functions

Radical functions $\left(\text{e.g., } y=\sqrt{x}\right)$ are easily recognized thanks to the presence of the radical sign. Since the x in $y=\sqrt{x}$ cannot be negative, the graph of $y=\sqrt{x}$ only appears in the first quadrant.

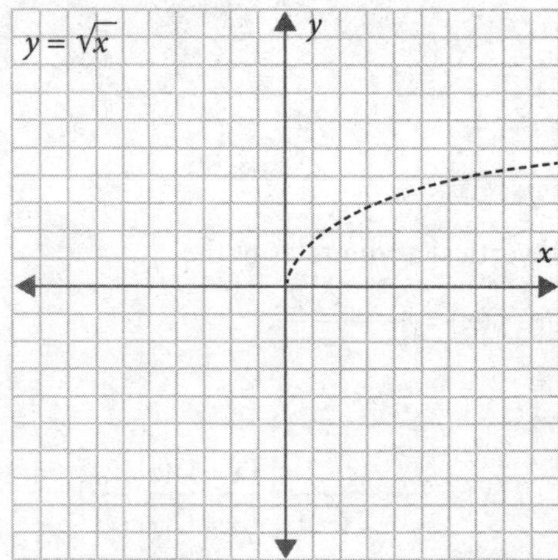

The image shows the graph $y=\sqrt{x}$. The graphs of all square root functions have this general appearance.

Some other characteristics of square root functions are as follows:

- The graph of $y=\sqrt{x}$ is the top half of a parabola that opens sideways.
- As you travel out along the graph of $y=\sqrt{x}$, the graph keeps going higher.
- The domain and range of $y=\sqrt{x}$ are both numbers greater than or equal to zero.

PRACTICE

Which of the following represents the parent function for the graph below?

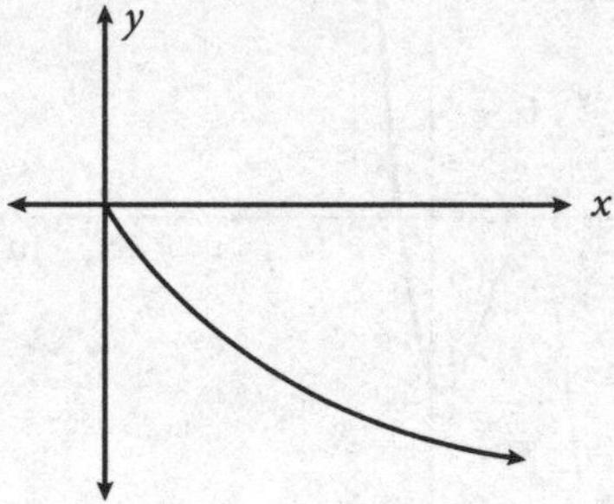

A. $y=Ax$

B. $y=Ax^2$

C. $y=Ax^3$

D. $y=A\sqrt{x}$

The correct answer is D. Even if you didn't immediately recognize that this graph of $y=\sqrt{x}$ is reflected over the x-axis, you can still answer this question using the process of elimination. Choice A can be immediately eliminated because it is a linear equation, and its graph would therefore be a straight line. Choices B and C can be eliminated because to yield a right opening graph, the x and y variables would need to be switched.

Absolute Value Functions

Absolute value functions ($y = |x|$) are easily recognizable due to the presence of the absolute value sign. The graphs of these functions are also distinctive due to their V shape.

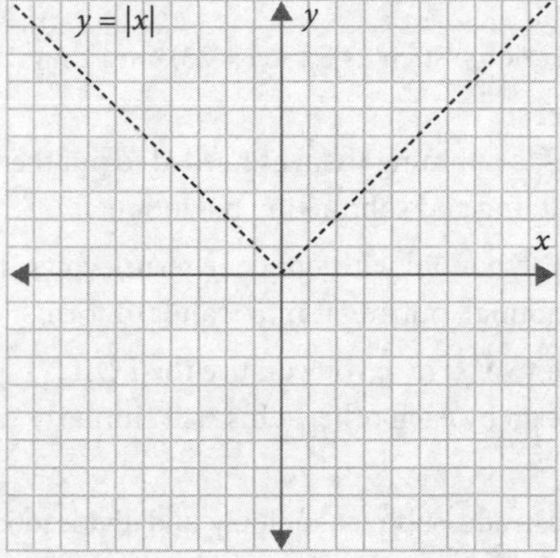

The image shows the graph $y = |x|$. The graphs of all absolute value functions have this general appearance.

Some other characteristics about absolute value functions are as follows:

- The graph of $y = |x|$ is symmetric over the y-axis.
- The domain of $y = |x|$ is all real numbers.
- The range of $y = |x|$ is limited to numbers greater than or equal to zero.

You should also be comfortable working with linear functions and inequalities involving absolute values. Solve these problems by writing them in equivalent forms involving basic linear equations and inequalities without absolute values, as follows:

Absolute Value Equation/Inequality	Solution
$\|x\| = a$	$x = a$ or $x = -a$
$\|x\| \geq a$	$x \geq a$ or $x \leq -a$
$\|x\| > a$	$x > a$ or $x < -a$
$\|x\| \leq a$	$-a \leq x \leq a$
$\|x\| < a$	$-a < x < a$

Use these definitions when x is replaced by some linear expression, and then solve the resulting equation(s) or inequality in the same manner that you would solve other more standard linear equations and inequalities. For absolute value equations, you will simplify within the absolute value brackets first, just as you would with parentheses. Removing the absolute value brackets then yields two equations or inequalities, as appropriate. Work through the following practice question to apply these concepts.

PRACTICE

Which of the following inequalities gives the complete solution set for the inequality $|2x - 3| < 8$?

A. $x < \frac{11}{2}$

B. $x > -\frac{5}{2}$

C. $-5 < x < 11$

D. $-\frac{5}{2} < x < \frac{11}{2}$

The correct answer is D. Express the absolute value inequality as the equivalent double inequality $-8 < 2x - 3 < 8$. Then add 3 to all parts of the inequality to get $-5 < 2x < 11$. Finally, divide all parts by 2 to get the solution set $-\frac{5}{2} < x < \frac{11}{2}$.

SUMMING IT UP

- A polynomial is one or more terms, each having a variable with a whole number (0, 1, 2, ...) as an exponent.
- Terms make up expressions (such as $5x + 3$) and equations (such as $5x + 3 = 23$), and they also are the building blocks of polynomials.
- Polynomials can be simplified by gathering like terms, combining them as needed to put them into standard form. This method is also used when adding and subtracting polynomials.
- When multiplying a polynomial by a monomial (a polynomial with only one term), you can often distribute the monomial throughout the polynomial, putting it into standard form.
- When multiplying two binomials (polynomials with two terms), you can use the FOIL operation (first, outer, inner, last) to multiply each term by each other. This will similarly result in an expression in standard form.
- A rational expression is a quotient of polynomials. You can add, subtract, multiply, and divide rational expressions in the same manner as fractions—you're now just combining algebraic expressions.
- The solutions of $ax^2 + bx + c = 0$ are given by the quadratic formula: $x = \frac{-b \pm \sqrt{b^2 - 4ac}}{2a}$.
- The discriminant of $ax^2 + bx + c = 0$ is $b^2 - 4ac$. The sign of the discriminant determines the number and nature of the quadratic equation's solutions.
- A function is a rule that associates to each input x a corresponding y-value. They are typically named using letters, like f or g. The notation $f(x)$ represents the functional value at x.
- The domain of a function is the set of all values of x that can be substituted into the expression and yield a meaningful output. The range of a function is the set of all possible y-values attained at some member of the domain.
- The sum $(f + g)(x)$ is defined as $f(x) + g(x)$. Likewise, the difference function $(f - g)(x)$ is defined as $f(x) - g(x)$, the product function $(f \bullet g)(x)$ is defined as $f(x) \bullet g(x)$, and the quotient function $\left(\frac{f}{g}\right)(x)$ is defined as $\frac{f(x)}{g(x)}$.
- The composition of f and g, denoted by $(f \circ g)$, is defined by $(f \circ g)(x) = f(g(x))$.
- The minimum of f is the smallest y-value in the range of f; it is the y-value of the lowest point on the graph of f. Likewise, the maximum of f is the largest y-value in the range of f; it is the y-value of the highest point on the graph of f.
- f is decreasing on an interval if its graph falls from left to right as you progress through the interval from left to right; f is increasing on an interval if its graph rises from left to right as you progress through the interval from left to right.
- An x-intercept of f is a point of the form $(x, 0)$. You determine the x-intercepts of a function by solving the equation $f(x) = 0$.
- A y-intercept of f is the point $(0, f(0))$.

TEST YOURSELF

ADVANCED MATH

12 Questions—19 Minutes

Directions: The questions in this section address a number of Advanced Math domain skills.

Use of a calculator is permitted for all questions.

Unless otherwise indicated:

- All variables and expressions represent real numbers.
- Figures provided are drawn to scale.
- All figures lie in a plane.
- The domain of a given function f is the set of all real numbers x for which $f(x)$ is a real number.

1. The expression $6x^3 (x^2)^3$ is equivalent to which of the following?

A. $6x^7$

B. $6x^8$

C. $6x^9$

D. $6x^{10}$

2. Which of the following is equivalent to the expression $\frac{3x^3y-9x^2}{xy^2}$?

A. $\frac{-6xy}{xy^2}$

B. $\frac{3x(xy-3)}{y^2}$

C. $\frac{3x^2-9x}{y}$

D. $3x^2 - 9x$

3. Which of the following expressions is equivalent to $(2 - 3x^2)(4x - 1)$?

A. $-12x^3 + 3x^2 + 8x - 2$

B. $-12x^3 + 2$

C. $-12x^3 + 3x^2 - 2$

D. $2x + 3x^2$

4. If x and y are positive numbers, $\frac{x}{5}-\frac{2}{y}$ is equivalent to which of the following?

A. $\frac{xy-2}{5y}$

B. $\frac{xy-10}{5+y}$

C. $-\frac{2x}{5y}$

D. $\frac{xy-10}{5y}$

5. What are the values of x for $x^2 - 2x - 15 = 0$?

A. 5 or –3

B. –5 or 3

C. –5 or –3

D. 5 or 3

6. What are the values of x in $2x^2 + 3x = 7$?

A. $x = \frac{3+\sqrt{65}}{4}, x = \frac{3-\sqrt{65}}{4}$

B. $x = \frac{-3+\sqrt{65}}{4}, x = \frac{-3-\sqrt{65}}{4}$

C. $x = \frac{3+\sqrt{47}}{4}, x = \frac{3-\sqrt{47}}{4}$

D. $x = \frac{-3+\sqrt{47}}{4}, x = \frac{-3-\sqrt{47}}{4}$

7. What is $z = 5x - 25xy$ in terms of x?

A. $\frac{z}{-20y} = x$

B. $\frac{z}{1-5y} = x$

C. $\frac{z}{5-25y} = x$

D. $\frac{z}{30y} = x$

8. What is $C = \frac{BA}{B-A}$ in terms of A?

A. $A = CB + (B + 1)$

B. $A = CB - (B + C)$

C. $A = \frac{CB}{B+C}$

D. $A = \frac{CB}{B+1}$

9. If $f(g) = \sqrt[3]{g-7}$, what is $f(-20)$?

A. $-\sqrt{27}$

B. –3

C. 3

D. 9

10. What is the domain of $f(x) = \sqrt[4]{6-2x}$?

A. $x < 6$

B. $x > -3$

C. $x < 3$

D. $x \leq 3$

11. Consider the function $H(x) = \frac{x}{4-x}$ where $x > 0$. For which pairs of functions $f(x)$ and $g(x)$ does $H(x) = (f \circ g)(x)$?

A. $f(x) = x$ and $g(x) = \frac{1}{4-x}$

B. $f(x) = \sqrt{\frac{x}{16-x}}$ and $g(x) = x^2$

C. $f(x) = \left(\frac{x}{4-x}\right)^2$ and $g(x) = \sqrt{x}$

D. $f(x) = \frac{x^2}{4-x^2}$ and $g(x) = \sqrt{x}$

12.

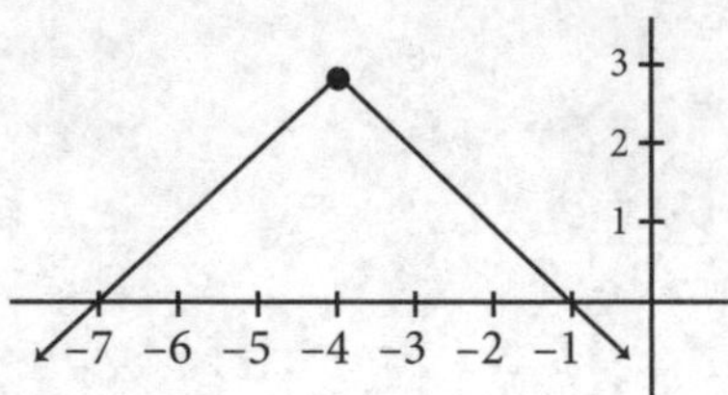

Which of the following functions represents the graph?

A. $f(x) = 3 - |x - 4|$

B. $f(x) = 3 + |x + 4|$

C. $f(x) = 3 - |x + 4|$

D. $f(x) = |x - 4| - 3$

ANSWER KEY AND EXPLANATIONS

1. C	3. A	5. A	7. C	9. B	11. D
2. B	4. D	6. B	8. C	10. D	12. C

1. **The correct answer is C.**

$$\begin{aligned}6x^3(x^2)^3 &= (6 \cdot x^3) \cdot (x^2)^3\\ &= 6 \cdot x^3 \cdot x^{(2 \cdot 3)}\\ &= 6 \cdot x^3 \cdot x^6\\ &= 6 \cdot x^9\\ &= 6x^9\end{aligned}$$

2. **The correct answer is B.** The variable x can be factored out of the all the terms in the numerator and denominator of the fraction:

$$\begin{aligned}\frac{3x^3y-9x^2}{xy^2} &= \frac{3x^2y-9x^1}{(1)y^2}\\ &= \frac{3x^2y-9x}{y^2}\end{aligned}$$

Factor the term $3x$ out of the expression in the numerator:

$$3x(xy - 3)$$

Because y appears in only one of the terms in the numerator, it cannot be factored out of either the numerator or the denominator. Therefore, $\frac{3x^3y-9x^2}{xy^2}$ simplifies to $\frac{3x(xy-3)}{y^2}$.

3. **The correct answer is A.** FOIL the binomials, as follows:

$$\begin{aligned}(2-3x^2)(4x-1) &= 2(4x)-2(1)-(3x^2)(4x)+(3x^2)(1)\\ &= -12x^3+3x^2+8x-2\end{aligned}$$

4. **The correct answer is D.** To simplify, you need a common denominator. The common denominator is 5y. Write the first fraction, $\frac{x}{5}$, as an equivalent one with a denominator of $5y: \frac{y}{y} \bullet \frac{x}{5} = \frac{xy}{5y}$. Likewise, rewrite the fraction after the minus sign as one with a denominator of $\frac{5}{5} \times \frac{2}{y} = \frac{10}{5y}$. Since the denominators are now the same, you can subtract: $\frac{xy}{5y} - \frac{10}{5y} = \frac{xy-10}{5y}$.

5. **The correct answer is A.**

$$\begin{aligned}(x-5)(x+3) &=\\ x &= 5 \text{ or } -3\end{aligned}$$

6. **The correct answer is B.** Write the equation in standard form:

$$2x^2 + 3x - 7 = 0$$

$$a = 2,\ b = 3, \text{ and } c = -7$$

$$x = \frac{-3 \pm \sqrt{(3)^2 - 4(2)(-7)}}{2(2)}$$

$$x = \frac{-3 \pm \sqrt{65}}{4}$$

The solutions are:

$$x = \frac{-3+\sqrt{65}}{4} \text{ or } \frac{-3-\sqrt{65}}{4}$$

7. **The correct answer is C.** Factor out an x from both terms on the right side of the equation:

$$z = x(5 - 25y)$$

Divide both sides by $5 - 25y$:

$$\frac{z}{5-25y} = x$$

8. **The correct answer is C.**

$$C = \frac{BA}{B-A}$$
$$C(B-A) = BA$$
$$CB - CA = BA$$
$$CB = BA + CA$$
$$CB = A(B+C)$$
$$\frac{CB}{B+C} = A$$

9. **The correct answer is B.** Substitute for the variable g to get $f(-20) = \sqrt[3]{-20-7} = \sqrt[3]{-27} = -3$.

10. **The correct answer is D.** Because the index, 4, is even, the radicand, $6 - 2x$, must be nonnegative. Hence $6 - 2x \geq 0$. Subtract 6 from both sides to get $-2x \geq -6$. Dividing both sides by –2 and reversing the inequality (because of division by a negative number) yields $x \leq 3$. Choices A and B are not correct because the domains include values greater than 3 that result in a negative number under the radical. Choice C is incorrect because it excludes $x = 3$, which is an allowable value in $f(x)$ $f(x): \sqrt[4]{6-2(3)} = \sqrt[4]{0} = 0$.

11. **The correct answer is D.** The most direct approach is to compute $(f \circ g)(x)$ which is $f(g(x))$ for the given pairs to see which one works. Keep in mind that the order of this composition matters.

Using the pairs in choice D yields $\frac{\left(\sqrt{x}\right)^2}{4-\left(\sqrt{x}\right)^2} = \frac{x}{4-x}$, as desired.

12. **The correct answer is C.** The idea is to use the translation results with the basic absolute value graph, as follows:

Step	Action	Equation
1.	Start with basic absolute value graph.	$y = \lvert x \rvert$
2.	Reflect over the x-axis.	$y = -\lvert x \rvert$
3.	Move the above graph left 4 units	$y = -\lvert x+4 \rvert$
4.	Move the above graph up 3 units	$y = -\lvert x+4 \rvert + 3$

This equation can be written equivalently as $y = 3 - |x + 4|$. All the distractor choices involve sign changes on the constant terms, which change the direction of the translation or if the original graph is reflected over the x-axis. While it is recommended to be familiar with the function translation facts stated above, sometimes the "trial and error" method may be quicker or your only alternative if you forget the facts. In this case, any point on a graph must make the equation true. Choosing either x-intercept (–7, 0) or (–1, 0) proves true for choice C alone.

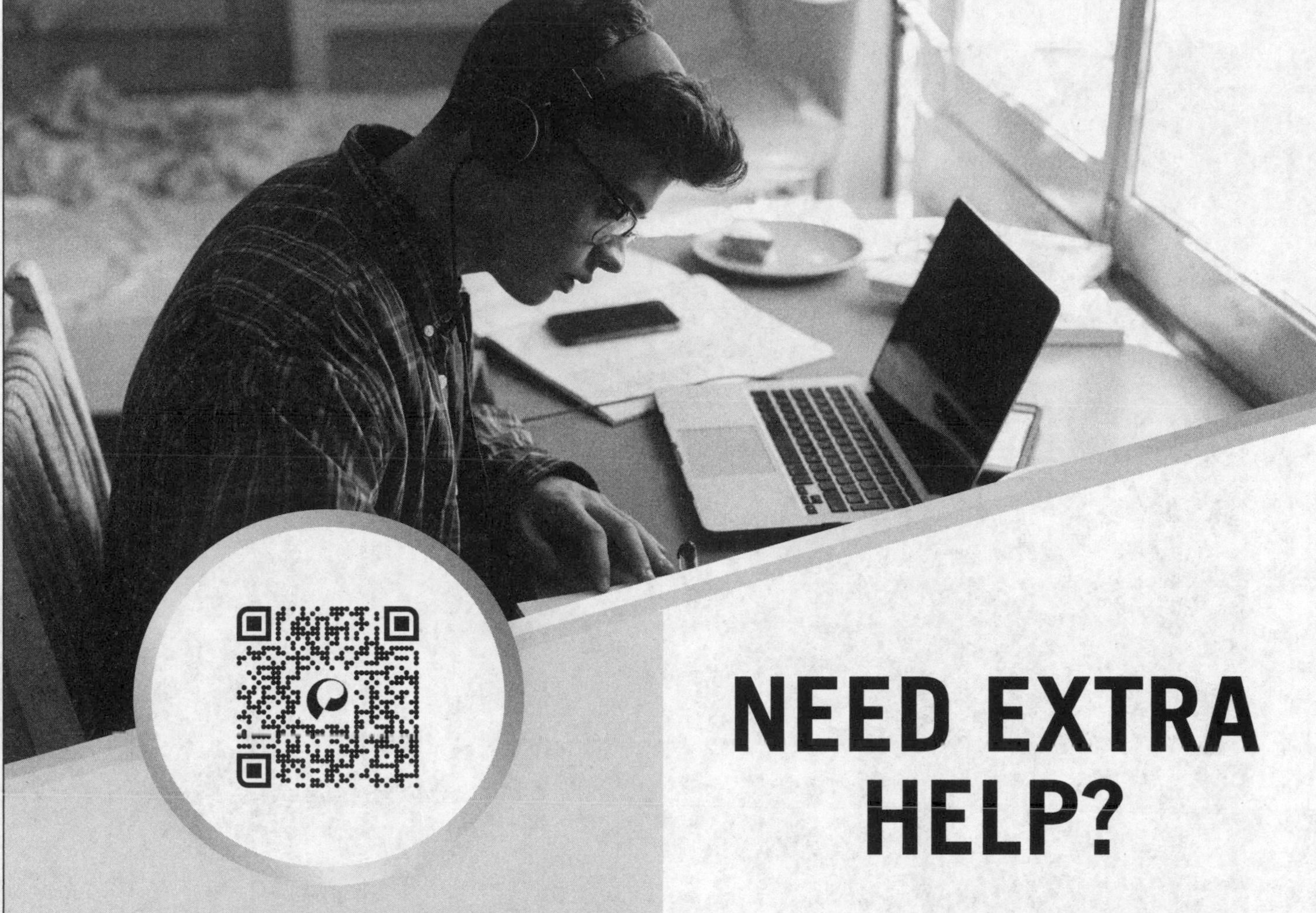

CHAPTER

Data Analysis, Statistics, and Probability

DATA ANALYSIS, STATISTICS, AND

OVERVIEW

The Problem-Solving and Data Analysis question domain for SAT Math includes a variety of topics and often situates the concepts in real-world scenarios, offering various graphical and tabular displays of data. In Chapter 10, you saw things such as the basics of measures of center, ratios and proportions, unit rates, and basic probability, all of which are covered by the Problem-Solving and Data Analysis domain. Here, we'll revisit some of those topics while going into greater depth for others. Use the practice questions throughout the chapter to check your understanding and the Test Yourself at the end to see how well you're performing with SAT Problem-Solving and Data Analysis questions in general.

DATA ANALYSIS AND STATISTICS

Analyzing data and applying statistical concepts on the SAT can take a variety of forms. You might be asked to make an inference from a graph obtained by "fitting" data to a curve.

PROBABILITY

14

Or, you might be asked to compute or interpret a numerical measure (like mean, median, or range) of an actual data set in an applied context. Different still, you might be asked to make an inference about the nature of large populations based on data obtained from a sample.

Measures of Center

Questions related to data sets may ask you to use or determine various numerical measures. The measures of center and spread that you'll encounter include arithmetic mean, median, and mode. Recall the following from Chapter 10:

- To compute the mean of a list of numbers, add the numbers and divide by how many numbers you added.
- To find the median, arrange the numbers in increasing order; if there is an odd number of values, the middle number is the median; if there is an even number of values, average the values in the two middle positions.
- To find the mode, find the data value that occurs most frequently in the set. If there are two such values, the data set is bimodal. If no value occurs more than once, the data set has no mode.

EXAMPLE

What is the average of the following set of numbers?

5, 23, 46, 98, 403

Solution

Recall that to find the average (arithmetic mean), you find the sum of the values in the set and then divide by the number of values in the set, as shown:

$$\text{Arithmetic Mean} = \frac{\text{sum of values}}{\text{number of values}} = \frac{5+23+46+98+403}{5} = 115$$

The average for this set is 115. Notice how the average is skewed by outliers in the data. Only one value in the set is higher than the average.

Another type of arithmetic mean problem gives you the arithmetic mean and asks for the missing term.

EXAMPLES

If a student averages an 89% across five test scores, what score would they need to reach an average of 91% across six tests?

Solution

To determine their final score, they would make the following calculations:

$$\frac{89(5)+x}{6} = 91$$
$$89(5)+x = 546$$
$$x = 101$$

The only way the student can achieve their desired average of 91% would be to score 101% on the final exam.

What is the relationship between the mean, median, and mode of the following data set?

12, 8, 14, 17, 3, 5, 9, 8, 11, 8

Solution

Place the values in sequence: 3, 5, 8, 8, 8, 9, 11, 12, 14, 17.

You can see that the mode is 8.

Find the median by averaging the two middle values: $\frac{8+9}{2} = 8.5$.

To find the mean, add the terms and then divide by 10:

$$\frac{3+5+8+8+8+9+11+12+14+17}{10} = 9.5$$

From these values, you can state that mode < median < mean.

Weighted Average

If asked to find the arithmetic mean of a group of numbers in which some of the numbers appear more than once, simplify the computation by using the weighted average formula. For example, suppose the question asks for the average (arithmetic mean) age of a group of 10 friends. If four of the friends are 17, and six of the friends are 19, you can determine the average in the usual way:

$$\text{Average age} = \frac{17+17+17+17+19+19+19+19+19+19}{10} = \frac{182}{10} = 18.2$$

However, the computation can be done more quickly by taking the *weights* of the ages into account. The age 17 is weighted four times, and the age 19 is weighted six times. The average can then be computed as seen in the following example.

EXAMPLE

Andrea has four grades of 90 and two grades of 80 during the spring semester of calculus. What is her average (arithmetic mean) in the course for this semester?

Solution

Calculating Using Average Formula	Calculating Using Weighted Average Formula
$\frac{90+90+90+90+80+80}{6} = \frac{520}{6} = 86\frac{2}{3}$	$\frac{(90 \cdot 4)+(80 \cdot 2)}{6} = \frac{520}{6} = 86\frac{2}{3}$

Be sure not to average 90 and 80 since there are four grades of 90 and only two grades of 80.

$$\text{Average age} = \frac{4(17)+6(19)}{10} = \frac{182}{10} = 18.2$$

Range

The range, or the spread, of a data set is the difference between the greatest and least data values. To find the range of a set of data, first write the values in ascending order to make sure that you have found the least and greatest values. Then, subtract the least data value from the greatest data value.

EXAMPLE

Celia kept track of the average price of a gallon of gas over the last 10 years. Her data is shown in the table below. What is the range in the average price of gas?

Solution

Year	Average price/gallon in US dollars
2006	2.00
2007	2.08
2008	2.44
2009	3.40
2010	2.85
2011	2.90
2012	3.50
2013	4.20
2014	3.80
2015	3.25

Write the data in order from least to greatest:

2.00 2.08 2.44 2.85 2.90 3.25 3.40 3.50 3.80 4.20

Subtract the least value from the greatest value:

$$4.20 - 2.00 = 2.20$$

$2.20 is the range or spread of the data.

Measures of Center and Spread in Context

On the exam, data will usually be presented within an applied context. The data may be presented within a frequency table, as in the following example.

EXAMPLES

Bowlers in an amateur league play six games during a weekend statewide bowling tournament. The following table displays the number of "turkeys" (three strikes in a row) scored by all players during the games they played that weekend.

Number of Turkeys Bowled	Frequency
0	19
1	15
2	2
3	8
4	9
5	7
6	0
7	6
8	0
9	4
10	0
11	0
12	2

How many bowlers participated in the tournaments, and what are the mean and median number of turkeys bowled that weekend?

Solution

The number of bowlers is the sum of the numbers in the right column, which is 72. Since there are 72 total scores, the median of this data is the average of the 36th and 37th outcome, which is 2.5. The mean is computed as a weighted average, as follows:

$$\frac{19(0)+15(1)+2(2)+8(3)+9(4)+7(5)+0(6)+6(7)+0(8)+4(9)+0(10)+0(11)+2(12)}{72}=\frac{216}{72}=3$$

The data in the preceding example could have been displayed using the following graph:

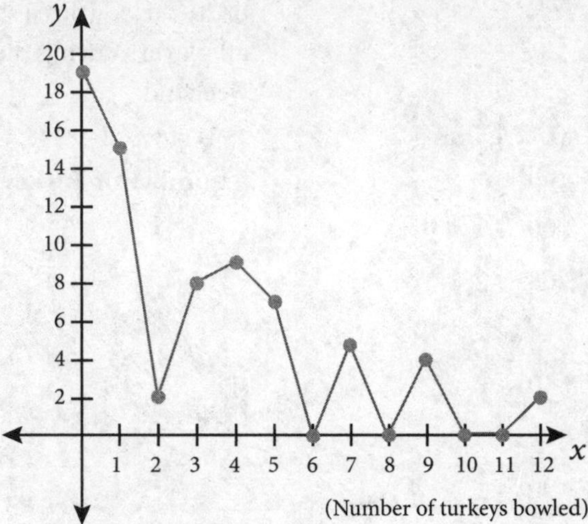

With the graphic presentation, the answer to the question is the same, but the way you initially extract the information is different. Specifically, the frequency of each "number of turkeys bowled" is the height of the points in the graph. Once you have this information, you can proceed as previously shown.

In a data set comprised of at least five values, every data value is 20 except for one value, which equals 1. What can be said about the median of this data set?

Solution

If the values are placed in order, the first value will be 1 and the values thereafter will be 20. There would simply need to be three data values in the data set to ensure the median is 20. And so, since there are at least five data values, the middle value must be 20. This is true if the data set has five values or 500 values! So, we conclude that the median of such a data set is 20.

Sometimes, a question straddles the line between data analysis and algebra, as in the following example. Questions like this, which require you to use multiple skill sets together, are among the more difficult questions on the exam.

EXAMPLE

A botanist's lab notebook shows the average percentage levels of carbon dioxide in a closed chamber kept at a constant temperature of 75 degrees Fahrenheit, inside of which tomato plants are being grown using a newly developed nutrient solution. The following table shows the recorded levels.

Day	%-Level of Carbon Dioxide
Monday	6.5
Tuesday	6.1
Wednesday	
Thursday	5.1
Friday	5.3
Average for the Week	5.5

There is a blank in the lab notebook in the place for the Wednesday reading. What was this reading?

Solution

Let x represent the missing reading. To compute the average of five readings, add them and divide by 5. For the moment, we drop the percent sign, and affix it to the final value of x.

$$\frac{6.5+6.1+x+5.1+5.3}{5}=5.5$$
$$\frac{23+x}{5}=5.5$$
$$23+x=27.5$$
$$x=4.5$$

So, the missing reading is 4.5%.

Comparing Data Sets Using Shape, Center, and Spread

Statistics questions on the SAT require using measures of central tendency, and so you will need to be familiar with the shape, center, and spread of data. The shape of the data refers to the normal distribution curve, which we examine in what follows. The center could be the average (arithmetic mean) or the median of the data values in the set. The spread is the range of the data, or the standard deviation of the data that describes the distance between values in a data set.

Standard Deviation—Normal Distribution

A standard deviation describes how far the data values in a set are from the mean or how much they "deviate" from the mean. The graphs below are both normal distribution curves. In the graph on the left, since much of the data clusters closely around the mean, there is a small standard deviation. In the graph on the right, since the data is more spread out, there is a larger standard deviation. If these were sets of test scores for Class A and Class B on a math exam, most of the scores in Class A would be very close to the average score, but, in Class B, the scores would be more varied.

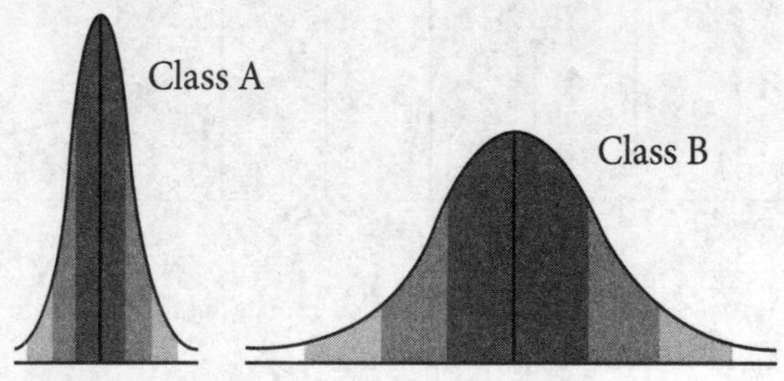

What You Really Need to Know About Standard Deviation

You won't have to calculate the standard deviation, but it is important to understand how to use it. If data has a normal distribution, the empirical rule states the following:

- Approximately 68% of the data falls within 1 standard deviation of the mean.
- Approximately 95% of the data falls within 2 standard deviations of the mean.
- Approximately 99.7% of the data falls within 3 standard deviations of the mean.

Let's see how this works with a table of data. The following table lists the number of students enrolled in six different sections of algebra, A, B, C, D, E, and F, offered by a college. First calculate the mean.

	A	B	C	D	E	F
Number of Students	18	23	15	19	28	11

$$\text{mean} = \frac{18+23+15+19+28+11}{6} = \frac{114}{6} = 19$$

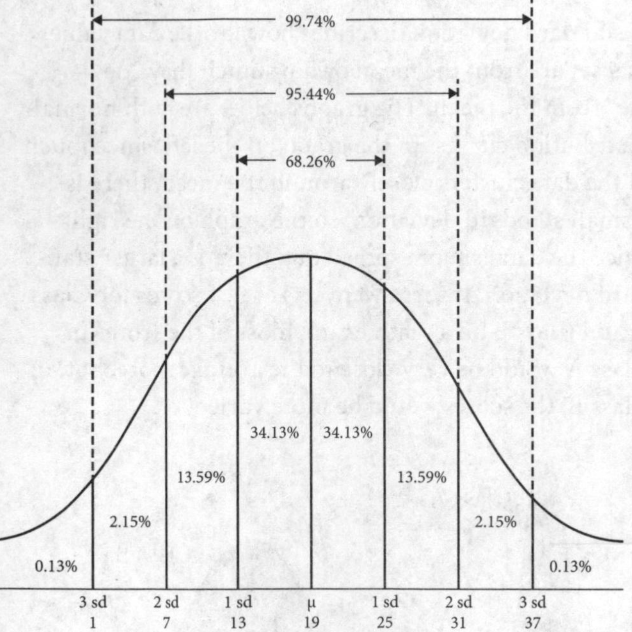

The mean is always in the middle. Here, it is 19, and the standard deviation is approximately 6.

In this example, the standard deviation of 6 means that approximately 68% of the algebra sections have between 13 (19 – 6) or 25 (19 + 6) students, plus or minus 1 standard deviation. Approximately 95% of the algebra sections lie within 2 standard deviations, meaning the sections have between 7 and 31 students.

Comparing Data Sets Using Mean and Standard Deviation

You may have two sets of data with similar means and ranges but different standard deviations. For the data set with the greater standard deviation, more of the data are farther from the mean.

PRACTICE

A coach is deciding between 2 baseball players to recruit to his team. He is looking at player performance over the past 10 seasons. Both players have the same mean batting average of 0.270 and the same range of batting averages (0.080) over the past 10 seasons. However, Player A's batting averages have a higher standard deviation than Player B's batting averages. What does this indicate about each player?

A. Player A is more likely to hit better than his mean batting average.

B. Player B is more likely to hit better than his mean batting average.

C. Player A's batting average is more erratic.

D. Player B's batting average is more erratic.

The correct answer is C. A greater standard deviation in a data set means that the data values are more spread out, or erratic, meaning performance varied more. Essentially, Player B's batting average is more dependable; he more frequently batted close to his batting average than did Player A. So, if the manager is looking for reliability, he may want to choose Player B for his team.

Confidence Intervals and Margin of Error

Measurement or sampling errors will usually occur when data cannot be collected about an entire population. If, for example, we are trying to determine the mean salary of people living in a city with 3.5 million people, we would probably use a smaller random sample of several hundred to several thousand people that was representative of the population. The maximum difference between the mean salary of the actual population and that of the sample population is called the margin of error. The sampling error decreases as the sample size increases, since there is more data that should more accurately reflect the true population. Here's an example:

A packaging company is gathering data about how many oranges it can fit into a crate. It takes a sample of 36 crates out of a total shipment of 5,540 crates. The sample mean is 102 oranges with a margin of error of 6 oranges at a 95% confidence interval.

What does the confidence interval mean? A confidence interval tells you how close the sample mean is to the actual mean of the entire population. In this case, it means that based on the sample, you can be 95% confident that the true population mean for the entire shipment is 102 ± 6, or 96 and 108 oranges per crate.

Making Inferences Using Sample Data

Frequently, a population is too large for every data value to be measured. Instead, a random sample of the population is used to make inferences about the true population.

PRACTICE

An online retailer wants to determine the average dollar value of an order that it receives on a daily basis. Based on a random sample of 200 orders, the mean dollar value is $72 and the standard deviation is $5.

The normal distribution curve would look like this:

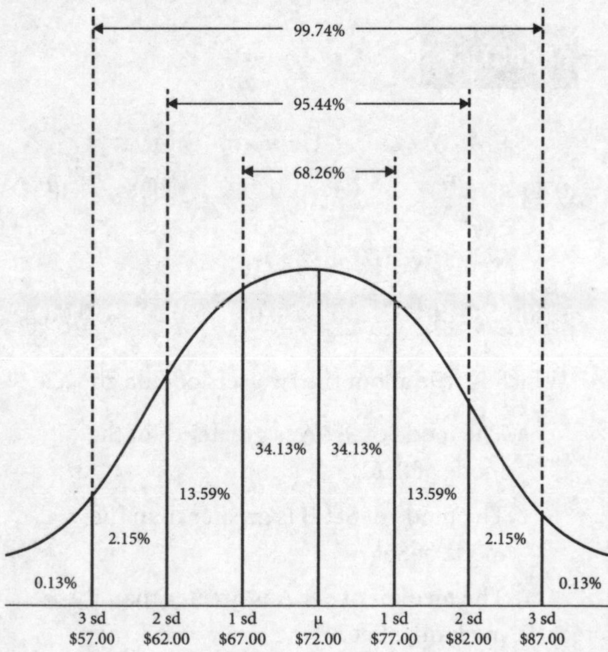

If the sample used is representative of the true population, what can be concluded about the true population of shoppers?

A. The mean of the true population is $72.

B. Most shoppers spend between $62 and $82.

C. All shoppers spend between $57 and $87.

D. The mode of the size of an order is $72.

The correct answer is B. Shoppers who spent between $62 and $82 fall within 2 standard deviations of the mean of the sample population. Approximately 95% of the shoppers fall within 2 standard deviations of the mean. Thus, it can be concluded that most shoppers spend between $62 and $82. Though the sample is representative, it does not indicate that the mean of the true population is equal to the mean of the sample population, so choice A is incorrect. Approximately 99.7% of the population lies within 3 standard deviations of the mean, which, in this case, is between $57 and $87—but this is not all shoppers, so choice C is not fully supported. We don't know the mode of the data, so choice D is not correct.

Comparing Data Sets Using Spread

Spread in data sets represents the differences between different values, including the least and greatest values as well as distances between values and the median and mean of a set. Different measures of spread can be used to come to conclusions about data variability.

PRACTICE

Todd's meteorology class researched weekly precipitation (measured in inches) in a tropical region during two 6-week periods. The data in Set A covers a period from January through mid-February, and the data in Set B is from July through mid-August. The results appear in the tables below.

Set A: Weeks 1–6 (January–February)					
0.43	1.73	1.93	0.28	0.08	1.18

Set B: Weeks 27–32 (July–August)					
0.20	0.01	0.00	0.08	0.04	0.00

Given that Data Set A and Data Set B have approximate standard deviations of 0.79 and 0.08, respectively, which of the following statements is true?

A. Data Set A shows more variability in data values than Data Set B, as evidenced by both the range and standard deviation.

B. Data Set A shows more variability in data values than Data Set B, as evidenced only by the range.

C. Data Set A shows less variability in data values than Data Set B, as evidenced by both the range and standard deviation.

D. Data Set A shows less variability in data values than Data Set B, as evidenced only by the standard deviation.

The correct answer is A. To calculate range, write the data values in order from least to greatest for each set:

Set A: 0.08; 0.28; 0.43; 1.18; 1.73; 1.93

Set B: 0.00; 0.00; 0.01; 0.04; 0.08; 0.20

Find the difference between the least and greatest value for each set:

Set A: Range = 1.93 – 0.08 = 1.85

Set B: Range = 0.20 – 0.00 = 0.20

The range in Set A is greater. Since a higher standard deviation indicates more variability in data values about the mean, Data Set A has a higher level of variability than Data Set B. So, both measures of spread indicate that Data Set A shows more variability in data values.

Comparing Data Sets Using Median and Mode

Using the same data sets about tropical precipitation, let's look at problems involving median and mode.

PRACTICE

Set A: Weeks 3–8 (January–February)					
0.43	1.73	1.93	0.28	0.08	1.18

Set B: Weeks 29–34 (July–August)					
0.20	0.01	0.00	0.08	0.04	0.00

Which is true about the two sets of data above?

A. The mode of Set A is greater than the mode of Set B.

B. The mode of Set B is greater than the mode of Set A.

C. The median of Set A is greater than the median of Set B.

D. The median of Set B is greater than the median of Set A.

The correct answer is C. In this case, Set A does not have a mode because there is no data value that appears more than once. So we cannot make any statements involving the mode of Set A.

Calculate the median of both sets of data. The median is the number in the middle of a data set when all the values are written in increasing order:

Set A: 0.08, 0.28, 0.43, 1.18, 1.73, 1.93

Here, the two middle numbers are 0.43 and 1.18, so we take their average:

$$\text{Median of Set A: } \frac{0.43+1.18}{2}=\frac{1.61}{2}=0.805$$

We perform the same set of calculations for set B:

Set B: 0.00, 0.00, 0.01, 0.04, 0.08, 0.20

$$\text{Median of Set B: } \frac{0.01+0.04}{2}=\frac{0.05}{2}=0.025$$

From this we can see that the median of Set A is greater than the median of Set B.

Evaluating Reports and Surveys

To evaluate a report about a set of data, it is important to consider the appropriateness of the data collection method. Random sampling ensures that every member of the population has an equally likely chance of being chosen. This data collection method type reduces bias and measurement error. There are different types of random sampling techniques that a researcher may use.

PRACTICE

A local politician wants to gauge how her constituents feel about the installation of a gas pipeline that will border her district. Which of the following would allow the politician to make a valid conclusion about the opinions of her constituents?

A. Survey a random sample of local Democrats

B. Survey a sample of citizens who volunteer to provide responses

C. Survey an intact group of senior citizens at a local event

D. Survey a random sample of citizens at a local library

The correct answer is D. Let's analyze each of these options. First is the random sample of local Democrats in Choice A. This may seem like a good choice. However, it excludes members of other parties and their opinions. Choice B may seem okay at first, but such a sample will likely promote bias of the data since the individuals responding will likely have strong viewpoints that may not be shared by others in the district. Choice C also seems like an acceptable choice at first, but this sampling method excludes other age groups. Data obtained from this sampling technique cannot be generalized to the population as a whole. Choice D would allow for a valid conclusion (or generalization to the population) since a random sample is used and a library will likely have patrons who have varying beliefs, backgrounds, ages, and so on. Choice D does not exclude any age or party and will result in the smallest sampling error.

When considering whether the data in a report is representative of a population, it is important to consider the demographics of the population being studied. Their habits, behaviors, and perhaps incomes will influence their decisions and even their ability to be included in the report. The type of survey that will include the widest range of habits, behaviors, and incomes of the people being studied is likely the most representative. As discussed previously, the use of random sampling reduces the sampling error and bias and results in sample data that may be used to represent the population from which the sample came.

DATA INTERPRETATION

Problem-Solving and Data Analysis questions in the SAT Math section will have you draw on tabular and visual displays of data to draw inferences about small data sets and samples that can lead to insights for populations. Data may be presented in a variety of forms, including bar graphs, charts, scatterplots, and tables. With those different forms you'll have to apply what you know about measures of center and spread to breakdown data presented by questions.

Working with Data in Tables

Some SAT exam questions ask you to solve mathematical problems based on data contained in tables. All such problems are based on problem-solving techniques that have already been reviewed. The trick when working with tables is to make certain that you select the correct data needed to solve the problem. Take your time reading each table so that you understand exactly what information the table contains. Carefully select data from the correct row and column. As you will see, things are even trickier when a problem involves more than one table.

In order to illustrate problem solving with tables, consider the following two tables. The three questions that follow are based on the data within these tables.

Paul, Mark, and Bob are computer salespeople. In addition to their regular salaries, they each receive a commission for each computer they sell. The number of computers that each salesperson sold during a particular week, as well as their commission amounts, is shown in the following tables.

NUMBER OF COMPUTERS SOLD

	M	T	W	Th	F
Paul	9	3	12	6	4
Mark	6	3	9	1	5
Bob	8	4	5	7	8

COMMISSION PER SALE

Paul	\$15
Mark	\$20
Bob	\$25

EXAMPLE

What is the total amount of the commissions that Bob earned over the entire week?

Solution

This problem concerns only Bob, so ignore the information for Mark and Paul. Over the course of the week, Bob sold $8 + 4 + 5 + 7 + 8 = 32$ computers. The second table tells us that Bob earns \$25 per sale, so the total amount of his commission would be $\$25 \times 32 = \$800$.

What is the total amount of commission money earned by Paul, Mark, and Bob on Thursday?

Solution

To solve this problem, focus only on what happened on Thursday. Ignore the data for the other four days. Be careful not to add the number of computers sold by the three people, since they each earn a different commission per sale.

- On Thursday, Paul sold 6 computers and earned a \$15 commission for each computer sold, so Paul earned $\$15 \times 6 = \$90$.

- Mark sold 1 computer, so based on his \$20 commission, he earned \$20.
- Bob sold 7 computers and earned a \$25 commission per machine, so he made $\$25 \times 7 = \$175$.

Overall, the amount of commission on Thursday is $\$90 + \$20 + \$175 = \$285$.

On what day did Paul and Mark earn the same amount in commission?

Solution

You can save yourself a lot of time if you look at the tables before you start to compute. Note that Mark's commission is larger than Paul's, and so the only way they could have earned the same amount is if Paul sold more computers than Mark. The only days that Paul sold more computers than Mark were Monday, Wednesday, and Thursday, so those are the only days that need to be considered. On Thursday, Paul made much more in commission than Mark, so eliminate Thursday. On Monday, Paul earned $\$15 \times 9 = \$135$, and Mark earned $\$20 \times 6 = \$120$. This means that the answer must be Wednesday. To be certain, note that on Wednesday Paul earned $\$15 \times 12 = \$180$, and Mark earned $\$20 \times 9 = \$180$ also.

Correlation and Scatterplots

If two variables have a relationship such that when one variable changes, the other changes in a predictable way, the two variables are correlated. For example, there is a correlation between the number of hours an employee works each week and the amount of money the employee earns—the more hours the employee works, the more money the employee earns. Note that in this case, as the first variable increases, the second variable increases as well. These two variables are positively correlated.

Sometimes, when one variable increases, a second variable decreases. For example, the more that a store charges for a particular item, the fewer of that item will be sold. In this case, these two variables are negatively correlated.

Sometimes, two variables are not correlated; that is, a change in one variable does not affect the other variable in any way. For example, the number of cans of soda that a person drinks each day may have no correlation with the amount of money the person earns.

One way to determine whether two variables are correlated is to sketch a scatterplot. A scatterplot is a graph in which the x-axis represents the values of one variable and the y-axis represents the values of the other variable. With scatterplots, any evident pattern of data points (or lack of a pattern) is of interest; it tells you something about the relationship between the two variables. When reviewing a scatterplot, you should ask yourself whether the points are close together or far apart and if they are clustering around a certain part of the graph or a line (or if they aren't). Several values of one variable and the corresponding values of the other variable are measured and plotted on the graph:

- If the points appear to form a straight line, or are close to forming a straight line, then it is likely that the variables are correlated.
- If the line has a positive slope (rises up left to right), the variables are positively correlated.
- If the line has a negative slope (goes down left to right), the variables are negatively correlated.
- If the points on the scatterplot seem to be located more or less at random, then it is likely that the variables are not correlated.

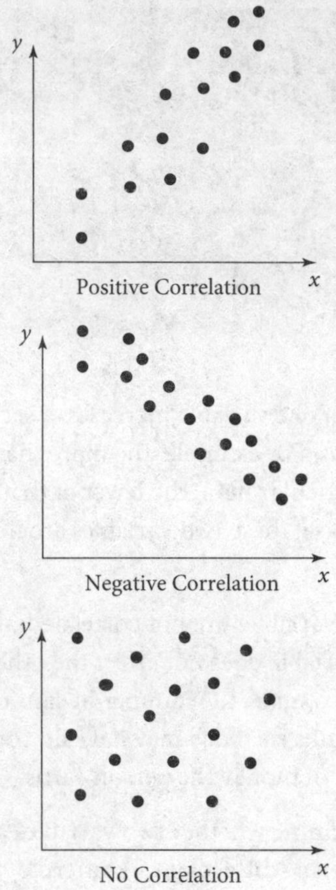

It is rare that the points on a scatterplot will all lie exactly on the same line. However, if there is a strong correlation, it is likely that there will be a line that could be drawn on the scatterplot that comes close to all of the points. Statisticians call the line that comes the closest to all of the points on a scatterplot the line of best fit (also called a regression line). Without performing any computations, it is possible to visualize the location of the line of best fit, as the following diagrams show:

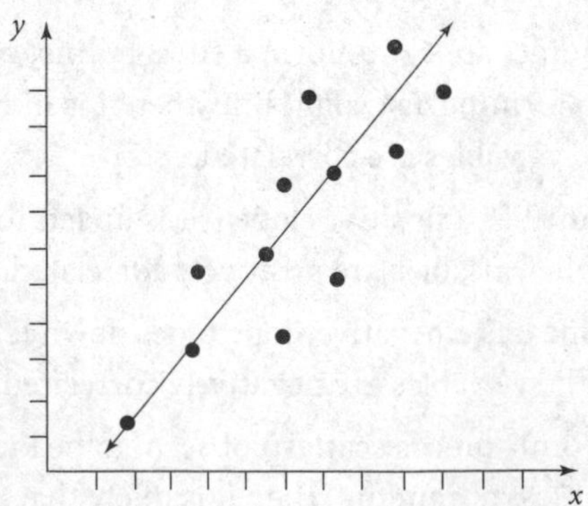

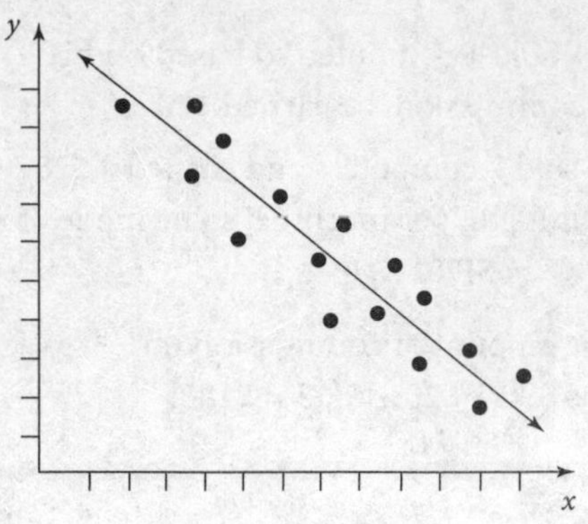

PRACTICE

Which of the following slopes is the closest to the slope of the line of best fit for the scatterplot shown here?

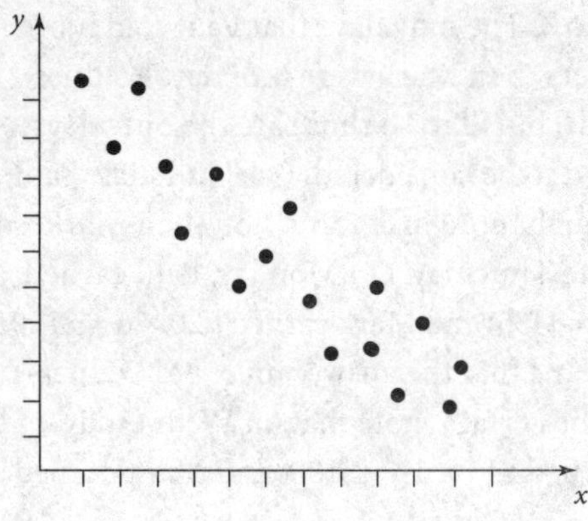

A. 3

B. 1

C. 0

D. −1

The correct answer is D. Begin by sketching in the line of best fit in its approximate location.

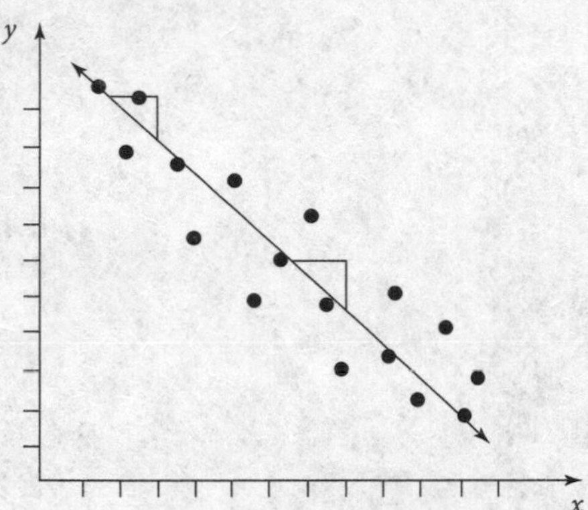

This line has a negative slope since it decreases from left to right. In addition, the slope appears to be about –1 because if you move one unit horizontally from a point on the line, you need to move one unit vertically downward to return to the line. Choice D represents the only negative slope.

Imagine you hear about a study that investigates the question, "Is the value of an extended warranty on electronics worth the cost?" One hundred middle-aged people were asked how much they spent on extended warranties in the last five years and their satisfaction level (on a scale of 0 to 10, where 0 represents "extremely unsatisfied" and 10 represents "extremely satisfied"). The following scatterplot describes the relationship between the amount spent on purchasing extended warranties and satisfaction level. Describe any pattern in the data.

From this scatterplot, we can infer that, generally, people who spent more on extended warranties had greater satisfaction. This is clear as the points are tightly packed together and rise from left to right as the dollar amount increased from 200 to 400. This trend can be described even more precisely by fitting a regression line to the scatterplot.

For this scatterplot, the points are in a positive correlation because they are close together and traveling toward the right as the x-values increase. That is, as the x-values increase, so do the corresponding y-values.

Satisfaction Level versus Amount Spend on Warranties

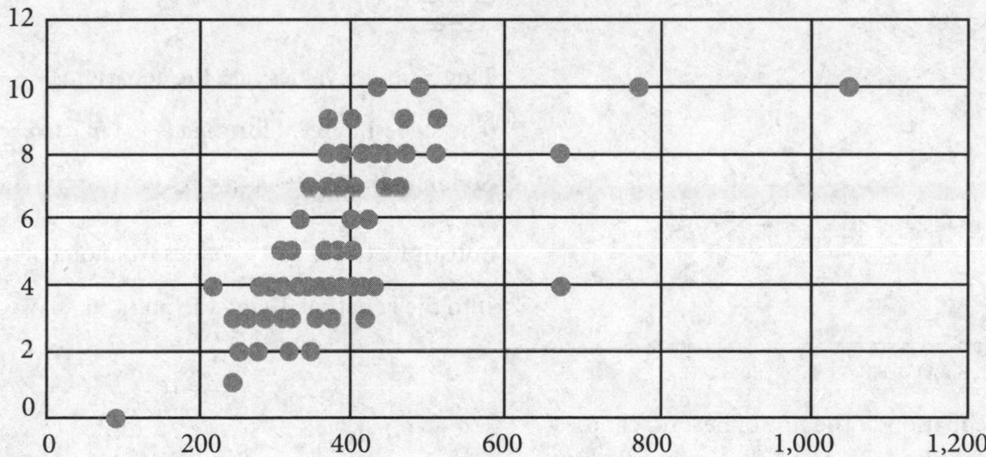

Equation of Line of Best Fit

You may see questions that ask you to create a line of best fit and give the equation for this line. Again, there is some approximation involved in determining a line of best fit. Look at the following scatterplot. Imagine a line that would come closest to all the data points and include an equal number of data points on either side of the line.

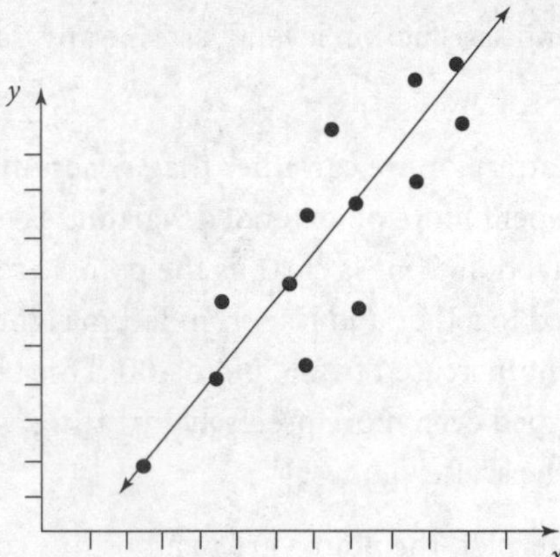

Look at the scatterplot below. Notice that the line of best fit has 8 points above and 8 points below the line. The line of best fit does not have to cross any of the data points. In this case, the line of best fit goes through the middle of the data and does not include any of the actual data points.

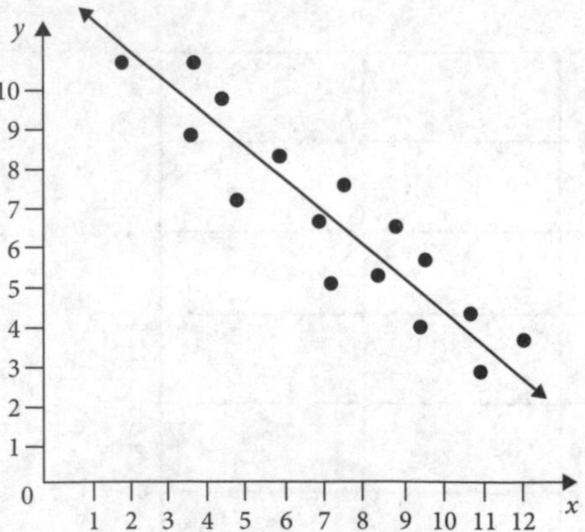

To determine the equation of the line of best fit, choose two points that lie on the line of best fit. You may have to approximate points if the line does not have points that are exactly on an intersection. The line appears to have points at (6, 8) and (12, 3). Use these two points to

determine the equation of the line of best fit.

First, calculate the slope, m, using the slope formula $\frac{y_2 - y_1}{x_2 - x_1}$.

Plug x- and y-values into the equation: $\frac{3-8}{12-6} = -\frac{5}{6}$.

The slope-intercept formula is $y = mx + b$.

So far, we have $y = -\frac{5}{6}x + b$.

Substitute the x- and y-values from one of the points into the equation. Using the point (6, 8), we can write:

$$8 = \frac{-5}{6}(6) + b$$

$$8 = -5 + b$$

$$b = 13$$

The equation of the line of best fit is $y = \frac{-5}{6}x + 13$.

Making Predictions

The following scatterplot shows the average number of books borrowed on a weekly basis for years 2000–2009 at a local library.

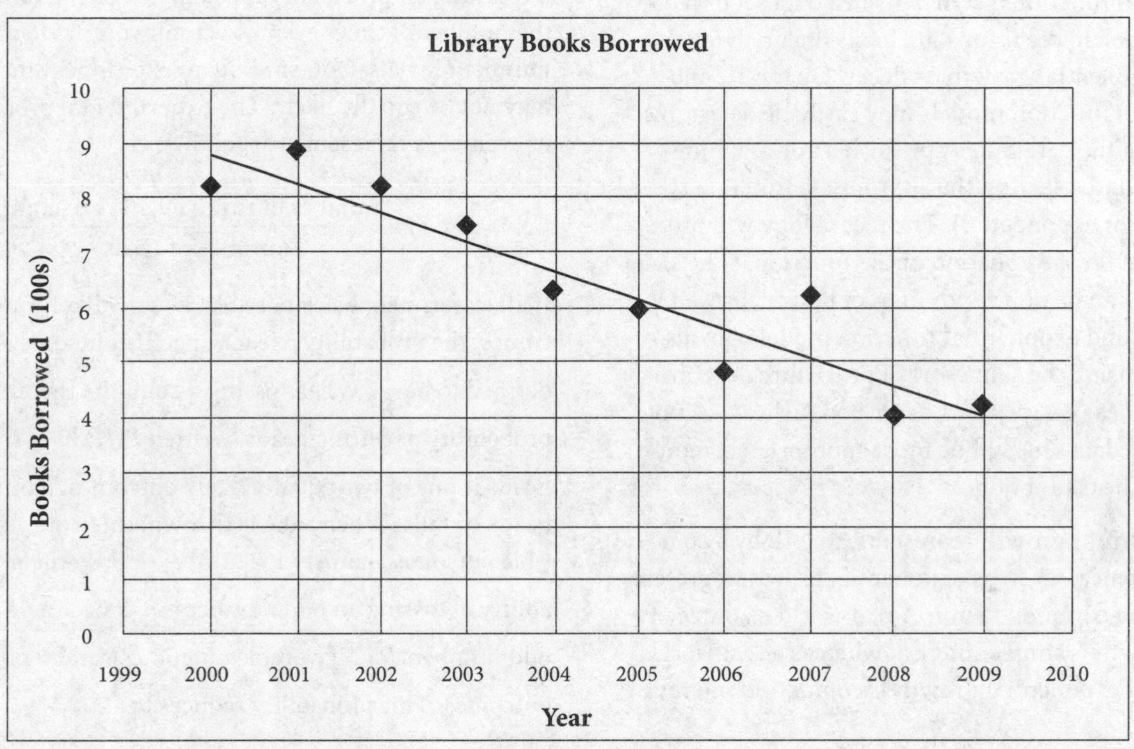

EXAMPLE

If the trend continued, approximately how many books were borrowed in 2010?

Solution

Use the slope of the line to make predictions about data points that are not shown. According to the slope, the average number of books borrowed weekly goes down approximately $0.6 \times 100 = 60$ books every year. Multiply by 100 because, according to the label of the vertical axis, the numbers are in the 100s. The expected value for the number of books borrowed in 2009 was 400. The slope says we should expect that number to decrease by 60 every year, so you can predict that there were 340 books borrowed in 2010.

You have seen data that show a linear correlation, which may be represented by a line of best fit. In other cases, data may be better modeled by quadratic or exponential functions. When given a data set or plotted data, look to see if the data looks linear, parabolic, or like exponential growth or decay. Quadratic and exponential function models may easily be determined by entering the data into a spreadsheet or graphing calculator and selecting the appropriate function type (quadratic or exponential). The technology will provide output for the equation of the function. (The same procedure can be done with lines of best fit, as well.) Quadratic and exponential function models can also be estimated using the same sort of procedure described with the linear correlations described earlier. Just note that not all data sets will be most appropriately modeled by a linear function.

Note that linear growth represents growth by a common difference, whereas exponential growth represents growth by a common factor. A real-world example of linear growth is simple interest, whereas a real-world example of exponential growth is compound interest.

PROBABILITY

Probability is a numerical way of measuring the likelihood that a specific outcome will happen. The probability of a specific outcome is always a number between 0 and 1. An outcome with a probability of 0 cannot possibly happen, and an event with a probability of 1 will definitely happen. Therefore, the nearer the probability of an event is to 0, the less likely the event is to happen, and the nearer the probability of an event is to 1, the more likely the event is to happen.

There are two types of probability: theoretical probability and experimental probability. Theoretical probability is defined by theory, whereas experimental probability is defined by outcomes of actual trials.

Theoretical probability is calculated as the ratio of the number of favorable outcomes to the number of possible outcomes (i.e., sample space). This type of probability is independent of the outcomes of any trials. The theoretical probability of event *A* is represented as follows:

$$P(A)=\frac{\text{number of favorable outcomes}}{\text{number of possible outcomes}}$$

Experimental probability is calculated as the ratio of the number of times event *A* actually occurs to the number of trials. Outcomes in an experiment may or may not be equally likely. The experimental probability of event *A* is represented as follows:

$$P(A)=\frac{\text{number of times event A occurs}}{\text{number of trials}}$$

If an experiment has *n* possible, equally likely outcomes, the probability of each specific outcome is defined to be $\frac{1}{n}$. When tossing a coin, the theoretical probability of getting heads, written *P*(*H*), is $\frac{1}{2}$ since heads is one of two equally likely outcomes, namely heads or tails. When a die is thrown, there are six possible outcomes, namely 1, 2, 3, 4, 5, or 6, so the probability of tossing an odd number is $\frac{3}{6}$ since there are 3 odd numbers (or 3 favorable outcomes), and 6 possible outcomes. This probability reduces to $\frac{1}{2}$.

Conditional Probability

The probability of an event occurring after another event has already occurred is called conditional probability. The notation for conditional probability is $P(B \mid A)$, which is read as "the probability of *B* given *A*."

If both events *A* and *B* are independent, where the result of *B* is not affected by the result of *A*, then the conditional probability of *B* given *A* is equal to the probability of *B*.

$$P(B \mid A) = P(B)$$

Likewise, if both events *A* and *B* are independent, where the result of *A* is not affected by the result of *B*, then the conditional probability of *A* given *B* is equal to the probability of *A*.

$$P(A \mid B) = P(A)$$

If both events *A* and *B* are dependent, where the result of *B* is affected by the result of *A* (or the result of *A* is affected by the result of *B*), then the conditional probability of *B* given *A* or *A* given *B* may be calculated using a few different methods. In probability situations involving dependent events, the way in which the question is asked will determine which equation to use.

The Multiplication Rule for dependent events states the following:

$$P(A \text{ and } B) = P(A) \bullet P(B \mid A)$$

or

$$P(A \text{ and } B) = P(B) \bullet P(A \mid B)$$

Using algebra, the following equations can be derived:

$$P(B|A) = \frac{P(A \text{ and } B)}{P(A)}$$

$$P(A|B) = \frac{P(A \text{ and } B)}{P(B)}$$

EXAMPLE

Of 100 people who work out at a gym, there are 45 people who take yoga classes, 55 people who take weightlifting classes, and 15 people who take both yoga and weightlifting. What is the probability that a randomly selected person takes weightlifting, given that the person also takes yoga?

Solution

This question is asking you to find the probability that a person is taking weightlifting, given that he or she is also taking yoga (or $P(A|B)$). This probability is found by writing the following equation:

$$P(A \mid B) = \frac{P(A \text{ and } B)}{P(A)} = \frac{15}{45} = \frac{1}{3}$$

The conditional probability that a person who takes weightlifting also takes yoga is $\frac{1}{3}$.

It may be helpful to use letters that more closely represent the pieces of the problem. For example, you may wish to use $P(Y)$ to represent the probability of taking yoga classes and $P(W)$ to represent the probability of taking weightlifting classes. The probability of taking both would be written as $P(Y \text{ and } W)$.

Independent Events

If events A and B are independent, then the probability of event B is not affected by the result of event A.

EXAMPLES

Adam tosses a coin and then tosses another coin. What is the probability that he gets heads or tails on the second toss, given that he gets heads on the first toss?

Solution

We are going to use H to denote heads and T to denote tails. Since the events are independent, we can write the following:

$$P(H \text{ or } T \mid H) = P(H)$$

Since $P(H) = \frac{1}{2}$, we know that the probability of getting heads or tails on the second toss, given that the first toss gives heads, is also equal to $\frac{1}{2}$.

Again suppose that Adam tosses a coin and then tosses another coin. What is the probability that he gets heads on the first toss and tails on the second toss?

Solution

Since the events are independent and the tosses can be distinguished, the probability can be represented as:

$$P(H \text{ and } T) = P(H) \bullet P(T) = \frac{1}{2} \bullet \frac{1}{2} = \frac{1}{4}$$

If Adam tosses two coins at the same time (and the toss that gives either result doesn't matter), the probability of getting heads and tails is $\frac{1}{2}$ because making a list would show that there are two favorable outcomes out of a sample space of four (i.e., the list *HT*, *HH*, *TH*, and *TT* shows that *HT* and *TH* have heads and tails, in some order). The ratio $\frac{2}{4}$, reduces to $\frac{1}{2}$.

Dependent Events

If events *A* and *B* are dependent, then the probability of event *B* is affected by the result of event *A*.

EXAMPLE

What is the probability of choosing a black 5, not replacing the card, and then choosing a red 5 from the same standard deck of cards?

Solution

There are two red 5s and two black 5s in a standard deck of 52 cards. Removing a black 5 from the deck will leave only 51 cards in the deck, so the probability can be found like so:

$$P(A \text{ and } B) = \frac{2}{52} \times \frac{2}{51} = \frac{1}{663}$$

Two-Way Tables and Probability

Data on the exam is often represented in two-way tables like the one in the example below. Be careful to read the correct row or column that represents the information in the problem.

EXAMPLE

Hattie is a member of the honor society. All members of the society are polled to determine how many hours they spend studying per week and whether they prefer math or science classes. The results are shown in the table below.

	Science	Math	Total
0–3 hours per week	4	2	6
4–6 hours per week	6	7	13
Total	10	9	19

What is the probability that an honor society member selected at random prefers math, given that the member studies 4–6 hours per week?

Solution

There are a total of 13 students who study 4–6 hours per week, and 7 of them prefer math. So the probability is $\frac{7}{13}$.

SUMMING IT UP

- The mean of a data set is the arithmetic average of the data values. To compute the median, arrange the values in the data set in numerical order, from smallest to largest. If there are an odd number of data values, then the median is the data value in the middle of the set. If there is an even number of data values, then the median is the arithmetic average of the middle two values. The mode of a data set is the value(s) that occur most frequently.
- When determining weighted average, multiply each data point by its weight (how often it occurs in the data set), sum the values, and divide by the number of data points, as you would for arithmetic mean.
- Range represents the difference between the maximum and minimum values in a data set.
- A standard deviation describes how far the data values in a set are from the mean or how much they "deviate" from the mean—think of it as the average distance of each data point from the average of the data set.
- Margin of error represents the range in which the average value of a sample of a population could fall.
- Not all problems that deal with averages will ask you to solve for the average of a set of quantities.
- The trick when working with tables is to make sure you select the correct data needed to solve the problem. Take your time reading each table.
- Correlation describes an apparent relationship between two variables. There may be no correlation (in which plotted data appear to have no relationship), positive correlation (wherein as one variable increases so does the other), or negative correlation (wherein as one variable increases the other decreases).
- In a scatterplot, the relationship between x and y is linear if the trend between x and y can be described by a line (known as the line of best fit). If there is another curve that more reasonably describes the relationship, the relationship is nonlinear.
- Observe trends with scatterplots, and use lines or curves to predict unknown values.
- Pay attention to sampling methods when you evaluate survey data. If a sample space contains N outcomes, then the probability of any one of them occurring is $\frac{1}{N}$. This can be extended to events in the sense that if A contains k elements, then $P(A) = \frac{\text{Number of outcomes in } A}{\text{Number of possible outcomes}} = \frac{k}{N}$. To find the probability of a compound event, use $P(A \text{ or } B) = P(A) + P(B) - P(A \text{ and } B)$.

TEST YOURSELF

PROBLEM-SOLVING AND DATA ANALYSIS

12 Questions—19 Minutes

Directions: The questions in this Test Yourself address some of the testing points in the Problem-Solving and Data Analysis domain.

Use of a calculator is permitted for all questions.

1. The costs of five different airlines' tickets from Dallas to Boston are shown in the table below.

Airline	Ticket Cost
A	$356
B	$298
C	$312
D	$304
E	$283

A sixth airline also offers flights from Dallas to Boston. The median price of the tickets from the six airlines, including those shown in the table, is $308. The range of the ticket prices is $77. What is the cost of the sixth airline's ticket?

A. $385

B. $360

C. $279

D. $231

2. Susan has an average (arithmetic mean) of 86 on three examinations. What grade must she receive on her next test to raise her average (arithmetic mean) to 88?

A. 90

B. 94

C. 96

D. 100

3. The ages of 14 US presidents at inauguration are listed here in order of their presidencies. Which of the following correctly compares the average (arithmetic mean), median, and mode of their ages?

54 51 60 62 43 55 56 61 52 69 64 46 54 47

A. Mode $<$ mean $<$ median

B. Median $<$ mode $<$ mean

C. Mode $<$ median $<$ mean

D. Median $<$ mean $<$ mode

4. Salena buys seven tickets in a raffle in which 50 tickets are sold. There are three prizes given: first, second, and third. What is the probability that she wins both first and second prizes?

A. $\frac{7}{50}$

B. $\frac{3}{175}$

C. $\frac{36}{2,401}$

D. $\frac{49}{2,500}$

5. The two-way frequency table below shows the results of a poll regarding video game play. The poll asked 150 randomly selected people the amount of time they spend playing video games each week and the type of game they most like to play. The table shows frequencies of each category.

	1–3 hours	3–5 hours	5+ hours	Total
Role-playing	12	15	16	43
Platform	24	19	18	61
Action	33	35	28	96
Total	69	69	62	200

What is the probability that a person plays 3–5 hours of games per week, given that they prefer platform games?

A. $\frac{19}{35}$

B. $\frac{19}{42}$

C. $\frac{19}{61}$

D. $\frac{19}{69}$

6. A hockey team roster has 20 players on it. There are 12 forwards, 6 defenders, and 2 goaltenders. If three players are selected at random without replacement, what is the probability that all three are defenders?

A. $\frac{1}{57}$

B. $\frac{2}{57}$

C. $\frac{27}{1,000}$

D. $\frac{3}{20}$

7. A sample of athletes was chosen, and the time it took them to complete an obstacle course was recorded. Mean time was 35 minutes, and the standard deviation was 4.25 minutes. If the sample is representative of the population of all athletes attempting the obstacle course, what conclusion can be drawn about the population of all athletes attempting the course?

A. All athletes complete the course in no more than 47.75 minutes.

B. The median completion time is 35 minutes.

C. Most athletes finish the course in between 26.5 minutes and 43.5 minutes.

D. No athlete completes the course in less than 25 minutes.

8. A researcher wants to measure the opinions of university students regarding global climate change. Which of the following poll results would most likely provide reliable data about the opinions of the entire population of university students?

A. The researcher interviewed 60 students selected at random at a political rally attended by about 16% of university students.

B. The researcher interviewed 55 students in a physics laboratory on campus.

C. The researcher randomly selected 100 students from the complete roster of registered students and emailed an interview invitation. Twelve percent participated.

D. The researcher randomly selected 100 students from the complete roster of registered students and emailed an offer of $5 to participate in an interview. Fifty percent participated.

9.

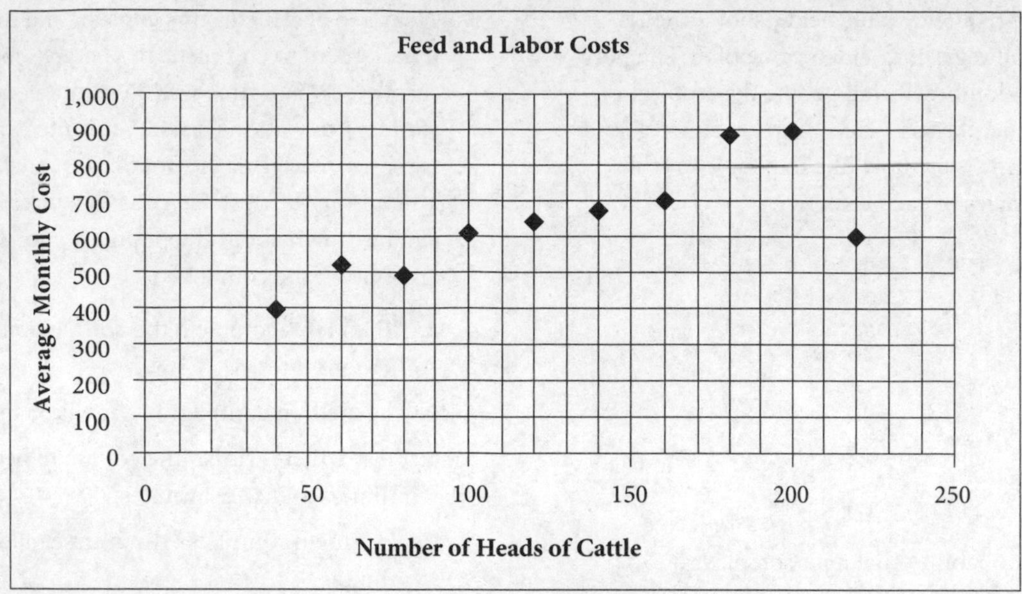

The scatterplot above shows average monthly feed and labor costs in dollars to raise different numbers of heads of beef cattle.

If the trend continued, what would be the average monthly feed and labor costs to raise 500 heads of beef cattle?

A. $1,380

B. $1,000

C. $880

D. $600

10.

Geographic Area	Attended College	Did Not Attend College	No Response	Total
Northeast	72,404	68,350	29,542	170,296
Northwest	88,960	125,487	48,960	263,407
Southeast	115,488	96,541	65,880	277,909
Southwest	79,880	65,874	13,840	159,594
Total	356,732	356,252	158,222	871,206

A survey was conducted in different geographic areas of a large state, covering the entire state population, pertaining to college attendance for people over the age of 30. The table above displays a summary of the survey results.

Of the people living in the northeast who reported that they did not attend college, 1,000 people were selected at random to do a follow-up survey in which they were asked if they were interested in attending adult education classes. There were 665 people who said they were interested in attending adult education classes. Using the data from both the initial survey and the follow-up survey, which of the following is most likely to be an accurate statement?

A. About 48,149 people living in the northeast who did not attend college would be interested in adult education classes.

B. Most people in the state are not interested in taking adult education classes.

C. About 19,645 people living in the northeast who did not attend college would be interested in adult education classes.

D. About 45,453 people living in the northeast who did not attend college would be interested in adult education classes.

11.

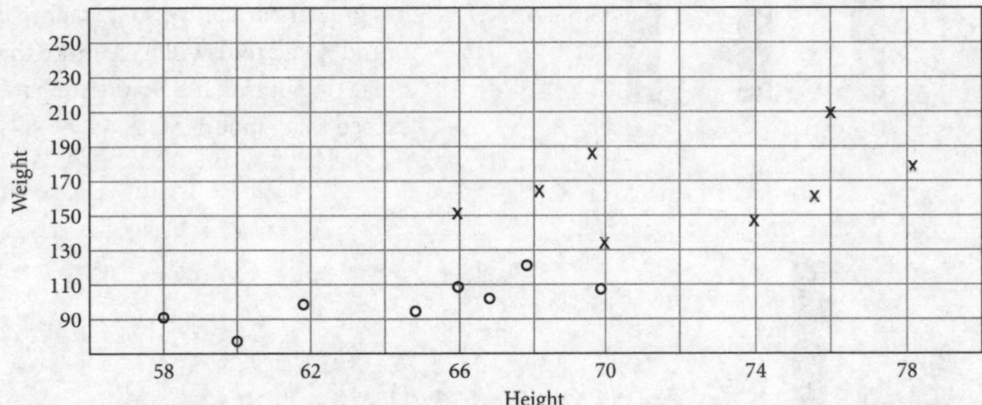

The scatterplot above shows the heights, in inches, and weights, in pounds, of 16 women and men at a health club. The women are represented by o's. The men are x's.

Which of the following is a true statement about the data?

A. The heights and weights are more strongly correlated for women than for men, and the slope of the line of best fit for women is greater than the slope for men.

B. The heights and weights are more strongly correlated for women than for men, and the slope of the line of best fit for men is greater than the slope for women.

C. The heights and weights are more strongly correlated for men than for women, and the slope of the line of best fit for women is greater than the slope for men.

D. The heights and weights are more strongly correlated for men than for women, and the slope of the line of best fit for men is greater than the slope for women.

12. The A public health group investigates a claim that Brand Y cigarettes have less than 18 milligrams of tar per cigarette, and that this is less tar than what Brand X cigarettes have. The group tests 16 randomly selected cigarettes from each brand. The findings are shown in the following charts.

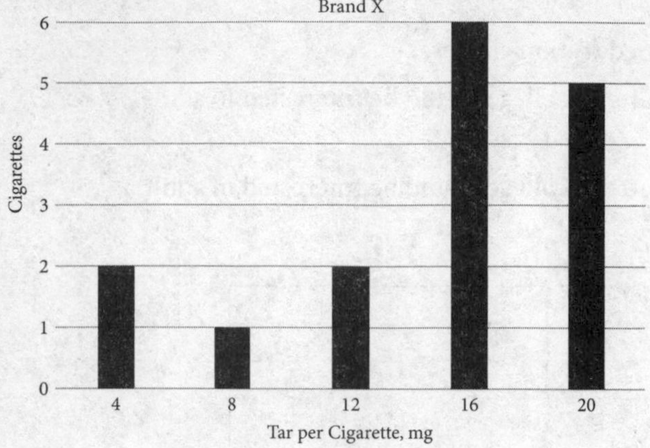

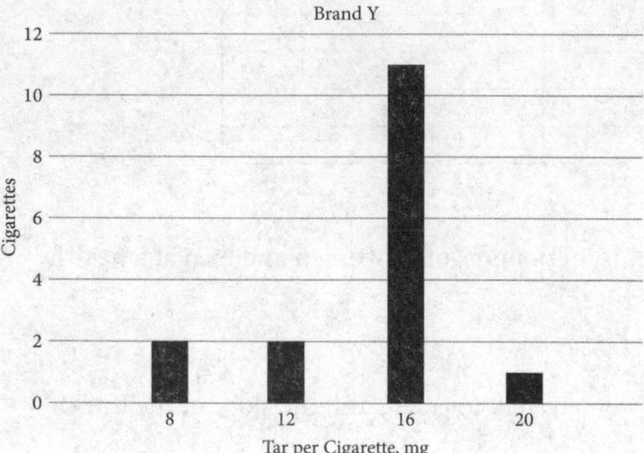

Which conclusion is supported by the data?

A. The average (arithmetic mean) tar per cigarette is higher for Brand Y than for Brand X, although the average is less than 18 milligrams for Brand Y.

B. The average (arithmetic mean) tar per cigarette is higher for Brand X than for brand Y, although the average is less than 18 milligrams for both brands.

C. The average (arithmetic mean) tar per cigarette is higher for Brand X, and it is greater than 18 milligrams.

D. The average (arithmetic mean) tar per cigarette is the same for the two brands. Brand X has greater variability, so it is more likely that a Brand X cigarette will have more than 18 grams of tar than it is that a Brand Y cigarette will exceed that amount of tar.

Answer Key and Explanations

1. B	3. C	5. C	7. C	9. A	11. B
2. B	4. B	6. A	8. D	10. D	12. D

1. **The correct answer is B.** List the given ticket costs from least to greatest:

   $283, $298, $304, $312, $356

   Add $77 to the least cost to determine if the unknown cost is also the greatest cost:

   $$283 + 77 = 360$$

   Use the value to find the median of the tickets:

   $283, $298, $304, $312, $356, $360

   Find the average (mean) of $304 and $312, which is $308. The unknown ticket cost is $360.

2. **The correct answer is B.**

$$\begin{aligned}\frac{3(86)+x}{4} &= 88\\ 258+x &= 352\\ x &= 94\end{aligned}$$

3. **The correct answer is C.** First, put the ages of the presidents in order.

   43, 46, 47, 51, 52, 54, 54, 55, 56, 60, 61, 62, 64, 69

   The mode of their ages is 54, which is the only repeated age.

   The median of their ages is the middle number, which is the average of 54 and 55, or 54.5.

   The average or arithmetic mean is found by adding their ages and dividing by 14.

$$\frac{43+46+47+51+52+54+54+55+56+60+61+62+64+69}{14}$$

$$\begin{aligned}&= \frac{774}{14}\\ &= 55.3\end{aligned}$$

   Now order the three values: 54 < 54.5 < 55.3, which means that mode < median < mean.

4. **The correct answer is B.** The probability of Salena winning first prize is $\frac{7}{50}$. Once that prize is awarded, that winning ticket is discarded from the original lot of 50 tickets, and the next one is selected for second prize. The probability of Salena winning second prize is $\frac{6}{49}$. The probability that she wins both first and second prizes is the product of these two numbers:

$$\frac{7}{50} \bullet \frac{6}{49} = \frac{3}{175}$$

5. **The correct answer is C.** There are 61 total people who play platform games. Of those 61 people, 19 play for 3–5 hours, so the probability is $\frac{19}{61}$.

6. **The correct answer is A.** The probability that the first selection is a defenders is $\frac{6}{20}$. The second selection is made from a lot of 19 players, 5 of whom are defenders; the probability that the second selection is a defenders is $\frac{5}{19}$. Finally, the third selection is made from a lot of 18 players, 4 of whom are defenders; the probability that the third selection is a defender is $\frac{4}{18}$. The probability that three defenders are selected is the product of these probabilities:

$$\frac{6}{20} \bullet \frac{5}{19} \bullet \frac{4}{18} = \frac{1}{57}$$

7. **The correct answer is C.** The interval containing 95% of the data is 35 – 2(4.25) = 26.5 to 35 + 2(4.25) = 43.5. This is the majority of the time, so statement C is true.

8. **The correct answer is D.** Although the interview at the rally would yield the greatest number of respondents, the population of political-event attendees—only 15 percent of all students—probably differs from the general population of students in their opinions about public policy issues, including climate change. Similarly, in a physics lab, the students interviewed are more likely to be science students; their opinions, though possibly more authoritative, could be expected to differ from the larger population of university students. Random selection from the entire student body is most likely to provide a sample that represents the general population, and the larger sample in choice D makes it more reliable than choice C. There is no reason to think that the offer of a small incentive would bias the sample.

9. **The correct answer is A.** Use the equation of the line of best fit to make predictions. Plug in 500 for the *x*-value:

$$y = 2(500) + 380 = 1{,}000 + 380 = 1{,}380$$

10. **The correct answer is D.** Extrapolating from the second survey, we can predict that $\frac{665}{1{,}000} = 66.5\%$ of the total population of the northeast will likely be interested in taking adult education classes. Applying this to the total northeast population who reported that they did not attend college: $68{,}350 \times 0.665 = 45{,}453$ people in this population are likely to be interested in adult education classes.

11. **The correct answer is B.** See the estimated lines of best fit for women (W) and men (M):

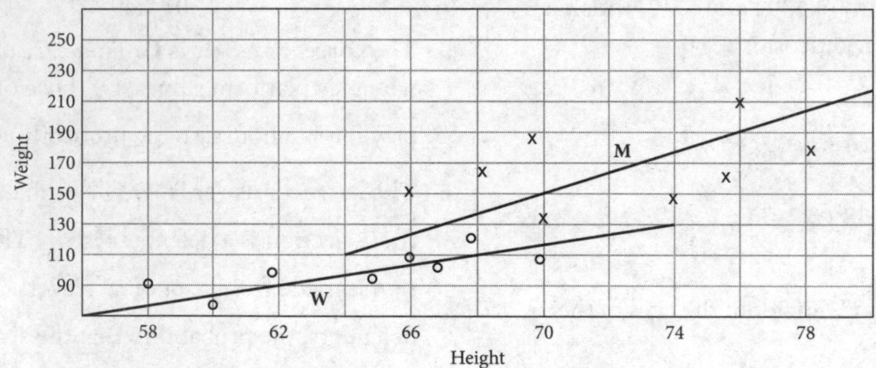

The o's generally are closer to line W than the x's are to line M, so the correlation is stronger for women. The slope of line W is about $\frac{1}{3}$; for M it is roughly $\frac{2}{3}$.

12. **The correct answer is D.** To calculate the mean tar per cigarette for Brand X, divide the total amount of tar in all Brand X cigarettes by the number of cigarettes, 16. Based on the bar chart we have the following (note: inside the parentheses is the amount of tar multiplied by the number of cigarettes with that much tar):

$$\frac{(4\times2)+(8\times1)+(12\times2)+(16\times6)+(20\times5)}{16} = \frac{236}{16} = 14.75$$

For Brand Y the corresponding calculation is:

$$\frac{(8\times2)+(12\times2)+(16\times11)+(20\times1)}{16} = \frac{236}{16} = 14.75$$

The average tar per cigarette is 14.75 milligrams for both brands. Only choice D correctly states that this average is the same for both. The statement that tar in Brand X is more variable than in Brand Y is also correct. Note as well that 5 of 16 tested Brand X cigarettes had more than 18 mg of tar, but only 1 of 16 Brand Y cigarettes exceeded that amount.

CHAPTER

Math Tips and Strategies

MATH TIPS AND STRATEGIES

OVERVIEW

When it comes to performing well on the SAT Math section modules, it helps to know the math. But even when you know the math (and sometimes when you don't), there are steps that you can take to improve your speed, make strategic guesses, and help you solve questions when what you need to do isn't perfectly apparent.

We've spent the last few chapters helping you review the math skills you'll need to perform your best on the SAT Math section. Now, we'll fill you in on some strategies that can help you make the most of the time you're provided to maximize your score. This chapter contains lots of advice on how to approach the Math section and save time as you work through it.

15

REFLECTING ON YOUR DIAGNOSTIC TEST SCORE

Just as we had you do for SAT Reading and Writing, start this section by revisiting your score charts from Chapter 2: Diagnostic Test and your reflections on your Mathematics test performance in Chapter 3. The process of reflecting on your diagnostic test performance is useful because it provides information about who you are as a learner and test taker. With this information, you can make thoughtful decisions about how to select and apply strategies for the SAT Math section. Take a few moments to reflect on your performance when you first started studying for the Math section. You can do so in your head, take notes on your own, or use this table to jot down some ideas.

DIAGNOSTIC TEST REFLECTION: MATH	
Math Diagnostic Section Score: __________	**Math Section Scoring Goal: __________**
Reflection Question	**Notes**
What went well for you during the diagnostic test, and which skills were easiest for you to use?	
What did you struggle with during the diagnostic test, or which skills were harder for you to use?	
Did you feel rushed? Did you have time left over?	
How close were you to your goal?	
After reviewing math skills in the last few chapters, what are some things you might like to keep in mind as you study further?	
What are some aspects of approaching the SAT Math section for which you are hoping to build strategies?	

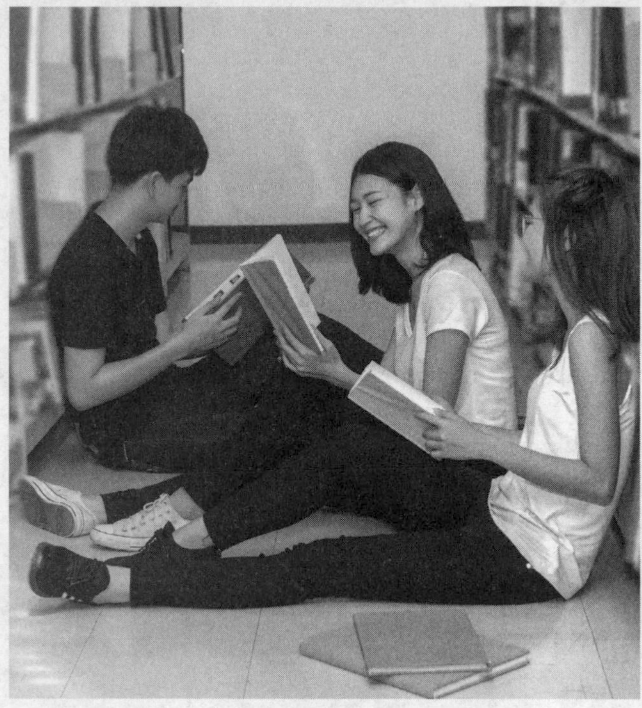

Reflecting on these questions should give you some useful feedback that you can now apply to determining your goals for the Math section. Test takers hoping to achieve a perfect score will have to approach things differently than those who want to outperform the average score. Your goal does not have to stay fixed but rather should change as you continue to build your math knowledge and practice. SAT Math largely depends on what you know. Your goal and your past performance should direct what math subjects you study, how much you study, and how you approach the questions in the test section.

GENERAL SAT® MATH TIPS AND STRATEGIES

In general, you have a considerable amount of time for each question in the SAT Math section. That doesn't mean that time management isn't important, but it does mean that your focus should be on accuracy. That comes down to a combination of using all the time you have to think through questions carefully and knowing how to use the design of the test and the style of the questions to your advantage.

SAT Math Section Key Details

To decide how you'll approach questions in the SAT Math section, you'll need to consider your performance on the diagnostic test in Chapter 2 as well as a few key characteristics of the test, as listed below:

- For each module, you have 35 minutes to answer 22 questions—roughly 1 minute and 40 seconds to answer each question.
- Using the Bluebook interface, you can cross out answers for multiple-choice questions and mark questions to review later.
- About 75% of the questions will be multiple choice while 25% will be student-produced responses (SPR), where you'll have to fill in an answer.
- In each module, questions generally progress from easier to harder—or simpler to more complex (in terms of question length, steps, and complexity level of subject matter).
- Most of the questions in each module will be focused on algebra (linear equations and inequalities) and more advanced math (functions, quadratics, polynomials, etc.). Some questions focus on problem-solving, data analysis, and geometry, but these are less common.
- If you perform well with the first module, then the second module, on average, will be harder. If you perform poorly with the first module, the second module, on average, will be easier.
- Your section score is capped below a certain level if you end up in the easier second module (perhaps as low as 600) because of how many questions you have already missed for the section.
- Answering around 60% of the questions correctly (about 26 questions) will put you around the average score for test takers.
- When multiple-choice questions have numbers for answers, the answers are put in order from lowest to highest or highest to lowest.
- All figures are drawn to scale unless otherwise stated.

15

SAT Math Goals

To maximize your score on the SAT Math section as a whole, you'll want to strive to do the following when taking your test:

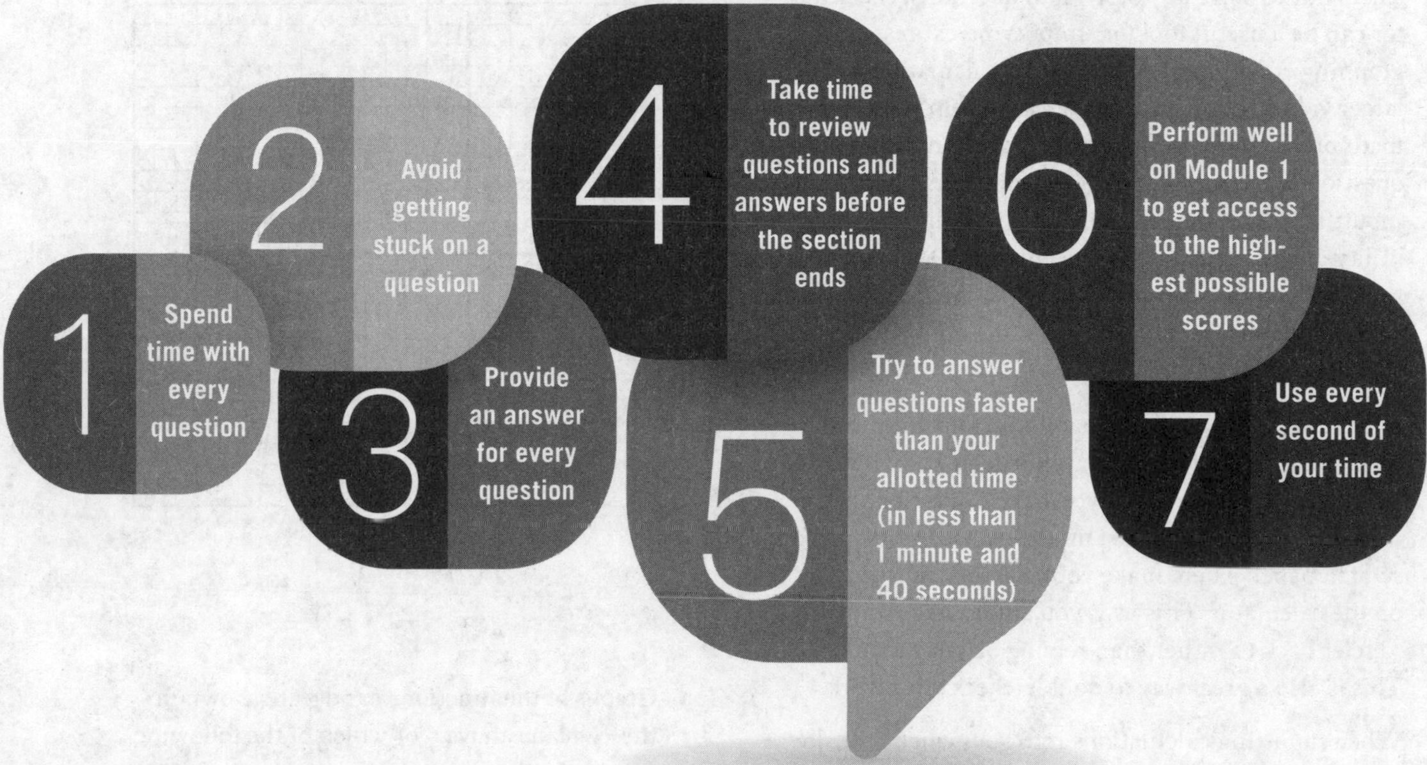

1
Spend time with every question
2
Avoid getting stuck on a question
3
Provide an answer for every question
4
Take time to review questions and answers before the section ends
5
Try to answer questions faster than your allotted time (in less than 1 minute and 40 seconds)
6
Perform well on Module 1 to get access to the highest possible scores
7
Use every second of your time

All of that information can inform how you approach the Math modules, depending on your goals, your strengths, and your weaknesses. In general, you'll want to adopt a step-by-step process that not only makes use of the time you have for each question but also minimizes the kinds of simple errors that test takers often make. Ultimately, your performance depends on your math knowledge and skills, but take time to practice and develop awareness of how the SAT presents its questions so you can maximize your score.

SAT Math Question Steps

Given what you know about the Math section, as you work through questions in the modules, you'll want to do the following:

1. Read the question.
2. Identify the question's goal, any given information, and any applicable concepts.
3. Solve the problem—either through calculation or with specific strategies.
4. Track your work on paper and check it with a calculator.
5. Record your answer.
6. Reread the question after recording your answer.
7. If you're unsure of an answer and you've used up most of your time for a question, guess, mark the question, and return after answering all other questions.

This process will change depending on the type of question you're dealing with (multiple choice or SPR) and other traits that you encounter. However, this general approach ensures that you take time to understand the question, check your work, and identify when you feel confident and when you need to spend more time to reach your scoring goals.

Use Your Calculator Strategically

Even though you can use a calculator for all of the SAT Math questions, keep in mind that you don't *need* a calculator to solve any SAT math questions. A calculator can be a useful tool for simplifying expressions, graphing equations, or performing calculations with larger values, but it won't necessarily help you solve a math problem if you don't first understand what the question is asking you to find. Sometimes, though, inputting equations and functions into the graphing utility of your calculator or the built-in Desmos calculator in Bluebook can reveal information that may help you better conceptualize the question and work toward a correct answer.

In general, try making it a habit to set up your work on paper first, and then plug the information into the calculator. For example, if you have a question that deals with an equation, set up the equation first on your scratch paper. Then, make your number substitutions on the calculator. This way, you always have something to refer back to rather than relying on your memory. This is also a great way to double-check your work.

When inputting calculations into your calculator, do the following:

- Check the display each time you enter numbers to make sure you entered them correctly.
- Clear the calculator between different calculations to avoid confusing outputs.
- Make appropriate use of parentheses to avoid issues with order of operations.
- Record your steps on paper for easier tracking.

Your Eye Is a Good Estimator

Figures in the standard multiple-choice math section are always drawn to scale unless you see the warning "Note: Figure not drawn to scale." That means you can sometimes solve a problem just by looking at the picture and estimating the answer. Let's look at a question from Chapter 2: Module 2, Question 7 rewritten as multiple choice for an example.

EXAMPLE

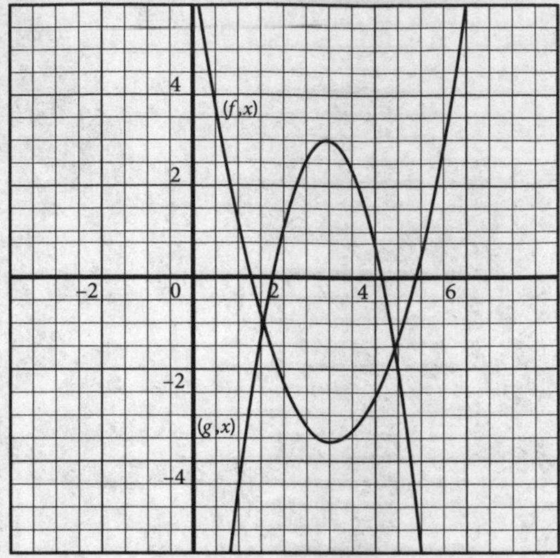

$$f(x)=(x-3)^2-3$$
$$g(x)=-2(x+3)^2-3$$

Graphs of the functions f and g are shown in the xy-plane above. For which of the following values of x does $f(x) + g(x) = 0$?

A. 1

B. 2

C. 3

D. 4

Solution

The sum of the function values is 0 when the function values for f and g are opposites. That appears to be true at $x = 3$. **The correct answer is C.** If you plug in that value into the sum of the functions and set them equal to zero, you can see that it is correct.

15

MULTIPLE-CHOICE TIPS AND STRATEGIES

The majority of SAT Math questions are easier than those on the math tests you take in class because the answers are right there in front of you. As you know from taking other standardized tests, multiple-choice questions always give you the answer—you just have to figure out which answer is the correct one. So even if you aren't sure and have to guess, you can narrow down your choices and improve your odds of being correct. The following section contains plentiful tips and strategies that can help you eliminate answers. Some of these strategies will also apply to Student-Produced Response questions but are easier to conceptualize for multiple-choice situations.

Solving Multiple-Choice Math Questions

While content knowledge plays a key role in your performance, there are steps you can take to make sure that you use your time to read and understand a question and that you did everything that a question asked you to do. Let's apply the general question steps from earlier in the chapter to some multiple-choice questions with some small tweaks:

1. Read the question.
2. Identify the question's goal, any given information, and any applicable concepts.
3. Solve the problem—either through calculation or with specific strategies.
4. Track your work on paper and check it with a calculator.
5. Eliminate wrong answers and record your answer.
6. Reread the question after recording your answer.
7. If you're unsure of an answer and you've used up most of your time for the question, guess, mark the question, and return after answering all other questions.

Now let's try out these steps on a couple of SAT-like multiple-choice math questions.

EXAMPLES

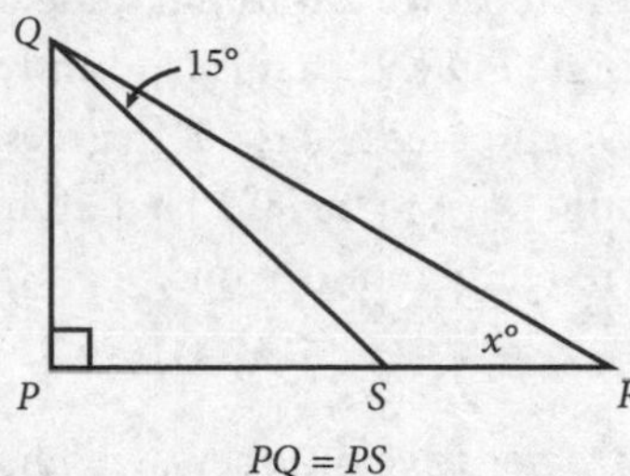

$PQ = PS$

What does x equal in the figure above?

A. 15°

B. 30°

C. 60°

D. 75°

Solution

This problem asks you to find the measure of one angle of right triangle PQR.

From the diagram, you know a few things about triangle PQR:

- $PQ = PS$
- Triangle PQR is a right triangle, as is triangle PQS.
- One angle in triangle SQR is 15°.

Two math principles apply:

1. The sum of the measures in degrees of the angles of a triangle is 180°.
2. 45-45-90 right triangles have certain special properties.

Since $PQ = PS$, PQS is a 45-45-90 right triangle. This means that angle $PQS = 45°$ and angle $PQR = 45 + 15 = 60°$. So angle $x = 180 - 90 - 60 = 30°$. Now look to see if 30° is among the answer choices. Indeed, it's listed in choice B. **The correct answer is B.** None of the other choices satisfy the principles for triangles, so they can be eliminated.

Before we move on, let's consider one more thing: did we answer the question? We can evaluate our steps: we found the value of x, 30°, in triangle PQR. If that is true and x, angle S, equals 30° and angle Q is 60° degrees, then angle P would have to be 90°. That all makes sense. You're ready to move on.

If x and y are negative numbers, which of the following is negative?

A. xy

B. $(xy)^2$

C. $(x - y)^2$

D. $x + y$

Solution

This problem asks you to pick an expression that is a negative number when the values of variables x and y are negative numbers. The principles that apply are those governing operations with signed numbers, leading us to the following:

- Since x and y are negative, choice A must be positive.
- As for choices B and C, as long as x and y are not equal to each other, both expressions must be positive. (If they're equal, the expression equals zero, and any number other than zero squared gives a positive result.)
- Choice D is negative since it represents the sum of two negative numbers.

If you are having trouble working with the letters for the variables, try substituting numbers for x and y to see which answer option is negative, but you should use the method that is easiest for you. Regardless, at this point, you've evaluated each answer choice and have found reasons to eliminate three of the four answers.

The correct answer is D. In rereading the question, did you find an expression that results in a negative number when both variables are negative? Yes, so you can move on.

Answer the Question Being Asked

SAT Math questions can test not only your math knowledge but also your attention. Sometimes, you may not be finished with a question even though you've done the bulk of the calculations required. Some SAT Math questions will have you solve for a value and then modify your work in some way. Suppose that you were asked to solve the following problem.

EXAMPLE

If $5x + 11 = 31$, what is the value of $x + 4$?

A. 4

B. 6

C. 8

D. 10

Solution

The first step is to solve the equation $5x + 11 = 31$.

$$5x + 11 = 31 \quad \text{Subtract 11 from both sides.}$$
$$5x = 20 \quad \text{Divide both sides by 5.}$$
$$x = 4$$

Your solution is among the given answer choices, choice A, but remember the goal of the question. The problem does not ask for the value of x; it asks for the value of $x + 4$, so the answer is actually 8. **The correct answer is C.** Make certain that the answer you select is the answer to the question that is being asked. To do so, take a few seconds to reread the question before moving on.

The Question Number Often Tells You How Hard the Question Is

Within each module, SAT Math questions will generally move from easier to harder as the test goes along. The first module will tend to have a relatively even distribution of difficulty. Easier questions will appear more regularly early in the module, and harder questions will appear more frequently toward the end. This same logic will apply for the second module, but due to the newly adaptive nature of the SAT Digital Test, what you see will depend on your performance.

If you score particularly well on the first module, the questions in the second module will have a higher difficulty level on average, but they will still adhere to the same difficulty pattern of easier to harder questions. Think of it as the difficulty floor being raised at the start. Similarly, if your first module needs some improvement, the second module will have a lower level of difficulty on average.

In order to reach higher scores, you will have to be able to successfully answer the majority of the questions, and this includes some of the more difficult ones. Knowing what to expect as you move through the questions is a key strategy in planning out your time and efforts. Take a look at these three examples. Don't solve them yet; just read the questions to get a sense of how the difficulty level changes from question 1 to question 12 to question 18.

EXAMPLE

1. If $\frac{a+5}{6}=m$ and $m = 9$, what is the value of a?

   A. 24

   B. 49

   C. 59

   D. 84

12. Line a intersects the x-axis at (3, 0) and the y-axis at (0, –2). Line b passes through the origin and is parallel to line a. Which of the following is an equation of line b?

   A. $y=\frac{3}{2}x$

   B. $y=\frac{2}{3}x$

   C. $y=-\frac{3}{2}x$

   D. $y=-\frac{2}{3}x$

18. Fernand averaged a score of 182 for 6 games of bowling. His scores for the first three games were 212, 181, and 160. Of the remaining three games, two scores were identical, and the third was 20 points higher than one of these two games. What was the second highest score of these 6 games?

   A. 173

   B. 181

   C. 182

   D. 193

Easy Questions Have Easy Answers—Difficult Questions Don't

Earlier (and thus easier) questions are straightforward, emphasizing isolated concepts and fewer steps. For instance, for question 1, once you substitute 9 for m and solve for a, your answer is clear and no further work is required. You can easily discern that $a = 49$, choice B, with limited calculations and conceptual knowledge.

As you progress through the module, however, you find that the complexity of the questions grows. You may see the level of the math jump from pre-algebra concepts to trigonometry. The number of math concepts required to answer the question can increase. The length of the questions and your calculations can double. In general, you'll find that the information is complex and the answers aren't obvious. If it seems too easy to find the answer on a difficult question, you can bet that simple answer is wrong. To see this theory in action, let's take another look at Question 18.

EXAMPLE

18. Fernand averaged a score of 182 for 6 games of bowling. His scores for the first three games were 212, 181, and 160. Of the remaining three games, two scores were identical, and the third was 20 points higher than one of these two games. What was the second highest score of these 6 games?

A. 173

B. 181

C. 182

D. 193

Solution

Not only will this question take a little longer to think through, but there are also some complexities embedded in details of the question along with an unintuitive goal (the second highest score, not the highest).

To start, you've read the question, identified the goal, and considered the given information (the different scores) and applicable mathematical concepts (calculating average and set items with algebra). You might be able to guess that choices B and C are not going to be the answer as they appear in the question itself. However, we don't need to eliminate them right now.

Set up a calculation for finding the arithmetic mean, or average, of a set of data points. Let x represent the score of one of the two games in which Fernand scored identically. Then, the score of the third game is $x + 20$, indicating that the game was 20 points higher than one of the unknown games. Since the average of all six games is 182, solve the following equation for x:

$$\begin{aligned}\frac{212+181+160+x+x+(x+20)}{6}&=182\\ \frac{573+3x}{6}&=182\\ 573+3x&=1{,}092\\ 3x&=519\\ x&=173\end{aligned}$$

You've found the value of x. Remember, though, that you're looking for the second highest score, not the value of the two identical games, as represented by x in your equation. Therefore, the second highest score is $x + 20$, or $173 + 20$, which equals 193. **The correct answer is D.**

Notice how the question is designed to draw your attention to both information from the question (choices B and C) as well as an answer choice that acts as a key part of your calculations but isn't the final answer. Such things are not uncommon in SAT Math section question design.

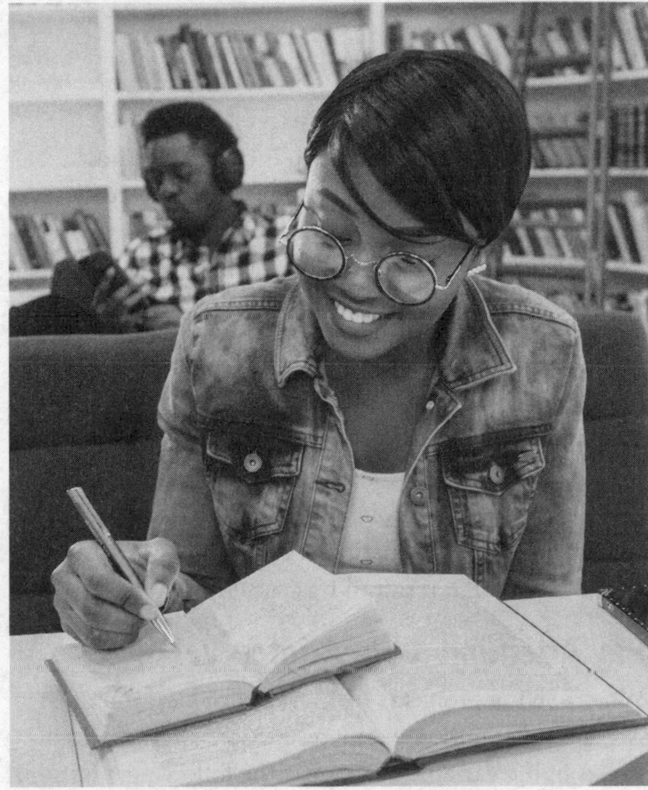

When Guessing at Hard Questions, You Can Toss Out Easy Answers

Now that you know the difficult questions won't have easy or obvious answers, use a guessing strategy. Remember, you are not penalized for incorrect answers, so guessing can't hurt. Start by scanning the answer choices and eliminating the ones that seem easy or obvious, such as any that just restate the information in the question. Then, depending on your time and knowledge, you can work through the question or take your best guess and return to the question later.

Try Working Backwards

Every multiple-choice math problem includes four answer choices. One of them has to be correct; the other three are incorrect. In certain situations, this means that you can plug each choice into the problem and sooner or later you'll find the one that works. Testing answer choices can sometimes be a much easier and surer way of solving a problem than attempting a lengthy calculation.

When working on multiple-choice math questions, remember that all of the numeric answer choices are presented in order—either smallest to largest or vice versa. As a result, when working backwards, it is better to begin with a middle option, choice B or choice C. This way, if you start with choice C and it's too large, you'll only have to concentrate on the smaller choices. With that, you've eliminated two choices quite quickly.

Let's try this process with a higher-level question from Chapter 2: Math Module 2.

EXAMPLE

In the *xy*-plane, the line determined by the points (8, *c*) and (*c*, 18) passes through the origin. Which of the following is the value of *c*?

A. 10

B. 11

C. 12

D. 13

Solution

Start with choice C because it may be easier to compute since it is an even number. The line through (8, 12) and (12, 18) is $y = \frac{18-12}{12-8}x + b$. This equation simplifies to $y = \frac{3}{2}x$, if the line passes through the origin.

Plug (8, 12) or (12, 18) into $y = \frac{3}{2}x$, and both sides will be equal.

$$12 = \frac{3}{2}(8) \quad \text{or} \quad 18 = \frac{3}{2}(12)$$
$$12 = 12 \qquad\qquad 18 = 18$$

The other values of *c* will not result in an equivalent equation. **The correct answer is C.**

Work with Numbers Rather Than with Letters

When a question hinges on variables and their relationships, it can be helpful to substitute numbers in for the letters rather than trying to work in the abstract. Consider the following examples.

EXAMPLES

If $x - 4$ is 2 greater than y, then $x + 5$ is how much greater than y?

A. 3

B. 7

C. 9

D. 11

Solution

Choose any value for x, but it's best to select a value that's easy to work with, such as $x = 4$.

Start by solving for x in the first equation. If $4 - 4 = 0$, and 0 is 2 greater than y, then $y = -2$.

In the second equation, if $x = 4$, then $4 + 5 = 9$.

Therefore, $x + 5$ is 11 more than y. **The correct answer is D.**

The cost of renting office space in a building is \$2.50 per square foot per month. Which of the following represents the total cost c, in dollars, to rent p square feet of office space each year in the building?

A. $c = 2.50(12p)$

B. $c = 2.50p + 12$

C. $c = \dfrac{2.50p}{12}$

D. $c = \dfrac{12p}{2.50}$

Solution

Let p, the number of square feet rented, equal 100. The rent for one month is then \$250 and the rent for one year is \$3,000. The only equation that will provide answers close to that value needs to be multiplicative in nature, $c = 2.50(12p)$. **The correct answer is A.**

If a question restricts the possible values for variables to an odd or even integer, then you can pick any integer that fits those constraints. In general, try to select values that make calculations easy. Avoid using 0 and 1 values as they can result in inaccurate outcomes.

Pay Attention to Restricted Values

When solving problems involving variables, you must pay careful attention to any restrictions on the possible values of the variables. Consider the following question.

EXAMPLE

If $x \geq 2$, which of the following is a solution to the equation $x(x - 3)(x + 4)(x + 2)(3x - 5) = 0$?

A. 2

B. 3

C. 4

D. 5

Solution

This equation has five solutions, but the goal is to look for a solution that is at least 2. Set each of the factors equal to 0 and solve for x. The only answer that is greater than or equal to 2 is 3. **The correct answer is B.**

Now, consider this slightly different version of the same problem.

EXAMPLE

If $x < -2$, which of the following is a solution to the equation $x(x - 3)(x + 4)(x + 2)(3x - 5) = 0$?

A. -3

B. -4

C. -5

D. There is more than one solution.

Solution

The solutions to the equation can be found by setting each of the factors equal to zero.

$$\begin{aligned} x &= 0 \\ x-3 &= 0 \\ x+4 &= 0 \\ x+2 &= 0 \\ 3x-5 &= 0 \end{aligned}$$

These lead to the solutions $x = 0, 3, -4, -2$, and $\frac{5}{3}$ respectively. Of these five solutions, only -4 (choice B) is less than -2. **The correct answer is B.**

Look Out for Extraneous Solutions

The procedure for solving equations involving square roots or algebraic fractions occasionally results in what are known as extraneous solutions. An extraneous solution is a number that is correctly obtained from the equation-solving process but doesn't actually solve the equation. Be sure to check your answer.

EXAMPLE

What value of x makes the equation $\sqrt{x+4}+15=10$ true?

A. -29

B. -21

C. 21

D. There are no solutions.

Solution

First, solve the equation.

$$\begin{aligned} \sqrt{x+4}+15 &= 10 \\ \sqrt{x+4} &= -5 \\ \left(\sqrt{x+4}\right)^2 &= (-5)^2 \\ x+4 &= 25 \\ x &= 21 \end{aligned}$$

It appears that the solution is choice C. However, if you check the solution $x = 21$ in the original equation, you will see that it does not make the equation true.

$$\begin{aligned} \sqrt{x+4}+15 &= 10 \\ \sqrt{21+4}+15 &= 10 \\ \sqrt{25}+15 &= 10 \\ 5+15 &\neq 10 \end{aligned}$$

The correct answer is D.

STUDENT-PRODUCED RESPONSE TIPS AND STRATEGIES

Now we will briefly examine the other kind of question you will see in the SAT Math section: Student-Produced Response (SPR) questions. These questions are distinct because you have to do the calculations and find the answer on your own; there are no multiple-choice answers from which to choose. Instead, you will enter your own answer into an input box.

Many students are intimidated by SPR questions, but they should not bring you significant concern. SPR questions test the exact same mathematical concepts as the multiple-choice questions. The only difference is that there are no answer choices with which to work. While this does prevent you from using some of the earlier strategies, such as eliminating incorrect answers and working backwards, it is worth noting that these questions are in the minority in each module. Overall, SPR questions make up around 25% of the questions in any given module. In other words, you will see around 5–7 SPR questions in a module, and they will be mixed in with the multiple-choice questions.

SPR questions also increase in difficulty over the course of the module, so you can plan accordingly just as you would with the multiple-choice questions. You can expect them to touch on each of the four domains, and the questions themselves will be structured very similarly to their multiple-choice counterparts. This does mean that you will have to have a confident grasp of the mathematical concepts at hand to correctly answer these questions. That said, if you have worked through the preceding chapters on math and then review them again before test day, you will be in a great place to succeed.

You can use the same general approach to questions that was introduced earlier in the chapter. The only real additional concern is that you take time to make sure you're entering your answers according to the rules for SPR questions.

Answering SPR Questions

In previous versions of the SAT, you would have had to mark these answers in special grid-in sections, bubbling in the correct numbers and writing them in boxes

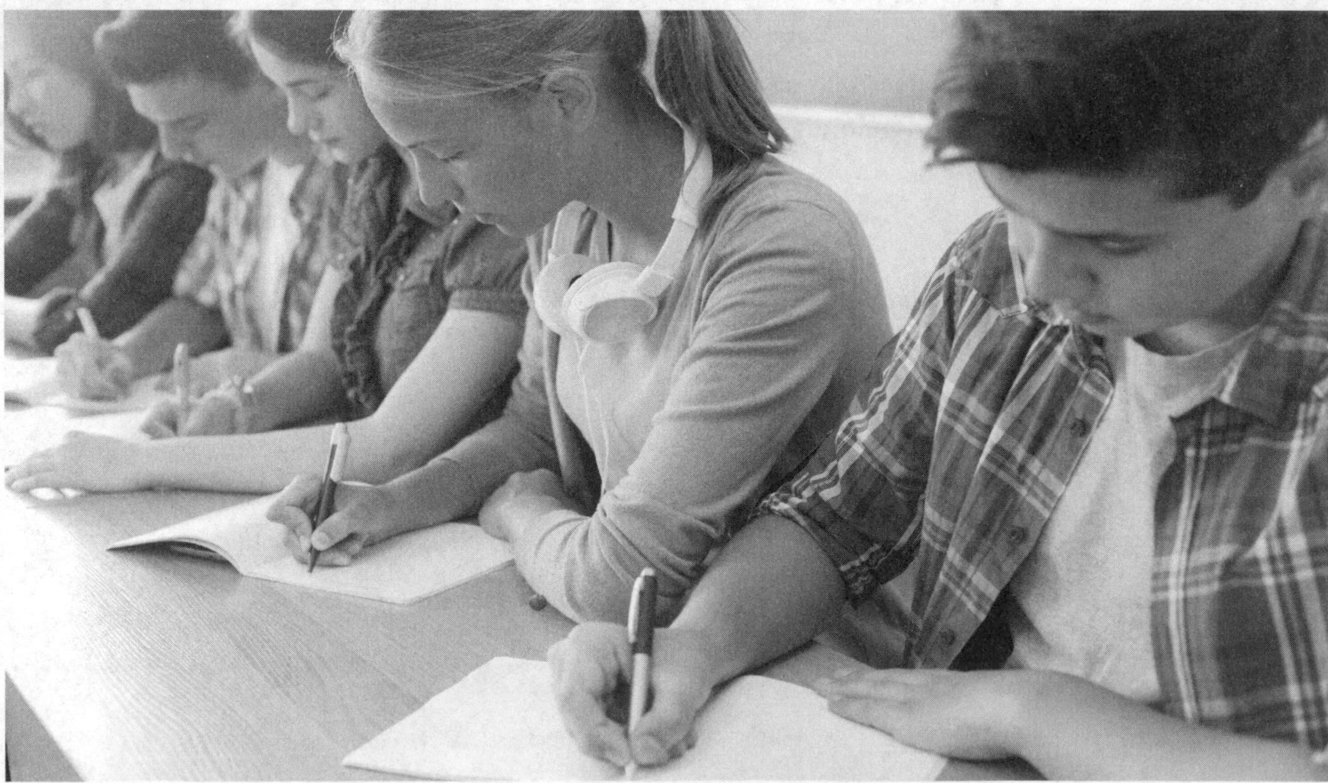

above. With the new SAT Digital Test, this system is no longer used. If you take the SAT Digital Test on a computer, there will be a small box under the question in which you can type your answer. This is the answer on which you are scored, so make sure to double-check for any errors or common typos (misplaced decimals, swapped digits, etc.) before moving on. Note that you are only allowed to enter a single answer, even if there may be more than one correct response to the question. In this case, you would choose one of the correct responses and type it into the box, as long as it meets the parameters of the question.

If you take the paper variant of the SAT Digital Test, the requirements have been similarly simplified. All you have to do is write your answer into your booklet beneath the question itself and circle it. You must circle your answer. If you do not, your answer will not be scored and will be counted as a missed point. As such, make sure to clearly circle your one, *and only one*, answer to the question. If you circle multiple possible answers, these will likewise not be scored. You are also free to use the space to write out your calculations, so make sure to distinctly circle what you intend to be your response.

Learn the Rules for SPR Question Answers

SPR questions also have a set of specific rules that dictate how you are allowed to type or write them in. Your test window or booklet will contain a reminder of these rules at the start, but it is worth briefly describing them here.

Answer Length

SPR answers have a strict cut-off of 5 characters for positive answers and 6 characters for negative answers, including the negative sign itself. This means that you cannot write any more than this at the risk of having your response marked as incorrect. If your answer is a particularly long decimal, you must cut it off or round it at the fourth digit after the decimal point. As a hidden benefit to this rule, it does mean that you will never be asked to work with particularly large numbers!

Mixed Numbers

SPR questions may involve fractions, both in the questions themselves and the answer that you provide. If your answer turns out to be a mixed number, meaning a combination of a whole number and a fraction (such as $4\frac{1}{2}$), you must instead write it as an improper fraction or a decimal equivalent. For the mixed number $4\frac{1}{2}$, its improper fraction form would be 9/2, and its decimal form would be 4.5.

No Symbols

SPR answers must not include symbols such as percent signs or even commas. It is likely that a question will ask you about a percentage or an amount in dollars, for instance. Just type or write the numerical answer without the related symbols and remember not to include a comma if the answer is one thousand or more. For example, rather than writing 11,254, your answer would simply be 11254.

Answers to SPR Questions Will Always Be Numerical

If you see an SPR question with algebra involving two unknowns, you know that you'll be able to eliminate one of the variables during your calculations. The reason for this is that all answers to SPR questions are numbers, whether integers, fractions, or decimals, and thus no expression with a variable can be a correct answer. You can use that information to help you determine how you should work through the question.

SUMMING IT UP

- Some of the SAT Math section's formatting and constraints can help you make decisions about how you work through the test:
    - You have about 1 minute and 40 seconds to answer each question. You should use all of your time in the section but should try to work a little faster on each question so that you have time to review your guesses or uncertain answers before time expires.
    - The Bluebook app lets you cross out answers. Use this feature to narrow down the answers you're considering.
    - Questions get progressively more complex as you move through the section, so keep this in mind for your use of time. If you spend too much time on the earlier questions, you may find yourself running behind later on.
    - If you perform well on Module 1, then Module 2 will be on average harder. Doing well on Module 1 is the only way to get access to the higher score range.
    - You can use a calculator for every question, but that doesn't always mean that you should.
- Develop a step-by-step system for working through each question. Doing so can focus your attention and help you avoid some of the traps SAT Math questions set out. Here are the steps we suggest, but you'll find that you may modify these as you practice to fit your specific strengths and weaknesses (or certain question types):
    1. Read the question.
    2. Identify the question's goal, any given information, and any applicable concepts.
    3. Solve the problem—either through calculation or with specific strategies.
    4. Track your work on paper and check it with a calculator.
    5. Record your answer.
    6. Reread the question after recording your answer.
    7. If you're unsure of an answer and you've used up most of your time for a question, guess, mark the question, and return after answering all other questions.

- Use a calculator where it can help the most: on basic arithmetic calculations, when calculating square roots and percentages, when comparing and converting fractions, and when dealing with graphs (checking equations and systems in the graphing utility).
- Figures in the math section are always drawn to scale unless otherwise stated. If you need to do so, use your eye as an estimator.
- Set up your work on paper, then enter the numbers in your calculator. This will help you in the event your calculation goes awry. This way, you don't have to try to replicate your setup from memory.
- Math questions are generally sequenced from simpler to more complex. The question number will clue you in as to how hard the question will be. Keep in mind that some of the difficult questions may be easier for you, and vice versa, depending upon your strengths and weaknesses.
- When it is more efficient and effective to do so, work backwards from the answer choices when they're numerical. When you do, start with choice B or choice C, which will allow you to eliminate answers that arc too high or too low.
- When you're working with variables and aren't sure how to solve, try to work with numbers instead of letters. This will help you avoid unnecessary algebraic calculations and abstract setups.
- Student-Produced Response (SPR) questions test the same fundamental mathematical concepts, but they do not have multiple-choice answers. However, the answers are always numerical.
- Make sure to type SPR answers into the provided input box on the digital test or circle your final answer on the written variant.
- SPR answers have a set of specific restrictions: positive value answers are limited to five figures; negative value answers are limited to six figures (including the negative sign); decimals must be cut off or rounded to their fourth digit after the decimal point; no special symbols are allowed (percent signs, dollar signs, commas, etc.).
- SPR answers are always numerical in form, even when questions are algebraic and involve multiple variables. Look for variables that can be eliminated.
- Check your work for SPR answers by plugging in your answer when it makes sense to do so.

PART V

PRACTICE TEST

CHAPTER

SAT® Practice Test

SAT® PRACTICE TEST

PRACTICE TEST

This practice test is designed to help you recognize your strengths and weaknesses. The questions cover information from both sections of the SAT. Use the results to help guide and direct any further study time and to measure your progress since the diagnostic test.

16

SAT® PRACTICE TEST ANSWER SHEET

Reading and Writing

Module 1

1. Ⓐ Ⓑ Ⓒ Ⓓ 7. Ⓐ Ⓑ Ⓒ Ⓓ 13. Ⓐ Ⓑ Ⓒ Ⓓ 19. Ⓐ Ⓑ Ⓒ Ⓓ 25. Ⓐ Ⓑ Ⓒ Ⓓ
2. Ⓐ Ⓑ Ⓒ Ⓓ 8. Ⓐ Ⓑ Ⓒ Ⓓ 14. Ⓐ Ⓑ Ⓒ Ⓓ 20. Ⓐ Ⓑ Ⓒ Ⓓ 26. Ⓐ Ⓑ Ⓒ Ⓓ
3. Ⓐ Ⓑ Ⓒ Ⓓ 9. Ⓐ Ⓑ Ⓒ Ⓓ 15. Ⓐ Ⓑ Ⓒ Ⓓ 21. Ⓐ Ⓑ Ⓒ Ⓓ 27. Ⓐ Ⓑ Ⓒ Ⓓ
4. Ⓐ Ⓑ Ⓒ Ⓓ 10. Ⓐ Ⓑ Ⓒ Ⓓ 16. Ⓐ Ⓑ Ⓒ Ⓓ 22. Ⓐ Ⓑ Ⓒ Ⓓ
5. Ⓐ Ⓑ Ⓒ Ⓓ 11. Ⓐ Ⓑ Ⓒ Ⓓ 17. Ⓐ Ⓑ Ⓒ Ⓓ 23. Ⓐ Ⓑ Ⓒ Ⓓ
6. Ⓐ Ⓑ Ⓒ Ⓓ 12. Ⓐ Ⓑ Ⓒ Ⓓ 18. Ⓐ Ⓑ Ⓒ Ⓓ 24. Ⓐ Ⓑ Ⓒ Ⓓ

Reading and Writing

Module 2

1. Ⓐ Ⓑ Ⓒ Ⓓ 7. Ⓐ Ⓑ Ⓒ Ⓓ 13. Ⓐ Ⓑ Ⓒ Ⓓ 19. Ⓐ Ⓑ Ⓒ Ⓓ 25. Ⓐ Ⓑ Ⓒ Ⓓ
2. Ⓐ Ⓑ Ⓒ Ⓓ 8. Ⓐ Ⓑ Ⓒ Ⓓ 14. Ⓐ Ⓑ Ⓒ Ⓓ 20. Ⓐ Ⓑ Ⓒ Ⓓ 26. Ⓐ Ⓑ Ⓒ Ⓓ
3. Ⓐ Ⓑ Ⓒ Ⓓ 9. Ⓐ Ⓑ Ⓒ Ⓓ 15. Ⓐ Ⓑ Ⓒ Ⓓ 21. Ⓐ Ⓑ Ⓒ Ⓓ 27. Ⓐ Ⓑ Ⓒ Ⓓ
4. Ⓐ Ⓑ Ⓒ Ⓓ 10. Ⓐ Ⓑ Ⓒ Ⓓ 16. Ⓐ Ⓑ Ⓒ Ⓓ 22. Ⓐ Ⓑ Ⓒ Ⓓ
5. Ⓐ Ⓑ Ⓒ Ⓓ 11. Ⓐ Ⓑ Ⓒ Ⓓ 17. Ⓐ Ⓑ Ⓒ Ⓓ 23. Ⓐ Ⓑ Ⓒ Ⓓ
6. Ⓐ Ⓑ Ⓒ Ⓓ 12. Ⓐ Ⓑ Ⓒ Ⓓ 18. Ⓐ Ⓑ Ⓒ Ⓓ 24. Ⓐ Ⓑ Ⓒ Ⓓ

Math

Module 1

1. Ⓐ Ⓑ Ⓒ Ⓓ	6. ________	11. ________	16. ________	21. Ⓐ Ⓑ Ⓒ Ⓓ
2. Ⓐ Ⓑ Ⓒ Ⓓ	7. ________	12. Ⓐ Ⓑ Ⓒ Ⓓ	17. Ⓐ Ⓑ Ⓒ Ⓓ	22. ________
3. Ⓐ Ⓑ Ⓒ Ⓓ	8. Ⓐ Ⓑ Ⓒ Ⓓ	13. Ⓐ Ⓑ Ⓒ Ⓓ	18. ________	
4. Ⓐ Ⓑ Ⓒ Ⓓ	9. Ⓐ Ⓑ Ⓒ Ⓓ	14. Ⓐ Ⓑ Ⓒ Ⓓ	19. Ⓐ Ⓑ Ⓒ Ⓓ	
5. Ⓐ Ⓑ Ⓒ Ⓓ	10. Ⓐ Ⓑ Ⓒ Ⓓ	15. Ⓐ Ⓑ Ⓒ Ⓓ	20. Ⓐ Ⓑ Ⓒ Ⓓ	

Math

Module 2

1. Ⓐ Ⓑ Ⓒ Ⓓ	6. Ⓐ Ⓑ Ⓒ Ⓓ	11. ________	16. Ⓐ Ⓑ Ⓒ Ⓓ	21. ________
2. Ⓐ Ⓑ Ⓒ Ⓓ	7. ________	12. Ⓐ Ⓑ Ⓒ Ⓓ	17. Ⓐ Ⓑ Ⓒ Ⓓ	22. ________
3. Ⓐ Ⓑ Ⓒ Ⓓ	8. Ⓐ Ⓑ Ⓒ Ⓓ	13. Ⓐ Ⓑ Ⓒ Ⓓ	18. Ⓐ Ⓑ Ⓒ Ⓓ	
4. Ⓐ Ⓑ Ⓒ Ⓓ	9. Ⓐ Ⓑ Ⓒ Ⓓ	14. Ⓐ Ⓑ Ⓒ Ⓓ	19. Ⓐ Ⓑ Ⓒ Ⓓ	
5. Ⓐ Ⓑ Ⓒ Ⓓ	10. Ⓐ Ⓑ Ⓒ Ⓓ	15. Ⓐ Ⓑ Ⓒ Ⓓ	20. Ⓐ Ⓑ Ⓒ Ⓓ	

READING AND WRITING

Module 1

27 Questions—32 Minutes

Directions: The questions in this section address a number of important reading and writing skills. Each question includes one or more passages, which may include a table or graph. Read each passage and question carefully, and then choose the best answer to the question based on the passage(s).

All questions in this section are multiple-choice with four answer choices. Each question has a single best answer.

1. It wasn't until 1983, when Sally Ride became the first American woman in space, that future astronaut Mae Jemison truly set her sights on NASA. She applied a few times to the astronaut program before finally being accepted in 1987. After two years of ___________ training, Jemison was slated to join the STS-47 crew, who would head to space in 1992 aboard the space shuttle *Endeavour*, making her the first African American woman in space.

   Which choice completes the text with the most logical and precise word or phrase?

   A. rigorous

   B. superfluous

   C. ephemeral

   D. obnoxious

2. Maize, or corn, is indigenous to the areas of Central America the Maya had inhabited. It was not only a staple of the Mayan diet but also a critical symbol of the Maya people's spiritual relationship with the earth. Perhaps most importantly, the Mayans believed that humankind itself had come from maize since their creation folklore included the idea that humans had been ___________ by the gods using white and yellow corn. In short, maize was linked to virtually all aspects of Mesoamerican culture.

   Which choice completes the text with the most logical and precise word or phrase?

   A. illustrated

   B. fashioned

   C. imagined

   D. destroyed

CONTINUE

3. This text is taken from the 1891 story "A Scandal in Bohemia" by Arthur Conan Doyle.

   To Sherlock Holmes she is always "the" woman. I have seldom heard him mention her under any other name. In his eyes she eclipses and predominates the whole of her sex. It was not that he felt any emotion akin to love for Irene Adler. All emotions, and that one particularly, were abhorrent to his cold, precise but admirably balanced mind.

   As used in the text, what does the phrase "abhorrent to" most nearly mean?

   A. found in

   B. lost from

   C. loved by

   D. hated by

4. Astronomers around the world who contributed to the Event Horizon Telescope (EHT) collaboration celebrated in May 2022 when they achieved the impressive feat of finally capturing an image of Sagittarius A* (Sgr A*), the supermassive black hole at the center of the Milky Way. While it may seem shocking to learn that there is a black hole so close to home, scientists have long suspected there was such an object in the center of our galaxy. They based their suppositions about the existence of Sgr A* (which is pronounced "sadge-ay-star") on their observations of gases and objects orbiting that spot at the center of the Milky Way.

   As used in the text, what does the word "suppositions" most nearly mean?

   A. guesses

   B. locations

   C. facts

   D. statements

5. Family is very important in Bedouin culture. Since tribes are not tied to plots of land, it is the tribal family unit that helps Bedouins establish a sense of place and belonging. Most of Bedouin life is organized around a patriarchal structure that includes large, extended families wherein the head of the family is often called the sheikh. Certainly, the sheikh wields a great deal of power in deciding matters for the tribe, but other elders get a say in tribal matters as well, usually by participating in a tribal council.

   Which choice best states the main purpose of the text?

   A. It criticizes Bedouin culture for being too patriarchal.

   B. It explains the structure and role of family in Bedouin tribes.

   C. It clarifies what a nomad is and why Bedouin tribes are considered nomadic.

   D. It defines the Bedouin term *sheikh*.

6. In roller derby, two teams each skate laps around a track for two 30-minute intervals called "jams." While a roller derby team consists of fifteen skaters, each team only has five players on the track at a time—one "jammer" designated by a star on their helmet and four blockers who help protect the jammer. To score points for their team, the jammer must lap members of the other team, meaning complete a full loop to pass them on the track. <u>This means that blockers are uniquely tasked with both offense and defense since they must assist their own jammer in lapping opposing teams while also blocking the opposing jammer from passing them.</u> As a result of all the jostling and jockeying to pass, derby is known for its physical skirmishes, a trait reflected in derby participants' colorful nicknames, such as "Helmet-Bash Heidi" and "Debbie Destructor."

Which choice best states the function of the underlined sentence in the text as a whole?

A. It explains how the jammer may score points in roller derby.

B. It defines the multiple roles of the blockers in roller derby.

C. It illustrates the roller derby teams' uniqueness and creativity.

D. It provides examples of jammer and blocker plays that are most effective.

7. Jenny Holzer is a conceptual artist who frequently explores art as social commentary. The content of her text-based works is usually observations about human nature and everyday life. For instance, one famous work is called "By Your Response to Danger" (1980–1982). In one iteration, it is a bronze plaque that reads, "BY YOUR RESPONSE TO DANGER IT IS EASY TO TELL HOW YOU HAVE LIVED AND WHAT HAS BEEN DONE TO YOU. YOU SHOW WHETHER YOU WANT TO STAY ALIVE, WHETHER YOU THINK YOU DESERVE TO, AND WHETHER YOU BELIEVE IT'S ANY GOOD TO ACT." Holzer's intentional use of capital letters is designed to make an impact as capital letters tend to affect readers more than traditional letters. The sense of danger or urgency one feels when looking at a message in all caps is reflected in Holzer's assertion that you can learn a lot about someone based on how they act when alerted to danger.

Which choice best states the main purpose of the text?

A. To argue for Jenny Holzer's superiority over other conceptual artists

B. To provide insight into Jenny Holzer's creative process

C. To introduce biographical information on Jenny Holzer

D. To provide an example of how Jenny Holzer uses art as social commentary

CONTINUE

8. A large proportion of the people who are behind bars are not convicted criminals but are people who have been arrested and are being held until their trial in court. Experts have often pointed out that this detention system does not operate fairly. For instance, a person who can afford to pay bail usually will not get locked up. The theory of the bail system is that a person who gives bail will make sure to show up in court when they are expected to show; otherwise, their bail will be forfeited, meaning they will lose the money they posted for the bail. Sometimes, a person who can show that they are a stable citizen with a job and a family will be released on "personal recognizance" (without bail). The result is that the well-to-do, the employed, and those with families can often avoid the detention system. The people who do wind up in detention tend to be the poor, the unemployed, the single, and the young.

   Which choice best states the function of the underlined sentence in the text as a whole?

   A. It proposes an alternative to the use of the bail system as a means of operation.

   B. It supports the methodology of using bail in the detention system.

   C. It criticizes the use of the bail system in judicial practices.

   D. It specifies the premise of the bail system and its function.

9. At the forefront of new discoveries in the field of psychology and neurobiology is the recognition that the brain experiences grief as a form of emotional trauma, meaning that significant grief experiences are akin to post-traumatic stress disorder (PTSD). Like PTSD, grief experiences can activate the fight-or-flight mechanism, causing people to behave in ways that may seem irrational, unprompted, or confusing to onlookers. This is because when the fight-or-flight mechanism is activated in a person, their heart rate and blood pressure tend to increase, and their body releases specific hormones, like cortisol and adrenaline, that affect how they behave.

   Which statement can most logically be inferred from the text?

   A. PTSD can cause a fight-or-flight response.

   B. Grief feels more intense for those who have already experienced PTSD.

   C. Grief feels less intense each time a person grieves.

   D. Grief is a primary cause of PTSD.

10. Invasive species are those introduced into a habitat outside of their origin, most often through human-created means. This process could occur by introducing exotic animals as pets into a new environment, from animals traveling undetected on cargo vehicles, or even from trading new species of plants for agriculture. Unfortunately, there is ample evidence of many invasive species causing deleterious effects in their new environments. However, some scientists note that restoring or preserving the "original" ecosystem is nearly impossible because after hundreds of years of human impact, the precise nature of the original ecosystem is unclear. Further, they have also observed that some introduced species provide food or develop habitat for native species, even rare or important ones. These scientists therefore claim that ___________________

Which choice most logically completes the text?

A. despite the inherent difficulties, humans should strive to restore the ecosystem to a state as close to its original form as possible.

B. it is not a certainty that all invasive species directly harm their new ecosystems.

C. in essentially every case, invasive species are a benefit to their new ecosystems.

D. all endemic species have the capacity to adapt to invasive presences in their environments.

11. The following text is taken from Edith Wharton's 1927 novel *Twilight Sleep.*

> All [Lita] asked was that nothing should "hurt" her: she had the blind dread of physical pain common also to most of the young women of her set. But all that was so easily managed nowadays: Mrs. Manford (who took charge of the business, Lita being an orphan) of course knew the most perfect "Twilight Sleep" establishment in the country, installed Lita in its most luxurious suite, and filled her room with spring flowers, hot-house fruits, new novels and all the latest picture-papers—and Lita drifted into motherhood as lightly and unperceivingly as if the wax doll which suddenly appeared in the cradle at her bedside had been brought there in one of the big bunches of hot-house roses that she found every morning on her pillow.

According to the text, you can infer that Lita likely attended the "Twilight Sleep" establishment for assistance with which concern?

A. Major surgery

B. Childbirth

C. Drug rehabilitation

D. Psychiatric care

CONTINUE

12. Climate change presents today's scientists with numerous unique questions, not the least of which involves how to take advantage of alternative resources as traditional resources dwindle. To utilize more ocean-based resources, some scientists foresee entire cities on the ocean. At first, they will be built close to the shore. Later, floating cities might be located hundreds of miles at sea. These cities could serve many functions. Some of the people living there could harvest fish and sea plants, like farmers of the ocean. Others could operate oil and gas wells or work in undersea enclosures mining the ocean floors. Additionally, the floating cities could serve as terminals or stations for international travel, where ships could stop for refueling or repairs.

Which choice best states the main idea of the text?

A. Floating cities on the ocean are being considered as an alternative way of life that utilizes ocean resources.

B. Climate change is causing damage to the ocean's resources and ecosystems.

C. Ocean cities will work well in the future when we have more international travel.

D. Farmers can convert their traditional techniques to harvest fish and sea plants.

13. Atoms with very similar electronegativities form molecules that are nonpolar. The electrons of these atoms are shared equally, and their molecules are said to be electrically symmetrical. Atoms with moderately different electronegativities form polar covalent bonds. The electronegativity of elements can also be quantified into a numeric form and compared this way. If observed on the periodic table, elements are arranged in vertical columns called groups, or families, and in horizontal rows called periods. When looking at electronegativity values of a small section of the periodic table, one can conclude that ________

Electronegativities of Groups 1A–7A

1A	2A	3A	4A	5A	6A	7A
H 2.2						
Li 1.0	Be 1.6	B 1.8	C 2.5	N 3.0	O 3.4	F 4.0
Na 0.93	Mg 1.3	Al 1.6	Si 1.9	P 2.2	S 2.6	Cl 3.2
K 0.82	Ca 1.0	Ga 1.8	Ge 2.0	As 2.2	Se 2.6	Br
Rb 0.82	Sr 0.9	In 1.8	Sn 1.8	Sb 2.0	Te 2.1	I 2.7
Cs 0.79	Ba 0.9	Tl 2.0	Pb 2.3	Bi 2.0	Po 2.0	At 2.2

Which choice most effectively uses data from the chart to illustrate the claim?

A. Lithium (Li) and Calcium (Ca) would likely form a polar covalent bond.

B. there is little correlation between electronegativity and an element's period.

C. Hydrogen (H) and Barium (Ba) would likely form a nonpolar molecule.

D. electronegativity tends to increase from left to right in a given period.

14. Wind speed is influenced by the obstacles the wind confronts on the earth's surface. Scientists have classified various types of Earth's terrain into roughness classes: the higher the roughness class, the rougher the terrain. Roughness Class 0 represents water surfaces, roughness Class 2 represents sparsely populated agricultural land, and roughness Class 4 represents very large cities with tall buildings. The table below shows mean wind speeds observed at three different heights above Earth's surface, in three different roughness classes. Observation heights are represented in meters (m), and wind speed is represented in meters per second (m/s). According to this data, as the height above the ground decreases, wind speed ____________

Table 1

Height Above Ground (m)	Roughness Class	Wind Speed (m/s)
50	0	13.73
50	2	10.7
50	4	8.1
100	0	14.4
100	2	11.7
100	4	9.39
150	0	14.8
150	2	12.29
150	4	10.14

Which choice most effectively uses data from the table to illustrate the claim?

A. increases more rapidly in rougher terrain.

B. declines more rapidly in rougher terrain.

C. increases more rapidly in smoother terrain.

D. declines more rapidly in smoother terrain.

15. The sprawling Blue Ridge Mountains cover the Eastern United States, running northeast from Georgia to southern Pennsylvania and spanning more than ________________ is part of the larger range known as the Appalachian Mountains. When viewed from afar, these tree-covered geological wonders have a bluish tint that gives them their name. Just over a billion years old, the Blue Ridge Mountains are among the oldest in the world, providing a home for human, plant, and animal life for millennia.

Which choice completes the text so that it conforms to the conventions of Standard English?

A. 500 miles and the mountain range

B. 500 miles; but the mountain range

C. 500 miles, the mountain range

D. 500 miles. The mountain range

SAT® PRACTICE TEST

CONTINUE

16. A quokka's most charming feature is its face; with round ears and a habit of looking like they're grinning from ear to ear, quokkas always seem happy to make your acquaintance. This appearance is matched by a tendency to trust and be curious ______________ exerting great effort to remind tourists that it's still best not to feed or interact too closely with these wild animals! Nonetheless, visitors to quokka habitats like Rottnest Island, home of the largest quokka population in Australia due to its lack of predators, have been known to pose for pictures with the smiling animals.

Which choice completes the text so that it conforms to the conventions of Standard English?

A. about humans a tendency that has conservationists

B. about humans! A tendency that has conservationists

C. about humans? A tendency that has conservationists

D. about humans—a tendency that has conservationists

17. The Jones Act, also known as the Merchant Marine Act of 1920, was established to require all import and export marine traffic to originate or terminate in the continental United States. This creates a problem for Caribbean territories of the US as it requires that any foreign-bound cargo must first stop in the mainland and then venture toward locations such as Puerto Rico and the US Virgin Islands. Many feel this contributes negatively to ______________ and other costs relating to foreign commerce.

Which choice completes the text so that it conforms to the conventions of Standard English?

A. their economic development: because it adds unnecessary tariffs

B. their economic development; because it adds unnecessary tariffs

C. their economic development, because it adds unnecessary tariffs

D. their economic development because it adds unnecessary tariffs

18. The Australian actor and writer Paul Hogan, formerly a bridge painter for the Sydney Harbour Bridge, is credited with bringing the country of Australia to the global mainstream viewing audience when he wrote and starred in the 1986 film *Crocodile Dundee*. The film became ________________ Australia's appeal as a worldwide travel destination.

Which choice completes the text so that it conforms to the conventions of Standard English?

A. a global and pop culture phenomenon: furthermore, it established

B. a global and pop culture phenomenon furthermore, it established

C. a global and pop culture phenomenon; furthermore, it established

D. a global and pop culture phenomenon, furthermore, it established

19. Between 1936 and 1938, Stalin's Soviet government executed around 750,000 people and interred another million in gulags. For authors like Anna Akhmatova, this period—known by historians as the Great Purge or Great Terror—was a particularly precarious one since any evidence of criticism toward the government could be used against them. So, what did Akhmatova do to make sure she and her poetry survived this period? She never kept a single written word. Instead, Akhmatova would create lines of poetry on paper, memorize them, then burn the scraps of paper. She regularly recited the parts she had already memorized so she could keep building on the poem over time. Akhmatova titled the poem "Requiem," and it ________________ one of the only surviving pieces of Russian literature written about Stalin's Great Purge while it was occurring.

Which choice completes the text so that it conforms to the conventions of Standard English?

A. became

B. becoming

C. is becoming

D. was becoming

CONTINUE

20. Divided into 17 autonomous communities, Spain is a European country that, along with Portugal, makes up the majority of the Iberian Peninsula. Often stereotyped as a nation of flamenco dancers and bullfighting, the reality is this country has varying cultural identities and traditions that are geographically separated by their self-governing, albeit limited, regions. Most are aware that Castilian Spanish is the origin of the Spanish language, which spread across Latin America as colonialism advanced during the 16th, 17th, and 18th centuries. Be that as it may, ______________ are three other major languages spoken in Spain: Basque, Galician, and Catalan, which carry the same name as their respective autonomous region. These languages are intrinsically linked to the cultural heritage that encompasses a land with thousands of years of history.

Which choice completes the text so that it conforms to the conventions of Standard English?

A. their

B. there

C. they're

D. they

21. Many so-called Baby Boomers remember where they were on November 22, 1963—the day President John F. Kennedy was assassinated in Dallas, Texas. On that tragic day, JFK and First Lady Jacqueline Kennedy rode through downtown Dallas in their motorcade when Lee Harvey Oswald shot and killed the president from the sixth floor of the Texas School Book Depository building. Oswald ______________ the scene, leaving his rifle behind, but he was apprehended 70 minutes later in a nearby theater. While being escorted in police custody, Oswald was shot and killed days later by Jack Ruby, a Dallas nightclub owner. There are many theories surrounding the details and intentions behind Kennedy's assassination that are still topics of debate today.

Which choice completes the text so that it conforms to the conventions of Standard English?

A. would flee

B. flees

C. had fled

D. fled

22. Often, mushrooms are considered notable because of their beauty, such as the veiled lady mushroom (*Phallus indusiatus*), which produces a fragile net that drapes down over its cap like a bridal veil. Examples of vividly colorful mushrooms are abundant: the amethyst deceiver (*Laccaria amethystina*), a striking purple mushroom usually found in forests; the white-speckled red mushroom known as fly amanita (*Amanita muscaria*), often depicted in illustrated children's books; and the vibrant indigo milk cap (*Lactarius indigo*), which oozes a milky blue substance when you cut into it. ________________, there are 80 different species of bioluminescent mushrooms that glow in the dark to attract insects. Like the devil's fingers mushroom, which does so through scent, such species have this adaptation to attract insects who can help the sporing process along.

Which choice completes the text with the most logical transition?

A. Clearly

B. Previously

C. Additionally

D. Whereas

23. Emerald ash borers are an invasive species in the US and Canada, killing up to 99% of ash trees in their path. ________________ adult emerald ash borers don't do much damage, the larvae feed on the inner bark, making it difficult for the trees to get the proper nutrients. Signs of an emerald ash borer infestation include D-shaped exit holes, woodpecker feeding holes, bark deformities, yellowing foliage, and more.

Which choice completes the text with the most logical transition?

A. While

B. Besides

C. Alternatively

D. As such

24. The most astounding thing about the human-like stone figures and other carvings erected at the Turkish archaeological site known as Göbekli Tepe is that they predate the invention of pottery and metal tools, making it difficult to conceive how prehistoric people were able to produce such a volume of artifacts with stone tools alone. ____________, discoveries made at the site offer incredible insights into how hunter-gatherers may have begun settling more permanently around seasonally significant landmarks, leading to the development of agricultural civilization.

Which choice completes the text with the most logical transition?

A. Moreover

B. Despite this

C. As a result

D. In summation

SAT® PRACTICE TEST

CONTINUE

25. Most of the early research on the microbiome–gut–brain axis has been conducted in rodents. Germ-free mice—which are born in sterile conditions and free of all microorganisms—are popular for gut flora research because scientists can inoculate the mice with specific microbes and observe the results. Experiments with germ-free mice have yielded intriguing clues about the possible influence of the gut microbiome on behavior and neurodevelopment. ___________, it is still unclear whether these findings are relevant to humans.

Which choice completes the text with the most logical transition?

A. Firstly

B. Finally

C. However

D. Above all

26. While researching a topic, a student has taken the following notes:

- Sojourner Truth was an American women's rights activist and abolitionist.
- She led an anti-racist and anti-slavery movement during the 19th century.
- Truth was born into a life of slavery but escaped to freedom in 1826.
- Truth gave speeches on the evils of slavery, championed women's rights and temperance, helped enslaved people to freedom, and assisted those recently freed with their transition to a new life.
- In 1851, at a women's rights conference in Akron, Ohio, Truth delivered her most memorable speech, "Ain't I a Woman?" The speech encompasses her passion for racial and gender equality and inspires resistance to the status quo.

The student wants to compare Sojourner Truth's life experiences before and after gaining her freedom from slavery. Which choice most effectively uses relevant information from the notes to accomplish this goal?

A. After gaining popularity as a civil rights activist, Sojourner Truth spent time later in life helping enslaved people to freedom and, once gained, assisting them with navigating their new lives.

B. As an enslaved person for the first part of her life, Sojourner Truth showed determination and resilience, risking her life for freedom; she continued this legacy of resistance by aiding and advocating for those who were just like her after she escaped to freedom.

C. Sojourner Truth was a powerful voice in the anti-slavery and anti-racism movements of the 19th century, never resigning herself or others to suffer under societal views and institutions that clashed with her ideologies.

D. Sojourner Truth delivered many speeches on her views about abolition, as well as women's rights and civil rights; her most famous speech is titled "Ain't I a Woman?"—first delivered at a women's rights conference in Akron, Ohio.

27. While researching a topic, a student has taken the following notes:

- The ancient supercontinent Pangea is believed to have split into two large landmasses over millions of years, eventually being separated by the Tethys Ocean.
- The southern formation that separated from Pangea, Gondwana, was proposed in the late 1800s by Austrian scientist Eduard Suess.
- Gondwana is thought to have included the Indian subcontinent, the Arabian Peninsula, South America, Antarctica, Africa, Australia, and Zealandia.
- The giant landmass to the north, Laurasia, included what is today North America, Europe, and parts of Asia.
- Laurasia was first postulated by South African geologist Alexander Du Toit in his work *Our Wandering Continents* (1937).

The student wants to present a timeline of the formation of the supercontinents. Which choice most effectively uses relevant information from the notes to accomplish this goal?

A. The supercontinent Gondwana, posited in the late 19th century, included the Indian subcontinent, the Arabian Peninsula, South America, Antarctica, Africa, Australia, and Zealandia.

B. The supercontinent Laurasia, postulated in 1937, encompassed what is today North America, Europe, and parts of Asia.

C. The giant supercontinent Pangea was formed millions of years ago and eventually split into two landmasses separated by the Tethys Ocean: Gondwana to the south and Laurasia to the north.

D. The two giant landmasses that split from Pangea were designated Gondwana by Austrian scientist Eduard Suess and Laurasia by South African geologist Alexander Du Toit.

STOP.

If you finish before time is up, you may check your work on this module only.

Do not turn to any other module in the test.

READING AND WRITING

Module 2

27 Questions—32 Minutes

Directions: The questions in this section address a number of important reading and writing skills. Each question includes one or more passages, which may include a table or graph. Read each passage and question carefully, and then choose the best answer to the question based on the passage(s).

All questions in this section are multiple-choice with four answer choices. Each question has a single best answer.

1. Shen Zhou was a Chinese artist who lived from 1427 to 1509, during the Ming dynasty. Zhou is best known for his landscapes, which are considered a revelation because they demonstrate an expertise and confidence that can only come from years of dedicated study. Even when working primarily with ink on paper, art historians note Zhou's skillful understanding of how to capture the qualities of light. Zhou tended to avoid being overly ostentatious, focusing instead on the subtleties of his subjects. One of his most famous works, a long handscroll entitled "Autumn Colors among Streams and Mountains," exhibits a sprawling landscape of delicate trees, rocks, and mountains elegantly rendered in textured brushstrokes.

As used in the text, what does the word "ostentatious" most nearly mean?

A. extravagant

B. modest

C. dull

D. vibrant

2. The following text is from Willa Cather's 1905 short story "The Sculptor's Funeral."

> The young Bostonian, one of the dead sculptor's pupils who had come with the body, looked about him helplessly. He turned to the banker, the only one of that black, uneasy, stoop-shouldered group who seemed enough of an individual to be addressed.
>
> "None of Mr. Merrick's brothers are here?" he asked uncertainly.
>
> The man with the red beard for the first time stepped up and joined the group. "No, they have not come yet; the family is scattered. The body will be taken directly to the house." He stooped and took hold of one of the handles of the coffin.

As used in the text, what does the word "scattered" most nearly mean?

A. overly depressed

B. widely dispersed

C. irate

D. currently fighting

3. The following text is taken from Camille Mauclair's 1903 book *The French Impressionists.*

As regards design, subject, realism, the study of modern life, the conception of beauty and the portrait, the Impressionist movement is based upon the old French masters. . . It has resolutely held aloof from mythology, academic allegory, historical painting, and from the neo-Greek elements of Classicism as well as from the German and Spanish elements of Romanticism. This reactionary movement is therefore entirely French, and surely if it deserves reproach, the one least deserved is that leveled upon it by the official painters: disobedience to the national spirit. <u>Impressionism is an art which does not give much scope to intellectuality, an art whose followers admit scarcely anything but immediate vision, rejecting philosophy and symbols, and occupying themselves only with the consideration of light, picturesqueness, keen and clever observation, and antipathy to abstraction, as the innate qualities of French art.</u>

Which choice best states the function of the underlined sentence in the text as a whole?

A. It clarifies common misconceptions about the Impressionist movement.

B. It illustrates the author's personal feelings about Impressionist artists.

C. It provides an overview of the guiding philosophy behind Impressionist art.

D. It praises the French masters for being the only ones to truly understand Impressionism.

4. The following text is taken from Frederick Douglass's 1881 essay "My Escape from Slavery."

I have often been asked how I felt when first I found myself on free soil. There is scarcely anything in my experience about which I could not give a more satisfactory answer. A new world had opened upon me. If life is more than breath and the "quick round of blood," I lived more in that one day than in a year of my slave life. It was a time of joyous excitement which words can but tamely describe. In a letter written to a friend soon after reaching New York, I said: "I felt as one might feel upon escape from a den of hungry lions." Anguish and grief, like darkness and rain, may be depicted; but gladness and joy, like the rainbow, defy the skill of pen or pencil.

According to the text, what is true about the narrator's experience?

A. He wants his figurative language to convey that the feelings he experienced were difficult to put into words.

B. He wants to compare his experience to those of great minds who came before him.

C. He deploys detailed imagery because he wants the reader to be able to imagine the scene exactly as he does.

D. He writes abstractly because he does not believe anyone will be able to understand what he experienced.

CONTINUE

5. **Text 1**

Unless completely deprived of a source of carbon, soil is packed full of microorganisms. Of the seven types of microorganisms found in soil, fungi account for the largest amount of relative biomass in soil, followed by bacteria and actinomycetes. Algae, protozoa, and nematodes are also present in soil to varying, much smaller degrees of relative biomass. Scientists collectively refer to these seven microorganisms as the "living" portion of soil organic matter (SOM).

Text 2

While scientists can predict that soil microbiomes are likely to survive the effects of climate change, the frustration comes in their inability to predict how. Much of this uncertainty stems from the complexity of soil microbiomes themselves. The intricate threads of life that exist between fungi, protozoa, bacteria, and other elements of active soil organic matter are so dense and complex that scientists have only just begun to unravel them. Since there is so much that is still unknown about how soil microbiomes operate, many scientists worry that our understanding of them is too elementary to effectively make predictions about or respond to how climate change will affect them.

Based on the texts, how does Text 2 relate to the information in Text 1?

A. Text 2 provides a current issue related to the general study of soil organic matter as described in Text 1.

B. Text 2 gives examples of different types of microbiomes found in soil organic matter.

C. While Text 1 explains the functions of microorganisms in soil organic matter, Text 2 describes the effects of climate change on these microbiomes.

D. While Text 1 hypothesizes the significance of soil organic matter in the future, Text 2 criticizes the lack of information on these microorganisms.

6. **Text 1**

Researchers are hopeful that further clinical research will highlight the potential benefits of psilocybin use for the therapeutic treatment of suicidality, post-traumatic stress disorder, addiction, and depression, among other conditions. One can expect that as psychedelic advocacy increases among medical researchers, so too will the potential for a wide range of therapeutic treatments that have heretofore been cut off from potential discovery. As the benefits of such therapies become clearer and demand for psychedelic therapy increases, we can expect the pace of clinical psychedelic research to accelerate accordingly.

Text 2

Even proper therapeutic applications of Schedule I psychedelics are not without dangers of abuse by patients and non-patients alike. Should Schedule I drugs like psilocybin become available, there is a strong likelihood that some who take them will form addictions and that the drugs will be more accessible for those who wish to abuse them recreationally. This is not to say that the likelihood of abuse precludes the potential benefits of clinical investigations into the therapeutic positives of such drugs, only that those who enthusiastically endorse more widespread access to these substances may unintentionally gloss over these dangers in their quest for scientific innovation. Any approach to research on use of psilocybin and other psychedelics for medicinal purposes would do well to take a long view rather than rushing to make these treatments widely available immediately.

Based on the texts, how would the author of Text 2 most likely describe the view presented in Text 1?

A. This view is problematic because it overstates the dangers of psilocybin use in therapeutic settings.

B. This view is problematic because it fails to acknowledge the potential dangers of psilocybin use in therapeutic settings.

C. This view is limited by a stringent adherence to existing research protocols regarding psilocybin.

D. This view does not adequately account for structural issues that would hinder psilocybin research.

CONTINUE

7. **Text 1**

At the beginning of 1990, the Berlin Wall had just been demolished. In its wake, the cities formerly dubbed East and West Berlin were tasked with knitting themselves back together into a unified urban space. During this period, decrepit ruins at what was now the city's center became a playground for students, artists, and activists working in commune-style collectives who shared a common drive. These groups wished to remake Berlin in their own image by squatting deserted spaces along the Wall's former path and transforming them to match their vision for the New Berlin. Though the main activity by squatting groups took place throughout 1990, the impact of the post-Wall squatters is still visible in Berlin more than three decades after the fact.

Text 2

As of 2022, a very small number of post-Wall squatter groups still occupy houses in Berlin. The commune at Rigaerstrasse 94 in Friedrichshain still exists, as does the punk-rock squatter's commune lovingly dubbed "Köpi" at Köpenickerstrasse 137 at the edge of Mitte; this space is known for being welcoming and artistic. However, the powers that be continue to target post-Wall squatter groups for evictions; for instance, one of the original squatting groups, Liebig 34, which had occupied Liebigstrasse 34 since 1990, was not evicted successfully by authorities until 2020 after a series of high-profile attempts during which the group forcefully resisted their mandated removal.

Based on the texts, which choice best characterizes the relationship between Text 1 and Text 2?

A. Text 1 presents a modern-day update to the historical information presented in Text 2.

B. Text 2 offers a modern-day update to the historical information presented in Text 1.

C. Text 1 critiques the claims made by the author of Text 2.

D. Text 2 critiques the claims made by the author of Text 1.

8. Around 66 million years ago, a huge asteroid struck Earth just off the coast of what is now Mexico. The impact would have super-heated the atmosphere, generated an earthquake 1 million times stronger than the strongest ever recorded, blasted 5,000 cubic miles of dust into the atmosphere, and released huge amounts of carbon dioxide (CO_2) into the air. Over the next few months, dust would blot out the sun, causing freezing temperatures and complete darkness. Highly acidic rain, formed from reactions in the heated atmosphere, would have fallen into the seas, killing marine organisms. After the dust cleared, the released CO_2 would have caused extreme global warming for as long as tens of thousands of years. All of these environmental effects could have caused organisms to go extinct relatively quickly in geological terms, over thousands of years. This hypothesis therefore implies that ________

Which choice most logically completes the text?

A. long-term effects on global temperatures were caused by carbon dioxide.

B. CO_2 caused a short-term decrease in the amount of sunlight reaching Earth's surface.

C. the extinction-triggering event took place over the course of many years.

D. environmental stresses following the extinction-triggering event were subtle.

9. When activist Malala Yousafzai, often known simply as "Malala," was growing up, the Pakistani Taliban instituted a prohibition on educating girls. As the daughter of an activist and educator, Malala's parents supported her when she decided to oppose the prohibition. During this time, the Taliban was routinely attacking girls for attending school or criticizing their policies, bombing schools that dared to educate girls and actively restricting women's rights. Despite the danger her activism posed, Malala continued her vocal opposition, blogging for the British Broadcasting Corporation (BBC) under an assumed name and making television appearances. While her efforts were recognized internationally, it didn't protect her from being targeted by the Taliban. Malala was shot in the head by a gunman from the Pakistani Taliban on October 9, 2012, while walking home from school. Miraculously, Malala survived this brutal attack, and it only made her more dedicated to her cause.

According to the text, what can you infer caused Malala to write for the BBC under an assumed name?

A. Since Malala was from Pakistan, she needed to assume a British identity to write for a British publication.

B. The BBC asked her to do so to avoid drawing attention to the paper.

C. As a young person, she assumed the identity of an older person to be taken seriously.

D. Malala wanted to protect herself from the Pakistani Taliban, who would have used the articles to target her.

CONTINUE

10. "The Slave Mother" is an 1854 poem by Frances Ellen Watkins Harper. In the poem, the author describes the agony of an enslaved mother whose child is being taken from her.

Which quotation from Frances Ellen Watkins Harper's "The Slave Mother" most effectively illustrates the claim that the poem is narrated by a witness to the event?

A. "Saw you the sad, imploring eye? / Its every glance was pain, / As if a storm of agony / Were sweeping through the brain"

B. "Saw you those hands so sadly clasped— / The bowed and feeble head— / The shuddering of that fragile form— / That look of grief and dread?"

C. "His love has been a joyous light / That o'er her pathway smiled / A fountain gushing ever new / Amid life's desert wild"

D. "No marvel, then, these bitter shrieks / Disturb the listening air: / She is a mother, and her heart / Is breaking in despair."

11. *Beyond Good and Evil* is an 1886 philosophical work by Friedrich Nietzsche.

Which of the following quotations from *Beyond Good and Evil* best supports the claim that Nietzsche used the work to argue that those with power are subject to corruption?

A. "To talk much about oneself may also be a means of concealing oneself."

B. "Love brings to light the noble and hidden qualities of a lover—his rare and exceptional traits: it is thus liable to be deceptive as to his normal character."

C. "The dangers that beset the evolution of the philosopher are, in fact, so manifold nowadays, that one might doubt whether this fruit could still come to maturity."

D. "He who fights with monsters should be careful lest he thereby become a monster. And if thou gaze long into an abyss, the abyss will also gaze into thee."

12. Heart rate, a measure of the number of heart beats per minute, rises as the body strives to meet the demands of physical activity. As one's resting heart rate decreases and as the degree of change in heat rate during exercise increases, fitness is said to increase. Recovery rate is the decrease in the number of beats per minute calculated for each minute following the cessation of physical activity until heart rate returns to normal resting levels. Greater fitness correlates with higher recovery rates. A high school swimmer and a high school basketball player participated for 10 continuous minutes in their respective sports while an electronic device measured their heart rates in beats per minute (bpm) over the course of their exertions. Both began with their heart rate at normal resting levels. Both athletes ceased physical activity after 10 minutes, whereupon the devices continued to monitor their heart rates during 5 minutes of subsequent inactivity. The results are indicated in the figure.

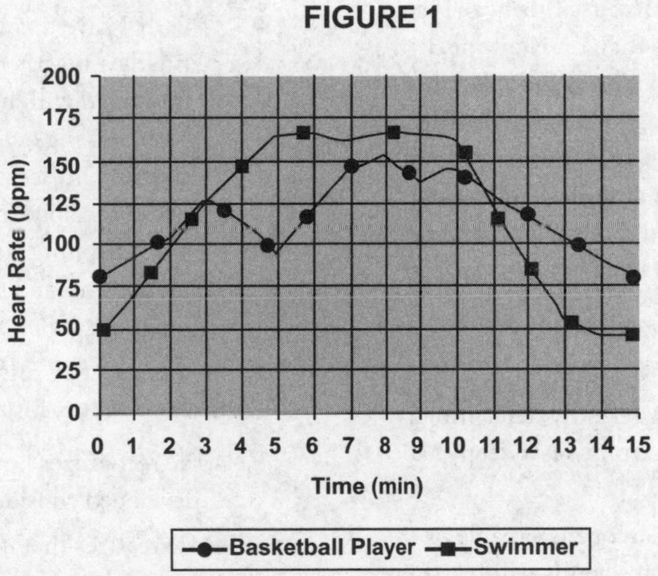

Which choice most effectively uses data from the graph to illustrate the claim?

A. The swimmer is fitter than the basketball player.

B. The basketball player is fitter than the swimmer.

C. Swimming is a more strenuous activity than basketball.

D. Basketball is a more strenuous activity than swimming.

CONTINUE

13. Why are Neptune and Uranus different colors despite being compositionally similar celestial objects? In 2022, scientists finally landed on a working hypothesis that could answer this question. Namely, observations taken from three different telescopes (Gemini North, the Hubble Space Telescope, and the NASA Infrared Telescope Facility) allowed scientists to create models of the two planets' atmospheres. What scientists found is that Uranus has a much thicker version of a particular type of atmospheric haze that is found on both planets. Because this haze is so much denser on Uranus than on Neptune, it tends to make Uranus's color appear blanched, such that it reads more as a deep cyan or turquoise than a true blue, like Neptune. Researchers suspect that were it not for this whitening haze, both planets would indeed appear to be about the same shade of blue.

    Which choice best states the main idea of the text?

    A. Scientists from NASA recently determined for the first time that Uranus is a deep shade of cyan.

    B. The Hubble Space Telescope is capable of discovering things that scientists didn't think were observable before.

    C. Scientists believe that the reason Neptune and Uranus are different colors despite being compositionally similar has to do with a certain haze that is thicker on Uranus.

    D. Scientists believe that the reason Neptune and Uranus are different colors despite being compositionally similar has to do with Neptune being much larger and colder than Uranus.

14. The following text is taken from Charles Darwin's 1887 book *The Autobiography of Charles Darwin*. The excerpt is taken from a section in which Darwin reflects on his time working as a naturalist aboard the HMS *Beagle*.

    > Looking backwards, I can now perceive how my love for science gradually preponderated over every other taste. During the first two years my old passion for shooting survived in nearly full force, and I shot myself all the birds and animals for my collection; but gradually I gave up my gun more and more, and finally altogether, to my servant, as shooting interfered with my work, more especially with making out the geological structure of a country. I discovered, though unconsciously and insensibly, that the pleasure of observing and reasoning was a much higher one than that of skill and sport.

    Based on the text, which of the following most accurately summarizes the narrator's key takeaway about his time aboard the HMS *Beagle*?

    A. He recognizes how his abilities as a scientist developed considerably during this time.

    B. He realizes that it was a job he was reluctant to undertake but glad to have.

    C. He identifies this point in his life as the time at which his interest in science began to supersede all his other interests.

    D. He remembers being bothered by his duties aboard the ship for interfering with his scientific research.

15. Today, the Vietnam Veterans Memorial is viewed as a groundbreaking and deeply moving structure. Historically, war had been seen as a necessary evil, one that required sacrifice and heroism in the face of death ________ toward war have changed. Monuments such as the Vietnam Veterans Memorial convey a complex relationship between the public and the necessity and purpose of modern warfare. Maya Lin's memorial, with its reflective black granite surface, places viewers' faces among the names of the dead, evoking a deeply private and personal connection with those who were lost. Prior to Lin's work, most memorials focused on the victors. But Lin's design shifted the focus to individual soldiers, both capturing America's shifting attitudes and forcing viewers to continue the reimagination of the relationship between our country and armed conflict.

Which choice completes the text so that it conforms to the conventions of Standard English?

A. and, destruction, however American attitudes
B. and destruction; however, American attitudes
C. and destruction however, American attitudes
D. and destruction? However American attitudes

16. One of the most important discoveries in quantum mechanics is the uncertainty principle, which was first proposed by Werner Heisenberg in 1927. The principle states that it is impossible to precisely measure certain properties ________. This means that the act of measurement itself changes the state of the particle, making it impossible to predict with certainty where a particle will be or how it will behave. The uncertainty principle has far-reaching implications for our understanding of the world, challenging our intuition about how things work.

Which choice completes the text so that it conforms to the conventions of Standard English?

A. of particles such as their position and momentum at the same time
B. of particles, such as their position and momentum at the same time
C. of particles, such as their position and momentum, at the same time
D. of particles, such as their position, and momentum, at the same time

CONTINUE

17. Fidel Castro seized control of Cuba in 1959 after six years of military and political conflict aimed at overthrowing the US-backed head of state Fulgencio Batista ___________ the Cuban Revolution. Once in power, Castro ruled Cuba under a communist regime for 49 years until 2008, stressing relations with the US as he demonstrated anti-imperialist ideologies and aligned with the Soviet Union. While some view him as a socialist and revolutionary hero, others see him as a dictator who drove Cuba's economic and social decline.

Which choice completes the text so that it conforms to the conventions of Standard English?

A. during the time period known as
B. during the time period, known as
C. during the time period; known as
D. during the time period: known as

18. In today's digital age, the internet has become an essential part of our lives. With the click of a button, we can access vast amounts of information and connect with people from around the world. However, it's important to remember that not everyone has the same level of access to these resources. In many parts of the world, especially in developing countries, there is a significant digital divide. ___________ prevent millions of people from fully benefiting from the internet's potential. Bridging this divide requires concerted efforts from governments, organizations, and individuals to ensure that everyone has equal access to the opportunities and knowledge the internet offers.

Which choice completes the text so that it conforms to the conventions of Standard English?

A. Limited infrastructure high costs and lack of digital literacy skills
B. Limited infrastructure, high costs and lack of digital literacy skills
C. Limited infrastructure; high costs; and lack of digital literacy skills
D. Limited infrastructure, high costs, and lack of digital literacy skills

19. The Mexican Muralist movement emerged around 1920, after the Mexican Revolution. A new government settled into power and contracted artists, or muralists, to paint large murals with the intention of spreading information without written texts to the Mexican people, many of whom were illiterate. The murals were intentionally painted in public places to spread the government's messages and promote pride in Mexican culture, history, and politics, yet unavoidably, the murals also included the ________ own ideas, which sometimes defied artistic and political norms. During the latter half of the 20th century, the influence of Mexican muralism spread throughout Latin America to portray and defy the oppression carried out by these nations' governments and leaders.

Which choice completes the text so that it conforms to the conventions of Standard English?

A. artist

B. artist's

C. artists

D. artists'

20. As with many old texts, the exact date of the composition of Shakespeare's *King Lear* is uncertain. However, there are records that indicate that the play was first staged around 1604. There were a number of sources for Shakespeare's version of the Lear story, although there is debate over which ones Shakespeare had actually read. He most likely ________ familiar with the basic story—a folk tale about a daughter who tells her father that she loves him as much as salt, but then she must prove that this means he is indispensable to her. Other sources included the anonymous play *King Leir*, Spencer's *The Faerie Queene*, and Higgins's *A Mirror for Magistrates*.

Which choice completes the text so that it conforms to the conventions of Standard English?

A. had been

B. was being

C. would have been

D. would be

CONTINUE

21. Victoria Falls, __________, is considered to be one of the seven wonders of the natural world for good reason. Visitors to the falls can spot columns of spray from up to 25 miles away, as millions of cubic meters of water per minute plunge 100 meters over a cliff. Anyone who witnesses this wonder will understand how it got the nickname "Smoke That Thunders." The roaring falls send up soaking billows of spray so enormous that they seem to defy reason.

Which choice completes the text so that it conforms to the conventions of Standard English?

A. which is a cataract composed of five actually separate falls

B. which is a cataract composed of actually five separate falls

C. which is actually a cataract of five separate falls composed

D. which is actually a cataract composed of five separate falls

22. Levittown, New York is largely considered the first major modern suburban settlement in the United States. Based on a prefabrication model created by the Levitt brothers, the community set the tone for American suburban development throughout the middle of the 20th century. It was lauded for its appeal and affordability, spawning the construction of new Levittowns in states across the country. __________, accessibility to the Levitt brothers' suburban dream was, at the time, limited to white families. Levittown housing covenants explicitly forbade people of color from buying homes. Once an African American family did eventually move into a Levittown in Pennsylvania in the 1950s, they were harassed and threatened. Even after decades of racial integration, many Levittowns are still predominantly occupied by white families to this day.

Which choice completes the text with the most logical transition?

A. In fact

B. Consequently

C. However

D. Accordingly

23. Goffman's dramaturgical model is a sociological theory proposed by Erving Goffman in his 1959 book *The Presentation of Self in Everyday Life*. The term dramaturgy, which is usually associated with the world of theatre, means "the practice and theory of composing drama." Goffman borrowed from his study of the dramatic arts, saying that theatrical drama is a good metaphor to represent the way people play-act to present themselves a certain way to the rest of society. ___________, social interactions are like scenes of dialogue in which the actors (humans in a society) are constantly acting and reacting to the norms and values communicated to them by others. Whether they follow norms or not is a matter of character, manner, and temperament, all of which are curated by the individual at both the conscious and subconscious levels to create a particular version of the self to present to society.

Which choice completes the text with the most logical transition?

A. At the time

B. In this model

C. As demonstrated

D. By contrast

24. While researching a topic, a student has taken the following notes:

- Gabriel García Márquez (1927-2014) was a Colombian writer and Nobel laureate known for his works incorporating magical realism.
- His most famous work is the novel *One Hundred Years of Solitude,* which brought magical realism into the literary spotlight.
- The novel is comprehensive tale of generations of the Buendía family in the fictional town of Macondo, Colombia.
- The novel incorporates magical realism through a narration style that portrays absurd and bizarre characters and events as normal and ordinary, interweaving fantasy with reality.
- The film *Encanto* (2021) channels magical realism through its enchanting storyline with subtle nods to García Márquez along the way.

The student wants to emphasize the importance of magical realism in Gabriel García Márquez's work. Which choice most effectively uses relevant information from the notes to accomplish this goal?

A. Gabriel García Márquez featured the Buendía generational tale in the fictional town of Macondo, Colombia, in his most popular magical realist work, *One Hundred Years of Solitude.*

B. The movie *Encanto* features magical realism and Colombia, both closely related to the world-renowned author Gabriel García Márquez.

C. The Colombian author Gabriel García Márquez wrote one of the most critically acclaimed magical realism novels of the 20th century: *One Hundred Years of Solitude.*

D. As a writer, Gabriel García Márquez was a master at interweaving fantasy with reality, resulting in what is called magical realism, a literary genre that put him on the map.

CONTINUE

25. While researching a topic, a student has taken the following notes:

- The deep ocean is considered as such once it goes beyond 200 meters in depth and very little light is available; once past 1,000 meters, it becomes devoid of all light.
- Roughly 95% of the unexplored ocean is deep and mysterious to humans as the harsh conditions make it virtually impossible to traverse without highly advanced technology.
- Once considered uninhabitable by any life forms due the lack of sunlight, new research has shown that there are organisms living in the deep ocean, including marine life such as fish and coral.
- At 11,034 meters (almost 7 miles) below sea level, the Mariana Trench is the deepest known oceanic trench on Earth and a prime location for exploration and research of the deep sea.
- Only around 20% of the ocean floor has been mapped, and only an estimated 10% of the ocean's species have been identified.

The student wants to clarify why studying the deep ocean is challenging for researchers. Which choice most effectively uses relevant information from the notes to accomplish this goal?

A. The deep ocean becomes devoid of all light once past 1,000 meters, and the Mariana Trench is the Earth's deepest known oceanic trench at 11,034 meters (almost 7 miles) below sea level.

B. The harsh conditions of the deep ocean make it virtually impossible to traverse without highly advanced technology; therefore, only around 20% of the ocean floor has been mapped and roughly 95% of the unexplored ocean is classified as deep sea.

C. New research of the deep ocean has shown that there are organisms able to sustain life there, including fish and coral.

D. At 200 meters below sea level, the term *deep ocean* is used to describe an area with very little available light; going to depths of 1,000 meters reveals an area that is completely bereft of light and difficult to navigate.

26. While researching a topic, a student has taken the following notes:

- Japanese artist Yayoi Kusama, often known for her incorporation of polka dots in her style and work, has been producing contemporary art since the 1950s.
- Kusama is one of the most influential and successful artists in the world, creating impactful paintings, sculptures, performance art, installations, literature, and even fashion.
- Her avant-garde work over the decades has included movements such as abstract and pop art, minimalism, and surrealism with feminist and environmental themes.
- Millions of people flock to museums and touring exhibitions around the world to get a glimpse of Kusama's talent and imagination as embodied in her art.
- Much of her work reflects trauma from childhood and World War II; Kusama has been open about her struggles with mental health, choosing to live daily in a psychiatric hospital since 1977.

The student wants to emphasize the topics from which Yayoi Kusama draws inspiration. Which choice most effectively uses relevant information from the notes to accomplish this goal?

A. Yayoi Kusama's avant-garde style has included feminist and environmental themes derived from her own struggles with childhood and war trauma, as well as mental health.

B. Every year, millions visit museums and exhibits to see firsthand Yayoi Kusama's work with its use of elements from abstract and pop art, minimalism, and surrealism.

C. Often known for her incorporation of polka dots in her style and work, Japanese artist Yayoi Kusama has been producing contemporary art since the second half of the 20th century.

D. Yayoi Kusama is one of the most influential and successful contemporary artists in the world, creating impactful paintings, sculptures, performance art, installations, literature, and even fashion since the 1950s.

CONTINUE

27. While researching a topic, a student has taken the following notes:

- Creating a geographical border between northern India and the southern edge of the Tibetan Plateau, the Himalayas of Asia are home to the highest mountains on Earth.
- At over 29,000 feet, Mount Everest, which is part of the Himalayan range, is the highest peak in the world.
- With exceptionally tall mountainous regions like the Himalayas, an effect called a rain shadow occurs where one side of the mountain range gets very little rainfall, resulting in desert-like conditions.
- The drier climate occurs on the leeward side of the range, which faces away from prevailing winds on the opposite, or windward, side.
- In the case of the Himalayan mountains, the arid rain shadow desert occurs along the Tibetan Plateau and continues through Central Asia for 2,400 km.

The student wants to focus on the magnitude of the Himalayan mountain range. Which choice most effectively uses relevant information from the notes to accomplish this goal?

A. A dry, arid area called a rain shadow forms on the leeward side of large mountain ranges like the Himalayas.

B. The Himalayas span a range of 2,400 km across Central Asia, hosting the highest mountain peaks in the world—including Mount Everest at 29,000 feet.

C. The Tibetan Plateau side of the Himalayan mountains faces away from prevailing winds on the opposite, windward side, creating a drier climate called a rain shadow.

D. The Himalayas form a geographical border within Central Asia between northern India and the Tibetan Plateau.

STOP.

If you finish before time is up, you may check your work on this module only.

Do not turn to any other module in the test.

16

SAT® PRACTICE TEST

MATH

Module 1

22 Questions—35 Minutes

Directions: The questions in this section address a number of important math skills.

Use of a calculator is permitted for all questions.

Unless otherwise indicated:

- All variables and expressions represent real numbers.
- Figures provided are drawn to scale.
- All figures lie in a plane.
- The domain of a given function f is the set of all real numbers x for which $f(x)$ is a real number.

Reference:

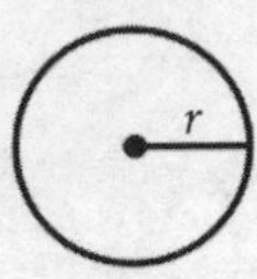

$A = \pi r^2$

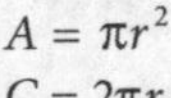

$C = 2\pi r$

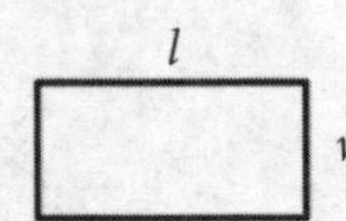

$A = lw$

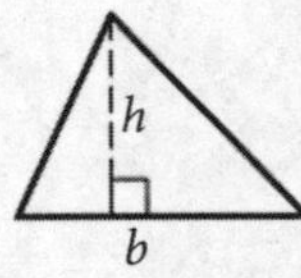

$A = \frac{1}{2}bh$

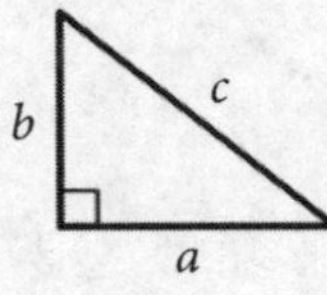

$c^2 = a^2 + b^2$

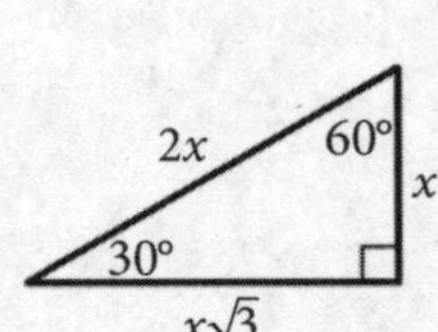

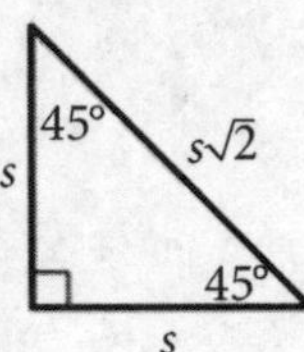

Special Right Triangles

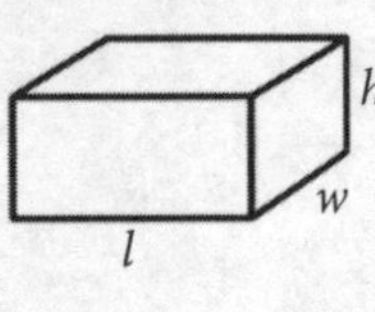

$V = lwh$

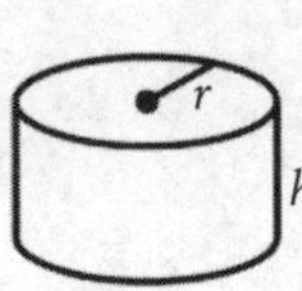

$V = \pi r^2 h$

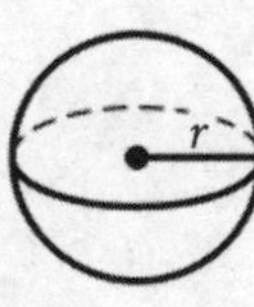

$V = \frac{4}{3}\pi r^3$

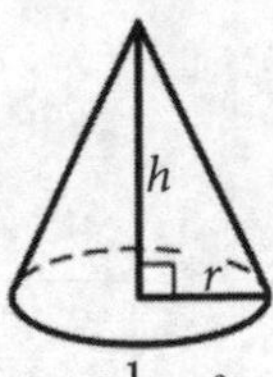

$V = \frac{1}{3}\pi r^2 h$

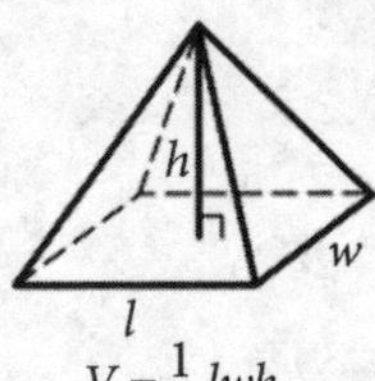

$V = \frac{1}{3}lwh$

The number of degrees of arc in a circle is 360.

The number of radians of arc in a circle is 2π.

The sum of the measures in degrees of the angles of a triangle is 180.

For **student-produced response questions**, your answer can be up to 5 characters for a positive answer and up to 6 characters (including the negative sign) for a negative answer.

If you find **more than one correct answer**, write only one answer in the blank provided.

If your answer is a **fraction** that is too long, write the decimal equivalent.

If your answer is a **decimal** that is too long, truncate it or round at the fourth digit.

If your answer is a **mixed number**, write it as an improper fraction or its decimal equivalent.

Don't include **symbols** such as a percent sign, comma, or dollar sign in your answer.

1. Nadia spent 7 more hours on math homework last month than Peter. If they spent a total of 35 hours doing math homework last month, how many hours did Peter spend on math homework?

A. 7

B. 14

C. 21

D. 28

2.

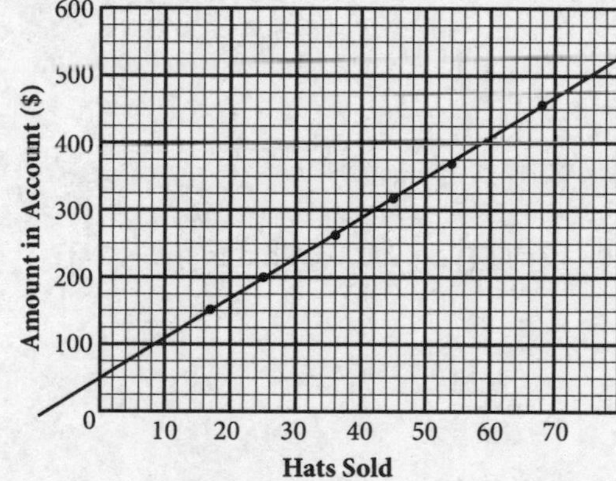

According to the graph, which of the following best approximates the number of hats that must be sold for the class to have raised a total of \$400?

A. 54

B. 58

C. 64

D. 68

3.

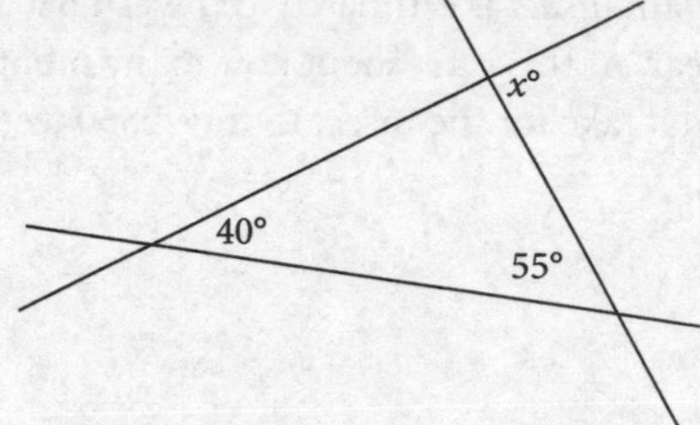

Three lines intersect to form a triangle. What is the value of $x°$?

A. 55°

B. 75°

C. 85°

D. 95°

4. If $w = \frac{2}{3}$ and $z = -\frac{1}{9}$, what is the value of $\frac{w+z}{2(w-z)}$?

A. $-\frac{1}{3}$

B. $-\frac{5}{14}$

C. $\frac{5}{14}$

D. $\frac{1}{2}$

CONTINUE

5. A certain insect is estimated to travel 1,680 feet per year. At this rate, about how many months would it take for the insect to travel 560 feet?

A. 0.75

B. 3

C. 4

D. 5.5

6. The length of a rectangle is 2 cm less than 4 times its width. If its perimeter is 36 cm, what is its area?

7. What percent of 40 is 18?

8. If c is 22 percent of e and d is 68 percent of e, what is $d - c$ in terms of e?

A. $90e$

B. $46e$

C. $0.9e$

D. $0.46e$

9. 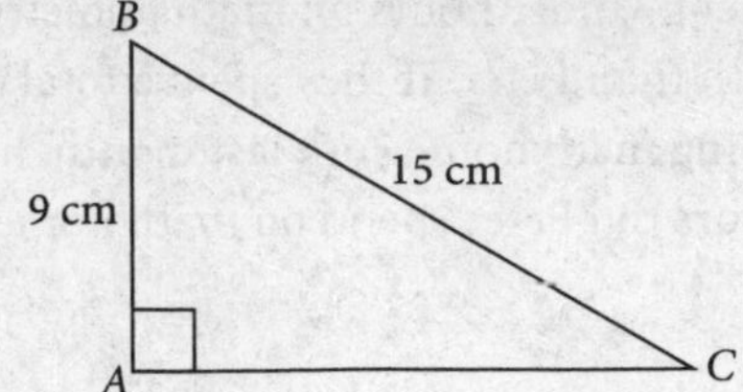

What is the area of right triangle ABC in square centimeters?

A. 12

B. 36

C. 54

D. 108

10. Let $h(x)=1-\frac{2}{3x}$. What is $h=\left(-\frac{4}{x}\right)$?

A. x

B. $\frac{x+24}{x}$

C. $\frac{2x+1}{12}$

D. $\frac{x+6}{6}$

11.

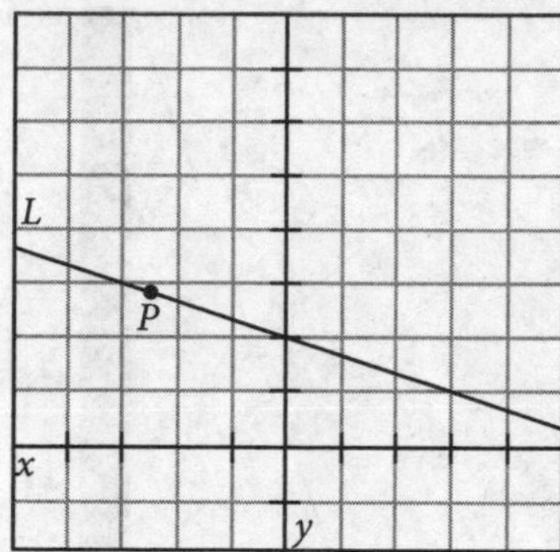

A line drawn through point P perpendicular to line L will have what slope?

12. At a township meeting, thirty residents are asked how many robocalls they received, on average, in a typical evening during election season. Each respondent indicated the number of calls they received as follows:

5	1	0	8	5	4
2	4	1	8	0	5
2	1	0	0	7	8
1	5	1	2	7	1
1	4	4	1	3	1

What is the relationship between the mean, median, and mode of this data set?

A. Mean < median < mode

B. Mean < mode < median

C. Mode < median < mean

D. Median < mean < mode

13.

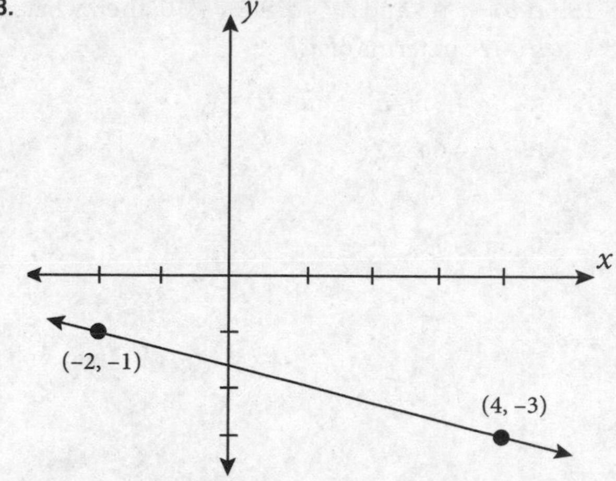

What is the equation of the linear function shown in the graph?

A. $f(x) = -3x - 7$

B. $f(x) = -\frac{1}{3}x - \frac{5}{3}$

C. $f(x) = -3x - 2$

D. $f(x) = -\frac{1}{3}x - 2$

14. The center of a circle is (–4, 3). If the point (2, –2) lies on this circle, what is the equation of this circle?

A. $(x + 4)^2 + (y - 3)^2 = 61$

B. $(x - 4)^2 + (y + 3)^3 = \sqrt{61}$

C. $(x + 4)^2 + (y - 3)^3 = 11$

D. $(x - 2)^2 + (y + 2)^2 = \sqrt{61}$

SAT® PRACTICE TEST

15. If $b = a + 3$ and $c = -a^2 + 3a + 10$, then what is $b^2 - 2c$ in terms of a?

A. $2(a + 3)^2(-a + 5)(a + 2)$

B. $3a^2 - 6a - 2$

C. $-a^2 + 6a + 29$

D. $3a^2 - 11$

16. What are the solutions of the equation $3|x| + 2 = 9|x|$?

17.

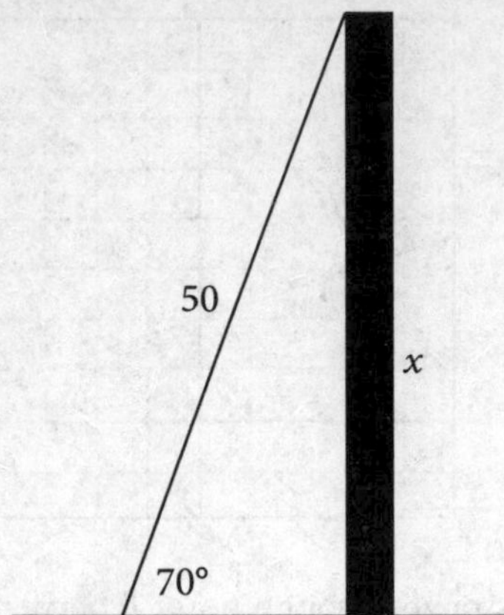

A 50-foot wire is attached to the top of an electric pole and is anchored on the ground. If the wire rises in a straight line at a 70° angle from the ground, how any feet tall is the pole?

A. 50 sin 70°

B. 50 cos 70°

C. 50 tan 70°

D. $\frac{\cos 70°}{50}$

18.

$$2x + 3y = 7$$
$$ax - 12y = b$$

According to the system of equations above, what is the value of ab that will make the system of equations have an infinite number of solutions?

19. Which of the following is the graph of $j(x) = 3^x - 2$?

A.

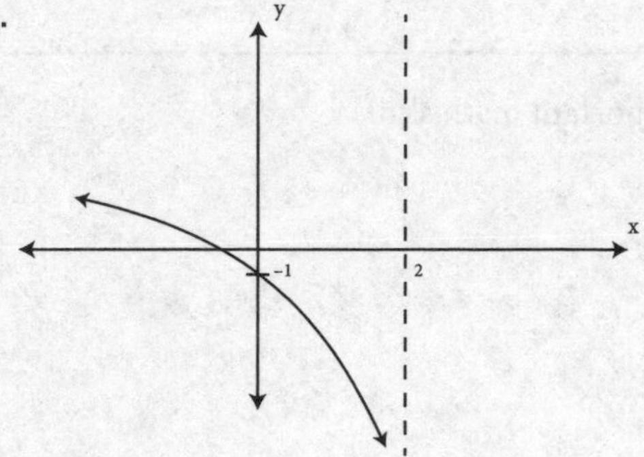

B.

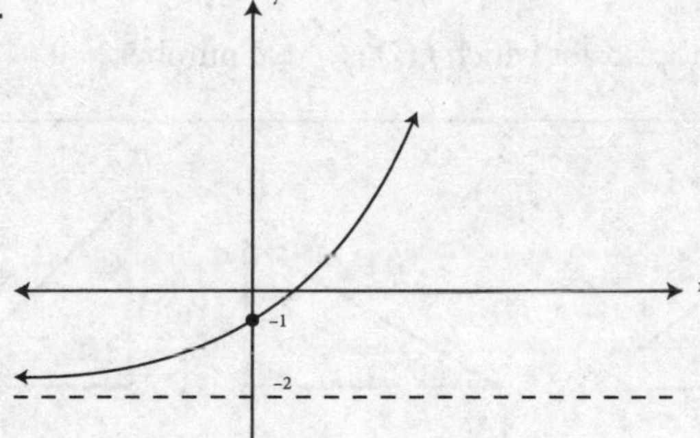

C.

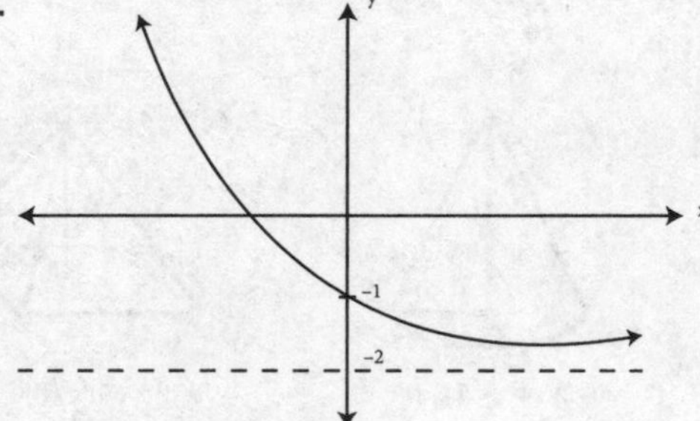

D.

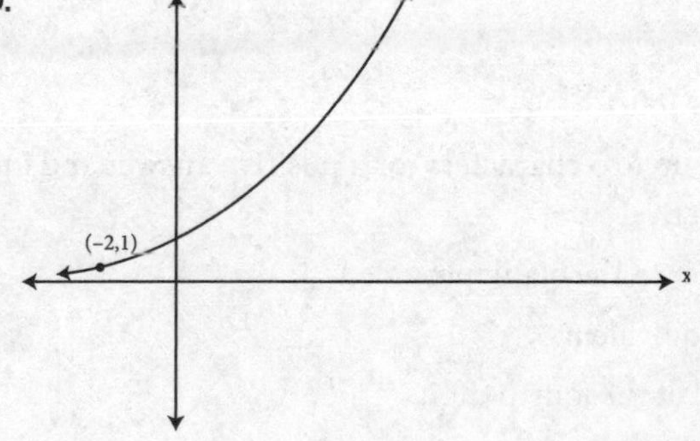

20. Which of the following expressions is equivalent to $2(y^2 - z^2) - 3(z - y)(2z + y)$?

A. $-8z^2 + 5y^2$

B. $3y^2 - 4z^2 - yz$

C. $4z^2 + 3yz - y^2$

D. $5y^2 + 3yz - 8z^2$

21. What are the solutions of the quadratic equation $2x^2 - x + 3 = 0$?

A. $x = \frac{1}{4} \pm i\frac{\sqrt{5}}{4}$

B. $x = \frac{1}{4} \pm i\frac{\sqrt{23}}{4}$

C. $x = \frac{1}{4} \pm \frac{23}{4}$

D. $x = -\frac{3}{2}, 1$

22. The only factors of the function f are $(x + 3)^2$ and $(3x - 2)$. What is the product of its three zeroes?

STOP.

If you finish before time is up, you may check your work on this module only.

Do not turn to any other module in the test.

MATH

Module 2

22 Questions—35 Minutes

Directions: The questions in this section address a number of important math skills.

Use of a calculator is permitted for all questions.

Unless otherwise indicated:

- All variables and expressions represent real numbers.
- Figures provided are drawn to scale.
- All figures lie in a plane.
- The domain of a given function f is the set of all real numbers x for which $f(x)$ is a real number.

Reference:

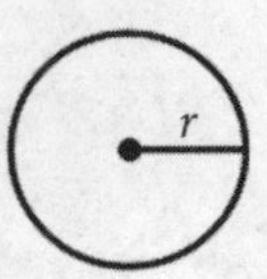

$A = \pi r^2$
$C = 2\pi r$

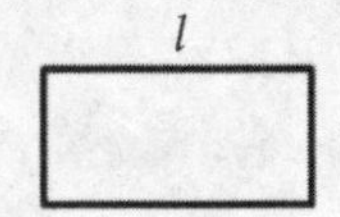

$A = lw$

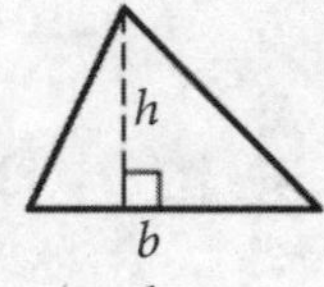

$A = \frac{1}{2}bh$

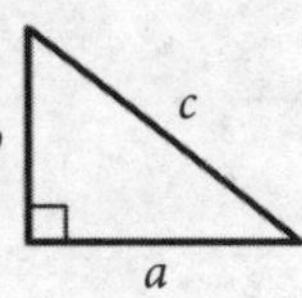

$c^2 = a^2 + b^2$

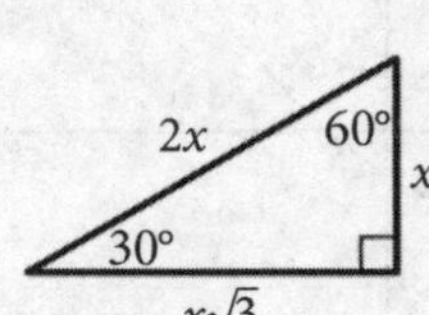

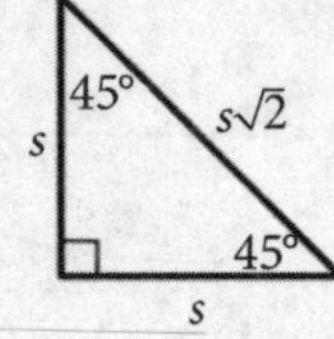

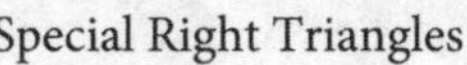

Special Right Triangles

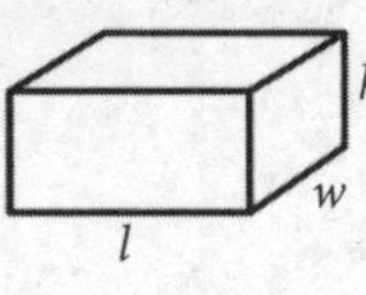

$V = lwh$

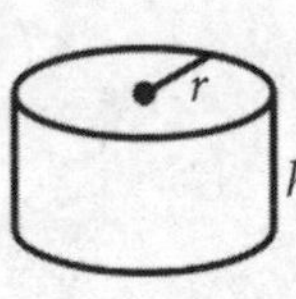

$V = \pi r^2 h$

$V = \frac{4}{3}\pi r^3$

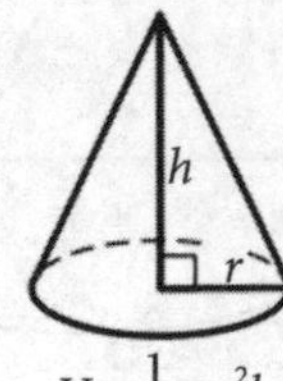

$V = \frac{1}{3}\pi r^2 h$

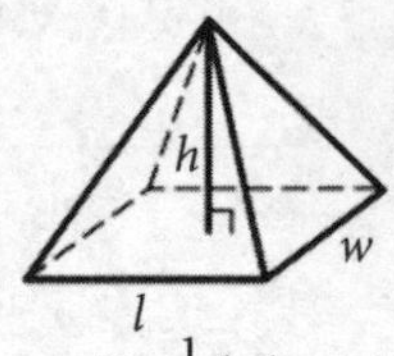

$V = \frac{1}{3}lwh$

The number of degrees of arc in a circle is 360.

The number of radians of arc in a circle is 2π.

The sum of the measures in degrees of the angles of a triangle is 180.

For **student-produced response questions**, your answer can be up to 5 characters for a positive answer and up to 6 characters (including the negative sign) for a negative answer.

If you find **more than one correct answer**, write only one answer in the blank provided.

If your answer is a **fraction** that is too long, write the decimal equivalent.

If your answer is a **decimal** that is too long, truncate it or round at the fourth digit.

If your answer is a **mixed number**, write it as an improper fraction or its decimal equivalent.

Don't include **symbols** such as a percent sign, comma, or dollar sign in your answer.

1. If $f(1) = 3$, $f(3) = -1$, $g(3) = 1$, and $g(-1) = 3$, what is the value of $f(g(3))$?

A. –3

B. –1

C. 1

D. 3

2. Jared is beginning to track the number of steps he walks each day. Yesterday he walked 950 steps. He set a goal of increasing his steps per day by 125, with an eventual goal of walking at least 3,000 steps per day. Which of the following functions can be used to determine the number of steps Jared plans to take d days from yesterday?

A. $f(d) = 3{,}000 - (950 + 125d)$

B. $f(d) = 3{,}000 - 125d$

C. $f(d) = 950 + 125d$

D. $f(d) = 950 - 125d$

3. If $n = 7$, what is $2m(16 - 6n)$ in terms of m?

A. $-52m$

B. $-15m$

C. $-14m$

D. $32m$

4. Glen earns $10.25 per hour and pays $12.50 per day to commute to and from work on the bus. He wants to make sure that he works long enough to earn at least three times as much as he spends commuting. Which of the following inequalities best represents this situation?

A. $10.25h \geq 3(12.50)$

B. $3(10.25) \geq 12.50h$

C. $3(10.25h) \geq 12.50$

D. $h \geq 3(12.50)(10.25)$

5. If $\frac{x}{12} + \frac{x}{18} = 1$, what is the value of x?

A. $\frac{23}{8}$

B. $\frac{36}{5}$

C. $\frac{114}{9}$

D. $\frac{67}{5}$

CONTINUE

6.

HOUSE STYLE

House Style	Town A	Town B
Ranch	75	62
Colonial	25	65
Cape Cod	53	43
Victorian	20	32

A sample of the population in two neighborhood towns, Town A and Town B, was surveyed in order to determine the most popular types of house styles. The results of the survey are shown in the table.

According to the table above, what is the probability that a randomly selected house in Town B is a colonial house?

A. $\frac{65}{202}$

B. $\frac{25}{62}$

C. $\frac{31}{45}$

D. $\frac{17}{18}$

7.

$$y = 2x + 5$$
$$y = -2(x+1)^2 + 3$$

If (x, y) is a solution to the system of equations above, what is one possible value of y?

8. A recent national poll of adults in the United States found that 64% favor stricter emissions on power plants. The margin of error for the poll was ±4% with 95% confidence. Which of the following statements is a conclusion that can accurately be drawn from this poll?

A. The true percentage of people who oppose stricter emissions of power plants is definitely between 32% and 40%.

B. The true percentage of people who support stricter emissions of power plants is definitely between 60% and 68%.

C. The pollsters are 95% confident that the true percentage of people who oppose stricter emissions of power plants is between 32% and 40%.

D. The pollsters are 95% confident that the true percentage of people who support stricter emissions of power plants is between 60% and 68%.

9.

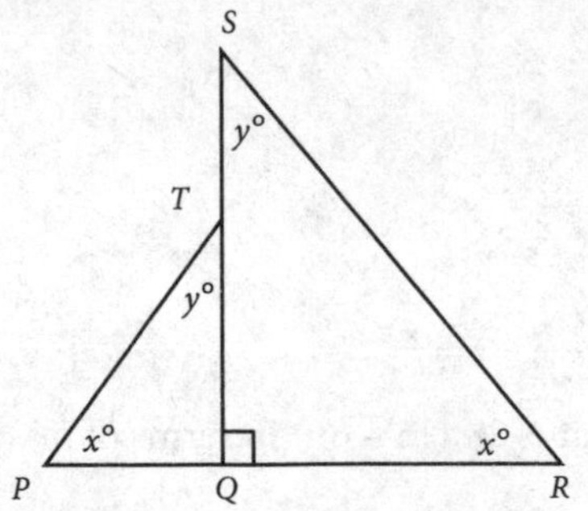

S
$y°$
T
$y°$
$x°$
$x°$
P
Q
R

Note: Figure not drawn to scale.

In the figure above, if $QP = 11.5$, $TQ = 15$, and $QR = 46$, what is the value of SQ?

A. 65

B. 60

C. 49.5

D. 42.5

10. Which of the following is the equation for the graph of a parabola that has a vertex at (3, –5) and a y-intercept at 13?

A. $y - 28 = (x - 3)(x + 5)$

B. $y = 2(x - 3)^2 - 5$

C. $y = (x - 3)^2 - 13$

D. $y = x^2 - 6x + 13$

11. If $4s - 3 < 2$ and s is an integer, what is the greatest possible value of $4s + 5$?

12. If a represents a real number, what condition must a satisfy so that the graph of $f(x) = 2(3a - x) - (5 + ax)$ does not intersect Quadrant III?

A. $a < \frac{5}{6}$

B. $-2 \leq a < \frac{5}{6}$

C. $a > \frac{5}{6}$

D. $a \leq -2$

13.

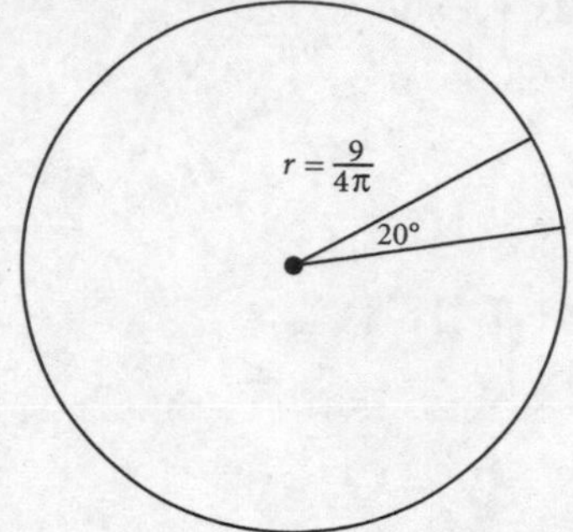

Note: Figure not drawn to scale.

Given the circle shown above, what is the length of the arc formed by the 20° angle?

A. $\frac{45}{\pi}$

B. $\frac{\pi}{4}$

C. $\frac{1}{2}$

D. $\frac{1}{4}$

14. $$y = 2(x - 5)^2 - 2$$

Which equation, where the x-intercepts appear as constants, is equivalent to the equation above?

A. $y = 2x^2 - 20x + 48$

B. $y = 2(x^2 - 10x + 24)$

C. $y = 2(x - 4)(x - 6)$

D. $y = (2x - 8)(x - 6)$

SAT® PRACTICE TEST

CONTINUE

15. If $f(x) = 4x^3 - 2x + 1$ and $g(x) = -x^2 + 5$, what is $2f(x) - xg(x)$?

A. $9x^3 - 4x - 3$

B. $8x^3 - 4x + 2$

C. $4x^3 + x^2 - 2x - 4$

D. $9x^3 - 9x + 2$

16. The equation for the graph of a circle in the xy-plane is $x^2 + y^2 - 10x + 4y = -20$. What are the coordinates of the center of the circle?

A. (5, –2)

B. (–5, 2)

C. (10, –4)

D. (–10, 4)

17.
$$2x - 5y < 6$$
$$x + ay < -3$$

Which of the following must be true if the system of inequalities above has solutions only in Quadrants II and III?

A. $a < 0$

B. $a = 0$

C. $0 \leq a \leq 2.5$

D. $a > 2.5$

18. If w is a negative constant less than –1 and v is a positive constant greater than 1, which of the following could be the graph of $y = a(x + w)(x + v)$?

A.

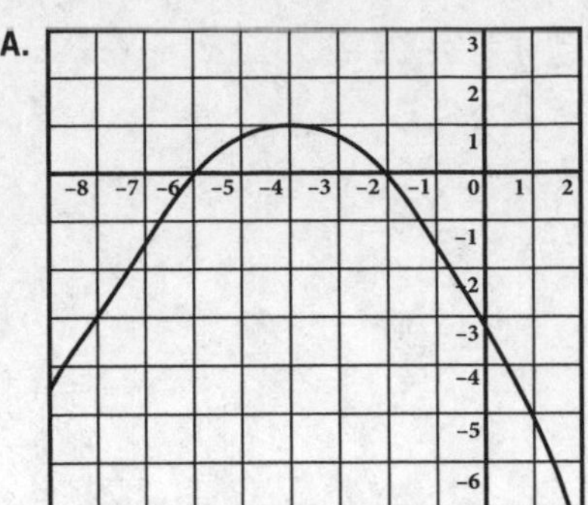

B.

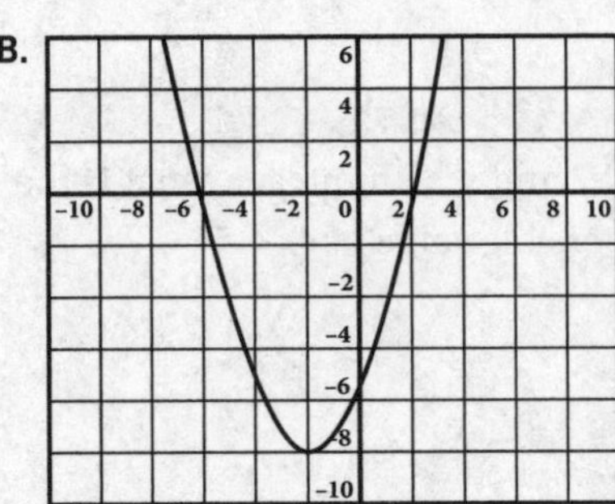

C.

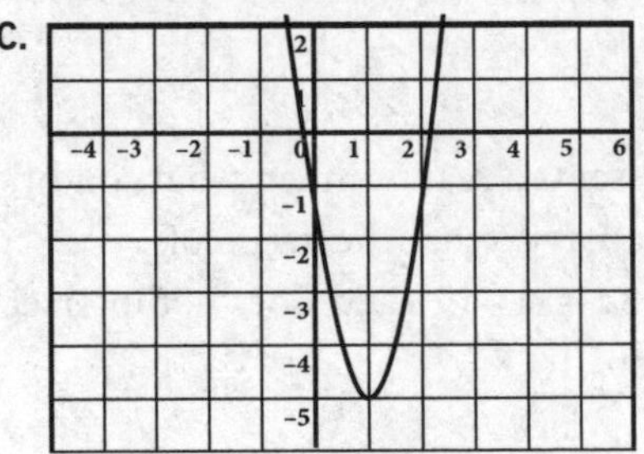

D.

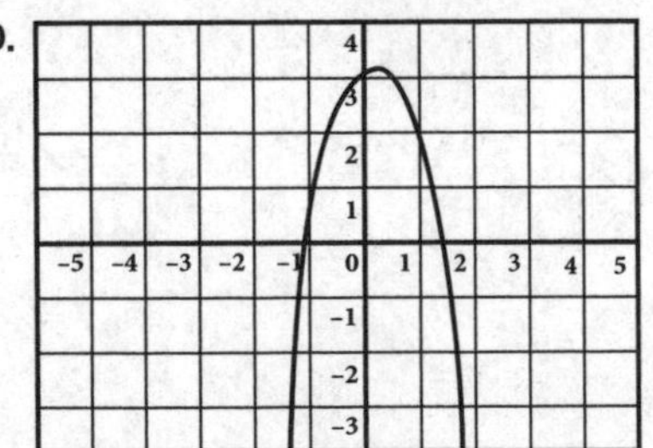

19. A certain type of weather radar, known as a Base Reflectivity Radar, has a circumference of 572π miles. The central angle of a sector of the circle that the radar makes is $\frac{3\pi}{4}$. What is the area, in square miles, of the sector of the circle?

A. 858π square miles

B. $\frac{429\pi}{4}$ square miles

C. $\frac{61,347\pi}{2}$ square miles

D. $81,796\pi$ square miles

20. If $f(x) = |x|$ and $g(x) = -\frac{1}{x}$, then for $x < 0$, what is $g(f(x))$?

A. $-\frac{1}{x}$

B. 0

C. $\left|\frac{1}{x}\right|$

D. $\frac{1}{x}$

21. The current population of a certain type of organism is about 100 million. The population is currently increasing at an annual rate that will make the population double in 18 years. If this pattern continues, what will the population be, in millions, 54 years from now?

22. Let b be a real number. For what value of b does the function $f(x) = x^2 - 2bx + (b^2 + 2b - 1)$ have only one x-intercept?

STOP.

If you finish before time is up, you may check your work on this module only.

Do not turn to any other module in the test.

ANSWER KEY AND EXPLANATIONS

Reading and Writing: Module 1

1. A	6. B	11. B	16. D	21. D	26. B
2. B	7. D	12. A	17. D	22. C	27. C
3. D	8. D	13. D	18. C	23. A	
4. A	9. A	14. B	19. A	24. A	
5. B	10. B	15. D	20. B	25. C	

1. **The correct answer is A.** The context of the passage calls for a word that means something like "intense" or "challenging." Only *rigorous* fulfills this purpose.
2. **The correct answer is B.** The word *fashioned* means "created, formed, or constructed."
3. **The correct answer is D.** The word *abhorrent* means "causing or deserving strong dislike or hatred."
4. **The correct answer is A.** Saying that the scientists had "suppositions" is a way of saying that they had assumptions or theories about black holes, meaning they had guesses.
5. **The correct answer is B.** The main purpose of the text is to explain the structure and role of family in Bedouin tribes. The definition of the term *sheikh* (choice D) only relates to part of the text. Choices A and C are not represented in this text.
6. **The correct answer is B.** The underlined sentence clarifies that blockers have more than one responsibility in roller derby when it says they must play "both offense and defense."
7. **The correct answer is D.** The main purpose of the text is to provide an example of how Jenny Holzer uses art as social commentary, as demonstrated by the words "for instance," to introduce the work "By Your Response to Danger." The insight provided into Holzer's creative process (choice B) only relates to part of the text. Choices A and C are not represented in this text.
8. **The correct answer is D.** The underlined sentence defines the idea behind the bail system in that it is supposed to motivate the person who has paid money for their release "to show up in court when they are expected to show" or risk losing "the money they posted for the bail."
9. **The correct answer is A.** The second sentences states that "Like PTSD, grief experiences can activate the fight-or-flight mechanism." This question is asking you to make a reasonable inference based on what the author more or less states, drawing an implicit conclusion from an explicit statement.
10. **The correct answer is B.** It is important to note that this passage offers two divergent observations. On one hand, the passage presents the fact that some invasive species have caused harmful effects to their environments. On the other hand, it highlights that some scientists have observed beneficial effects from some invasive species. Therefore, one can infer that there is still relative uncertainty about how invasive species interact with their ecosystems. Since this is the case, only choice B aligns with this perspective, acknowledging the implication that there might be cases wherein invasive species offer positive effects.
11. **The correct answer is B.** The passage describes Lita's visit to the establishment to give birth, which we can infer from the statement "Lita drifted into motherhood" as well as the figurative description of the infant as a "wax doll which suddenly appeared in the cradle at her bedside."
12. **The correct answer is A.** The main idea of the text is that floating cities on the ocean are being considered as an alternative to our traditional way of life and use of resources. Ocean cities as an advantage to international travel (choice C) and ocean farmers (choice D) both relate to parts of the text and

support the main idea, but those choices do not fully encompass the main idea. Choice B is not represented in this text.

13. **The correct answer is D.** This is the only claim that is supported by general data trends in the chart. If you chose any particular row, you would see electronegativity values increase from left to right in various intervals. Hydrogen (H) stands alone as a period in this particular table excerpt, but it is not enough to fully disrupt the general trend seen in the other periods. The key phrase in this claim, therefore, is "tends to," as there is strong enough evidence to support the claim made in choice D. The other three choices make claims that are either in direct opposition to the information from the passage or what is presented in the chart.

14. **The correct answer is B.** There are two important things to notice that help answer this question. First, we're asked to notice something about what happens when height above the ground decreases, and second, we're looking to compare the magnitude of wind speed changes in various kinds of terrain. In all three terrains, wind speed decreases as height above the ground decreases. For example, follow the numbers for Class 4 at 150 meters, then 100 meters, then 50 meters; you'll see that the wind speeds decrease. That observation eliminates choices A and C from consideration. The issue is now the rate of the decrease—do the numbers drop more quickly in rougher terrain or in smoother terrain? Let's use the figures in the table to determine this. In the roughest terrain, Class 4, wind speed drops from 10.14 at 150 meters above ground to 9.39 at 100 meters and 8.1 at 50 meters. This is a drop of approximately 0.7 and 1.3, respectively. In a less rough terrain, Class 2, the corresponding decrease is from 12.29 to 11.7 to 10.7, which represents a drop of roughly 0.6 and 1.0. This drop is less dramatic, and the decrease in roughness Class 0 even less so—from 14.8 to 14.4 (a drop of 0.4) to 13.73 (a drop of 0.67). Therefore, the drop-off in wind speed as height above ground decreases is more rapid in rougher terrains.

15. **The correct answer is D.** A period should be used to avoid a run-on sentence.

16. **The correct answer is D.** The sentence contains two separate clauses that should be separated by an em dash. The em dash signifies that the following clause expands the meaning of the first. Choice A has no punctuation to indicate the separation of clauses. Choices B creates a sentence fragment as the following clause cannot stand on its own. Choice C misuses a question mark; the independent clause is not interrogative.

17. **The correct answer is D.** Here, the subordinating conjunction *because* joins an independent clause and a dependent clause without the need for punctuation. Choices A, B and C use unnecessary punctuation to separate the clauses that are already separated by a conjunction.

18. **The correct answer is C.** The semicolon is used between related independent clauses connected by conjunctive adverbs, such as the word *futhermore* used here.

19. **The correct answer is A.** As written, choice B contains an inappropriate use of a present participle verb, *becoming*, that would also require a linking verb, and choices C and D contain the present and past tense forms of the linking verb "to be" but do not make sense within the context of the sentence. The sentence requires the past tense, *became*, so choice A is the best choice.

20. **The correct answer is B.** Choice A, *their*, is a possessive pronoun, which is not needed. Choice C is a contraction of the words *they are*, and *are* has already been used in the sentence, making *they are* redundant and contextually illogical. Choice D is the subject pronoun *they* and is inappropriate for the syntax. Only choice B, *there*, is logical in the sentence as an adverb preceding the verb *are*.

21. **The correct answer is D.** As written, choice A contains an inappropriate use of the future conditional, *would flee*, that does not make sense in the historical context of the text. Choice B indicates the present tense, *flees*, which does not match with the

past tense previously used in the text. Choice C uses the past perfect, *had fled*, which changes from past tense and disrupts the flow of the text. The sentence requires the past tense, *fled*, so choice D is the best choice.

22. **The correct answer is C.** The author intends to provide another reason that mushrooms are beautiful, so the transition word *additionally* is the most logical choice here.

23. **The correct answer is A.** The most logical transition is *while* because it separates the activities of the adult emerald ash borers from those of the larvae.

24. **The correct answer is A.** Since the context suggests that the author is using the last sentence to note another reason that Göbekli Tepe can be considered astounding, you want a transition word of phrase that conveys an additive relationship. *Moreover* is the only option that fulfills that purpose.

25. **The correct answer is C.** The most logical transition is *however* because it counters the previous information about the study of germ-free mice in that there is little information as to the relevance to humans.

26. **The correct answer is B.** The sentence compares Sojourner Truth's life experiences before and after gaining her freedom from slavery by describing her life as an enslaved person and then using the word "continued" to connect her character to her activities after gaining freedom. Choices A and C focus on her activist ideologies after her freedom only. Choice D only focuses on her speeches.

27. **The correct answer is C.** The student presents a timeline of the formation of the supercontinents by listing the order in which they emerged. The sentence states Pangea's formation as occurring "millions of years ago" and uses the word "eventually" to indicate appropriate temporal relationships. Choice A describes only the southern supercontinent, and Choice B describes only the northern one. Choice D explains who first postulated each of the three landmasses.

ANSWER KEY AND EXPLANATIONS

Reading and Writing: Module 2

1. A	6. B	11. D	16. C	21. D	26. A
2. B	7. B	12. A	17. A	22. C	27. B
3. C	8. A	13. C	18. D	23. B	
4. A	9. D	14. C	19. D	24. D	
5. A	10. D	15. B	20. C	25. B	

1. **The correct answer is A.** The word *ostentatious* means "extravagant, garish, over-the-top, or gaudy."
2. **The correct answer is B.** Saying that the sculptor's family is "scattered" is a way of saying that they are living in different places far from the town, meaning they are widely dispersed.
3. **The correct answer is C.** The underlined sentence outlines the ideas related to the Impressionist art movement by stating what it is ("immediate vision," and "light, picturesqueness, keen and clever observation,") and is not ("does not give much scope to intellectuality [. . .], rejecting philosophy and symbols [and having] antipathy to abstraction").
4. **The correct answer is A.** The narrator uses figurative language to express feelings he cannot put into words, such as comparing his joy to an escape from a lion's den as he declares that "words can but tamely describe" these feelings. He illustrates his emotions by comparing them to a rainbow, as they "defy the skill of pen or pencil."
5. **The correct answer is A.** Text 2 provides a current issue surrounding how the complex soil organic matter described in Text 1 will survive the effects of climate change.
6. **The correct answer is B.** Text 2 indicates the potential dangers of psilocybin use for therapy, such as addiction and recreational use. Text 2 also states "those who enthusiastically endorse more widespread access to these substances may unintentionally gloss over these dangers in their quest for scientific innovation," which supports choice B.
7. **The correct answer is B.** Text 2 describes the current situation of the few remaining squatter groups. It therefore updates the historical information about these collectives that is presented in Text 1.
8. **The correct answer is A.** In this hypothesis, large amounts of carbon dioxide (CO_2) were blasted into the atmosphere by the impact of an asteroid. It further implies that this increase in CO_2 caused long-term global warming, or a long-term global temperature increase. Choice B is incorrect because the hypothesis claims that a cloud of dust, not CO_2, caused a short-term decrease in the amount of sunlight reaching Earth's surface. Choice C is incorrect because the hypothesis claims that the asteroid impact, an extinction-triggering event, happened in an instant. Choice D is incorrect because the passage argues that an asteroid impact led to dramatic environmental changes and stresses.
9. **The correct answer is D.** The only answer one can infer based on the details given in the passage is choice D. Since the passage states that the Taliban targeted girls who pursued education or criticized them, it would make logical sense for Malala to have hidden her name to make it easier to publish ideas that were critical of the Pakistani Taliban, something she was able to do because the BBC was published in a different country.
10. **The correct answer is D.** The quotation addresses the claim that the narrator witnessed the event of a child being taken from their mother by hearing the child and/or mother scream ("No marvel,

then, these bitter shrieks / Disturb the listening air:") and observing the mother's sorrow ("She is a mother, and her heart / Is breaking in despair."). The fact that the shrieks are coming from somewhere else that the narrator can hear tells us that the poem is not narrated by the mother directly. Choice C is incorrect as the "her" mentioned in the lines is not identified as the mother.

11. **The correct answer is D.** The quotation describes how those in conflict are likely to take on some of the traits their adversaries possess. For those in power, the exercise of power against "monsters" represents the possibility of corruption, "thereby [becoming] a monster."

12. **The correct answer is A.** The passage indicates that, as a general rule, increased fitness correlates with lower resting heart rates, a greater degree of change in heart rate during exercise, and greater recovery rates. The swimmer wins on all three counts. The swimmer's resting heart rate sits under 50 while the basketball player's is over 75. The swimmer's heart rate increases faster during exercise than does the basketball player's (note the swimmer's steeper curve as their heart rate shoots from under 50 to around 160 at the 5-minute mark). Finally, the swimmer's steep downward curve from 10 to around 13 minutes when their heart rate is back to normal indicates a higher recovery rate than that of the basketball player. All of these clues allow us to deduce that the swimmer is fitter, which both confirms choice A and eliminates choice B. Choices C and D are incorrect because the graph provides data only on the heart rates of these two individuals. That, by itself, is not enough to state that one sport is more demanding overall. Observing a single individual participating in both sports might shed light on this issue, but the graph alone is insufficient to do so.

13. **The correct answer is C.** The main idea of the text is that scientists believe that the reason Neptune and Uranus are different colors despite being compositionally similar has to do with a certain haze that is thicker on Uranus. Uranus being a deep shade of cyan (choice A) and the Hubble Space Telescope (choice B) are both related to the main idea, but these statements do not represent the main idea. Choice D is not represented in this text.

14. **The correct answer is C.** The narrator's key takeaway when reflecting on his time aboard the HMS *Beagle* was identifying this point in his life as the time in which his interest in science became more important to him than any of his other interests. For instance, he states, "my love for science gradually preponderated over every other taste." *Preponderated* means "outweighed" or "exceeded in importance." He goes on to provide an example of giving up hunting animals for sport and becoming more of an observer and intellectual, saying "the pleasure of observing and reasoning was a much higher one than that of skill and sport."

15. **The correct answer is B.** Here, your best option is to end one sentence with a semicolon and start the next with the conjunctive adverb *however.* Only choice C executes the grammar in this manner. The other choices misuse or misplace at least one punctuation mark.

16. **The correct answer is C.** Commas are needed to separate nonessential and parenthetical elements from the main clause. Nonessential and parenthetical elements provide extra information that is not necessary for the meaning or grammatical correctness of a sentence. In this case, the phrase "such as their position and momentum" is nonessential for the grammar of the sentence. Choice A lacks both commas needed and therefore can be eliminated. While choice B includes one comma to separate the first part of the nonessential and parenthetical elements from the main clause, it is lacking the second one at the end. Choice D adds an unnecessary comma within said element.

17. **The correct answer is A.** No punctuation is needed to separate this prepositional phrase as it modifies the independent clause that starts the sentence.

18. **The correct answer is D.** The statement lists three items in a series, requiring the use of commas to separate each item in the list. Choice A uses no punctuation. Choice B is missing the serial comma

before the final item of the list, and choice C incorrectly uses semicolons.

19. **The correct answer is D.** The apostrophe goes after the s to indicate the possessive case of the plural noun *artists*, as the text is describing the ideas of the artists across multiple murals. The *'s* is only used to show possession after nouns not ending in s.

20. **The correct answer is C.** As written, choice A indicates certainty, yet the text indicates some uncertainty. Choice B does not make grammatical sense using the past progressive tense of "to be." Choice D uses the conditional tense to indicate a possible future context, which is not relevant with this text. Only choice C correctly uses the conditional perfect form, *would have been*, to indicate that something likely would have happened if it turned out that certain conditions had been true (where the condition in this case is that Shakespeare would have been familiar with a story that was popular at the time).

21. **The correct answer is D.** Choice D contains the correct sentence structure using the adverb *actually* to modify the verb phrase *is composed*. Note that while choice C also places *actually* correctly, it inappropriately shuffles the word order in the rest of the statement.

22. **The correct answer is C.** You are looking for a term that represents how what follows will be a contrast to what was stated before since the context of the passage tells you that the lack of accessibility for non-white families is a departure from the view of Levittown as an ideal community. First, eliminate *Accordingly* (choice D) since it implies a continuation of the thought before. Of the choices that remain, only *However* fits the context of the sentence. *In fact* (choice A) suggests that the following sentence will somehow be illustrative of the preceding thought. *Consequently* (choice B) indicates that the following sentence will be a logical consequence of the preceding statement.

23. **The correct answer is B.** "In this model" uses a logical link from the sentences before it (which mentions Goffman's dramaturgical model) to begin the sentence that explains the dramaturgical model as it relates to society.

24. **The correct answer is D.** The sentence emphasizes the importance of magical realism in Gabriel García Márquez's work by describing him as a "master" and stating that his use of magical realism "put him on the map." Choice A elaborates on a specific and famous work. Choice B connects his work to contemporary film. Choice C provides historical information.

25. **The correct answer is B.** In choice B, the student clarifies why studying the deep ocean is challenging for researchers: " harsh conditions of the deep ocean make it virtually impossible to traverse." The sentence goes on to support that claim with statistics that prove how little research has been successfully conducted to date. Choice A explains the nature of the deep ocean and the deepest known area. Choice C summarizes new research that has been conducted. Choice D defines the term deep ocean.

26. **The correct answer is A.** The student emphasizes the topics from which Yayoi Kusama draws inspiration by stating that the themes of Kusama's art were "derived from her own struggles," meaning they were based upon her experiences. The sentence lists "childhood and war trauma, as well as mental health" as sources of motivation. Choice B describes the popularity of the artist and her art. Choices C and D provide background information on the artist.

27. **The correct answer is B.** This question relies on your recognition that the term *magnitude* refers here to the size and scope of the Himalayan mountain range. The student focuses on the magnitude of the Himalayas by using descriptions like "span a range of 2,400 km across Central Asia" along with mention of the elevation of the range's tallest peak (Mount Everest). Choice A describes the general nature of rain shadows. Choice C describes the rain shadow of the Himalayas in relation to the Tibetan Plateau. Choice D focuses on the geographical location of the mountain range.

ANSWER KEY AND EXPLANATIONS

Math: Module 1

1. B	6. 56	11. 3	16. $-\frac{1}{3}$ or $\frac{1}{3}$	20. D
2. B	7. 45	12. C		21. B
3. D	8. D	13. B	17. A	22. 6
4. C	9. C	14. A	18. 224	
5. C	10. D	15. D	19. B	

1. **The correct answer is B.** If Peter spent x hours, then Nadia spent $x + 7$ hours on math homework, and together they spent $x + (x + 7) = 35$ hours. Solve for x:

$$\begin{aligned} x+(x+7)&=35 \\ 2x+7&=35 \\ 2x&=28 \\ x&=14 \end{aligned}$$

2. **The correct answer is B.** Read the graph and look for where the line has a vertical coordinate of $400. The closest approximation is 58 hats.

3. **The correct answer is D.** The sum measure of a triangle's interior angles is 180°, so the missing interior angle measures 180° – 40° – 55° = 85°. Since this angle is supplementary to the angle measuring $x°$, $x = 180 - 85 = 95$. Choice A is incorrect because the angles labeled x and 55 in the diagram are not congruent alternate interior angles. Choice B is the likely result of an arithmetic error; you should be computing 180 – 85. Choice C is the measure of the third angle in the triangle, not the one labeled x.

4. **The correct answer is C.** Substitute the values for w and z into the expression and simplify:

$$\frac{\frac{2}{3}-\frac{1}{9}}{2(\frac{2}{3}+\frac{1}{9})}=\frac{\frac{6}{9}-\frac{1}{9}}{2(\frac{6}{9}+\frac{1}{9})}=\frac{\frac{5}{9}}{2(\frac{7}{9})}$$

$$=\frac{\frac{5}{9}}{\frac{14}{9}}=\frac{5}{9}\div\frac{14}{9}=\frac{5}{9}\cdot\frac{9}{14}=\frac{5}{14}$$

In choice A, you added fractions incorrectly; you must first get a common denominator. Choice B has the wrong sign. In choice D, you canceled terms, not factors, common to the numerator and denominator.

5. **The correct answer is C.** We must first determine how many feet the insect travels in an average month. Then we can determine how many months it will take for the insect to travel 560 feet. To determine the number of feet the insect travels per month, we divide the yearly total by 12:

$$\frac{1,680}{12}=140$$

The insect travels 140 feet each month. To determine how many months it would take the insect to travel 560 feet, we divide the total number of feet (560) by the number of feet that the insect travels in a month (140):

$$\frac{560}{140}=4$$

Traveling at a rate of 140 feet per month, it would take the insect 4 months to travel 560 feet.

6. **The correct answer is 56.** Let x stand for the width of the rectangle. Then, $4x - 2$ is its length. So, the perimeter of the rectangle is $2x + 2(4x - 2) = 2x + 8x - 4 = 10x - 4$, and we are given that this equals 36. Equating these two quantities and solving for x yields $10x - 4 = 36$, so that $10x = 40$ and $x = 4$. As such, its length is $4(4) - 2 = 14$ cm. So, the area is $4(14) = 56\text{ cm}^2$.

7. **The correct answer is 45.** The statement "x% of 40 is 18" is equivalent to the equation $\frac{x}{100} \cdot 40 = 18$. Solving for x yields:

$$\begin{aligned} \frac{x}{100} \cdot 40 &= 18 \\ \frac{2}{5} \cdot x &= 18 \\ x &= \frac{5}{2} \cdot 18 \\ &= 45 \end{aligned}$$

As such, 18 is 45% of 40.

8. **The correct answer is D.** Since c is 22 percent of e, c equals ($e \times 0.22$), or $c = 0.22e$. Likewise, because d is 68 percent of e, d equals ($e \times 0.68$), or $d = 0.68e$. To find the value of $d - c$ in terms of e, we can set up an equation:

$$\begin{aligned} d - c &= (0.68e - 0.22e) \\ d - c &= 0.46e \end{aligned}$$

9. **The correct answer is C.** The area of a triangle is $\frac{1}{2}bh$. We already know the height of the triangle, 9 centimeters. To find the base, use the Pythagorean theorem, or recognize this as similar to a 3-4-5 right triangle:

$$\begin{aligned} 9^2 + AC^2 &= 15^2 \\ 81 + AC^2 &= 225 \\ AC^2 &= 144 \\ AC &= 12 \end{aligned}$$

Since the base of the triangle is 12, the area of the triangle is $\frac{1}{2}(12)(9) = 54$ square centimeters. Choice A is the length of the unknown side, in centimeters. Choice B is the perimeter of the triangle, in centimeters. Choice D is double the area, which may result from forgetting the $\frac{1}{2}$ in the area formula.

10. **The correct answer is D.** Calculate as follows:

$$\begin{aligned} h\left(-\frac{4}{x}\right) &= 1 - \frac{2}{3\left(-\frac{4}{x}\right)} \\ &= 1 - \frac{2}{-\frac{12}{x}} = 1 + 2\left(\frac{x}{12}\right) \\ &= 1 + \frac{x}{6} = \frac{6+x}{6} = \frac{x+6}{6} \end{aligned}$$

Choice A is incorrect because $\frac{x+6}{6} \neq \frac{x+\not{6}}{\not{6}}$. Choice B is incorrect because you did not simplify the complex fraction correctly. Choice C is incorrect because $\frac{2x}{12} + 1 \neq \frac{2x+1}{12}$; you must first get a common denominator.

11. **The correct answer is 3.** The slope of line L is $-\frac{1}{3}$, as can be determined by selecting any two points on the line and calculating the ratio of the difference in the y-values to the difference in the corresponding x-values. Using the points (–3, 3) and (0, 2), we can represent the slope as:

$$m = \frac{2-3}{0-(-3)} = -\frac{1}{3}$$

The slope of *any* line perpendicular to the line L will be the negative reciprocal of the slope of L. The negative reciprocal of $-\frac{1}{3}$ is 3. So, the slope of a line perpendicular to the graphed line will have a slope of 3.

12. **The correct answer is C.** Construct a frequency table:

Data value	Frequency
0	3
1	9
2	3
3	1
4	4
5	5
6	0
7	2
8	3

The mode is the most frequently occurring data value, which is 1. The median is the average of the 15th and 16th data value, namely $\frac{2+3}{2}=2.5$. The mean is the average of all the data values:

$$\frac{0(3+1(9)+2(3)+3(1)+4(4)+5(5)+6(0)+7(2)+8(3)}{30}$$

$$=\frac{97}{30}=3\frac{7}{30}$$

Thus, the mode < median < mean.

13. **The correct answer is B.** Use the two labeled points to determine the slope of the line:

$$m=\frac{-3-(-1)}{4-(-2)}=-\frac{2}{6}=-\frac{1}{3}$$

Using point-slope form with the point (–2, –1) yields the following equation:

$$y-(-1)=-\frac{1}{3}(x+2)$$
$$y+1=-\frac{1}{3}x-\frac{2}{3}$$
$$y=-\frac{1}{3}x-\frac{5}{3}$$

14. **The correct answer is A.** The radius is the length of the segment connecting the two given points:

$$\sqrt{(2-(4))^2+(-2-3)^2}=\sqrt{6^2+5}=\sqrt{36+25}=\sqrt{61}$$

Using the center $(h, k) = (-4, 3)$ and radius $r=\sqrt{61}$ in the standard form for the equation of a circle $(x-h)^2+(y-k)2=r^2$ yields the equation $(x-(4))^2+(y-3)^2=\sqrt{61}^{\,2}$, which simplifies to $(x+4)^2+(y-3)^2=61$. Choice B has the signs of the center wrong, and the right side should be squared. In choice C, you did not square the differences in the *x*- and *y*-coordinates when computing the distance between the given points. In choice D, you used the wrong point for the center and should square the right side.

15. **The correct answer is D.** Substitute $a + 3$ for b, and $-a^2 + 3a + 10$ for c, into the expression $b^2 - 2c$ and combine terms.

$$(a+3)^3-2(-a^2+3a+10)$$
$$=a^2+6a+9+2a^2-6a-20$$
$$=a^2+2a^2+6a-6a+9-20$$
$$=3a^2-11$$

16. **The correct answer is** $-\frac{1}{3}$ **or** $\frac{1}{3}$. Gather the $|x|$-terms on one side and the constants on the other, and then divide by the coefficient of $|x|$. Then, use the definition of absolute value to conclude what the values of x must be:

$$3|x|+2=9|x|$$
$$2=6|x|$$
$$\frac{1}{3}=|x|$$

So, $x=-\frac{1}{3},\frac{1}{3}$.

17. **The correct answer is A.** The height of the pole, *x*, is opposite a 70° angle, and the hypotenuse of the triangle is 50. Sine equals opposite divided by hypotenuse:

$$\frac{x}{50}=\sin 70°$$

$$x = 50 \sin 70°$$

Choice B is the length of the unlabeled leg of the triangle. In choice C, you used an incorrect definition of tangent. In choice D, you used an incorrect definition of cosine.

18. **The correct answer is 224.** The system will have an infinite number of solutions when the two equations are equivalent. In order to make the *y* coefficients the same in the two equations, we can multiply the first one by –4. So multiply each term in the first equation by –4 to find the values for *a* and *b*, then find their product:

$$-4(2x+3y)=-4(7)$$
$$-8x-12y=-28$$

For the two equations to be equivalent, a must be –8 and b must be –28.

$$\begin{aligned} -8x-12y&=-28 \\ ax-12y&=b \\ a&=-8 \\ b&=-28 \\ ab&=-8(-28)=224 \end{aligned}$$

19. **The correct answer is B.** This is the graph of $y = 3^x$ shifted down 2 units. The shape remains the same and the horizontal asymptote goes from $y = 0$ to $y = -2$. This results in the graph of choice B. Choice A is incorrect because this is the graph of a log function; exponential functions do not have vertical asymptotes. Choice C is incorrect because the graph should increase from left to right. Choice D is incorrect because the horizontal asymptote should be $y = -2$.

20. **The correct answer is D.** First, FOIL the two binomials. Then, distribute the 3 through all of the resulting terms, as well as 2 through the binomial in the first expression. Finally, combine all like terms:

$$\begin{aligned} 2\left(y^2-z^2\right)-3(z-y)(2z+y)&=2\left(y^2-z^2\right)-3\left(2z^2-yz-y^2\right) \\ &=2y^2-2z^2-6z^2+3yz+3y^2 \\ &=5y^2+3yz-8z^2 \end{aligned}$$

Choice A is incorrect because you did not FOIL the second expression correctly. Choice B is incorrect because you dropped the 3 that is in front of the product of two binomials from the calculation. Choice C is incorrect because you did not distribute the negative across all terms of the second expression after FOILing.

21. **The correct answer is B.** Use the quadratic formula directly to get:

$$x=\frac{-(-1)\pm\sqrt{(-1)^2-4(2)(3)}}{2(2)}=\frac{1\pm\sqrt{-23}}{4}=\frac{1\pm i\sqrt{-23}}{4}=\frac{1}{4}\pm\frac{i\sqrt{23}}{4}$$

Choice A is incorrect because the radical portion of the quadratic formula is $\sqrt{b^2-4ac}$, not $\sqrt{b^2-ac}$. Choice C is incorrect because you forgot i; note that $\sqrt{-23}=\sqrt{-1}\bullet\sqrt{23}=i\sqrt{23}$. Choice D is incorrect because you computed the radicand portion of the quadratic formula incorrectly since it should have been negative.

22. **The correct answer is 6.** The factor $(x + 3)$ occurs twice. As such, the zero –3 should be counted twice. Also, $(3x - 2)$ is a factor, making $\frac{2}{3}$ a zero. Therefore, the product of the three zeros is $(-3)(-3)\left(\frac{2}{3}\right)=6$.

ANSWER KEY AND EXPLANATIONS

Math: Module 2

1. D	**6.** A	**11.** 9	**16.** A	**21.** 800
2. C	**7.** 1 or 3	**12.** C	**17.** C	**22.** $\frac{1}{2}$ or 0.5
3. A	**8.** D	**13.** D	**18.** B	
4. A	**9.** B	**14.** C	**19.** C	
5. B	**10.** B	**15.** D	**20.** D	

1. **The correct answer is D.** Use the correct order of evaluating functions. First evaluate $g(3) = 1$, then substitute in $f(g(3))$ as $f(1)$ to find that $f(g(3)) = 3$.

2. **The correct answer is C.** The question asks for Jared's goal in steps per day after d days. He increases his goal by 125 steps each day, so after 1 day it will go up 125(1), after 2 days it will go up by 125(2), and after d days it will go up by $125d$ from his original amount of 950.

3. **The correct answer is A.** The question is asking us to substitute the value that we are given for n and then to simplify the expression. We're asked to provide an answer in terms of m or, in other words, an answer that contains the variable m. Let's see what we get when we substitute 7 for n:

$$\begin{aligned} 2m(16-6n) &= 2m\left[16-6(7)\right] \\ &= 2m(16-42) \\ &= 2m(-26) \\ &= -52m \end{aligned}$$

4. **The correct answer is A.** The total amount that Glen earns in one day is $10.25h$ where h is the number of hours Glen works, and 3(12.50) is three times what he spends commuting. If he wants to earn at least three times what he spends commuting, then the inequality in choice A is the only answer that represents the situation.

5. **The correct answer is B.** Begin by multiplying all terms of the equation by the LCM of 36:

$$\begin{aligned} 36\left(\frac{x}{12}\right)+36\left(\frac{x}{18}\right) &= 1(36) \\ 3x+2x &= 36 \\ 5x &= 36 \\ x = \frac{36}{5} &\text{ or } x = 7.2 \end{aligned}$$

6. **The correct answer is A.** To find the conditional probability that a randomly chosen house in Town B is a colonial house, first find the total number of houses that are in Town B:

$$62 + 65 + 43 + 32 = 202$$

Then write and simplify (as needed) a ratio of colonial houses in Town B to the total number of houses in Town B in the survey:

$$\frac{65}{202}$$

7. **The correct answer is 1 or 3.** First, combine the equations by substituting $2x + 5$ for y in the second equation. Then solve for x. Next, substitute the x-values back in and solve for y:

$$\begin{aligned} 2x+5 &= -2(x+1)^2+3 \\ 2x+5 &= -2x^2-4x-2+3 \\ 0 &= -2x^2-6x-4 \\ 0 &= -2(x+2)(x+1) \\ x &= -1, -2 \\ y &= 2(-1)+5 = 3 \\ &\text{or} \\ y &= 2(-2)+5 = 1 \end{aligned}$$

8. **The correct answer is D.** The 95% confidence that the margin of error is ± 4% is important, and choices A and B ignore the confidence interval. Choice C is not correct because there are likely people who don't know or have no opinion on whether there should be stricter emissions standards for power plants. Only choice D accurately uses the confidence interval and the data given in the problem.

9. **The correct answer is B.** The key to solving this geometry problem is to recognize that the figure contains two similar triangles. We know that the triangles are similar because their corresponding angles are equal ($x = x$, $y = y$) and the two right angles at point Q are equal. Since the triangles have equal corresponding angles, we know that the sides are in proportion to one another.

   We want to determine the ratio between the corresponding sides in the larger triangle, SQR, and the smaller triangle, TQP. We can do this by comparing the two corresponding sides for which we have measures. We're given the length of QP in the smaller triangle as 11.5. We're also given the length of its corresponding leg from the larger triangle, QR, as 46. How many times larger is QR than QP? If we divide 46 by 11.5, we see that QR is 4 times larger than QP.

   The question asks us to determine the length of SQ, which is a side of the larger triangle, SQR. We know that the measure of its corresponding side in the smaller triangle, TQP, is TQ, which measures 15. We also know that all corresponding sides in the larger triangle, SQR, are 4 times longer than the ones in the smaller triangle, TQP, so SQ measures 4 times longer than TQ, or $4 \times 15 = 60$.

10. **The correct answer is B.** The equation for a parabola with a vertex at (h, k) is $y = a(x - h)^2 + k$, and if the y-intercept is 13, then (0, 13) is a point on the parabola, and $13 = a(0 - h)^2 - k$. Since $13 = 2(0 - 3)^2 - 5$, the equation shown in choice B is correct.

11. **The correct answer is 9.** Solve for the expression requested in the inequality, then interpret the answer in the context of the question asked:

$$4s-3<2$$
$$4s<5$$
$$s<\frac{5}{4}$$

   We want an integer value for s that will maximize the value of $4s + 5$. The greatest integer less than $\frac{5}{4}$ is 1. Substitute 1 for s:

$$4s + 5 = 4(1) + 5 = 9$$

12. **The correct answer is C.** First, put the function into slope-intercept form:

$$\begin{aligned} f(x) &= 2(3a-x)-(5+ax) \\ &= 6a-2x-5-ax \\ &= -(2+a)x+(6a-5) \end{aligned}$$

   In order for the graph to not intersect Quadrant III, $(2 + a)$ must be nonnegative so that the slope of the line is negative or zero and the y-intercept $(6a - 5)$ must be positive. This gives two conditions:

   $-(2 + a) \leq 0$ and $6a - 5 > 0$.

   Solving these inequalities yields:

   $a \geq -2$ and $a > \frac{5}{6}$

   Both conditions must hold. So it must be the case that $a > \frac{5}{6}$.

13. **The correct answer is D.** First, we convert 20° to radians: $\frac{\pi \text{ radians}}{180°} \text{ x } 20° = \frac{\pi}{9}$ radians. Then, we use the formula for the length of an arc, s, formed by an angle of θ radians on a circle of radius, $r : s = r\,\theta$. Evaluating this formula for the given radius and central angle measure, in radians, gives $\frac{9}{4\pi} \bullet \frac{\pi}{9} = \frac{1}{4}$. So the length of the arc that intercepts the given central angle is $\frac{1}{4}$.

14. **The correct answer is C.** Distribute, combine like terms, and factor to identify the x-intercepts (4 and 6) as:

$$\begin{aligned} y &= 2(x-5)^2-2 \\ &= 2(x^2-10x+25)-2 \\ &= 2x^2-20x+48 \\ &= 2(x^2-10x-24) \\ &= 2(x-4)(x-6) \end{aligned}$$

Answer choices A, B, and D are equivalent to the given equation, but they do not directly reveal that 4 and 6 are the x-intercepts.

15. **The correct answer is D.** Simplify each portion of the expression and then combine like terms:

$$2f(x)=2(4x^3-2x+1)=8x^3-4x+2$$
$$xg(x)=x(-x^2+5)=-x^3+5x$$

So,

$$\begin{aligned}2f(x)-xg(x)&=(8x^3-4x+2)-(-x^3+5x)\\&=8x^3-4x+2+x^3-5x\\&=9x^3-9x+2\end{aligned}$$

Choice A is incorrect because you did not distribute the 2 or x across all terms of the quantity. Choice B is incorrect because this is just $2f(x)$. Choice C is incorrect because this is $f(x) - g(x)$; you ignored the multiples of 2 and x, respectively.

16. **The correct answer is A.** Use completing the square to find the coordinates of the center of the circle. Separate the equation x- and y-terms:

$$x^2+y^2-10x+4y=-20$$
$$x^2-10x+y^2+4y=-20$$
$$(x^2-10x+25)+(y^2+4y+4)=-20+25+4$$
$$(x-5)^2+(y+2)^2=9$$

The center is (5, –2) because the standard form of the circle is $(x-h)^2+(y-k)^2=r^2$.

17. **The correct answer is C.** If you try values of a that are (1) less than zero, (2) greater than zero but less than 2.5, and (3) greater than 2.5, then you will be able to select the correct answer from among the choices provided. To graph more easily, note that the line corresponding to the first inequality is $y=\left(\frac{2}{5}\right)x-\frac{6}{5}$, and the line corresponding to the second inequality is $y=\left(-\frac{1}{a}\right)x-\frac{3}{a}$. The cases where $a = -1$, $a = 1$, and $a = 6$ are shown at the end of this explanation. Only in the second graph, where $a = 1$, is the dark-gray solution completely within Quadrants II and III (left of the y-axis). So among the choices, $0 \le a \le 2.5$ must be correct.

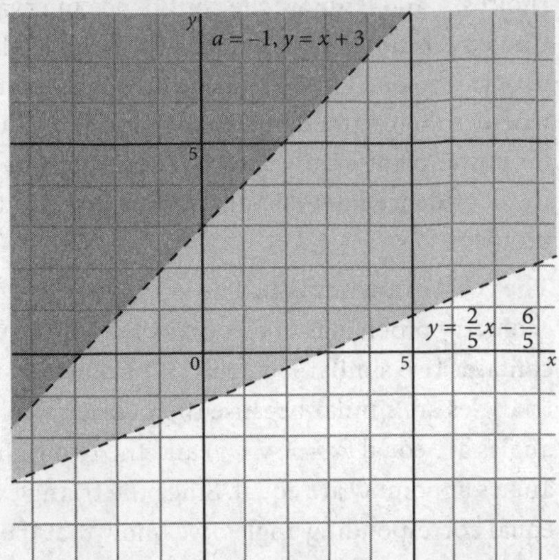

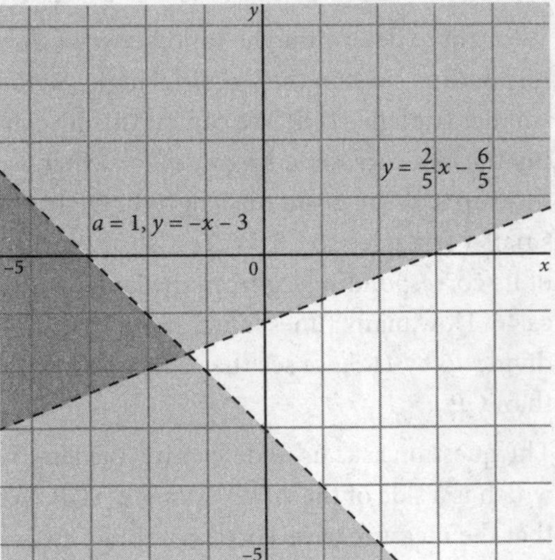

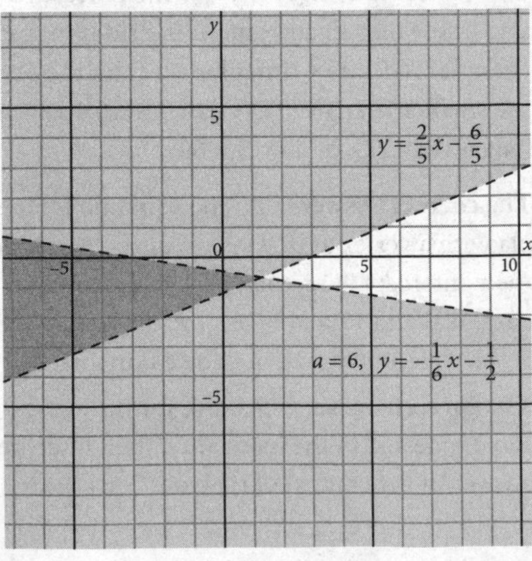

18. **The correct answer is B.** If $w < -1$ and $v > 1$, then the x-intercepts of the graph must be greater than 1 and less than –1. Choice D is incorrect because the graph shows an x-intercept exactly at (–1, 0).

19. **The correct answer is C.** Use the circumference of the circle to find the radius.

$$C = 2\pi r$$
$$572\pi = 2\pi r$$
$$286 = r$$

Then use the measure of the central angle and the radius to find the area of the sector. The area of a sector is the product of the ratio $\dfrac{\text{measure of the central angle in radians}}{2\pi}$ and the area of the circle:

$$A = \frac{\frac{3\pi}{4}}{2\pi}\pi(r)^2$$
$$A = \frac{3}{8}\pi(286)^2$$
$$A = \frac{61{,}347\pi}{2}$$

20. **The correct answer is D.** If $x < 0$, then $f(x) = |x| = -x$. Then, $g(f(x)) = g(-x)$. Finally, $g(-x) = \left(\frac{1}{-x}\right) = -\frac{1}{x}$.

For instance, assume $x = -3$: $f(-3) = 3$ and $g(f(-3)) = g(3) = -\frac{1}{3}$.

21. **The correct answer is 800.** The formula for population growth is given in terms of n, the number of years. In order to solve this problem, plug the value of n, in this case 54, into the formula and calculate the value of the expression $100(2)^{\frac{n}{18}}$:

$$\text{Population (in millions) after } n \text{ years} = 100(2)^{\frac{n}{18}}$$
$$= 100(2)^{\frac{54}{18}}$$
$$= 100(2)^3$$
$$= 800$$

22. **The correct answer is $\frac{1}{2}$ or 0.5.** Complete the square on the function so that the vertex is readily identifiable:

$$f(x) = x^2 - 2bx + (b^2 + 2b - 1)$$
$$= (x^2 - 2bx + b^2) + (b^2 + 2b - 1) - b^2$$
$$= (x - b)^2 + (2b - 1)$$

The vertex is $(b, 2b - 1)$, and the parabola opens upward. The graph will have one x-intercept, which coincides with the vertex, if and only if $2b - 1 = 0$. That is, when $b = \frac{1}{2}$.

SCORING CHARTS

Mark missed questions and then calculate the total number of questions you answered correctly for each question domain, module, and test section

READING AND WRITING			
Question Domains	**Question Numbers**	**Module Totals**	**Raw Scores**
Craft and Structure	**Module 1:** 1, 2, 3, 4, 5, 6, 7, 8	**Module 1:**_______/8	_______/15
	Module 2: 1, 2, 3, 4, 5, 6, 7	**Module 2:**_______/7	
Information and Ideas	**Module 1:** 8, 9, 10, 11, 12, 13, 14	**Module 1:**_______/6	_______/13
	Module 2: 8, 9, 10, 11, 12, 13, 14	**Module 2:**_______/7	
Standard English Conventions	**Module 1:** 15, 16, 17, 18, 19, 20, 21	**Module 1:**_______/7	_______/14
	Module 2: 15, 16, 17, 18, 19, 20, 21	**Module 2:**_______/7	
Expression of Ideas	**Module 1:** 22, 23, 24, 25, 26, 27	**Module 1:**_______/6	_______/12
	Module 2: 22, 23, 24, 25, 26, 27	**Module 2:**_______/6	
			Total Raw Score: _______/54

MATH			
Question Domains	**Question Numbers**	**Module Totals**	**Raw Scores**
Algebra	**Module 1:** 1, 8, 11, 13, 14, 15, 19	**Module 1:**_______/7	_______/16
	Module 2: 1, 2, 3, 4, 5, 7, 11, 12, 17	**Module 2:**_______/9	
Advanced Math	**Module 1:** 4, 10, 16, 18, 20, 21, 22	**Module 1:**_______/7	_______/13
	Module 2: 10, 14, 15, 18, 20, 22	**Module 2:**_______/6	
Problem-Solving and Data Analysis	**Module 1:** 2, 5, 7, 12	**Module 1:**_______/4	_______/7
	Module 2: 6, 8, 21	**Module 2:**_______/3	
Geometry and Trigonometry	**Module 1:** 3, 6, 9, 17	**Module 1:**_______/4	_______/8
	Module 2: 9, 13, 16, 19	**Module 2:**_______/4	
			Total Raw Score: _______**/44**

Use the raw-to-scaled score conversion charts on pages 117 (Reading and Writing) and 257 (Math) to see your estimated score range. Then, record the values in the table below. Combine your section totals to calculate your total SAT score.

SAT TEST SECTION AND FINAL SCORES	
Test Section	**Scaled Scores**
Reading and Writing	_______/800
Math	_______/800
SAT Total Score	_______**/1600**